Dionysus Writes

Dionysus Writes

The Invention of Theatre
in Ancient Greece

Jennifer Wise

Cornell University Press
Ithaca and London

First published 1998 by Cornell University Press.

Printed in the United States of America.

Library of Congress Cataloging-in-Publication Data
Wise, Jennifer.
    Dionysus writes : the invention of theatre in ancient Greece / Jennifer Wise
        p.   cm.
    Includes bibliographical references and index.
    ISBN 0-8014-3459-9 (cloth : alk. paper)
    1. Theater—Greece—History. 2. Greek drama—History and criticism—Theory, etc. 3. Written communication—Greece—History. 4. Literacy—Greece—History. 5. Dionysus (Greek deity) 6. Literary form. I. Title.
PA3201.W57 1998
792'.0938—dc21   97-52393

Cornell University Press strives to utilize environmentally responsible suppliers and materials to the fullest extent possible in the publishing of its books. Such materials include vegetable-based, low-VOC inks and acid-free papers that are also either recycled, totally chlorine-free, or partly composed of nonwood fibers.

Cloth printing 10 9 8 7 6 5 4 3 2 1

For my parents,
Ben and Sheila Wise,
and for
Nicholas Seiflow

Contents

Acknowledgments

MANY SCHOLARS HAVE GIVEN GENEROUSLY OF THEIR TIME AND ADVICE BY reading this manuscript at various stages of its development. I am glad to have this opportunity to express my thanks to Benjamin Bennett, David Blostein, Ronald Bryden, Derrick de Kerkhove, Mechtilde O'Mara, Domenico Pietropaulo, and Colin Visser. I owe a particular debt of gratitude to David Blostein and Mechtilde O'Mara for their thorough, meticulous, and always entertaining commentary on and correction of the whole, and to Benjamin Bennett, both for clarifying my thinking in Chapter 1 and for encouraging me to turn the manuscript into a book. Gordon Shrimpton read parts of the manuscript very thoughtfully when he had little time to spare, and my thanks go to him, as to Michael Sidnell, whose graduate seminar in Theory of Drama at the University of Toronto inspired me so many years ago to embark on this project in the first place. For wrestling my chaotic bibliography into shape and for rectifying countless other inconsistencies, Amanda Heller deserves a citation for bravery, as does David Everard for his labors in the University of Victoria Library.

Excerpts from *The Complete Greek Tragedies,* ed. David Grene and Richmond Lattimore (Chicago: University of Chicago Press, 1991), are reprinted by permission of the publisher.

J. W.

Introduction:
The Theoretical Problem

Concepts, just like individuals ... harbor a
kind of homesickness for the place of their
birth.   Kierkegaard

*A*T LEAST SINCE THE START OF THE TWENTIETH CENTURY, WHEN JANE
Ellen Harrison hypothesized that drama arose in Greece out of "orgiastic religion,"[1] students of theatre and drama have looked to ritual for answers to perennial questions about the origins and essence of the art of the
stage. According to Harrison's ritual hypothesis, it is only by an illusion of
historical forgetfulness that the theatre has come to appear as a storytelling
genre, a genre of myth. On the contrary, or so the argument goes, the myths
of the ancient theatre were religious observances in disguise, and Nietzsche
was right after all: the ancient theatre was at root a Dionysian ritual that the
literary genres of tragedy and comedy have since only obscured.

By her own admission, Harrison was neither a historian of the theatre
nor a theorist of art. Like that of Nietzsche, which it resembles in some
ways, Harrison's theory of drama was not a historical account of the emergence of the genre—although it has often been treated as though it were. As
many scholars have since demonstrated, Harrison and Nietzsche were
equally guilty of distorting the historical evidence.[2] Nietzsche, for his
part, eventually came out from under Wagner's influence, abandoned his
Dionysian polemics, and finally admitted the "heresy" that "the Athenians
went to the theatre *in order to hear beautiful speeches.*"[3] Harrison never did
test her hypothesis against the historical evidence for drama's emergence.
Nevertheless, the ritual hypothesis was taken up with gusto and eagerly im-

1. Harrison 1991:568 (orig. pub. 1903).
2. Vickers 1973; Silk and Stern 1981; May 1990; Ackerman 1991; Fowler 1991; Schlesier
1991.
3. Cited by Ober and Strauss 1990:259; my italics.

ported into theatre studies, where it has remained in some quarters to this day.[4]

To her own field, Harrison made an invaluable contribution. By refocusing attention away from the Olympian heights and onto the orgiastic rituals practised in the valleys below, Harrison showed that ancient religion was not a matter of doctrine or rational moral codes, but mainly the observance of concrete rites and symbolic actions based on "fear and deprecation" (Harrison 1991:7).[5] Efforts to unearth similarly ritualistic roots for theatrical practice came up empty-handed however. Lacking any concrete historical evidence, Harrison's followers have even been accused of fabricating proto-theatrical rituals that never existed.[6] In fact, classicists who have since examined the evidence have found the ritual hypothesis for theatre to be "crude and unworkable" and ultimately simply "false."[7] But as Robert Ackerman noted as recently as 1991, the "news" of the discrediting of the ritualists has somehow failed to reach the ears of their followers (189).

For the theory and practice of theatre in our own century, the widespread adoption of the ritual hypothesis has meant the perpetuation of a kind of hermeneutic circle, one that continues to deform our understanding of both the history of the theatre and its destiny as an art form. A good example can be seen in official textbook accounts of drama's emergence in Christian Europe. The ritual hypothesis presupposes that evidence crucial to theatre's appearance must be sought within the sphere of religious activity. As a result, historians studying theatrical activities during this period tend to focus mainly on religious and ritual behavior: liturgical drama, biblical cycles, Christian morality plays. The many theatrical and proto-theatrical activities that went on outside of religious contexts—within the spheres of law, rhetoric, education, and commerce, for example—tend to be ignored in favor of demonstrably ritualistic ones.[8] The bias inherent in this historical

---

4. Bert O. States introduces a 1985 study of the phenomenology of theatre with bald statements of theatre's "probable" ritual origins (1–2), and a popular college textbook, the *HBJ Anthology of Literature* (Stott et al. 1993), introduces the drama section with a description of Greek theatre's "pre-literate," religious, ritualistic roots (682).

5. See esp. Fowler 1991:79.

6. See Taplin 1978:161, 191 n. 3; Pickard-Cambridge 1962:16. Also Burkert 1966:87–121 and Harrison 1991:568.

7. Kirk 1985:248, 223. See also Kirk 1970. Brian Vickers devotes a useful chapter to the "picturesque and attractive theory" built by the ritualists "on no historical basis" (1973:38). Surveying the "modern scholarship . . . [which has] demolished the flimsy and inconsistent evidence" presented by Harrison et al. (33ff.), Vickers concludes that "this whole complex of false ideas, so widely disseminated, must finally be abandoned . . . because there is no actual evidence for any of its assumptions" (42).

8. There are of course exceptions to this trend; see, for example, Jody Enders's *Rhetoric and the Origins of Medieval Drama* (1992).

method would be bad enough by itself; but what is more dismaying is that the findings from these investigations are then taken, in a kind of self-fulfilling historical analogy, as confirmation for the ritualist scenario in Greece. In fact, plentiful evidence exists for medieval Europe that the rise of theatre had other spurs, namely, the spread of literacy and, with it, the ability to write down the tales of bards and minstrels for the first time. Evidence of this kind exists for Greece as well, but the fixation on ritual origins has long obscured it, especially from nonspecialists, to whom it would not occur to seek alternate historical sources. For according to the premises of the ritual hypothesis, nonreligious behavior—such as the literate activities of minstrels, scholars, and law clerks—would have little bearing on theatre practice anyway.

But it does; and the conviction that such nonreligious behavior bears directly on theatrical activities serves as the central premise of this book. My intention here is to recover, for theatre history and dramatic theory alike, some of the evidence for the emergence of theatre which has been neglected as a result of a century-long enchantment with ritual. For too long, theatre history has been written in accordance with a hypothesis which, if not inappropriate to begin with, has in any case been discredited. Not only has the legacy of ritualism been a cart-before-the-horse approach to theatre history; but also ritualism has bequeathed us a faulty theoretical conception of the nature of theatre art itself, particularly insofar as its place within literature is concerned. A better procedure would be to follow the lead of Friedrich Schlegel,[9] to build a theory of genre on the foundation of history rather than the reverse. For to do so is to discover a startling fact about the theatre in ancient Greece, and one that, besides possessing huge theoretical significance for us today, would otherwise remain invisible. Simply put, the fact is this: theatre emerged as the first text-based art in the Western poetic tradition, as an art form whose central generic features depended on the alphabetical literacy of its first practitioners. Theatre may originally have been a Dionysian art form, for there is no denying the identity of drama's patron deity; but this particular god presided over theatre only because, by the time of theatre's appearance in Greece, Dionysus could read and write.

Historically speaking, drama cannot be traced further back in Greece than the sixth century, perhaps to 600 B.C.E. if we believe Herodotus' story about Arion and his addition of verse-speaking satyrs to his choral lyrics. Had theatre been practised earlier, there would surely be some indication of it, for evidence of various other types of performance art—dance, poetry,

---

9. See Schlegel 1957:20 and 1968:19, 60, 76, 78; Peter Szondi provides a useful discussion in "Friedrich Schlegel's Theory of Poetical Genres" (1986:75–94).

solo and choral singing—has survived from before 600, giving a pretty full picture of the diversity of art forms practiced in the Archaic period. But it is not until the sixth century, when alphabetical literacy had been employed in Greece for almost two hundred years, that the first references to theatrical form appear. The historical moment of theatre's appearance thus coincides with Greece's literate revolution, a coincidence that has not escaped the notice of a number of scholars.

One of many thinkers of recent years to draw a causal link between Greece's alphabetical literacy and its cultural and intellectual achievements,[10] Derrick de Kerckhove was perhaps the first to focus directly on theatre. In 1981 he argued that "Greek theatre was one of the developments of the phonetic alphabet" (23). In asserting that "the theatre was to oral epic what writing was to speech" (24), de Kerckhove was, on one level, simply making a historical observation: as Greece shifted from an oral to a literate culture, the stories once narrated in epic performance came to be theatrically performed in the written art of drama (Aristotle *Poetics* 1449b7–9).

That the epic was an oral genre, composed without writing, and that theatre, the genre that replaced it, was a written one, composed by literates, are not in themselves contentious ideas. The orality of the Homeric epics is attested almost universally;[11] and the literacy of the ancient theatre is denied

10. Most important among these for theatre research is Havelock 1963, 1977, 1986; Ong 1982; Segal 1986; and de Kerckhove, who in several journal articles explores the relation between alphabetical literacy and the theatre (1979, 1981, 1982, 1983). Charles Segal (1986) touches on the effect of writing on the mythological material of tragedy, and Walter Ong (1982) and Alfred Burns (1981) mention theatre in passing as one of the products of Athenian literacy. Jesper Svenbro (1990) sees the theatre as itself contributing to the literacy of fifth-century audiences. De Kerckhove has argued that theatre not only reflected but in its first appearance actually advanced the epistemological revolution begun by the alphabet. My approach differs radically insofar as I am interested not in the ancient theatre's effects on audiences, but rather in its sources in literate activities outside the theatre. Segal's approach comes close to my own in places, but his focus is on Greek tragedy exclusively; he does not discuss writing from the point of view of drama as a genre. Ong and Burns only make offhand, isolated suggestions about theatre's dependence on writing, which they do not follow up. And while I have greatly benefited from Svenbro's discussion of the *ABC Show*, I think his conclusions are illogical. De Kerckhove has made an interesting case for the theatre as an agent for the transmission of the alphabet's effects, but I remain unconvinced that, as Svenbro suggests, spectators can improve their reading by watching plays. For additional scholars of Greek literacy who connect their findings with the theatre, see footnote 12.

11. See esp. Lorimer 1948; Lord 1960, 1991; Havelock 1963, 1986; Nilsson 1968; Parry 1971, 1989; Ong 1977, 1982; Nagy 1981, 1986; Foley 1981, 1986, 1990, 1991; Goody 1987; Willcock 1990; Powell 1991; and Thomas 1992:12.

by virtually nobody.[12] But de Kerckhove's theory of tragedy is more radical in its implications. It suggests not just that theatre "happened to be" a literate phenomenon, but that it *owes its existence* to the alphabet.

To acknowledge the literate nature of the ancient theatre is one thing; to suggest that the alphabet was responsible for its invention is another altogether. Does a mere scriptory system have the power to create an art form that would not have existed otherwise? After all, a great deal had happened in Greece between the epic and dramatic periods besides the adoption of the alphabet. For a start, society at large had transformed itself from a heroic aristocracy to a mercantile democracy, and this shift in itself could plausibly account for even major changes in a nation's artistic practices.[13] Furthermore, there is something especially paradoxical in the suggestion that an art of real bodies, real voices, and real presences could have been affected in any substantive way by *writing,* which signifies the absence of all these things.

Whether literacy seems capable of having influenced the invention of theatre will therefore depend in the first place on how we choose to view writing. Now, in traditional linguistics from Aristotle to Saussure, writing is seen as an inert medium for representing speech. In a sort of Platonic hierarchy, writing and speech are viewed as related to each other as shadow to substance, false image to primary living reality. As a mere record of speech, writing of any sort is not imagined, within this purview, to have any effects on actual speech practices (besides occasionally "perverting" and masking them).[14]

This view of writing has, however, been replaced in our time by a more dialectical understanding of the way writing systems affect the languages they record. There is no question that, ontogenetically and phylogenetically, speech precedes writing, and may very well continue happily in its absence. But writing is a technology; and as with any technology, its use by humans sets up a dialectical relationship between itself as artifact and the natural entities it represents. As Don Ihde suggests in his *Philosophy of Technology* (1993), the introduction of such "historic" technologies as writing, the map,

---

12. See Page 1987; Turner 1951, 1971; Davison 1962; Harvey 1966; Woodbury 1976; Ong 1982; Kirk 1985:105; Segal 1986, 1992; Harris 1989:35; Vernant and Vidal-Naquet 1990; Svenbro 1990; and Cole 1992.

13. This is essentially the line of argument pursued by Meier (1990), Vernant and Vidal-Naquet (1990), and Goldhill (1990).

14. See Derrida's discussion in *Of Grammatology* (1976) of the evils attributed to writing systems by Saussure, Lévi-Strauss, and Rousseau; a related discussion appears in Thomas (1992:128), and throughout Steiner (1994).

and the clock marks the beginning of a gradual transformation of available ways of seeing the natural phenomena they measure, encode, or record. Just as the clock not only marks time but also alters our perception of it, so too does writing penetrate and transform linguistic communication even while representing it. First, writing freezes the ordinarily ephemeral flux of spoken language in a form that can be "returned to and repeated" (59). By making language into a fixed artifact, writing both distances verbal meaning from its speakers and makes it available for objective analysis, measuring, and comparison. With the existence of the measured artifact come new standards— of intelligibility, accuracy, evidence, proof, and so on—which derive not from the "natural" course of direct involvement in "immediate environments" (59) but from the artifact. As Ihde observes, these artifactual standards—established, for example, by an exactly clocked "minute"—open up a "dialectic" or "difference" between themselves and naturally perceptible standards. This difference brings with it two related consequences. Either "the sheer repeatability of the standard within the artifact [will] be taken as a kind of ideal which nature [can] only approximate" (59), or the differences established between natural and artifactual will provide a set of abstract values against which phenomena begin to be judged, evaluated, and specially privileged.

A good example of the first of these technological effects can be seen in Platonic philosophy. Without appearing to have recognized what he was doing, Plato latched on to the representational structure of writing and built a whole metaphysics around it. In representing verbal material in a fixed and decontextualized form, writing established new standards of ideality, repeatability, and sameness for words, abstract qualities that spoken language, tied as it is to particular instances of utterance and engagement with unique constellations of perceptual data, never attains. As Eric Havelock argued in *Preface to Plato* (1963), the existence of these new decontextualized standards made it possible for Plato to conceive of, and then privilege, the single, repeatable entities of thought we know as the "forms." [15]

In short, Plato takes writing's fixed artifactual standards of noetic purity and semantic stability as *the* standard with which to judge *all* entities. Natu-

---

15. For Plato, intellectual entities are "always the same in all respects," whereas "the many" objects available to natural perception, "by showing themselves everywhere in a community with actions, bodies, and one another" (*Republic* 5.476a), "wander about, driven by generation and decay" (6.484b). For abstract, decontextualized contemplation, "an *idea* of the beautiful itself . . . always stays the same" (5.479a); "the lovers of hearing and the lovers of sights," by contrast, are "unable to see and delight in the nature of the fair itself" (5.476a–b). These translations are by Allan Bloom (1968).

rally occurring entities, however, which are always in flux and subject to the shifting dynamics of perception, cannot live up to the standards of fixity and repeatability set by writing. As a result, the whole perceptual world of sights and sounds must be devalued in Platonic philosophy, demoted to the status of mere imitations of transcendental signifieds.[16]

The second of Ihde's technological effects might be well exemplified in the Enlightenment semiotics of G. E. Lessing, who imagines a kind of polar continuum, with the "artificial" signs of written language at one end and the "natural" signs of body language at the other. Value here is given to activities, such as poetry and theatre, which "naturalize" phenomena (i.e., move them along the continuum away from their arbitrariness as manufactured signs and toward the naturalness of the living body).[17]

Now, the idea that the two poles in any sort of nature/culture difference will always stand in a mutually constitutive, interdependent relation is an obvious one to any student of dialectics. But in the case of the relation of writing to speech (or texts to phenomena), the dialectical interpenetration of one by the other has not always been self-evident. According to Jack Goody (1986), writing's effects on thought and cultural practices first became apparent when a historical dialectic, usually applied to questions of economic production, was adopted for use in studies of communication practices. In our century, Harold A. Innis (1951) and Marshall McLuhan (1964) were the ground-breakers in exploring the effects of communication systems on cultural life. The enormous popularity of Jacques Derrida's work has contributed further to the general awareness that writing may have been a significant "absent cause" in our intellectual history. Since the 1960s, innumerable books and articles about the consequences of literacy have appeared, and thus even the most skeptical readers today are not likely to deny that a technology as pervasive as writing has had *some* effect on cultural life. More controversial is the question of what those effects are, and how writing brings them about.

Some theorists have seen writing's causality as direct. For example, Robert Logan, who claims membership in the Toronto school of communication theorists along with Innis, McLuhan, and de Kerckhove, credits the alphabet directly with all of the products of Western civilization: codified law, monotheism, abstract science, deductive logic, individualism, democracy, mass education, and capitalism (1986:18ff.). While the alphabet cer-

---

16. This metaphysics is elaborated most fully in Books 5 and 10 of the *Republic*.

17. Useful analyses of Lessing's semiotics can be found in Wellbery 1984:129, and in Wellek 1981 1:165.

tainly had an important role to play in all of these developments, the idea
that literacy, or one variant of it, can by itself "cause" anything directly has
been criticized for its idealism and mechanistic determinism.[18] As David
Olson cautions, writing alone cannot "simply cause social or cognitive
changes" (1985:4). The Ashanti warriors in Africa, for example, used writing
not to represent speech or to pursue Aristotelian philosophy, but to decorate
their war coats (Goody 1968:264). And in ancient Sparta the alphabet was
known, but its use was actively discouraged for most purposes except the
sending of military messages.[19] The historian of science G. E. R. Lloyd
(1990) has mounted an especially trenchant critique of the idea that a whole
society, such as that of the sixth-century Greeks, can in truth be said to possess a single "mentality," literate or otherwise.[20] What Lloyd demonstrates is
that it is not directly in the psychology or biology of whole historical groups
that technological change manifests itself. Rather, technologies are mediated
by the concrete "styles of discourse" practised in particular locales at particular historical moments, and especially by the socially and politically specific
"contexts of communication" in which these discursive styles are embedded.
Rosalind Thomas, the foremost expert on Greek literacy, agrees: it is necessary to accept that the implications of literacy "are culturally determined"
(1992:28) and are not by any means automatic or directly physiological.

But even having shown the uselessness of deterministic models (insofar
as they are unable to take due account of "the importance of political factors—both as necessary conditions and as positive stimuli" [134]), Lloyd
must finally make a pivotal acknowledgment. And what he is forced to con-
fess for language generally can also be said of the various media available for
representing it: that different systems *do* have inherent traits, and these traits
will naturally be either more or less conducive to the expression, and therefore the development, of certain ideas (136).

Long before McLuhan and Derrida, Wilhelm von Humboldt made it
his business to analyze the inherent traits of different writing systems, and
he drew a number of conclusions about the relation between writing and
civilization. For its ability to signify sound without the added baggage of an

18. For critiques of technological determinism, see Scribner and Cole 1981; Olson
1988; Olson and Hildyard 1985; Finnegan 1977; Taylor 1988; and Thomas 1992:28ff.

19. Cartledge 1978:25–37; Thomas 1992:136–37.

20. Rosalind Thomas (1989, 1992) has demonstrated this general argument at length
by showing that Greek society retained many oral features even during periods when writing was used; that levels of literacy were extremely varied, and in some cases probably
nonexistent; and that attitudes toward literacy varied throughout the Greek states depending on other sociopolitical factors such as the extent of democracy.

already constituted, value-laden reality of meanings and things, alphabetic writing struck Humboldt as more conducive than other scripts to certain abstract noetic functions. Although Humboldt's Eurocentrism rings hollow today, his main insight has only gained in authority: "Even though we write as we do because that is the way we speak, it is also the case that we speak as we do because that is the way we write."[21] Since Humboldt's time, writing has indeed been observed to affect the speech practices of its users in many concrete ways. In spoken Japanese, for example, written borrowings from Chinese have led to what Florian Coulmas has called a "creolization by writing." As Coulmas explains, spoken Japanese has been shaped in part by the "massive influx of Chinese loan words" which came into the language through the written register (1989:122–24). The large number of homophones that exist today in the Japanese vocabulary can be traced directly to the borrowed writing system and the process of its adaptation to Japanese phonology (127).

But because writing systems are modes of representation which, along with language, get internalized for use in all types of thinking, writing's effects will inevitably manifest themselves even beyond the domain of speech.[22] Consider the nature of scientific inquiry. Eastern and Western historians of science agree that despite comparably magnificent achievements in antiquity, alphabetical Greek and logographic Chinese investigations did take slightly different forms (Lloyd 1990:11). Whereas the abstract, analytical, isolating operations of alphabetical script are clearly reflected in the nature of Western science, Chinese science manifested itself in ways that reproduce the characteristics of Chinese script: in practical, applied inventions directly connected with concrete activities and carried out under rigid hierarchies (125). If writing systems are capable, albeit in a socially mediated way, of influencing their users' speech practices, habits of thought, and scientific activities, there is no reason to suppose that artistic practices alone will somehow remain immune.

Art forms are, after all, concrete social practices too. In heightening our sensitivity to the material dimension of even ordinary speech practices, students of literacy from Havelock (1963) through Ong (1982), Goody (1987), and Thomas (1992) have added greatly to our understanding of just how vulnerable such practices are to technological change. In particular, the work of these scholars has emphasized that real consequences accrue from

21. Humboldt cited in Christy 1989:344.

22. For valuable discussions of the process whereby representing systems are psychologically "internalized," see Olson 1988:423–25; Vygotsky 1978, 1992; and Luria 1981:27–87.

such subtle technological variables as how cultural material is preserved and how it is transmitted. Depending on what technologies are available, not only the "how" of cultural communication but also the "why" of it can change from one social context to the next. The research on which this book is based suggests, likewise, that the society that records its culture in books, teaches it in schools, and transmits it verbatim will function according to different standards and values—and be apt to indulge in different sorts of behaviors—than the society that uses none of these things and depends instead wholly on the embodied wisdom of elders and bards. And a culture like that of the sixth-century Greeks, which records, criticizes, teaches, and transmits its stories and laws through the written medium, is one that is likely to indulge, specifically, in those behaviors that have since been ranged under the heading of "theatre."

This study of the relationship between literacy and the theatre in ancient Greece is divided into four chapters, each of which explores theatre's dependency on the technology of alphabetical writing from a different point of view. Chapter 1, "The ABCs of Acting," outlines the significance of the use of the alphabet to record stories once confined to the oral register. The second chapter, "The Student Body," details the consequences of learning and teaching such narrative material through the agency of the literate classroom rather than through oral instruction. In Chapter 3, "Courtroom Dramas," I show how the writing down of law effected changes to social behavior in the public sphere which further reinforced the shift toward a theatrical style of storytelling. Chapter 4, "Economies of Inscription," contains a discussion of a number of related literary activities—the inscription of city coinage, letters, wills, and ostraka—which together consolidated the shift away from a contextually embedded model of information exchange and toward the kind of highly mobile, cosmopolitan economy of exchange on which the theatre depended.

Although this inquiry ranges widely among social spheres, from poetic performance to education and legal procedures to political economy, the separate investigations are united by the question of alphabetical literacy and the consequences of its earliest uses in ancient Greece. Each chapter is based on a concrete practice or practices for which the evidence is secure. We know for certain that in the sixth century B.C.E. and earlier, the Greeks used the alphabet (Chapter 1); that they learned to write in schools (Chapter 2); that they had public, written law codes (Chapter 3); that they wrote letters, poetry, citizen lists, and wills, and that they used coins and ballots with written inscriptions on them (Chapter 4). While strictly sequenced, each chapter takes its own view of the ways in which the literate practices of ancient Greece would have shaped the mode of representation we know as theatre.

In tracking the generic shift between epic recitation and theatrical representation, we must however take care to conceive of these genres with as much historical accuracy as possible. Without a precise picture of the characteristics of each genre in its time, we will hardly be able to appreciate the nature of the shift from one to the other. And a false impression of each is more likely than not, for our understanding of the relationship between epic and theatre has been so muddled by ritualistic thinking that its distinctive features are often misconstrued. As John Herington has shown (1985), the shift from epic to dramatic poetry was not the generic revolution it is often supposed to be. For theatre is widely assumed to have *introduced* features that in fact it only *retained* from the genres of predramatic poetry: corporeal performance in person before large audiences, impersonation of narrative figures, costumes, music, dance. In addition to Herington, Charles Segal (1992) and Rosalind Thomas (1992) have reminded us that multi-medial corporeality was a defining characteristic of *all* poetry in Greece—before, during, and after the dramatic age of the fifth century.[23] Theatre did introduce certain new generic features into the performance of poetry in Greece, as we shall see. But none of them is connected with the musical, multi-medial corporeality which, in the popular imagination—and thanks in part to Nietzsche—theatre alone embodies.[24] By emphasizing the gradual emergence of dramatic form out of epic and lyric recitation, Herington has almost single-handedly repaired the damage done to theatre studies by the assumptions of ritualism. Unfortunately, Herington does not consider the use of writing in his account of this generic shift, an omission that finally leaves it incomplete. He does show that drama appeared as an incorporating fulfillment of a long tradition of competitive epic and lyric recitation; but because he does not consider the impact of literacy, he cannot explain how or why this happened as it did.

In searching for the stimuli for Greece's shift from epic to dramatic performance, one must therefore isolate sufficient causes, and separate them

23. The Homeric epics give us clear pictures of the singing, dancing, and emotional identification that accompanied predramatic performances. Segal (1992:4–29) provides a complete list of scenes of bardic performance from both the *Iliad* and the *Odyssey* with discussion. The lyric poems of Archilochus evince a similar performance style (see Ayrton 1977).

24. In connecting the "birth of tragedy" to the "spirit of music," Nietzsche has given many students of drama the mistaken impression that music was somehow uniquely typical of drama, that music did not also characterize the predramatic genres of epic and lyric, which it did.

from impulses that, although probably buried irretrievably in human pre-history, produce poetic performance itself. Theatre was not the first genre of poetic performance; it was simply the first genre of poetic performance in Greece which made use of unmediated enactment by a number of nonspe-cialist performers, verbatim memorization, and a dialogic style. This generic profile was new to Greece, and all of the performative innovations that went into it, constituting it as the new art of the theatre as distinct from its epic antecedent, are demonstrably dependent on the use of writing.

The evidence suggests that a knowledge and use of writing enabled the first playwrights to manipulate poetic materials in ways that had been un-available to oral bards. In terms of its creation by an individual *reader* of inherited material; in terms of its public submission and transmission by arbitrary and anonymous signs; in terms of its performance by nonspecialist and "other" actors; and in terms of its democratic and nonconservative function in relation to its audience, the dramatic text no less than theatrical performance represented a radical departure from epic narrative, the main genre of poetry practised in Greece before "tragedy and comedy came to light" (*Poetics* 1449a13).

As for the date when writing was first used for poetic composition in Greece, creating the conditions for this gradual generic shift from epic bard to theatrical actor, the archaeological record is clear: alphabetic writing was used to record verse as early as the eighth century B.C.E. For this reason, the dramatists of the fifth century B.C.E., despite what Walter J. Ong has said,[25] were not so much innovators in their use of writing for poetic composition as they were revolutionary in the degree to which they exploited the poten-tialities of literate modes and, in so doing, made use of writing as "text" rather than as a mere reminder of a spoken performance.

Accordingly, the story I tell of theatre's emergence begins with the writ-ing down of archaic stories—stories that had once been confined to the "winged words" of oral recitation. Barry Powell (1991) may be right that these epic stories were written down as early as the late eighth century B.C.E.; or perhaps the most scrupulous of scholars are right when they em-phasize the lateness of the evidence for these early literary activities, and in-sist that we postpone the date of a literary Homer into the sixth century B.C.E. But the extent of textual criticism that is detectable in the sixth cen-tury—as practiced by writers such as Xenophanes, Theagenes, and Stesicho-rus[26]—gives us good cause to say with confidence that a written Homer,

---

25. Ong 1977:72.
26. In addition to Pfeiffer 1968:5–26, see the discussion of Homer's earliest critics in Richardson 1992:30–39, which supports Powell's case for the earliest possible date for a writ-ten Homer. Similar arguments can be found in Segal 1992.

and literary criticism of the works attributed to him, were components of Greek poetic life during the lifetime of Thespis—that is, before the flowering of dramatic form under Aeschylus in the early fifth century B.C.E. The immediate progenitors of Aeschylus were therefore not the orgiastic congregations of goat sacrificers so dear to ritualists, but individual readers of Homer. If Aeschylus was able, by his own admission, to develop his art of drama by cutting thick slices from the Homeric feast (Athenaeus *Deipnosophists* 8.347e), he was able to do this slicing precisely because history had placed into his hands an appropriate tool: a writing implement. For just as the bard is always represented wielding the instrument of his trade, the lyre,[27] fifth-century representations of the playwright, both on vases and in the theatre itself, depict him clutching the instrument of *his* chosen genre—the book roll.[28]

After outlining the technological conditions under which theatre first emerged—and to which it must, as both an art form and a social practice, be considered indebted—I conclude with some suggestions about what these findings might mean for literary and theatrical theory today.

More than a century ago Gilbert Murray expressed his belief that what "enabled Athens to create the drama" was a peculiar sympathy for both sides in any conflict, a sympathy learned from the epics of Homer. In a Homeric world, both Priam and Achilles, both the Trojans and their enemies, both vanquished and victor are invested with equal humanity and honored with equal esteem. And in this Homeric genius for portraying human conflicts in a two-sided way, Murray saw a generic germ of the dramatic style. He was right to do so. But whether this Homeric attitude toward storytelling would, by itself, have created dramatic form is another matter altogether. As David Olson reminds us, "what the mind can do depends on the *devices* provided by culture," not just on how that culture thinks.[29] It is my view that without the advent of a new technology for poetic composition, epic recitation might well have retained its supremacy as a storytelling form and never have produced the drama at all. For in the absence of writing, nothing more highly "theatrical" would have been possible.

27. *Iliad* 9.188, 18.567–604; *Odyssey* 22.340f.; Segal 1992:4, 25.
28. See esp. the Pronomos Vase as reproduced in Winkler and Zeitlin 1990, plate 1; Aristophanes describes Euripides as a writer (frag. 676b Edmonds 1957) and his plays as available to readers aboard ships (*Frogs* 52–53).
29. Cited by Scinto 1986:164.

CHAPTER I

The ABCs of Acting

> This ABC and grammar of acting are . . . not
> difficult. Without them, it is impossible to live
> on the stage. Stanislavski

*I*N AN UNKNOWN YEAR IN THE FIFTH CENTURY B.C.E., POSSIBLY AT THE end of the 430s, when Euripides' *Medea* and Sophocles' *Oedipus Tyrannos* were performed, the Athenian poet Kallias wrote and presented a play about the alphabet. Sometimes translated as the *ABC Show,* and sometimes as the *ABC Tragedy,* the *Grammatike Theoria* of Kallias[1] is provocative even in its title: a "theory" for the Greeks was literally a "looking at" (*theoria*), and what is seen (*theasthai*) by the spectators (*theatai*) of this show is a play about letters, about language made visible in the alphabet. A *theoria* of letters thus finds its natural platform on the stage of the theatre (*theatron*), the place for viewing. The etymological and even the practical connections between theatre and theory in general are numerous and provocative, and have often been remarked on before.[2] The *ABC Show,* in thus "showing" writing to its audiences, confirms theatre's theoretical connections, and provides a most bracing opportunity for analyzing the special kinship between an alphabetical and a theatrical manner of making things visible.

The Chorus of this fifth-century play is made up not of Theban elders or the women of Trachis but of the twenty-four letters of the Ionian alphabet, from Alpha through Omega. The prologue consists of a sung list of all the letters in order ("Say Alpha, beta, gamma, delta, and then The God's epsilon,[3] zeta, eta, theta, iota. . . ."); and when the Chorus splits into pairs,

---

1. Frag. 31 A, B, C, D Edmonds 1957. Both Svenbro (1990:381–82) and Harvey (1966:632 n. 13) provide valuable discussions of this fragment. I am in their debt.

2. See esp. Svenbro 1990:383 and Reinelt and Roach 1992:3–4.

3. Svenbro (1990:381–82) restores the original *ei* of the manuscripts, which Edmonds (1957) alters into "epsilon" in his translation; both explain that *ei* was inscribed on the temple at Delphi and was thus known as Apollo's letter.

what is sung is the combinations of consonants and vowels: "Beta alpha: ba. Beta epsilon: be. Beta eta: bē. Beta iota: bi. . . ." The second half-chorus answers: "Gamma alpha: ga. Gamma epsilon: ge. Gamma eta: gē. . . ." Dialogue in the *ABC Show* includes a conversation between what appears to Jesper Svenbro (1990) to be a teacher and two female pupils:

> You must pronounce *alpha* by itself, my ladies, and secondly *ei* by itself. And you there, you will say the third vowel!
>
> Then I will say *eta*.
>
> Then *you* will say the fourth one by itself!
>
> *Iōta*.
>
> The fifth—
>
> *O*.
>
> The sixth, *U,* say alone.
>
> *U*.
>
> But the last of seven vowels, ŏ, I will pronounce for you. And then put all seven into verse. When you have pronounced them, say them to yourself.[4]

Unfortunately, little more of this fragment has survived. But properly read, it is a pithy lesson in much more than the alphabet. It is a lesson in theatrical theory, too, and a demonstration of the debt owed by theatre to the alphabet.

Now, the phonetic principle of the Greek alphabet is not normally a subject we would associate with the ancient theatre festivals. And yet Kallias was not alone in choosing it as the subject of a play. Even in the earliest extant dramas of the fifth century, dramas ostensibly devoted to a retelling of the stories of mythology and Homeric epic, a concern with alphabetic literacy is palpable everywhere. Including Kallias' *ABC Show,* at least eighty-one separate references to writing can be found throughout the extant plays and fragments; and at least eleven fifth-century plays have plots that depend on the literacy of the characters and their use of texts.[5] And these numbers appear all the more impressive when we remember that the vast majority of

---

4. Svenbro's translation is used here in the main (1990:382).

5. *Seven Against Thebes, The Women of Trachis, Antigone, Hippolytos, Iphegenia in Aulis, Iphegenia in Taurus, Frogs, Clouds, Birds, Knights.* We might also include Cratinus' *Wineflask* (frag. 195–96 Edmonds 1957), for Niall Slater thinks that this play may have been about a character "writing a comedy"; but the play survives in too fragmentary a form to say whether the episode that features this activity was an isolated one or typical of the whole work (1996:108–9).

plays written in the period have not survived.[6] In both stage action and narration, dramatic characters are represented reading books, sending and receiving letters, writing wills, interpreting written oracles and laws, studying scholarly texts, and keeping expense account records and records of testimony in court. In the Greek dramas, everyone from Athenian dogs (*Wasps* 959–60) to Olympian gods (*Eumenides* 275, *Frogs* 52–53) is depicted as knowing, and using, their ABCs. In conspicuous contrast to the mythic gods and heroes as depicted in Homeric epic, the dramatic characters of the fifth-century theatre inhabit a world where writing is a more or less everyday fact of life.

Within these eighty-plus references, writing is occasionally integral to the plot; sometimes it is used merely as a metaphor, with characters instructing one another to "inscribe" something on the "tablets" of their minds; and sometimes the alphabet is brought visibly onto the stage. In the remaining bit of the Kallias fragment, one of the female writing students physically acts out the shape of the letters *psi* and *omega,* with an effect that was apparently obscene.[7] In this, too, Kallias was in good company, for Sophocles, Euripides, Aristophanes, and others are also reported to have used this same

---

6. None of my sources has attempted to amass a complete list. I count eighty-one references to reading, writing, books, inscription, letters, and waxed tablets. Organized by author only, my list contains the following: Aeschylus *Eumenides* 273–75; *Prometheus Bound* 788–89, 459–61; *Seven Against Thebes* 647, 660; *Suppliants* 178–79; 991–92, 944–49; *The Libation Bearers* 450; *Aitnai* [?] frag. 530 as cited by Pfeiffer 1968:26; Sophocles *Antigone* 450–55, 499, 707–9; *Philoctetes* 1325; *Triptolemus* frag. 540 Nauck 1964; *The Women of Trachis* 46, 155–63, 680–83, 1167; frag. 742 Nauck; *Amphiaraos* (satyr play) (Athenaeus 10.454f. as cited by Svenbro 1990:383); Euripides *Hecuba* 293, *Hippolytus* 452ff., 857–65, 880, 953–54; *Iphigenia in Aulis* 108–23, 891; *Iphigenia among the Taurians* 584–85, 641–42, 763; *Melanippe* frag. 506 Nauck; *Palamedes* frag. 578 Nauck; *Suppliants* 431–37; *Theseus* frag. 382 Nauck; *Trojan Women* 661; Agathon frag. 4 Nauck; Akhaios *Omphale* frag. 33 Nauck; Theodectes frag. 6 Nauck; Aristophanes *Babylonians* frag. 64 Edmonds 1957; *Banqueters* frag. 217 Edmonds; *Birds* 974–91, 1024, 1036, 1277; *The Broilers* frag. 490, frag. 676b Edmonds; *Clouds* 18–24, 30–31, 759–74; *Ecclesiasusae* 1012–20, 1050; *Frogs* 52–53, 1114, 1407–10; *Gerytades* frag. 157 Edmonds; *Knights* 188–89, 190–92, 1256; *Thesmophoriazusai* 768–84; *Triphales* [?] frag. 623 Edmonds; *Wasps* 959–60; Cratinus *The Laws* frag. 122 [?], frag. 274 Edmonds; *The Thracian Women* frag. 71 Edmonds; *The Wine Flask* frag. 195, frag. 196 Edmonds; Kallias, *Grammatical Play* frag. 31A, B, C, D Edmonds; Hermippus *The Porters* frag. 63 Edmonds; Eupolis *Exempt from Service or the Workmen* frag. 35, *Flatterers* 149–153, *Maricas* frag. 193, unknown work, frag. 304 all Edmonds; Plato *The Poet* frag. 114, *Phaon* frag. 173, *Daedalus* [?] frag. 194 all Edmonds; Philonides, unknown work frag. 7 Edmonds; Aristomenes *Wizards* frag. 8–10 Edmonds; Theopompus frag. 77 Pfeiffer 28 n. 2; Nicophon frag. 19. 4 Pfeiffer 28 n. 2.

7. See Edmonds 1957:181; Svenbro 1990:382.

theatrical device.[8] Sophocles' satyr play *Amphiaraos* includes a scene in which an actor dances out the shapes of letters (Athenaeus *Deipnosophists* 10.454f.); and Akhaios, in a fairly lengthy fragment, has a satyr name all the letters in an inscription for the audience, which together spell D-I-O-N-U-S-O-U ([I belong to] Dionysus; frag. 33).[9] In Euripides' *Theseus* (frag. 382), an illiterate rustic, a herdsman, describes what he sees, but cannot himself read, on the side of a ship: "T-H-E-S-E-U-S." The alphabet was also "staged" by Agathon in his *Telephus* (frag. 4) and by Theodectes (frag. 6), and was ultimately parodied by Aristophanes in the *Thesmophoriazusae* (768–84). Spelling out "Euripides," Mnesilochus exclaims, "What a horrible 'R' !"[10]

Why were the Athenian playwrights so taken with the theatrical and thematic possibilities of the alphabet? To begin with, the alphabet was relatively new. From surviving samples of Archaic writing, specifically from inscribed objects such as cups, vases, and tombstones, scholars have dated the earliest use of alphabetic writing in Greece to the middle of the eighth century, circa 740 B.C.E.[11] This means that writing had been in use in Greece for only two hundred years before Thespis won the first known prize for a drama. Now, two hundred years may sound like a long time to us, used as we are to rapid technological change; but Archaic Greek culture functioned so well on an exclusively oral basis that the acquisition of literacy was a slow, uneven, and in some spheres of life barely perceptible process.[12] Even in the fifth century, when schools were widespread and the functioning of the democratic state and its legal institutions depended on writing, country folk may have remained unlettered (Harvey 1966:620), and even some city folk, like Aristophanes' sausage seller, could read and write little, and that with difficulty (*Knights* 188–89, 636, 1030–89). Alphabetical inscriptions that have survived from the eighth and seventh centuries are rarely more than a few lines long, and often betray writing skills of a very rudimentary nature. Indeed, as William Harris (1989) and Rosalind Thomas (1989, 1992) have argued at length, the advance of literacy in Greece was so gradual until the sixth century, and so spotty even thereafter, that many aspects of Greek life remained primarily oral in practice until well into the fourth century B.C.E.[13]

8. Harvey 1966:604; Cole 1981:149 n. 20; Bowra and Higham 1950:459; and Svenbro 1990:383 provide useful discussions of these fragments.

9. This and following fragments are from Nauck 1964; see Svenbro's discussion (1990:377).

10. See Harvey's discussion (1966:632 n. 13).

11. The evidence is discussed at length by Stroud 1989:103–19; Harris 1989:vii; Jeffrey 1990:21; Powell 1991:144ff.; and Thomas 1992:53ff.

12. See esp. W. Harris 1989:vii–115; Thomas 1989, 1992; Steiner 1994.

13. See also Lentz 1989:6ff.

Nevertheless, given the prevalence of references to literate activities in the dramas of the early fifth century, and given the fact that many of these pass without special comment, one might be inclined to distrust the archaeological record and assume that literacy must have been more fully entrenched in Greek life than surviving artifacts would suggest. And there are indeed good reasons to do so, since much of the evidence for literacy in the Archaic period is certain to have disappeared without a trace for purely physical reasons. Leather, wood, and waxed tablets are among the writing materials used by the Greeks which were not durable enough to survive; and their absence in the archaeological record must surely distort to some extent our impressions of the extent of predramatic literacy.

Luckily, however, there is another source for the commencement of literary activities in Greece. This source is the Homeric epics,[14] long recognized by scholars as a "modern and up to date" picture of life in Homer's historical period.[15] Barry Powell's comprehensive survey of the internal and external evidence for dating these poems puts their composition no later than the end of the eighth century B.C.E. And when we examine these predramatic poems, this storehouse of mythic tales from which the early dramatists drew in creating their plays, we are struck by an inescapable realization: Homer's epic heroes, unlike their dramatic embodiments, were illiterate.

Taken together, the *Iliad* and the *Odyssey* constitute a "vast encyclopedia" (Havelock 1986:79) of life during war and during peace, a comprehensive panorama of life as the epic singers knew it. No sphere of human life escaped portrayal in these songs, from the most heroic to the most homely; everything from the proper method of steering a chariot on the battlefield to the domestic arrangements in Penelope's bedroom is honored with representation. Given the completeness of these poems as what an ancient observer called "a fair mirror of human life,"[16] and given especially their penchant for anachronism,[17] one would expect writing to be represented within them if it was known. But in the tens of thousands of lines of Homeric verse, there are no references to alphabetic writing at all, neither as a thing done nor as the subject of a trope.

14. As Gilbert Murray pointed out, many more epics were attributed to Homer, or considered "Homeric," in the ancient world than have come down to us (1907:8–53). I will be using Homer's name to refer to that body of works which, while exemplified to us mainly through the *Iliad* and the *Odyssey*, also included the many stories connected with Thebes, or the *Thebais*, and others, such as the *Cypria, The Sack of Ilion, Homecomings*, and *Telegoneia*.

15. See Bowra 1969:32; more recently Powell 1991.

16. Alcimadas as cited by Pfeiffer 1968:50.

17. Nilsson 1968:211.

The closest encounter with any kind of inscription occurs in the story of Bellerophontes in Book 6 of the *Iliad* (168–170). The "baleful signs" (*semata lugra*) that Bellerophontes takes with him to Lykia could be described as a kind of writing insofar as they are "inscribed in a folding tablet"; but they are also said to have magical powers "enough to destroy life." As Powell has shown, the "fatal letter" motif was inherited into the epics from the ancient East, where such folding tablets were used from an early date (1991:199). Yet the eighth-century singers of the Greek epics evidently had no idea how writing actually worked: the word *semata* is used again in Book 7 of the *Iliad* when the warriors draw lots, and it becomes clear that it is not writing that is being referred to. Each hero puts a mark on his own lot, but these marks are illegible to everyone but the marker (181–89); they are in fact little more than paw prints. Indeed, neither Bellerophontes' symbols nor the warriors' marks are intended to *represent* anything at all; in one case they *are* their own magical effects, in the other they are meaningless scribbles. Clearly, the bards are not here depicting writing in the ordinary sense, as a device for representing speech. Because of this obvious ignorance of the capabilities of the alphabet, readers of Homer since the eighteenth century have concluded with justification that the composer of the *Iliad* and the *Odyssey* was a strictly oral poet who knew nothing at all about the technology of writing.[18]

The picture we get from the epics of a strictly oral society thus confirms the archaeological evidence, which suggests that the widespread use of writing which we see reflected in the fifth-century dramas was a radically new development, and absolutely unprecedented before the end of the eighth century.

Between the later eighth century and the time of Thespis, surviving written artifacts are few and far between; and although these artifacts show that writing was being used before Thespis' time for a wide range of recording activities—dedications, graffiti, private letters, laws—the sample is too small for us to guess at the numbers of people using it at this time. But while scholars continue to disagree about the exact literacy levels of the Greeks at various historical periods, it is certain that at least *some* ordinary citizens, craftsmen, poets, mercenary soldiers, and philosophers were using writing in the seventh and sixth centuries. It is also a near-certainty that by the end of the sixth, its use had become "virtually universal amongst the

---

18. Robert Wood (1976; orig. pub. 1769 and 1775) must be named as the earliest of these; since then, see Lorimer 1948; Parry 1971:xxvii; Willcock 1990; Powell 1991:200; Thomas 1992:12, 50.

men who made up the political and social elites" (W. Harris 1989:29).[19] From this point forward we can more easily watch the advance of literacy in the images painted on the sides of pots, jugs, and vases, which by the beginning of the fifth century have started depicting inscribed scrolls, many in scenes populated by female Muses and women.[20] Three of these that have survived can be dated to before the birth of Aeschylus; and by Sophocles' time, in the early years of the fifth century, the famous Sphinx was already being depicted in visual art as reading from a book between her paws (Pfeiffer 1968:27)—an image that we should keep in mind when considering this playwright's treatment of Oedipus' cleverness in solving her riddle. And on the Pronomos Vase, which remains the most detailed iconographic representation of theatrical activities from the end of the century, the poet is clearly portrayed as a writer, in possession of two book rolls.[21]

Although the spread of the alphabet may initially have been slow, by Kallias' time (i.e., later fifth century) literacy had become widespread enough among the Athenian citizenry at large for Aristophanes to joke that every member of his audience carried his or her own book into the theatre to check the literary allusions (*Frogs* 1114). Between the end of the eighth and the end of the fifth centuries, then, Greece had undergone something approaching a literate revolution, having been transformed from a place in which alphabetical writing was unknown to one where everyday life was so overrun with books and bookmongers (see especially *Birds*) that cheap editions of philosophy could be picked up from the bookstalls for a drachma (Plato *Apology* 26d), and whole shiploads of texts were being exported abroad (Xenophon *Anabasis* 7.5.14). Indeed, in the market of fifth-century Athens, as Eupolis tells us, one was as likely to find books as onions, garlic, and incense for sale (frag. 304 Edmonds 1957). No wonder, then, that the Athenian playwrights were keen to represent writing and its uses: in the period between Homer and Kallias, Greek culture had been transformed by it.[22]

But it is not primarily as a relatively new subject for poetry that the presence of the alphabet is worthy of note in Kallias' play—and, for that matter, in the dozens of other fifth-century dramas, tragedy and comedy alike, that feature writing as a subject. Rather, whether the early dramatists

19. See also W. Harris 1989:48, 56; also Turner 1951; Davison 1962; Harvey 1966; Pfeiffer 1968; Woodbury 1976; Burns 1981; Cole 1981; Stroud 1989; Thomas 1989, 1992; Robb 1994.

20. Pfeiffer 1968:27; Cole 1981:133.

21. See Winkler and Zeitlin 1990 plate 1.

22. See Robb 1994:4–21, 255 for analysis of this transformation.

were aware of it or not (and the likelihood is that they were not), the use of the alphabet had provided them with both the motive and the means to change the nature of poetic performance itself, to revolutionize it along the same lines that writing had altered their culture at large.

Before 534 B.C.E., when Thespis' first documented performance of a drama took place, there is nothing in Greek verbal art that exhibits the style used by Kallias to tell his story.[23] Kallias is not telling a story using his own voice, as the epic bards or their heirs the rhapsodes did; nor has he cast his speakers in roles that are identical to their own real-life identities, as the choral lyricists did. Rather, Kallias' piece, even in its fragmentary condition, exhibits all the salient generic features that we associate with dramatic form: dialogue, real people standing in for fictional characters, a visible enactment of the story rather than a narrative telling of it, and a tendency both toward colloquial speech and away from formulaic diction. Before Thespis' tragic victory in the sixth century, the Greek verbal arts were dominated by a Homeric storytelling style; and while all predramatic poetry was character-ized by the same spectacular performative elements that we find in tragedy and comedy—music, dance, costume, poetic meter, large festival audi-ences[24]—there is nothing in their single-voiced narrative style to prepare us for the genres of enactment which were to emerge out of them and which, by Kallias' time, were to have practically replaced them. In the *ABC Show*, as in all fifth-century drama, what we find is a type of poetic storytelling that represents visually, as the alphabet does; and like the alphabet, in which let-ters arbitrarily signify the sounds of speech, it is a mode of representation in which one thing is given to stand in arbitrarily for something else—actors for letters of the alphabet, young men for female writing students. And un-like any type of narrative that had been seen before, plays were stories that could be taught to and performed by anybody, and this as easily as Kallias' grammar students are shown learning the alphabet. Kallias' grammatical characters, given written letters to repeat, can tell the story by themselves, free from mediation by the skilled narrator who had dominated all previous genres of storytelling, and whose dependence on oral memory had made his poetic speech into a stylized, homogeneous monologue.

That Kallias' mode of representation was a new one, unknown in Greek

23. There is an ancient tradition that holds that it was in fact not Thespis but the choral lyricist Arion of Methymna who, over half a century earlier, had invented the dra-matic style by adding speaking satyrs to his choral songs (Herodotus 1.23). I will be dis-cussing his contribution in Chapter 2. For Thespis' dates, see Pickard-Cambridge 1968:72.

24. See especially Herington 1985 and Gentili 1988 for the "spectacular" qualities of Archaic poetry.

verbal art before the rise of the alphabet, is clear from antique sources. The Homeric epics, for example, provide detailed descriptions of the various performance arts that were practiced in the prealphabetic period of Greek civilization. And while there are many references to the performance of epic lays and to dance (*Iliad* 18.604–5; 24.720–22; *Odyssey* 4.17–19; 8.248–62, 370–80, 470ff.; 23.143–45), there is nothing that remotely resembles drama. Instead, the poetic arts represented in the *Iliad* and *Odyssey* are confined to the performative genre which these works themselves embody: a single bard sings, to his own lyre accompaniment, of the "acoustic renown" of heroes. Later, in the seventh and sixth centuries, when poets such as Alcman, Archilochus, Sappho, and Alcaeus augmented the Greek poetic repertoire with their lyric songs, the focus shifted somewhat away from the legendary deeds of heroes and toward the poet's personal concerns and feelings; but the performance procedure of these lyric singers remained essentially the same as Homer's had been, for their poems are generally intended for one voice,[25] and stylistically they never break away—in neither metrical structure, Homeric formulas, nor modes of thought—from the bardic tradition that preceded them.[26]

Thus, despite drama's maintenance of the luxuriant combination of song, dance, instrumental accompaniment, costume, and verse that had characterized these earlier poetic genres, its many formal and substantive innovations were profound enough for it to be considered a new art in its time.[27] As John Herington in particular has shown, the tradition of performed poetry has a long and vital history in Greece, one that stretches far back into the Bronze Age and defined Greece very much as a "song culture" until the fourth century, when it was transformed, under the influence of literacy, into what Rosalind Thomas has called a culture of "oratory" (1992).[28] The predramatic genre of epic has the longest documented history: current scholarship dates the composition of the Homeric epics to the end

---

25. The exception to this rule, and one to which we will be returning, is choral lyric, which was written either for performance by a specific group of celebrants (see, for example, Alcman's Maiden-Songs, where the singers are actually named; Edmonds 1952:51ff.), or for the celebration of a particular ritual event, such as a wedding (see Sappho's Epithalamies in Edmonds 1952:283ff.). The choirs for whom such choral lyrics were written are believed by Murray to have been highly trained professionals (1907:95–97).

26. For detailed discussion of this essential point, see Gentili 1988:16, 19, 20; and Miller 1994:20–95.

27. Aristotle *Poetics* 1449b11, 1449b7, 1449a13; Else 1965b; Gernet 1981:57, 17; Vernant and Vidal-Naquet 1990:23–25, 185.

28. See also Havelock, who was the first to describe this shift toward literate modes and the corresponding decline in the cultural primacy of poetic performance (1963, 1986).

of the eighth century B.C.E., although the earliest strata of these poems date back hundreds of years before that.[29] And lyric song, while closely related, is well attested throughout the seventh and sixth centuries.[30] Nevertheless, the traditional dominance by these two predramatic genres of the musical and poetic life of the Greeks—and especially of their musical competitions—was increasingly threatened by the parallel advances of the alphabet and drama. Although the upstart arts of tragedy and comedy were given official recognition at different times,[31] they shared enough formal and functional features, and differed from their poetic forebears in sufficiently similar ways, for them to be considered together as two faces of the new art of the theatre (*Poetics* 1448b12). A fourth-century B.C.E. writer named tragedy "the most people-pleasing and hypnotizing branch of poetry."[32] Such was its success, and comedy's, that even by the fifth century, "no first-rate poet in any of the traditional nondramatic genres was composing in Greece" (Herington 1985:99). As Aristotle remarks, "When tragedy and comedy came to light, poets were drawn either to one or to the other" (*Poetics* 1449a13). That is, whereas poets had in "ancient" times practised other genres (1448b11), particularly heroic epic and iambic lyric, they had turned almost en masse to tragedy and comedy, since these dramatic arts, while containing all the elements of the earlier forms, improved upon them in a number of ways, becoming "in each case a higher kind of art" and more valuable, especially in their appeal to audiences (1449a13; 1462a1–1462b16). Given the frequency among ancient sources of references to the fact, observed by Aristotle, that in drama, for the first time, the audience could "actually see the persons of the story" (1460a16), Herington speculates quite rightly that the generic novelty of drama in its time must have approximated that of the first cinematic spectacles in our century.

From a strictly chronological perspective, then, it is beyond dispute that the emergence and swift poetic hegemony of drama coincided with the advance of the alphabet in Greece. And yet, how many contemporary theorists of drama would be willing to take this coincidence a step further and entertain the idea that Western theatre, which seems to bear a family resemblance to the performative practices of preliterate societies, might be causally connected with a writing system—and a *particular* writing system at that? Surely there is something counterintuitive in the idea that an art so corpo-

29. Powell 1991:114.
30. Edmonds 1952, vols. 1, 2; Davison 1962:149–50; Nilsson 1968.
31. *Poetics* 1449a3–1449b4; Pickard-Cambridge 1968:72ff.
32. *Minos*, cited by Herington 1985:98.

real in nature, so oral in practice, could owe its central generic outlines to something as bookish as literacy. Nevertheless, the appearance of the alphabet in ancient Greece set in motion a whole host of changes in the nature of verbal life. Although these changes are related and were to some extent simultaneous, they can be analyzed separately, and I shall attempt to do so here. Together, and in the space of two hundred years, these literacy-sponsored changes succeeded in eliminating the conditions under which the monologizing poetry of oral epic was composed, and replacing them with ideal cultural circumstances for the creation of dramatic form.

In the first place, the existence of writing changed the nature of memory, and this by itself was almost sufficient to guarantee that the nature of poetry would change accordingly. In the absence of any written records, memory must remain a very approximate thing. In the absence of a (verbatim) written record, there is, in fact, no way to tell if something *has* been memorized or not. Consequently, in periods and places that lack writing, the very concept of exact repetition has no meaning. As I. M. L. Hunter has noted, "The human accomplishment of lengthy verbatim recall arises as an adaptation to written text and does not arise in cultural settings where text is unknown."[33] As the fieldwork of anthropologists and psychologists of memory has confirmed, societies without writing have a different concept of memory than do literates, and do not memorize things exactly.[34] Even oral bards' seemingly virtuoso feats of memory have been observed in our time to consist, in fact, of often radically dissimilar versions of a given narrative, which, however, are "experienced" by the bards themselves as "exactly the same."[35] As Clanchy (1979:233), Goody and Watt (1968:31–34), and Goody (1986:12) have noticed, members of oral societies *perceive* continuity where change is in fact the norm. Mythic narratives, laws, and customs are believed by those who repeat them orally to have been preserved intact for generations, whereas in fact all have undergone enormous changes without anyone noticing.

The continual shedding, without trace, of memories, history, laws, and customs which no longer have present relevance has been called a "homeostasis of orality" (Ong 1982:46): without written records of the progress

33. Cited in Goody 1987:294.

34. Ruth Finnegan (1977, 1990, 1992) is the one dissenting voice here; but as her examples are very brief Inuit poems, they should not be counted as genuine counterevidence. Thomas (1992:39–51) discusses Finnegan's objections usefully, but alas does not analyze the evidence they are based on. See also W. Harris (1989:31–33) against the common assumption that the memory of illiterates is simply better than that of literates.

35. Nilsson 1968:184–205; Lord 1960:17ff.; Goody 1987:86–88.

and change of actuality, a difference between "remembered" and "forgotten" cannot come into existence.[36] Without writing to control its vagaries, the human memory embellishes, deletes, transposes, and forgets altogether, and does so without any awareness of these changes. Recent findings in neurobiology have confirmed Walter Ong's view: memory is but the "storage of fragmentary but 'relevant' features."[37]

Accordingly, the culture dependent on memory will remain at the mercy of memory in maintaining itself. Unable to rely on books, libraries, and archives to keep track of information pivotal to its sense of identity and material well-being, an oral culture must seek and find its knowledge, truth, skills, history, and wisdom about itself in the living memories and speech of its members. Those members of an oral society whose memories stretch back farthest will necessarily be most valuable to the community at large, as will their ability to remember well and pass on what they know in memorizable form to others.

Oral cultures have thus been described as "conservative," in every sense of the word (Ong 1977:119). Given the ephemerality of the spoken word, and the mortality of the oral community's ultimate authorities, its elders, a number of strategies tend to be used in preliterate societies for performing this culturally essential job of conservation. Central among these is the use of constant repetition—of stories, songs, rituals, genealogies, ancestry lists, formulas, phrases, epithets. Ivan Kalmár has written about contemporary West Africans who still sit together throughout the day reciting ancestry lists from memory (1985:156); in oral cultures, the recital of genealogies constitutes a distinct speech genre (Halpern 1990:301–21). And in ancient Greece throughout its oral period, as in so many unlettered societies throughout the world, it was primarily through the recitation of poetry that culture was conserved. As J. A. Notopoulous pithily describes the situation, "the poet is the incarnate book of oral peoples."[38]

In the predramatic poems of Homer and Hesiod, we find perfect examples of the use of poetry as an aid to cultural memory. The catalogues of ships and gods and rivers and the lengthy genealogical lists surely functioned in their time as more than rhetorical ornamentation: they served the practical function of preserving knowledge and history. The stylistic peculiarities of these poems are also comprehensible only if understood as stemming directly from the limitations of an orally dependent cultural memory.

36. Thomas provides a useful discussion of this "structural amnesia" for ancient Greece (1989 passim; 1992:108–12).
37. Changeux 1988:49; see also Loftus 1979, 1980; Finkel 1988:62.
38. Cited in Havelock 1963:57 n. 21.

Not only in Homer and Hesiod, whose works are dated to the eighth century, but also in the lyrics of the seventh century, we find a poetic style that bears all the distinctive traits of an oral composition-in-performance process.[39] As with other oral poetry around the world—from ancient Sumeria, through the former Yugoslavia and into pre-contact North America—the language of the Homeric epics exhibits a "formulaic" linguistic style.[40] Features common to verbal compositions which, like Homer's, were carried out without the aid of writing include a rigid poetic meter, a ring-like, episodic structure, the use of memorable epithets, stock similes, and other such formulaic expressions which can be plugged in whole, as metrics allow, plenty of repetition, and the joining of phrases with principal conjunctions ("and . . . and . . .").[41] These features are common throughout the world to poetry composed in and for oral recitation, and have been observed in North American aboriginal verse as well (Petrone 1990:19–22).

With this oral-formulaic method, it is possible for a singer of tales to recite poems thousands of lines long without the aid of a fixed copy. Rather than memorizing anything verbatim, the *aoidos* or bard learns a vocabulary of formulas and a technique for manipulating and recombining them within metrical constraints. As C. M. Bowra explains:

> The art and the technique of poetry are passed from generation to generation by a strict training in the needs of oral composition and recitation. The young bard learns from his elders the main outlines of stories, the names and personalities of characters, the rules of metre, the appropriate epithets for things and places and people, and, above all, an enormous mass of formulaic phrases, which are his main mater-

39. Many scholars have devoted book-length studies to demonstrating that the Archaic poets, particularly Homer, composed their verses orally, without the aid of writing. These include Lorimer 1948; Lord 1960, 1991; Havelock 1963, 1986; Nilsson 1968; Parry 1971, 1989; Ong 1977, 1982; Nagy 1981, 1986; Foley 1981, 1986, 1990, 1991; Goody 1987; Willcock 1990; Powell 1991. Of the more recent discussions of the orality of Archaic poetry, Parry 1989:198–264, Powell 1991:113–200, and Thomas 1992:50ff. are the most critically minded and thorough. Even Thomas—who has made it her business to carry on Finnegan's (1977) work of problematizing the image of oral poetry as popularized in the early days by Lord (1960)—has concluded that "whether or not Homer knew the art of writing, he would have remained an 'oral' poet by any meaningful sense of the word" (1992:50). The same point has been made about the other predramatic poets, notably by Gentili 1988:19–20, 56.

40. See Lord 1960, 1981, 1990, 1991; Parry 1971, 1989; Hatto 1980; Foley 1981, 1986, 1990, 1991; Bauman 1986; Duggan 1990; and Nagler 1990.

41. For this last feature of oral composition, see Fowler 1987:27. Aristotle calls it "parataxis" (*Rhetoric* 3.9.1409a24).

ial in composition and his abiding resource to meet almost any need. Once a phrase has been formed and tested and proved its worth, it commands respect because it is established and comes from the past. It is expected and even demanded in the appropriate context. (1969:4)

In the absence of a written version of any of their materials, then, the oral singers in effect stitched their poems together during performance, plugging their internalized stock of phrases and formulas into appropriate metrical slots. Unlike modern literary texts, which are generally composed once and then perhaps performed many times thereafter, the epic songs that we attribute to Homer—and which he had inherited from a long chain of bards and immortalized under his own name[42]—were in effect created anew each time they were performed, improvised with the aid of a vocabulary of ready-made blocks of utterance which could be "regularly used under the same metrical conditions to express a given essential idea" (Parry 1989:30).

From the Bronze Age down to the end of Greece's strictly oral period, this formulaic compositional style was alone responsible for preserving the valuable "winged words" not just of poetry but of all culturally significant discourse—which were, through these years and beyond, basically one and the same thing.[43] And it did its job well. The oral style, however, for all its efficiency in preserving important cultural materials in the absence of writing, had a number of specific consequences for storytelling.

First among these was that the mythological characters portrayed in poetry could not be represented as individualized, particularized speakers. Consider the representation of speech in the *Iliad* and *Odyssey*. Homer's heroes are simply not characterized by their speech; or rather, if speech is a guide to personality, their personalities are virtually interchangeable. What distinguishes Agamemnon from Odysseus, or Hektor from Menelaus is not a distinctive word choice or the use of characteristic constructions or

42. The question of how we came to attribute these songs to a virtual unknown named Homer has long plagued classical scholarship and continues to be the subject of controversy. The literature on the subject is vast, and the issue too complex to go into here. Powell's (1991) contribution to the debate supports my own view that Homer's name ended up on these stories because he was the foremost singer of them at the time when they were written down, or perhaps that they were written down in his time precisely because the alphabet was available and he was such a masterly singer of them. These hypotheses gain support from twentieth-century researches into oral poetry, particularly those conducted by Lord (1960), which indicate that the notion of authorship, of poetic property, first came on the scene with literacy and when attempts were made to commit poems to writing.

43. See esp. Jaeger 1960, vol. 1, and Havelock 1963, 1978, on the cultural function of poetry in Greece.

metaphors in what they say. Not only does an oral bard think nothing of giving identical speeches to a variety of unlike characters, but his poetic procedure actively encourages him to do so. As M. M. Willcock (1990:10) has shown, the exact same words are spoken by Agamemnon in one place and by Odysseus in another (*Iliad* 9.122–57, 264–99).[44] Roughly the same soliloquy is spoken on one occasion by Odysseus (11.404–10) and on another by Menelaus (17.91–105),[45] and the selfsame formula is used to express the thought of Agenor (21.553–70), Hektor (22.99–130), and Achilleus (22.378–94).[46] In the *Odyssey*, Penelope and Eumaios deliver themselves of the exact same words as well (17.41–44 and 16.23–24),[47] and the list goes on. What distinguishes characters in epic is primarily the bard's use of descriptive epithets: the brilliant Odysseus, the glorious Hektor, the warlike Menelaus. And Hesiod, who rarely attempts to represent the speech of his figures at all, relies similarly on epithets to characterize them: wide-seeing Zeus, glorious Hermes, golden Aphrodite. This use of formulas to particularize and differentiate characters often fails altogether, however, as we see in Hesiod, when for example two or more unlike figures end up with the same epithet ("trim-ankled" for both Medea and Clymene; and Hera, Aglaia, and Ariadne are all indifferently described as someone's "fertile wife" [*Theogony* 497–529; 907–68]).

Because the representation of speech in epic is controlled by the metrical and formulaic consistency demanded by an oral mode, a fictional character, in the hands of an oral storyteller, can be represented as saying only what the available metrical units in a line will permit, and all speeches are

44. This is the thirty-five–line offer of treasure that begins, in Lattimore's translation, with "seven unfired tripods; ten talents' weight of gold; twenty shining cauldrons; and twelve horses, strong, race-competitors who have won prizes in the speed of their feet. That man would not be poor in possessions, to whom were given all these have won me, nor be unpossessed of dearly honoured gold." The two speeches end with "All this I will bring to pass for him, if he changes from his anger," and they are identical except that Odysseus says "he," "Agamemnon," and "you" instead of "me," "I," and "him."

45. It is the internal debate weighing two evils which begins "And [or 'deeply'] troubled, he spoke to his own great-hearted spirit: 'Ah me, what will become of me?' " and ends "Yet still, why does the heart within me debate on these things?" and "Then why does my own heart within me debate this?" There are small differences within the two versions of the speech, but the pattern is the same.

46. All three fighters say, "Yet still, why does the heart within me debate on these things?" and two begin with similar utterances: "Ah me! If I run away before the strength of Achilleus," and "Ah me! If I go now inside the wall and the gateway. . . ."

47. Both speeches begin "You have come, Telemachos, sweet light; (and) I thought I would never see you again, when you had gone in the ship to Pylos," and end "But come now. . . ."

largely determined in advance by the existence of tried-and-true schemes. For this reason, speech as represented by the oral means of the epic is not particularized beyond the point of basic pragmatics: the uttering of a threat, the offering of thanks, the announcement of a wish to die at once.

Furthermore, the homogeneity of speech as represented in epic is but a kind of symptom of the fact that the bard speaks in his own voice for all characters. In Homer and Hesiod a single speaker delivers all utterances, both his own narrative and the sayings of the represented figures. To indicate transitions between the two modes, formulaic phrases are used here as well: "So she spoke," "So he spoke," "Then in answer again spoke brilliant swift-footed Achilleus," "Then in answer again spoke powerful Agamemnon." Thus, both in the sameness of speech style from one represented character to the next, and in the fact that in performance, all speech is literally of a single piece—that is, it belongs to one speaker—epic diction turns all speech diversity into a formulaic monologue. And owing to the demands of an oral composition-in-performance style, it could not possibly have done otherwise.

In addition, the partly improvisatory, partly obedient technique of composition-in-performance was not an easy one to learn or master. Requiring a lifetime of practice or apprenticeship, expertise in the oral style of poetic performance was rare. Although, as Kevin Robb puts it, oral poetry is always "hoarded by the entire community," it nevertheless remains in the hands of specialists: "It is everywhere in oral societies discovered to be the special preserve of tribal singers and reciters" (1994:33). In times before writing, traditional narratives had no existence "outside" of the bards who knew how to tell them, and in consequence they remained the exclusive property of those who knew the technique. As we see from a number of contemporary contexts, oral traditional stories and songs are collective property through time (from one generation to another), but they tend to be the monopolized possession of certain specialized individuals or groups at a given moment. In aboriginal Canadian culture, for example, only "certain initiated elders" have the right to tell some stories (Petrone 1990:11), and to this day families possess particular songs over which they have exclusive control. Either one must be a member of a special society, such as the Medewin of the Ojibwa (11), or have learned the special skills of an *aoidos* from apprenticeship to one who has already mastered and internalized them. The esoteric nature of much oral material is obscured by the communal nature of its reception; but all members of the collective are not equally authorized or able to produce it. Accordingly, in the *Odyssey* (17.382ff.), the bard is described as a specialist, a craftsman; and both through the epithets attached to him and through his traditional blindness, the oral singer is always depicted as one of the Muses' special elect, a rare and divine creature (1.335, 7.62–64). Hesiod, too, describes his special initiation into poetry by the Muses (*Theogony* 20–40), a process of divine selection that was assumed to create all poets. Similarly, in contemporary Africa, the *izibongo* singer believes that his skill is "inspired by God[;] it is a gift" (Whitaker 1996:205–7). Thus we can begin to see that traditional poetry's monologic character was, like the formulaic style itself, tied directly to its orality, its confinement to the world of sound. That is, in an oral context, the monological form of poetry is all but guaranteed by the esoteric nature of the technique needed to remember it: the bard *had* to speak for all his characters, for only he knew how to keep the story going.

At some point between the eighth and the sixth centuries, however, the Homeric poems were written down. This event, despite continued uncertainty as to exactly when it took place, was to have incalculable consequences for the history of the performing arts in Greece. In addition to signing the death warrant of the oral style, so to speak, it was to prove the first significant step toward the invention of theatre.

Lamentably, scholars have yet to reach anything approaching a consensus about when Homer was "alphabeticalized." And yet this is hardly to be wondered at, given the fragmentary and circumstantial nature of the evidence. Eric Havelock believed that the epic stories were written down at some point between 700 and 650 B.C.E. (1963:115); Rudolf Pfeiffer can say with confidence only that a text of these works must have been in existence by the sixth century at the latest (1968:8). In 1987, Robert Fowler wrote that "most [scholars] now accept" that a Homeric text existed at the end of the seventh century (33); more recently, however, Barry Powell has argued that the Homeric poems were written down in the earliest days of Greek literacy, that is, toward the end of the eighth century (1991). Depending on whom one wishes to side with, this means that a fixed, written version of Thespis' narrative inheritance either had been available for generations, or was a relative novelty at the time of the first dramatic performances.

Briefly summarized, the evidence is as follows: during the seventh and sixth centuries, the Greeks' love of poetry and competition manifested itself in "numerous and much frequented" contests in the recitation of Homer and Hesiod.[48] Hesiod (frag. 357) and the Homeric *Hymn to Apollo* tell us of the contests held at the festival of Apollo on Delos; Herodotus in *The His-*

48. Gentili 1988:156; Bowra 1969:54; also Powell 1991:216.

tory (5.67) tells of choruses sung at Sicyon; Pausanias (10.7.3) saw a tripod inscribed in commemoration of the musical competitions at the Pythian games in 586; and from Dodona, we have a surviving inscription by a competing rhapsode named Terpiscles, who dedicated a tripod to Zeus in celebration of his victory.[49] The competitive recitation of poetry is also known to have taken place at the Panathenaia, which was believed by the ancients to have been either instituted or expanded by Peisistratos around 566.[50]

The fact that artisans from all over the Greek world were representing "Homeric"[51] episodes on their jugs and pots as early as the seventh century does seem to suggest that epic lays were being recited before large festival audiences at least in the century before Thespis (Myres 1958:15). The seventh century also recommends itself as the date for this phenomenon through the evidence of the poetry being written at the time: Callinus (ca. 660) mentions the *Thebais* as Homer's work; Semonides (ca. 630) quotes a line from the *Iliad* and attributes it to "a man of Chios" (said to be Homer's birthplace); and the poets Alcman, Archilochus, and Stesichorus, all of whom were active in the middle years of the seventh century, clearly knew Homer's poetry well.[52] Given that these poets came from different cities, they would have been exposed to Homer either through festival recitations—to which audiences came from far and wide—or through written copies, which themselves could have circulated far and wide. Powell argues that the Homeridai, a society devoted to the preservation and performance of Homer's works, possessed the first manuscript, or copies of it, that went right back to Homer's time (1991:232). But the earliest concrete evidence that we have for the existence of a written version is the rule, datable to the sixth century, which specifies that the reciters at these contests must deliver the stories in their proper order (Plato *Hipparchus* 228b). As Pfeiffer concludes, this contest regulation strongly suggests that "a traditional text must have been available to which the rhapsodes were compelled to keep" (1968:8). And he is probably right. As we see from both Homer's description of bardic procedure in the *Odyssey* (1.340; 7.97; 8.500), and from Albert Bates Lord's fieldwork with oral poetry in the former Yugoslavia (1960:30), unlettered singers are not naturally inclined to think of their repertoire of

49. Gentili 1988:156; Bowra 1969:54.

50. Dillon and Garland 1994:102.

51. These representations seem to have been based most often on mythic narratives other than the *Iliad* or the *Odyssey.*

52. Murray 1907:8; Fowler 1987:8–37. Fowler provides useful lists of the many quotations and imitations of Homer and Hesiod in the seventh- and sixth-century lyric poets, and analyzes them for the probable extent of their reliance on a fixed text.

stories as a continuous, chronological whole. On the contrary, they select an episode to suit the mood of or fulfill a request from the particular audience they happen to be addressing; and they rarely sing any of these discrete, decontextualized episodes to the end, for events that take place within the audience in the palace or the café are allowed to interrupt the performance. As Homer sings at the start of the *Odyssey,* "Begin it, goddess, at whatever point you will." Epic lays were thus liable to start and stop in a random, episodic way that is quite alien to literates, who are accustomed to thinking in terms of beginnings, middles, and ends, and in terms of an uninterrupted narrative line from cover to cover.[53] Thus, any rule about chronological continuity where Homer is concerned is a probable sign of the presence of literate thinking. C. M. Bowra agrees: the predramatic reciters of Homeric works "must have learned [them] by heart from written texts" (1969:54).

According to Fowler, the existence of a written Homer in the very early sixth century is proved incontrovertibly by internal textual evidence from sixth-century lyric poetry (1987:33–37). That a written Homer existed in the time of such poets as Ibycus and Solon is also suggested by the sixth-century controversy about textual tampering by the Athenians. There was a belief among the ancients that, as a way of justifying their political claims on places such as Salamis, the tyrants of Athens had inserted into the epics passages that were not authentic.[54] This sort of controversy certainly seems to smack of literate thinking.[55] For, as G. S. Kirk observes, "with the concept of the fixed text comes the concept of the correct text" (1985:110), and such anxieties about the authenticity of an official version are not likely to have emerged unless there was in fact a single version that could be held up as the true one. Clearly, by the sixth century, the Homeric poems were being treated as "canonical," "not susceptible of expurgation or amendment" (Myres 1958:20), which does argue in favor of their reduction to writing by this time. And although the evidence here is getting later and later, Cicero repeats an earlier—and, according to Robb, "fairly reliable" (1994:255)—anecdote which credits Hipparchus' father, Peisistratos (born ca. 605–600) with having collected the "scattered songs" of Homer and with having "arranged in their present order" the Homeric works which had previously been sung only in fragments (Gentili 1988:18).

In light of the lateness of such evidence, some scholars are skeptical that

53. Murray provides a lucid account of how the epics, originally sung in self-contained episodes, came to achieve the literary, unified form in which we read them today (1907:20–22).

54. See Murray 1907:11–12; Myres 1958:31.

55. See, for example, Herodotus *History* 5.67, 7.161.

this so-called Peisistratid recension of the epics actually took place. And yet, as John Myres argues, even if such editing did take place under the sponsorship of the Peisistratid tyrants, it is not likely that this would have been the first time the epics were written down (1958:15–16). Were it not for the existence of a few additional scraps of evidence, we should probably have to say simply that the date of the first inscription of the epics is undecidable.

Foremost among these scraps is the lively literary activity of the Ionian philosophers and rhapsodes of the sixth century. From Plato's (later) portrait of the rhapsode Ion, we know quite a lot about what these reciters did. Like actors, they wore beautiful costumes; and like actors, they performed before large festival audiences. But unlike actors, they performed the older, by this time classic poetry of Homer, Hesiod, Archilochus—in short, the monological poetry of the archaic bard. And that they did so from fixed, written copies of these works, at least in the fifth century, is made quite clear by Xenophon, who describes these rhapsodes as "very precise about the exact words of Homer, although very foolish themselves" (*Memorabilia* 4.2, 10); he also reports that a contemporary of Socrates, Euthydemos of Chios, possessed a complete text of Homer with all verses intact (4.2, 10). Plato's depiction of the rhapsode as a mere second-hand "interpreter" (*Ion* 535a) points up nicely the extent to which poetic performance had changed since the days of the oral bards: because he need know nothing himself but how to memorize a particular text, the rhapsode is no longer the kind of expert craftsman that the oral bard was. And Socrates criticizes him for this reason, saying that he possesses no special art or craft (*techne*).

But it is clear from the *Ion* that the rhapsode did in fact have a specialty—albeit not one with which Plato was likely to be impressed. This specialty was *textual interpretation*. Although Socrates quickly denigrates even this skill, since it is evidently not transferable to the work of other poets, Ion is quite proud of his ability to explain and analyze Homeric texts. Now, the criticism of Homer had become something of a minor industry by this time.[56] In his *History of the Peloponnesian War*, Thucydides remarks on the textual inconsistencies in Homer (1.10), as does Herodotus, who claims, after citing lengthy passages from the *Iliad* and the *Odyssey*, that some of these discrepancies are serious enough to cast doubt on the authorship of works traditionally attributed to Homer (i.e., the *Cypria* and *Epigoni*; *History* 2.116–117, 4.32). By the end of the fifth century, such literary debates about the age, origin, authenticity, meaning, and correctness of words in

56. See Lamberton and Keaney 1992.

Homer and elsewhere were raging among Sophists such as Prodicus, Gorgias, Protagoras, and Hippias; and these critics, who, like rhapsodes, wore purple robes and performed at festivals, were equated wherever they went with books and bookishness.[57]

But when Aristotle, in passing, refers to these hair-splitting literary disputes among the "ancient critics of Homer" (*Metaphysics* 1093a26), there is evidence that by "ancient" he meant sixth-century, and that the practice of literary criticism dates back to Thespis' time at least. Pherecydes, a philosopher active in the middle of the sixth century, is the earliest certain writer of prose who can be credited with what we would today call literary criticism. In his book, which Diogenes Laertius (1.119) says was still in existence in the third century C.E., Pherecydes discussed aspects of the epics etymologically, substituting unusual grammatical variants for the names of Homeric gods as a way of explaining their origins (frags. 42, 44, 49 Kirk, Raven, and Schofield 1987). Even if he had not been specifically credited with having been "the first to bring out a book in prose" (Diogenes Laertius 1.116), there would still be little doubt that Pherecydes was a user of texts, since etymological activities of this type would depend on the evidence of letters.[58] The next important pre-Thespian literary critic was Xenophanes of Colophon (born ca. 570). Xenophanes was perhaps the first great skeptic produced by the literate age, and something of a scientific empiricist, too, judging from his surprisingly advanced studies of fossils and his explanatory theory of cyclical ocean levels (Herodian frag. 37).[59] He seems to have been most famous, though, for his criticism of the epic poems, particularly in their representation of gods, which Xenophanes found implausibly anthropomorphic, and immoral.[60] As Diogenes Laertius tells us, Xenophanes wrote not only against Homer and Hesiod, but also against the opinions of a number of philosophers of his own time as well (9.18).[61] Xenophanes' mocking criticism of Homer was not left unchallenged, however. Accordingly, the last of Homer's sixth-century critics who deserves mention here is Theagenes of Rhegium, a little-known writer and rhapsode who is said to have been among the first to defend Homer's works on allegorical grounds.[62] He ar-

57. See esp. Plato *Theaetetus* 162a, *Protagoras, Gorgias;* Aristophanes *Broilers* frag. 490 Edmonds 1957; see also O'Sullivan 1996:115–27.

58. Kirk, Raven, and Schofield doubt that his book would have been the first prose work to be published; but they speculate that his book, and the book of Anaximander—which they think may have been roughly contemporary with it (ca. 547)—may simply have survived in a more substantial form than earlier works (1987:52).

59. Number 184 in Kirk, Raven, and Schofield 1987.

60. Numbers 166, 167, 168, 169 ibid.

61. Number 161 ibid.

62. Pfeiffer 1968:9; see also Myres 1958:34; Richardson 1992:31.

gued that Homer's gods were intended as symbolic representations of the forces of nature, not as literal deities. Thus it was not only by Ion in the fifth century but also by the contemporaries of Thespis in the sixth that textual criticism of Homer was being practiced.

About the works of Thespis almost nothing is known. But the tradition of textual criticism inaugurated in his time, while probably more familiar to us in its late fifth-century, Sophistical incarnation, is one that was to bear its most distinctive fruits in the works of the early tragedians, Aeschylus, Sophocles, and Euripides. For these dramatic works, with their often radical reinterpretation, revision, and alteration of Homeric myth, represent a kind of sustained textual critique of the poetic repertoire of the time.[63] In order to view Thespis' historic performance of a dramatic work in 534 B.C.E. in its proper light, therefore, it must be borne in mind that he lived in a time when the defining performative materials of Greek culture were no longer exclusively oral, but were subject instead to the scrutiny of readers.

Can we imagine the moment when the epics were written down for the first time? To do so requires that we understand just how well suited the alphabet was for recording Greek poetry. As G. E. Lessing pointed out with respect to the artistic media of painting and poetry, a representing medium is likely to have innate potentialities and characteristic weaknesses; and this is true for representing media such as scriptory systems, too. A nonphonetic type of writing, in the form of Linear A and B, was known in Greece before the alphabet; but the samples of Linear B that have come down to us show that it was not a subtle and sensitive recording device like the alphabet.[64] On the contrary, it was so cumbersome and specialist that, in Pylos for example, all writing seems to have been done by the same thirty or so scribes (Stroud 1989:109). Given its characteristics, it is not surprising to find that Linear B seems to have been used only for recording things like inventories (for metalworking, wool production, agricultural produce, defense, trade in imported luxuries, and so on) (108). Most significantly for our purposes, no poetry has been found in this script. As C. M. Bowra describes it, Linear B was "unusually inefficient, even by the standards of its own time." There is

---

63. See Chapter 2, in which these innovations and alterations are discussed with examples. Segal (1986, 1992) also provides excellent discussions of the critical spirit of early drama in comparison with earlier poetry.

64. A convincing solution to the puzzle of Linear A has still not been proposed. See Chadwick 1990:156.

"no sign that the script was used for anything that might be called literature, and if it was, it would have done its task abominably" (1969:4).[65]

In bold contrast to the uses to which Linear B was put, however, the alphabet was used to record poetry almost instantaneously. In fact, the incredible speed with which it was put to this end is so striking that some scholars have been led to hypothesize that the Greek alphabet "might have been invented as a notation for Greek verse" (Wade-Gery 1952:11–14).[66] This does not seem very likely, really, as the Greeks learned phonetic letters from the mercantile Phoenicians in the course of trade: its earliest use in Greece is therefore liable to have been connected with commerce and property (Jeffrey 1990:7–13). Nevertheless, it must be admitted that no commercial uses for writing are actually attested in the writing samples that have survived from the eighth century. On the contrary, nearly all the earliest artifacts show that writing was first used in Greece to record short snatches of hexameter verse, the language of epic poetry (Powell 1991:221). Among these eighth-century inscriptions, which are only a few lines long, the artifact known as "Nestor's cup" (ca. 740–20) constitutes, as Barry Powell points out, the first known literary allusion in the Western tradition, for it refers directly to a royal drinking vessel as described by Homer. The early use of alphabetic writing for recording Greek poetry, and then the Homeric epics, was not coincidental. Both in the phonetic principle itself and in the way the alphabet is learned, there are many clues to be found which explain why the Greeks only started inscribing their oral poetry after they had developed an alphabet.

We can see the characteristics of the Greek phonetic system most vividly when we contrast it with the systems in use elsewhere in the ancient world. In the Chinese system, for example, then as now, the written unit is the morpheme, and there are tens of thousands of them (guesses have been made at fifty thousand; Taylor 1988:203). Since these legions of signs do not code sound directly, they must simply be memorized. As a result, the Chinese system, like Egyptian hieroglyphics, was practically destined to remain in the hands of a specialist elite. Aided neither by an alphabet to organize words along predictable lines, nor by a thoroughgoing phonetic principle, students of such scripts need to be very learned even to use a dictionary properly. Under such learning conditions, Egyptian script could easily be

---

65. See also Chadwick 1990 passim for detailed description of the ambiguities and peculiarities of Linear B.

66. See also Pfeiffer 1968:23; Powell 1991 passim.

kept a "sacred language" indefinitely; and Chinese writing, too, was used exclusively for "ritual and magic purposes" for over a thousand years (Hagège 1988:79). The illiteracy rate in China even at the beginning of the twentieth century has been estimated at 80 percent (Taylor 1988:207). In short, logographic scripts tend by nature to remain in the hands of a small elite of the specially initiated, for much study is needed to acquire them.

It should be noted, however, that languages "choose" their own most efficient writing system; there is no such thing as a better or worse type of script. As a monosyllabic language with no inflected endings, a number of separate "tones," and an unusually heavy proportion of homophones, Chinese could not efficiently be represented with an alphabet. By the same token, the Greeks modified the Semitic consonantal alphabet into a fully phonetic system complete with vowels because their language demanded it.[67] As Eric Havelock has stressed, however, the Greeks' (necessary) discovery of the vowel made it possible for them to reduce the ambiguity of syllabic writing systems, and in so doing eliminate the dependence on specialist scribes that inhibited the spread of writing elsewhere. With the invention of vowels, writing became genuinely phonetic, and for the first time even nonspecialists were able to read and write (1963:129 n. 6). Consequently, (alphabetic) writing could be, and was, used in Greece immediately for private purposes and by obviously untrained individuals. Eighth-century inscriptions include the personal messages and graffiti of ordinary people (Jeffrey 1990:63); and as writing became more widespread in the following centuries, "the skill was certainly not confined to aristocrats or a class of specialists" (W. Harris 1989:48).[68] Scribal specialists, who in so many other ancient cultures reserved writing for their own exclusionary purposes, did not do so in ancient Greece.[69]

And they could not have done had they tried, for the phonetic principle guaranteed that even unschooled sausage sellers could learn to read and

---

67. Taylor 1988:203–10; Hagège 1988:76; DeFrancis 1989.

68. The question of exactly, or even roughly, how many people were literate in ancient Greece at any given point in the advance of literacy, although interesting in itself, is irrelevant to the present discussion. Regardless of whether there were thirty or thirty thousand literates in the eighth century B.C.E. in Greece, surviving artifacts dated to that period show distinctly that within the same century that the alphabet was developed, it was already being used to record poetry by unskilled hands. William Harris devotes a book to the sensitive question of how many literates Greece possessed, and what level of literacy was likely to have been attained by them (1989:vii–115); Jeffrey 1990, Stroud 1989, Powell 1991:119–86, and Thomas 1992:56–88 discuss the archaeological evidence from the eighth and seventh centuries which proves that early Greek writers were ordinary amateurs.

69. Goody 1986:17; Thomas 1992:57.

write with minimal study. With the acquisition of a mere twenty-four signs (other alphabets have between twenty and thirty-seven), students of the Greek alphabet can transcribe any and every word in their spoken vocabulary without special study. They may not spell these words "correctly," but the phonetic principle will guarantee the decipherability of their writing by anyone who knows the same twenty-four signs. What is more, it is possible with an alphabet to transcribe words one doesn't even know, such as foreign or archaic words, specialist jargon, or words disguised by dialect—a fact which will prove significant for the development of theatre, as we shall see. This connection between phoneticism and ease in transcribing oral material is further demonstrated by the modern Chinese example, where mass education has not been able to proceed without the adoption of the phonetic pinyin script. The creation in Japan of the phonetic Kana scripts between the eighth and twelfth centuries C.E. has helped guarantee the extremely high literacy rates there (although socioeconomic factors have undoubtedly contributed as well; cf. Taylor 1988:210).[70]

As Powell (1991) has demonstrated at length, use of the alphabet was an absolute precondition for the recording of Homer: the artificiality of epic diction, plus the essential role played in it by lengthened and shortened vowels, all but ensured that the Greeks could not have recorded their hexameter poetry without a phonetic system. But there is more to say about the nature of the alphabet than that it was an appropriate recording device for epic verse. One of the first linguists to emphasize the inherent traits of the alphabet was Wilhelm von Humboldt (1767–1835). Through a comparison of the functioning of foreign, logographic scripts with his own culture's alphabetical writing, Humboldt was able to isolate some of the latter's key defining characteristics, and his observations remain valid today. In his treatises "On Alphabetic Writing and Its Connection with the Structure of Language," and "On the Connection of Writing with Language,"[71] Humboldt notes that alphabetic script is distinguished by its tendency to represent sound separated from meaning (Christy 1989:339). In this tendency Humboldt saw more than a mechanical operation; he saw the alphabet's sound/sense separation as effecting a profound change in the relationship between people and their language. To begin with, the use of the alphabet

---

70. William Harris argues that the high literacy rate in countries such as contemporary Israel and Japan is not proof that mass literacy is unrelated to the writing system: modern industrialized nations have remedies for the absence of phoneticism (such as the printing press, dictionaries, textbooks, and mass education) which Archaic civilizations certainly lacked (1989:46).

71. Cited by Christy 1989:339ff.

requires the breaking down of the sounds of speech into their smallest units. These sounds, called phonemes, are in turn represented by a minimal number of signs—letters—whose main distinguishing feature is that they have no referential function. What a letter represents is not a meaning but just a sound, or range of sounds, which is meaningless in itself. Whereas, for example, Semitic signs such as *bet, mem, 'ayin, yod,* and *rosh* stood originally for "house," "water," "eye," "hand," and "head," the Greek equivalents after the phonetic revolution—*beta, mu, omicron, iota, rho*—have no meaning at all; they represent only sounds (Naveh 1988:84–89). Alphabetic writing thus represents speech by "hearing it"; alphabetic writing acts as the "ear" of speech. And because what is heard must be aurally atomized into representing letters, the sounds of speech become the "subject" of alphabetic writing, a subject requiring analysis.

Logographic writing, on the contrary, could be said to remain comparatively "deaf" to speech. Characters in Chinese, for example, do have a phonetic portion, but it notes only certain features of the word and not its pronunciation. That is, a sign in Chinese may represent a sound, but may also represent a totally different sound in another context. In Chinese, and in the logographic part of Japanese, there are no characters that have "a fixed phonetic value for all elements of the language" (Hagège 1988:77). Because they are disconnected in this way from the sounds of spoken language, logograms, according to Julia Kristeva, encode speech "without hearing/understanding it: without hearing/understanding its ideal and phonetic autonomy as separate from what it designates." In "dissociat[ing] the spoken chain from what it expresses" and encoding only its sounds, alphabetic writing on the contrary frees language up from its referential, world-ordering functions and reveals it as a subject for abstract, acoustical analysis (Kristeva 1989:93–94). In Humboldt's view this promotes a detached, objective contemplation of language because, with the alphabet, it is possible to think of constituent linguistic forms without simultaneously invoking what Kristeva has called the whole "semantic and cosmic classificatory" system which each logogram encodes. For logograms function by actually constituting the speaker's semantic relation to the world. A logogram makes inextricable "the concept, the sound, and the thing"; a Chinese word, for example, "doesn't lose the thing; it only transfers it to a plane where it becomes ordered with others in a regulated system. In this way *la langue* and 'the real' are one and the same thing" (Kristeva 1989:94).

To visualize the alphabet's "speech-centrism" as clearly as possible, we might try the following somewhat silly but effective experiment. Imagine an itinerant Chinese bard singing a long traditional poem about legendary or historical personages and deeds. If the script available to his listeners is a lo-gography, he need only sing the word *ma* with a less than perfectly distinct tone for them to fail utterly to know whether they should write the charac-ter for "agate," or the character for "weights," or for "ant," "masurium," "mother," "clamp," "sacrifice," "scold," or "question particle" (DeFrancis 1989:103). In everyday speech, such extreme ambiguity would not occur; but in poetic speech, surprising words often appear in unexpected places. This is especially true of traditional oral poetry, which preserves archaic forms and accumulates terms and idioms from widely separated geographic locations. If the logographer/spectator of this epic performance heard an unfamiliar word, say "petard," and he did not know the character for it, he would have no choice but to put together a sequence of characters chosen for their pho-netic value. Such a stringing together of characters whose phonetic associa-tions approximate the sound of an unknown spoken word is obviously cumbersome. But its inefficiency lies mainly in the fact that there would be nothing to prevent the next reader of his manuscript from decoding the signs *semantically* and reading, in place of "petard," "creek him two beans" (*pu ta er dou*).[72] This demonstration is fanciful and actually somewhat un-fair, for "petard" is an English, not a Chinese word. But by contrast to the ease with which the Homeric epics could be written down, the unwieldiness of a nonalphabetical system is significant. Having learned twenty-four let-ters, an ancient recorder of a Homeric performance could write down every single word that he heard, even if he had never heard half of them before.

In light of the logographic system's lack of interest in the sounds of speech, it should not be surprising to discover that Chinese verbal culture has no epic (Hsu 1985:378; Lu Hsun 1959:19). Although Tao-ching Hsu in-vokes a political explanation for this "well-known" anomaly—state suppres-sion during the Chou dynasty (1122–255 B.C.E.)—it is equally likely that this absence of a unified body of popular mythology has its source in the writing system. Or, more accurately, one should say "seeming absence," for the Chi-nese writing system may simply never have recorded an epic. Given the likely number of ancient Chinese literates, and given the sacred/hierarchical nature of their involvements, it is plausible that popular Chinese legends and myths from earlier oral times were never recited to anyone who knew enough characters to write them down. In fact there is a story that palace of-ficials in the Chou dynasty were sent into the streets to collect the people's myths and legends; but as a writer from the Han dynasty (206 B.C.E.–220

72. DeFrancis makes this same point, albeit much more effectively, in *The Chinese Language* (1989 passim); Coulmas discusses similar problems in Japanese (1989:127).

C.E.) reports, this was done more as an attempt at surveillance, to learn how the other half lived: "The ancient kings who wanted to know local customs appointed these officers to report on them" (Hsun 1959:23). Thus, if Chinese myths were at any point written down, it would have been by official state scribes, not by the people who actually told and enjoyed these stories themselves. Without accessible and widespread written records of it, traditional material could simply disappear over time. In Greece, by contrast, as the amateurish quality of early hexameter inscriptions shows unmistakably, the means for recording traditional poetry rested in the hands of its audiences from the very beginning of literacy.

In the failure of a Chinese epic to emerge during this time, we find an important indication that the artistic speech practices of the logographic East were headed along a different developmental track than those in the alphabetical West. Whereas the existence of a body of fixed, repeatable narratives provided the Greeks with both the impetus and the raw material for developing an art of enactment in their literate period, the absence of epic material all but guaranteed that the performative arts of music and dance in China would remain tied to (essentially nonnarrative) ceremonial court rituals during an analogous historical period (sixth century B.C.E.).[73] Even thousands of years later, observers from both East and West are still remarking on the profound dissimilarities between the performing arts of the two cultural worlds.[74]

As Tao-ching Hsu notes, a popular storytelling theatre did not emerge in China when it did in the West. Despite ten centuries in which impersonation and dialogue were known,[75] and despite the magnificent spectacles, elaborate dance forms, brilliant musical invention, and stylized ritual performances that may date back to the second millennium B.C.E.,[76] a theatre of plays did not come into being until the thirteenth century C.E. (Hsu 1985:230–301; Dolby 1976:13–15). Although far ahead of the Greek in many ways in the fifth century B.C.E., Chinese culture had nothing that could be compared with the plot-based theatre of repeatable plays by Aeschylus, Sophocles, and Euripides. Chinese performance arts of the time were dis-

73. Although Chinese writing is much older than the alphabet, it was not until the thirteenth century C.E. that anything like repeatable plays emerged; a real storytelling tradition is not marked in China until the Ch'ing dynasty, 1644–1911 of our era (Hsu 1985:301, 230).

74. For example, see Artaud 1958; Barba 1990; and Weijie 1990.

75. The first recorded use of a human mask is circa 380 C.E. (Hsu 1985:208).

76. The last emperor of the Hsia dynasty is said to have had "strange and spectacular shows staged by jesters and dwarfs," although Hsu thinks the source unreliable (1985:202).

tinctly nonlinguistic: they showed a lack of interest in human speech and left no written records of things said. Chinese court jesters, who were perhaps the closest historical analogues to Thespis and Aeschylus, are reported, in historical documents, to have mimicked the speech of certain individuals—the governor of Hsuan-Chou, for example—on particular ceremonial occasions.[77] But in the absence of a really flexible mode of transcribing exactly what their verbal imitation consisted of, such impersonations, as Hsu reports, remained tied to the particular moment of their utterance: they did not outlive their original context or produce repeatable plays, let alone a body of dramatic literature. The repeatable elements of Eastern performance arts thus consisted in the ancient world, and still consist to an extent, of nonlinguistic elements: costumes, gestures, dance steps, melodies, and stylized character types.[78]

The "deafness" of logographic script to speech has its advantages: it enables speakers of related but mutually unintelligible languages to communicate by writing. But the result of this politically unifying potentiality in China was that the written register came to dominate Chinese intellectual life at a remarkably early date. As G. E. R. Lloyd puts it, the "widespread intelligibility" of the written script caused China to be "very much a culture mediated by the written, more than by the spoken, word" (1990:112). The early ascendance of the written register over the spoken in China was particularly acute in the sphere of poetry, and did much to determine the shape of Chinese performance arts. For as Oscar Brockett has noted (1982:102), Chinese verse forms before the time of the T'ang dynasty were determined by the number of characters written in a line. A poetic line thus oriented to writing cannot easily be made to fit the rhythms of music, and hence this poetry will tend to stay disconnected from oral performance. The disconnectedness of Chinese writing from the rhythms and sounds of speech is perceptible in traditional Eastern theatrical forms even today. Spoken elements are recessive in general, and those that are used are in some cases so disconnected from the living speech of audiences that it is not unusual for these words to be gibberish to audiences and performers alike (Hsu 1985:210). As Eugenio Barba says, it is in fact part of the "horizon of expectations" of the Eastern spectator that what she or he sees may be unintelligible in its verbal aspect (1990:33).

In Western theatre, by contrast, one sees a distinct and possibly defining focus on the spoken register. Whether capturing the sounds of a tyrant's

77. See Hsu 1985:212.

78. Thomas provides some interesting evidence for Greece that such performative elements can be preserved without the use of writing across the centuries (1992:122).

bombast or a politician's sophistry; whether ridiculing the jargon of a profession or the pretensions of the bookish; whether mimicking the quaint errors of a foreigner or the woeful effusions of teenaged balladeers; whether charting the oral habits of old speech, young speech, or speech between the sheets—that is, regardless of the particular character of the speech it records—it is certain that the Western theatre has kept both ears open to oral language since the genre first appeared. And the same speech-centrism that defines the alphabet, and that came to define the Western theatre, also defined Greek life in other areas. Even long after the introduction of writing into Greece, that is, into the time of Aristotle, culturally significant social discourse continued to be *spoken* discourse, with agonistic oral debate organizing and carrying out most social, political, and intellectual activities.[79] The equation this leaves us with is that the disconnectedness from speech effected by the Chinese writing system is replicated both within culturally significant discourse generally and within the representational style of Eastern performance art; and the sensitivity to spoken language exemplified by the alphabet similarly manifests itself within Greek discursive style overall as well as in the speech-conscious representations of Greek theatre.

Had alphabetic writing been available to ancient Chinese court jesters, there is obviously no guarantee that a body of epic writings, and then a literary theatre, would necessarily or automatically have materialized. Social and political factors were also at work.[80] But while some of these factors certainly created suitable conditions in Greece for a secular, popular, and poetic use of writing from an early date, and while others certainly discouraged it in the East, the practice of recording traditional oral narrative was itself made available to the Greeks owing to the inherently open-eared, "speaker-friendly" nature of the alphabet.

The sound-sensitivity of alphabet, coupled with the fact that it could be, and was, used for recording poetic performance by any ordinary Greek almost at once, thus enabled poets and performers to preserve their narrative legacy in an unusually copious form. Aeschylus is said to have described his plays as "slices from the great banquets of Homer"; Sophocles' use of Homeric material gained him the appellation *philhomeros* and *Homerikotatos* (Athenaeus *Deipnosophists* 8.347e; 7.277e). Indeed, numerous ancient sources, from Herodotus to Isocrates to Plato to Aristotle, leave little doubt that in their time, the dramatist's art was considered a continuation, through new formal means, of the telling of stories first told in traditional epic recitation (Herington 1985:103–4). As Eric Havelock notes, "The

79. See esp. Lloyd 1990 and Thomas 1992.
80. See Burn 1960:157; Harris 1989:61; and Hsun 1959:19ff. for some of these.

Athenian stage plays, composed closer to the native vernacular, became the Attic supplement to Homer" (1963:48). Aristotle leaves little doubt about the indebtedness of drama to the survival of Homeric epic: Homer provided the model of a "dramatic" "metrical representation of heroic action" for tragedy, and "was the first to mark out the main lines of comedy as well" (*Poetics* 1448b11–12; 1449b7ff.).

The alphabetical conservation of Homer also had the effect of ensuring that, while already ancient in the dramatists' time, these works would stay alive for contemporary audiences. With the alphabet, all kinds of archaic words could be preserved before their use died out and their meanings were lost forever. Because the forms and sounds of poetic words had been preserved in text, rhapsodic performers generations after Homer were given access to their meanings as well. Partly through etymology and partly as a result of having the whole poem before them in fixed form, performers of a written narrative could maintain access through time to the meaning of a word such as "phlegm," as Prodicus did (Pfeiffer 1968:40). In fact, from Aristotle we learn that "glosses" of rare or obsolete words were a common feature of epic texts (*Poetics* 1459a9f.); and Rudolf Pfeiffer considers the possibility that these glosses date back to the sixth century, although the word itself (*glossai*) first appears in the fifth (1968:12). Consequently, the recitation of even very old traditional material never could degenerate into a ceremonial incantation of meaningless sounds, as such material did in the East. What writing itself does for cultures generally, then, alphabetic writing did for Western performers: it enabled them to have access to the "real semantic history" of their performative material (Ong 1982:8). If the recorders of Homer had had instead a pictographic or logogrammatic system at their disposal, they would have been very seriously discouraged by it from even attempting to include the many unconventional or unfamiliar words of the traditional epic vocabulary.[81]

· The importance of this relatively easy, nonspecialist access to writing for the development of theatre is also suggested by events centuries later in Europe and England. Despite the alphabet, scribal elites retained control of writing, at least in part by associating writing with Latin, a language not spoken by the vast majority of people.[82] But as soon as writing started being used to record the vernaculars of Europe, the alphabet's "ear" for speech was as quickly exploited for recording poetic performances as it had been in ancient Greece. In fact, among the very first written documents in the vernac-

---

81. See Havelock and Hershbell 1978:5–10; Powell 1991:71–107.
82. See esp. Auerbach 1965.

ular to appear in Europe between the ninth and twelfth centuries were, conspicuously, jongleurs' manuscripts; and once performers with scripts replaced oral bards, actors were soon to follow (Auerbach 1965:280–94). If it is
fair to generalize from the evidence of only two such occurrences of theatre's
emergence in the West, it would seem that this chain of generic shifts—
from (nonliterate) oral bards, through individual jongleurs or rhapsodes
reciting from a written record of an epic performance, to groups of actors
with a common text written explicitly for them—amounts to a kind of rule.

Nevertheless, the mere survival of the Homeric narrative legacy would not
in itself have been enough to stimulate the invention of an art of enactment.
What created the conditions for the generic shift from epic to drama was
that Thespis and his heirs inherited these stories in a form that made them
visible to the eye. As perhaps the first poets ever to have before them complete texts of the epics from start to finish, the early dramatists were in a position to notice things that may never have been seen so clearly before. And
much of what they saw, they changed. Whereas oral audiences had previously had access to Homer's stories only through ephemeral performances of
them, the dramatists could scrutinize these works as critics and readers. And
their use of writing in the composition process gave them the means not
only to reflect their criticisms in their poetry, but also to regard their own
works with an equally critical eye, freed as they were from the demands of
oral compositional techniques.[83]

The first thing to go was the formulaic style itself. The mere existence
of writing meant that embodied memory was no longer needed for cultural
continuity, and the mnemotechnics of oral poetry were rendered obsolete.
Indeed, when we compare the language of oral epic with that of drama, we
find differences that could not be more pronounced. First among these is
the "paradox," noted by Walter Ong, that drama, while the first poetic genre

---

83. That the dramatists used writing to compose is suggested, of course, by their literacy, for which they provide ample enough proof throughout their plays (see note 6). Many
contemporary scholars are quick to remind us, however, that as late as Aristotle, playwrights were still being called the "makers" of their plays rather than the writers of them
(see, e.g., Page 1987:108). Aristotle, however, was clearly not intending to suggest that the
dramatists did not use writing; he was speaking of the construction, or making, of plots
and poetry generally. The fact remains that in the century before Aristotle, dramatists were
already and explicitly being represented as the *writers* of their plays (Cratinus *Wineflask*
frags. 195 and 196 Edmonds 1957; Aristophanes frag. 676b ibid.). K. J. Dover further tells us
that the dramatists had to submit their plays to the archon months in advance of their performance, which strongly suggests that they wrote them (1972:15).

to be controlled by writing from the start,[84] should also have been the first language genre to "make deliberate use of colloquial speech" (1977:72). In light of what has been said so far, however, it may not be so paradoxical at all. Given the tendency of writing to make obsolete the need for memorable, formulaic expression, and given the capacity of alphabetical script to encode speech-as-spoken, it would stand to reason that it was not in spite of but rather because of drama's literary character that it quickly distinguished itself as the genre of contemporary speech par excellence.

In providing an easy and responsive method for transcribing pronunciation, use of the alphabet opens up to poetic composition the ability to "hear" the speech of individuals. Cut loose by writing from the formulaic and metrical constraints of composition-in-performance, storytellers could begin to exploit this alphabetical potential to the full, and the early dramatists did. The representation of the idiosyncratic speech of individuals could not be pursued in epic speech beyond a very rudimentary degree, and seems to be atypical of non-alphabetical theatres as well. But in the dramas of fifth-century Greece, the accents, nuances, and social values inherent in each character's language are not only emphasized individually, but also brought into an even sharper relief through contact with the speech of other characters. In Bakhtinian terminology, the separate discourses of drama can be said to mutually illuminate and comment on one another.

Consider, for example, the unadorned, mocking verbal blasts of Sophocles' Antigone: "I knew it; of course I did. For it was public" (*Antigone* 492); "I know that I will die—of course I do. . . . I count that as a profit" (504); "Why do you wait, then? Nothing that you say pleases me; God forbid that it should" (545).[85] Her expressions, rhetorically spare and pointed, are characterized by a certain amount of aggressive overstatement and are rooted in intensely felt but often unreasoned emotion: "Oh, oh, no! Shout it out. I will hate you still worse for silence—should you not proclaim it to everyone" (99–101); "If you talk like this I will loathe you. . . . Let me alone and my folly with me, to endure this terror. No suffering of mine will be enough

84. Ong does not himself *prove* that drama was the first genre to use writing from the start, but all evidence does point in that direction. By "from the start," I assume he means that plays were written *before* they were performed, whereas the use of writing for the epic had been after the fact, that is, only for recording a performance. If epic was orally composed, we are left only with lyric as an alternate contender for the title of first literary genre. Less is known about the compositional methods of elegists and iambicists of the seventh and sixth centuries. They may still have been in the habit of composing their songs out loud, perhaps to lyre accompaniment, but there is no certain proof either way.

85. All translations of the tragedies are from Grene and Lattimore 1991.

to make me die ignobly" (109–14). The contrast with, say, the speech of another Sophoclean heroine, Deianira, could not be greater. Whereas an epic bard might have, in his own stereotyping voice, described Heracles' wife as "the gentle Deianira," the "long-suffering Deianira," or the like, Sophocles the playwright portrays the character through the qualities of her speech. Her meekness and lack of self-confidence are conveyed through her characteristic use of qualifications, a kind of continual verbal self-subversion: "Zeus of the contests made the end good—if it has been good" (*The Women of Trachis* 25–26); "For here I have taken on a girl—no, I can think that no longer—a married woman" (536–37); "Well, the move is made, unless you think I am acting rashly. If so I will stop" (586–87). She speaks with the unfocused wordiness of a young girl, with full self-disclosure, as if she were always aware of being answerable to someone else, of having to prove that she has been a good girl: "I do not speak of the manner of their struggles for I do not know. Someone who watched the spectacle unafraid could tell" (21–23); "Something has happened which, if I tell you, my friends, will seem a marvel such as you never thought to hear. . . . I want to tell you this in detail, so you may know the whole story" (672–79); "I neglected none of the instructions that the beast the centaur explained to me. . . . And I did only what I was told to do" (680–81); "And this is what I did" (688); ". . . as you saw" (692). Her many uses of the words "house" and "home," her tags of endearments ("dear friends," "my friends," "dear women," "O kindest of men") and easy resort to clichéd truisms (1–3, 92–93, 548–49) mark her speech with its distinctively sweet, trusting, domestic flavor, and contrast it with the speech of others. Or consider the language of Creon, with its heavy reliance on metaphors and images of control: Antigone is a horse to be broken (*Antigone* 522–23), his citizens growling animals who must be brought under the yolk (324); tongues must be kept under lock and key (200). People are described by him as animals and objects: Ismene is a viper (531), Polynices a meal for birds and dogs (207), Antigone a furrow for Haemon's plow (569). He is every inch the tyrant, and his distrustful, advantage-seeking nature manifests itself in an overwhelming number of profit, monetary, and bribery images (325–34, 343–46, 361, 1094–95, 1096, 1107, 1118, 1127, 1130). This high level of speech particularization, carried out with such consistency throughout a work, is unthinkable without the aid of writing. Oral composition cannot help but flatten out and homogenize the representation of individual figures' speech—and this regardless of the poet's own sensitivity and artistic genius, which in Homer's case were immense.

Individualized speech is manifested equally in tragedy and comedy, and was to remain a distinguishing characteristic of the dramatic genres throughout history. As we saw earlier, the alphabet's special relation to spoken language is evidenced especially in the ease with which it can represent even foreign, incoherent, or otherwise semantically opaque language. Exploiting the abilities of his writing system, Thomas Dekker would carry on the dramatic tradition by representing the sounds of Dutch speech (*The Shoemaker's Holiday*); Shakespeare would do the same for the sounds of French speech (*Henry V*). Earlier in the tradition, we find Aristophanes using the alphabet for inscribing the incoherent jargon of Persians (*Acharnians*),[86] and recording the imaginary dialect of frogs in his comedy of that name. In Euripides' *Orestes,* the alphabet proves its elasticity in transcribing foreign "babble" at length, as translated here into an equivalent mangling of English:

> Greekish sword—kill dead!
> Trojan scared, oh.
> Run, run.
> Jump in slippers, fast, fast,
> clop-clop clamber over roof
> Hole in beams, inside court,
> jump down
> *boom!*
> below.
> Oh, oh,
> Where can run, where go?
> Mebbe foreign ladies know?
> Up, up,
> Soar in air, him shimmer nothing?
> Swim in sea—mebbe? mebbe?—
> Where godbull ocean cradles world
> flowing water with?
> (1368–79)

As a final example of the subtlety and particularity of speech representation that could be attained by a poet who had learned his ABCs, we might look at the sentry's speech to Creon in *Antigone*. David Grene, who translated it, remarked on a number of features which may not be obvious to a reader of the English version: "He speaks with marked clumsiness ... the royal presence makes him think apparently that he should be rather

---

86. See the Athenian Society text (1931 1:106) for an English rendering of this foreign babble.

grand. . . . He uses odd bits of archaism or somewhat stale poetical passages, particularly in catch phrases" (1991:169). Here is the speech:

> My lord, I will never claim my shortness of breath
> is due to hurrying, nor were there wings on my feet.
> I stopped at many a lay-by in my thinking;
> I circled myself till I met myself coming back.
> My soul accosted me with different speeches.
> "Poor fool, yourself, why are you going somewhere
> When once you get there you will pay the piper?"
> "Well, aren't you the darling fellow! Stopping again?
> and suppose Creon hears the news from someone else—
> don't you realize you will smart for that?"
> I turned the whole matter over. I suppose I may say
> "I made haste slowly" and the short road became long . . . (242–53).

This speech—pompous, apologetic, and endlessly digressing—continues in this vein until Creon finally shouts, "For god's sake, tell me and get out of here!" (267).

As even these perfunctory examples should attest, the use of a written alphabet—for breaking up words and putting them back together in new ways, for catching exact rhythms and idiosyncratic constructions, for combining different styles and meters in the same work and maintaining the integrity of each—gave the poet a device for recording speech with vastly more individuality than was formerly possible. Unencumbered by the formulaic, mnemonic demands of oral recitation, the dramatic writer could, with the help of this new technological "ear" of speech, record human discourse with a freedom not to be matched until the invention of the wax cylinder.

This shift from the mnemonically oriented formulaic language of epic to a dramatic language of fixed, individualized vernacular speech did not happen all at once, of course. The grand hexameters of Homeric diction remained widely in use in lyric composition throughout the seventh and sixth centuries. Even between the heroic Aeschylus and the "bookish" Euripides one can see an ongoing movement, with the advance of literacy, away from the language of stereotype and toward a language of idiosyncratic contemporary speech.

In addition to particularizing their characters' speech far beyond anything that an oral bard could have managed, the early dramatists eliminated a number of other features of Homeric diction. Oral epic, composed as it was of blocks of formulaic utterance which were "stitched together" in performance, could be likened to ordinary speech in one respect. In oral discourse, as Wallace Chafe has shown, speakers tend similarly to stitch together "the relatively brief, relatively independent idea units" of their thought with the help of "flow-monitoring devices" such as "you know," "so," "anyway," "so I said," and so on (1985:12). In lengthy oral recitations of modern works such as the African "Bagre" (Goody 1987:79, 168) or the Canadian aboriginal story of "The Girl Who Married the Bear" (Petrone 1990:12), we find evidence for the universality of this method of composition in oral storytelling. By contrast, a composition that has been put together at leisure, in a spatiotemporal context *not* inhabited by a listening audience, has no need of these flow-monitoring devices; and indeed no direct references to "you," to the listener, can be found in any of the tragic texts that have come down to us (Taplin 1977:131).[87]

The elimination of vocatives to the audience is just one of the changes to composition that followed from the dramatists' use of the written medium. Because it both freed language from the demands of memory and arrested its course in visible space, writing also stretched its users' control over it. A writer can manipulate longer units than a speaker can, and indulge in more complex, multidimensional functions. The increased length of the units of language that the poet can master with the help of writing can be seen, first, at the level of the sentence: subordinate and relative clauses barely exist at all in Homer but flourish in the writings of the classic dramatists (Kalmár 1985:157). Increased complexity can also be seen at the level of the story as a whole. In oral composition, stories "are built up largely from self-contained episodes," and themes are abandoned after they have served their purpose in the individual locales (Bowra 1969:50–51). As a result, both the *Iliad* and the *Odyssey* contain what C. M. Bowra describes as "real contradictions" from episode to episode (1969:51). When it becomes possible to see the beginning, middle, and end of a composition simultaneously, however, the concept of an organic, unified structure comes into existence. Aristotle speaks of a poem as an animal whose head, body, and tail the eye takes in at once—a statement that could never have been made of poetry before the use of writing (*Poetics* 1451a). Nor, in an oral milieu, could one speak of a poetic composition as a visible design or "painting," a trope Aristotle also resorts to in describing tragic composition (1450b). But when all elements of a plot are set down on paper, the relationships among them

87. The situation is obviously different in Old Comedy, in which the chorus addresses the audience directly. See, for example, the *parabasis* of Aristophanes' *Frogs,* ll. 674–737.

can become apparent, visible at a glance (Ong 1982:148). In preliterate epic, language is confined to the "winged words" of oral speech; its parts must follow and actually replace one another in time. It is only when put in visible space that they can be co-present and available for comparison. With written texts come poetic questions of thematic and verbal consistency, and of relationships between part and whole.

From the appearance in their texts of an exact, continuous line of Homeric verse,[88] we can be fairly certain that the tragedians had before them a written copy of the epics (Pfeiffer 1968:111). As the first genre to benefit from the preexistence of stories that did not inhere in a particular speaker or in any live performative context, drama was also the first Western verbal art to be composed "as a self-contained, discrete unit, defined by closure" (Ong 1982:148)—that is, to exhibit a unified, non-episodic structure. As Charles Segal has stressed, the "deferred relation" between literate storytelling and audience reception also permits the composition to be worked on, in private, over time, and to be edited, corrected, reorganized, and constructed throughout with the tightness and thematic consistency that we associate with the works of all the fifth-century dramatists (1986:77). Examples of this feature of dramatic form are perhaps not necessary; but if we compare, with Aristotle, the unity of the *Oedipus* with the "several separate actions" that make up the epics, we cannot but be impressed with the extent to which the ability to see the whole plot at a glance enabled the dramatists to unify and concentrate their stories beyond anything that could have been achieved by an extemporizing bard (*Poetics* 1462b9–15).

Not only did relationships between the elements of a story become visible to Homer's literate followers, but also these same elements started to be viewed as possessing relationships that were not confined to their narratological function. As I noted earlier, alphabetical script sunders the palpable connection that exists in speech between word and meaning, between the signifier (the word "tree"), and the signified that it refers to in reality (the class of organic entities with roots, trunk, and leaves). Gerd Baumann (1986) maintains that in an oral culture, words represent the world indexically: to define the meaning of a word, one simply points to the object or state of affairs. Because orally dependent language must always be "sponsored" language (R. Harris 1989:100ff.) that is, sponsored by some speaker, language in a preliterate environment will always be embedded in some concrete context of actual use, engaged in an indexical pointing-to-the-world. But within the

88. Pfeiffer 1968 cites *Antigone* 29–30, *Hecuba* 1078, *Suppliants* 800f., and *Ion* 504f.

second-order symbolic system of writing, words begin to refer to other words within the system, to define one another outside of their indicating function. By becoming a static, visible object for sight—a "thing" to look at—language loses the illusion it has in speech of being a transparent referential medium. Writing distances words from their relation with reality and brings their relationships to one another into consciousness.

What results is a new awareness of a systematic dimension of language, of the fact that words define other words arbitrarily in addition to defining the world referentially. In culture generally, this abstracted view of language has been credited with the birth of abstract philosophy and of linguistic studies. But it was also one of the central driving forces at work in the new genre of drama, tragedy especially. In the dramatic rewriting of Greek mythic material, we find a "problematic of the signifier" which is noticeably absent by comparison in the epic versions. When the warriors of epic speech are said to be "god-supported" or "worthy of honor," these words refer unproblematically to the aid of the gods and the battle renown of fighting mortals which constitute the stuff of heroic legend. In the dramas, however, characters use words that are explicitly ambiguous; the same word means one thing to one speaker, something else entirely to another. In tragic speech, words have lost their Homeric transparency of meaning and have become question marks that must be negotiated within the linguistic system itself. Accordingly, the number of words and concepts in drama which are semantically uncertain, intentionally ambiguous, is notably high. In the *Oedipus* alone, there are fifty words whose meanings are made problematic;[89] and although few dramas can lay claim to that statistic, all are marked by an actively questioning attitude to the meaning of words.[90] What *is* honor? A convention of war or a virtue in itself? If a virtue, what kind? What is "love?" What are the different kinds? Does the word "love" contain within it certain inherent contradictions—a love of family bound to conflict with a love for the polis? And what of "polis"? What is its relationship with smaller units? With the nonhuman realm? What is "law?" Is it the opposite of "nature," or do the two words have some other relationship than as simple contraries? Words in drama have been unmoored from a certain and stable relationship with extraverbal reality and have instead become objects in their own right, objects whose limits, powers, and peculiarities as meaning-generating entities can be explored.

89. J. P. Vernant 1978:175 refers to the number collected by Arnold Hug.
90. Vernant analyzes occurrences and types of ambiguity in the *Agamemnon* and *Antigone* (1978:175–76).

This distancing of speech from speakers, which theorists today commonly call alienation, has determined the form and function of drama in a number of ways, some of which we shall explore in Chapter 4. For the moment I will only point out that alienation does not so much introduce new features into language use as it makes old ones apparent and available for conscious reflection. To alienate language through writing is simply to *see* linguistic mechanisms that were invisible previously. Words *do* define one another systematically, and always have; but contextually embedded speech gives them the *illusion* of referring directly to the world of our experience. Like Brecht's decision to let the lighting apparatus of the stage be seen by the audience, writing's alienation of language simply shows what was always there in speech, but which the directness and diaphanousness of spoken language tended to disguise.[91]

Evidence of this new problematic of language spawned by writing can be seen in nearly all fifth-century drama. The conflict in *Antigone* stems directly from mutually incompatible definitions of law and duty. No single and certain referent for *nomos* (law, custom) is attainable; the word has become an abstract problem for analysis.[92] The same can be said of *kratos* (might, power, rule) in the *Suppliants,* of *omma* and *phainesthai* (eye, to make visible, bring to light) in the *Women of Trachis,* of *dike* (justice) throughout the *Oresteia,* and *sophia* (wisdom) in the *Bacchai,* or of the semantic relationship between *eidos* (that which is seen, known) and *agnoia* (want of perception, ignorance) in the *Oedipus.*[93] As Jean-Pierre Vernant and Pierre Vidal-Naquet observe, this linguistic indeterminacy marks a profound shift from the "stable realities" of earlier forms, and defines the particular character of dramatic language (1990:186, 38–64).

The abstract, analytical relationship to mythic material that we find in the dramatic rewritings of it stems from the fact that the eye had begun to take over many of the functions once performed exclusively by the ear. A linguistic record of experience, previously communicated from mouth to ear in the form of myths, elders' maxims, and ritual recitations, could now be made in "visual space" instead: on stone, pottery, animal skin, papyrus, or even, as at Delphi, on the surface of a bean. And as early as the sixth century, as Frances Yates implies, this technique for encoding information in visual space had been internalized, providing a model for representation in "mental" or imaginary space as well. In *The Art of Memory,* Yates points out

91. This aspect of writing in its relation to speech is described with uncharacteristic lucidity by Derrida in *Speech and Phenomena* (1973).

92. Vernant adds *dike, philos* and *philia, kerdos, time, orge,* and *deinos* to the list of problematic words in the *Antigone* (1978:495 n. 5).

93. Discussion of some of these terms can be found in Seale 1982:211 n. 3.

that, by Simonides' time in Greece, memory had become associated not with the sounds of words, but with the visualization of fixed images (1966:1ff.). In an oral context, as witnessed by the *Iliad* (3.250–325), events are remembered and described through the order in which people speak; memory has the paratactic structure of oral syntax ("and then . . . and then . . . and then"). By Simonides' time, however, things are being remembered through their physical disposition in space.[94] Rather than being associated with a temporal sound sequence, memory is experienced in terms of simultaneous spatial arrangement—a habit of thought that would, of course, be encouraged by the ability of writing to subordinate clauses, hold related concepts in view simultaneously, and arrange them. As Havelock, Ong, de Kerckhove, and Segal have argued, this shift from sound to sight, from a mental soundscape to a visible landscape or "scene," is modeled on the example set by the existence of visible written records. It is a shift for which the tragic texts and fragments provide direct evidence in their many references to memory as a writing on the mind.[95]

We also find evidence of this "hypervisualized noetic world" (Ong 1982:127) somewhat later in Platonic philosophy. Continually exhorting his interlocutors and readers to imagine visual images of "ideas" which have an eternal (i.e., non–temporally linked) "form," Plato actively reflects this literate shift from temporal "hearing" to spatial, static "viewing." The mode whereby knowledge was received and disseminated had shifted from remembering what one heard to "seeing" the truth. In Plato's intellectual "scenes," such as the Cave of Book 10 of *Republic,* no less than in the fifth-century practices of theatregoing and reading itself, we see evidence of a move to visualization. And by Aristotle's time, memory is directly equated with the order of letters in the alphabet (*On Memory and Reminiscence* 452b16–25).[96] Theatre's emergence at a time when this shift from sound to sight was under way cannot be a mere coincidence. Nor is it likely to be coincidental that the most elaborate of the memory systems that developed out of Simonides' technique were to take the form of "Memory Theatres."[97]

94. Instead of recollecting the events at a banquet by saying which guests spoke in what order, as Homer would have done, Simonides reconstructs the event by saying where everyone was located in the room (Yates 1966:1).

95. Pfeiffer provides a useful list of the relevant passages in plays and fragments (1968:26 and notes).

96. See Yates 1966:35.

97. In de Kerckhove's view, Simonides "may have been the first Greek thinker to conceptualize the interiorization of visible space" and imagine memory as "a container, a mental box to store and classify representations and abstractions" (1981:32). See the Memory Theatres of Giulio Camillo and Robert Fludd as reproduced and discussed by Yates 1966:129–72, 320–67.

This heightened emphasis on the visual manifested itself in Thespis' time in a preference for *seeing* a story rather than simply *hearing* it narrated by a bard. This generic shift, between the aurality of epic and the visibility of the new theatrical forms, is given unmistakable expression by one of Euripides' characters in *Iphigenia among the Taurians:*

> I have heard marvelous tales from story-tellers,
> But nothing to compare
> With this event which my own eyes have seen.
> (900–903)

In preliterate storytelling, it was in the acoustic chain of sung or spoken incidents that a plot inhered. Despite the musical, instrumental, performative *mode* of epic recitation, a performing bard's stories were verbally given, temporally arranged, and taken in by the ears. With the advent of theatrical form, a story came to be something that one sees. These words from *Iphigenia among the Taurians* are spoken immediately after a discussion about the nature of writing, and are delivered to a group of characters who are themselves lettered. But the passage is also "addressed" to Euripides' theatrical audience. In juxtaposing the hearing of tales from storytellers with the seeing of an event with one's own eyes, Euripides is undoubtedly making a metatheatrical statement about the virtues of his chosen genre. That storytelling had, by Euripides' time, come to be associated with sight rather than sound is also reflected in Aristotle's later writings on poetics. Indicative of a notable departure from oral compositional methods, Aristotle advises the aspiring playwright to "keep the scene before his eyes" while writing (*Poetics* 1455a14ff.). As Aristotle explains, physical impossibilities and visual contradictions are "not noticed" in epic because "we do not actually see the persons of the story" (1460a15–17). The dramatist, on the contrary, must concern himself with moving speakers around visibly before the audience's eyes; he cannot simply dispense with a character once he finishes speaking, as the epic singers did.[98]

This shift from oral hearing to literate seeing has been studied for medieval Europe as well. Through his work on the period between 1066 and 1307, M. T. Clanchy (1979) has found that the spread of literacy in Europe had consequences for communication practices which were strikingly analogous to those that took place in Greece between the turn of the millennium and the classic age of Athens. Whereas preliterate Europeans would custom-

---

98. See Bowra 1969:50 on the "real contradictions" that are possible and inevitable in oral compositional methods.

arily have remembered a dying man's last will and testament by having "heard" it themselves at his bedside, they began to remember having "seen" a seal placed on a document, and to consider this as evidence for the genuineness of the will (203). The technological effect of writing on wills, knowledge, stories, and other information is thus to make them all, for the first time, objects for the eye rather than for the ear exclusively.[99] And once the possibility existed of making what was formerly only "heard" actually "visible," the Greeks were liable to have jumped at the chance: from the Archaic into the classical period, Greek usage records a highly valued distinction between hearing and sight. What was "heard [from another]" had the value of mere "hearsay"; what one saw with one's "own eyes" was more worthy of trust.[100] For this reason, it comes as no surprise to learn that drama was the most "people-pleasing" genre of poetry in antiquity; for in the words of one member of the ancient theatre audience, drama meant that Homer's stories could at last be not "merely heard, but also seen" (Herington 1985:103–4).[101]

In addition to making things visible, the evidence of letters will also tend to reveal the difference between myth and history, and to bring the category of fiction into existence for the first time. Especially from the Platonic texts, it is clear that the Homeric poems had customarily been expected to provide more than just pleasure and a disinterested sort of edification. On the contrary, in Havelock's words, they were viewed as a "vast encyclopedia" (1986:79). They were seen as handbooks for proper conduct, or *paideia*, since time immemorial, storehouses of true statements about men and the gods.[102] But in functioning as a continuous series of factual historical and ethical exempla, the epics perpetuated a situation in which the lines between history and myth were blurred.[103] This was because an oral culture's lack of

99. The emphasis here is on the word "exclusively," since reliance on acoustic evidence did not by any means disappear altogether. See Thomas 1989, 1992 for Greek evidence about the continued reliance on oral modes.

100. *Odyssey* 3.93–95; *Oedipus* 105; Herodotus 2.99, 147, 156; Thucydides 1.20.1, 73.2; 6.53.3, 60.1; cf. Thomas 1989:3 n. 3; Segal 1986:86.

101. It is interesting to note that this relationship between newfound literacy and theatrical representation is evident also in the emergence of aboriginal theatre in Canada. The use made by Native poets of actors and theatrical form, starting in the 1970s, has been described by one expert as "giv[ing] the oral tradition a *three-dimensional* context" (Petrone 1990:180).

102. Xenophanes frag. 10 (Lesher 1992); Jaeger 1960:35–56; Robb 1994:67.

103. The same point has been made for other oral cultures as well. In Canadian aboriginal society, for example, oral myths and legends and folk tales were not experienced as fictional. On the contrary, they functioned as indispensable repositories of cultural values

"hard copy" compels it to satisfy its need for the conservation of information by means of a medium that is by nature prone to continual change. As an inevitable result, an event such as the Flood, or the Sack of Troy, will enter the realm of myth nearly as soon as it occurs—that is, at the very moment of its entry into the unstable medium of oral tradition. As Rosalind Thomas has shown for family and state history as perpetuated in Greece (1989), factual material told and retold orally becomes very distorted. With no written account to refer to, even genuine memories of real events get "simplified" by oral modes of transmission. Acquiring "conventional or idealized elements, clichés and stereotyped form," they are gradually transformed into legendary material that bears "slight relation to the original material" (284). These falsifications are cumulative, and thus the telescoping, distortion, and simplification of oral transmission is "irreversible" (284). Anachronism is common, as is the tendency to endow events with a more "colourful" narrative character than they really possessed (285). The past is commonly altered to fit in with present values and beliefs, and whole blocks of history disappear altogether. Although such distortions are occasionally deliberate, in general they are a function of the mode of communication itself (284). Above all, it is exaggeration that is responsible in oral record keeping for turning historical fact into what Thomas calls "a timeless catalogue of heroic deeds"—in short, into myth (232).

Goody (1986, 1987) and Ong (1977, 1982) have found that this tendency toward the narrativization of experience is a feature common to all oral milieus, and it is easy to see why. Not until a fixed record, such as that of a Thucydides, can exist, will true history be able to detach itself from oral lore. As William V. Harris points out, Thucydides included actual transcriptions of key texts, and thus was able to separate history from the mythologizing tendencies of oral history, tendencies that are still very much present even in the work of Herodotus, who was content to record and accept as fact "what was said" (1989:80).[104] Thucydides, however, explicitly and repeatedly ridicules those who believe everything they hear, and proudly advertises himself, by way of contrast with such mythographers, as a contemporary of and eyewitness to many of the events he recounts. Moreover, because he was writing, he did not have to rely on the stylizations

---

and teachings (Petrone 1990:10). Songs and stories served as applied science, historical record, and religious practice all rolled into one: certain songs were used to heal the sick, others to attract animals, others to strengthen the hunter (10–19, 121). When Petrone lists the genres unknown in native Canadian culture before contact with writing, she tellingly names "fiction" along with drama (183).

104. The same point is made by Thomas 1992:112.

that had been the oral singer's only cure for forgetting.[105] In Thucydides, as Harris puts it, the logic of performance and invention was replaced by the logic of writing and documents (80), and history is differentiated from storytelling as a special kind of activity with its own rules and procedures.[106]

Writing for this reason has been credited with the emergence not only of historiography but also of fiction, as distinct, intentional activities separable from mythic recitation (Segal 1986:90). For as soon as a difference between tradition and truth can become perceptible, fiction cán emerge as a distinct way of speaking about the world or the past. In Theagenes' sixth-century defence of Homer on allegorical grounds, we see the first awareness of this category of fiction in Greece: as Theagenes argued, a story may have value *even though* it is not literally true. And by Kallias' time, storytelling had detached itself so far from the record-keeping function of epic poetry that a play could be written about something as patently fictional as talking letters.

To Aristotle, in whose time literacy was much more deeply entrenched, the distinction between fiction and history was fairly obvious (*Poetics* 1451bf.). In the *Poetics* we see him drawing boundaries between such specialist disciplines, distinguishing poetry from history and history from philosophy. The category of fiction, of a poetic making which is altogether free from the record-keeping function of oral epic, was also securely established by this time, as we see from Aristotle's reference to the fact that, like Kallias, some dramatists make up their stories from scratch (1451b19–26).

In what Bowra calls "the strict tradition" of epic recitation, "any manifestation of individual idiosyncrasies" is usually rejected (1969:56).[107] But

105. These mnemotechnical stylizations included conventional formulas and epithets, parallel structures, regular meter, and exaggeration. Now, the memorable qualities of a statement such as "In fourteen-hundred and ninety-two, Columbus sailed the ocean blue" do not, it is true, seem to interfere with the historical accuracy of the saying. But in the recording of more complex and detailed historical verities, conventionality and exaggeration will seem to have their way. As proof of this, we need only remember the mythical qualities of Homer's telling of the events surrounding the Trojan War. So thoroughly did history become myth through oral transmission that scholars before Schliemann did not believe that there was any historical truth behind Homer's tales of Mycenae (see Chadwick 1990:6).

106. As Gordon Shrimpton (1997) has shown, however, Thucydides organized his history according to a seasonal principle in order to facilitate memorization, and thus still assumed that his readers read as a prelude to memorizing, not as a substitute.

107. Finnegan 1977 and Thomas 1992 stress that oral singers do tend to embellish stories and stamp them with their own style; deliberately changing meanings, however, is impermissible.

once the conservative function of storytelling was obviated by the existence of writing, "variation came to be accepted for its own sake" (Kirk 1985:103), a change that would further reinforce the emergence of fiction as a distinct linguistic category. Speaking about the "fresh meanings" introduced into traditional material by Aeschylus, Sophocles, and Euripides, G. S. Kirk says that "such drastic . . . reinterpretations usually presuppose a literate culture, both in Greece and elsewhere" (1985:109). For as long as stories function as collective memory, writes Albert Bates Lord, deliberate changes in the telling of them would be counterproductive, even dangerous to the survival of the tradition: oral bards accordingly always look on innovative interpretations or alterations as "wrong or awkward, or . . . a 'mistake' " (Lord 1960:130).[108] As Lord goes on to suggest, it is only in a literate context that conscious changes and departures are felt to be "right" and desirable (130). Thus, in what must have seemed a radical departure from the long-established rules of storytelling, the dramatists began to change the epic stories to suit their own personal intentions. In his fourth-century guide to the practice of playwriting, Aristotle confirms that the rules of poetry had changed in precisely this way: he says not that the dramatist "may," but that the dramatic poet "*must* show invention" in his use of the tradition (1453b11; my italics). The innovative, and in some places downright subversive, character of the tragedians' treatment of epic material can thus be attributed to a great extent to the freedom given them by a written version of traditional material: they were free to alter and criticize as much as they wanted without imperiling the survival of the tradition itself.

As a particularly powerful symbol of this new literate concern with narrative novelty, competition in drama, unlike rhapsodic contest, demanded the creation of large quantities of brand new poems, year after year. The oral poet must conserve; the literate poet, as Aristotle nagged, must show invention; he must offer his audience something *new*. And the very structure of the theatre festival, where original plays were expected every year, reflects this literate freedom from conservation, this freedom to change, innovate, rewrite stories of the past, even to invent new ones that have nothing to do with conservation at all.

Had the dramatists confined their innovations in storytelling to their irreverent handling of tradition, however, their art, while certainly much altered from oral epic, would not have differed from it in more than content.

108. Finnegan 1990:247 makes the same point.

Instead, they changed the mode of performance, too, and in so doing created an art that departed from its antecedent along fundamental generic lines.

The shift from a narrative to a dramatic mode was made by Thespis through his introduction of the mask. This was a radical innovation, and it must have left no doubt in the minds of sixth-century audiences that a new type of storytelling was being introduced. For masks had never been used in any epic or lyric performance up until that time; before Thespis, all narrative performance had been delivered *in propria persona*. Neither epic reciters nor dithyrambic choral singers wore masks, for neither had any need of disguise. Predramatic singers always spoke as themselves: as revelers, worshippers, inspired bards, or members of a competing tribe.[109] Thespis' radical departure from traditional poetic practice was so notable, in fact, that classicists were once at a loss to explain it. Some, like Jane Ellen Harrison, looked outside poetry to the sphere of religion, hoping to find in the common ritual use of animal and god masks an explanation or source for Thespis' unprecedented move toward corporeal impersonation (1991:568).[110] But the true explanation is both more obvious and more mundane. Thespis needed a mask for purely practical reasons, since storytellers had never before attempted what he was about to attempt: the telling of a story not through *propria persona* narration, but through *visual representation*.

It should be noted that even the predramatic rhapsode was expected to be something of an impersonator. From the *Ion* (530cff.) and from Aristotle (*Poetics* 1462a6–7), we know that Homer's reciters typically got carried away with the representation of their fictional characters' speeches, and were as apt to overdo their gestures in the process as actors. When rhapsodes such as Ion recited sections of the *Iliad* and the *Odyssey* at the Panathenaia, they, like actors, wore special costumes and impersonated the speech of their fictional characters. In fact, as John Herington has shown with a number of ancient sources, a good deal of what we have come to think of as "histrionic technique" had already been worked out by the rhapsodes of the sixth century (1985:7–13). Because of their impersonations, and because their perfor-

109. Flickinger 1973:10–11; Pickard-Cambridge 1962:50; Vernant and Vidal-Naquet 1990:23–24.

110. Harrison was of course a student of religion, not theatre, so her misguided efforts are understandable. By her own admission, Harrison was interested neither in art nor in theatre (Peacock 1991:173). She was similarly unapologetic about what she called her "dislike for history" (Schlesier 1991:201). Her "ritual hypothesis," that drama took its rise from orgiastic religious practices, has been discredited. See esp. Pickard-Cambridge 1962:189; Else 1965b:7; Vickers 1973:33ff.; Kirk 1985:223ff.

mances consisted of interpretations of poetic texts (*Ion* 530c3–4), Herington is justified to some extent in considering the actor's art a continuation of, rather than a radical break with, earlier genres of poetic performance.[111] But he is justified only to a certain extent, for there is a generic leap between merely reporting the various characters' speeches, as the rhapsode did, and actually pretending to stand in for one of them visually, as the actor came to do. The rhapsode did not change his identity or appearance: he always performed visually "as" himself, a rhapsode, merely telling his audience, with appropriate gestures, what other fictional figures said.

In drama however, and for the first time in poetry in Greece, the performer now pretended to have traded his own identity for the identity of a fictional figure. And because the direct physical representation of fictional characters was unprecedented in his time, Thespis had to think of something to show unequivocally that his performers were not mere rhapsodes, narrating the story, but were rather a new poetic species, performers whose own appearances and identities were to be ignored in favor of whatever visual illusion they might create of representing Homer's Achilleus, or Odysseus, or Clytaemestra, Medea, or Ajax. So Thespis experimented, first using white lead as a disguise, then flowers; but evidently these were not adequate, and he settled on a plain linen mask as a sign to the audience that they should focus not on the performer's own face or persona but instead imagine someone else's in its place.[112]

Thespis' experiments with disguise and eventual settling upon the mask were therefore probably a case of necessity being the mother of invention: the theatrical performer visually represents something other than himself, so the actor needs a disguising device. Yet it is still not clear how it came to pass that the actor became this kind of performer. Why had Thespis abandoned a narrative style in the first place? Why didn't he retain the *propria persona* voice of the rhapsode and bard?

It is distinctly possible that, having internalized the alphabet's mode of representation, the inventors of drama were able to conceive of an "alphabetical" representational style for performance too: as letters represent, so might the performer. Because it breaks the sounds of speech down into units on the individual or "atomic" level, alphabetical writing has been connected with the trend toward "atomization" in the Western intellectual tra-

111. Havelock makes the same point: "Whether recited and mimed by an epic rhapsodist who himself 'does' all the characters, or split up into parts done by different reciters who became actors," the two types of performance "differed in degree rather than in kind" (1963:48).

112. See Pickard-Cambridge 1968:190 for Thespis' experiments.

dition generally. In science, for example, this trend is visible in the fifth-century writings of Leucippus and Democritus, who conceived of individual "atoms" which "are compounded together and entangled . . . [to] create something" (Aristotle *On Generation and Corruption* 1.7, 325a30ff.).[113] Such thinking clearly reflects the alphabet's procedure of dividing unities into small, mobile units. This breakdown of speech into individual letters has also been associated by some cultural theorists with the breaking down of monolithic social and political structures. As Kristeva sees it, whereas "the ideogrammatical type of writing was often accompanied by a mode of production said to be 'Asian' (large productive and interdependent collectives, managed by a central organization without isolated, urban and 'democratic' . . . units . . .)," alphabetical systems tend to be accompanied by social systems in which the individual is given an autonomy analogous to that afforded to individual letters: "The Greek alphabetical system had as its correlative, on the sociological level, units of production that were isolated and closed on themselves, a development of individual consciousness in ideology, and a logic of non-contradiction in science" (1989:95). In the aesthetic sphere, the same analogy is visible: the "emancipation of the signifier" typical of alphabetical representation is echoed in the emancipation of the narrative figures typical of theatrical representation. Just as the alphabet represents speech by dividing the verbal world into a small number of repeatable visual shapes, or letters, so too does the dramatist proceed by dividing the storytelling world into a number of discrete, visible "characters."

In the *ABC Show* in particular, we see the continuity of activity between inscribing speech in writing and performing stories through the bodies of actors. For in the same way that the letters of the alphabet could be freely used in combination to represent the words of speech, so too were the bodies of actors—or young men singing in the chorus—given over to the task of representing the letters of the alphabet. We recall from my earlier discussion that the novelty of the alphabet was that letters represented sounds arbitrarily, unconnected to any meaning, and that it was this semantic indeterminacy that gave phonetic letters such flexibility in representing speech. Theatrical performers thus function like letters in this respect as well: their freedom from their own identities, or any particular identity, gives them the freedom to represent any other thing. This absolute representational mobility is ultimately what separates the actor from the bard or rhapsode, who remains always Homer or Ion even when he is relating what Achilleus said or did.

113. As translated by Kirk, Raven, and Schofield 1987:407.

The body of the actor, which functions explicitly as an unmotivated "letter" in the *ABC Show,* functions implicitly as an unmotivated sign (for a fictional character) in every other play. Unlike the epic *aoidos,* who sings the Muse's song in his own person, the theatrical performer has the semiotic freedom to stand in for anyone and anything. Whether representing a mythic hero or a contemporary Athenian slave, a god, or a frog, actors, who explicitly represent letters in Kallias' play, are those performers who, like letters, function primarily *by* representing, and have the semiotic freedom to represent potentially any meaning.

In this way, the stage could be said to have absorbed the signifying, alienating practice of writing, for the semiology of phoneticism was transferred from the letters of the alphabet to the bodies of performers on the stage. In theatrical representation, the performer is liberated from the bardic or rhapsodic "as-himself" and endowed with an (arbitrary, alphabetical) "as-anything." In all dramatic literature, there is perhaps no better description of this semiotic freedom than the analysis of the particular "manner" of theatrical "showing" provided by Shakespeare's Launce:

> Nay, I'll *show* you the manner of it. This shoe is my father; no, this left shoe is my father: no, no, this left shoe is my mother; nay, that cannot be so neither:—yes, it is so; it is so; it hath the worser sole. This shoe, with the hole in, is my mother, and this my father . . . this staff is my sister . . . : this hat is Nan, our maid: I am the dog; no, the dog is himself, and I am the dog,—O! the dog is me, and I am myself: ay, so, so.
> (*Two Gentlemen of Verona* 2.3.15–26)

Like Launce's shoes, the actor has the representational freedom to stand in for *anything* on the theatrical stage—even inanimate objects like Kallias' letters. Furthermore, the basic principle of semiotic mobility extends also to objects on the stage, where shoes and hats can stand for parents and maids.

The use of a body as a sign for something else obviously has predramatic precedents; but it is in drama that this basic semiotic activity is exploited consciously and fully for artistic ends. For example, in the *Odyssey* alone there are numerous cases of corporeal impersonation,[114] although it is usually the prerogative of a goddess, Athena, to arrange for someone's disguise (1.105, 2.383, 2.401, 8.8, 13.429–30). Not only does the fictional Odysseus dress up as a beggar as part of his homecoming scheme, but also the historical Solon, we are told, impersonated a mad messenger to deliver a

---

114. These cases of corporeal impersonation were not, of course, aesthetic performances, but rather functional expedients to accomplish a practical goal.

political poem in the marketplace (Else 1965b:41). In addition, the use of the body to represent animals or gods has been seen to accompany religious rituals and dances around the world.[115] As Aristotle suggested (*Poetics* 1448b5ff.), and as contemporary neurobiology confirms,[116] imitative role-playing comes naturally to humans and serves the practical function of adapting us to our cultures and teaching us how things are done in them. Children do it even before they have done much else, and continue to use their bodies to imitate other things throughout their lives. Humans apparently learn by imitation and role-playing, the utilitarian benefits of which always seem to include a measure of inherent pleasurability. So the use of the body and things for representing *other* bodies, things, or states of affairs clearly did not come into existence with the advent of dramatic form (let alone writing). But before theatre, there is no evidence that such role-playing had been fused with storytelling, nor had it emerged as a poetic genre proper. Before writing, storytelling was the province of a single speaker and that speaker's own deictically grounded identity. The various characters represented in his tale were all controlled and motivated by his single identity as composing/performing servant to the Muse. When the appearance of writing fractured this oral unity of composition and performance into two separate activities, the poet emerged as a writer who tells his story through the use of arbitrary signs rather than through his presence. And this semiotic method of storytelling, observable at the stage of poetic composition in the activity of inscription, was extended to the activity of performance as well, with actors rather than letters doing the representing. Arbitrary representation of this kind was not new to life, in other words, but new to the phenomenology of storytelling.

As a further consequence of the dramatist's ability to divide performance up alphabetically, it became possible to delegate storytelling to non-specialists. In a literate world, performers were suddenly able to memorize a story written from start to finish by someone else, and to do so conceivably overnight, with no apprenticeship whatever. This in itself would have supported the move toward atomization in storytelling. With the contribution of each performer determined in advance and recorded in text, a communal storytelling effort would have become much easier to manage. But most significant of all, the preexistence of the story in written form made it possible for performative power to be delegated to those who had no special skills in improvisation or oral-formulaic technique. Once scripts exist, paradoxically

---

115. Hsu 1985:196–208; Lévi-Strauss 1982; Petrone 1990:17; Beck 1993.
116. See esp. Finkel 1988:66.

enough, the performer does not even need to know how to read (although it helps), because the fixity and repeatability of a written text makes rote memorization possible even for those who must learn their parts with help from another reader.[117] And so it is not insignificant that the earliest Greek actors were amateurs: in a notable departure from epic practice, actors had no specialized skills, nor were they in possession of a specially monopolized traditional style. Although actors' guilds and clubs, schools and techniques, were eventually to emerge and a "histrionic tradition" eventually to appear (and sometimes be passed on within families), none of these existed in the early days of dramatic performance (Slater 1990:385ff.).

This de-specialization of performance is fundamental to the representational style of the theatre, and has remained a distinguishing characteristic of dramatic performance to this day. For, in the final analysis, all the "methods" and theatrical families in existence cannot outweigh one fact: that more plays are enacted by amateurs than professionals. Whether in school plays or church plays or plays performed at home or at some local community center (Brownies, summer camp, Boys' and Girls' Clubs, and so on), ordinary citizens participate in thousands of theatrical performances every year throughout the Western world. Even individuals who have never set foot in a professional theatre are likely to have performed some part, in some play, at some time.

The liberation of the performer from the need to belong to an exclusive sect or special caste was achieved through the detachment of performative material from the body and physical memory of the initiate. Before writing, traditional stories existed solely within the mind and personal performance of culturally sanctioned specialists. Within the newly literate world, these songs now existed "on the outside," where they could be picked up and performed by "anybody." That this democratizing alienation of mythological material represented an alarmingly new state of affairs, at least to some observers, can be seen in Plato's *Ion*. Here the philosopher raises his concerns about the propriety of performances of important traditional material by those who had no legitimate or obviously special claims on it. Because Ion was just an "anybody" with a script,[118] Plato cast doubt on his legitimacy by

117. This is an important point, for it suggests that not all participants in a literate theatre would necessarily need to be skilled readers, or even literate themselves. See W. Harris 1989 for very conservative estimates of the number of readers in the various Greek periods.

118. Ion was clearly a very talented reciter of Homeric epics, so he was not just "anybody" in that sense. Plato's objections revolve rather around the fact that Ion was demonstrably not an expert in anything other than the memorization of another man's words. For evidence that rhapsodes like Ion used written texts, see Xenophon *Memorabilia* 4.2, 10; Sandys 1958:30; and Thomas 1992:119.

saying that he had neither sufficiently specialized *episteme* nor authentic *techne*, neither knowledge nor craft. What rhapsodes like Ion inaugurated by performing material that did not belong exclusively and properly to them, actors developed even further.

It is worth noting that Plato's resistance to amateurism in public performance cannot be wholly attributed to his particular philosophical outlook. Wherever performance has traditionally been the preserve of specialists, the figure of the actor, every inch the amateur, is bound to be welcomed onto the storytelling scene with all the warmth extended to the parvenu at the yacht club. As we see in Europe some centuries later, this was precisely what did happen when the popularity of amateur plays began to challenge the privileges of the professional minstrel. The monopoly on storytelling previously enjoyed by the minstrels was in fact so seriously threatened by the script-bearing amateur actor that the minstrels tried to have amateurs prohibited from giving performances (Child 1912:8). The ability of written stories to take storytelling out of the hands of a specialized group is thus attested both in antiquity and in the early days of secular drama in Europe.

But there is an additional issue here: in a theatrical performance, the story is not merely detached from the body of the tradition's proper representative, the *aoidos* or minstrel. It is detached also from the body of *any* single performer. In contrast to both bardic and rhapsodic performances, the story in a dramatic presentation is shared among a number of separate performers. As Niall Slater points out, it is when the story can no longer be told by the single body of any one performer (specialist or otherwise) that the actor is born (1990:385). Rather than embodying in himself the locus and control center of a single unified poetic monologue, as did the bard or rhapsode, the performer in drama becomes, like a letter, an atomized element in a larger semiotic structure, a systematic collective.[119]

Returning to Kallias' grammatical theory, we can now see the natural affinity of the actor for the alphabet, and vice versa. Instead of creating meaning for an audience through who he *is*—an *aoidos* inspired by the Muse of memory, or a rhapsode inspired by the memory of the *aoidos*—the actor creates meaning through whom or what he can arbitrarily *represent*: a

119. Gordon Shrimpton has suggested in conversation that the nature of rhapsodic competition may *itself* have suggested a dramatic style. Indeed, the sixth-century rule about sequential recitation determined that each competing rhapsode would, in effect, have been cooperating in telling a bigger story, and thus would have functioned as an actor in this respect—or in any case would have had a performative experience akin to the systematic storytelling of theatre. This is an intriguing possibility that had not occurred to me. Nevertheless, the contest rule that would have inaugurated this practice—the demand for sequential recitation of a "single" story by separate reciters—was itself a product of a literate approach to storytelling, as we saw earlier in this chapter.

Trojan woman, a cloud, the letter *O*. But the use of writing for poetic composition had also created a situation in which the story to be told no longer inhered within the performer's body and his specialist technique. Instead, it existed in a written version, a fixed, external form, separate from any particular performance technique. Although this disconnectedness from technique meant that a written story could be learned easily by anyone, it *did* have to be learned—from scratch—because the literate demand for "invention" in storytelling meant that each story now had to be a *new* one. Unlike the specializing bard, who was a bard precisely by virtue of the fact that he already knew how to tell all the old stories, the amateur actor was the performer called upon to learn all the new ones. The actor's part had to be "taught" to him, and new ones were taught each year.[120] And so it is altogether fitting that, in the *ABC Show,* the actors should be cast in the role of *students.*

The alphabetical division of the story into separate characters determined that the poet could no longer tell it by himself; but the literate bias in favor of originality guaranteed that no performer already knew it. The poet now needed actors; but actors needed the poet's instructions. For this reason the playwright was called *didaskalos,* the teacher of his poems, for his original stories could be properly told only by being taught to performers who would not otherwise have known what to say or do.[121] In this way did the alphabet bring the actor into existence and determine that he would be a species of performer new to Greece: the grammar student, the memorizer of text.

120. See Taplin 1977:12–14; also *Frogs* 1249ff.; *Birds* 749.
121. Taplin 1977:13; also *Thesmophoriazusae* 30, 88, and *Frogs* 1021.

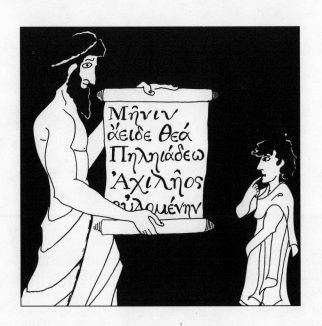

CHAPTER 2

The Student Body

> Yes, my dear, when you have first shown me
> what it is you have in your left hand, under
> your cloak. For I suspect you have the actual
> text.
>
> Plato

> The abdomen is the reason why man does not
> easily take himself for a god.
>
> Nietzsche

O NE FINE DAY IN FIFTH-CENTURY ATHENS, OUTSIDE THE THEATRE OF
Dionysus, the great philosophy teacher Socrates was delivering a lecture, and Plato chanced to hear him. Now Plato, barely twenty years old,
was already something of a poet by this time, having composed dithyrambs
and other lyrics; he had also just written a tragedy, and was planning to submit it to the upcoming contest in drama. Our source for this story does not
reveal the subject of Socrates' talk; but whatever it was, it must have had a
sensational effect on Plato, for as a result of it, he renounced playwriting
forever. We know nothing about what happened to Plato's work in the predramatic genres of choral and solo lyric; but the tragedy he had written for
submission to the theatre festival suffered a remarkable fate under Socrates'
pedagogical influence: Plato consigned it to the flames (Diogenes Laertius
Plato 3.5–6).

Plato went on, of course, to make his name as a writer of dialogues, a
literary form whose connections to drama are intriguing to say the least.
Like drama, the philosophical dialogue focuses on the speech of speakers at
the expense of almost all surrounding lexical and narrative material. Like
drama, its "stories" are cast in terms of an interlocutory situation. But the
difference between drama and the dialogue, as far as literary form goes, is
perhaps ultimately more significant still: what is implied by all dramatic
texts, the bodies of performers, is not required by the Platonic dialogue. Regardless of what Plato may have intended in composing them, his dialogues

have survived as objects for classroom study and private reading, and function self-sufficiently as pure literary texts—something that cannot be said of texts intended for performance in the theatre.

For theatre people, there is no more revealing story about the relationship between students and teachers than this one. In becoming a student, Plato had found it necessary to renounce not *all* aspects of dramatic form but only the bodies of performers. In burning his tragedy and composing dialogues instead, Plato is a powerful symbol of the trend in literate culture toward increasingly de-corporealized communication practices. For as Aristotle noted, the history of artistic genres, from oral epic through drama and toward the novel, is a gradual movement away from the body and toward communication "in bare prose" (*Poetics* 1447b). Under conditions of orality, verbal communication in the absence of a body is not an option; but when writing came on the scene, the choice could be made to do away with it and communicate by language alone. In short, with literacy came a new problem: what role should the body be given in a particular act of communication? Now, there is much in Socrates' own philosophy that could explain his student's decision to eliminate corporeality from his artistic output. Throughout the Socratic metaphysics as related by Plato, there is a generalized devaluation of the "sights and sounds" of sensible reality, sensory phenomena of which a performing human body would naturally be a prime example. But, as we shall see, there is something in *all* literate learning and teaching that separates itself from the body in this way. It was not only by virtue of his being Socrates' student that the body became a problem for Plato; it was by virtue of being a student, period.

The first thing we notice, however, when cogitating upon the nature of the fifth-century student is how closely theatrical practices resembled scholarly ones. Had Socrates' lecture taken place within the Theatre of Dionysus rather than outside it, he might have looked, to all appearances, like an actor rather than a teacher; and we know from Aristophanes' *Frogs* that plays were expected to *teach* as well as delight. Not only did fifth-century teachers of rhetoric and philosophy such as Lysias, Protagoras, and Prodicus dress in special costumes when they appeared before large festival audiences, but they are also known to have delivered their lessons from memorized written scripts.[1] In so doing, they performed much in the manner of actors, who similarly delivered written works to the public in an oral form. Like Plato's unperformed tragedy, the plays of the ancient theatre did not reach their public unless the text was learned and memorized by actors. For this reason the playwright was

1. *Phaedrus* 227d–228, 228d–229, 230e; *Theaetetus* 162a; Diogenes Laertius 9.50. See also O'Sullivan (1996:115–27) for the written nature of Sophistic teaching.

called *didaskalos* (*Thesmophoriasuzae* 30, 88; *Frogs* 1021), a teacher, and he must have functioned very much as did the fifth-century schoolmaster. "And as soon as his boys have learned their letters, and are in a condition to understand what is written . . . [the teacher] sets before them on their benches the works of good poets to read, and compels them to learn them by heart" (Plato *Protagoras* 325d–e). Indeed, as Richard Green and Eric Handley remind us, the word normally used to say that someone produced a play, *edidasken,* is the very same one used to describe teaching youngsters in a school (1995:33). If the playwright is the teacher of his poems, presumably that makes the actor his student; and learning a written text by heart certainly does seem a scholarly thing to do. When we consider the fact that, before writing and book-based schools, such activities were utterly unknown, the actor's likeness to the student becomes especially pronounced.

In fact, no matter where we look in stage history or dramatic literature, a connection between theatre and scholarship is visible. From Aristophanes' "Thinkery" to Molière's schools for husbands and wives, students and teachers are omnipresent in the repertory. As early as the century after Aristotle, theatre is explicitly singled out among the genres as having a special connection with attendance at school. In Herondas' mime *The Schoolmaster,* an irate mother complains that her truant son skips school so often that he cannot even recognize the letter *A;* and the proof of his delinquency is that he hasn't memorized a single line from a play!

> But when asked to say something from a play,
> As anybody might ask a schoolboy,
> . . . What trickles out, as if from a cracked jug?
> *Apollo the bright, a hunter was he!*
> Your old granny, I say, can recite that
> Without being able to read or write![2]

In other words, while even the schoolmaster's granny—or the student's great-grandmother—might have committed to memory a line of oral-formulaic poetry, like "any Phrygian slave in the street," it was a mark of a book-learned student that he would also know lines from a *play.*

The natural affinity Herondas sees between the theatre and the classroom has only strengthened through time. After centuries of the near-total abatement of organized theatrical activities in the Christian era, theatrical form was to make its first reappearance (ca. 900) in the school plays of Hroswitha, written for performance by her students. And the reemergence

2. From the Davenport translation (1981).

of a theatrical tradition in the Renaissance is unthinkable without the early experiments of scholars and schoolmasters whose adaptations of the classics for the classroom not only reminded Europe that such works were meant to be performed, but also stocked the nascent professional theatres with boy actors used to memorizing and acting in plays. From Hippolytos to Hamlet, Pheidippides to Faustus—and including such later-day students as Tesman, Constantine, and Oleanna—the Western stage has abounded with characters who are cast in obvious ways as book-toting students, and whose fates are intimately connected with their scholarly vocations. The grammar student of Kallias' dramatic imagination has clearly gone on to become one of the perennial images of our theatre.

Even for Antonin Artaud, centuries later, to whom the theatre's alliance with bookishness seemed an unholy one, the connection was nonetheless evident: because the Western theatre is built on a respect for "what has been written," its practitioners are vilified as "grammarians" and "graduate students" (1958:41). Theatre, for Artaud, is *too much* like school, and we find similar complaints about theatrical didacticism in twentieth-century theorists from Edward Gordon Craig (1956:35) to Patrice Pavis (1982:141). Judging from what we have seen so far of the shift from bardic expertise to actorly amateurism, such concerns do not seem altogether unfounded. In trading a virtuosic composition-in-performance technique for a mere "teacher's" text, the literate performer does seem, at least at first sight, to have lost creative autonomy in direct proportion with the adoption of scholarly models. For all the hysteria of his attack against the Western theatre's textual didacticism, Artaud may have been on to something.

Whether the theatre is indeed, as Artaud feared, too much like school is one of the questions toward which we will be working throughout this chapter. In answering it, we will also see something of what is at stake in Plato's schooldays rejection of theatre altogether. But for now we need to set the scene, historically, for the appearance of the first schools in Greece; for it appears that the first playwrights, beginning with Aeschylus, were among the very first poets in the Western tradition ever to go to school.

The archaeological record for schools in Greece is not easy to interpret, and there remains some uncertainty about when exactly it was that classroom instruction began. A very early wax-covered writing tablet has survived (ca. 650) with the alphabet written across the top as if for a student (Powell 1991:155 fig. 55), but there is nothing specifically to connect this teaching device to use in a school. A tradition does exist that dates schools in Greece all the way back to this time, the seventh century B.C.E., but the sources for it are late and have been deemed untrustworthy by some (cf. Beck 1964:77). Evidence for schools in the sixth century takes the form of the school laws attributed to Solon of Athens and Charondas of Catana; these stipulated that schooling was mandatory for all citizens' sons, and that the city must foot the bill (W. Harris 1989:21). The problem with these laws is that the sources for them, again, are centuries after the fact, by which time it had become something of a national pastime to attribute to Solon laws that actually came later. Concrete references to specific grammar schools (in Chios ca. 496, Astypalaea ca. 490) do not appear until the first decades of the fifth century. As William Harris notes, however, none of this evidence suggests that the teaching of letters in a classroom was any sort of innovation (1989:57). Herodotus refers only casually and in passing to the 119 children who were killed when the roof of their school collapsed on them while they were "learning their letters" (6.27). From such evidence, scholars such as Harris conclude that "there must already have been some [schools] in the sixth century" (57), and his opinion is shared by most of his colleagues.[3] By the 490s, it is fairly certain that "practically all prosperous Greeks, and some who were not, sent their sons to school" (58). The Douris Cup (ca. 485) represents a typical school scene from this period, and confirms iconographically the literary evidence, such as it exists. In summary, then, though in some ways ambiguous, the available evidence suggests one thing unmistakably: that the first grammar schools cannot be dated to any point after the 490s, since they were already widespread and well established by this time; and it would be wrong to date them much earlier than the birth of Aeschylus in the 520s, since there is no concrete proof of their existence so early. It appears, in other words, that book-based schooling came on the scene at some point between the end of the sixth and the beginning of the fifth centuries B.C.E., which means that Aeschylus may have been among the very first students ever to creep like snail unwillingly to school.

Is it really possible that poets before Aeschylus had no experience of classroom instruction? Was not Sappho famous for her school for girls in the Archaic period? As Susan Pomeroy reminds us, the image of Sappho as a schoolmistress is a modern invention, and one that is belied by both her poetry and all the stories told about her in antiquity (1975:53). The case of Sappho is nevertheless revelatory, for it reminds us how profoundly education was changed with the introduction of formal schooling. If Sappho's poems are "teachings," they are all addressed to the teacher's intimates, lovers, and

---

3. See Beck 1964, 1975; Burns 1981:375; Immerwahr 1964:17; cf. Havelock 1977:386 n. 4, who alone disagrees, dating schools somewhat later.

friends. Her love songs to Anactoria, Gongyla, Atthis, her daughter Cleis[4]—all these bespeak the kind of "passionate involvement" (53) that typified all learning and teaching before the advent of schools.

For book-based study radically altered the nature of learning in Greece. As Frederick Beck (1964) has pointed out, the word *didaskaleion,* or "school," does not exist at all in Homer, nor can it be found anywhere else in predramatic poetry. It makes its first appearance in the sense of "school" in the fifth century, in Herodotus (6.27), Sophocles (frag. 799), and Thucydides (7.29).[5] In predramatic literature it is more common to come across references to individual teachers, whose actions are described with the verb *trepso,* to "rear" (Beck 1964:49). Both from the context of Homer's and Hesiod's discussions of this brand of teaching, and from the word itself, it is clear that this preliterate "rearing" is a rather different thing from that which happens in schools. Speaking of the relationship that prevailed between a Cheiron or a Phoenix and his pupil, Beck summarizes as follows. The "rearer" in Homer and Hesiod "was responsible for the whole development of his pupil, moral, physical and intellectual, and not merely or solely for the imparting of specific aspects of knowledge" (49).

The preliterate teacher began his involvement with his charge more or less from birth, and might continue it for nearly a lifetime. Phoenix, for example, "reared" Achilleus "to be both a speaker of words and a doer of deeds" and did so "with [his] heart's love" (Iliad 9.435–43, 485). In preliterate education, as Beck describes it, "the pupil learns by imitating his teacher in all their joint activities" (60–61). Consequently, between such "rearers" and their charges there is a strong emotional bond, and learning is but the outcome of their intimate ongoing relationship and shared experience. Phoenix bounced Achilleus on his knee, cut up his meat into little pieces at table, and fed him wine (*Il.* 9.490ff.). As a result, the service of a preliterate teacher such as Phoenix is, in Werner Jaeger's words, "only a continuation of the almost paternal love which has always bound him" to his charge (1960, 1:28). The poems of Sappho confirm that this intimate relationship, this passionate lifelong attachment between teachers and their pupils, continued beyond the Homeric period and into the "lyric" age of Greece.[6]

A legendary teacher like Cheiron—evidence of whose reputation has come down to us through literary and archaeological material from the Archaic period—is, however, never represented as a teacher of letters (Beck

4. *Lyra Graeca* (Edmonds 1952), Sappho, 1.38, 45; 2.48, 81, 82, 83, 86, 108; 6.130.

5. See Beck 1964:78.

6. The Suda *Lexicon* is not sure what to call the subjects of Sappho's poems and affections, and so names them "pupils or disciples." See Edmonds 1952:147.

1975:10). For literacy was to put an end to the kind of one-on-one relationship that such teachers represented. Predictably enough, representations of Cheiron in Greek art begin to disappear with the establishment of formal literary schooling (Beck 1975:10). Whereas teachers and students had formerly enjoyed each other's company "in all their joint activities," fifth-century students were trundled off to learn their letters only for certain specific hours of the day. And when they arrived for their lessons, they appear, by all accounts, to have sat in classrooms in anonymous groups of between sixty and one hundred or more.[7] And whereas the tutor had formerly shared all the student's activities, Athenian grammar students apparently had separate specialist instructors for each class.[8]

From the fifth-century dramatists and from Plato we have learned a few general things about the nature of education in a newly literate world. From Sophocles and Euripides, who both feature *pedagogoi* in their *Elektra* plays, we learn that the rearing function of a Homeric teacher seems to have been taken over by a household servant called a *pedagogus;* he was a kind of nanny, caring for the children and taking them to school, but apparently not responsible for instructing his charges himself (Plato *Lysis* 208c). In Aristophanes' school in the *Clouds,* an actor representing the "Right" argument waxes nostalgic about the good old days when boys walked to school together decorously, when discipline in the classroom was strict, and the students learned good old-fashioned poetry by heart (961ff.). Right Argument describes the regular school curriculum of earlier fifth-century education as consisting of music and/or letters and gymnastics—an educational program that is confirmed in other literary sources as well.[9]

In Kallias' *ABC Show,* however, we are treated to an especially intimate portrait of the kind of book learning that the dramatists would have experienced themselves as boys.[10] They repeated. And they repeated verbatim: "Beta alpha: ba. Beta epsilon: be. Beta eta: bē." They did as the teacher bade them do: "You must pronounce alpha by itself, and secondly epsilon by itself. And you there, you will say the third vowel!" (frag. 31 Edmonds 1957). As archaeological evidence confirms, students learned their lessons in precisely this way. A piece of pottery has survived with grammar lessons in-

7. Herodotus 6.27.2; Thucydides 7.29; *scholion* on *Laws* 629a as cited by Burns 1981:375 and Beck 1964:77–89.
8. Jeffrey 1990:63; Burns 1981:375; Beck 1964:81.
9. *Knights* 188–90; Plato *Protagoras* 325d–e; also Harris 1989:57 n. 56.
10. From a few surviving vases and terra-cottas, we see that it was not only boys but also perhaps girls who went to school (Cole 1981; Beck 1975 plates 69 and 71 esp.), as Kallias' play suggests.

scribed upon it—"rha, rhē, rhi, rho, rhou, rhō, sa, sē," and so on—complete
with a mistake and the teacher's correction (Beck 1975:16). From literary references and contemporary representations in visual art, we know that poetry, largely Homer's, was a major component of the student's educational
diet (Beck 1975:14). And as the passage cited earlier from Plato shows, poetry was memorized the same way that the alphabet was: the student learned
it by heart from a written text placed before him on his bench (*Protagoras*
325d–e). Plato's account of epic memorization in the classroom is further
confirmed, iconographically, by the Douris Cup. It shows a student studying a (now lost) poem, the first line of which—"Moisa moi amphi Skaman-
dron eurron archom' aeindein"—is depicted on the scroll held by the
onlooking, seated teacher (Beck 1975:14).

In the year when the Douris Cup was decorated with this charming
teacher-student scene, Sophocles was nine years old. He would have been in
school himself at this time. An iconographic image from Aeschylus' school
days is unfortunately not available; can we perhaps provide one for ourselves? The teacher says, "You there, Aeschylus, recite this passage from Sappho's love poem." And the diligent student does, knowing all the while that
he is not a Sapphic lover, his teacher is not the beloved, nor is the classroom
either a festival or a symposium to which the other pupils have come for entertainment. In short, what is repeated by the student in the process of book
learning is not connected with his "here-and-now" experience in the classroom. In the preliterate one-on-one relation between tutor and friend, the
recitation of poetry would normally have had some direct grounding in the
interlocutors' shared experience. In Homer, songs about battle or home-
coming are sung in related circumstances; Sapphic poems about love and
friendship were sung to lovers and friends. But between a roomful of students and an instructor who may be a virtual stranger to them, and a paid
professional to boot (Beck 1975:14), any direct relation between the content
of the lesson and the social context in which it is learned is precluded. Consequently, book learning demands the repetition of contextually irrelevant
material, material that is unmotivated by the context in which the speaker
finds himself. It requires the student to "bracket" or ignore the present being
lived—ignore, that is, the concrete social relations inherent in the present
interlocutory situation.

This tendency of literate study to detach readers from the concrete circumstances that surround them is comically demonstrated by Aristophanes
in the *Frogs*. Reading from a written text of Euripides' *Andromeda* while
aboard a ship, Dionysus loses all sense of context and proper action. He is
supposed to be fighting the enemy under his captain Cleisthenes, but is carried elsewhere by his reading, first mentally, and then physically, as he basi-

cally deserts the fleet in order to seek out the author (52–53). A similar loss of contact with the physical "here-and-now" is attributed by Aristophanes to the bookish Sophists: in the *Clouds,* Socrates is presented as so oblivious to his immediate surroundings that he wouldn't notice a lizard sitting over his head unless it actually shat in his eye (160ff.). And in the *Phaedrus,* Phaedrus' book is likened to a drug which makes its readers heedless of their surroundings: like the mythical Oreithyia, whose preoccupation with Pharmacea got in the way of her noticing a dangerous wind, so too may a reader of books have his senses distracted from prevailing physical circumstances.[11]

In conditions of orality, it is hard to imagine anything teachable that would not be taught within a concrete sphere of action: fishing is taught to the apprentice in midstream, religion to the initiate during a ceremony, recitation to bards-hopeful during a recitation, proverbs to grandchildren in contexts to which the proverb applies. But learning a poem by heart in a classroom is clearly not of this kind. Like all other book-based classroom activities, it is characterized by a high degree of abstraction and decontextualization. As Werner Jaeger has pointed out, students before writing learned everything in situ and by physical imitation in a 360° context of action (1945 1:29); a student who is learning from a book, by contrast, is confined to a specialized "abstract" space and encouraged to develop a unidirectional gaze at a writing tablet or book roll.[12] What were the effects of this new pedagogical model on its first students? Might their exposure to this novel teaching style have influenced their poetic output as adults, particularly insofar as their contributions to the nascent art of drama is concerned? For as we have seen in our time, it is largely through their experiences in the classroom that literates absorb the kinds of practices and models which mark them as "literate" in comparison with their "oral" counterparts. Modern psychological studies and tests have demonstrated that it is an individual's exposure to the classroom that, more than any other factor, causes the changes in his or her attitudes and mental habits which we have come to associate with the effects of literacy.[13]

For a start, the *Phaedrus* suggests that the decontextualizing of book-

11. This reading of the myth is suggested by Steiner (1994:213–14).

12. This point was made to me by Derrick de Kerckhove in a personal exchange. Jesper Svenbro takes the idea further by suggesting that this readerly, scholarly disposition—passive, unidirectional viewing in an autonomous, abstract space—is precisely the one that theatre assumes and calls upon in its audiences. Svenbro (1990:365–84), however, does not connect such skills to schooling per se. His concern is with the skills acquired through reading itself, particularly *silent* reading.

13. See esp. Scribner and Cole 1981; also Taylor 1988.

based study is a bit of an effort, not the natural impulse when students and teachers get together. But apparently it is an effort that needs to be made if literate teaching and learning are to proceed. In order to avoid succumbing to the charms of his student's physical presence, immersing himself in the present context, Socrates finds that he must go so far as to keep his head and eyes covered (237a5). Socrates is determined to compete as a teacher with Lysias and discourse upon the subject of love. But Lysias, "the cleverest of present writers," has worked on his composition "at his leisure" and over a long stretch of time (228); in order to compete in cleverness with such a polished speech, Socrates must immunize himself against the physical realities of the interlocutory situation in which he finds himself.

Phaedrus begins by reading out the written lecture of Lysias in the hope of convincing Socrates of its excellence. Expecting, no doubt, to prove his theory about the weaknesses of writing and the superiority of oral modes of instruction, Socrates counters by attempting to improvise a speech on the same subject orally. But what he finds is that oral performance *cannot* compete with the special kind of teaching that writing makes possible, that in fact oral performance interferes with thought. Before he knows what has happened, he has started speaking "in hexameters," the language of epic poetry (241e). He has become "possessed," not just by his student but by the beauties of the place to which his student has "exposed" him (241e). He gets carried away by his talk about the appetites of love, and, perhaps noticing the extent to which the content of his speech and the social context of its delivery have coincided—for Phaedrus is many times referred to as a bewitching creature—Socrates stops his speech in the middle, unable or unwilling to go further (241d–e). In allowing the present situation to intrude upon his lesson, Socrates has not only lapsed into the language of the inspired bard but has also replicated the bard's compositional style: he recites episodically, with no proper structure, no ending, and he interrupts his discourse with vocatives to his audience (238c–d). Worse still, he has missed the mark of truth. In speaking extemporaneously about the interestedness of a lover, he has become interested himself *as* a lover, and in consequence delivers a "dreadful speech" of which he is ashamed and for which he refuses to take responsibility (242c–d). So completely did the presence of his interlocutor determine his lesson that he thrice attributes the speech to Phaedrus, his student and listener, rather than to himself (238d, 242d, e).

Like Lysias' written speech, which asserts the superiority of the disinterested lover (231–34d), the dialogue as a whole has many positive things to say about the advantages of disinterestedness in learning and teaching. Bodily based conversation, with its immersion in present contexts, is shown to risk "[leading] us in a wrong direction" (265b–c), taking us astray "like an animal" (235e). By contrast, the disinterested, phenomenally disengaged character of literate study is shown—and not just in this work but throughout Plato's oeuvre—to have enormous advantages over a practically embedded model of learning. Taking utterances and information out of contexts enables one to reflect on them consciously and at leisure, to view their premises and hidden assumptions, to expose the prejudices that support them and the illogicalities that they hide. Mental structures, social paradigms, and inherited values can be pulled into the light of abstract reason, and inconsistencies, contradictions, and injustices drawn out. By "bracketing" the sights and sounds of sensible reality, one is less likely to mistake fleeting desires, illusions, or mere opinions for truth. This literate bracketing of one's physical context is also associated in the *Phaedrus* with the qualities that make for clear thinking and speaking generally: self-consistency, synthesis, clarity, definition of terms, the breaking up of entities into constituent parts, "divisions and collections," and especially a unified organic structure (264c, 266c). Although these are qualities that "even . . . the worst writer" is not likely to fail in mastering (235e), they prove to be qualities beyond the reach of the oral improviser, whose involvement in his context must siphon attention away from his proper study. As the representative of the "old school" remembers in the *Clouds,* the proper learning of the boys' lessons meant "on *no* account pressing their thighs together" while memorizing epic texts, nor leaving bum prints in the sand during gym class (969ff.). When it comes to study in the classroom, the body just gets in the way.

In Platonic philosophy, particularly as explained in the *Republic,* this effortful detachment from sensible reality is described as a precondition for freeing oneself from mere opinions about the world and approaching ideal forms of thought. But poetry, too, was a beneficiary of this bookish practice of detachment from contexts, for dramatic form no less than philosophy reflects the "drawing away" or abstraction of the body from engagement in acts of performance.

In Chapter 1 we looked at some of the changes to poetic composition that followed on the use of the alphabet. The literate poet, freed of the conservative function of the oral bard, suddenly had greater leeway in making his own contribution. Instead of being expected mainly to preserve the tradition, he came to be expected to "show invention" in his use of it (*Poetics*

1453b11). Unburdened by text of his obligation to serve the Muse of memory, the poet came to be viewed as an inventor of fictional stories instead.[14] The ability to see the beginning, middle, and end of a composition simultaneously further reinforced the emergence of the literate category of fiction: narrative closure, thematic structure, and organic form became poetic virtues in their own right, connected with compositional skill but not with the needs of any particular audience.[15] Having been reduced to writing, the epic tradition of the Greeks came to be redefined as a storehouse of stories amenable to division and alteration, criticism and innovation. Whereas the lyric poet Stesichorus was believed to have been struck blind in punishment for having "sinned in matters of mythology" (*Phaedrus* 243), the dramatists of the fifth century had gained the freedom through literacy to treat the epic tradition more or less as they pleased.

The alienating atmosphere of literacy puts inherited mythology, and the formulas that contained it, at a distance from poets and performers alike. For this reason, a general "interrogatory" stance—both toward inherited material and toward the values carried by it—has been linked by many scholars to the use of writing.[16] The development of a generalized skepticism is especially dependent on the use of writing, for without written records that can be accumulated and compared, doubts about inherited wisdom cannot be followed up and will tend to be overwhelmed by the longevity of the tradition itself (Goody 1986:31). The strength of the tradition over and against the individual derives mainly from the fact, observed

14. From the descriptions in the *Odyssey* of the practice of Phemios (1.325) and Demodokos (8.43ff.), it is clear that the bard's song was not considered fictional: it was history and news in one. Telemachos, hearing reports of Orestes' matricide, says it will soon be a "theme for bards," confirming that the instantaneous passage between history and myth that I mentioned previously was a smooth one (*Od.* 1.350–52; see also Beck 1964:29). The bards were "the historians of their time, having the double function of recording and teaching history" (Beck 1964:30). What they sang was inspired by the Muse, authorized by the collective memory over which she presided, and was therefore true. By the literate dramatic age, however, traditional material had become simply the "raw ingredients" of fiction, to be divided up and used for various pleasurable effects which were unrelated to any record-keeping function (*Poetics* 1450b8–1451b3).

15. A performance of epic material, on the contrary, was shaped according to the needs of the audience. As we see from the opening invocations of the *Iliad* and the *Odyssey*, and from Demodokos' own procedure (*Od.* 8.500), the singer starts up at potentially any point in the cycle, and ends equally arbitrarily, usually when someone interrupts him, as Alkinoos and Penelope do (7.97; 1.340). In fact, as Albert Bates Lord found from his field research in the former Yugoslavia, stories are rarely sung to the end; they simply stop for one reason or another (1960:30).

16. See esp. Winchester 1985:34; Goody 1987:279.

in Africa by Jack Goody, that the "embeddedness of speech and action" in concrete contexts produces an atmosphere in which meanings, norms, and values tend to be immanent in one's way of life. Until ideas and practices take on an existence outside a particular lived context (i.e., when they get written down in texts), they tend not to be experienced as having any existential limits or boundaries. Until a practice is "drawn away" or abstracted from the doer by being written down, it is not an "object" for a "subject" to view but a constituent of his being (Bauman 1986:44). With no difference delineated between speaker and spoken or actor and thing done, members of a nonliterate society have been observed to have no experience of, for example, religious ritual as a distinct category of action. As Goody puts it: to be an Asante is to be necessarily in an existential state where such-and-such things are said and done (1986:3–12). Ritual doings, such as mimetic sacrifice, and traditional sayings, such as mourning songs and prayers, are ontologically merged with the doer and sayer's own identity. It is consequently a feature of many preliterate practices that they are compulsory. Any question as to whether or not something culturally mandated should or should not be performed or said by an individual will tend not to emerge.

Greek poetry before drama is clearly marked by these two oral features: identity between speaker and spoken and the presence of compulsory ritual elements. The Homeric bard is described as a "divine singer" whose special identity as the gods' elect is affirmed throughout, both in epithets and by his blindness, as a sign of his sacred office (*Odyssey* 1.335; 7.62–64). In the choral lyrics that are said by Aristotle to have given rise to drama, poetic content is identical to performative context: a song about Agido and her cousin Hageschora is sung by Agido and her cousin Hageschora (Alcman 1 35–95 Edmonds 1952). Epic recitation is also marked by the presence of a compulsory ritual element: the invocation to the Muse at the start. A fixed ritual invocation is also included at the beginning of many modern Yugoslavian songs as well (Lord 1960:45).

These features of predramatic performance can also be seen in more recent examples of oral practices. A piece of oratory has been recorded from a West Coast Native tribe of Canada which is cast in the form of a responsive choral song. A bereaved chief exhorts his tribe not to mourn any more; they repeatedly respond, "We do not mourn any more" (Petrone 1990:22). A modern reader or anthropologist might be inclined to see in this dialogue between chief and tribe a dramatic speech practice. But to do so would be to take literacy practices so much for granted as to forget that, in this mourning ritual, speaker and spoken are ontologically merged. These words are not "performed" for viewers, in the dramatic sense. They are a necessary consequence of who the speakers are (a mourning chief and his tribe). Similarly in Greece, the predramatic poetic genres were a direct expression of the identities of the speakers. Brides sang bridal songs, and the descendants of Homer's heroes sang the praises of their forefathers. For the epics, too, functioned as affirmations of the identities of the singers and their audiences. To be a post-Mycenaean Greek was necessarily to sing the praises of one's ancestors, to celebrate one's own lineage as recorded in the epic catalogues of men and their illustrious deeds.

In literate contexts, however, Goody has found that speech practices become decontextualized to the point where they are optional; not only does the compulsion of ritual disappear, but also performance is no longer an extension of identity.[17] Accordingly, in drama all compulsory ritual sayings and doings have disappeared. Despite what Arthur Pickard-Cambridge has called the "unscrupulous" fantasies of members of the myth-and-ritual school, classical scholars have been unable to find any evidence of fixed and compulsory ritual elements in the ancient Greek plays.[18] And as we saw in Chapter 1, the identity of speaker and spoken which typically characterizes nonliterate practices is visibly sundered in theatrical representation: a chorus of Trojan women is performed by Athenian ephebes (Winkler 1990:20–62); young boys represent women who represent letters of the alphabet. Plato could choose to compose a tragedy or not, go to the theatre festival, or attend a Socratic lecture instead.

These new freedoms in performance—from the duty of conservation and its attendant constraints, from the constraints of proper identity, and from the compulsion of ritual—can all be connected in one way or another with the existence of fixed texts. It is certainly paradoxical that textual fixity should have such liberating effects. But both in Greece and again in the

17. Goody 1986:14; 1987:69.

18. I am speaking here about the contents of the plays. The only religious ritual performed in the theatre was apparently the immolation of a piglet to purify the space; but as this action was also performed in the Assembly to purify the seats of the Prytanes, it can hardly be considered a ritual with any special connections to theatrical performance. See Else 1965b:3–17; Pickard-Cambridge 1968:x–58; Taplin 1978:161, 191 n. 3; Gernet 1981:57; Herington 1985:5–7; Segal 1986; Vernant and Vidal-Naquet 1990:16–23; Csapo and Slater 1995:103–7. Winkler's hypothesis that the chorus was made up of young men in military training is not evidence for the existence of ritual elements in the plays themselves; even if this does connect tragic performance to a rite of passage for some, it was hardly a ritual, since only the best singers were chosen, and thus not all ephebes would have gone through it (1990:57–60). A ritual in the sense I mean is compulsory and must be repeated exactly the same way every time to function properly. See Vickers for the absence of ritual elements in the earliest drama (1973:33–42). The theatre festival itself staged a number of civic and military rituals in addition to the dramas; these will be discussed in Chapter 4.

Middle Ages, book-based study tended to loosen up ossified poetic habits: not only was its unprecedented control by writing what allowed drama to be the first poetic genre to make deliberate use of colloquial speech (Ong 1977:72), but also it was the most "sophisticated . . . schoolmen" who pioneered the use of vernaculars in the poetry of the Middle Ages (Clanchy 1979:170).

When a customary saying or practice gets written down, a number of things happen. First, it loses its "invisible" or transparent and borderless equivalence with life as lived. It is made a visibly concrete, distinct thing on the page, but it also becomes an intellectual challenge insofar as it becomes a thinkable thing with limits. In an oral society man stands, in Walter Ong's words, at the center of a 360-degree sound-life: he is part of it and contained within it. Once aspects of this sound-life are put on paper, they can be viewed, as it were, from without. The individual's unidirectional gaze at a page—be it papyrus, parchment, or waxed tablet—puts him in a new relation to cultural material. No longer contained "within" a speech or social practice, he is availed of the position of an "outsider," a viewer whose gaze is separated from involvement.

This outsideness of a literate's relation to a text not only introduces the possibility of taking an individualized stance toward the language or custom, be it dissent or active endorsement, but also to some extent necessitates a redefinition of oneself as an individual, perceiving subject. For as long as engagement is one's mode of being in relation to a given practice, the practice is equivalent with one's participation as a member of the group. It is probably for this reason that even elementary literacy has been tied to the likelihood of an individual's separating himself or herself from local traditions, imagining an alternative reality, and actually seeking it elsewhere (Winchester 1985:47), just as Dionysus does after reading the *Andromeda*. Literacy's tendency to separate individuals from their unexamined immersion in cultural practices and to encourage their individualized responses was implicitly recognized by Plato, who criticized literates precisely for their tendency to be difficult to manage (*Phaedrus* 274–75). In the *Clouds*, Aristophanes exaggerates this tendency, suggesting that students are prone to reject traditional ways of life to the extent of beating their parents!

The separation of speaker and spoken that writing accomplishes means that epic material now exists "outside" the poet, and he stands outside of it. This "outsideness" can be credited directly with one of the central poetic innovations that dramatic form represented in its time. Oral epic is a genre that praises the past deeds of heroes. The epic bard had a single rigid mandate: to preserve and increase "the glories of men" (Jaeger 1945 1:40). The bard Phemios is described as "the speaker of fame," and the glorifying function of the epic singer is made clear elsewhere as well (*Od.* 1.338, 8.73; *Il.* 9.189). As Jaeger observes, epic is so strictly limited to praise that "everything low, contemptible, and ugly is banished from the world of the epic" (1945 1:42). In the words of the ancient rhetor Dio of Prusa: "Homer praised almost everything—animals and plants, water and earth, weapons and horses. He passed over nothing without somehow honouring and glorifying it. Even the one man whom he abused, Thersites, he called a *clear-voiced speaker.*" [19]

As Gregory Nagy has shown (1986:89–102), the genre of praise poetry to which the Homeric epic belongs is practised around the world. Ruth Finnegan has described the context of this genre as practised in parts of Africa: the bard travels from town to town, taking up his position in the marketplace and singing the praises of a rich or influential townsman until he gets money or some other gift (1990:250). From descriptions in the *Odyssey,* we find confirmation of this practice: Demodokos is fetched by a herald to come and sing the praises of an illustrious house and be fed (8.43ff.). And Pindar, too, made his living by peripatetic flattery: "My plainest rule, when I arrive in this isle, is to shower it with praises" (*Isthmians* 6, 20f.).[20] Now, in African praise poetry the panegyric turns to invective if the singer is ignored. As we see here clearly, praise and abuse are related as antithetical speech types; but most important is the fact that both are motivated directly by the context in which the performance occurs. One praises in expectation of one's supper and abuses when it is not provided.

In a preliterate milieu there is no sustained abstraction possible of content from context: to sing the epics is necessarily to be performing a particular concrete action, namely, praising heroes. But when writing allows composition to be separated from performance, poetry comes out from under the control of specific performative contexts. It can be composed outside of these contexts (alone and at home, for example), and new options can emerge. In predramatic poetry each genre had its own specific performative function and its own distinctive musical meter. The praise poetry of a Pindar, for example, would be written in the appropriate meter, such as Aeolic or dactylo-epitrite. Epic praise was confined to dactylic hexameters and invectives to iambics. Within oral performance, this melopoetic consistency served both the needs of the singers and dancers and the pragmatics of the song itself, whose function had to be made manifestly clear. In praising

19. Dio Prusensis *Or* 33,2, cited in Jaeger 1960 1:42.
20. As cited and translated by Kirk 1985:102.

an athlete in an epicinian ode, for example, one could not very well lapse into iambics, the meter used for invective. But because the advance of literacy was increasingly making poetry an object for analysis rather than contextual performance alone, it became possible to contemplate these compositional norms and to overturn them.

Thus, whereas predramatic poetry was locked by orality into the use of a single homogenizing musical and metrical mode, drama became, under literacy's tutelage, the first genuinely heterogeneous genre. In dispensing with dactylic hexameter and introducing iambics (among other meters) in its place, dramatic composition was able to exploit the potential of the alphabet for recording speech. By including iambics in its storytelling, drama was able to bring poetry closer to the sounds and rhythms of everyday speech, as Aristotle acknowledged (*Poetics* 1449a18).[21] But equally pronounced was the effect that this hybridizing must have had on the nature of the story and of performance itself. Singing the legendary deeds of one's ancestors in *iambics?* This was new indeed. What must the poet think of Homeric material if he writes about it in the meter reserved for invective?

According to a well-known anecdote, Solon berated Thespis for standing in front of so many people and telling such blatant lies in his play (Plutarch *Solon* 29). Now, this story is usually interpreted to mean that Solon was shocked at the duplicity inherent in Thespis' chosen form, that is, in pretending to be someone he was not. But a closer look tells us something else. It was certainly not Thespis' *impersonation* that shocked him, for Solon was in fact well known for at least one such poetic impersonation of his own (*Solon* 8.2). A more plausible explanation lies elsewhere.

Unfortunately, we have none of Thespis' plays. But drama from Aeschylus onward is specially marked by its tendency to set inherited material on its ear. All the plays that treat of mythological material (and that is most of them) share a distinct taste for criticizing, altering, questioning, and transforming the traditional stories they treat. Dramatic texts tell the story of a Greek military victory from the point of view of the losers, who turn out not to be "barbarians" at all; Iphigenia was never actually sacrificed on the altar by the Greeks, as legend had it, but got a job elsewhere, sacrificing the Greeks themselves; the glorious hero Ajax is portrayed in the theatre as a demented and decidedly unheroic torturer of sheep; the great and famous archer Philoctetes is depicted as a smelly, pathetic, whining invalid; Helen is portrayed with any number of contrasting personalities, and flies off to Egypt instead of Troy; Orestes is delirious, if not clinically insane; the mur-

---

21. See also Herington 1985:119–20.

der of Agamemnon was masterminded and carried out not just by the tyrant Aegisthus but by Agamemnon's own wife; heroes are exiled or executed for political reasons rather than dying magnificently in battle, or simply go about in "rags and tatters" rather than in the shining armor and strong greaves that Homer dresses them in. The all-seeing Zeus is portrayed as a paranoid, typical sixth-century tyrant, Athena as a recognizable fifth-century citizen, casting her ballot capriciously in the *dikasteria*. As G. S. Kirk notes, Euripides' Princess Elektra is married off to a "virgin peasant" and herself becomes a "condescending psychopathic shrew"; Jason is both cowardly *and* unfaithful; and the god Apollo is a bungler (1985:103–4). On the theatrical stage, as Geoffrey Bakewell (1997b) has shown, traditionally awe-inspiring figures such as the Eumenides and Oedipus are demoted to the status of metics, the fifth-century Athenian equivalent of green card holders; the stories of such gods and kings are recast in drama and described partly in terms of decidedly inglorious immigration problems. In drama, Homeric deities and heroes are no longer the extratemporal, godlike stuff of praise poetry but, essentially, contemporary Athenians subject to ridicule and abuse, and to representation in iambics. If Thespis' plays were anything like this, it is no wonder that Solon was shocked.

Comedy's connection with iambics, or lampoons, was well known to the ancients (*Poetics* 1448b10ff.); but rarely do scholars today accept how close tragedy, too, must have been in its early days to the humor of the lampoon. Because one of the novelties of tragedy was to represent even epic heroes in nonheroic meters, tragedy can be seen today, as the ancients themselves saw it, as sharing a common origin with comedy. As G. F. Else records, Plutarch wrote in his *Proverbs of the Alexandrians* (30) that tragedy and comedy both arose "out of laughter" (1965b:24), and Aristotle clearly shared this view, for he says that tragedy only "acquired seriousness late," being initially composed of "short plots and comical diction" (*Poetics* 1449a17–18).

The tendency of orality to lock composers into a single poetic mode and meter also afflicted performers, of course. As far as the worldview and technique of epic is concerned, this remained the case even after writing had replaced the improvising bard with the reciting rhapsode. In the *Ion*, it is clear that even as late as the fifth century B.C.E., the performer of epic material remained confined to a contextually embedded pragmatics of praise. Throughout this dialogue the rhapsode describes his activity, and is described by Socrates, as *praising* Homer, even when he is explaining him (536c–d, 541e). In fact, Plato speaks of both poets and performers in *all* the predramatic genres as "in bondage" to a single metrical muse:

Each is able to do well only that to which the Muse has impelled him—one to make dithyrambs, another panegyric odes, another choral songs, another epic poems, another iambs. In all the rest, each one is poor. . . .

So the worshipping corybantes have a lively feeling for that strain alone which is that of the deity by whom they are possessed, and for that melody are well supplied with attitudes and utterances, and heed no others. (534c; 536c–d)

Like Ion and Homer, predramatic performers and poets of all kinds are each "held" by a single muse (536b). Ion is skilled "only in regard to Homer" and the speech genre of praise (531). As we shall see, this "bondage" of the performer to his poetic material disappears in the actor, who, like the dramatic poet, is freed by writing from immersion in any particular type of contextual speech.

In separating spoken content from speech context, literacy makes shocking and socially unconventional speech acts more likely to occur. Whereas heroes must, so to speak, always be praised in oral epic recitation, they can be subjected to novel interpretations when creation has been separated from performance. Indeed, in the hybrid literary art of the fifth century, what Solon called "lies" were not merely tolerated but actually sanctioned. As Simon Goldhill (1990) has shown, ancient drama expresses its nature—its rewriting of tradition and subversion of norms—both within the plays and between the plays and the festival context in which they were performed. According to Goldhill, tragedy and comedy were "genres of transgression" in the most expanded definition of the term, for their targets were not only the heroic values of the Homeric worldview,[22] but also the norms and values so grandiloquently displayed at the Great Dionysia itself. The performative context of the theatre festival—with its display of allied tributes, its awards to citizens for outstanding service to the polis, and its parade of the orphans of war—was meant to celebrate Athenian civic-military virtues and to advertise them abroad. Considering the dramatic festival as a "speech act" of a global kind, one could say that it was a genre of praise for Athens. But the plays themselves actively probe and even undermine the civic and military virtues that are championed by the social setting in which they appeared (Goldhill 1990:97–129). For this reason, Goldhill is almost alone among classicists today in maintaining that there was in fact a more than circum-

22. See Goldhill 1986: chap. 6.

stantial connection between theatre and its patron deity, Dionysus.[23] Contrary to the ancients' own favorite dictum, that it had "nothing to do with Dionysus,"[24] Goldhill suggests that it was this specially theatrical transgression of context by content that made dramatic performance an "essentially Dionysiac event" (129).

But in addition to its daring use of iambics for singing of heroes, drama distinguished itself from previous poetic practice by combining in itself practically all the meters that had traditionally been kept distinct. As M. S. Silk and J. P. Stern remind us, the various poetic meters available in Greece from the eighth century B.C.E. to the birth of drama were roughly equivalent not only to the various rhythms of Greek music, but to separate poetic genres as well (1981:139–40). Add to this the fact that these poetic species had associations with separate localities and even different dialects (Herington 1985:112–13), and we can begin to get an idea of the radical heterogeneity that drama introduced. Before drama, the poetic and musical modes had not been allowed, as it were, to "converse" with one another; with writing they could be brought into contact, into a hybridized state of mutual interanimation. Speaking of drama's incorporation of previously unrelated poetic material, Aristophanes wrote in the *Frogs:* "What is this phlatothrat? Was it from Marathon that you collected these rope-winder's songs, or from where?" (1296). Of Euripides he writes: "He gets his honey from anywhere—from porn songs, from the drinking songs of Meletus, from Carian oboe tunes, from keenings, from the dance-halls" (1301). In Aristoxenus' words, tragedy was "a *mixture*" (Herington 1985:110).

Drama's thoroughgoing language heteroglossia shows just how complete a disjunction literacy had effected between speech content and speech context. Euripides could put porn songs and ritual lamentations into "dialogue" in a single poetic composition, and put them both together on the

23. Compare the more representative conclusion of Louis Gernet that there is "no primary and fundamental relationship" between "Dionysus and the literary genre which circumstances ended up placing under his patronage" (1981:57). See also Jaeger: "Tragedy, too, owes both its traditional material and its ethical and educational spirit to epic, not to its own Dionysiac origin" (1960 1:42). Vernant and Vidal-Naquet write similarly: "The 'truth' of tragedy is not to be found in an obscure, more or less 'primitive' or 'mystical' past secretly haunting the theatre stage" (1990:185). Rather, it is "a literary genre with its own rules and characteristics" which must, "from the point of view of art, social institutions, and human psychology, be regarded as an invention" (23). Or, as R. C. Flickinger writes, it is only by "transgress[ing] good philological practice" that one could trace tragedy back to any sort of religious ritual (1973:6).

24. This motto was originally uttered in connection with either Epigenes' tragic composition, or Thespis'. See Flickinger 1973:11.

stage, because thanks to literacy's alienation, both had lost their necessary connection to particular performative actions and contexts. A Sapphic love poem, when recited in the classroom, is no longer an *instance* of love but just a poem of a certain genre in a certain meter. The existence of such poetic genres in writing meant that a "keening" was no longer something that was necessarily and exclusively done over a dead body; it was now just one poetic language among many. As an alienated (decontextualized) language with no inviolable connection to any particular action, it could be "staged" in juxtaposition with a porn song without excessive impropriety. Standing outside of direct involvement with any concrete speech context, the literate playwright could bring languages into novel combinations, representing them freely on the stage as objects for contemplation.[25]

Throughout his oeuvre Mikhail Bakhtin argues that it is only when discourses are seen from "without" that they lose their sacrosanct and inviolable character. When this happens, social languages, and the practices that go with them, are relativized to the point where they can no longer lay claim to any absolute metaphysical truth. They are forced instead simply to compete with one another in the "marketplace" of heteroglossia. The emergence of this condition of linguistic free enterprise in Greece cannot, of course, be attributed solely to the study of poetry in school. Certainly Athens's growing cosmopolitanism under the Peisistratids, as well as Greek colonialism and commerce generally, would have made their own contributions to this process by "physically" bringing various languages into relativizing contact with one another. But the radical heteroglossia of language that drama reflects is also liable to have been encouraged in the classroom, where poetry was abstracted from its normal contexts and studied in a disinterested, objectifying way.

Book-based study is also characterized by a tendency toward debate and contest. At least this is what we see in the *Phaedrus* and the *Protagoras,* both of which dialogues show Socrates, with surprisingly little success, competing against rival teachers and their interpretations of various subjects. And it should not be wondered at that bookish pursuits should lead to such intellectual contests. For not only does the cutting loose of discourse from its embeddedness in contexts of action give rise to an individual "subject" who can treat a discourse as an "object", but by the same token, it also must lead to the possibility of conflicting views of that same object. For this reason,

25. Vernant and Vidal-Naquet stress the difference between doing something and staging it: on stage, a ritual lamentation or sacrifice becomes "simply a representation" (1990:16).

the emergence of an individual perspective on, as opposed to a group participation within, cultural activities has also been linked with a shift "from worldview to ideology." As Goody notes, "writing, the presence of the text of the word in addition to its utterance, favours a partly independent role for ideology, giving it a measure of 'structural autonomy' which it doesn't possess in oral societies" (1986:22).

The most significant consequence of the emergence of an independent ideology is that by its nature it will be perceived in opposition to other ideologies. For example, in fixing the worldview of Homeric orality in writing, the technology of script detaches its value system from particular lived performative contexts (the celebration of the deeds and *arete* of heroes), and establishes it as an abstract, non–context dependent "universal" dictate. Through the now visible dialectical difference between textual universals and lived particulars, an ideological conflict emerges. But writing goes further: it establishes what Goody calls a "semi-permanent platform" (1986:31) for those aspects of experience that conflict with these now universalized ideas. In so doing, writing allows the dissenting voice of the ideological "other" to be heard over longer stretches of time, long enough to establish itself as a different interpretation of reality. For example, we begin to hear, in the poetry of Archilochus (ca. 650), the occasional challenge sent out to the traditionally esteemed Homeric notion of the glory of a hero's death in battle. In Archilochus a coward proclaims *his* virtue, the love of life. This is a proclamation that thumbs its nose at an entire worldview—the Homeric culture of *kleos* (acoustic renown). But in Euripides, Archilochus' personal, lyric rejection of the heroic ideal has been detached from the mouth of any one singer and instead appears within the context of multiple views of the same subject. When in drama a character says that "it is better that we live ever so miserably than die in glory" (*Iphigenia at Aulis* 1250), one competing point of view among many is receiving a generalizable expression, and one that does not depend on the identity of any particular speaker. In short, interpersonal conflict is now ideological in nature, and discourse is its medium. And because each discourse is equally alienated, and representative of a different interpretation of reality, there is no resolution possible, only winning and losing.

As we have seen, the Homeric worldview did not exist in a fixed written version for long before ideological debate over its values appeared: Xenophanes attacked it on a number of grounds; Stesichorus (ca. 640–555) denied the veracity of Homer's version of events;[26] and rhapsodes performing the textual

---

26. As we learn from his *Palinode;* see Plato *Phaedrus* 243a.

Homer were, accordingly, forced to defend him ideologically, some resorting to allegorical arguments. From at least the sixth century on, Greek poetic and intellectual life was dominated by this polemical spirit, this
agonistic claim and counterclaim by individuals against other individuals.
Stories of the famous "contest" of Homer and Hesiod go back to the sixth
century (Pfeiffer 1968:11), as does the institution of contests in epic, dithyrambic, and dramatic poetry.[27] In the fifth century, Sophists attacked one
another, philosophers attacked the Sophists, and by Aristophanes' time,
playwrights were accusing one another on stage of being "frauds" (*Frogs*
909). These polemics only escalated into Aristotle's time, when arguments
"Against X" were the order of the day (Pfeiffer 1968:49–131). In other words,
Homeric praise was increasingly replaced by ideological contest, a discursive
shift that also manifested itself in the innovations of theatrical form. As Vernant and Vidal-Naquet put it, "The legendary hero, extolled in epic, becomes a subject of debate now that he is transferred to the theatrical stage"
(1990:186).[28]

The agonistic style of literate Greek discourse has been usefully discussed by G. E. R. Lloyd (1990), who finds the conflictual ad hominem argument at work in spurring on many of the finest humanistic achievements
of Greek science and philosophy. But where storytelling is concerned, the
literate shift from worldview to ideology proved equally productive. Between the eighth and the sixth centuries B.C.E., as writing began to be used
for increasingly elaborate poetic compositions, the idea emerged that a poet
of mythological material could be a single creative individual. Consistent
with the earliest uses to which it was ever put,[29] writing thus became a mark
of poetic "personal property." In the fifth century, as we see from Aristophanes' *Frogs*, storytelling had become a site of personal ideological conflict. By contrast, the rhapsode, as depicted in Plato's *Ion*, was but one link
in a chain of inspiration which bound the performer to an impersonal tradition. But the dramatist was expected to fight it out personally, bringing to
bear not just his poetic technique but the full weight of his individualized
interpretation of the world. As a powerful symbol of the ad hominem nature of this contest in theatrical performance, the central seat in the Theatre

27. See Csapo and Slater, who point out that whereas dithyrambic singing has a long
history as a choral genre, it seems not always to have been a *competitive* genre (1995:106–7).

28. See also Peter Arnott, who notes that "debate" predominates in both tragedy and
comedy, even at the expense of "action," and serves "more often than not [as] the heart of
the play" (1989:105).

29. See Schmandt-Besserat 1989:27–42 for writing generally, W. Harris 1989:46 for
eighth-century Greece.

of Dionysus was decorated on both sides with an image of fighting cocks (Winkler 1990:49). For John J. Winkler, the cockfight captures perfectly the "zero-sum" reckoning system of the Greek agon in this period, for to win always meant to defeat one's opponent. And indeed, when the teachers go head-to-head in the *Protagoras,* surrounded by "partisan" students on chairs and benches egging their favorites on and even applauding the nice hits (337–38), they exemplify the same kind of agonistic spirit that enlivened the battle of poetic identities staged every year at the theatre festival.

Dramatic form reflects this shift to ideological contest in two crucial ways. In the first place, poetry in the theatre had become ideologized insofar as it had become *dialogic.* I have spoken of the poetic heteroglossia that drama inaugurated by combining within itself meters and dialect characteristics that had been used only separately before (see Herington 1985:114). There is one poetic feature, however, that drama does not appear to have borrowed from anywhere: the stichomythia (Herington 1985:140). This rapid-fire interchange of statement and counterstatement is the epitome of the special kind of ideological debate that writing fosters. Swift but sustained dialogic exchanges between speakers was not used anywhere that we know of in predramatic poetry—and could not have been practiced in poetic composition without the aid of writing. This is because, in stichomythia, meaning is created between speakers. In isolation, the utterances are incomplete; the meaning of each is absolutely dependent on its position in the two-part exchange. The locutions of dialogue are interrelated, codependent on one another to the extent that the whole exchange stands or falls on the inclusion of each and every element in sequence. This is not the kind of poetic composition that one can improvise spontaneously in the manner of an oral bard. The verbal fabric is so tight that every word, in exact sequence, counts for the intelligibility of the whole. In other words, its exact verbatim repeatability is a precondition of stichomythian dialogue, which means, in effect, that the use of writing is a precondition for both its creation and its performance.

Stichomythia is an interchange not only of utterances but also, necessarily, of *voices.* Dramatic dialogue, which thus marks the breakup of the unified time-space context in which poetic discourse used to be located, is for this reason a clear aesthetic reflection of the ideologically conflictual tenor of literate society. By using writing in the first place, the dramatist is untying his discourse from the time-space context in which he produced it. But in using dialogic form in particular, the playwright goes further. The dramatist is the poet who can no longer perform his own work by himself, and thus the very act of writing is inclusive of others, and of the separate time-space contexts which they inhabit. Dramatic poetry not only implies others but needs them as well.

The contest that writing opens up between inheritors of the same poetic tradition is thus reflected, on the level of dramatic form, by a textual gap—and, potentially, another contest—between creator and performer. Just as two literate poets will differ in their interpretation of the same mythological material, and pit these differing visions one against the other on the stage as the fifth-century dramatists did, so too may the poet and his performers come into conflict over the interpretation of the role as written. Stories of such interpretive contests between actors and playwrights are numerous in our time; but even in Aristotle's time there is evidence that, as Plato predicted, literacy would make students—and the actors who were their aesthetic corollaries—"difficult to get along with."

The contest between performers and poets that written study helps make possible is an important one to keep in mind. For it is not just the literate poet such as Aeschylus who accrues to himself all the benefits of literate decontextualization; the performer benefits in the same way. Critics of text-based learning and teaching from Plato to Artaud—and there is no shortage of them even today—presuppose that a system of verbatim memorization will inculcate a superficial, parrot-like mentality and discourage true wisdom, real art, all good things in proportion as it is adopted. No longer accustomed or allowed to improvise in the manner of an oral bard, the performer is imagined to have lost all creative freedom. The text, which must be memorized word for word, is seen as a tyrant, a dictator, bringing to bear on performers all the authority of a bad teacher.

The actor's textual lesson, however, is not of this kind. Both for reasons having to do with the historical context of drama's emergence, and because of certain features of all writing, the student of a dramatic *didaskalos* enjoys, if anything, greater liberty in his performance than his poetic antecedents. Representing a radical contrast to the "bondage" of the rhapsode, who is magnetically "held" in obedience to Homer and compelled always to "praise" him (*Phaedrus* 534e, 536d–e), the actor's study snips the chain of "possession" that enthralled previous performers, and puts debate, disagreement, and even opposition in its place.

Unlike the oral bard, the student-actor repeats verbatim. But because the words he repeats come from a book and not from another performer's mouth, what he repeats has a special character. Like musical notation, written speech cannot record the performance itself. As theorists of language such as Mikhail Bakhtin (1981, 1986) and Paul Ricoeur (1981) have taught, writing cannot even record *meaning* by itself (i.e., without interpretation).

In speech, linguistic meaning derives mainly from extraverbal factors: from conditions prevailing in the context of the utterance; from the inner intentions, knowledge, and beliefs of the speakers; from the nature of their relationship in terms of social status; from their gestures, tones of voice, and facial expressions (Lakoff 1972:926). In speech, in fact, the verbal component constitutes a relatively small percentage of all meaning-generating elements.

To use the speech act vocabulary of J. L. Austin (1975; orig. pub. 1962) and J. R. Searle (1992; orig. pub. 1969), writing can record only the locution of the said. The locution gives us, essentially, a string of syntactically arranged words whose *possible* individual meanings can be looked up in a dictionary. But that, of course, does not give us a meaning for the utterance as a whole. This is because writing has no means of recording either the illocutionary intentions of the speaker (a desire to frighten, inform, or to arouse the listener), or the perlocutionary effects the utterance was meant to generate (causing the listener to do, feel, or think something as a result of the utterance). The dramatic text, composed as it is almost exclusively of direct first-person utterances without surrounding lexical material, is therefore especially ill equipped to convey the meaning of its locutions.

Nicholas Udall, who with *Ralph Roister Doister* wrote perhaps the first genuine comedy of the English Renaissance, understood the inherent ambiguity of such texts. As headmaster of Eton, he appears to have written the play at some point between 1534 and 1541 for performance by his students. The play features the famous letter incident, where Ralph Roister Doister's (purchased) love letter is read aloud on stage, twice, each time with an opposite meaning. In terms of the pedagogical relation between Udall and his actor-students, the play would have provided a superb example of what the decontextualization of language in writing can do. Indeed, when one of Udall's students went on to publish his own book, *Rule of Reason* (1553), he inserted Ralph's letter into the text as an example of ambiguity.

Udall's pupil Thomas Wilson certainly learned this lesson well, whether from his classroom studies or his acting one cannot say. But Ralph's delightfully ambiguous letter is a paradigmatic document for the theatre as well as the classroom. Before speaking what has been written, one needs to decide what type of speech act it is: is it a humble and charming love letter, or the offensive blather of a self-aggrandizing blockhead? As Robin Lakoff puts it: "It is normally true in all languages that one must somehow make clear the type of speech act involved: are you asking a question, making a statement, or giving an order?" (1972:926). Are you being ironical, or serious, professing your love, or merely being kind? In written speech, the "type of speech act involved" is not provided.[30]

When a performer learns a poem from the mouth of an oral bard, language comes complete with its bodily dimension intact. Words are accompanied by appropriate gestures, and the "type of speech act involved" is implicit in the context. In memorizing a text, however, one can internalize only what the text provides. And what the text provides is the locution. In order for the text to be spoken, to make sense as an act of speech, the actor must decide what type of speech act it is. In other words, per- and illocutionary intentions must be added. Consequently, in turning a decontextualized locution into a speech act, the actor must contribute "more" than he is given.[31] Not only must he decide what type of speech act to supply, but he must also add all the extraverbal elements which in life would normally accompany a speech act of the kind he has decided to perform. These extraverbal elements, without which the actor may be uttering just a list of ambiguous words, will range from rate of delivery, to tones of voice, to facial expression, to physical action and deportment, even through to an imaginary positing of a "context," which may involve appropriate clothing and the use of objects.[32]

The difficult position into which writing thrusts its performers has been effectively described by David Olson: "While writing solved the problem of storage of information, it created . . . the 'meaning' or 'interpreta-

30. This deficiency of written language is of course less apparent in inflected languages such as Greek, which goes further than English in expressing the mood of an utterance.

31. Interpretive contributions of this kind are obviously not literally quantifiable. But as the example of Ralph's letter (or, better still, very bad acting) proves, it is possible to reduce the comprehensibility of a written utterance to near zero—a fact which suggests that the actor's contribution must be accepted as decisively large.

32. The situation is of course made even more complex by the fact that the speech act which the actor has devised on the basis of the written locution is not in fact destined for reception by the listener to whom the locution is addressed in the text. That addressee is a fictional character, and exists only as another textual locution or set of locutions. Rather, the speech act is destined, initially in rehearsal, for reception by the actor's fellow performer(s), and ultimately in performance for an audience of spectators, many of whom may be barely within earshot. Therefore, in addition to creating a meaningful corporeal speech act, the actor must devise a way to communicate his conception to a great many people who may be watching and listening from a distance. Depending on the circumstances, this may require that he add features to the conception, amplify it, or modify the whole in some other way. It is clear, then, that the verbatim memorization of a textual locution is in fact but the very beginning of a complex interpretive process which far exceeds the model on which it is based.

tion' problem" by inaugurating a visible distinction "between what a text says and what it means" (1988:425, 429). Out of this difference comes the possibility of taking a variety of different mental attitudes to verbal content: "One can hear the propositional content and then decide whether to believe or doubt it, or one can hear an utterance and then think whether it was meant literally or metaphorically. One can, as we say, begin to reflect on text rather than merely remembering it" (435). Thus, compared to the type of repetition an oral performer might practice, that of the text-bearing actor is more philosophical and ultimately more personal: philosophical because it involves the interpretation of an abstracted, decontextualized locution, personal because textual locutions are by nature ambiguous and will admit of divergent interpretations. Interpretation not only gives scope for an individual's own tastes, values, beliefs, and desires, but in fact demands that the full range of these personal criteria be brought to bear. In short, verbatim repetition, when used in the service of performance, is not at all the same thing as parrot-like copying, and may in fact discourage it.

In his discussion of the nature of writing, Plato implicitly acknowledges this feature of written speech. In a much-discussed passage in the *Phaedrus,* Socrates laments the fatherlessness of all writing. Cut off from its author, a text "has no power to protect or help itself" when "ill-treated" (275e). By ill-treatment, Plato did not of course have in mind the interpretive liberties that actors are wont to take with their texts; but because their study is a written one, actors learning a role are dealing not with the tyrant of Artaud's imagination but with the "orphan" of Plato's. While the text's inability to "answer back" disables it, to Plato's mind, as an effective teacher, this same fatherlessness gives the actor performative liberties not enjoyed by his poetic antecedents. The members of the Homer Society were not by accident called the "sons" of Homer, for the rhapsode's allegiance to his bard approaches the filial in its irrational exclusivity. Ion confesses that Homer alone inspires his love, obedience, and reverence; Hesiod and Archilochus only make him fall asleep (530–31). The fifth-century actor, by contrast, was the heir of no one poet, being instead assigned to dramatic poets randomly, by the luck of a drawn lot. And this disconnectedness of the actor from any one poet was made even more palpable in the fourth century, when the best actors were required to appear in all three dramatists' plays.

Whereas the most that a rhapsode might do in personalizing his recitation of Homer was to "overdo his gestures" (*Poetics* 1462a6), the ancient actor quickly distinguished himself, and became notorious, for playing fast and loose with his text. As Denys Page suggests, surveying the hundreds of known or suspected changes made to tragic texts in performance, "We can be certain that actors made themselves free of the play and altered it repeatedly" (1987:10). They appear to have added lines, cut speeches, altered stage directions, written their own prologues, changed sad endings to happy ones, transposed speeches from one character to another and even from one play or other written work to a separate piece. Aristotle mentions, among other things, the penchant of actors such as Neoptolemos and Theodorus for deliberately giving "new significance to old sentences" (Page 1987:16), and Theodorus apparently "would not allow any other actor . . . to enter before himself," regardless of the order of entrances called for in the text (*Politics* 1336b27). Aristotle also mentions the tendency of actors to "put in something of their own" (*Poetics* 1461b3–4). The actor who was to play the Phrygian slave in *Orestes* is believed to have flatly refused to jump off the roof for his entrance as the text demands, evidently insisting that lines be added to support his preference for entering normally, through the door (Page 1987:42). Given the penchant of the ancient theatre's "students" for thus contradicting the "teachings" of their texts, Page concludes that our founding thespians may have been almost as cavalier with their texts as Garrick was with *Hamlet* or Hamlet was, for that matter, with *The Murder of Gonzago*.

In fact, the kind of textual liberties attributed by Aristotle to Neoptolemos were apparently taken so often and so generally that the Athenians actually felt compelled to pass a law against such irreverent behavior.[33] Copies of the three great tragedians' work were installed "in public," presumably in the city archives or Metroön, and actors were legally bound not to deviate from them. Now, the act of installing plays in the archives is symptomatic of a typically literate tendency to endow certain much-beloved works with a "classic" status and to protect them from any changes thereafter. This happened to the Homeric poems soon after they were written down, as we saw in Chapter 1, and performers of Homer from that point forth were bound to be "very precise about the exact words" (Xenophon *Memorabilia* 4.2, 10). Once a consciousness of the canonical nature of a given text has set in (as we know, with the passing of the Lykurgan law, that it had by the fourth century in Greece), it does indeed become increasingly difficult to alter a text in performance. Or does it?

One need not look very long or hard at theatre history to see how futile are all attempts to protect the integrity of even the most canonical texts. Father Shakespeare never could say anything about the happy endings added to *Lear* and *Romeo and Juliet* by later actors, and not just because of his

---

33. Plutarch *Lives* 10, *Orat. Lyc.* 841f. as cited by Thomas 1989:48.

death. Nothing prevented the first performers of *A Doll's House* in Germany from abusing the play, within Ibsen's lifetime, to the point where Nora decides not to leave her husband after all. If the actors of the ancient theatre took advantage of the fatherlessness of their texts in performance, they were certainly not doing anything that all actors haven't made a profession of doing since.

The formal feature of drama which all but guarantees the taking of such liberties—a textual separation between composer and performer—has also determined the subject of many plays. Mention of the Lykurgan law puts us instantly in mind of the many plays of Shakespeare which, like *Hamlet,* depict a character's attempts to control his actors, forestall nonauthorial additions, or make alterations to a given play. The clearest example of all, of course, is *Measure for Measure,* which shows Angelo as a Renaissance Lykurgus, trying to legislate the citizen body into obedience. But as he learns, the body, always outside the text, in one way or another resists all such attempts at didactic proscription. Neither Angelo's legal text, nor Isabella's religious text, nor ultimately the Duke's dramatic text proves able to bring the performing body into obedience: Barnardine's body refuses to obey the schedule and die at the prescribed time (4.3.59); Angelo's sex organs fill up with "strong and swelling" blood in the middle of an anti-sex lecture (2.2.142ff.); and Isabella's body can barely be stopped from further seducing and "breed[ing]" with practically the first man she sets eyes on when on furlough from the nunnery (2.2.40ff.). Everyone's "codpiece," as Lucio puts it, will "rebel" of itself, irrespective of all discursive dictates (3.2.124).

We can be quite sure that Lykurgus' law against textual liberties on stage was about as effective as Angelo's law against fornication out of wedlock. The proof of this is to be found in the ancient plays themselves, which are forever reinforcing the idea that the body escapes all written prescript.

Although it is not about texts specifically, the *Philoctetes* provides a useful introduction to the nature of didacticism as a fifth-century dramatist saw it. As a story about a *didaskalos,* it may tell us something about how Sophocles viewed his role in this capacity. The play begins with Odysseus giving Neoptolemos some very schoolmasterish, decontextualized instruction, teaching him in the manner of a Sophist what to say and how to say it. As we know both from Aristophanes' *Clouds* and from Plato's *Protagoras,* the Sophists were marked as teachers precisely by their skill in teaching citizens how to use words for "gain;" and Odysseus, in justifying his teaching, defends his lesson in just this way, in the name of "gain" (111). He in fact directs his student in an elaborate play-within-a-play, explaining the actor's objectives, and even offering him a possible "motivation" with which to make his performance appear more credible.

Neoptolemos goes on to give an excellent recitation for the poor susceptible Philoctetes—at least initially. He begins by doing as all obedient student/actors must: he "brackets" his own contextual reality, suppresses his own motivatedness *in propria persona,* and functions like a sign in Odysseus' story. He represents the embittered warrior, wronged by the Atridae, on his way home. But his cooperation in Odysseus' plan to "ensnare the soul of Philoctetes with . . . words" ultimately crashes to the ground like a stack of writing tablets when the bottom is pulled out. The bottom, literally, for what he faces is that against which no lesson is proof: the grotesque body of his interlocutor. As is the case elsewhere in Greek literature, it is the foot and not the buttocks which takes on the burden of all that is lowest in man; and Philoctetes' foot is as grotesque as can be imagined. Gushing pus and foulest stench, it reduces the body connected to it to that powerless state of surrender to biological reality so typical of physical illness or decay. This is human life before civilization, during that period of servitude to a "state of nature" wherein life is but the grinding round of pain, sleep, the struggle to feed oneself and drag one's imprisoning carcass into shelter. Face to face with this suppurating flesh, this man as "the thing itself," Neoptolemos, from the point of view of his own physical, experiential reality, must reevaluate his semiotic intentions in the midst of his performance. He takes off his mask, speaks unscripted lines, and shows *himself.* And Sophocles criticizes the "shabby, slit-eyed soul" of Odysseus precisely for its life-denying didacticism: he criticizes him for teaching Neoptolemos "step by step" how to act "against his nature" (*Philoctetes* 1013).

What we find here is a contest between teacher and student in which the battle lines are drawn between the content of the lesson and the lower bodily reality of the performer's own experiential context—the student's "gut" reaction. We have already had a glimpse of this text-body contest in the *Phaedrus.* When Socrates greets the book-toting Phaedrus by asking what he's got protruding from under his cloak, he sounds rather like Mae West demanding to know whether the bulge in her interlocutor's trousers is a pistol or a sign that he's "happy to see" her. When he wants to subvert the loftiness of his ascent into tales of mythic nymphs, Socrates brings the discussion down to the level of his feet (230b7). In fact, he uses foot-related tropes twice in this dialogue (250e4–5), both times referring either to "descent" into animalistic pleasures ("surrendering himself to pleasure does his best to go on four feet") or a descending return to the physical reality of the present context ("to judge by my foot"). Whereas, according to Socrates, bookish pursuits elevate writers to the status of immortal gods (258c), face-to-face instruction thrusts speakers down to their lower bodily parts. In fact, the whole dialogue is an implicit comparison between the elevation of texts, the high-minded pursuit of disinterested truth, and the downward pull of the lower body—sexual appetite, impregnation, birth, eating, sickness. By the dialogue's end, Plato has come down in favor of entry, impregnation, and the propagation of one's ideas, or "seeds," in the physical body of a listener (276–7b). Although real knowledge, for Socrates, can perhaps be gained only through physically disengaged means, to stay alive it must keep planting itself physically into present bodies. If we plant our ideas only in books, he says, we will be sowing them ineffectually, that is, our words will bear no fruit (276e). We must on the contrary sow what we know physically in our listeners, keep seducing them in the flesh and impregnating them with a love of wisdom. The superiority of face-to-face instruction therefore ultimately rests on the fact that it is *procreative* (276e).[34]

The same association between texts and sterility is drawn in the *Hippolytos,* a play that features a student second in fame only to Phaedrus. Hippolytos is introduced as a "pupil" (11), an obsessive reader of books (953–54); but his bookishness has immunized him to the calls of the flesh. Not only has he forsworn the flesh literally, in the vegetarianism which he flaunts so shamelessly (952), but he scorns Aphrodite too, spurning the bed of love and marriage (14). His hatred of women (612–52) and allegiance to chastity, even his devotion to the hunt, are all presented in this play as consequences of his bookish "high heart" (730). And because of all of these denials of bodily life, "the doors of death" must open for Hippolytos (56): Aphrodite, or love itself, will "lay [him] by the heels" (9), crush him to death under the feet of trampling horses.

In both the *Phaedrus* and *Hippolytos,* we find similar conceptions of book-based study. Books are associated with height and high-mindedness, but also with barrenness, and contrasted with "lower" realities of the body, particularly the feet. In Aristophanes' lampoon of the Air-worshipping residents of the "Reflectory" in the *Clouds,* we again see this association of scholarship with elevation and height: Socrates flies onto the stage suspended aloft from the god's machine, and walks around with his head in the clouds (200–235). When Aristophanes wants to criticize the physical gag

34. Oral teaching is described as "taking a fitting soul" and planting and sowing in it "words accompanied by knowledge, which are able to help themselves and the man who planted them, and are not without fruit but contain a seed, from which others grow in other soils."

artistry, the reliance on giant phalloi, that characterizes the comedy of his competitors, he explicitly contrasts the lowness of such techniques with the highness of his own, more bookish ones (*Clouds* 520–64; *Wasps* 65). And when he wants to ridicule the pretensions of high-mindedness, he lowers the discussion to "the lowest reaches" (192) of the student anatomy, the asshole (185–95). In fact, once we have seen the outlines of this contest between high texts and low bodies, we begin to find it everywhere, functioning as a central organizing principle of many fifth-century plays.

For example, Oedipus may not often be associated with scholarship, but we should remember that in Sophocles' lifetime, the Sphinx was depicted iconographically as reading from a book. In solving her riddle, Oedipus would thus have been seen by Sophocles as exemplifying, if not a skill for textual exegesis, then at least a general kind of literate braininess. But Oedipus knows nothing about himself physically, cannot recognize his father's body, his mother's womb, the truth about his own desire. And, as we might expect from the reliance we find elsewhere on the feet as symbols for low corporeality, Oedipus' high textual mastery is explicitly contrasted with the brute lowness of his "swollen foot."

In fact, the lower body "puts its foot down" against high textual aspirations throughout the plays of the fifth century. Like Odysseus' didactic stratagems, which are thrust earthward by a disgustingly odoriferous disease in the archer's foot, the high justice of written law in the *Oresteia* is contested and opposed by the grotesque bodies of the Furies, who ooze bodily fluids on the ground. In the *Women of Trachis,* overweening confidence in the interpretation of oracular texts is countered with grisly physical agony. In the *Antigone,* Creon tries to set "written laws" over and above the needs of a dead body, but Antigone, answering instead to the call of the lower, chthonic orders, will not be instructed. In another typical subversion of textual height by bodily lowness, Philocleon of the *Wasps* starts the play addicted to writing out sentences and penalties in the law courts, and ends the play, cured, dancing drunkenly around the stage with a naked flute girl. This play is an especially interesting example, since the low-bodily triumph over textuality refers directly to the performance of drama itself: the debased dikast speaks distinctly of "the feet of Euripides" (1414) and the dance steps, leg kicks, belly slaps, and bum splits of Thespis and Phrynichus (1480, 1492, 1524–25). In the *Knights,* the reading of oracle books is brought into direct contrast on stage with the guzzling of a bellyful of wine. Pentheus' official state cleverness is also "taught a lesson" by the low animalistic forces of physical ecstasy in the *Bacchai.* And what, in the end, is the great answer to the Sphinx's riddle? It is of course the *feet* of man as he ages, his physical reality, which, like Oedipus' "swollen foot," can be punctured and wounded, which decays and really dies—but only once.[35]

What all these dramatic characters learn to find "below" their written lessons is the body, for better or worse. And it is a discovery that dramatic characters were still being forced to make centuries later. Beneath their religious and legal dictates, Angelo and Isabella, too, discover what "the flesh . . . shall better determine" (2.2.273–75): that to be frozen into textual absolutes (1.4.58–67; 2.2.45; 3.2.106) is to "be absolute for death" (3.1.5, 118). All attempts to legislate the body into strict obedience must fail. The "voice of recorded law" (2.4.61) may attempt to control the body, but short of "geld[ing] and splay[ing] all the youth of the city," they "will to't" nonetheless.

The contest between high and low that we see in these plays is characteristic of literate cultures everywhere. As scholars of literacy such as Jack Goody (1968, 1986, 1987), M. T. Clanchy (1979), and Gerd Baumann (1986) have shown, even in newly and only partly literate societies, bookish activities quickly establish themselves as "higher" than orally embedded ones. Goody describes how schools and/or religious sects—be they of the Egyptian temple scribes, medieval scriptoria, or other types of academy—actively perpetuate this high/low binarism, this socially polarized high/low "diglossia" (Baumann 1986:42). Characteristic of this valued split is its tendency to spread out both horizontally and vertically: it will have the effect of classing occupations as well as gender in a social hierarchy. Those who work and learn with their hands, or speak only the "mother tongue," will lose status proportionately as scholarship establishes itself.

Where does this high/low binarism come from, and why does literacy tend to introduce it? Historical explanations might be found, such as the early use of writing for charting the movements of heavenly bodies, or the fact that a given culture is likely to have learned writing from one that seems to be "superior." In some places it might seem attributable to the use made of writing by the "upper levels" of a given social hierarchy (government, clergy). These explanations will not do for ancient Greece, however. Not only did the Greeks believe themselves culturally superior to all of their lettered neighbors (Steiner 1994), but writing was first used in Greece by private individuals, and never appeared to be the prerogative of any elite, religious or governmental. It may rather be the case that the high/low con-

35. See Vernant's discussion of the riddle (1978:485).

test originates in a more fundamental and universal experience in the bodily life of literates.

Just as all people must experience their head, eyes, and brain as "higher" than their lower regions of feet, anus, gut, and genitals, so too, perhaps by a kind of primal existential analogy, will intellection, sight, and imagination be deemed higher functions than walking, making, copulation, digestion, and defecation. Peter Stallybrass and Allon White (1986:3) have provided a useful description of how, in general, "cultures 'think themselves' in the most immediate and effective ways through the combined symbolisms" of a geographic hierarchy (mountaintop versus valley), a corporeal hierarchy (upper versus lower orifices, protrusions, and organs); a hierarchy of the so-cial plane (king versus beggar) and of psychic forms (high philosophical, theological, or "classic" literary genres versus low physical crafts, "popular" entertainment, etc.)[36]

In one of his characteristic attempts to interfere with such rigid binary thinking, Nietzsche famously claimed that the only thoughts worth having come *while walking;* but the communication of thoughts through writing is by definition an activity of the "upper" realms. With no alphabetical equiva-lent for the physical presences of speech, what writing leaves out is, in Roland Barthes's words, "quite simply, *the body*" (1985:5). It is still a body that writes, and a body that reads; but reading and writing cannot be corpo-real in the same way that speaking and listening are. Passionate readers and writers might disagree. After all, as Euripides shows in *Iphigenia in Aulis,* even writers moan, wail, and pull out their hair in the act of writing a letter. But there is a limit to the extent to which writing can serve as conduit for the body. Punctuation and other graphic and lexical devices can substitute themselves somewhat for the signs the body uses in speaking (grimaces, eye movements, hand gestures); but there is one side of bodily input into speech for which there is absolutely no analogue in writing. How does one even de-scribe it in writing? Following Walter Benjamin, Barthes refers to the "aura" of an individual body, the obtuseness and uniqueness of its brute surfaces, none of which can be mechanically reproduced or even properly contained within language at all. But Bakhtin possibly puts it more usefully by speak-ing about the "grotesque body," the body experienced as full of secreting orifices and pregnant protrusions, the body that burps and farts, laughs and

36. A writer in the twelfth century C.E. contrasts the lowness of "trifling mummers in vulgar rhymes" with the height of literary works such as the *Aeneid* (Clanchy 1979:157); Aristophanes elevates his intellectual writings over "vulgar low comedy" (*Wasps* 66).

gets pregnant, putrefies and dies. In terms of the symbolically generative hierarchy just mentioned, this is the *low* body, the body as lower order, the body as base. In eliminating all traces of this grotesque aspect of bodily life from written communication, writing "elevates" itself over speech. Writing thus makes all texts appear "high" in comparison with the grotesque bodily realities of speech. But of course Plato has as much as suggested this explanation already: in the absence of a real speaker's body, physical entry and fecundation cannot take place.

The high textual/low bodily polarity pursued so far owes a great deal to Bakhtin's concept of the carnivalesque (1968). In Bakhtin's view, the grotesque body represents the body of "the people" which resists all attempts by official culture to control its actions and centralize its verbal-ideological reality. Bakhtin conceives of "carnivalesque degradation," which manifests itself in popular-festive forms of social interaction such as theatre, as subversive of the attempts made by the high forces of serious, literate culture to impose their sacred books and transcendent doctrines throughout the verbal-ideological world:

> The carnivalesque spirit . . . destroys this limited seriousness and all pretense of an extratemporal meaning.
>
> The essential principal of [this] grotesque realism is . . . the lowering of all that is high, spiritual, ideal, abstract; it is a transfer to the material level, to the sphere of earth and body. (20)

For Bakhtin, carnivalesque degradation is a double movement down: it both "bring[s] down to earth," and "turn[s] [its] subjects into flesh" (20). In the cosmic dimension, "downward" is earth, "upward" is heaven, while in the bodily aspect, "which is not," according to Bakhtin, "clearly distinct from the cosmic, the upper part is the face or the head and the lower part is the genital organs, the belly, the buttocks" (21). Or the feet, we might add, which were and which remain in many Mediterranean countries the "lowest," rudest part of the anatomy. Bakhtin was chiefly interested in the incorporation of carnivalesque imagery by the novel, and he did not pursue the relation between carnival and theatre.[37] But like Nietzsche's Apollonian/Dionysian contest, by which it was certainly influenced (Wise 1989), Bakhtin's high/low binary has obvious uses in theatrical theory. Indeed, all the plays we have looked at in this chapter are carnivalesque in the Bakhtinian sense, even the tragedies. For no matter whether the end is a happy or sad one, an ecstatic drunken dance or an ecstasy of death and de-

37. See Bristol 1985, who did.

struction, the body always wins. All high textual aspirations are turned into flesh by the end.

Literally: for drama is a genre in which real grotesque bodies are always given the last word. Theatre is itself a kind of generic acknowledgment of the lesson about literacy taught in the plays I have described: that the body must have some input into any interpretation of what is good and right, human or inhuman, virtuous or evil. The lesson about literate study that these plays teach thus amounts to a kind of critique of literacy, a warning about its dangers. Many such critiques of didactic prescription appear in the repertory, and all of them, when performed, must succeed in a way that cannot be matched elsewhere in literature, even by the most self-critical of novels. We cannot say, of course, whether the actor Neoptolemos was inspired by the Sophoclean hero of that name, but what we learn from each of these pupils is the same: the literate student body will rebel. As a literary form, drama is uniquely well equipped to teach this lesson again and again, to actors, poets, and audiences alike.

The actor who has conned his part considers himself "off book," an accurate description if ever there was one. In his analysis of the actor's interpretive procedure, David Cole (1992) argues that the actor interprets his text while alone, and then defends his reading against the solitary readings of other actors in rehearsal. In reality, the process is not as masturbatory and "readerly" as that. For in the particular type of textual understanding that characterizes the actor's work, the bodies of others actively enter into the interpretation process, where they become both hermeneutical device and final court of appeal. In the theatre, the creation of meaningful utterances out of textual locutions happens in a context of direct intercourse between bodies. Meanings generated from play texts are thus the products not solely of isolated literary interpretations, but also of the actual effects that bodies have on one another. In rehearsal no less than in performance, the ear for speech that the text provides is augmented by an eye for what the grotesque body *does*. A suddenly dilated pupil or rush of blood to the skin tells the actor something new about the relation of this language to these bodies; perspiration, revulsion, or desire may come unbidden and add to understanding. The actor, as memorizer and repeater of already written texts, thus starts out like the Athenian grammar student with a poem set on his bench. But as a performer who speaks to listeners in person, he is also like Phaedrus, the lover who affects his interlocutor with his lower body. To borrow the imagery that Plato used throughout his dialogue about writing and teaching, a performer of this type is thus subject to both decontextual *and* sexual models of communication. If the theatre is a classroom, it is therefore one in which the student learns as much from bodies as he does from texts.

As a performed art of texts and bodies, drama can reveal the limitations of textuality and *mean it*. What dramatic critiques such as *Philoctetes* or *Measure for Measure* represent, in writing, is also necessarily what actors do themselves in rehearsal and performance: they both study their parts *and* show themselves in ways that may contradict textual dictates. Dramatic texts as lessons thus have a built-in generic safeguard against the possibility that any text may turn out to be the product of a "slit-eyed soul" in light of new physical evidence. All actors may begin like Neoptolemos, dutifully learning their lessons, but they are also generically sanctioned, nay, forced, to do as he does in going beyond and "below" them.

What does an actor find "below" his text? In Bakhtin, the textually repressed lower order is characterized, to use Michael Bristol's words, as "insistently cheerful and hopeful" (1985:23). It is the fecundating principle of the Platonic body as described in the *Phaedrus*. To Bakhtin's mind, the lower material bodily realm is forever affirming the indestructible vitality of life, the indomitable spirit of the people, the ever-regenerating power of nature. In carnival as Bakhtin sees it, the barriers separating man from man are joyfully broken down and a spirit of universal brotherhood prevails. Not surprisingly, Bakhtin's vision of bodily life has since been characterized as "naively idyllic, vague and even silly" (Bristol 1985:23).

But Nietzsche, who first sketched in the outlines of this theory, knew better. The populist orgiastic rituals which for Nietzsche represented the antithesis of high Apollonian control threatened even their participants with savage violence and death. If we can trust Euripides' account in the *Bacchai*, Nietzsche was closer to the ancients' own view of the matter. Indeed, the blind destructiveness of the bacchantes' revels in the *Baccha* stands as a perpetual caveat against any temptation to view the body and its low domain in simplistic, idyllic terms. The bodily principle in *Hippolytos, Oedipus, Antigone,* and *Women of Trachis* is similarly shown to bring painful disfigurement, entombment, and death.

As far as the history of literate culture is concerned, Bakhtin was largely right. Populist corporeal doings *do* tend to be banished, denigrated, and ideologically demonized by high, official culture in its efforts to establish itself as sovereign over cultural life. And all texts do banish the grotesque body, naturally and inevitably, from the elevated spheres of writing and reading. Historically, the theatre certainly has suffered, over lengthy stretches of time, from just such attempts to repress the lower bodily realm. These attempts have taken the form not only of the antitheatrical tracts written in such numbers by the early Church Fathers, but also of the many hierarchizing statements by modern literary theorists who demote theatre in status as a vulgar or "impure" form.

But it would be wrong to reverse the snobbery, so to speak, and view all nonliterary activities as transcendently, transhistorically true, good, and humane. As Stallybrass and White remind us, carnivalesque orgies are just as likely to manifest their grotesque bodily impulses in the stoning of pigs, or Jews, or adulteresses, in the slaughtering of animals, or "witches," or Turks, or in the ideologically motivated destruction of any other group marked out for a ritualistic "cleansing." Pentheus was not the first nor will he have been the last to be ripped apart by reveling mobs.[38]

The lower material bodily stratum certainly stands opposed to literate modes, insofar as it marks the limit of what texts can represent and what they can compel. But there is no justification for positing the existence of any single bodily truth, from "universal harmony" to "the fecundating goodness of nature." If we are to take the body seriously in the theatre, and the genre obviously demands that we do, we must take it seriously on its own terms. To do so means taking it as, primarily, a material substance in human history. And just as any other aspect of material nature is affected by culture and reflects its ongoing changes and trends, so too must the body be seen as subject to more or less precisely locatable historical values and assumptions.[39] The female body for example, as I think most would now agree, has been perceived throughout history in various different ways. Images of "womanhood," however they are generated, become the lenses through which spectators view female bodies on the stage, even through which actors view their own bodies (Diamond 1992:390ff.). The body is *also* a "medium of culture,"[40] and it will be perceived and even experienced according to available models. To take just one example, T. B. L. Webster noticed that seventh-century B.C.E. sculptures of the human form were to some extent determined by literary models. The Homeric body, with its emphasis on eyes and knees, is what artists came to see when looking at real bodies: their human forms privilege eyes and knees accordingly (1959:44). Such historically determined perceptions of the body may be invisible at the time, and those who represent the body through history may claim that they are simply seeing the body as it really, or naturally, is. But the verbal-

38. To say nothing about the more prosaic fact that the lower body can also be, and in our time especially has been, a carrier of disease, suffering, and death.

39. In particular, see Purdy 1992:5 for a discussion of the body as "a primary site for ideological inscription."

40. Susan Bordo as cited by Forte 1992:249.

ideological content of such representations (i.e., "eyes and knees")[41] becomes increasingly obvious over time. In short, the relation between "the 'material' body and the body in representation" is not a simple one (Forte 1992:249).

The relation between text and body is rather a dialectical one which the theatre simply keeps alive. In the *Philoctetes,* Sophocles all but admits to the undecidability of the contest between high and low by bringing on a deus ex machina at the end of the play. The battle between Odysseus' clever mouth and Philoctetes' grotesque foot, in the midst of which the actor-student Neoptolemos finds himself, is not the kind of contest that should be decided once and for all in favor of either. Neither foot nor mouth has a greater claim to truth as far as the human anatomy is concerned: an absolute decision either way is amputation, or censorship, of the most arbitrary kind. As far as the theatre as sociohistorical institution is concerned, Philoctetes' foot, as a stage image, will take its meaning for audiences and actors alike from the historical context in which they are all embedded. For the Greeks—who in spite of their many cures for diseases (*Antigone* 398) had no antibiotics or CAT scans—the decay of the archer's flesh would probably have represented a genuine threat to bodily health and a descent, ultimately, into the realm of the inhuman. To us today, it might represent no more than a quaint reminder that we are composed of flesh and blood after all, in spite of our many machines. The important thing is that, as both a literary and a corporeal art, drama can explore the text/body dialectic without peremptorily annulling the "lower" half—something that obviously cannot be said of the philosophical dialogue. Having ruled out a role for the performing body in his writings, Plato ensured that in Platonic texts the body is never grotesque and rebellious. All that is left is an abstract literary *idea* of the body.

The spread of literacy, both in post-Homeric Greece and in early Renaissance Europe, does seem to have inaugurated precisely the kind of split in cultural life that both Bakhtin and Nietzsche describe: on the one hand, urban, Apollonian forces tend to put centripetal pressure on cultural life, textualizing and universalizing it; on the other hand, rural, Dionysian involvements, with their popular oral traditions and orgiastic rituals, dances, and animal acts, tend to function centrifugally, pulling it apart and down to the lower regions of the grotesque body. In such periods of transition from

---

41. The "eyes and knees" of Homeric epic might be compared to the "tits and ass" of the modern American musical comedy; see the song of that name in *A Chorus Line.*

oral-traditional to high-literate culture, when centrifugal and centripetal forces are both simultaneously at peak levels of vitality and influence, a special species of art could be said to emerge. The period between Homer and Socrates must number among these transitional times, as must that between late medieval and early Renaissance Europe. And the genre of poetry that emerges under these conditions is one that could not have been produced by either oral or literate modes by themselves, but is rather a kind of offspring that, as Nietzsche would say, requires the participation of both parents.

Furthermore, what has been said about literate culture in the Renaissance could be said with equal justification about the context of drama's birth (and of other literate civilizations as well): that literacy is a city phenomenon (Goody 1987:300). It is to the cities that intellectuals and poets gravitate, and it is from the city that writing emanates in the form of decrees, laws, levies, treaties, books. To inhabitants of the city—with its tendencies toward enlightenment, erudition, and verbal-ideological centralization—the country—with its illiterates, its stronger connections with ancient rituals, animal life, and other bodily doings—often appears base, backward, low. At Athens, a ham actor is told to take his small verbal technique and big bodily brawn to the rural festivals, where a "lower" form of art prevailed.[42] Socrates had no use for the country; the only thing that could lure him beyond the city walls were "speeches in books" (*Phaedrus* 230d5–230e). Illiterates represented in the dramas and fragments are generally from the country, as I mentioned earlier; and Socrates of the *Clouds* dismisses his hopeless old student as an ignorant rustic (628). And when characters try to escape the city in the *Birds,* the city comes after them in the form of books and more books. Peisistratus is said to have brought poets from all parts of Greece to the Athenian city court, within which urban literate milieu drama was developed (Herington 1985:61).[43]

We have already seen something of this marriage of high and low in the intrapoetic dialogue that drama established between the praise of epic and the blame of iambics. To this carnivalesque generic novelty we might also

---

42. Pickard-Cambridge 1968:168; Aristotle *Rhetoric* 3.12.1413b12f.; cf. Dover 1972: 12 n. 3.

43. Similar circumstances can be seen to have been instrumental in the development of aboriginal theatre in Canada. Theatre was "foreign" to aboriginal culture before writing (Brask 1992:142; Brask and Morgan 1992:x, xii, xiv; Wheeler 1992:43), but playwright Tomson Highway, born in rural Manitoba, says that it first occurred to him to dramatize traditional Native stories during his sojourn, after a university degree, on the city streets of Toronto (quoted in Morgan 1992:130).

add the story about Arion of Methymna, who, although supposedly rescued at sea by dolphins, was also believed, by Herodotus at least, to have written a tragedy before Thespis. If true, the legend supports my depiction of drama as a generic combination of high and low. For Arion is said to have come up with the idea of tragedy by bringing some low, concupiscent satyrs—the embodiment of everything bodily, rural, and debased—onto the stage in the middle of a high choral praise poem.[44]

But whatever intermediate stages poetic performance went through on the way to the invention of dramatic form, there is no doubt that a "satyric," or carnivalesque, lowering of all that is high has remained the main distinguishing characteristic of theatre among the literary genres. This has tended to brand it with a more or less disreputable image within high-literate culture.[45] Always implicitly threatening the highest ideals of scholarship with "debasement," the theatre has also had a checkered career as far as its membership in the hierarchy of genres is concerned. In ancient Greece as in Renaissance Europe, however, literary standards were very high, but never so all-encompassing as to foreclose inclusion of the grotesque body in literate compositions. For this reason, despite their various historical distortions and idealizations, both Nietzsche's and Bakhtin's generic theories are not altogether wrong in connecting the birth of genres to precise historical moments.

For the inventors of drama, bookish elevation was still something of a novelty. When Aristophanes quips that "either Prodicus, or a book, has been the ruin of *him*" (frag. 490 Edmonds 1957), he is giving voice to a widespread belief that books are just bad news, and bad for the city.[46] In fact, nearly all Aristophanic scenes that feature writing criticize it as a "nuisance" of one form or another (*Birds* 1037). Whether maligned for its sterility (Plato), its secrecy (Herodotus), its tendency to effeminize citizens (*Clouds*) or empower the rabble (*Birds*), it is clear that in the fifth century, in the first "round" of this contest between the student body and text, the text was *not* the favorite.[47]

44. Herodotus *History* 1.23; Webster 1959:68, 76 n. 36; Else 1965b:17–24; Pickard-Cambridge 1962:131f.

45. The most exhaustive study of the theatre's low reputation within literate culture is Jonas Barish, *The Antitheatrical Prejudice* (1981).

46. See Steiner 1994, who makes the same point for Herodotus.

47. Rosalind Thomas confirms the non-controlling nature of writing as used by the Greeks through all phases with much discussion and evidence (1992:128ff.). Turner (1951:15–23) discusses fifth-century critiques of writing; Slater discusses those of Old Comedy (1996:99–112).

For the fifth century was still a period of literary history in which what was said and done mattered more than what was written. This is especially true of poetry. Playwrights, we must remember, won or lost on the basis of what happened on stage during performance; their plays were not judged in the festival as texts (Page 1987:108). When Dionysus, in Hades, has settled on the poet best equipped to save the city and the theatre festival, he does not want merely to bring a text back up with him; he wants a poet in the flesh (*Frogs* 1419). As Rosalind Thomas (1989, 1992), William Harris (1989), and Deborah Steiner (1994) have shown, Greek society in the fifth century continued, despite the presence of a growing number of literate activities, to be organized primarily around face-to-face communication, whether in the form of speeches in the Assembly, testimony and argument in the law courts, gossip in the marketplace, or poetic performance, which was still the expected method of disseminating verbal art. From Aristophanes' depiction of Dionysus sitting on board a ship reading his own copy of Euripides' *Andromeda,* and from other remarks about everyone having a book "in his hands" (*Frogs* 52, 1114), we have to conclude that plays were available to the public in written form, at least from the end of the fifth century. But available not as holy writ, as it were, for bodily performance was still the main goal. By contrast, literate activities in our time have come to dominate civic and artistic life to an extent that would have been unimaginable to the first playwrights. And so a historical leap is required to imagine what "the text" meant for the inventors of drama: it was not an ossified dictator but a part of an ongoing oral process.

What the playwright presented in competition on stage obviously consisted of the performers' own corporeal speech acts. And since, for all we know, the first published version of a given play was based on one specific and highly interpolated performance, such actorly input may itself have *become* the official text.[48] In the context of theatre's emergence, the literate preference for authorized versions, canonical texts, and narrative closure had

---

48. As for the difficult question of exactly how the dramatic texts were copied and circulated among the public, very little is known for certain. L. D. Reynolds and N. G. Wilson find enough evidence to date the existence of a "book trade" to the middle of the fifth century (1968:2). References to the part of the Athenian market where books could be bought (Eupolis, frag. 304 cited by Reynolds and Wilson 1968:2), plus Socrates' statement about the price of philosophy texts (*Apology* 26), would lead us to assume that the public got copies of plays by likewise buying them. Whether the copies were made by the playwright, the actors, or entrepreneurial booksellers and scribes is not known. See Page 1987 and Hadas 1954.

not yet taken the extreme form to which students are accustomed today.[49] Intending both memorization *and* performance, the dramatic text that emerged under these conditions of literacy has, as a result, retained what Bakhtin would have called a "loop-hole," a bodily escape hatch which ultimately distinguishes plays from other products of literacy. It should not therefore be surprising to find that classicists are in agreement that the texts of the three great tragedians have come down to us in irredeemably "corrupt" versions. And what was true of ancient Greek tragedies is true of Shakespeare and plays in modernity as well: Which text could lay claim to being the "authorized" Shakespeare (see esp. Orgel 1988:1)? Which version of a Beckett play is the "original"? Although playwrights such as Jonson[50] and Shaw[51] have occasionally appeared as exceptions to this rule, it is more typical of dramatic writing from Aeschylus to the present that the dramatic text does not possess the kind of textual purity and fixity up against which scholarized standards for "original authority" and "absolute allegiance" can meaningfully be held.

It is fascinating to see that the particular attitude to text that we find in the fifth century has managed to survive within the theatre to this day, and perhaps there alone, despite all pressure from other spheres of literary endeavor to enshrine texts as unchangeable. Even the actor's book bespeaks the irreverent attitude of theatre to its texts. Unlike the books of many other types of students, the actor's text looks more like a scroll than a book from spending so much time in a pocket during rehearsal; it is covered with markings on every page, from the arrows and squiggles that indicate blocking, to coffee stains, to underlinings, to marginal notes of every kind. It quickly becomes a fairly dog-eared palimpsest of the actor's physical experience during the preparation of the show. Used book stores tell the same tale in another way. Except perhaps for gift-box sets of Shakespeare, the volumes in the play section are invariably smaller, cheaper, and in general more disreputable-looking than the objects one sees on the history, religion, and

49. Thomas provides copious evidence that improvisation was still highly valued in the fifth century and beyond (1992:124), and that written records never developed the kind of "controlling" power over Greek life that some moderns associate with literacy (129ff.). Thomas cites Lévi-Strauss as an example (128), a modern writer whose misunderstanding of literacy's effects parallel Artaud's almost exactly.

50. Jonson supervised the printing of his plays and cared deeply about the published version.

51. Shaw's obsessiveness about the printing of his plays extended even to the spelling of particular words and included an almost novelistic concern with the finer details of decor and clothing.

philosophy shelves. This may seem a trivial point, but it is an accurate reflection of the theatre's relation to its books. That is to say, even the theatre's high texts are somewhat base, grotesque, "corrupted" by traces of lower, material, bodily life. When we consider players' manuscripts from the late Middle Ages, we see just how significant this fact is. The oldest extant secular play in English, the *Interludium de Clerico et Puella,* written in approximately 1260—and abducted from the British Museum in 1971—survived into our century in a tiny, palm-sized roll (Clanchy 1979:113). Like other players' manuscripts of the time, it is a physical record of the contexts in which it was used. As Erich Auerbach points out, these texts, written for use by actors, survive so sparsely in libraries precisely because they were actively, physically carried around in palms and pockets and simply fell apart. Those that survived are generally poorly executed and very badly worn (1965:288–89).

As Jiri Veltrusky remarked about the possibility of a genre's remaining "the same" over time: "A literary genre is not 'timeless' because it does not change but because it preserves its identity through all the changes it undergoes" (1977:7). The identity of drama as a literary genre thus resides in its maintenance of a certain freedom from itself *qua* literary text. As Thomas (1989 and 1992) suggests, the standard of absolute textual authority which the scholarly community was destined eventually to champion, and which in art we are more justified in associating with novels than with plays, had to wait for its fulfillment for the invention of the printing press. By Artaud's time, theatre's scholarly associations had come to seem shameful and constricting. So "high" indeed had bookishness become over the centuries that bodily performance itself had been eliminated entirely from many spheres of public and scholarly life. But the tyrannical text of the twentieth-century theorist's diatribes, while perhaps always a fear, was never a reality for fifth-century playwrights and performers, who esteemed a dramatist's belly slaps and bum splits on an equal level with his words.

Two conclusions are inevitable. First, if the theatre involves a kind of learning in which the student profits equally from an intercourse with texts *and* with bodies, then theatre as a literary genre is not one that is likely to endear itself to teachers convinced of the inviolability of textual messages. Scholarly anxieties about textual spuriousness and corruption are bound to be at their most acute in studies of drama, for it is a type of writing that does not lose its contact with bodily realities, with new performative contexts that leave their marks upon it. If literate culture must cast the body as low, theatre is almost guaranteed to retain its somewhat disreputable position as far as the hierarchy of literary genres is concerned.[52] We have seen how the decontextualizing atmosphere of the newly established classroom may have facilitated fresh operations on poetic material, operations that determined both the generic form and many of the perennial thematic concerns of drama. But as literacy and scholarship went on to entrench themselves as increasingly sovereign over cultural life, the very decontextualizing activities that brought theatrical form into existence in the first place became ever more well positioned to banish theatre's "Neoptolemean" inclinations from the ranks of serious study.

The second conclusion is that the dramatic text, by a felicity of history, is not the bad teacher that Artaud imagined it to be, for it is both written and "unfinished" at the same time.[53] Because it intends performance by contemporary bodies, the dramatic text must be weighed in the corporeal scales of actors' lived experience of the present, and made answerable to their live speech contexts on an ongoing basis. If its wedding gowns are experienced as ideological straitjackets, or its heroic-militaristic ideals as paralyzing suits of armor, then the actor can exercise his or her generically mandated prerogative for casting such textual garments off. Using a Bakhtinian figure, we might say that drama is a kind of textual acknowledgment that, when it comes to the student-performer's body and the fabric of the text, "all existing clothes are always too tight" (1981:37). Despite the fact that drama has surely benefited from its high intellectual standards, the practice of book learning has not made the theatre too much like a school. For unlike Plato's preferred literary genre, the philosophical dialogue, the dramatic text does *not* "always say the same thing" (*Phaedrus* 275d).

And so we return to Plato, whose rejection of theatre launched our inquiry into the nature of the student. The final message of the *Phaedrus* is that while intellectual errors will no doubt come of our surrender to live speech acts, it is a risk that must be taken, for the very madnesses and transports that produce poetry and wisdom in the first place cannot feed but on real flesh. Too bad this teacher did not heed his own lesson. Had he done so, he'd have written plays.

52. Sir Thomas Bodley's thinking when it came to establishing his library at Oxford in 1612 is typical: all plays were to be excluded from his collection of books. He considered them all unworthy "baggage" (Stone and Kahrl 1979:168).

53. It is fascinating, if perplexing, to observe the frequency with which literary theorists arrogate this quality of "unfinishedness" to the novel, a genre that, more completely than any other, reflects the fixed and finished tendency of print literacy. See Bakhtin 1981 and 1986, and the discussions of Friedrich Schlegel's theory of genre in Szondi 1986:75–94.

CHAPTER 3

Courtroom Dramas

> This can't be Athens; I don't see any law courts.
> Aristophanes
>
> For the law of writ and the liberty . . .
> Shakespeare

W HEN THE HEROES OF HOMER'S WORLD COLLIDE, THEY SULK IN THEIR tents, nurse grievances, steal one another's prizes, go on strike, slaughter the suitors. They receive embassies of reconciliation, advice from elders, offers of settlement from rivals and kings; but they feel free to reject all such arbitration in their disputes, preferring to take justice into their own hands and arms against their troubles. Had Homer's heroes lived in the literate age of drama, they would have taken one another to court.

For the Athens of Aeschylus' time was a highly litigious place. Aristophanes never tired of ridiculing his fellow Athenians' mania for public prosecution, their addiction to jury trials. And with six thousand citizens registered for jury duty every year, Aristophanes' quip in the *Birds* appears less hyperbolic than simply descriptive: if they're Athenians, they must be jurymen (108–9). Like Shakespeare's London, always noisily "buzzing with lawyers and their litigious clients" (Thomson 1994:84), fifth-century Athens was a hive of disputatious wasps from which no one was safe. Having been hauled before the courts himself "for having ridiculed magistrates . . . as well as Kleon, in the presence of foreigners" (*Acharnians* 377–82), Aristophanes knew the workings of the city's legal system from painful firsthand experience. But in this he was not alone among his playwriting predecessors and contemporaries: Phrynicus was tried and found guilty of insulting the city with his play *The Capture of Miletus,* for which crime of bad taste he was fined one thousand drachmas; Aeschylus was prosecuted, but acquitted, for violating secrecy laws of the state religion (Aristotle, *Nicomachean Ethics* 3.1.1111a6–10); and Sophocles was accused of incompetence by his son, although the charges were read and dismissed after the preliminary hearing

(Bieber 1961:28–29). Born into a world newly altered by books and class-rooms, the playwrights of the fifth century B.C.E. grew to adulthood in a city not long since revolutionized by the courtroom. As a result, disagreements between fathers and sons, sons and suitors, suitors and wives, wives and husbands were no longer occasions for private revenge, curses, murder, and abduction, but had come to be seen as public matters, requiring public legal redress. Unlike disputes in Archaic times, human conflicts in the fifth century were resolved at law, staged in public before an assembled citizen jury.

Like the book-based school, the *didaskalion,* the law court is a social phenomenon that is conspicuously absent from the world of the epic. But the law court, again like the literate classroom, is highly visible in both the dramatic age at large and in dramatic works in particular. Aeschylus, Sophocles, Euripides, and Aristophanes each wrote at least one play on the subject of written law and the jury system; of Aeschylus' surviving works at least four are concerned with it. If Athens's democratic legal system was so often discussed on the stage of the theatre, this was the case for a simple reason: the theatre, as a mode of public speech, was organized along the same lines as the popular jury courts, and is in fact unthinkable without them. Without the advent of written law, Athens's particular brand of litigiousness could not have emerged; and in the absence of this peculiarly *literate* attitude to conflict resolution, neither would the storytelling style of the theatre.

Of course, legal processes of one sort or another exist in most human societies that have been observed and described throughout history; but legal procedures in preliterate societies do appear to share certain features that distinguish them from the practice and function of law in societies with writing (Gagarin 1986:8, 9). The workings of preliterate justice have often been studied before, both as depicted throughout the Homeric epics and as manifested in a variety of nonliterate cultures around the world.[1] The many obvious parallels between Homer's version of oral law and the proto-legal procedures typical of other oral cultures suggest that the bard's picture of justice before writing is a reliable source of information about conflict resolution in Greece during the oral period.[2] In comparing the representation of human conflict in the epics with the theatre's treatment of such discord, however, we see a number of significant differences—differences that accurately reflect the generic shift from epic to dramatic form.

---

1. O'Barr 1982:10; Beck 1993; Humphreys 1985:316; Gagarin 1986:2–6, 23, 29–30.
2. Bowra 1969:32; Humphreys 1985:316; Powell 1991.

The picture that Homer provides of the workings of preliterate justice is also corroborated by Hesiod, who was himself involved in a legal wrangle with his brother Perses. Both from Homer's most detailed descriptions of conflict resolution (*Iliad* 18.497–508 and *Odyssey* 11.568–71) and from Hesiod (*Works and Days* 27–39), we find a conception of justice as "straight *dike*," as a "straight" settlement that is spoken by the noble elders, called kings (see *Il.* 23.571–95). These hereditary kings are described as sitting in judgment, either individually or in an elders' circle, and suggesting mutually agreeable compromises to the disputants. From Hesiod (*Theogony* 80–93 and *Works and Days* 213–85), we know that proposing solutions of this kind was one of the central duties of the hereditary kings, and that giving such judgments was largely a matter of persuading the parties to accept the offered solution. From Homer's description of the arbitration of the blood feud on Achilleus' shield, we see that the elder who proposed the "straightest *dike*" was rewarded with "two golden measures," a prize or gift paid by the disputants. Not surprisingly, these kings were also said to be "gift-devouring" (*Works and Days* 27–39), for favorable judgments had to be paid for in gifts. In the absence of a code of written law, justice thus resides within the body of the king or magistrate, and the judge's authority derives also from his body, as it were, for he is a king and spokesman for justice by virtue of blood ties and class inheritance.

Other features of preliterate justice can be found throughout the *Iliad* and *Odyssey.* Among the most important from our perspective is that legal redress was not available universally, and in many respects remained a private (as opposed to a public) affair. In the case of homicide, for example, it was the duty of the victim's family to enforce the traditional punishment, which was generally exile (or possibly blood money; cf. *Il.* 18.497ff.). The epics show that this reliance on family meant that murder went unpunished in many cases. For example, as Michael Gagarin points out, Heracles could kill a foreigner without legal consequences, for a foreigner has no family to enforce the customary penalty (1986:14; *Od.* 21.24–30). Or, as Gagarin further reminds us, Homer's Oedipus could commit patricide with impunity, and continue to rule Thebes even after knowledge of his deed had come to light (1986:14; *Od.* 11.271–80; *Il.* 23.679–80). With legal process a private, familial affair, it was, in effect, optional and dependent on the existence of individual families, and on their will and power to enforce punishment. This meant that suppliants, women, noncitizens, or any other members of society without strong kinship or clan ties would necessarily find themselves excluded from the customary avenues for legal action. Moreover, because justice in the absence of legal codes consists of mutually acceptable compromises (Gagarin 1986:105), disputants are in a sense free to determine whether even customary legal rules will pertain or not. For example, Eurymachus suggests a settlement in the *Odyssey* (22.54–59) which Odysseus appears to be at liberty to reject; he accepts no restitution from the suitors and slaughters them instead. All the Achaians agree that Agamemnon should accept the ransom offered by the priest as settlement for Chryseis, but he rejects the proposal out of hand (*Il.* 1.20–34). The private and personally discretionary character of preliterate justice is also evidenced in Achilleus' rejection of Nestor's proposed settlement in Book 1 of the *Iliad* and in other disputes throughout the same work (23.543–54, 571–95, 787–92).[3]

Indeed, the narrative of the *Odyssey* as a whole validates the ad hoc workings of private hereditary justice. Odysseus is presented as praiseworthy in his murder of the suitors, and, as Richmond Lattimore reminds us, the example of Orestes, in his decisive murder of Aegisthus, is held up to the procrastinating Telemachus as a positive one (Grene and Lattimore 1991:8). In the absence of written laws of the state, blood ties will tend to empower individuals to make their own family-rooted rules: as legitimate hereditary kings, Odysseus and Orestes can also claim "legitimacy" for any bloody deeds that preserve their royal houses. The dispute between Achilleus and Agamemnon which forms the plot of the *Iliad*, despite the proposals of men in council, is also finally settled on a purely personal basis: Achilleus simply refocuses his wrath toward the enemy, and gives up punishing his own co-combatants. As Gagarin points out, in the absence of systematic legal rules and binding penalties, disputes will tend to be settled in a way that leaves the conflict itself intact (105). For example, the "resolution" of the conflict between Achilleus and Agamemnon makes no decision for the future about rival claims for status; within the heroic worldview, each combatant had little choice but to assert his own. Similarly with homicide: if families are obligated to exact extralegal justice for such crimes, then they are obligated to take turns in doing so ad infinitum—a point made by Aeschylus throughout the *Oresteia*. As long as blood crimes are resolved as if they were private offenses against individual families, there is no end to murder.

Gagarin, who has analyzed all of these Homeric disputes (and others in Hesiod), concluded that it is not an exaggeration to say that law as we understand it came into existence with writing. There existed, to be sure, many traditional maxims and orally repeated codes of conduct before writing. But as our Homeric examples show, traditional proto-legalistic sayings have the illocutionary force of pieces of advice; they are invoked to justify a certain

---

3. See Gagarin's excellent analyses of these episodes (1986:39–41).

line of conduct, but do not have the force of determining behavioral choices in the first place (55). They are statements of what people usually do, or have traditionally done, and are used as rhetorical support for advice. Unlike written laws, they do not apply necessarily and universally; and they are, in any case, sponsored by particular speakers whose advice may well be rejected.

The one exception to the notion that law is equatable with writing is often said to be the case of the Icelandic "lawspeakers." Like the early Irish bards, who are said to have memorized and recited collections of laws, the Icelandic lawspeakers possessed a body of laws which they recited in full every three years. But as the historian Knut Gjerset has shown (1924:29–48) and Gagarin has argued (10), in places where such "law" is confined to the oral register and remains in the possession of specially authorized individuals (lawspeakers or hereditary magistrates), it fails to produce "legal behavior." Such laws, because they remain connected with the body of the king or lawspeaker, do not inspire general obedience. As Gjerset notes, civic life in preliterate Iceland continued to be ruled by private custom, for regular citizens did not view this arcane specialist knowledge as having any relevance to them personally (46). Most significantly, when the Icelandic laws were written down circa 1118 C.E., they were still subject to a kind of private possession, the consequence of which was that for several centuries no official version of them existed. Between the various copies possessed by individual lawyers for their own use, there were substantive variations. The net effect of this condition, of course, is that justice remains "oral" in principle: the voice of the law is still rooted in a particular speaker's body.

The physical rootedness of (preliterate) legalistic utterances in the concrete circumstances of their delivery is reflected in their formal structure. Traditional spoken maxims will tend to take the form of a second-person imperative: "Do unto others," for example (Gagarin 1986:55). Speech of this type implies a close physical proximity between "me" and "you," between the giver and receiver of the oral counsel. Interestingly, the implied co-presence of speakers which characterizes proto-legal advice also characterizes epic speech. The epic singer addresses the Muse directly in a second-person imperative: "Sing, goddess, the anger of Peleus' son"; "Tell me, Muse, of the man of many ways."[4] This is speech from "me" to "you," and the deictic structure of the opening invocation is repeated in the works themselves, with the characters sometimes taking on the position of the "you" (e.g.,

---

4. Lattimore trans. (Grene and Lattimore 1991). Cf. the imperative mood of the line of epic verse inscribed upon the Douris Cup (see Chapter 2).

"Then, O swineherd Eumaios, you said to him in answer . . ." *Od.* 14.165, 360, 442; *Il.* 20.2). The speech act of epic could thus be described as "I sing to you about him," or "You (the Muse) sing to me about him." But in either case it is a speech exchange between a present "me" and a present "you."

In the type of speech that structures written law, however, the situation is different. Unlike oral advice, a law generally takes the form of a third-person conditional statement: "If anyone does X, Y will happen" (Gagarin 1986:55). In the first place, the utterance is in the conditional: "if . . ." or "when . . ." Who is now speaking? The lack of deictic grounding for the speaker in a conditional utterance is further emphasized by the lack of a specific addressee: Who is the intended listener or receiver? The subject of the legal utterance is "anyone" or "the man who . . ." Whereas both proto-legal advice and epic song are grounded in a specific speech situation—between "me" and "you"—and refer to the identity of a specific absent "him"— Orestes and his exemplary deed—a written legal utterance is abstracted away from any and all particular speakers, listeners, and subjects. Like the dramatic text as I described it in the previous chapter, written laws are thus "nonspecialist" utterances: they are addressed to anyone and everyone, but no one in particular. According to Dennis Kurzon's speech-act analysis of legal utterances (1986), the illocutionary force of a law is "to enact." But since the law being enacted depends upon future conditions (*if* anyone commits X), such utterances may more accurately be called "potential performatives" (40). To enact themselves, they depend on the fulfillment of certain "post-conditions." Kurzon claims that such potential speech acts do not occur outside of legal texts. But as a global speech act, the dramatic text stands as an exception to this rule, if it is one. Precisely like a legal text, the dramatic text as a whole is a conditional third-person utterance: "If anyone performs this play, this is what the actors shall say." As in the case of such legal performatives as wills and marriage ceremonies, which depend on future actions for their legal enactment (death or consummation), the dramatic text is a potential enactment contingent on future extratextual events. Like traditional maxims and proto-legal advice, the Homeric epic has an "I" declaring to a "you" what has happened in the past; like literate legal utterances, the dramatic text is a third-person "potential performative" awaiting enactment in the future by "anyone."

The earliest extant written law, found in Dreros, Crete, has been dated roughly to the middle or second half of the seventh century (Jeffrey 1990:311). It begins with the formula "the city has thus decided," and goes on to stipulate that if a man has held a certain public office, he shall not be able to hold the same office again for ten years. Carved in stone on the wall of a temple, this law is our earliest record of the growing trend toward public legislation that was soon to manifest itself throughout Greece. Whether written on *axones,* or wooden blocks, as they were initially in Athens (Jeffrey 1990:58–59), or cut in stone, as in Crete, the law codes of seventh- and sixth-century Greece had a number of features in common: they were self-consciously public, they applied to everyone, they were specifically *legal* in nature, and they were officially authorized and recognized as such by the polis as a whole. The homicide law of Draco (ca. 620), of which some fragments have survived (Gagarin 1986:52), is especially interesting in this regard. As perhaps the very first law on murder, the Draconian statute, merely by being written down, made murder a public offense.[5] As Kurzon says about such criminal codes, they are really "laws" only when they are addressed to everyone; "the *publication* of statutes is [thus] an integral part of the promulgation of legislation" (27; my italics). Or, as the legal theorist George M. Calhoun puts it, it is only with written law that legal rules and changes "become distinctly perceptible, and when made have to be made consciously and intentionally. . . . And so begins a long process which matures in a fully developed system of statute law, with permanent legislative machinery and provisions for periodic revision, and gradually transforms the esoteric legal lore of the aristocracy into legal science" (1944:22–23).

The first steps toward the establishment of a truly legal order seem to have been taken by the writing down of "ancestral *thesmia*" by lawgivers, *thesmothetai,* who recorded decisions for their own use.[6] But with the publication throughout Greece of written laws, or *nomoi,* law took on a different character. Their detached, public status, and the fact that highly specific penalties were stipulated, took such laws out of the hands of individuals and removed them from the sphere of personal discretion. With the establishment of an abstract entity such as "the city" as the agent of justice, a genuinely legal atmosphere was in effect inaugurated. As we saw in the Homeric examples, a crime might come to light yet remain unpunished in the absence of an aggrieved relative. But in a *legal* dispute there must necessarily be two parties. With the city now speaking the law rather than an individual, even those crimes that were suffered privately, because the plaintiff

---

5. Because, even after the reforms of Ephialtes, murder continued to be tried by the closed hereditary court of the Areopagus, one could argue that homicide continued to be a "private" suit (cf. Humphreys 1985). But the laws of Draco, which made legal procedure *compulsory* and closely regulated by public statute, had the effect of removing homicide remedies from the private realm of family self-help, making them in essence a "public" issue (Gagarin 1986:114).

6. Aristotle *Constitution of Athens* 3.4, 16.10; Gagarin 1986:56, 130.

had no champion, were brought within a public legal sphere. With laws now officially authorized by a *place,* they were for the first time addressed to everyone who lived in that place. Thus, even crimes within various "non-city" spheres, such as the family or religion, were soon brought under the Solonian "shield" of such universal city laws (Ostwald 1986:139, 145).

As Gagarin points out, the very act of enacting a set of laws for a particular place would have had the effect of redefining individuals as *citizens* rather than merely as members of families (1986:80). Aeschylus clearly acknowledges this effect in the *Suppliants:* individuals are now subject to the laws of their states, which, despite ancestral customs, may be different from one place to the next ("According to laws at home you must plead . . ." 390). And this new conflict between state law and family custom is featured prominently in other dramas as well (*Antigone,* the *Oresteia*). In fact, there seems to be a relationship between *all* theatre and this consciousness of citizenship. As Per Brask and William Morgan have observed of Amerindian, Inuit, and other aboriginal communities, theatrical performance "seems to have evolved in the context of the rise of state-level societies" (1992:x). Of the appearance of drama in Greek antiquity, Jean-Pierre Vernant and Pierre Vidal-Naquet have similarly observed (paraphrasing Walter Nestle), "Tragedy is born when myth starts to be considered from the point of view of a *citizen*" (1990:33).

The public inscription of law had another, equally significant effect: social rules were now visibly separated into laws and non-laws. This is important, for as Gagarin notes, societies without writing have rules, but no method for recognizing rules, no legal infrastructure for distinguishing rules from other types of social utterances. For this reason, it is fair to say that the Greeks' decision to write down a set of laws "was in effect a decision to enact legislation" (1986:136).

With written law, an abstraction—"the city"—now regulates the behavior of "everybody," another abstraction. Somewhat surprisingly, however, public prosecutors were unknown. With the city now authorizing the law but not actually representing it in court, it might appear that the legal rule requiring two parties in any dispute could not be upheld. But Solon enacted a law code in the first decade of the sixth century at Athens which was to have the effect of guaranteeing public prosecution. He introduced "the right of any person to take legal action in behalf of the injured party" (Ostwald 1986:9; *Constitution of Athens* 9.1). Legalizing an action of this sort, which came to be called a *graphé,* meant that legal redress became available even to those who, either by citizenship laws or by some other obstacle, were prevented from pleading their case in person. By permitting injured parties to be *represented* in this way by written accusations, the Solonian code changed the whole nature of justice. Because litigants no longer had to be *embodied* litigants, that is, particular flesh-and-blood litigants, justice was now something that even an abstract litigant could claim. This representational structure proved to be a democratizing one, for now cases could be submitted on behalf of "the people" as a whole, and crimes by magistrates or other civic officials could be prosecuted with "the people" as the injured party (Ostwald 1986:9; Gagarin 1986:69).

With even magistrates now subject to prosecution, the Homeric scenario, where two disputants bring their case before the judge, was rewritten. The judge was no longer the outside arbiter of private conflicts who possessed legal procedure within himself. He was now pulled within the legal sphere as a potential disputant. As a corollary of this new state of affairs, Solon enacted a law of impeachment (*Const. Ath.* 8.4.), and established what appears to have been a public law court, the *heliaia,* and an appeals procedure for hearing disputed judgments of the magistrates (*Const. Ath.* 9.1).[7]

There is a great deal of uncertainty about the finer details of the Solonian reforms, for the sources for them, Aristotle and Plutarch, are very late. But the written laws of the seventh and sixth centuries, whether intentionally or not,[8] indisputably started a shift toward an increasingly democratic legal system (Ostwald 1986:203). By establishing an appeals procedure and a public court composed of regular citizens chosen by lot irrespective of wealth, Solonian law sketched in the main outline of the populist jury courts of the fifth century which Aristophanes immortalized in the *Wasps.* Aristotle considered these law courts, or *dikasteria,* the main repositories of popular power in Athens.[9] The right of *isegoria*—the right of every citizen to have his say regardless of social position—was only further enshrined by Solon's followers, Cleisthenes and Ephialtes.[10] Although I have so far spoken of Athens as a cosmopolitan meeting ground for poetic dialects and metrical types and the place where the "mixed" genre of drama was invented, Athenians were even prouder, perhaps, of their other "mixing" policies: the mixing of the speech of rich and poor, powerful and powerless, in a single voice of binding legal authority.[11]

---

7. See Ostwald 1986:9.

8. That these legal reforms probably did not intend to have the effects they did is a point made repeatedly by Ostwald (1986) and Gagarin (1986). We shall be returning to this idea shortly.

9. *Politics* 2.12.1273b35–74a5; *Const. Ath.* 9.1, 41.2.

10. Ostwald 1986:48, 203, 461–62.

11. *Const. Ath.* 21.4; Ostwald 1986:15–20.

This pride in *isegoria,* in the mixed speech of the whole people, was surely shared by Aeschylus, whose *Suppliants* is a kind of sustained celebration of the glories of popular sovereignty. Performed, it seems, in 463 B.C.E.,[12] this play shows how, in a country where law has admitted into itself the principle of representation, even weak noncitizens can receive a fair public hearing. The suppliant women from Egypt seek refuge in Argos (which is really fifth-century Athens disguised), and throw themselves on the altars of the local deities for protection. But as Aeschylus shows, it is not by customary religious practices that the suppliants are saved but by a legally binding vote of the assembled people. The daughters of Danaus are described as exiles from a less democratic state, to whom the notion of popular sovereignty is quite alien. They know nothing of the empowerment of the people to make authorized decisions for the polis as a whole. Reflecting a prelegalistic concept of kingship, the Chorus, urging King Pelasgus to make a judgment in his own person, says: "You are, yes, the city, the people / A prince is not judged. / The land, the hearth, the altar you rule / With the single vote and scepter" (369–72). But Pelasgus, king in a democracy, must "share all with the citizens"; he refuses to "act / Alone, apart from the people" (367–68, 398–99). By "representing" the suit of the daughters of Danaus before the assembled citizens of Argos, Pelasgus wins for them an authorized *city* remedy against the customary violence of their pursuing cousins. As I mentioned before, a suppliant escaping the "self-help" of a family in its private disputes would have had no hope of protection from any higher public law before the Draconian code. In the *Suppliants,* this victory for the weak through legal means is a double one, however. Not only are otherwise helpless plaintiffs given protection from family vengeance, but also women, shown throughout Homer to be mere chattels or "prizes" for men to dispose of as they wish, are legally protected in their desire not to be "household-slave[s] to Egyptus' sons" (334). As the Chorus stresses, the citizen jury of Argos honored them even as women, not "cast[ing] their votes / On the side of men" (643–44), as would have been customary.

Although the publication of the Draconian and Solonian law codes did not necessarily intend this, the effect of writing on legal process was to give the Greeks a distinct taste for the precise kind of public accountability that Aeschylus celebrates in the *Suppliants.* In Ronald Stroud's words, the early Greeks were in fact "obsessed" with public accountability (1989:103–19). At the base of many Greek legal inscriptions we find the phrase "So that anyone who wishes may read" (Harvey 1966:600). That writing (in a script that

12. Podlecki 1966:43.

could be easily read by the public at large)[13] was the precondition for such juridical accountability is not merely the view of modern historians and theorists of law such as Gagarin, Kurzon, Ostwald, and Calhoun; it was the belief of the ancients themselves.

We find direct causal connections drawn between written law and democratic government in Aristotle[14] and implicitly in Aeschylus.[15] But Euripides perhaps stated it best: the public inscription of law is the great equalizer.

> In early days, before laws were common,
> One man has power to make the law his own:
> Equality is not yet. With written laws,
> People of small resources and the rich
> Both have the same recourse to justice. Now
> A man of means, if badly spoken of,
> Will have no better standing than the weak;
> And if the little man is right, he wins
> Against the great. This is the call of freedom:
> "What man has good advice to give the city,
> And wishes to make it known?"
>
> . . . .
>
> For the city, what can be more fair than that? (*Suppl.* 432–43)

This speech explicitly compares written law with preliterate conflictual speech: written law upholds the rights of weaker individuals, and does so by validating their verbal claims. Before writing, the rich man could be "badly spoken of" by one with "small resources," without effect. Writing comes to the aid of speech, under this view, for without it, disputes remain contests of identities in which the great will win.

The abstracting of justice away from the body of the judges and disputants alike made personal conflicts into decontextualized "cases" for public hearing. In the legal context that bred drama, conflicts and kingly decisions which were once hidden from common view went public: they became theatricalized.[16] Etymologically, the theatre was a place for viewing, the place

---

13. For estimates of how many members of the Greek population were able to read these inscriptions, see W. Harris 1989 and Thomas 1992.

14. *Politics* 1270b28ff.; Thomas 1989:60.

15. *Suppliants* 942–49; see also Burns 1981:377.

16. Vernant and Vidal-Naquet make a similar point when they write that tragedy "could be said to be a manifestation of the city turning itself into theatre, presenting itself on stage before its assembled citizens" (1990:185).

where citizens went to see, to contemplate and judge the musical *agones,* or competitions. What they saw on stage once dramas were performed there was very similar to what they saw on Athens' other public stages, in the Assembly and the law courts. In the courts they watched as cases were argued, self-justifications offered, events recounted, and verdicts passed on the guilty. They heard the claims and counterclaims of witnesses and the mutually contradictory statements of the litigants. They heard cross-examinations and denials, and observed the relentless drive to get to the bottom of things, to the truth. Judging from the earliest extant dramas of the fifth century, that is also precisely what they saw in the theatre in its glorious first century. In the Theatre of Dionysus no less than in the *dikasteria,* regular citizens watched as "great men" faced public prosecution, interrogation, and indictment on various charges. In drama, the great figures of mythology and public life were forced, like ordinary criminals, to stand public trial and justify themselves in speech. Orestes must defend himself against murder charges; Oedipus must prosecute "anyone" guilty of crimes against the state, with "anyone" proving inclusive even of himself; Antigone must stand interrogation for violating the state's written laws by Creon, who must in turn justify his own lawlessness; and Prometheus, sentenced to a term in the stocks for traitorous actions against a tyrant, justifies his man-loving crimes in a fashion at once typically dramatic and typically forensic: in speech, in argument, in rebuttal and explanation. That Prometheus is immobilized on a rock makes his recourse to verbal self-justification especially poignant.[17] But in appearing on stage before the assembled citizen audience as an accused criminal whose "case" is being heard, Prometheus is not in principle different from any other dramatic figure. And just as it was written law that gave the public the ability to bring even the strong man to justice, so too is Prometheus' criminal case connected with writing in the theatre. Prometheus' crime involved giving writing to mankind, an act conceptualized explicitly as a democratizing threat to the lawlessness of the tyrant Zeus, who rules without public accountability ("he . . . rules without having to give account" Aeschylus *Prometheus Bound* 324).

As Werner Jaeger has observed, the climaxes of the action in the *Iliad* are always "Tales of Prowess," or *aristeiai* (1960 1:44). Similarly, all the episodes in the *Odyssey* are aimed toward the *aristeia* in which Odysseus, together with his son, at last vanquishes the suitors. In Homer, the consequences of such great deeds are never so important as the doing of them. But even in the earliest dramas, we see a wholly different attitude to human

17. But not unusual in theatrical literature; see esp. Samuel Beckett's *Play.*

action. Here, the climax of the action is not the deed but the verbal justification of it after the fact. When Aristotle lists all the possible permutations of a tragic plot, he admits that there can be only these: either the deed was done or it was not, and if done, either knowingly or not (*Poetics* 1453b15–16). The focus in a tragic plot, in other words, has shifted away from a recounting of the prowess of deeds and toward a determination of their lawfulness. Did the doer have criminal intent? Did he in fact even commit the crime of which he stands accused? The types of plots Aristotle specifies for drama, based as they all are on retrospective investigation of the mental state of a protagonist, are of course completely incompatible with epic storytelling, in which such deeds are long anticipated and then at last simply celebrated. But when the action in drama begins, Ajax has already slaughtered the sheep, Oedipus has already broken all the laws, the Danaids have already disobeyed, and the Persians have long since built their unholy bridges. In some cases, it is true, the crime is not actually committed until the second scene or, as in *Medea,* much later. But delays in these cases usually exist only to establish that the doer is acting knowingly and on purpose. Antigone and Clytaemestra, for example, make their first entrances as purposeful criminals, despite having not yet actually committed the crime. Dramatic form put all such mythic heroes on stage, not to watch them in action but to cross-examine them.[18]

The startling similarities between public hearings in the legal sphere and those that were staged before citizens in the theatre have often been remarked on.[19] Court cases were heard before mass audiences of hundreds or thousands of listeners;[20] the audiences at dramatic presentations also numbered in the thousands, as we see from the size of surviving theatres. Furthermore, many scholars believe that even the seating for both types of "hearings" was arranged according to the same rules.[21] The casting of a ballot by judges was the climax toward which both legal and theatrical specta-

18. The number of plays in the theatrical repertory that feature actual cross-examination scenes is of course noteworthy in itself: the *Eumenides, Pierre Pathelin, Merchant of Venice, Much Ado, Measure for Measure,* Kleist's *Broken Jug, The Bells, Caucasian Chalk Circle, Saint Joan, Our Country's Good* (to say nothing of *Witness for the Prosecution, Inherit the Wind, Twelve Angry Men,* and other courtroom dramas).

19. See esp. Ober and Strauss 1990:237ff.; Henderson 1990:271–313; and Vernant and Vidal-Naquet 1990:32–33, who write: "Tragedy is not only an art-form; it is also a social institution that the city, by establishing competitions in tragedies, set up alongside its political and legal institutions."

20. Humphreys 1985:316, 357 n. 20; Sommerstein 1983:xvi; Ostwald 1986:205.

21. Winkler 1990:22–23; Henderson 1990:286; Ober and Strauss 1990:238. See also Pickard-Cambridge 1968:269–70.

cles aimed: both agonistic performances aimed toward a majority decision about the winner. Furthermore, playwrights and oratorical speech writers were described by their contemporaries as doing the exact same thing: both were writers of "tetralogies," a term that originated in reference to the delivery in court of four speeches concerned with the same case (Pickard-Cambridge 1968:80). The Greek word *agonizomai* refers equally to "going to law" and competing on stage for the prize in a play.[22] And finally, the length of the contestants' speeches was regulated at law *and* on stage (before the fourth century) in the exact same way: by the water clock (*Poetics* 1451a12).[23]

Philokleon of the *Wasps* describes the courts as "a mighty power that allows us to mock at wealth" (575); Euripides describes writing as an aid in this process of criticizing the "great man." In legal procedure of the fifth century, writing was used for this purpose in a particularly concrete way. The "complaints" that formed the preliminary hearings of a court case were submitted to the *anakrisis* in the form of writing, *graphé:* "to hand in an accusation" against someone was *graphen apopherein.*[24] This use of writing to criticize the great was equally palpable in the sphere of fifth-century poetry, for the dramatists *also* brought their work to an archon for a "preliminary hearing" prior to the theatre festival. This poetic *anakrisis* would likewise determine whether the case would receive a public hearing or not. For this reason, the act of submitting a play for performance was identical in structure to the act of submitting a legal complaint for trial: when Euripides handed in, say, the *Hippolytos* or the *Medea* for consideration for the theatre festival, he was in effect "handing in an accusation" against these noble-blooded mythological figures, these great men and women. To my earlier conclusions about the "unfinished" nature of the dramatic text, one might add this insight, drawn from legal procedure of the time: the dramatic text remains open precisely because, like the *graphé* of a complaint against the great, it awaits its day in court. It is the written accusation, not the judgment itself. Is Hippolytos an insufferable misogynist prude, or an innocent victim of a false *graphé* (in this case a literal one, submitted by his stepmother)? Is Medea a victim of a monstrous society or a monster herself? Is

22. See Liddell and Scott (1983:10): "to contend for the prize on the stage, act" and "to contend against in a law suit."

23. There is a problem with the manuscript at this point in the *Poetics;* Rudolph Kassel in his 1965 text marks it with obelisks. If the text as we have it is correct, however, it was believed by Aristotle's contemporaries that plays were "once in other days" regulated by the water clock, a device that unquestionably was used in the courts. For evidence of the practice in pre–fourth-century theatre, Aristotle cites only common opinion ("they say").

24. *Wasps* 846; Thomas 1989:42; Stockton 1990:99.

Orestes guilty as charged or innocent? What about Oedipus? Antigone? Verdicts of this type are made on the basis of performance alone. The case is not decided until it comes to court—and may, in any case, not make it past the preliminary hearing.

If and when such cases did come before the public, the audience, whether of jurors or of playgoers, was conscious of its role as a decision maker. And both in the theatre and in the law courts, Athenians relied on writing as an aid in reaching their decisions. Philokleon comes home from the law courts "plastered with wax beneath his fingernails" from marking the litigants' penalties on writing tablets (*Wasps* 109, 165); and when Bdelykleon acts the part of juror, he calls instantly for his writing tablets so that he might make a note of the main points of the testimony (538, 559, 576–77: "That's now the second point of yours I'm writing down."). Likewise, in the "great debate" that Aristophanes says took place in the theatre, and which he gives us a glimpse of in the *Frogs*, the "jurors" apparently came "armed for action" as well: "Everyone's holding his little book, so he can follow the subtle points" (1114). Whether he meant, by "little book," the texts of the plays being judged or tablets for writing down the good points of the debate is impossible to tell.[25] But certainly when it came to the final decision, theatrical judges voted by inscribing the name of their chosen poet in writing.[26]

Nevertheless, and despite the use made of writing by jurors and theatregoers alike, contests at law and in the theatre were decided primarily on an oral basis, at least in the fifth century. Admittedly, the role of writing in the jurisprudential process grew thereafter: from 378–77 B.C.E., witnesses merely confirmed their prepared written testimonies, and cross-examination was eliminated (Humphreys 1985:316). And by Aristotle's time, playwrights, too, were showing signs of retreat into pure textuality, writing plays "suitable for reading" alone.[27] But before this time, legal and dramatic trials were won or lost on an oral basis, according to the speakers' ability to win the audience's favor. When we remember that the six thousand jurors who passed judgment in the Athenian law courts were ordinary nonspecialist citizens who had received no training in law whatsoever, we can appreciate the full extent of the similarity between dramatic and forensic speech: "The presiding magistrate did not sum up the arguments made by the two parties or give authoritative rulings on legal issues" (Humphreys 1985:323). Nor did

25. See Pickard-Cambridge, who discusses the ambiguity of the line and the difficulty in determining exactly what Aristophanes meant by *biblion* in this context (1968:276).

26. See the evidence about literate voting practices in Csapo and Slater 1995:160.

27. Aristotle *Rhetoric* 3.12.1413b12f.; see also Pfeiffer 1986:29 and Taplin 1977:13 n. 1.

the jurors deliberate; they heard the oral performances and dropped their voting pebble in an urn. Similarly in the theatre, the judges listened, and voted then and there. Thus we see why her study of Athenian legal procedure led Sally Humphreys to conclude that the law courts and theatre were related "urban institutions": "Both put the audience in the position of judge; both made extensive use of competitions in argument" (323).

The same went, of course, for the popular Assembly, where arguments were similarly staged, put in contest, and voted on. The Theatre of Dionysus near Munychia was used on at least one occasion for such political Assembly meetings (Ostwald 1986:394), and of course the Theatre of Dionysus at Athens was used every year as an assembly hall, as a place for hearing complaints about behavior during the festival, after the plays had all been seen.[28] As in the law courts and theatre, performative speech in the Assembly, too, was preceded by a written document;[29] but the "end" of all these activities was an oral performance whose aim was to gain a lay audience's favor, that is, to *win*.

The chorus in the *Frogs* addresses the whole citizen audience as the "judge" of the musical competition. And, like the jurors of Athens' legal system, the judges of the theatre festival were chosen by lot.[30] In the theatre, admittedly, only ten spectators were officially allowed to perform the judging function, to pick the winners and cast written ballots on behalf of the whole audience; but Simon Goldhill is convinced that their voting was deeply affected by general audience response, by the sympathies of the mass theatrical "jury" as a whole (1990:100). Eric Csapo and William Slater similarly conclude on the basis of available evidence that theatrical judges not only were swayed by the crowd, but were expected to be swayed (1995:160). And as the story about Alcibiades' unpopular victory over Taureas shows, the audience made its preferences clear.[31] One ancient but much later writer reports that the audience at the *Clouds* shouted to the judges, "Write no other name but Aristophanes!"[32] In writing the winner's name, or voicing their approval or condemnation in the form of shouts, applause, or footstomping, theatrical audiences thus functioned essentially as jurors in a court of law. And as Jeffrey Henderson has demonstrated at length

28. Demosthenes *Against Meidias* 8–10, as discussed in Pickard-Cambridge 1968:64–68.

29. That is, by draft proposals prepared by the Council; see Stockton 1990:88; Ostwald 1986:77.

30. Pickard-Cambridge 1968:95–96; Ostwald 1986:462.

31. Pickard-Cambridge 1968:273.

32. Aelian *Varia Historia* 2.13, as cited and discussed by Csapo and Slater 1995:160.

(1990:271–313), the identity between these two activities was obvious even to the participants at the time.

Of course, what similarities there are between the "hearing" of a text-based case in the theatre and Pnyx or *dikasteria* conceal one major difference. A successful speech in the Assembly may send thousands of men off to their deaths in battle, whereas a successful tetralogy in the theatre causes nothing directly to happen outside of the addition of the victors' names to the list of winners.[33] But as a "literacy event,"[34] theatrical performance is structured like a jury trial, where a written accusation is judged by a mass audience in performance.[35]

The new written status of law thus created a social atmosphere, for plaintiffs and poets alike, in which the "great men" of public life and mythology could be conceived of as susceptible to public prosecution for their crimes. The stories told by the fifth-century dramatists clearly reflect this reconceptualization of human behavior, crime, and conflict. Heroes who in Homer get off scot-free are called to justice in drama. But they are called to justice in a particular way. For the future-oriented, conditional structure of properly legal utterances guaranteed that the mere accusation of guilt cannot be the end of the story. Oral, proto-legal utterances, with their first-person imperative structure and reference to the past, tend to exhaust themselves within the present context of their delivery. But the potential performatives of written law and theatre, with their conditional, abstracted structure, *require* a future trial, both for determining whether the "conditions" have in fact been met, and for applying the abstract rule about "anyone" to this particular case, these particular litigants. And because written law is authorized as law by the city as a whole, its application to particular cases through trial must involve the city, must take a civic form. A secret trial would have been as pointless and objectionable in Athens' literate legal system as would a private performance of the plays written for the theatre, and for the same reasons. Not only has the structure of written law deter-

---

33. Although basically valid and worth making, this distinction, between the real consequences of forensic speech and the unreal consequences from dramatic speech, is not absolute. Some of Aristophanes' poetic suggestions seem actually to have been instituted in reality. See Henderson 1990:271–313.

34. Brian Street discusses Heath's definition of a "literacy event" as "any occasion in which a piece of writing is integral to the nature of the participants' interactions and their interpretive processes" (1988:61).

35. The Greek preference for a mass decision over that of an individual gets powerful corroboration from Aristotle's insistence, even in the more bookish and specialist fourth century, that the opinion of a mass audience is more valuable than the judgment of a single critic (*Politics* 3.1281b7). See Pickard-Cambridge 1968:277.

mined that the city itself must hear and judge each new application of legal abstractions to particular individuals, but also the nature of written law, having made possible equitable representation for both plaintiff and defendant in any dispute, has guaranteed that hearings in the literate age will, and must, consist of dialogic argument.

Unfortunately, most of the works that originally made up the full tetralogy of the dramatic accusations are lost. Had more complete dramatic case hearings survived, it is certain that the legalistic essence of early theatre would be more readily apparent. Discussions of ancient tragedy in our time are more likely to emphasize Aristotelian notions of "catharsis" and "tragic flaws." [36] But the legal associations even of these terms have somehow been obscured in modernity. By Aristotle's time, the former had come to have strong associations with medical practice; by our time, the latter in particular has come to be associated with anachronistic Christian values. In the century before the invention of drama, however, in the legal inscription from Dreros, Crete, we find that *katharos* has something to do with the kind of purification one achieves by swearing an oath in court (Gagarin 1986:86). And *hubris* as we find it in Hesiod is not a tragic flaw, moral failing, sin, or any other abstract or merely personal ethical trait, but the bad outcome of a crooked lawsuit (*Works and Days* 224–85). The opposite of *hubris* is not modesty or goodness but *justice* and straight settlements in the arbitration of disputes (Gagarin 1986:49). When Aristophanes was indicted by Kleon with a crime against the state (*demos*), he was charged specifically with having committed "an act of *hubris,*" an "outrage" against the people.[37] From Demosthenes' remarks somewhat later, it is clear that *hubris* for the ancients was practically synonymous with "anything illegal": "If anyone commits an act of hubris against anyone else, whether child, woman, or man, whether free or slave, or does anything illegal against any of these, let anyone who wishes, of those entitled, lay an indictment." [38] Anyone might bring such a lawsuit, not just the one wronged, because, as Isocrates declared at the end of the fifth century, "the matter of hubris [is] a matter of *public concern.*" [39] We cannot hope to grasp the meaning of hubris today unless we recognize

36. Brian Vickers discusses the widespread misinterpretation and mistaken use by modern theorists of critical terms from antiquity (1973:26–31).

37. *Scholion* to *Acharnians* 378, as translated and discussed by Csapo and Slater 1995:178.

38. *Against Meidas* 31–33, mid-fourth century, translated by Csapo and Slater 1995:180.

39. *Against Lochites* 20.2–3, as translated by Csapo and Slater 1995:180; my italics.

that written law had made such outrages "a matter of public concern," and that hubris was therefore primarily a *legal* problem.

In the prosecution of Aeschylus for impiety we find further confirmation of how much more the early theatre had in common with law than with religion. Not only have the specifically legal meanings of *hubris* been eroded in modernity, but the extrareligious nature of the theatre itself is often denied by moderns altogether. Along with Megacles, Aeschylus shares the distinction of having been the first citizen to be charged with a religious crime against the state. He was accused of revealing religious secrets of the Eleusinian mysteries in a play, secrets that should have been known only to initiates.[40] Aeschylus was apparently acquitted by a *dikasterion;* his defense, according to Aristotle, was that he did not know they were secrets when he staged them in a play.

So far from "being" a religious spectacle, tragedy was legally prohibited even from *staging* religious mysteries. In the dramatic age, religious cults, which had traditionally been under the control of the old families, came under the jurisdiction of the state. The hereditary priesthoods were upheld by public legislation (Ostwald 1986:145), but their essentially private and secretive character was affirmed as well. In fact, in the first years of the fifth century, two particular family-run priesthoods were ordered by public decree to perform initiations *individually;* initiating in groups would be punishable by a fine of one thousand drachmas (Ostwald 1986:140). Therefore, while true religious practices were supposed to be individualistic, private, and secret in nature, what dramatists such as Aeschylus did in staging plays was the virtual opposite: public, communal, open, unhidden.[41] Theatre was not an initiation "into" anything; it was, like a legal spectacle, a public bringing-to-light, a show, a "hearing." Aeschylus' surviving three-part "case" against Orestes gives us perhaps the best glimpse we have of the legalistic nature of dramatic composition; and in subjecting his tragic hero to public prosecution in a play, Aeschylus was making use of a ready-made model for investigating public crimes and solving conflicts, and one to which he had been subjected himself.

As had so many dramatists: Herodotus (*History* 6.21.2) reports that the tragedian Phrynicus was also forced to stand trial in the courts, where he was

40. Aristotle *Nicomachean Ethics* 3.1.1111a6–10; Ostwald 1986:528. This anecdote reminds one instantly of the trouble Mozart is said to have gotten into for revealing secrets of the Masonic temple cult in his *Magic Flute.*

41. See esp. Padel 1990:336ff. and Seale 1982 passim for discussions of Greek drama as that which reveals, brings to light, makes public.

not as lucky as Aeschylus. In 492 B.C.E. or thereabouts, he was sentenced to a fine of one thousand drachmas and prohibited from re-performing his *Capture of Miletus* on the grounds that it had reminded the Athenians of their recent and traumatic loss of that city. It seems that there were limits to what could be shown on stage: religious secrets were taboo, as were, apparently, too-fresh miseries. Sophocles was publicly charged by his son with incompetence; the accusation was read in court and the playwright was acquitted (Bieber 1961:28–29). After a performance of the *Babylonians* at the City Dionysia in 426, Kleon submitted a *graphé* against Aristophanes "for having ridiculed magistrates . . . as well as Kleon, in the presence of foreigners" (*Acharnians* 377–82).[42] This action seems not to have made it beyond the preliminary hearing; nevertheless, Aristophanes says that the filthy suit almost killed him anyway (370–82).[43] Aristophanes really seems to deserve some sort of prize, in fact, perhaps a Golden Wasp, as the poet most often "stung" at Athens. If we can trust our sources, he was also charged with "wrongful acquisition of citizen rights," a false accusation against which he was nevertheless forced to defend himself a second and a third time.[44]

That a particular legal system will tend to suggest, to the poets living under it, a corresponding type of storytelling is confirmed by Sally Humphreys's (1985) study of the social relations implicit in various legal systems. In China, for example, where magistrates were brought in from elsewhere to judge cases in social contexts that were unfamiliar to them, bringing the truth to light in court was a labyrinthine and hazardous task. To Humphreys it is therefore not surprising that the detective story, which explores the "outsider's" navigation through an alien, clue-strewn environment, was invented in China (315). But in Athens, where citizens sat in public judgment over fellow citizens, a forensic form of storytelling was invented instead.[45] In Greece's dramatic age, and under the influence of literacy, interpersonal conflict had become legalized and theatricalized, and dramatic form represents this state of affairs in its very structure.

In addition to its organization as a third-person conditional utterance oriented toward a public, performed "hearing," dramatic form reflects the legal atmosphere in which it materialized in other ways as well. Foremost among these is the stichomythia, which, while absent from epic speech, is

---

42. See esp. Henderson 1990.

43. Ostwald 1986:207 n. 33; see also Henderson 1990.

44. Scholion to *Acharnians* 378 and *Life of Aristophanes* 19–26, as translated by Csapo and Slater 1985:178.

45. See also Padel, who says that in Athens "the assembly and the law courts were a kind of theatre, and the theatre an assembly-place, a court" (1990:338).

typical of drama. In the dispute between Achilleus and Agamemnon in the *Iliad,* for example, the epic bard represents the speech of each disputant as separate and self-contained. In the space of 132 lines, only nine monologic speeches are represented, and each one is fairly long, ranging from seven to twenty-three lines of uninterrupted discourse. In epic storytelling, verbal contest consists of autonomous set speeches which do not intersect directly at any point. Because the bard introduces each speaker in the bard's own voice, the characters speaking never respond to one another directly; their speeches do not come into contact but are buffered by transitional narrative segments spoken by the bard.

In drama, however, a new type of verbal debate makes its appearance. The paradigmatic example comes from the interrogation of Orestes in the *Eumenides:*

> Chorus: Say first, did you kill your mother or did you not?
> Orestes: Yes, I killed her. There shall be no denial of that.
> Chorus: There are three falls in the match and one has gone to us.
> Orestes: So you say. But you have not even thrown your man.
> Chorus: So. Then how did you kill her? you are bound to say.
> Orestes: I do. With drawn sword in my hand I cut her throat.
> Chorus: By whose persuasion and advice did you do this?
> Orestes: By order of this god, here. So he testifies.
> Chorus: The Prophet guided you into this matricide?
> Orestes: Yes. I have never complained of this. I do not now.
> Chorus: When sentence seizes you, you will talk a different way.
> Orestes: I have no fear. My father will aid me from the grave.
> Chorus: Kill your mother, then put trust in a corpse! Trust on.
> (587–99)

In thirteen lines, thirteen separate statements, each responding directly and inextricably to the one before. I spoke earlier about why this type of interchange would require the use of writing, for both composition and performance. As a poetic mode of representing human speech, however, it owes an equal debt to the model of forensic speech which developed out of written law. Aeschylus was of course deliberately staging a legal cross-examination in this scene, as Aristophanes was to do later in the *Wasps,* where a trial of the family pet is staged with kitchen utensils for witnesses (908–80). Nevertheless, a forensic speech style is exhibited also by dramatic characters who are not visibly competing in a court of law. In a grove outside Argos, the daughters of Danaus are challenged to provide verbal proof of the "truth" of their "tale" that they claim Argive ancestry (*Suppl.* 270–80):

Chorus: Wasn't Io once in Argos charged with Hera's temple?
King: Io was, the tale is prevalent.
Chorus: And wasn't Zeus to a mortal joined?
King: Which was from Hera unconcealed.
Chorus: How end these royal jealousies?
King: A goddess changed a woman to a cow.
Chorus: And Zeus, did he approach the horned cow?
King: Zeus became a bull, they say.

. . . .

Chorus: But what did Hera appoint for ill-omened Io?
King: A gnatlike goad it was, or driving sting.
Chorus: That the Nile-dwellers call the gadfly.
King: That drove her from Argos.
Chorus: It confirms my tale.
(291–310)

When Aristotle was later to draw up rules for the effective interrogation of opponents in his *Rhetoric,* it was to the dramatists he looked for examples of forensic speech no less than to the orators themselves. He would have approved of the Chorus's strategy here of leading the witness by asking a series of short questions. As he puts it, interrogation is an effective device "when one premise of an argument is obviously true, and you can see that your opponent must say 'yes' if you ask him whether the other is true" (1419a6ff.). He goes on in this vein, advising further that, as the audience will be unable to follow "a series" of questions posed at once, the successful orator will ask one compact question at a time—precisely as the Chorus does here (1419a17–20). This forensic dialogue structure is apparent throughout Sophoclean drama as well. One sees a lengthy cross-examination, made up of short questions and replies, in the *Oedipus* (986–1045), *Ajax* (95–120), *Antigone* (786–815), and *Philoctetes* (100–122); the very terse dialogic exchange between the sisters in *Oedipus at Colonus* (1957ff.) is also structured as an interrogation.

Even when modern theorists acknowledge the forensic style of theatrical speech, rarely does it seem to occur to anyone that there might be concrete historical reasons for this peculiarity of theatrical form. For example, Manfred Pfister's *Theory and Analysis of Drama* is a thoroughgoing account of the special structure of the dramatic text. Pfister notes here that the direct speech of characters, especially their dialogical speech, "constitutes the predominant verbal matrix used in dramatic texts" (1988:5). Pfister quite rightly also notes that this primary truth about dramatic texts often goes unacknowledged; even Aristotelian poetics obscures it by focusing instead on abstractions such as "the plot." The question Pfister leaves unanswered, and unasked, is: *Why* does discourse in drama consist mainly of direct dialogical debate?

We have begun to see how writing would have played a part in making obsolete the mediating voice of the narrator, or bard, whose function before writing was to remember and with his own voice report what all the characters said and did. But the emergence of this characteristically dramatic "verbal matrix," this direct dialogical speech, may have been equally beholden to the agonistic free-for-all of Athenian jurisprudence. In the absence of an authoritative judge in the legal sphere, human disputes became precisely what we see in drama: direct dialogical speech without interruption, without narrative manipulation, and with judgment passed only by an ordinary listening audience at the end of the performance.[46] In our time, on the contrary, even jury trials are regulated by an authoritative judge, whose specialist knowledge and impartiality are supposed to ensure that justice is properly administered. In such forensically mediated atmospheres as ours today, it is not surprising that the main storytelling arts of our time are the heavily mediated genres of novel and film. Indeed, it is only in our time that the presence of the guiding hand of some outside authority has come to be expected even in the theatre (i.e., the director).[47] In short, the potentially unmediated verbal agon of all dramatic form may derive from the forensic style of Athens's literate legal system.

It is not, however, only the nature of discourse in drama that is traceable to Athens's literate legal system; the identity of the *speakers* is equally indebted. In the long speech from the *Suppliants* cited earlier, Euripides also equates written law with an expansion, to more types of speakers, of the freedom to speak and give "good advice" to the city. The phrase he uses toward the end of the speech is actually a quotation from ordinary civic proce-

46. The audience at the theatre was judging the performance of a play, whereas the listeners at a trial were supposed to be judging the merits of the case. This might seem to suggest that the type of judging being done was different in each case. As we shall see, however, the difference between the two is not as great as it might appear. As Bettyruth Walter (1988) and Dennis Kurzon (1986) have shown, speakers in legal contexts win the support of their audiences mainly on the basis of their *performances,* which in many cases means that acting coaching is required even by those litigants who are "innocent." *Being* innocent is never enough; one must *appear* to be innocent as well, which sometimes means *acting* innocent.

47. See esp. Pavis 1982 for uncritical acceptance of the mediating role of the director in theatre art, and unexamined assumptions about the existence of such mediators in theatre practice throughout history.

dure. The Athenian Assembly always opened with a herald asking: "What man has good advice to give to the *polis* and wishes to make it known?" (Finley 1983:139). With the existence of the "shield" of written law, not only does the speech of the poor have protection,[48] but so does that of the younger members of the community. Euripides' speaker goes on (after the quoted section) to discuss the plight of the "youthful townsmen," who, like "ears of corn in a spring field," are likely to be cut off by their power-jealous elders (*Suppl.* 291–310). But with the publication of written laws, the legal decision-making process, and speech itself, is "liberat[ed] . . . from its attachment to immediate reality" (Meier 1990:86), and "good advice" can for the first time be judged without reference to or prejudice against the speaker's own identity. As Humphreys puts it, legalized debate meant that those who would not otherwise have been called upon to speak in public found themselves addressing large audiences for the first time, and doing so in a context where attention had to be paid to "the way in which opposing views were argued rather than [to] the status and achievements of the proponents" themselves (1985:317). In the oral world of the epics, as in oral societies generally,[49] we see clearly how the speech of the young is devalued in favor of that of the elders (*Il.* 9.53–54; *Od.* 3.21–24, 125, 362–63; 4.205; 7.155–58). In the tragedies, on the contrary, as Robert Garland (1990) has pointed out, elders are not depicted as having any innate monopoly on wisdom, and have moved mainly to the periphery of the action. In the written world of drama, even youths such as Neoptolemos can speak with more wisdom than their elders, such as Odysseus, and elders are themselves often portrayed as crotchety and conventional in their thinking.[50] The growing power of the younger members of society is amply demonstrated by Aristophanes throughout his oeuvre, especially in the *Knights, Acharnians, Clouds,* and *Wasps.*[51] Martin Ostwald has amassed considerable evidence connecting the increasingly visible presence in public life of the young to use of the law courts (1986:229ff.). For this empowerment of more types of citizens to have their say, Euripides credits writing.

And the theatre, of course, reflects this widened speech community. In marked contrast to the epic, the drama of literate Athens gives power of

48. Solon said that he "stood covering both [rich and poor] with a strong shield, allowing neither to triumph unjustly over the other" (Solon frag. 5.5–6 as cited by Gagarin 1986:138 and Finley 1983:1).

49. Clanchy 1979:150.

50. For example, the chorus of old men in *Agamemnon,* Tiresias in *Oedipus Tyrannos,* and Oedipus and Creon in *Oedipus at Colonus;* see Garland 1990:266–67.

51. *Knights* 225–26, 731; *Acharnians* 676–718; and the whole of *Clouds* and *Wasps.*

public speech to slaves, women, children, cripples, foreigners—even the insane. I have already mentioned some examples of dramatic presentations of the speech of foreigners (*Orestes, Persians*); Aeschylus also put publicly before the ears of the assembled Athenian citizenry the broken Greek of a foreigner in the *Suppliants* (835–950). In the story of Clytaemestra as told by Homer, the woman is peripheral to the story. She is given power neither of action nor of speech (*Od.* 529ff.). By Agamemnon in the *Iliad* she is compared, unfavorably, to his new slave Chryseis (1.111–14); but from neither woman do we hear a thing.[52] The innovations represented by drama are perhaps nowhere more pronounced than here: written drama gave the women of Greek mythology a chance to speak. In delegating the performative power of public speech to female figures, the Suda reports that Phrynicus led the way (Flickinger 1973:4); but Aeschylus was not far behind. In the *Agamemnon*, Clytaemestra has become one of the main actors in the mythological story of Agamemnon's murder; she has joined the lists of verbal combatants, and her entry into the public order of speakers is explicitly recognized: "My lady, no grave man could speak with better grace. I have listened to the proofs of your tale, and I believe" (351–52). The epic singer, by contrast, confined his song largely to the deeds of Achilleus and Odysseus and their fellow warriors.[53] The speechwriters, or *logographoi*, of the theatre wrote instead for Antigone and Clytaemestra and Iphigenia and

---

52. The justly famous exchange between Hektor and his wife is often cited as evidence of Homeric sympathy for female speakers, and for the importance of their place in the heroic world. The scene itself, however, shows Hektor telling Andromache to go back to her knitting and her womenfolk and not to trouble her head with thoughts about war, which are the business of men (read "loom and distaff" for my knitting: *Il.* 6.486–90). Helen is indeed given "the last word" (nearly) at the end of the *Iliad,* but in proportion to the length of this vast work, that is precisely what she gets: a word. In a work tens of thousands of lines long, Helen's fourteen-line speech in Book 24 (762–75) is negligible, particularly in light of the fact that the war was supposed to have been about her in the first place.

53. Women are not, of course, *absent* from the world of the epics. Odysseus does meet some interesting females on his way home, and Penelope is never long out of his mind, nor ours. But Homer's women are chiefly instruments in plots about men, or reflect the desires, actions, and aspirations of the men who are the real subjects of both stories. As Werner Jaeger has suggested, the virtues of a Penelope, Helen, Arete, or Nausicaa—loyalty, chastity, beauty, and good advice—are enumerated and praised mainly insofar as they reflect well on the men who are associated with them (1960 1:23). Epic women all remain "prizes" on a certain level, and do not pursue their own actions and agendas. On the contrary, a dramatist's treatment of the tale about Odysseus' return home would doubtlessly have cast Penelope as her *own* protector and murderer of the suitors—or of her unfaithful husband! This hypothesis is amply confirmed by Aeschylus' treatment of the homecoming theme: in Homer, it is Aegisthus who slaughters Agamemnon; in Aeschylus, Clytaemestra is clearly the mastermind.

Lysistrata; for Hecuba and Elektra and Medea; for Helen and Andromache and Alcestis; for suppliant women and Trojan women and women of the Assembly.

As in the law courts and Assembly, however, women were not allowed to appear on the stage in person. Their speech could be represented in writing, but not performed in the flesh. Nevertheless, given the ability of writing to outlive the context of its production, these represented discourses could at least survive, perhaps to be more properly incarnated in the future. For this reason, we might add to writing's virtues a certain measure of immunity from the social conventions regulating public speech at a given moment.[54]

Access to public speech was evidently widened in the age of drama, but speech *in propria persona* was still limited, by the Athenian concept of citizenship, to landowning males. And it is here that writing's connection with *isegoria* shows its most interesting face. For while foreigners such as Lysias and women such as Aspasia could not speak publicly themselves, they were enabled, by the existence of written forms of communication, to write speeches for others to deliver.[55] Such writers, or *logographoi,* wrote speeches for others to memorize and deliver in public, guaranteeing that their own voices could, in some manner, be heard. So popular were such written speeches that by the fourth century, "court speeches were—in the company of dramatic texts and mimes, with which they have much in common . . . —the light reading of the period" (Humphreys 1985:318, 320).

Women, foreigners, and slaves did not enjoy the same rights of public speech as landowning males in Athens of the fifth century B.C.E. Neither, of course, were blacks, Indians, and immigrant Chinese allowed to testify as witnesses in court in California as recently as the nineteenth century.[56] The disempowerment of some speakers in public is not, however, just a political issue. Speech contexts often do exclude many potentially wise speakers for technical legal reasons, for example, for lack of proper credentials such as citizenship or membership. But *all* speech contexts disempower *some* members of society "naturally" or inevitably. Isocrates was evidently a case in point in Athens. He had much good advice to give the city, but apparently was not gifted by nature as a pleasing speaker (Rowe 1986:215ff.). There is

54. I do not mean to suggest that the dramatists themselves hoped that women would one day perform their female roles. That writing accumulates meanings and performative possibilities through time which were not intended by the author is a matter to which I shall be turning shortly.

55. Stockton 1990:18; Cole 1981:135.

56. L.-W. Doo cited by Humphreys 1985:356 n. 1.

also a funny story told by Aristophanes about the book-loving Thucydides, who became suddenly tongue-tied, "paralysed in the jaws," when he was called upon to speak in a trial (*Wasps* 945–48). Not all members of a given speech community will be effective speakers, but some may not be able to speak at all. For example, at a moment just before writing had revolutionized the legal sphere in Europe, an unexpected case came before a medieval English court with remarkable results. In a judicial system where testimony and proof still had to be authorized by speech in person, a certain Agnes, a deaf-mute, was denied all legal rights because she could not speak on her own behalf (Clanchy 1979:222). Her case could not be *represented,* either by writing or by someone else's speech, as it could have been in literate Athens: she either spoke for herself or was disqualified from receiving legal redress. Without a technology for representing speech, citizens like this English mute cannot enjoy the rights of *isegoria,* even in places where they do exist.

From Aristophanes in particular we know that playwrights were valued largely for the advice they gave to the city; but not everyone who has a valuable contribution to make is gifted by nature with prizewinning charm. As we see from the inscription on a statue erected in the Theatre of Dionysus, actors won audience favor above all for "the charm of their speech" (Herington 1985:126), and apparently they still do. According to the New York theatre critic John Simon, charm is the one quality an actor cannot do without (1975:216–18). Socrates, who was said to be the ugliest man at Athens, may have lacked this particular quality himself—a detail that might help to explain his sardonic treatment of crowd-pleasers such as Ion. With the existence of writing, however, the public platform is opened up to anyone who merits an audience, regardless of his or her natural physical equipment and prevailing social taboos. Foreigners and women, such as Lysias, Isocrates, and Aspasia, were allowed to have their day in court, so to speak. In a world of speech without writing, the pragmatics of performance will tend to accentuate the speaker's identity and the degree of his personal charm over and above the substantive qualities of his argument. Without the need to appear in person, the dramatic logographer, by the same token, is free to make his or her contribution on paper, and leave the public communication of these ideas to those best suited by nature to win an audience's approval.

Nevertheless, like the switch from oral-intensive instruction to book-based schooling, which we looked at in Chapter 2, the writing down of law has a cost. The loss of their lived, context-bound particularities made disputes into abstract cases rather than contests of identities, which was a decidedly good thing as far as justice and fairness were concerned. But this loss of context, which always accompanies writing to some extent, means a corresponding loss of meaning. Although some degree of interpretation is required even in speech, interpretation takes on a much greater burden in deciphering meaning when communication is done in writing. I spoke earlier of the ease with which alphabetical writing can transcribe speech; but newer technologies of communication, such as film, video, and tape-recorders, have revealed just how much of speech is in fact *not* recorded by writing. In ancient writing up to the invention of the printing press, this was especially true. Since then, we have developed a detailed and more consistently used system of nonverbal signs to take the place, in writing, of the gestures, inflections, tones, pauses, emphases, and so on that organize and give meaning to our verbal utterances in oral delivery. But punctuation, paragraph breaks, italics, and font size can go only so far as substitutes for the sounds and gestures which in oral communication have enormous semantic value even though they have no alphabetical equivalents. It is for this reason that, in literate communication, interpretation comes to the forefront in the search for meaning.

Using Paul Ricoeur's words, we might say that writing can fix only the "noema" of speech, the "saying as said" (1981:203); what the alphabet is not equipped to represent is the "noesis" of a given speech act, the communicative intention in the mind of the speaker. In direct oral interlocution, nonverbal gestures and other bodily signs carry most of the burden of communicating intentions. For words themselves are inherently ambiguous. They possess only more or less strictly delineated *potentialities* for meaning; it is *how* they are used that determines what is meant. And so with written law such questions arise as "What exactly did Solon *mean* when he wrote that 'anyone' can submit a *graphé?*" It is context alone that tells us that when he wrote "anyone," he did *not* mean women and slaves. Meanings such as these, which are more or less directly manifested to listeners located within the historical and psychological context of the utterance, must be actively supplied by readers. For readers are by definition those receivers of verbal message who inhabit contexts separate from those in which the messages are produced. The contextual difference between conditions of production and of reception may be one of space or time, but is usually both.

The difficulty of interpreting such written locutions is often faced directly by our ancient sources. To the Solonian rule about the ability of "anyone" to submit a *graphé* on behalf of an injured party, Demosthenes adds the qualifying "of those Athenians entitled." [57] But the identity of even these "entitled" Athenians was obvious to Demosthenes' contemporaries in a way

57. *Against Meidas* 31–34; 47, as translated by Csapo and Slater 1995:180.

that it is not to readers from other contexts. Lysias also acknowledges the difficulties of interpretation that come with writing when he points out that a legislator who refers in writing to a person who "killed" someone is also intending to refer to a "murderer," even though he may not actually have used that particular word. To eliminate all ambiguity in writing, the legislator would have to accompany each written word with every single one of its synonyms, which would obviously be too much work.[58] Instead, continues Lysias, the legislator assumes that readers will interpret his writing by augmenting what he *says* (the saying, or noema), with what is being "signified" or intended (the noesis).[59]

As a decontextualized communication, writing thus makes the need for interpretation explicit. But interpretation was not unknown before writing. In Homer, for example, we notice that interpretation was widely practiced. Given the naturally decontextualized nature of dreams, omens, oracles, and other ambiguous phenomena, meaning must be actively supplied by anyone interpreting these phenomena if it is to be had at all. The interpretive reading of signs assumed to be significant was described by the verb *hupokrinesthai* (Svenbro 1990:373). In contrast to the *manteis,* whom Plato describes in the *Timaios* as the soothsayers or oracular mediums who themselves *produce* the ambiguous phrases, a *hupokrites* is one who (only) *interprets* such "words and enigmatic signs" (72a–b). Interpretive practices of this kind—be they aimed at the cryptic sayings of a Delphic oracle, the flight of birds, the cracks on heated animal bones, or the entrails of beasts—are widespread in early societies from Newfoundland to China. Judging from the occurrences of references to interpretation in Homer,[60] the meaning of the activity for the ancient Greeks is fairly clear: a *hupokrites* is one who suggests the "real meaning" of a verbal or visual sign. What oracles, entrails, and the flight of birds have in common with writing is that all are experienced as autonomous, meaning-laden sign systems which are cut off from ordinary, explanatory embeddedness in a communicative context.

With the advent of written law, a new kind of decontextualized utterance makes its appearance, and interpreters are required. Accordingly, orators or lawyers quickly come into existence with the advent of written law, joining the ranks of Greek culture's other interpreters. Given their function, it should not be surprising to learn that the Greeks used *hupokrinesthai* and

58. Although some legislators do try!
59. *Against Theomnestos,* 1–12, as translated by Csapo and Slater 1995:183.
60. *Il.* 8.407 and 12.228; *Od.* 2.111, 15.170, and 19.535; Hymn to Apollo 171.

related words to describe the public speech of orators (Pickard-Cambridge 1968:127).

Like law, poetry too needs interpreters once it is written down. In conditions of orality, poetry does not exist in a decontextualized state. Poetry is manifested only in concrete conditions of utterance, where producer and receiver are co-present. When a poetic utterance comes through the mouth of the bard, jongleur, or griot, there is no textual "locution" to interpret; the "real meaning" intended by the speaker is present in the context. But once poetry is composed directly in writing, outside of a physically engaged communication event, interpretation—both the possibility and necessity of it— is built into poetry from the start. Even the poet must to some extent be the interpreter of his own work, for production and reception cannot coincide absolutely. And so, predictably enough, a class of interpreters quickly sprang up in writing's wake within the sphere of poetry, too, and one that was analogous to that of orators in the legal sphere. And the interpreters of poetic texts, of course, were those performers called *hupokritai,* "actors." From the official lists of victors in poetic contests,[61] and from Aristophanes (*Wasps* 1279), we know that *hupokrites* was the proper word to describe the dramatic actor from at least the fifth century on. Distinguishable from the rhapsode and from other types of performers through the use of this special name, the actor for the ancients was first and foremost that performer who, like a lawyer, *interprets.*

Although theorists of drama today are likely to emphasize the actor's role-playing capacity[62] or physical presence as the essence of the actor's art, it must be remembered that these ways of distinguishing actors from other performing artists would have had no meaning in antiquity. It would have been meaningless to say that the actor was the one who danced or sang in person, or impersonated other men, for in the time and place of drama's invention, *all* poetry, not just drama, was performed, sung, and danced and involved impersonation. As John Herington (1985) has shown at length, epic and lyric and dramatic poetry were all, equally, arts of musical, corporeal performance. Plato speaks of both theatrical actors and epic rhapsodes as

---

61. Pickard-Cambridge 1968:132 cites *Inscriptiones Graecae* 2.2.2325.

62. Cf. Svenbro 1990 and Pickard-Cambridge 1962:110 for other interpretations of *hupokrites* among moderns (the "answerer," for example, was briefly popular but was discredited by Ingram Bywater and Pickard-Cambridge). I accept H. W. Parke's definition of the word as "one who suggests a meaning" (1967:17), and I trust it mainly because, as a scholar writing on a subject other than theatre, Parke can be assumed to be disinterested.

"out of their proper minds" when impersonating mythological characters; and Arthur Pickard-Cambridge provides good evidence that lyric recitation involved impersonation as well (1962:41–43). According to Herington, the main shape of histrionic performance, which came increasingly to be associated with actors, had in fact already been worked out by rhapsodes before the invention of dramatic form proper. Working from his written "reminders" of Homeric texts, the rhapsode was essentially the same kind of performer that the actor became. Differences between rhapsodic and theatrical performance do exist, but they do not pertain to questions of impersonation or corporeal presence.

One of these differences has to do with the nature of their respective texts. Once writing was available for recording Homeric poetry, rhapsodes used written reminders. This determined that their function—like that of the actor—would be "to interpret the meaning of the poet to the audience" (*Ion* 530c3–4). But the rhapsode's script was essentially a record of an oral performance, a written version of a poem that had originally been oral, untouched by writing. In Ricoeur's terms, it was not yet a "text." For Ricoeur, a decisive break is made when writing is not just used to record preexistent spoken utterances in a fixed form, but is chosen from the start, *before* the commencement of spoken communication or *in place* of it. Text takes over from "reminder" when writing ceases recording discourse and starts creating it. The birth of text is what brings the actor as *hupokrites* into existence, for he is the first performer ever who comes *after* a writing, a writing that antedates any corporeal performance of it, and must therefore be interpreted prior even to its first performance. Whereas the rhapsode interprets an oral singer, the actor interprets a *text*.

The actor's performance, like that of the rhapsode or lyricist in so many ways, thus distinguishes itself from theirs insofar as what is performed by the *hupokrites* is already an interpretation of ambiguous signs (as the name suggests). Common parlance even among actors today confirms this interpretive function. In order to understand the meaning of their "words and enigmatic signs," actors must supply the illocutionary and perlocutionary intentions and effects that are missing from the textually fixed locution. They must decide what a given locution "really means" in a given context—which, as we saw earlier, is tantamount to deciding what it *does* in the context of the utterance: issues a threat, makes a promise, changes the subject, and so on. The actor must also decide what perlocutionary effects this illocutionary act is able, or is intended, to achieve: bring the conversation to a halt, attain the interlocutor's trust, and so on. Actors ordinarily speak, in

Stanislavskian terms, of "motivation," "through-line of action," and "objective" instead of illocutionary and perlocutionary acts, but as the foregoing discussion should indicate, these are effectively the same things.

Of course, actors and lawyers are not the only interpreters that writing spawns. Textual scholars and exegetes, literary critics, historians, and theorists of various kinds are also called into being with the separation of utterance from context. What actors and lawyers do at the level of individual sentences (what Medea or article 10 of the Constitution says *here* . . .), textual critics, historians, and theorists do at the level of utterances taken as wholes (what Euripides' works say in their totality; what the law intends or effects generally). As far as theatre and the law are concerned, there appear to be two main consequences of this growing reliance on textual interpretation.

The first is a potential for seeing meaning as static and singular.[63] Partly because, before print, text had to be copied laboriously by hand, word for word, the "truth" of the text could easily be equated with its "literal" accuracy. Furthermore, an assumption that such "literal meaning" is a property of language itself could ensue. An assumption of this kind is what Per Linell has called the "myth" of literal meaning. It is a myth, of course, because "there are no fixed 'literal' meanings which are invariably activated when utterances containing certain specific words are processed, no invariant features constituting the subject matter every time a particular word is used. In each single case different things are, or may be, known and understood" (1988:47). Words themselves are "dynamic, only partly determined"; it is their use in particular contexts that decides what they mean. What Manfred Pfister has said of dramatic utterances is equally true of speech acts of any kind: they do not "just consist in [their] propositional expressive content alone, but also in the way [they are themselves] the execution of an act— whether in the form of a promise, a threat," and so on (1988:6).

Textual interpreters have been known in our tradition to fall into this literate trap of forgetting about the context-bound, action-oriented nature of linguistic utterances. Particularly in interpretive spheres where texts are not integrally attached to action and performance, there is potentially nothing to prevent equations between meaning and "literal" truth. For example, where interpretation is modeled on scribal letter copying, meaning may seem to be decidable only with reference to the exact letters of an "original,"

---

63. I have already referred to the appearance of this literacy effect in Platonic philosophy. Compare also G. S. Kirk's observation that writing will tend to encourage the establishment of a standard authorized version: "With the concept of the fixed text comes the concept of the correct text, and incongruous versions are gradually eroded" (1985:110).

and verifiable only with a textually based true or false. Meaning, in short, can be confused with textual qualities, and be assumed to have the fixed and single form of letters. Nevertheless, those interpreters of texts whose interest is explicitly performative—such as actors and lawyers—know in principle that the letters of a literal locution may reflect very little of the "real meaning" of a given utterance.

A literacy-sponsored belief in the existence of single, "literal" meanings is, however, an extreme case even in modernity and was certainly not typical of fifth-century Greece. Although our culture does know of them, literate activities so divorced from life as to become breeding grounds for such hermeneutical mistakes or "literacy myths" are rare. Even rarefied religious exegesis is on guard against the letter which killeth. A more common and representative effect of textual analysis on language practices is rather the reverse: that writing actively encourages the *multiplication* of meanings.

Meanings are multiplied in two ways. In the first place, it is possible for an utterance on the page to suggest a variety of mutually contradictory referents and connotations. Such overdetermination is possible and to some degree inevitable in writing because written locutions are intentionless, as we have seen. In speech, however, a locution so lacking in intention would be impossible to understand: What is this speaker trying to say? For example, as Howard Felperin (1985) has argued, echoing a sentiment that we might associate with Hazlitt, even a single Shakespearean word such as "virginalling" cannot be delivered orally without the loss of many of the meanings that attach themselves to it as long as it remains written down.[64] Whoever wishes to turn an ambiguous textual locution into meaningful speech simply has no choice but to rule out *some* of its potential meanings in advance.

But in addition to the greater polysemy of written language at a given moment, there is also the fact that texts accumulate meanings over time. As Ricoeur points out, this is the "positive significance" of writing's *Verfremdung* (alienation). For while writing deprives documents of the intentions of their creators, it also releases documents from the *limitations* of those intentions; and meanings that were either not available to writers in their present contexts, or were even expressly foreclosed or "censored" by them, can be discerned and contributed by readers from other temporal contexts. In artificially extending the life of a given utterance, writing thus extends the *range*

---

64. Felperin writes: "The impossibility of rendering theatrically the suggestive force of the word 'virginalling' must stand as a perennial caveat to those who maintain the primacy of performance over text" (1985:7).

of that utterance's meaningfulness, making it available to more receivers in more contexts. And writing extends the *depth* of an utterance's meaningfulness as well, permitting it to be interpreted in light of *previous* readings. To take an example from the legal sphere, the reforms of Solon and Cleisthenes were hardly intended to put political and legal power into the hands of the *demos* (Ostwald 1986:15ff.). *Isegoria* was the eventual result of written law, not its motivation (Gagarin 1986:123–24). The same could be said about the Constitution of the United States when it was drafted. The survival of such locutions in textual form has been accompanied by continued reinterpretation of them, and a gradual accretion around them of additional meanings: that government by "the people" should by right include the enfranchisement of women, naturalized immigrants, and landless citizens; that "equality" among citizens includes equality among races; and that "anyone" means more than landowning males. Equality among the genders or races was always contained in and justified by the concept of equality among citizens, but it was a dormant and invisible meaning which had to await later readings. As Carol G. Thomas puts it, social inequities of these types are brought into consciousness largely on the basis of the decontextualized analysis of terms: "Although written codes were a precondition for the eventual perception of inequities, such a perception was surely the result, not the cause, of the codification" (1977:455). Pressure for concrete social reform may come out of such perceptions (458), and this sometimes in spite of the writer's own intention.

After centuries of interpretation of the Greek plays, there is no doubt that some of the meanings available to us today were scarcely visible to Sophocles' audiences and not intended by Sophocles himself. But that does not mean that they were not there as potentials. In the case of the Greeks and even Shakespeare, a huge time span and great lack of documents would prevent us from even attempting to distinguish "intended" from surplus meanings. For a concrete example of this accretion of meanings around dramatic texts, we might be better off looking closer to home, say, to the nineteenth century. Erckmann-Chatrian's *Le Juif Polonaise* was performed in London in 1871 in a stage adaptation called *The Bells*. It was a big success and consolidated Henry Irving's fame. In its original context, the play's meaning had to do with a greedy father's guilty conscience and the psychology of guilt generally. Interpreted by us today, after ovens actually were used in Europe to dispose of Polish Jews after they had been robbed, the play reads as a much more sinister document and even as a work in some way "about" Auschwitz. This meaning, which is now undoubtedly "in" the play, would obviously not have been available to its first audience or to its author.[65] Some truths, invisible to contemporary speakers, come back to pester later readers.

As Peter Szondi (1986) and Paul Ricoeur (1981) have demonstrated, textual interpretation involves a special kind of analysis, and cannot be thought of as merely a variant of the interpretation of speech. The textual utterance, already decontextualized, provokes readers to different sorts of mental operations, for their understanding needs to be *constructed.* In speech, understanding is guided by the speaker's present intentions. In writing, an experience of authorial intention fades, and the focus shifts to the reader's own internal repertoire of available meanings. Attributing meaning to texts thus inevitably sends readers into a kind of self-reflexive process through which their own world-making and world-imagining apparatus is brought into active operation.[66]

Thus, despite its orality in performance, the language spoken by actors on the stage has been shaped by textual properties and properties of textual interpretation. One of the effects of writing on speech, as I discussed briefly earlier, is the infusion into discourse of an abstract ideological dimension. For conflictual forensic and dramatic speech, this means that spoken debate will take on a "principled" quality. In forensic speech we can see with great clarity how disputes in a literate context have come to be inhabited by larger, more general social and political issues. In marked contrast to pre-legal arbitrations, "the formal hearing of a dispute essentially dramatizes power relations between opposing *groups* within a society" (Humphreys 1985:315; my italics). As we see from the *Wasps* and the *Knights* in particular, public debates in fifth-century Athens took on social dimensions larger than the individualities of the disputants themselves: they were experienced as representative of power struggles between rich and poor, old aristocracy ver-

65. The climax of this play is the famous courtroom scene in which the Jew's murderer is tried and found guilty of the crime through verbal cross-examination.

66. Note, however, that I am speaking here about the textual interpretation accomplished by actors, not about the experience of listeners in the audience. Theatre audiences are placed in a position vis-à-vis meaning that is fundamentally different from the position in which actors find themselves. The process of shuttling back and forth internally between intentionless signs and self-supplied interpretations is a hermeneutical process alien to the listener of live speech acts. The listener in the theatre is instead given a continual supply of already constituted verbal meanings and intentions which he or she is, instead, called upon to internalize, let resonate there, and organize into patterns and conclusions. For this reason, it makes no sense to attribute "readerly" responses to theatre audiences, as have so many theorists in our time (esp. Bennett 1987; Cole 1992). The actor, like the lawyer, is a textual interpreter; but listeners, both in the law courts and in the theatre, are subject instead to oral models of interpretation.

sus nouveau riche, young Sophists against old democrats, and so on. In epic speech, by contrast, stories about Agamemnon, Clytaemestra, Orestes, and Antigone are told without reference to generalized ideological conflicts. Epic disputes always seem to be contained comfortably within a unified worldview where heroic and familial or dynastic values are taken sufficiently for granted not to need expression. Eumaios does not tell us how he likes being a faithful servant; Penelope has nothing to say about her position in the heroic society—she goes quietly upstairs when her son tells her to get lost. But these same basic stories, when staged, became the vehicles for exploring power relations between societal groups: Antigone's conflict with Creon is explicitly cast as a "gendered" one (*Antigone* 70–73), and representative of social tensions between the *oikos* and the *polis* in general; the effects of the Trojan War on Clytaemestra are also conceived in terms of the inequities of a gendered social hierarchy (*Agamemnon* 859, 940). The investigation of Orestes' bloodguilt is similarly conceived as a problem of power relations, a contest between fathers and mothers for status under customary justice, and between customary justice and Athene's city court for status as legitimate law. In Homer, on the contrary, Achilleus' wrath runs its course oblivious to underlying social conflicts. The dispute is not, for example, a principled disagreement about whether women are appropriate tokens of status, but only about who gets which one. According to Jack Goody, the kind of ideologized debate that one sees emerging in drama is not "based exclusively on a particular political system, nor upon [a] clash of cultures in a general sense"; rather, it depends "upon the framed opposition of theories set down on paper which permitted a different form of scrutiny, the analysis of text" (1987:77).

In addition to being shaped by this ideologizing tendency, dramatic speech is also characterized by a related literary impulse: the demand for logical proof. In opening up what Roy Harris calls the "autoglottic space" (1989:105) between utterance and sponsor, writing makes abstract, conceptual thinking practicable, as we have seen. But the putting down of ideas on paper leads to a particular form of abstract reasoning, and one that is especially dependent on the visual plane of the textual medium. I am thinking here of the syllogism, the noncontradictory proof. This noncontradictory syllogism—if all men are mortal, and Socrates is a man, . . . —tied by so many scholars to Greek literacy, is the bedrock on which both legal and dramatic thought processes are based.

The indebtedness of legalistic thinking to the syllogism reveals itself with especial clarity in the *Hecatompedon* (485–84 B.C.E.), one of the oldest extant legal texts from the period. This document revolves around the question of whether an offender against the law must have acted knowingly (*eidos*), or should be found guilty even if he acted in ignorance (*agnoia*), or despite himself, without criminal intent (*akon*).[67] The syllogistic problem posed here—"If a man breaks the law, but does so in ignorance, . . ."—is also, of course, an accurate synopsis of the plot of the *Oedipus*. Indeed, the tragedy as a whole is a kind of exercise in abstract, noncontradictory logic: if all men are prohibited from committing incest and parricide, and Oedipus is a man who did both of these things, then Oedipus is therefore a criminal, *despite* who he is in this particular case—a good king with no *mens rea* (criminal intent).

But it is not only the *Oedipus* that exemplifies this autoglottic concern with an abstract truth, demonstrable syllogistically. The organization of incidents in tragedy generally shows a like use of the noncontradictory proof, and could even be said to depend on the syllogism. For dramatic poetry, as Aristotle described it, is not about unrelated or mutually contradictory particulars (as history might be), but is about "demonstrable" truths of probability and necessity (*Poetics* 1451b36ff.). Like the conditional structure of the dramatic utterance as a whole—"if . . ."—the arrangement of incidents within particular plays is generally aimed at the eduction of the third term in a logical demonstration: "If Character X does/did Y, and Y is Z, then X is Z." As Aristotle says of all such tragic syllogisms, their possible outcomes are strictly limited in number by logic: "Besides these there is no other way, for they must either do the deed, or not, either knowingly or unknowingly" (1453b15–16).

Forensic demonstrations of this type, which first come into existence when law is extracted from personality and written down, manifest their connection with dramatic discourse again when literacy has its renaissance in Europe. From the point at which the monastic class begins to dominate our literary records in the Christian era, writing is not often used to record secular civic debate in Europe until around the ninth century.[68] But when secular documents do begin to appear, between the ninth and twelfth centuries, we notice that writing is used earliest for two significant and probably related purposes: for transcripts of juridical proceedings, and for the stage scripts of jongleurs.[69] Why the benefits of writing should be recognized so quickly for these two speech practices is clear: in both cases the exact wording is important to the outcome, as is the order in which the ut-

---

67. Vernant and Vidal-Naquet 1990:64; Ostwald 1986:23.
68. Clanchy 1979; Elsky 1989; Auerbach 1965.
69. Auerbach 1965:280–91; Clanchy 1979:225.

terances are delivered. Syllogisms about Socrates' mortality or Oedipus' guilt will fail to induce the final term if individual words are changed even slightly. Scripts, "whether for jongleurs or lawyers," enable their readers to see exactly what was said, or how they should speak, and "see the manner directly" (Clanchy 1979:225). And what is true for the jongleurs who learned vernacular romances by heart is even more true for the actors who replaced them after the thirteenth century. An oral bard, working alone and without anything to "prove," can deliver the episodes in nearly any order at all, without consequences for his recitation as a whole. Witness the invocation that starts the *Odyssey:* "Begin it, goddess, at whatever point you will." In the communal production conditions of drama, the order of incidents must on the contrary be known in advance: unexpected departures can result in pandemonium for everyone. But more importantly, if the order of incidents in a dramatic story is not strictly predetermined and adhered to, the syllogism will fall apart, fail to induce any logical conclusion. The same goes for proceedings at the bench: exact verbatim records of the litigants' and witnesses' testimonies are crucial to the outcome. This fact of forensic speech is recognized instantly by Bdelykleon: he writes down the key points in the defendant's argument verbatim (*Wasps* 576–77). Indeed, one could go so far as to assert that one of the earliest secular dramas of the European period was actually a lawyer's handbook, called *The Court Baron* and published in 1265. The lively, vernacular-style[70] forensic dialogue in this practical guide to pleading so closely resembles the speech of Shakespearean characters that one cannot help but appreciate the extent to which legal discourse, even the fictitious legal discourse of *The Court Baron,* provided a ready-made model for dramatic composition. (Asked a simple yes-or-no question by the crown, the naive poacher Walter de la More launches into a lengthy digression about how his wife, off her food for a month, was suddenly taken with a mighty longing to eat a tench—a speech that parallels, in nearly every aspect, Pompey's rambling discourse about Mistress Overdone's sudden "female" cravings for stewed prunes in *Measure for Measure.*)

The "reckoning all together" of syllogistic reasoning depends on an ability to arrange the major and minor premises simultaneously, and to see the relationship between them. For this reason, as Jack Goody has argued, formal operations such as the noncontradictory syllogism cannot be pursued beyond a very rudimentary point in the absence of writing (1987:77). In oral contexts, without the ability to arrange thoughts in simultaneously

70. Vernacular-*style* because it was written in French, the written language of the time, but intended as a lifelike representation of regular speech.

co-present configurations, contradictions are difficult to see. Writing for this reason is conducive to the invention of the formal proof; but perhaps even more significantly for science and the humanities, "it also accumulates and records these proofs (and what they prove) for future generations and for further operations" (68). Thus we are not surprised to find that the scientific method and empirical observation begin to replace ritual magic, shamanism, sacrifice, and belief in oracles and other supernatural agents in literate societies. As Goody suggestively describes it, it is only when one keeps a running, systematic record of the relation between one's dreams or horoscope and reality that one begins to discover for certain that the former hardly ever actually "foretells" the latter: "In oral memory the many misses tend to be forgotten in favour of the occasional hits" (69). Writing thus not only makes possible logical demonstrations and proofs, but also produces an atmosphere in which such methods of argument will tend to be expected.[71]

A good example of this expectation of rational argumentation can be found in Jocasta's speech to Oedipus against putting one's trust in oracles. Like any forensic speaker, she is of course partial: she has no desire to lose a loved one *again* to a husband's irrational fear of oracular predictions. But her demonstration nevertheless depends on abstracted, syllogistic reasoning: the future is by definition unknowable; oracles pretend to be able to predict the future; therefore they are necessarily untrustworthy (*Oedipus Tyrannos* 977–84). To say that Euripides was even more famous than Sophocles for such rationalist inquiries would be a serious understatement; as Aristophanes jokes in the *Frogs,* Euripides' characters walk around muttering, "*Is* life life?"[72] Euripides' "bookish" preference for what can be visibly proven true is also accurately reflected in a line from *Wise Melanippe* (frag. 286 Nauck 1964): "Zeus, whoever Zeus is, for I know him only by report."[73]

To be able to induce visible contradictions and logical deductions on papyrus is one thing, however; communicating one's true deductions in public is another thing entirely. The uttering of Euripides' line about Zeus in the theatre is reported to have caused such an explosion of disapproval from the

---

71. This is not to say that literate Greece did not remain a profoundly superstitious and religious society. People still put their trust in oracles and priests, and remained irrationally terrified of curses, symbolic acts, and religious gestures. But atheists, scientists, and other empirical observers began to appear in increasing numbers, and such "proofs" as the empiricists were developing came to be expected even in other spheres as well. See especially Lloyd 1990, but also Thomas 1992.

72. See Arrowsmith for the Euripidean sources of the joke (1962:97–98 n. 69).

73. See Ostwald for other "atheistic" statements of Euripides (1986:280–81).

audience that Euripides was forced to retract it (Ostwald 1986:281). And so at last we are brought to one of the central issues in our discussion of dramatic logography: What is the relation between the accusation and the public hearing? We have established so far that the former is written, "comes first," and possesses certain qualities, and that the latter is oral, follows it in time, and produces a popular judgment. What are the implications, for speech genres such as drama, of this hybrid use of two separate media, temporally thus configured?

The tragedians Aeschylus and Euripides are shown competing, in the *Frogs,* largely on the basis of what they wrote, for the honor of being judged best civic adviser; but all evidence shows that in the auditorium itself, it is the charming speech of the performers that will tend to carry off the prize. Socrates is reported to have cautioned that charming speech and good advice are two different things, and those blessed by nature with an abundance of the former are not necessarily the same people who have any of the latter to offer (Xenophon *Memorabilia* 3.6). A performer is by definition someone who seeks the spotlight, who desires and often needs recognition for his personal charms. But as Socrates of the *Phaedrus* sensibly warns, if we give our attention to those who *need,* rather than *merit,* our attention, we are putting ourselves into the hands of "not the best people but the most helpless" (233.d.5).[74]

Socrates' warnings about the hazards of trusting good advice to performers deserve our attention. For we have already seen at least one compelling reason why the pragmatics of performance will have a tendency to run counter to the pragmatics of dramatic speech writing, that is, giving good advice to the city: the need for public favor, the need to please and, by pleasing, to win. As Aristophanes warns his potentially "indignant" audience at a performance of the *Acharnians,* "What I say will be shocking but it will be right" (496–509). In other words, the poetic motive to speak about "justice" and what is "right" can be difficult to reconcile with the performative need to please. In fact, it appears that as long as it remains an oral process, the giving of public advice will tend to remain tied to the kind of audience psychology that "blames the messenger."

Herodotus reports that in the summer of 479, a messenger was dispatched to propose a peace settlement to the Athenians on Salamis. Lycides, who stood up before the Assembly and advised that the offer be accepted,

74. This suggests that there is good justification for a division of labor among writers and performers. Nevertheless, the existence of actor-playwrights such as Aeschylus, Shakespeare, and Molière suggests that Socrates may have been mistaken in this after all.

was stoned to death by his indignant audience (*History* 9.5.1–3; cf. Ostwald 1986:25). We begin to see what might have been at stake in Ibsen's revocation of his shockingly feminist ending to *A Doll's House* for the first performance Germany. In fact, the retraction of such "shocking" statements as Euripides wrote for the theatre may therefore be an inevitable consequence of arguing cases orally before a democratic, ideologized public. Athenian jurors normally dropped their stones harmlessly into urns rather than hurling them homicidally at the defendants, and the tomatoes we throw at our public speakers today are unlikely to result in mortal injury, but the pragmatics of audience response is the same in all such live speech situations.

According to Aristotle and Aristophanes in particular, public performance, for all its democratizing strengths, will tend to compromise the integrity of public debate in certain ways. Aristotle lamented this development thus: "And just as in drama the actors now count for more than the poets, so it is in the contests of public life, owing to the defects of our political institutions" (*Rhetoric* 3.1.1403b33). What he meant by the "defects in our political institutions" was fully articulated by Aristophanes in the *Wasps* and the *Knights,* both admirably analyzed by Martin Ostwald (1986:219–26). In the *Wasps,* we see how unfettered popular power in the law courts can produce a situation where the class interests of the jurors take precedence over abstract values of juridical fairness. When civic debate is itself ideologized, every case becomes an opportunity for the common man to bring the rich man down, and make him pay, and this regardless of the particulars of the case (*Wasps* 241). An ideologized text is one thing; a live public with an ideological axe to grind is a force not to be messed with. To such an audience, every defendant becomes an "enemy of the people," a "lover of monarchy," a "conspirator," or a "dictator" (463–500). Even wrangles in the marketplace over onions and salt fish are invested with ideological implications (488–99). Furthermore, the omnipresence of such ideological hostilities created a paradise for demagogues, who fanned the flames and, in Aristophanes' view, made the practice of truly blind, impartial justice an impossibility in Athens.

The resulting situation, at least in Aristophanes' view, is one in which the decision-making process is corrupted by the need to "feed" the audience, to bribe it with tasty treats. Successful public speech is thus presented in the *Knights* as a matter of flattering the audience with appeals to its stomach: here a sausage seller is the ideal orator, for he will know the most delicious recipes. He is advised to make his speeches, literally, palatable (*Knights* 214–16). The use of cookery images in Aristophanes' discussions of successful public speech reminds us, of course, of Brecht's warnings about "culinary theatre." The danger of "catering" to audience "tastes" is similarly warned against by Aristophanes in the *Acharnians* (370–74, 634–40). In the legal and political sphere in Athens, this need to flatter the audience in order to get a favorable judgment was epitomized by the sycophants, orators who grew rich by prosecuting wealthy men before hostile juries (Ostwald 1986:219–26).

Such weaknesses of a theatricalized judicial system are still of concern today. In her study of modern forensic speech and its effect on juries, Bettyruth Walter found that juries tend to have a built-in bias in favor of prosecutors (1988:vii), a proclivity that may be a holdover of the democratic ideal expressed earlier by Euripides—that common written law will bring the great man low. Walter calls the lawyer's final summation speech to the jury the "aria" of the performance (225), and concludes that the most successful lawyers are those who are most aware of their histrionic function (vii). Confirming Socratic and Aristophanic fears about the pragmatics of performance, Walter found further, from hundreds of case studies and interviews, that "much of what [lawyers] do and say during the trial, including summation, is directed towards getting the jurors to like them" (221).

And apparently, both today and in ancient Greece, the straightest route to a popular audience's heart is through its stomach, the organ most susceptible to emotion and ideology. What is most intriguing about Walter's findings is that in legal contexts where lawyers are not competing directly for a popular audience's affections—in appellate court, for example—they are less inclined to demagoguery, more inclined to demonstrate expertise in law. When arguing in appellate court before legal colleagues only, lawyers are equally constrained by audience response; but they are constrained in the direction of high (legal) standards and away from what we might call "low" emotional tactics and direct appeals to the audience's ideological sympathies (224). In ancient Greece, however, there was no appellate court, and all public speakers had to cope with the tastes of popular juries. From what we see in Aristophanes and Aristotle, these tastes have not changed. The pressure to appeal as directly as possible to the emotions is hilariously described by Philokleon in the *Wasps* (565–75). As for the need to cater to the audience's ideological sympathies, Aristotle complained in the fourth century that juries care more "for what is to the people's advantage than for what is just" (*Const. Ath.* 1.13). Walter concludes that even seemingly monologic forensic speech is "in fact a two-way communication" (viii), for argument in the presence of a judging audience will always perforce be a "response" to the audience's needs, wishes, tastes, and prejudices.

Theatrical analogues for these pragmatics of performance are not hard to find. Brecht's "culinary theatre" is of course one of them, as are the many hams, schmaltz mongers, and sycophants of stage history. Like Walter's lawyers, performing artists are probably equally likely to find their performances changed by their audience's perceived level of expertise. A Diana Rigg or a Christopher Plummer might think twice about using, before an audience of respected actors, certain histrionic devices which they would use with impunity before a popular audience of nonspecialists. The same could be said about musical performers: a "pops" concert is not above resorting to the kinds of bells and whistles that are thought "too low" to be offered for the delectation of expert musicologists. Like the high/low dynamic which I discussed in Chapter 2, there appears to be a high/low polarity in the cuisine of performance technique as well: one "caters" to expert taste with rarefied specialist knowledge and textual fidelity, and satisfies the lay audience with emotion and ideology. Speaking of the "low" tactics used on stage to win the favor of the mass festival audience, Aristophanes describes plays that feature "slaves scattering nuts from a little basket among the spectators" (*Wasps* 58). Such culinary tactics, although ridiculed as vulgar, were apparently quite common.[75]

There is evidence to be had, particularly from Denys Page's analysis of ancient actors' interpolations, that the pragmatics of performance will tend to have a number of other, related effects. Performers often appear to have "improved" their texts by making them, on the one hand, more conventional and repetitious and, on the other, more gratuitously spectacular and sensational. Tragic endings were often changed to implausibly happy ones, and the addition of redundant virtuosic ornamentation seems to have been common as well (Page 1987:43). There also seems to have been an urge to suit the presentation to the tastes of the audience, which in some cases may have led to the deletion of certain speeches or episodes that were crucial for the coherence of the plot (38–39).

What is perhaps most fascinating about such interpolations is that they appear to characterize oral speech practices generally. In oral speech as in performance, the pragmatics of action and effect on the listener take precedence over the syntactic coherence of what is said. I discussed this earlier with reference to Plato's equation between the oral speaker and the lover in the *Phaedrus*. In that discussion I suggested that, despite its weaknesses, writing does have the virtue of fostering greater disinterestedness and logical consistency. In Rosalind Thomas's study of Athenian family and state history as perpetuated by written and oral means, respectively (1989), we find

---

75. *Peace* 962; *Wealth* 794–801; and see Sommerstein 1983 4:157.

some interesting corroboration for the Platonic view that speaking in public "means frequently saying good-bye to the truth" (272e).

According to Thomas's findings, an oral version of a given event will tend to take a more "conventional and repetitious form" than will the same material recorded and communicated in writing (214). Furthermore, an oral history quickly becomes ideologically selective as well: historical events (and people) which do not explicitly confirm the basic ideological picture of Athens as a bastion of freedom and justice and a bulwark against enslavement get deleted from the account. Only the written documents retain traces of military defeats, shameful deeds, collusion with tyrants, bribery. The reason for this is clear: a speaker is always dialogically engaged in a concrete communicative context where some kind of real action is taking place. An orator delivering a funeral oration, for example, is not in a position to remind mourners that the battle in which their loved ones lost their lives was a disgraceful defeat, or that victory was gained by morally dubious means. When delivering obsequies, one must perforce be obsequious.

From this we might conclude that the same is likely to go for speakers in other contexts as well: the needs of the listeners and the context will tend to be given precedence over the internal completeness or accuracy of what is said to them. As Roland Barthes has put it, the needs of interlocution tend to "overwhelm" what is said. In speech situations, my body, as speaker, must respond to the needs of your body, as listener. In writing, the listener's body is absent, and so are its needs; in writing, in Barthes's words: "I think less for you, I think more for the 'truth'" (1985:6). Writing at home, Phrynicus must have thought *The Capture of Miletus* a great idea; within the festival context of dramatic performance, it was a disaster. Ditto for Euripides and his skepticism about Zeus, or his praise of money in the *Danae,* which also caused a riot in the theatre.[76] It would appear, then, that written logography and oral performance do seem destined to run at cross-purposes in this respect: truth pursued disinterestedly on the page must somehow be made palatable on the stage.

Not only are speakers likely to have the motive for glossing over certain unpalatable truths in a speech situation, but such is the ephemerality of the spoken word that these omissions and illogicalities will tend not even to be noticed. It is only when one writes down, say, a family genealogy that missing generations and impossible chronologies become obvious and undisguisable. Accordingly, it is only because Page has the text before him, in a written version that can be inspected with the eyes, that he can see that

76. Pickard-Cambridge 1968:274.

something important has dropped out of a plot. Similarly with Aristophanes' jurors and his festival audience: without the aid of some kind of written version of the case being argued, it is hard—if not impossible—to judge the truth of what is being said.

In stage history from antiquity to the present, we can easily find examples of all the types of distortions and falsification which Thomas discerns in oral versions of family and state history: dramatic characters are deleted or merged into composites, incidents are wiped out or get mixed up in performance with other incidents, complexities are simplified, time telescoped. Oral history's tendency to remember defeats as victories has a clear analogue in the stage's proclivity for turning sad endings into happy ones, as so many performers have done with *Romeo and Juliet, Lear,* and other plays. Oral history also has a habit of foregrounding and then remembering only sensational aspects of an event at the expense of its "substance." For example, a political reformer in ancient Greece is remembered not for his role in introducing radical democracy, but for the mysterious circumstances surrounding his death (Thomas 1989:203). Similarly in the modern theatre, a play such as *The Bells* enters stage history not as an alarming symptom of European anti-Semitism, but as a stunning spectacle in which Henry Irving slowly laced up his boots. Just as Thomas has found that the needs of the context of the *epitaphios*—the glorification of Athenian democracy—pragmatically dominated everything said there, so too do the performative choices made throughout theatre history often suggest that the audience's culinary and ideological needs are the altar on which abstract values such as logic, fairness, and truth may be sacrificed.[77]

In the previous chapter we looked at the crucial role played by the student/actor's "gut" reaction in the process of textual interpretation. But as we see from the behavior of Aristophanes' jurors and Athenian audiences alike, such live visceral responses are a mixed blessing: sometimes the one thing an audience cannot "stomach" is the truth. And the same may go for actors. In the final analysis, perhaps the most pertinent question to ask of a theatrical presentation of a written accusation is *not* whether it compromised the truth of the text, but whether it gave the case a fair hearing. And fairness is not

---

77. I do not mean to suggest that sad endings are better than happy ones or that catering to audience taste is necessarily a bad thing. As in other "free market" situations, the need to satisfy public demand creates competition and can produce brilliant and original results. For the other side of the coin—that is, for a more sympathetic account of the role played by performative forces that run counter to the "truths" expressed in texts—see Chapter 2.

easy to achieve through the medium of public speech. Students of linguistics generally claim that writing lags behind speech and tends to conserve outmoded forms. In the realm of public performance, however, where audiences may come to judge a case or a play already convinced about what is right and just and what is not, it is liable to be writing, not speech, that is more open-minded and progressive. Writing is able to imagine new kinds of speech long before they would be applauded in actuality. Not only do the writings of Aspasia and Lysias come to mind, but also those of Maria Stewart in nineteenth-century America. She gave the very first public speech by an American woman, in Boston in 1832. But her oration, about the need for higher education for blacks, particularly black women, met with an audience so hostile that she was forced to give up public speaking within the year (Safire 1992:562). So we cannot but be sympathetic, ultimately, to the actor in Germany who refused to outrage her audience by performing Nora's door-slamming departure at the end of the play. She may simply have known her audience well enough to know that Ibsen's indictment of Nora's marriage would never have received a fair hearing had she left it in. A theatrical audience, like Aristophanes' jurors *Philo*kleon and *Bdely*kleon,[78] often knows what it likes and what it hates—before even hearing the evidence.

The ability of writing to promote types of speech that would be hissed in public is of course witnessed whenever written episodes and sentiments are expurgated in performance for ideological reasons. This same feature of writing can be seen in the many female, "foreign," or otherwise ethnic roles that were written into the theatrical repertory by individual playwrights only to be performed in public for years, sometimes even centuries, by speakers less likely to be pelted with fruit.

As Rosalind Thomas has shown, oral performance tends to perpetuate stereotypes, whereas the greater detail and accuracy of writing tends to expose these stereotypes for what they are. Without the checks to their generalizing, simplifying tendencies provided by such written documents as, say, the written histories of Thucydides, oral accounts can take on "the quality of a timeless catalogue of heroic deeds" (Thomas 1989:232). An example of how dramatic texts may indeed function much like historical documents in recording the more "unsavory" or difficult truths of a given society can be seen if we compare Euripides' *Ion* with oral tradition on the subject of corruption at Delphi. Oral history, as Thomas shows, "forgets" the Alc-

---

78. *Philokleon* means "loving Kleon" and *Bdelykleon* "loathing Kleon."

maeonids' bribery of the oracle and remembers only that they were great enemies of tyranny. The "bookish" Euripides, by contrast, does not hesitate to call the oracle a "Delphian fraud."

Temporarily sheltered from the sting of voting pebbles and rotten vegetables, writers such as Euripides may be slightly freer than speakers of the obligation to cater to ideological stereotype. But they are hardly free of *all* motives, nor lacking in techniques for fulfilling them. Literate decontextualization extends only so far. Even the solitary writer is subject to personal agendas, and if skilled, can devise specious "proofs." As a character in Euripides' *Phoenix* says of this problem of truth and argument: "I've already been chosen to judge many disputes and have heard witnesses competing against each other with opposing accounts of the same event. And like any wise man I work out the truth by looking at a man's nature" (frag. 812 Nauck 1964).[79] In other words, in human conflicts it is sometimes not the written arguments that matter but the disputants' "natures" or intentions. And it is here, of course, that power shifts from the writer to the performer, from the intentionless written accusation to the trial. The arguments are fixed, but performers have considerable leeway when it comes to determining the disputants' natures and intentions. For example, Charles Macklin's decision to perform Shylock as a dignified character altered the nature of this disputant in *Merchant of Venice,* and as a result probably gave the play a fairer hearing in the eighteenth century that it had received formerly. But the controversy that continues to rage around this play, about whether it even deserves to come before the public at all, suggests that performative decisions can go only so far in tipping the scales of justice toward fair trials. Some dramatic accusations may simply be condemned, by history and the accumulation of interpretive readings, to appear irremediably corrupt over time, after which point all the textual tampering in the world is not enough to eliminate a contemporary audience's sense that the playwright has warped the evidence, disadvantaged one of the disputants, or perhaps even charged the wrong man. In such cases, the play in question will tend to fall permanently out of the repertory.

It would not be reasonable to imagine, in other words, that all written accusations, in the law or the theatre, are ideologically innocent or inherently fair or even equally deserving of a public hearing in the first place. But in neither of these two spheres of social life is the text intended to be an end in itself. Rather, legal and dramatic texts are meant to set in motion a dis-

79. See Humphreys 1985:323.

cursive process whose mode is *performance* and whose end is a *decision*.[80]
The reliance of law and theatre on performance *can* have deleterious effects
on the fairness of a given verdict, as we see both on the stage—when great
plays fail, or succeed only through bowdlerization—and in the courts, when
juries acquit or condemn defendants on the basis of ideological prejudice
rather than legal rules and evidence. But the reliance on performance has its
positive function, too, for it is an implicit acknowledgment that the law is
meant to serve the actual people living under it, not the other way around,
and that even good laws may need revision, while some may deserve to be
struck from the books altogether.

A nice example of the positive value of performance, despite the cost, is
provided by Aeschylus. After hearing testimony in the interrogation of
Orestes' crime in the *Eumenides,* Athene adds her ballot in favor of Orestes'
acquittal because, as she says with a feeble attempt at self-justification, she
identifies with men rather than women. This is hardly what one would call a
reasoned decision. Indeed, the biased nature of Athene's verdict is liable to
be so repellent to modern performers and audiences alike that it is hard to
imagine the *Eumenides* receiving a fair hearing today. According to Christian Meier (1990), however, there is actually something much bigger at stake
in this dramatic moment than the sexist ideology conveyed by Athene's acquittal. Understood in its proper historical and dramatic context, this gesture is less a piece of shameless prejudice than it is an affirmation of the
benefits of a public jury system, a celebration of a citizen's authority to make
such judgments, be they ever so capricious.[81] The preliterate system of
hereditary justice had, after all, guaranteed that bloodguilt be perpetuated
ad infinitum; if, in the transition to a properly legal sphere, one man must
go unpunished, then this is a compromise whose humanistic benefits for all
far outweigh the ideological drawbacks in this one case. As Meier describes
it, "what is presented here is, in a nutshell, the 'decisionist' insight" which
constitutes one of the main political advances of Athenian democracy.
Athene's vote, while poorly justified, is accepted as legitimate because it is a

---

80. In my comparison between the decision-making process in court and that which
takes place in a theatre festival audience, some readers may sense a qualitative difference.
They might object that judging the guilt of an accused criminal is fundamentally different
from judging the excellence of a play. As the case of David Mamet's *Oleanna* shows clearly,
however, audience reaction is intimately tied up with judgments about whether the characters are being justly or unjustly accused. Like the ancient dramas, *Oleanna* is structured as
an "indictment" of its characters, and audiences have loved or hated it depending on their
"verdicts" about the validity of the playwright's charges.

81. Compare Aeschylus' suppliants, who praise the jury of Argos for siding with them
as women rather than identifying with their male cousins.

valid contribution to the public decision-making process. She has heard the evidence, and votes on the basis of who she is at that particular moment, and Aeschylus makes no apology for the blatant partiality of her decision. The point of this scene, for Athenian law no less than for the aesthetic court of the theatre, is that the decision is accepted as valid *despite* its partiality, despite the fact that it "may not necessarily rest on compelling arguments" (107). As a decision taken within the living context of the decision makers' present reality, it may not embody "ultimate truth," but it will at least be an accurate reflection of one real moment in the community's ongoing *search* for it.

In short, the pragmatics of oral performance may produce legal and aesthetic decisions that seem arbitrary and poorly reasoned, especially when compared with the values endorsed by the texts that launched these live speech activities in the first place. The written submission remains, however, long after the ballots have been cast, as a standard against which to review the decisions taken within particular oral-performative contexts. A hearing on the stage, as in the courts, is always subject to appeal.[82] The case may be brought before the public again with different interpreters and different jurors, or perhaps when social conditions are more favorable to a fair hearing. Having read their texts in light of successive readings over time, later performers may be able to see aspects of the case that earlier performers missed, and bring new physical evidence. In performance, low culinary techniques may tend to "cook the books" according to ideological stereotype; but so long as these books *also* survive for reading and interpretation, their high intellectual and professional standards will keep such impulses in check—and vice versa. That is, as long as both written and spoken media are allowed to balance each other's weaknesses, there is a good chance that the decisions made in performance will be able to go on exemplifying democracy in action without straying too far from the abstract call of justice.

What could be said of a society with written laws *and* oral-performative jury courts could be said also of social contexts where written theatre thrives. If the decisions made by interpreters and their audiences in and through performance fall short of the standards set by writing, this shortfall represents less a miscarriage of justice than a guarantee of its responsiveness to the individuals who rely on it. For such decisions can inform the future, without binding it, about the experiential truth of one particular moment in the ongoing dialogue between speakers and their texts. And what is more,

82. Jury trials in fifth-century Athens were not actually open to appeal; but ours are today, of course.

the freedom to make such decisions, as Meier suggests, could even be described as a precondition of any genuinely liberal order, political or aesthetic (108).

When Aeschylus represented Athens's eponymous deity on stage in the *Eumenides,* he envisioned her as a democratic-minded but less than perfectly rational juror casting her vote according to her taste. This image is as fitting a tribute to Athens's populist legal system as it is to the theatrical stage on which it was displayed. Under the protection of a written law code and a city court, free democratized debate could be carried on at Athens—both at law and in the theatre.

Like the jury courts, theatre was a literate civic institution which owed its existence largely to written law and the *isegoria* which it made possible. But writing was responsible for expanding the freedom and mobility of human actors in other ways as well. Not only in legal disputes but in economic exchange, private communication, and in other personal spheres of action too, writing was instrumental in the creation of new types of social intercourse, of all of which theatre was an accurate aesthetic reflection. It is to these that we will be turning now.

CHAPTER 4

Economies of Inscription

Bring out the scales then, if my duty is to judge
two master poets like a grocer selling cheese.
Aristophanes

In death the creature got a voice; in life it had
none. Sophocles

THE EPIC PLOT OF THE *ODYSSEY* REVOLVES AROUND THE WANDERINGS OF
a husband and father, Odysseus, who has not been heard from in ten
years, and whose absence from home is becoming a serious problem. According to Homer, there is only one way available for Odysseus' news-
starved family to make contact with him: one of its members must step
physically into a ship, set out across the wine-dark sea, and seek out the absent father in the flesh. With a little exaggeration, it could be said that the
whole of the *Odyssey* ultimately boils down to one simple technological
problem: the epic hero's inability to write home.

For in Homer's time, no technology existed for representing human
speech in the absence of speakers: whoever wished to communicate with
someone, to hear or tell a story or news, had to bring himself physically
within earshot of an actual speaker. Before the spread and development of
alphabetical literacy in the seventh and sixth centuries B.C.E., communication was limited to face-to-face exchanges, and stories about such impoverished communication conditions—such as the *Odyssey,* in which characters
must physically travel to exchange valuable information—are almost
inevitable.

By the time of the playwrights, however, such stories had been technologically surpassed. As Aristotle was later to observe, the characters invented
during the dramatic age do not need to get into ships to communicate with
absent fathers and friends: unlike their epic embodiments, dramatic characters stay put and simply send letters, write last wills and testaments, pin
suicide notes to their chests. For in the hands of literate playwrights, mytho-

logical figures such as Agamemnon, Iphigenia, Heracles, and Phaedra are
writers, and can escape the physical constraints of time and distance by
sending written signs as their embassies to others. This new state of affairs,
in which disembodied signs can be exchanged in lieu of the things themselves, is clearly reflected in the altered plots of myths as treated by the literate poets of the fifth century; but this literate economy of exchange is
reflected also in the institution of the Athenian theatre itself, and helped to
bring it into existence.

In *Of Grammatology*, Jacques Derrida makes the following observation
about the nature of writing:

> Th[e] movement of analytic abstraction in the circulation of arbitrary
> signs is quite parallel to that within which money is constituted.
> Money replaces things by their signs, not only within a society but
> from one culture to another, or from one economic organization to
> another. That is why the alphabet is mercantile. It must be understood
> within the monetary moment of economic rationality. The critical de-
> scription of money is the faithful reflection of the discourse on writ-
> ing. In both cases, an anonymous supplement is substituted for the
> thing. (1976:300)[1]

Derrida's description of the mercantile nature of writing serves usefully to
emphasize that texts, like coins, *circulate,* move freely between people in a
way that people and things themselves cannot. His conception of the relation between money and writing is also surprisingly identical to the ancients' own view of it: like money, writing is an arbitrary currency, and those
who traffic in both are availed of behavioral choices that are denied those
who exchange goods and information by more direct and physically embedded means.

Within the world of the epic, for example, there is neither money nor
writing, and the behavior of Homer's heroes is constrained accordingly. Like
other preliterate milieus, the world of the Homeric epics reflects a "pre-
market society" (Donlan 1981:101). As Aristotle was to say later of "barbarian" economies, exchange in the absence of coinage meant the direct barter
of "useful objects for other useful objects" (*Politics* 1.9.1257a25). Strabo in his
Geography similarly spoke of the Albanians as "not like shopkeepers"; they
too did not use coins, but rather used "straightforward" barter to exchange

1. I have modified Gayatri Spivak's translation very slightly, for she does not use the
word "mercantile," which seems a more accurate choice than the two approximate terms
she puts together in lieu of Derrida's one.

goods (11.4.4).[2] Aristotle's and Strabo's descriptions of such pre-market systems suggest that while perhaps "barbarous" on one level, these systems were also more "natural" on another. Aristotle associates the use of coinage with "the other art of wealth-getting, namely, retail trade" (1257b). A look at the "natural" economy of the Homeric period shows, however, that the emergence of retail trade out of the barter system meant more than just the emergence of "the art of wealth-getting"; it also meant the growth of a traffic in *theatrical* signs.

We see the barter system at work in the epics when the Achaians obtain wine by exchanging bronze, iron, skins, oxen, and slaves (*Iliad* 7.472–75). But as Walter Donlan has shown in his study of such Homeric transactions, goods given and exchanged were valued *symbolically,* not according to strictly economic principles. Like the aboriginal inhabitants of the Queen Charlotte Islands of British Columbia, for whom the possession of coppers and blankets traditionally secured social prestige,[3] the Homeric society prized commodities in a way that was not commensurate with what we would call their "monetary" value. A cup, tripod, or item of clothing or jewelry, as a "treasured" status symbol or "prize," would not have a direct equivalent in common goods such as animals or other natural produce; hundreds or even thousands of oxen would be needed to make up the perceived value of a single item of "treasure" (Donlan 1981:106). In short, material transactions were stratified into two distinct levels of exchange, the "prestige" economy of "treasure" given and received among the warrior elites, and the substantive economy having to do with livelihood, and in which everyone participated: "Functionally, the social-symbolic sphere of the Homeric economy sustains and perpetuates a graded status-system, enabling those at the top to preserve their positions relative to those below" (109).

It was only by virtue of one's membership in the warrior class that one had access to the items with prestige value, and these were circulated within the elite class according to ritualistic and symbolic rules as opposed to economic ones: as gifts or signs of kingly hospitality. For this reason, Donlan describes the Homeric economy as being directly embedded in the "total social structure," where transactions are carried out according to non-economic motives (101–6). We can see this clearly in the agon between Achilleus and Agamemnon: the allocation of treasure goods is described as symbolic of the relative status of the warriors. And as Donlan explains further, the wealth of objects offered to Achilleus in belated recognition of his

2. As translated in Jones 1993:21.
3. Cole and Lockner 1993:52, 128–29.

status (*Il.* 9.160–61) serves as a "demonstration of the ranking figure's ability to exercise political dominance by controlling the movement of prestige goods" (110). With the adoption of coinage throughout the Greek world in the seventh century (Kraay 1976:25–27), however, the symbolic and socially stratified status system of Homeric exchange was replaced by a liberalized, independent economic sphere. As a result, the circulation within one group of prestige goods was displaced by the economic exchange of natural products between different groups, that is, by trade and commerce (Donlan 1981:110).

Written law, as we saw in the previous chapter, had the effect of replacing aristocratic social values with more democratic ones. In the economic sphere, precisely the same democratizing effect was achieved through the advent of coinage. As the tragedians described written law, so Plato and Aristotle described money: it was a great equalizer. Retail trade, as Plato remarks, had positive social benefits beyond the advent of shopkeepers: "For surely one who makes equal and similar the nature of goods of any kind, when it is dissimilar and unequal, does good; and we must agree that this is what the power of money also achieves" (*Laws* 11.918a–b). Money is an "instrument" (*Politics* 289a–b) which in Aristotle's words makes things equal: "Money is in fact a kind of measure which by making things measurable reduces them to equality" (*Nicomachean Ethics* 5.5.1133a–b). In a free market economy as opposed to a prestige one, exchanges must be able to occur among socially unequal individuals and between one social sphere and another. For in truly reciprocal economic relations, Aristotle writes, it is not always "two doctors [for example] that associate for exchange, but a doctor and a farmer, or in general people who are different and unequal; but these must be equated. This is why all things that are exchanged must be somehow comparable. It is for this end that money has been introduced, and it becomes in a sense an intermediate; for it measures all things . . . [and determines] how many shoes are equal to a house or to a given amount of food" (*Nic. Eth.* 1133a17–21). Money—called *nomisma* because it is a man-made custom or law (*nomos*) rather than a naturally occurring phenomenon—thus makes both goods and the individuals who exchange them commensurate and equal. As an abstract medium for fixing value outside of concrete social relations, *nomisma* gives shoemakers the same economic rights to purchase tripods as kings had monopolized in Homer, just as written *nomoi* had equalized their rights and freedoms in the settling of disputes.

The representational "law" of money was also recognized by the ancients as analogous to the representational structure of writing and language generally. Both are merely customary, have no real meaning or value in themselves, and function by convention in the absence of the thing itself.[4] The writer of the dialogue *Eryxias* (Plato?) wrote at length on the arbitrariness of money: "In Ethiopia they use engraved stones which would be useless to a Spartan"; the Carthaginians tie objects up in leather pouches and the Spartans use "iron weight as a currency." But all these systems are as mutually incomprehensible as foreign languages: "Among us the man who had the most of these would be no richer than if he had a number of pebbles from the mountain" (399e–400c). Like language and writing, which make it possible to discuss things and states of affairs in their absence and even in the absence of (one of) the speakers themselves, so money, by representing absent things arbitrarily, expands people's ability to exchange goods without reference to their own identities or status or to the presence or identity of the things exchanged.

We saw in the case of written law that the first step in the establishment of an independent public legal order was the writing down of ancestral *thesmia* by the *thesmothetai,* the hereditary lawgivers. These laws, although written, were still private property in effect; they had not yet been thoroughly abstracted away from the body of the king. In the history of coinage, we find that a similarly proprietary stage was gone through before money became a genuinely public, city phenomenon. The first issues of Greek coins, which Colin Kraay calls *Wappenmünzen,* or "heraldic coins," were connected with particular ruling families or other individuals who appear to have been personally responsible for minting them (1976:56–57). These coins were stamped with changing imagery (beetle, bull's head, horse, seal, lion, cock, goat, owl); and, like the early coinage of medieval Europe, these heraldic coins with their shifting types seem to have been recognized as valid only for short periods of time each (59). A half-stater from Ephesus, dated before 590 B.C.E.—contemporary with the Solonian law code and predating the first recorded contests in tragedy by several decades—has written upon it: "I am the badge of Phanes" (23). Coins of this kind were associated also with the Peisistratids of Athens, appeared in Ionia and Lydia as well, and functioned, in Kraay's words, as "personal devices of successive rulers or tyrants" (21–23, 25). Although he puts it forward only as a hypothesis, Kraay thinks that the change in types may have had some connection with the Panathenaic festivals.

4. Cf. Plato's description of money, where he uses the same terms he uses elsewhere to describe writing (*Republic* 3.416e–417a; also 2.371b); see also Plutarch: "The use of language resembles the exchange of coinage" (*De Pythiae Oraculis* 24.9406b, as translated in Jones 1993:12).

A connection between money and the festival atmosphere within which drama emerged was soon to be palpable, however. By the fifth century, anyway, Aristophanes could speak in the same breath about visitors to the festival and the money they brought with them in the form of tribute: "That is why they will come now from those states bringing you their tribute, eager to see that superb poet who took the risk of talking justice before the Athenians" (*Acharnians* 641–51). Pericles called Athens a "wage-earning city" (Kraay 1976:64); and Isocrates tells how Athens displayed those wages on stage every year at the Great Dionysia as one of the central civic activities of that festival: "They passed a decree to divide the funds derived from the tributes of the allies into talents and to bring it onto the stage, when the theatre was full, at the festival of Dionysus."[5] Theatrical presentations thus shared "top billing" at the festival, shared the stage, with money. What does this tell us about the nature of dramatic performance? The Greeks liked to point out that their theatre festivals had "nothing to do with Dionysus";[6] they clearly had something to do with coins, however. What exactly was the nature of the relationship between money and the theatre?

Sometime after 560, the heraldic coins with shifting pictographic types were replaced by new *fixed* type: the famous Attic owl with a helmeted head of Athena on one side and a standing owl, olive branch in the field, on the other. Most importantly, this coin featured a writing that did not refer to "ownership" by a sponsoring individual such as Phanes. These owls were stamped with an *alpha*, a *theta*, and an *epsilon*: Athens. A coin of this type, clearly marked with the city of its origin rather than the name of an individual patron, is explicitly *international* currency. Unlike the earlier heraldic coins, which have been found by archaeologists only in particular localities (Kraay 1976:58), these "owls from Laurium" (*Birds* 1106–8) circulated widely, ending up in places far away from Athens. Kraay concludes that "all these features suggest a change of function, from a coinage intended for internal needs to one designed for foreign trade" (60).

This new international status of coinage is in keeping with movements elsewhere in Greek social life, during the sixth century, toward greater cosmopolitanism. Many of the first writers of laws for Greek states were also foreigners (Gagarin 1986:60), and nearly *all* of the lyric poets who assembled in Athens around the time of drama's invention were from elsewhere.[7]

---

5. Isocrates *De Pace* 82, as translated by Goldhill 1990:101–4.
6. Flickinger 1973:11; Pickard-Cambridge 1968:131.
7. Pickard-Cambridge 1962:19–58; Herington 1985:61–81.

As I noted in Chapter 2, the poetic heteroglossia that distinguished drama from earlier forms accurately reflected this increased cosmopolitanism. With Athenian coinage now intended for use in foreign markets as well as at home, not only traders but also poets were encouraged to expand their sphere of activities beyond their local markets.

With international currency, economic interactions are extended in two ways at once: spatially and temporally. Plato recognized the first of these when he noted in the *Politics* that with money one can make exchanges indifferently in one's own marketplace at home "or traveling from city to city by land or sea, exchanging money for other things or money for money" (289e–290a). The ability to do so is inherently empowering to the individual: with money as portable as it is, a shoemaker from a land where shoes have no value can travel to a place where shoes are in short supply, trade his shoes for money, and return home to purchase the house that would otherwise have been unattainable.[8] For this reason, Aristotle rightly associated money with the existence of surplus goods (*Politics* 1257a–b) and its workings with the law of supply and demand. But the freedom from *local* conditions of supply and demand that money wins for its users is reinforced by money's abstraction from temporal conditions as well. In Aristotle's words, "money is also a kind of guarantee of *future* exchange," for while money is not always worth the same amount, "its value is more likely to be stable" than that of things themselves (*Nic. Eth.* 1133a–b). This is because a sudden drop in demand can render actual commodities valueless. Unlike money, real objects are subject to decay, damage, and seasonality, physical forces from which a representing medium such as coinage is all but immune.

Just as the Athenian owl represented exchange freed from temporal and spatial constraints, so too did the dramatic text, which came to prominence within the century, signify poetic composition liberated from time and space. With a written text "in his pocket," Aeschylus could restage a play in Sicily which had already been shown at Athens.[9] Aristophanes, too, could give repeat performances of the same play in different years,[10] and revise his texts after their performance,[11] as could Euripides.[12] Unlike the partly improvised recitation of the oral bard, the dramatic text outlives its context,

---

8. For similar reasons, Shakespeare could travel to London, exchange his talents for money, and return to Stratford to purchase the house that would have remained out of reach had he stayed at home.

9. *Life of Aeschylus* 18; see Csapo and Slater 1995:14, and Podlecki 1966:6.

10. Arrowsmith 1962:98 n. 70.

11. Sommerstein 1982–85 5:xix.

12. Segal 1986:78.

guaranteeing that, like a coin, it retains its value for the future—either for a re-trial at home or a remount abroad. Like city currency, the Athenian play both reflected a local origin and saw itself in cosmopolitan terms, was aware of itself, if you will, as an international commodity.

From this point of view, the presence on stage of foreign monies does seem to tell us something about the type of social institution that the theatre originally was. Perhaps the clearest image of theatre's essentially international, mercantile nature can be had by way of contrast with religious ritual. As Euripides shows in the *Bacchai,* Dionysian rites were explicitly *not* intended for "outside" viewers; like all religious and initiatory rituals, such rites were by nature *local* phenomena (Bynum 1981:142–63). While rituals of propitiation, sacrifice, and fertility and rites of passage are practised around the world, the details of their performance are not universal; on the contrary, rituals are a reflection of prevailing local conditions and do not travel well from one locale to another. Stories, by contrast, have a greater universalist appeal, and the mythological material on which drama was largely based had always had a strong "universalizing tendency" (Herington 1985:59). As songs about the ancestors of a variety of politically and geographically distinct peoples, the epics were not tied to a specific locality as rituals generally are.[13] Sacred aboriginal Canadian songs, for example, are performable in particular localities only; their export to outsiders in the form of a written version is explicitly forbidden (Filewod 1992:26).

The festival context within which drama first made its appearance had also at one time possessed local religious functions and attributes. But during the sixth century, the internationalizing power of money was exploited by tyrants who, according to Eric Csapo and William Slater, entered directly into competition with local aristocrats, re-minting their local, family-run religious activities into secular, centralized, *civic* phenomena (1995:103–4). "The city" thus became the focus of these festivals, which, like the Panathenaia, were reorganized as properly civic institutions in the early sixth century.[14] But the city, the unified political entity whose existence was, from the sixth century, celebrated at festivals such as the City Dionysia, was also that civic entity whose existence was demonstrated on every Athenian coin, whose existence was partly constituted in the first place by the advent of city coinage.

Drama was the sole genre of festival poetry to be invented within this

---

13. See Kirk 1970; Brask and Morgan 1992.

14. The reorganization of the Panathenaia is conventionally dated to ca. 566 B.C.E. (Thomas 1989:290).

new international money market. Epic recitation, with a long history as an oral form, was already a "festival phenomenon" by this time, involving the performance of acknowledged "classics" (Pfeiffer 1968:8). And lyric, too, was already being practised in the seventh century. Thespis, however, began competing in the musical competitions around 560–34, in what was then a new prize category of tragedy. Competitions in men's and boys' choruses were added to the festive *agones mousikoi* in 509–8 or 502–1, and comedy was added as a prize category in 486.[15] But whereas, for example, the dithyrambic choruses had entered the competitive lists already loaded with distinctly local, tribal associations—having had a long history as a (probably noncompetitive) tribal form[16]—the tragic chorus was a new type of performing group and was free of all such connotations and connections.[17] Both in its (probable) performance by ephebic hoplites and in its militarist dance formations and marching music,[18] the tragic chorus was a competitive art of the Athenian military state and thus had imperial or interstate associations from the start. The tributes of Athens's military allies thus shared the stage with tragic choruses for substantive cultural reasons. The *xenoi*, the strangers and allies who came to the City Dionysia to bring their tribute and watch the show (*Acharnians* 496–509), were by both actions participating, though as "outsiders," in Athens' cultural and military display—and in a sense *paying* for it. One does not perform one's local religious rituals for "wages" paid by foreigners. Yet at mercantile Athens the poets were paid (*Frogs* 367), as were the actors (Dover 1972:15–16), as was "wage-earning" Athens itself in the form of allied tributes. In religious rituals it is local gods, not cosmopolitan citizens, who get paid.

Reflecting its emergence within this mercantilist atmosphere, drama also appears to have been the first genre of Greek poetry to establish this practice of charging money for admission. Unfortunately, the details of the theoric fund are frustratingly vague; the sources say only that a fund was established by the city to help the poorer citizens attend the dramatic contests. Pericles is credited with, or perhaps accused of, instituting the *theorikon* to curry favor with the public, the poorer members of which apparently suffered when citizens of greater means bought up blocks of seats.[19] Evidently paid in cash to citizens whose names were written on citizenship lists, theoric funds were probably used primarily to buy theatre tickets, which are re-

15. Winkler 1990:49; Pickard-Cambridge 1968:82.
16. Csapo and Slater 1995:106.
17. See esp. Gernet 1981:17; Raschke 1988:79.
18. Winkler 1990:20–58.
19. See Pickard-Cambridge 1968:266–68.

ported to have cost two obols individually, or perhaps one drachma for admission to all plays performed over the three days.[20] The precise details and value of the theoric fund are ultimately much less important, however, than the simple fact of its existence, for it represents the first reference in antiquity to the practice of paying for the privilege of hearing a public poetic performance, and paying in a medium that is blind to the identity of the one who pays. As Demosthenes was later to say of the *theorikon,* "the sum of money . . . is small, but the habit of mind that goes with it is important."[21] It was an important "habit of mind" because it reflected a reconceptualization of poetic performance as a properly *economic* commodity to which, at least in theory, everyone had equal access. Not only is drama the first art to have been associated with money in this way, but it is also the first festival phenomenon that we know of to have put local audiences into a "free market" competition for seats,[22] and to have put both locals and visitors on par as ticket holders, and for all we know, ticket scalpers.[23] The religious prohibition against outsiders, with its ritual distinction between here and elsewhere, must be seriously eroded when everyone, both local and alien, has been transformed by money into an anonymous "paying customer."

As Isocrates wrote of the internationalist character of Greek institutions in the fifth century: "Those are called Greeks rather who share in our culture than those who share in our common race."[24] In other words, in this mercantile age of international currency, Athenian culture, too, had separated itself from locality and blood ties to become an international com-

20. Pickard-Cambridge's hypothesis (1968:267).

21. As cited by Pickard-Cambridge 1968:268.

22. The fact that the city eventually stepped in with its subsidy does not alter, and actually reinforces my point, that is, that monetary market forces were allowed to prevail, if only temporarily.

23. The number of seats set aside for foreigners (and women?) seems to have been relatively small, amounting perhaps to two thousand at the most, or two of thirteen wedges of seats (Pickard-Cambridge 1968:269–70). So foreigners were certainly not "on a par" in respect of numerical equality. Rather, foreigners were "equated" with locals in the same way that, according to Aristotle, coinage equated doctors with farmers: all were enabled through money to buy the same things, regardless of their social status.

24. *Or.* 4, *Panegyricus* 50, as cited by Pfeiffer 1968:50. See Jaeger's discussion of Isocrates' internationalist cultural ideals: "The economic exchange of goods by export and import is only the material expression of this spiritual principle. He makes the Piraeus [the port of Athens] the focus of the whole commercial life of Greece. And, similarly, he makes the Attic festivals the great social centre of the Hellenic world. In the immense throngs of strangers and in the many-sided intellectual intercourse which takes place there, both the wealth and the art of Athens and Greece are displayed and harmonized with one another" (1960 3:78).

modity suitable for "export" and expressly directed beyond its point of origin.

The rise in the use of coinage just prior to the appearance of drama helped determine that the theatrical stage was, and remains, a mercantile space. From Sophocles' Theban kings, to Aristophanes' Athenian jurors, to Dekker's and Lillo's London merchants, to Shakespeare's whole cosmopolitan crew and beyond, dramatic characters are forever talking about obols and drachmas and florins and ducats and dollars, and either visibly giving these objects to one another on stage as in *Twelfth Night,* or comparing their value to the worth of actual physical realities as in *The Merchant of Venice* and *Death of a Salesman.* As a perennial stage image the coin represents above all the mobility of signs that Derrida describes in *Of Grammatology,* and one that is integral to the kinds of stories that the Western theatre has told since its beginnings.

By detaching economic value from its former embeddedness in social relations, the coin allowed even Athenian slaves to get rich. Within a decade or so of Aeschylus' death, Pericles instituted pay for public service (Ostwald 1986:223), and his "commodification" of civic life meant that the poor could also take up powerful decision-making positions. As we are led to believe by Aristophanes, jurors were notoriously poor; they took the job mostly for the obols. In a social context not "alienated" by the use of money, only the privileged leisure class can afford to enter public life, which in Athens was almost synonymous with social prestige.

In an oral context, a citizen's perceived social worth will tend to remain tied to hereditary wealth. Homer's heroes are "valued" in precisely this way: a man is judged noble in terms of who his father is. Social worth is measured in vials of noble blood, so to speak. But by Sophocles' and Euripides' time, poetry shows a different sort of economy, and the worth of dramatic figures is measured in such "anonymous" scales as even a shopkeeper might use (Aristophanes accused Euripides of being the son of a greengrocer, but he was apparently just making a joke at the tragedian's expense).[25] In *Elektra,* family prestige is rejected as a reliable indicator of human nobility (367–90), and even the offspring of barbarian slaves will be judged of higher value than swaggering, asinine aristocrats like Agamemnon (*Ajax* 1225–1400). In drama, characters are "written in our hearts" as worthy (*Ajax* 1399) according to calculations other than hereditary lineage. For this we must give at least partial acknowledgment to the revaluation of worth that the anonymous coin effected.

25. *Acharnians* 475–79; see Csapo and Slater 1995:184.

The increasing reliance on such currency in the century before the rise of drama produced a situation in which not only social worth but also debt could be detached from blood-based realities. As a powerful symbol of this freeing up of value judgments, Solon outlawed the securing of loans on the person, probably in the year 594–93 (Ehrenberg 1975:64). In a pre-market economy, debt could be repaid only with a real thing, which, before Solon, often meant the debtor's own body. Victor Ehrenberg believes that many previously free Athenians became slaves as a result of this pre-Solonian equation between debt and actual bodies (62–67). Money, however, made other options possible: a debt could be represented rather than embodied. Where debts were concerned, this principle of representation amounted to a literal liberation of enslaved bodies; but as we saw earlier in the legal sphere, the ability to represent rather than only embody suits meant a comparable expansion of liberty to bodies, as even the grievances of noncitizens and slaves could be represented in court. And in the aesthetic sphere, of course, this literate abandonment of a demand for a thing-to-thing equivalence made it possible for the gods, kings, and heroic legends of mythology to be merely represented, and represented without apology, by ordinary mortals, regular Athenian citizens, young boys, amateurs.

This liberation of exchange from time/space categories, and from determined social relations, has noneconomic corollaries elsewhere in Greek verbal life. Now, dramatic texts, although certainly among the first books that Greek literacy produced, were probably not the very first, that honor apparently going to the works of the pre-Socratic philosophers.[26] But books of any kind are not likely to have been the most common manifestation of literacy at this time. The Greeks wrote on leather, papyrus, and waxed tablets, but samples of such writing could never have come down to us from the sixth century;[27] our sources for these writings are mainly literary and iconographic.[28] The majority of actual samples of writing contemporary with drama's appearance which have survived are inscriptions, both private and public, on the more durable materials of stone, pottery, marble, lead, household objects, and tombs. Let us turn now from coins to the other types of inscribed objects that made up the Greek information economy.

Solon described his written law code as a "shield." In a society where war is as common an occurrence as it was in Greece, a shield is bound to be a

---

26. Harvey 1966:587; Turner 1951, 1971; Burns 1981.

27. An actual sample of a waxed writing tablet has, however, survived from very early seventh-century northern Etruria, with an alphabet inscribed along the top, presumably as a prototype. Reproduced in Powell 1991:155 fig. 55.

28. See, for example, Herodotus 5.58–59; Burns 1981:374.

loaded image. In Book 18 of the *Iliad,* almost two hundred lines are devoted to the famous description of Achilleus' shield. Made by Hephaistos, this shield depicts scenes from the cosmic, natural, and social realms. Central among these painterly vignettes is a description of the workings of preliterate justice, where the blood feud between two men is arbitrated by the elders of the tribe. In *Seven Against Thebes,* Aeschylus takes up the Homeric image of the shield, but subjects it to a typically dramatic revision. In devoting an entire poetic work to verbal descriptions of the shields of Thebes' assailants, Aeschylus is harking loudly back to Homeric practice, to be sure.[29] But the shields of the Seven are not "epic," not image-laden tapestries or colorful murals of the sights and sounds of life, as Achilleus' was. Rather, they are modeled on Solonian literate practice, for they are shields of *writing.*[30]

The play is fairly static in terms of action, but it is nonetheless tightly wound around a central opposition from which it gains great tension. That opposition is between the written proclamations of the shield bearers who aim to sack the city, and the battle as it unfolds in actuality. No distinction is made here between the aggressors' writing and their speech: the written sayings on their shields are descried as "shouts" or "loud cries" (476–78) and "boasts" (437); the letters "declare" (434), are "threats" (436); the characters on the shields are even granted the power to "babble" (661) and utter "dreadful sayings" (678–79). These written sayings are in essence threats, or rather promises and predictions, about the impending destruction of Thebes. One forecasts, "I'll burn the city" (434); one promises that "Ares himself shall not cast me from the tower" (470); the last depicts Justice, personified as a woman, saying, "I will bring him home and he shall have his city and shall walk in his ancestral house" (647–49). Triumphant destruction is what these writings vaunt.[31] But the battle itself proves them false; the attack is repulsed and the city saved. Because we do not meet the war-

---

29. See Garner 1990:179–83 for other interpretive allusions to Homer in the tragedies.

30. It is worth mentioning here that what Barry Powell has described as the "first literary allusion" of the Western tradition, the poetry inscribed on "Nestor's Cup" (ca. 735–20 B.C.E. and still extant), presents us with another clear image of the changes that were made to Homeric practice under the impact of literacy. For whereas the famous Bronze Age cup of Nestor in the *Iliad* (2.632–37) is decorated with the forms of doves and with golden nails, a cup made in the late eighth century, and meant to refer to Homer's, is conspicuously inscribed with alphabetic writing, complete with punctuation for word, phrase, and line divisions (Powell 1991:163).

31. And, as Derrick de Kerckhove has rightly observed, each boast is an individualized utterance with its own attitude and point of view. By contrast, warriors subjected to epic treatment are typically given nonparticularized formulaic utterances, regardless of their personalities.

riors behind the shields, their writings become a kind of "character" in the play. The contest acted out within the drama becomes one between the promises of inscription and the temporal unfolding of real events.

Shoshana Felman (1983) and George Steiner (1977), following Nietzsche, have written about the paradoxical nature of promises of any kind, written and spoken. How can a physical entity such as a mortal person even make a promise at all? A promise implies a knowledge of the future, which no speaker has; or, let alone *knowledge* about the future, it assumes the mere existence of a future which the promiser may not even live into. That contingent, present-bound creatures such as men and women even dare to make promises at all strikes these two writers as perhaps a "scandal" in itself. But what is merely scandalous about the promises of speaking bodies becomes a kind of ontological emergency in their writing. For what *The Seven* suggests about Polyneices' writing is applicable to *all writing*. To write means to fracture a given act of communication into two or more temporal compartments, each of which is sealed off from the others to some extent. I write in *my* temporal present, a writing that will be read in *your* temporal future. When in that unpredictable future you read what I have written, it will speak to you from the past, since that is where it was written; but it will speak to you in a present which I as writer will not share, and of which I can know nothing. What is noticeably scandalous about oral promises is therefore even more pressingly the scandal of writing, for every writing is directed at the future, yet cannot respond to the changes reality is sure to undergo on the way there.

The inscriptions on the Seven's shields, no less than the inscription of laws on stelae or plays on papyrus, stand as implicit contracts or covenants between temporal contexts. In general, they intend control over the future—"All men shall . . ."; "Thou shalt not . . ."; "He shall have his city . . ."; "Ares shall not . . ."; "I will burn . . ."—and into whatever contexts they enter, they bring the future-controlling echoes of the past in which they were authored.

For an art form such as theatre, this "promissory" structure of writing— what Aristotle called money's "guarantee of future exchange"—has important theoretical implications. It suggests that theorists such as Peter Szondi (1987), who speak of drama as the genre of the "absolute present," are telling only a small slice of the tale. Using Bakhtin's category of the chronotope, we might agree that drama's *internal* representation of time is oriented toward and in favor of the present. Radically departing from epic speech in this respect, which always speaks of events that took place in the distant past, dramatic discourse inhabits the same temporal context as the story it speaks about. What in the epic is presented as legendary material, cut off from any experiential contact with the singer and his audience, is represented in drama as a contemporary event, unfolding in the same temporal context which the actors and audience themselves inhabit. As Bakhtin has persuasively argued, a discursive shift into the present and away from an illustrious but inaccessible past is loaded with political and ideological significance. The implicit message that epic speech sends to its audiences is, in effect: "Everything is already over and done with. Nothing is happening now; yours is just to marvel as a descendant." But by telling of tragic and comic events that are unfolding now, before the audience's very eyes, drama for its part acts as a kind of validation of the present. Contrary to epic speech, it says, in effect: "The great decisions are being made *now*, in your lifetime. This world is *your* world, these figures are your contemporaries, and these problems belong to you, to us." Or as Goethe noted in his 1797 essay on epic and drama (1986:192–94), "The epic poet describes an action as being altogether past and completed"; he speaks as one recollecting things that have happened, and that "belong absolutely to the past." The voice of the epic poet is "the voice of the muses in general." Against the epic word, Goethe contrasts the explicitly anti-transcendent, living contemporaneity of dramatic presentation: "With the stage player on the other hand, the position is exactly reversed. He comes before us as a distinct and determined individual. He wants to interest ourselves in him and his immediate surroundings." Even when the subject of a play is taken from the past, as the ancient dramas often were, it is still presented from the point of view of the still-evolving historical present being jointly lived by the actor and his audience, within the concrete present of the theatrical event. So Szondi is at least partly right to stress the "presentness" of drama in comparison to other modes.

But only partly right, since the structure of the written word has determined that this *internally represented* present, this dramatic chronotope, is already inhabited by the past—the past of the author's inscription. Because written works outlive this past, in performance they rather open up an intercourse between past and present which is infinitely renewable. And because they position themselves for unlimited future readings as well, the "present" of each performance is in fact merely a single juncture of temporalities in a potentially infinite series aimed toward the future. Anything written both comes from the past and positions itself as kind of promise toward the future.

This polytemporality of the dramatic text gives it the structure of a legal utterance, as I noted earlier. But it also reflects a feature of all linguistic communication that is not normally apparent in speech. What is rarely tangible to speakers is that even regular speech situations are inhabited by a complex of temporalities. Every here-and-now, in life as on stage, both is inhabited by the past and projects itself into the future. The thought of writing's "pastness" has been known to offend theatre theorists since at least Artaud, who called for the speedy destruction of texts after their first use. Insofar as Artaud was not talking nonsense, his view has the virtue of reminding us that writing cannot help but offend our purest notions about human communication: that it should remain fully alive and attuned to the present moment, be free of anything ossified, worn-out, stale. Living speech should not, like Polyneices' text, be so fixed and finished that it is unable to respond to changing realities as they unfold in present time. From an Artaudian perspective, the flaw in the assailants' inscriptions is the flaw of all writing: it dies as soon as it is inscribed, and tells lies thereafter.

By the same logic, however, even speech is guilty of importing dead forms into the present. For it is not only written words but all words which are already old when we use them. We are not, as Bakhtin wrote, Adams and Eves uttering the first words of speech. Even if each of us were able to freshly fabricate a brand new language for every new moment of our experience, we would still be the inheritors of thousands of years of meaningful verbal communication and all the established semantic and syntactical habits and patterns that have grown out of it. We are rather scavengers, taking words from wherever we find them—from previous contexts, past experiences, other people's mouths. Any act of speech requires that we breathe our own breath into these *mots trouvés,* that we make them adequate to our needs in a given context, that we make them *live* for us, and for our interlocutors. Like the dramatic actor who must take locutions from a text and new-fashion them into personal, living acts of speech, so too must every speaker off the stage work at bringing old language into the present, and into life. The difference between speaking a line of written text and making a "spontaneous" oral utterance is therefore *in principle* not as great as is sometimes imagined. Every word we use in speech is already a linguistic quotation from elsewhere, and thus even in its natural, spoken form, language possesses some of the scandalously ossified properties that we might more readily associate with writing.

Once having taken up a word for use, even speakers enter into a pact with the future. To speak at all is to promise implicitly that one's words will "hold," that they will remain adequate to one's intentions during the time it takes for them to travel to the other's ear, and on the following day as well.

Language itself has this structure of a promissory note; writing simply makes our verbal contracts with the future explicit.

The issue for the theatre, then, is not how written exchange may or may not sin against some illusory ideal of perfect presence—for not even speech achieves this[32]—but rather what it makes possible, given the inevitable polytemporality of all linguistic experience. As Derrida has argued throughout his work, human consciousness is always inescapably putting its faith in the mental signs, words, and images that extend consciousness beyond itself, into the future, merely as a function of its self-preservation. To write may perhaps simply be to have greater faith in the ability of meaning to survive the vagaries of this temporal slippage. But from the *Seven Against Thebes,* we can glimpse one thing that writing can do that speech cannot.

As we saw in Chapter 3, live speech situations in the present are hampered in ways from which writing is comparatively free. Being in the present means being subject to the needs of the present, the ideological blindnesses of the present, and so on. Because the present cannot, at any given point in history, accommodate all truths, writing, precisely because it is *not* contextually embedded in any given point in present time and space, can go on insisting on those ideas that present contexts have disowned or failed to hear. Like the inscription on Polyneices' shield, writing can uphold the rights of the losers, whose speech is silenced altogether in the decisions of real events. To the Theban hearers of Polyneices' sayings, his words were foolish "babblings"; and the fact that Thebes won the day confirmed them in this view. But were they really babblings just because present reality nullified them? Polyneices did have some rights to the Theban throne, after all. In writing about the justice of his claim rather than just speaking about it, Polyneices makes reality accountable for the partiality, one-sidedness, and occasionally arbitrary nature of its decisions.

An example from Aeschylus' own temporal context is illuminating here. In the 470s, coincident with the appearance of *The Persians,* the institution of the public funeral oration was established at Athens. So intent were the Athenians of the time on dismantling the old aristocracy and establishing in its place a "de-tribalized" democratic polis that legislation was passed prohibiting the singling out of individuals for praise (Nagy 1986:95). Speech at the public funerals of war dead had to confine itself to praise for the polis as a whole. Soldiers and generals alike were to be lauded simply as citizens who had communally, not individually, contributed to the glory and triumph of

32. See Derrida 1973.

Athenian democracy. After centuries of Homeric-style emphasis on ancestors and noble lineages, it became "politically incorrect" to refer to such things. Gregory Nagy has suggested that these legislated restrictions against a certain kind of speech may have led directly to the invention of a new written genre, the poetic epigram (1986:95). If so, this might provide a good illustration of the remedy that decontextualized, "non-present" writing can provide to speakers in literate milieus. Like written law, which traffics in hypothetical futures in order to better protect the liberties of those living under it in the present, the dramatic text stands also like a shield over performance, guaranteeing that what sounds like babblings to an audience today may be given a fairer hearing tomorrow.

Laws, coins, and written promises, like dramatic texts, are thus all covenants between temporal contexts. Like the written contract described by Euripides in the *Palamedes,* they are "medicine against forgetting" (frag. 572 Nauck 1964).[33] In this fragment Euripides praises writing for protecting truth as it travels into the future: "The tablet . . . does not allow lies." We will look shortly at the *Hippolytos,* which shows that things are not quite so simple: writing can preserve lies as well. For the moment, however, let us see what other insights for dramatic texts we can wrest from the structure of an inscription.

The next thing we find, unexpectedly, is that the earliest alphabetical inscriptions found so far in Greece by archaeologists are not public but private and fairly personal in nature. The thousands of clay tablets that have come down to us from the brilliant Mycenaean palace cultures of Knossos and Pylos, written by a handful of official scribes in Linear A and B, are generally palace inventories.[34] No private correspondence, poetry, or laws have been found in this writing. When alphabetical writing begins to appear in the eighth century, however, we find writing first put to rather different ends.

In the earliest alphabetical inscriptions now extant, writing is used to make objects speak. The objects in question are jugs, cups, vases, statues, and tombstones, and the speech is in verse, sometimes with punctuation included. An eighth-century cup, in dactylic hexameters, says: "I am the delicious drinking cup of Nestor. Whoever drinks from this cup, swiftly will the desire of fair-crowned Aphrodite seize him" (Stroud 1989:111–12). A seventh-century marble statue says, in three hexameters, "Nikandra, daughter of Deinodikes the Naxian, a maid beyond compare, sister of Deinomenes, now

33. Translated by Burns 1981:377.
34. Stroud 1989:108; Finley 1968:7–23.

wife of Phraxos, dedicated me to the far-darting goddess who delights in arrows" (112). A final example, analyzed most provocatively by Jesper Svenbro (1990), is most stunning in its relevance to theatrical practice: "I explain [*hupokrinomai*] the same thing to all men, whoever asks me, namely, that Andron son of Antiphanes dedicated me as his tithe."[35] This example is so provocative, of course, because *hupokrinomai,* "I interpret/expound/ answer/speak dialogue/reply," belongs to the word family used by the Greeks to describe their actors as well, who were *hupokritai.* This speaking object, in Svenbro's view, shows how, in sixth-century Greece, "the written word and the actor [were] analogous, interchangeable" (374). Andron's statue describes itself as a *hupokrites* whose textual message says the same thing to all men. And as Svenbro points out, this interchangeability of writing and acting becomes explicit in Plato, who criticizes *both* writing and acting on precisely these grounds—that they both "always signify the same thing" (378; *Phaedrus* 275d; *Ion* 532d). Both inscribed statue and actor are the agents for the transmission of someone else's textual message; both communicate a fixed message to all men indiscriminately. There are a few things about this use of writing that deserve attention.

In the first place, the inscriptions on these "speaking objects" mark what Paul Ricoeur might call the birth of "text," the birth of writing as an autonomous form of verbal communication.[36] Because jugs and statues do not actually speak, the utterances inscribed on them are not *records* of speech. They are not even really representations of it, for there is no conceivable model on which such a representation could be based. Writing here is not so much representational as it is *authorial.* This is someone writing, someone initiating communication through inscription as an alternative to speech rather than as an echo of it. A palace inventory in Linear B, on the contrary, was probably not experienced as autonomously communicating with its readers. Its contents were likely thought of as a mere potential to be actualized by the reader's voice.[37] But the inscriptions on the speaking objects are in the first-person singular; they present themselves as an "I" who

---

35. The verb *hupokrinesthai* in Homer denotes a spoken reply in the form of an interpretation (see Svenbro 1990:373). Svenbro translates it here as "answer" for convenience, but rejects "answer" as an unacceptable English equivalent for *hupokrinomai* in this context. As Svenbro does not himself supply a better alternative, I take the liberty of suggesting "explain."

36. Speaking of fifth-century funerary inscriptions, to which we will be turning momentarily, William Harris makes a similar point: writing of this kind clearly went beyond the function of transcribing a spoken message (1989:83–84); such writing is text rather than recorded speech.

37. See Svenbro 1990 on reading before *silent* reading.

speaks by itself. On the speaking objects, then, writing has the power to speak, or rather to communicate by itself *instead* of speech.

The speaking objects are also significant insofar as they represent the earliest extant use of writing for Greek poetic composition. Because pre-alphabetic Greek script seems not to have been used for poetry, these alphabetical inscriptions mark the detachment of poetry from the human mouth in ancient Greece. In their use of the personal pronoun, they anticipate the lyric practice of poets such as Archilochus, who for his unprecedented emphasis on the "I" in poetry has been described as "the first Western man whom we know as a personality" (Barnstone and McCulloch 1962:2). But there is a peculiarity of the use of the "I" on the speaking objects which brings it closer to dramatic practice than lyric. For the lyric poet generally speaks *for* himself in his poems; he uses the "I" with reference to his own identity, as does the epic singer occasionally.[38] The inscriber of the speaking object, however, uses the "I" without reference to himself or herself. It is the jug or statue to which the "I" refers, not the one writing. What this does, in a sense, is to create a hypothetical identity, the use of which declares: "*If* this cup could speak, this is what it would say." The relationship between inscribed speech and authorship in drama is the same. The "I" in dramatic speech refers not to the author, the one writing, but to hypothesized identities: "If the mythological figures of Homer could speak to us today, this is what they would say." For this reason, the inscribing of speech on these *oggetti parlanti* is already *dramatic* composition in the profoundest sense (Svenbro 1990:366–84).

Both dramatic texts and speaking objects are inscriptions of direct first-person speech which is unmediated, unmotivated, and decontextualized: unmediated because the writer is not "quoting" the speech within his own utterance, as an epic singer or novelist might; unmotivated because the "I" does not refer to the one writing; and unusually decontextualized because it is neither grounded in a concrete speech situation (an epic bard singing to an audience) nor constitutive of a real first-person address (what happens when a lyric "I" speaks/writes to a hearer/reader).

This use of writing, as mentioned earlier, is what Manfred Pfister has

---

38. The epic singer also uses the "I" in passages that quote the represented figures' speech, but he is always, in effect, telling us in his own discourse what "they" said. Such first-person speech in epic storytelling is never detached enough from the singer's own identity, as deictically grounded spokesman for the Muse, to become autonomous first-person speech. The "I" in epic, as I discussed in Chapter 3, is the bard; the "you" is the re-membering Muse, a character, or the listening audience. The speaking figures represented in epic normally remain at a third-person remove of "they."

called the predominant verbal matrix of the dramatic text. For the phenomenology of theatrical performance, writing of this kind has special consequences. As Pfister notes, it makes the story temporally immediate, which in
turn allows for its physical enactment. Following Thornton Wilder, whom
he quotes, Pfister notes that the dramatic story unfolds simultaneously with
its telling (1988:274). The writer interrupts the story neither with his own
"I" nor with any other temporally disjunct material, which means that the
story orients itself naturally to translation into real speech in the here and
now (performance) and does not need the teller/author at all. But there is an
additional consequence.

The direct first-person address inscribed on the speaking object "speaks
for itself." Not completely by itself, of course; it needs a reader. But that is
explicitly what it needs most. The voice of the performing poet, who used
to speak to the listener in his own voice, his own present "I," is not necessary in the presence of a speaking object. According to M. T. Clanchy
(1979), Martin Elsky (1989), and Svenbro (1990), writing did not always appear to speak directly to readers in this way. Medieval manuscripts were assumed to need the voice of a living speaker; the idea of silent reading was
practically unknown (Elsky 1989:115). The same could be said of writing in
Greece before speaking objects (Svenbro 1990:370). But here, as in the dramatic texts that were shortly to follow, the written "I" addresses its recipient
directly, regardless of whether it is performed out loud or read silently. This
is a feature of the dramatic text which is worth lingering on for a moment,
for while fairly self-evident, it argues strongly against Hegelian notions that
drama comes into "contradiction" with itself unless performed. Speaking
objects do not need to be performed to be understood, even though they are
inherently performable. So I agree with Pfister that the unmediated speech
that makes up the dramatic text accounts for its performability; but it *also*
accounts for its mere readability, and no less essentially—a fact of which
Dionysus of the *Frogs* might have reminded us himself, reading from the
Andromeda by himself on a ship, far away from all possible performers.

Recognition of the directness of first-person speech as represented in drama
actually takes us a bit further, toward a realization that the dramatic text addresses itself to any and all readers, to textual interpreters generally. This
would seem to go without saying, but it does not, to judge from a persistent
trend in theory away from the notion that what the dramatic text intends,
as preface to performance, is a *reading* experience. Hegel stands as a precur-
sor to this trend, by way of his proclamation that dramatic texts are not for
reading, period. More recently, J. R. Searle's Austin-inspired analysis of the

dramatic text stipulates that a dramatic text is like a recipe for baking a cake: "It is a set of instructions for how to do something, namely, how to perform the play" (1975:328). David Cole similarly describes the dramatic text as a "blueprint" (1992:215). Because "there are no general readers of blueprints," Cole extends the logic to the dramatic text, concluding that actors are the only intended readers of plays: "Theirs alone is the kind of reading invited and legitimized by dramatic texts" (215). That the dramatic text is neither a recipe nor a blueprint can be seen clearly from the Andron statue, which says the same thing to all readers, without discrimination.

A recipe tells one how to do something. From our previous look at what written speech does and does not contain, it is clear that the act, the "doing" part of speech, is precisely what the text leaves out. A given line of text can be "done," that is, performed, in any number of ways: it can be mumbled, sneered, shouted, sobbed; said quickly while knitting, drawn out slowly throughout the duration of a sword fight; it can be spoken as an aside to oneself, shared confidentially with the audience, laughed in the face of another actor, or "thrown away" into the wings as the set changes and another part of the forest is revealed. In short, the one thing a dramatic text *does not* tell its readers is "how to perform it." So it is clearly not anything like a recipe. A recipe in which action remained so completely undetermined would not be a recipe at all; it would produce a cake one day and a Waldorf salad the next, depending on who was following it. Actors, in any case, are not objects like the eggs, flour, and sugar which are combined according to the instructions of recipes. A text of written speech simply does not give instructions for action; it prescribes only that it be read, and if read by actors who intend to perform it, that it be memorized and spoken out loud by them.[39]

Searle is not primarily a theorist of drama, of course, and his view of a play as a recipe is not likely to be shared by anyone who has ever worked in the theatre. Nevertheless, proper theatre historians often make the same mistake. As Michael Kobialka (1988) has shown, the still-popular view that medieval drama "began" with the *Quem Quaeritis* trope is based precisely on this assumption: that theatre appears when action is prescribed. When put back in context within the *Regularis Concordia,* as Kobialka has done, however, the text of the *Quem Quaeritis* proves to be not a "play" complete with "stage directions," but simply a description of proper monastic practice— indeed, a recipe. For the *Regularis Concordia* is itself, first and foremost, a

39. Writing much more sensibly than Searle about the logical status of performative texts, Thomas stresses that the texts of archaic poetry demanded only that they be read and "learnt by heart as soon as possible" (1992:119). They did not, in other words, prescribe anything specific as far as *performance* is concerned.

rule book specifying how and when the monks should perform the actions of their daily duties: how and when to shave, change clothes, conduct church services. Because some of these concrete actions were properly executed in front of other people (i.e., during religious worship), "authorities" in theatre history call such actions "theatrical" and the texts regulating them "plays." Rather, they were codes of conduct, "recipes," instructions for monastic practice. Like all ritualistic documents, what they prescribe and regulate is, precisely, action, deeds, doings. The first-person direct speech of the dramatic text, on the contrary, does *not* say what to do.[40] For this reason, we can look neither to the *Quem Quaeritis* trope nor to any other set of ritual rules for the beginnings, or even a manifestation, of drama. Not only is there a paucity of instructions for *how* to do things in dramatic texts, but also there is a built-in preference in theatrical activities for doing them differently every time. If Mrs. X delivers a given line while lacing up her corset, Mrs. Y is obliged to give the speech while taking the corset off; and Mrs. Z, if she comes so late, has our sympathies, for she must come up with something altogether new. As Oliver Taplin has observed, ritual performances work in the opposite way: "The whole point about ritual is that it should always be the *same:* it is the aim of its performers to repeat the rigmarole as perfectly, as identically as possible."[41] In theatre, it is not continuity but invention and novelty that guide action: Hamlet on the beach, in the kitchen, in white, in black, with a dagger, with a rapier, in a Nazi uniform, in a skirt.[42]

Cole's blueprint idea is not much better than Searle's recipe. Aris-

40. In recognition of this cardinal rule of the theatrical text, Pavis (1982) goes so far as to claim that stage directions are not really part of the dramatic text at all. His view is that only what is pronounced by the actors on the stage is the dramatic text proper. This extreme position accurately reflects the fact that many dramatic texts have no stage directions, and all can do without them, since they tend to be ignored in practice anyway. I think this takes things too far. The representation of speech in such modern drama as that of Ibsen, Chekhov, and Shaw has focused on very subtle psychological nuances. The "written accusations" of modernity often indict stage figures with inner rather than outer crimes—crimes of thought and motive rather than of deed. With verbal conflict increasingly interiorized, stage directions must carry a larger burden, providing as they do useful aids in a sometimes baffling interpretation process. Statements made by Chekhov's characters, for example, are often so perfectly banal on the surface that extraverbal clues—for instance, that a character speaks while looking out a window at migrating birds—can be a decided help. Even where the author did not himself write them, stage directions are still part of the dramatic text—which is to say that like everything else in the play, they are fair game for the whims of performance.

41. Taplin 1978:161; see also Vickers 1973.

42. That this theatrical impulse toward novelty in performance is not a development of modernity or "postmodernism," but goes back to the ancients themselves, should be clear from my discussion in Chapter 2.

tophanes joked that everyone in the audience has his own *biblion,* which should serve to remind us that it is not by some antitheatrical error of modernity that plays are enjoyed by readers. Indeed, plays are naturally directed even toward *nonspecialist* readers: as the Andron statue remarks, direct written speech says the same thing to *all* men. All men who can read, of course; but they needn't know any arcane codes, as architects must, nor even be performers themselves. This is a key feature, since, as we saw earlier, the first actors were not professionals.[43] Unlike ritualistic and otherwise specialized documents which are meant for or are comprehensible only to the specially trained—blueprints, instructions for surgery, choreographic notation, and so on—dramatic texts are addressed to anyone who can read: military trainees, students, bellows menders. *A Midsummer Night's Dream* points this fact up nicely: even tradesmen with no specialized knowledge of theatrical conventions can respond immediately to the direct speech of their dramatic text just by reading it. And as their bizarre, albeit strangely affecting performance shows, their script does *not* provide instructions for *how* to perform it!

There is another set of speaking objects which sheds some light on this. These are the inscribed tombstones, of which there are numerous samples that predate drama by about a century. These show clearly how, when it comes to written speech, it is not a question of the loss or return of orality, but merely a matter of the fact that writing was chosen from the start *instead* of oral speech. One inscription reads: "Stranger, go back to Sparta and tell our people that we who were slain obeyed the code" (Barnstone and McCulloch 1962:136). This is not the hypothetical speech of a drinking cup but the hypothetical speech of dead people. Like the speech of an inanimate object or fictional character, this written speech cannot be referred back to an "earlier" occurrence of "situational discourse," for this utterance presents itself as the speech of people who are already dead. To communicate information to a living person from beyond the grave is a verbal act that *must* take written form, that can only ever be a written communication.

The advantages of this overtly textual form of verbal communication were as obvious in antiquity as they are today. Writing is especially valuable for recording wills, contracts, and any other vital information that may be in the private possession of one individual and therefore vulnerable to irreplaceable loss in case of death. Euripides celebrated these benefits in the *Palamedes:* "A man dying may write the measure of his possessions and tell his children, and he who receives may know" (frag. 572 Nauck 1964).[44]

---

43. See esp. Winkler 1990 and Slater 1990.
44. Translated by Burns 1981:376–77.

Sophocles explores the phenomenology of the written will in more detail in *The Women of Trachis.*

Deianira opens this play with the observation that "you cannot know a man's life before the man has died," a typically Attic sentiment which proves to have some relevance to writing. The play explores, among other things, the difference between knowledge available before and after Heracles' death, and does so partly through the agency of the writing he left his wife before he set out on his final labors. During more than a year there has been "no word" from him—no spoken word, that is: in his absence, his writing spoke to her instead. The tablet he left is both an oracle and a last will and testament, but it begins to function as a private letter might, communicating directly to one person in the physical absence of the speaker. In the quoted passage from *Palamedes,* Euripides names the letter along with the will as a written remedy for physical absence: "that one not present across the expanse of the sea may know how everything is at home." Deianira says of her absent husband that he sounds, in print, "as though he were no longer living" (161). Because the tablet contains instructions about what should be done with his property after his death, there is no surprise in finding that Heracles sounds "as though he were no longer living."

Deianira's remarks can be taken further, however. To engage in other kinds of writing is also to invoke one's death, structurally, since it is a peculiarity of written communication that it can continue to function and deliver its message in the absence, and even after the death, of the sender. In an oral speech situation there is, if not the illusion of immortality, at least the probability that one will live through the conversation, or expects to do so. Oral speech acts could even be said to be life-giving; at least this is suggested by the many stories performers know of the power of performance to keep illness and death at bay until the curtain falls. In common parlance, "curtains" means death; but until they fall, the actor lives and speaks. It is probably very rare that one of the interlocutors in any type of speech situation dies before the end of the exchange. If they entered the ongoing present of a speech act alive, chances are they both expect to leave it in the same state.

But it is when one thinks of death that writing suggests itself, and vice versa. The possibility that his death might be imminent sent Heracles for his writing instruments, not to his wife's ear. Wills can of course be delivered orally, as King Lear tries to do. But as Shakespeare shows in his play about a will, the oral register is incapable of handling such verbal content without disaster. Instead of signing and sealing his last testament in a decontextualized writing situation, as he might have done, Lear makes his beneficiaries perform for it. And by insisting on delivering his will in a situational present—rather than writing it up for posterity—Lear gives his heirs a cruelly mixed message. He speaks of death, but implies through his use of living speech that he is by no means resigned to its inevitability. Like all of Shakespeare's plays, *King Lear* abounds with scenes featuring the use of writing for communication, and can in fact be read as a sustained exploration of the contrasting characteristics of oral and written modes and the way they interact with one another.

Writing brings a whiff of death not only because much of the writing available to literates was written by people who have since died, but also because, for all a writer ever knows, his or her words may reach their very first reader only posthumously. To write is to defer the presentation of one's words or thoughts to a future date, and the ever-present risk is that one may not live to see it.

This connection between writing and death becomes especially pressing in Euripides, the most "bookish" of tragedians, and one who is rivaled only by Plato for the amount of thought he devotes to the impact of literacy. Three of his plays, *Hippolytos, Iphigenia among the Taurians,* and *Iphigenia in Aulis,* feature letters prominently in the action.[45] As in Sophocles' play about a will, the written messages sent within Euripides' families are all bound up with death in some way. In *The Women of Trachis,* Heracles writes to his wife out of fear that his death may be nigh; Phaedra writes to her husband as a direct result of her decision to commit suicide; Agamemnon writes to lure his daughter to a sacrificial death; and Iphigenia sends a letter to Orestes, written by a dead scribe, to "save [her] from dying" in foreign obscurity. Describing his daughter in death, Agamemnon uses the same phrase Plato would later use to describe a piece of writing: both types of offspring are "cut off and quite separated" from their respective parents (*Iphigenia in Aulis* 669; *Phaedrus* 275d–e).

I have already suggested some of the advantages of this cutting-off: escape from time and space restraints, and freedom from the adverse pragmatics of certain kinds of performances. For Plato, however, the decontextualized or orphaned status of writing is also a weakness. Separated from the explaining, self-justifying presence of its "father," a text can too easily be

45. See especially William Harris (1989) for the archaeological proof for the use of writing for such private communication over long distances. One particularly relevant artifact is the lead letter, found in the Black Sea area, and written at the end of the sixth century from a Greek colony of the period. Much like Iphigenia's letter in Euripides, it was written by someone in present danger of enslavement, and is a letter home for help (56). Harris takes Herodotus' mention of Polycrates' letters (520s B.C.E; 3:40–43) as the first existing evidence for letter writing; see also 57 n. 55).

"ill-treated and unjustly abused." It can be misunderstood, and perhaps even more dangerously, fall into the wrong hands. This is exactly what happens in *Iphigenia in Aulis,* when a letter meant for Clytaemestra is hijacked by Menelaus and read by him—an invasion of privacy which Agamemnon describes as "a thing which goes against all conscience" (304ff.). Like the speaking objects and tombstones, the letter is a message that communicates indiscriminately with everyone. For regardless of the intentions of the writer, whoever reads a letter becomes its receiver.

Speech, by contrast, can choose its hearers; it can also rule certain hearers out. This suggests that even private writings such as letters have something of a public character about them, which is paradoxical given the seemingly more private nature of the activity of writing. In *Iphigenia in Aulis,* a private message between husband and wife becomes news for the whole army. While writing's "promiscuity" with respect to its potential readers greatly alarms Plato, it is given a more balanced hearing by Euripides. The interception of the letter is unquestionably a bad thing for Agamemnon and family, but it is a clear boon for the stalled expedition. The inability of writing to control the circumstances of its reception can thus be viewed as either a detriment or a strength, depending on one's politics. To those, like Plato, who value the author's own intention above all, the fatherlessness of writing must weaken and even damn it to some extent; but to those who value the rights of the many potential receivers over and above the authorizing privilege of the sender, writing's orphaned state will be seen rather as one of its greatest strengths. (Given the communal nature of theatrical production, it can be assumed that the performers of plays will most often subscribe to the latter view.)

In *Iphigenia in Aulis,* Agamemnon's first letter has the power to transport his daughter to the sacrificial altar;[46] his second letter proves powerless to avert her transport to death. This theme of death and transportation is a common one in Euripides, appearing also in the *Ion, Helen,* and *Iphigenia among the Taurians* (Lattimore 1964:344). In the two Iphigenia plays, the theme is connected with the potentialities of writing. Because of its ability to transcend her physical conditions in Taurus and communicate with receivers in another time and place, Iphigenia's letter has the power to "save [her] from dying." In an oral context, such immorality can also be attained through the song of the epic bard and the muse of memory. But to achieve acoustic renown (*kleos*), and the immortality that it confers, in the absence

---

46. See Powell's discussion of the "fatal letter" theme (1991:199); see also Thomas for other evidence for the general Greek "distrust of writing" (1992:130).

of writing, one's deeds must already be known, must already have had their public impact. In *Iphigenia among the Taureans,* the writer is living in foreign obscurity, beyond the reach of *kleos,* and is believed dead. To read Iphigenia's letter will be, in her words, to "listen through my opening grave / And hear my living lips cry out" (641–42). Iphigenia's situation thus reminds us of the exiled, expatriate, or otherwise silenced writer—examples of which were as plentiful in antiquity as they are today.[47] Through her letter, as through texts generally, a message may still reach the ears of the community, if only posthumously. Iphigenia also evokes the situation of *receivers* of such written messages: like the many actors who were to speak Euripides' words after his death, she is aware that "[her] words were written down by one who died" (584).

And so the paradoxical nature of texts: at once more private *and* more public than speech, on one hand they imply the death of their authors, and on the other extend their lives almost indefinitely. In *Iphigenia among the Taureans,* writing proves doubly paradoxical in its effects. As long as they confined themselves to oral speech, brother and sister failed to recognize each other. Both believed the other to be dead, and this foreknowledge—or deception, as it turned out—determined that each perceived the other as a stranger. It is only when Iphigenia reads her letter out, verbatim (785), that the truth of their identities is revealed. Their co-presence in a phenomenally real context deceives them and blinds them to a truth only revealed in writing. That writing has the power to manifest a truth which a situational presence obscures is an idea that goes very much against the grain of one of the central myths of modern performance theory. But what this scene demonstrates is that phenomenal perception is never "naive," and the senses are not a tabula rasa on which the pure essences of things imprint themselves. According to Heidegger perception is, "in itself, something which already . . . interprets" (1962:189–90). Merely seeing an object is a presentation to oneself of "something *as* something" (207). Iphigenia presents Orestes to herself "as" a Greek stranger and sacrificial victim; Orestes presents the phenomenal being before his eyes to himself "as" Thoas' priestess. This scene must present audiences with a graphic account of the ineluctable interpenetration of "real" perceptions with the representing "foreknowledge" that structures and interprets them. As in the countless dramas in the repertoire which similarly traffic in stories of disguise, deception, last-minute reversals, and revelations, *Iphigenia among the Taurians* shows how internal cognitive processes can shape even our real perception of phenomenally present realities.

47. See note 45.

But once the writing in Iphigenia's letter has remapped the "as-structure" of her and Orestes' perceptions, the representation is rejected as a poor substitute for the reality it has revealed. The "dead" letters, written by a dead man on behalf of a woman believed dead, have paradoxically succeeded in revealing the living to the living. Speech unaided by writing could not have done this, for perception is ruled by the perceivers' assumptions about what they see and hear. But once a perceptual revolution is accomplished by the letter, the ecstasy of sensual contact follows:

> How can I look at letters! Let me look—
> Oh let me stare at you . . .
> Oh let me touch you with my hands and prove
> That you are real and hold you close, close! (793–96)

Writing can reveal new realities for perception, but the goal of such revelations remains bodily engagement. Writing, in this recognition scene, is shown to be an enabling device, not an end in itself. This goal—of real sensuous contact—is, however, shown to depend on a rerouting of the semiotic circuit within the bodies of the perceivers. This perceptual restructuring, at least as Euripides has it, could only be achieved by bypassing reality and intervening directly in the representational structures themselves (i.e., through abstract text). To use a Nietzschean image, we might say on the basis of Euripidean dramaturgy that the physical co-presence of man to man may not itself be sufficient to break down the dikes that separate them if each perceives the other "as" the enemy. Iphigenia and Orestes would not have embraced but for the ability of writing to remake their world in another image.

Like the coin, the letter is an object of exchange which had transformed human behavior in Greece just prior to the appearance of drama, and which continues to define the concerns of the genre. When Menelaus demands his purloined letter back in *Iphigenia in Aulis* ("give me the letter"), he may be the first speaker to be represented in verbal art as making such a request, but he is by no means the last (cf. *Lear* 1.2.41, for example). In fact, the number of extended incidents involving letters in the Shakespearean corpus alone rises to nearly forty. The very persistence of the image in Western theatre from its beginnings suggests that it is an essentially theatrical image, not just a convention of this or that particular stage.

In some cases, the "fatherlessness" of written messages is exploited by its users for the purpose of deception (Agamemnon's first letter, and those of Phaedra in *Hippolytos*, Edmund in *Lear,* and Maria and company in *Twelfth Night*). However, letters are used in equal numbers to communicate a truth whose utterance a hostile speech context prevents: Agamemnon's second letter, Iphigenia's, and those of Friar Lawrence and Romeo, of Malvolio, and nearly all of Shakespeare's comedic lovers, particularly Beatrice and Benedick, who are forced by the written evidence of their own hands to acknowledge a truth they would deny in speech. Not only are letters used for deception as often as for the revelation of truth, but speech is shown throughout the repertoire to be as effective in spreading falsehood as writing is. There are many Greek characters who, like Clytaemestra, Phaedra's maid, Hippolytos, Orestes, and Odysseus, pledge with their mouths while keeping their hearts unpledged; just as, on Shakespeare's stage, speakers may smile and speak fair while remaining villains. Speech, too, can obscure. If the persistence of images of letters on the stage tells us anything, it is that speech and writing are equally at home there. In literate contexts, speech and writing are, equally, modes through which individuals represent the world to one another; and as Iphigenia says of writing and speech in *Iphigenia among the Taurians*, "In any plan, two ways improve upon one" (759).

There is a final use of inscription at Athens that has bearing on theatrical practice. This is the writing or scratching of an individual's name on a piece of broken pottery, known as an ostrakon. The institution of the ostracism is believed to have been established by Cleisthenes, sometime between the end of the sixth and the beginning of the fifth centuries—that is, a decade or more before Aeschylus' first recorded win at the festival. The purpose of the ostracism—which was held yearly if the citizens voted in favor of holding one—was to rid the city for ten years of the one man whom most citizens wanted to be rid of. Scholars today describe the ostracism as a politically expedient, inverse substitute for voting, since Athenians did not elect many of their civic officials but drew names randomly by lot.[48] Over five thousand ostraka have been dug up by archaeologists—a drop in the bucket, since at least six thousand ostraka had to be submitted each year for the ostracism to go ahead.

The ostrakon functions like a secret ballot. The individual whose name is written most often by the voters wins—not a prize, as in the case of the *agones* of the theatre festival, but exile for ten years. The literate practice of voting by inscribing a name on some surface or other was a common one at this time in Greece: priestesses at the oracles recommended courses of action by scratching names on beans (Parke 1967:87), and theatrical judges wrote the contestants' names as a way of selecting the winner.[49]

48. Ostwald 1986:27, 118, 177; Vanderpool 1970.
49. See Csapo and Slater 1996:160, and Dover 1972:16.

To write a name on an ostrakon was to express one's opinion in public without having to answer for it personally, a practice that would have mixed consequences. On the one hand, it would protect genuine, honest desires that might otherwise shrivel into passivity (I might be afraid to ostracize Themistocles or vote for Euripides if I had to do it face-to-face). On the other hand, it could encourage an abdication of responsibility and poorly thought-out decisions. As Plato might ask of such anonymous written practices, from whence comes the writer's authority to vote for Themistocles? Can he defend his scrawl, or is what he wrote the extent of his knowledge? In protecting the writer's anonymity, the ballot may be protecting his ignorance; but it may by the same token be protecting the freedom of his speech. Aristophanes apparently submitted his first plays without revealing his identity (Dover 1972:15), and the option that he exercised in so doing, of making a public contribution anonymously, existed thanks to writing.

Not only did the selection of the winner in the theatrical contests depend on this literate practice, but also playwriting itself was a kind of aesthetic reflection of the institution of the ostracism.[50] In both cases a public event is going to take place; it is already scheduled. The ostracism has been voted upon and is imminent; similarly, the theatre festival is an annual occurrence whose date is set and known in advance. Both civic institutions represent for the individual citizen an *opportunity*, an opportunity to contribute something in writing. For both types of citizens, playwrights and ostracizers alike, writing is a mode of public participation. Although both types of written contribution concern, are in a sense addressed to, the citizen body at large, the immediate context of inscription is largely private, not public. One could always fill out ostraka in groups, of course,[51] and Sophocles, at least, is said to have taken the "natures" of his actors into consideration in writing for them.[52] Nevertheless, there are limits on the extent to which writing can ever be a social act. It takes only one hand to hold a writing instrument, whereas two people at least must be present for a conversation to take place.

The similarity between these two literacy events is evident also after writing's entry into the public sphere. For in both cases the bids for public

---

50. Humphreys thinks that the establishment of the ostracism coincided with the addition of comedy to the theatre festival, and that both institutions provided citizens with "an opportunity for the expression of public suspicions without formal trial or the possibility of defence" (1978:229).

51. See Vanderpool 1970:11–16.

52. See also Aristotle, who says that dramatists may write to please the actors (*Poetics* 1451b11f.) and/or the spectators (1453a12f.).

participation may amount to nothing, or to something other than was hoped for by the writer. One's inscription of the name of Pericles on an ostrakon may prove to be an isolated gesture, and Themistocles may be banished after all. Or one's inscription of a play about Heracles may be rejected by the archon and one about Oedipus performed instead. After his death, the name of Aeschylus on a submission was enough to guarantee that a chorus would be granted and the play produced. But otherwise, the plays submitted for performance might not reach the public at all (Dover 1972:15).

Now, the performance of a fictional play about a mythic personage such as Heracles may appear only superficially related to the banishment of a living contemporary citizen such as Pericles. But the two activities are in fact related. Tragedy, as we remember, was believed by the ancients to have been invented when a poet named Arion began to write choral compositions based on a *named subject*.[53] The act of *naming* is, of course, the essence of the ostrakon, as it is of the ballot generally. In filling out an ostrakon or ballot, the citizen must survey the whole social scene of competing interests and individuals; he must consider multiple scenarios and zero in on that single name which represents to him all that is rotten about the life of the city at that moment. Similarly, in writing their plays, the first Greek playwrights surveyed the great mass of mythological material and zeroed in on that single character whose story they felt was most germane to the current social scene. From the political relevance and topicality of subjects in tragedy and comedy alike, it is clear that the playwright's choice of a name was, in essence, his answer to a very specific question: Given the current state of Athenian life, a public hearing of whose case would be most pressing and apt at this year's festival?

For example, Aeschylus wrote about the bloodguilt of Agamemnon, Clytaemestra, and Orestes in the immediate aftermath of the Ephialtic reforms, which deprived the Areopagus of "all those accretions by virtue of which it exercised guardianship over the state" (*Constitution of Athens* 25.2; Ostwald 1986:203). The pacification of the Eumenides, about which Aeschylus could write in naming Orestes, had its direct civic correlative in the denuding of the Areopagus of all but one of its hereditary rights as law court, and in the empowerment of the popular city jury in its place. Plutarch has preserved a story which suggests that the topicality of Aeschylus' choice of names in the *Oresteia* was typical of his playwriting practice in general: "And so it befell, as the story goes, that when the verses composed

53. According to Solon in his *Elegies*, the Suda and John the Deacon's commentary on Hermogenes; see Csapo and Slater 1995:100–101; Flickinger 1973:8–9.

by Aeschylus upon Amphiaraus were recited in the theatre [he cites lines 952–54 of the *Seven Against Thebes* here] all the spectators turned their eyes on Aristides" (*Life of Aristides* 3.4–5).[54] At a time when Aristides was up for trial on bribery charges, Aeschylus' portrayal of the mythological Amphiaraus turned the spectators' thoughts to a contemporary citizen similarly fallen in with bad company (Podlecki 1966:39). Here, a mythological name is but a front for the name of a contemporary citizen. Scholars believe that Sophocles' Neoptolemos was meant to evoke thoughts of the young Pericles (Ostwald 1986:413 n. 4), and Anthony Podlecki provides evidence for the topicality of other character names in Aeschylus' tragedies as well.

The topicality of dramatic names is much more readily apparent in early comedy, of course. In his plays, Aristophanes names Kleon, Laches, Euripides, and Socrates directly; Eupolis named Alcibiades in the *Dippers,* and apparently got "dipped" in the sea by Alcibiades in return for this theatrical dipping.[55] Eventually, perhaps in the aftermath of Aristophanes' prosecution by Kleon, a law was passed against naming citizens directly in the plays inspired by them, and comic poets thereafter had to ridicule individuals "figuratively," through symbolism.[56] But before the advent of these slander laws, citizens were as vulnerable to being named by the dramatists of Athens as they were to being singled out by the inscribers of ostraka.

A closer look at the ostraka themselves shows additional similarities with playwriting. On many ostraka, it is true, there is nothing but a name, a fact which might seem to suggest that the comparison cannot be taken too far. Writing a play, which involves plot, characterization, and poetic and musical invention, is obviously a far more involved and exacting undertaking than the writing of a bare name. But some of the ostraka that have survived actually resemble artistic character sketches in miniature. In making their written contributions to the life of the city, some citizens expressed themselves by drawing caricatures of their named choices; some added insults and curses, and one, who submitted an ostrakon against Pericles' father in 484 B.C.E., wrote his accusation in the form of a little poem (Vanderpool 1970:15, 9). When we bear this in mind, the writing of plays and the writing of ostraka begin to seem surprisingly similar.

The *Iliad* and the *Odyssey,* which largely made up that Homeric "banquet" from which the tragedians selected their names,[57] were by nature *com-*

54. Translated by Podlecki 1966:37.
55. Scholion to Aelius Aristides *Orations,* 3.8, as translated by Csapo and Slater 1995:178.
56. Iohannes Tzetzes *Prooemium* 1.87–97, as translated by Csapo and Slater 1995:179.
57. Athenaeus *Deipnosophists* 8.347e.

posites of stories, catalogues of sailors' or warriors' tales which were built up through inclusion, accumulation. Dramatic plots, however, both comic and tragic, tend to move in the opposite direction, by exclusion. In writing a play about Socrates, for example, Aristophanes was in effect singling out the individual he thought was most blameworthy in Athenian political life at the time of the festival. Not all plays are about individuals, of course; some are about groups such as the women of Troy or the children of Heracles. But even a play about the daughters of Danaus has singled them out from a larger mythological scene. And as Geoffrey Bakewell (1997a) has demonstrated so convincingly, Aeschylus named the Danaids in response to current political events. In writing a play about the Danaids, Aeschylus had chosen the names that would enable him to address such topical issues as the status of metics at Athens and the logistics of housing them. Kratinos named Pericles in a comedy for similar reasons: this "squill-headed Zeus," this builder of the Odeion may have escaped ostracism, but he could still be named and criticized for his Olympian pretensions by a playwright in the theatre (Kratinos frag. 71 cited by Humphreys 1978:229).

In performing this kind of selective naming operation upon the narrative material available to them, the dramatists, as participating citizens, apparently chose their names for the festival each year in response to the same kinds of civic concerns that would have moved other citizens to fill out ostraka. Like the regular citizen who wrote a poem about Xanthippos, son of Arriphron, for submission to the ostracism, playwrights chose a name by way of making a written contribution to an upcoming civic event. And so we should not be surprised to find that while ancient papyri manuscripts lack many of the extraverbal markers we associate with writing, they do include character names.[58] A written composition about Iphigenia or Prometheus may not have included punctuation, word separations, or paragraph breaks, but it would *name names*.[59] The ability to write a name, and a colloquial or poetic comment, was apparently one literate skill that even the most backward hayseed was liable to have possessed at the beginning of the fifth century (Vanderpool 1970:9): and it was a skill on which the ostracism, no less than the theatre festival, depended.

This ability to write a single name, but also a list of names, is a literary practice on which the theatre depends for a number of reasons. Athenians often wrote lists of names: archon lists, victors lists, casualty lists, lists of cit-

---

58. This is a complex issue. The papyrus manuscripts are late copies, and often character names were abbreviated. But the fact that some character names were written is sufficient for our purposes here. See Dover 1972:10.

59. See Page 1962:74, 106, 169, and passim.

izens, of jurors, of assemblymen. Now, as I noted earlier, the recital of ancestry lists is a common feature of oral culture, amounting to a distinct poetic genre in some oral milieus.[60] But as Jack Goody (1987) observes with respect to emergent African literacy in the twentieth century, to write a list whose items one can *see* is a very different thing from an oral recitation of an acoustic series. The purpose of an oral list is to *remember* the series. Poetic meter and formulas are used to help the items stay glued in sequence, and the sequence must go on; to stop in the middle is to risk losing one's place. For this reason, the only types of relationships between terms that can emerge are those of sound and sequence. To alter the chronological sequence is tantamount to defeating the purpose of the list.

When the terms in a list are visibly co-present in space, however, they can admit of operations upon them which are neither acoustic nor chronological but abstract and conceptual. As Goody's case study among the Vai shows, people who have learned to make written lists soon begin to manipulate their contents along logical, categorical lines. To cite just some of Goody's examples, to write a list of fruit names is to begin to see the boundaries of abstract categories: Is tomato a fruit? Where do fruits end and vegetables begin? To write a list of supplies is to begin to wonder whether chicken belongs in the meat category: On what basis does one decide whether two items are of the same type? Similarly, a list of expenditures begins to suggest and allow a division into *types* of purchases, rather than just a temporal segmentation into *when* they were made. Goody found as well that a chronological ordering principle for names tended to be abandoned in favor of more useful organizing principles such as age, sex, initial syllable, and so on (213ff.).

In ancient Greece, as it happens, the use of the written list in the sixth century B.C.E. did have revolutionary results of precisely this kind. The citizen body was reconceptualized on paper. Whereas blood and ancient cult ties had traditionally been used as the organizing principle for individuals' names, these customary and naturally occurring categories were replaced by abstract conceptual ones. Ten new tribes (*phylai*) were artificially created, and individual citizens' names were inscribed under the new tribal list headings not according to ancestry (i.e., not according to a hereditary chronology), but according to domicile. By pushing names around on paper, Cleisthenes created new conceptual units, and new relationships between items were revealed. Whereas, for example, "Boutad" had formerly referred only to descendants of the noble Boutes, it became the name "of any per-

---

60. Halpern 1990:301–21.

son, however humble, who resided in the deme of that name" (Ostwald 1986:20). Accordingly, citizens' names begin to appear on ostraka without their patronymic, and modified by their demotics instead (Vanderpool 1970:6–8).

Not only were individuals reconceptualized and categorized according to deme rather than Dad, but the tribes, which had once been similarly organized according to blood ties, were reconceptualized as well, transformed into what Eric Csapo and William Slater have called "purely administrative units" (1995:107). Whereas tribes had formerly been dominated by a few powerful families with ancient religious affiliations, the tribe was reconstituted in writing according to an abstract principle, in this case the idea of "fair representation." Henceforward, each tribe consisted of inhabitants of spatially disjunct demes, which meant that for the first time, tribe affiliation was an abstraction without "natural," blood-based associations (Ostwald 1986:21). Whereas individuals used to belong to the collectivity—or be excluded from it—on the basis of their membership in hereditary brotherhoods, they were now free-floating items in a written list which could be moved around at will.

The consequences of these paper-based reconceptualizations for Athenian politics were huge, as David Stockton (1990), Martin Ostwald (1986), and Christian Meier (1990) have shown. By creating categories that existed only on paper, Cleisthenes broke up local connections based on religious cults, and for the first time established *citizenship* as the sole organizing principle for items in the community lists (Meir 1990:61, 60). Even the names assigned to the new tribes were arbitrary and detached from traditional connections. A list of one hundred hero names was submitted to the Delphic oracle, and a selection of winning names was made by the priestess in writing (60).

In a corresponding fashion, a poet to whom a list of mythological names is available is capable of performing different operations with and upon them than is a poet confined to the world of sound. In an oral context it is undoubtedly possible to "think" Odysseus separately from the stories told about him. But it is only through the agency of literate practices such as the list that a name like Odysseus will become an object for abstract, decontextualized contemplation (*theasthai*). To write a list of the Homeric hero names is to shake them loose from epic embeddedness in traditional songs—loose, that is, from the singers' traditional treatment of them. It is to be able to contemplate them with less semantic predetermination. Detached from their inherited oral-acoustic chains, character names were allowed to enter into new cognitive configurations. Anything put in a written list is given a new lease on life, as it were. Just as Cleisthenes was able to reconceptualize citizens on the basis of where they lived rather than, as formerly, on the basis of who their ancestors were, so too were the literate poets of the dramatic age able to rethink narrative figures along lines other than those established by traditional stories alone. In making use of epic tradition, as Aristotle advises, the dramatist "must show invention" (*Poetics* 1453b11). Before new interpretations of Odysseus can be imagined, however, his name must be abstracted away from the customary view of him as a many-wiled and always resourceful husband and fighter. Accordingly, in drama he has become a slippery smooth talker, a shameless manipulator, a politician.

The phenomenology of the dramatic text is most illuminating here. What we see when we look at a play today is unique in the verbal arts. At the beginning is often a name: Elektra, King Lear, Minna von Barnhelm, Uncle Vanya, Candida, Amadeus. Works from the other genres are often titled by names as well, of course. But in the dramatic text, the name or title is followed by another written element which is not technically speaking part of the story being told: a list of other names. Now, there is no way of knowing whether the ancient playwrights headed their plays with lists of characters as playwrights do today. Regardless, though, of *when* the practice of writing out a list of character names attached itself to playwriting, it became and remains one of the key distinguishing features of the dramatic text.

The significance of this phenomenological feature of the dramatic text for theatrical performance is enormous. The writing of character names *outside* the storytelling discourse signifies nothing less than the liberation of the mythological figures from their containment within the Muse's monologue. In epic storytelling there is only one speaker. The *aoidos* or rhapsode alone has the power of speech in performing the story, even though there is no limit to the number of characters who can be *spoken for.* This feature of epic speech—that all speech represented in the story is subsumed under and within the single voice of the speaker and the Muse of memory who inspires him—is fundamental to the genre. It is also a defining characteristic of (nonchoral) lyric and novelistic speech as well. When Thetis or Hephaestos, Penelope or Odysseus, Leopold or Molly or any other novelistic character speaks, his or her speech remains an utterance of a single controlling linguistic consciousness, that of the author, *aoidos,* or rhapsode. In drama, by contrast, the names of speakers signify the existence of x-number of autonomous speech positions, actual speakers (actors). The writing of character names in the dramatic text, whether in the list at the beginning or before each bit of speech, is therefore symbolic of narrative exotopy: these written elements remain perpetually outside of the story, just as the actors who stand in for these names remain outside the speech act of the storyteller (the playwright).[61]

The decontextualized list of character names thus stands at the entrance of the dramatic text like an engraved Delphic motto on the architrave above the gates: Speak for Thyself. Before the dramatist can delegate this power of speech to "outside" individuals as the genre demands, however, he must first determine who these individuals are. For nothing happens in drama until the speakers or their names are chosen (see the very start of rehearsals for the play-within-a-play in *Midsummer Night's Dream:* "Here is the scroll of every man's name" 1.2.4). Unlike epic and novelistic storytelling, which can get under way simply on the basis of an impulse to tell a story—"Once upon a time . . ."—the dramatic text *has no story* outside of the speech of its separate characters. Regardless of what stories it is based on or inspired by—and a very large percentage of dramas are based on preexistent stories—the text itself, phenomenologically speaking, consists almost exclusively of names and speech.[62] With the exception of the occasional stage direction,[63] the dramatic text contains the names of characters and what they say. Speaker and spoken, sayer and said: these are the materials out of which the dramatist makes his story.

This use of the speech of named figures to tell a story requires that the single beam of narrative discourse that was the bard's or novelist's be sent through a kind of prism, a prism that fractures it into the separate speech positions which are the separate characters and, ultimately, the actors who will perform them. The list of the dramatis personae is the basic expression of this fracturing, a kind of spectrogram or image of it. Or rather, the list of names may function in the first place as a spectrograph, an instrument for obtaining the kind of atomized image of speech that drama makes out of narrative material.

The visual orientation of this analogy of the spectrograph is apt, since ancient audiences of the first dramas appear to have been struck most by drama's making visible what was formerly only described by the voice of the

61. This point is an important one for theory, since it shows that the dramatic text is composed of non-spoken elements which are still integral to performance. See Pavis 1982, who says that the dramatic text must be defined as including only those elements that are actually pronounced by the actors.

62. See Pfister 1988:163ff. on the "limitation" of dramatic storytelling, that is, that figures appear only insofar as they speak, or fail to speak.

63. K. J. Dover thinks that some stage directions in ancient tragedy and comedy "go back to the author's own day" (1972:10).

rhapsode.[64] To liberate mythological characters from their containment in the Muse's song, and to allow them to step forward into the light of embodied day, amounts to a translation into visible space of what was formerly heard. But what is made visible is constructed as a speech spectrograph: the story is broken down into the speech of Antigone, of Ismene, of Creon, Haemon, Eurydice, the Elders of Thebes, and so on. With the whole burden of storytelling, or world-making, now devolved upon the speech of named subjects, a character's speech is no longer just one element in the story—as dispensable as, say, a description of the sunset—as was the case in epic speech. In oral tradition, the basic principles of variability and multiformity which we looked at earlier have been observed to extend even to the story's character names (Lord 1986:20). In the oral mode of storytelling, who says what is not important, nor is the name given to a particular character; in different versions of the "same" oral story, character names may change as well. The structure of drama, with its division of the world into specific speech positions, has determined on the contrary that only Hamlet can say "To be or not to be"; only Jocasta can say "God keep you from the knowledge of who you are."

To write a story based on a list of speakers means to divide the world up into speech positions. And just as one begins to see relations among colors in a spectrogram, or among items in a written list, so too will the relations among speech positions become manifest in a dramatic writing of mythic material. Where does Antigone's speech end and Ismene's begin? What determines which aspects of a story are given to one character for utterance rather than to another? This problem of who says what is for the playwright not just a logistical one. To decide, for example, whether chicken goes in the meat category involves asking questions about the essence of the abstraction "meat," and examining abstract relations among types of animals, methods of husbandry, of food preparation, and so on. Similarly, when the names Antigone and Ismene enter the lists, they can begin to be conceptualized in ways that make their relationship to each other visible. They are sisters: How do sisters speak to one another? To what extent do they speak the same language? To what extent will their age difference manifest itself in linguistic differences? In different values and outlook? And so on. Dramatic writing

64. See esp. de Kerckhove 1979, 1981, 1983; Segal 1986:75–86; Vernant and Vidal-Naquet 1990:185–86, 243. As Herington puts it: "For the contemporaries it must have been dazzling enough, especially in the early years, when each Dionysia might reveal to the audience for the first time ever an Orestes, say, or a Memnon, or a Niobe, or an Oedipus, who was no longer a mere mechanical component of a famous story, but who breathed, walked, and, above all, spoke for himself" (1985:136).

thus involves conceiving of individuals as loci of speech (or silence, as the case may be), and thinking of the world of actions and events in terms of verbal correlatives. In dividing the world up into separate speech positions, the dramatist is thus engaging in a kind of conceptual analysis of the verbal-ideological world.

Like the internal chronotope of the dramatic text, which shifts value from the finished past onto the ongoing present, this spectrographic division of narrative into exotopic speech positions carries social and political implications: characters are subjects who speak for themselves, not "objects" for containment within a single transpersonal discourse of tradition. Just as the institution of the ostracism gave ordinary citizens a voice in public affairs, so too did the shift from epic to dramatic form give the figures of mythology a voice in the telling of their stories. For this reason, dramatic form is democratic and clearly reflects the structure of political institutions such as the ostracism. Without lists of citizens, lists of candidates, and the ability to submit written names anonymously, democratic institutions of this kind cannot function properly, if at all.[65] For similar reasons, the ability to draw up a list of separate speakers and their speech, and to submit it for public hearing and performance by others, is a precondition of dramatic form.

65. See W. Harris 1989:115, 63.

Conclusion: Theatre and Technology

What should that alphabetical position
portend?   Twelfth Night

*I*N THE FOREGOING CHAPTERS WE HAVE LOOKED AT VARIOUS WAYS IN which both the dramatic text and the social practice that is theatre were dependent from their beginnings in Greece on the technology of alphabetical literacy. The practice of literary criticism, inaugurated by the writing down of Homer's epics; the decontextualized study of poetry, made possible by the literate classroom; the reconceptualization of conflict initiated by the writing down of law, and the emergence of a literate economy of exchange——all of these literate developments made crucial contributions to the rise of theatre and its displacement of an epic storytelling model.

On the basis of these findings, two things are clear from the outset: that from their inception, theatre and drama were structured according to the same set of social and poetic principles and therefore cannot be described as two separate art forms; and that we can no longer accept those theories which portray literacy and literacy practices as peripheral to, let alone destructive of, the art of the stage. As a genre dependent on the manipulation and exchange of decontextualized, arbitrary signs—in the form of written speech, lists of names, future-oriented contracts and coins, and the documents left by the absent and the dead—theatre is indeed an art of writing.

What these findings suggest for contemporary and future theatrical and dramatic theory still remains to be drawn out. In terms of its historical emergence, theatrical form does appear to be structurally beholden to writing; but in practice, theatrical activities are clearly neither exhausted nor explained by writing to the same degree, or even in the same way, as the other literary genres are. Indeed, the relationship that prevails between theatre practice and the use of texts is unusually complicated, not merely by the standards set up by other textual disciplines, but by any standards. Consequently, and unsurprisingly, no matter where one looks in modern theatrical theory, one finds that discussions of the relationship between writing and the theatre are marked by distrustful uncertainty amounting in some cases to hostile vexation.

The nature of the relationship between writing and the theatrical stage has been illuminated by the evidence from Greece insofar as alphabetical writing preceded the emergence of theatrical form and determined many of its characteristics. Writing introduced the practice of verbatim repetition, which in turn enabled poetry to dispense with the conservatism of previous speech genres, and to develop, both stylistically and functionally, into the actively innovative, critical, and self-consciously fictional art form of drama. The use of the alphabet also shaped theatrical poetry as a highly speech-sensitive genre, a genre of idiosyncratic contemporary speech. The forensic atmosphere created by written law codes shaped theatre in many ways, determining its accusatory civic function, its dialogic structure, and its split orientation toward, on the one hand, abstract textual values, and on the other, popular public judgments. The literacy of the Athenians ensured also that amateurism, internationalism, mercantilism, and ideological competitiveness defined the practice of Western theatre from the very outset.

Literate practices, as we have seen, set off a number of subtle dialectical chain reactions; and theatre, as both an art and a social practice, grew up within this technological force field and contains its tensions on a deep generic level. To reiterate but two of these twists that are sure to be of interest to theatre artists and theorists today, there is the fact that verbatim repetition proves itself, perhaps against expectations, to be a kind of precondition for creative advancements rather than an obstacle to them; there is also the fact that while literacy does tend to cast the body as culturally "low," it also permits readers and writers, through the detachment of meanings from actual contexts, to envision new interpretations of the body which may be more liberal in the long run.

Of all the aspects of theatrical form that have been illuminated by our look at the influence of literate modes, it is perhaps this relationship between texts and bodies which cuts most directly to the heart of theatrical art. As an issue of abiding concern to theorists and practitioners alike, it is unfortunately a theoretical problem that will not easily admit of a simple solution. As we have seen, the relationship between texts and bodies is a complex dialectical one which cannot be solved once and for all: a "final solution" to this most human of dilemmas would be neither possible nor even desirable. Rather, precisely by virtue of its dynamic constitution, the text-body relation is one that needs to be plumbed on an ongoing basis through time and historical change. And this, of course, is where theatre it-self comes in. We have already seen some evidence that theatre is ideally constituted as an art form to fulfill this measuring and testing function, so long as there are texts and bodies that use them. Consequently, it is the ac-tual practice of theatre, the concrete use made by real bodies of disembodied texts, that provides the only true theory of drama insofar as the relation of texts to performance is concerned. But because it is not just actors but *all* literates who are afflicted, and blessed, with this text-body dialectic, it would seem that drama's ability, rare among the arts, to stage and interro-gate this dialectic should be one in which all members of a literate culture retain a significant intellectual and physical investment.

For theorists of drama, this conclusion—that the text-body relation cannot be theoretically solved once and for all but must rather be tested afresh in every production—may be disappointing. But from the point of view of literate culture generally, and theatre's perennial role within it, this is a conclusion full of optimism and laden with positive implications. Never-theless, there are a few theoretical issues that remain to be addressed, and the remainder of this chapter will be devoted to them. For modern theatri-cal theory has tied itself into many unfortunate knots in its efforts to wrestle with this problem of the relation between writing and the theatre, knots which our evidence from ancient Greece has gone some distance toward untying.

Once upon a time, in classical aesthetics, the critical terminology was such that artistic genres as diverse as epic, drama, the novel,[1] and even dance and flute playing could be meaningfully discussed as related activities (*Poetics* 1447a–1448a). What these genres appeared to have in common was the goal of imitative performance. Their formal and substantive differences—the materials they used, the performative means they employed, and the objects they imitated—seemed theoretically insignificant compared with the shared telos which unified them within a single poetic collectivity.

But this theoretical aegis has disappeared over time: Romantic theories of art replaced *mimesis* with *poiesis*,[2] and the history of literacy, with its

---

1. Aristotle speaks about the genre "without a name" which "imitates by language alone" (*Poetics* 1447b). We would call such things novels.

2. Romantic theorists of art such as the Schlegels became disenchanted with the sepa-ration between form and content implied by classical *mimesis*. Rather than viewing art as a representation of external nature, they insisted that art should be judged as a made thing, as something that signifies only itself and is therefore creative rather than imitative. See Tzve-tan Todorov (1982a:151–76) for a good summary of the shift from *mimesis* to *poiesis*. See also Todorov (1982b:4) for the use of *poiesis* to describe the modern view, and Göran Sörbom (1966:208) for the use of *mimesis*.

"Gutenberg" practices and habits of mind, eliminated performance from many spheres of artistic life. Before writing, of course, all poetry was enjoyed exclusively through the bodily realities of performance; but for literates, verbal art came to mean "literature," things that are *read.* Once capable of contributing effortlessly and usefully to the study of theatre, theories of verbal art, under the impact of technological change, have shriveled into theories of pure textuality, leaving theatre and drama out in the theoretical cold.

In classical theories of poetics, drama—as the genre that incorporates *all* the arts of imitative performance—recommends itself as a kind of sovereign genre; in the *Poetics,* drama assumes a correspondingly central position. But modern poetics, which is concerned mainly with *textual* literature— that is, print-based, nonperformative poetry and prose—either cannot cope with drama at all, or must treat it as an anomaly. Is it a dead historical relic, the literary theorists wonder, an archaeological remnant of our oral past, a merely instrumental stage in the evolution of our supremest, purest literary form, the novel?[3] Drama's multi-medial, performed nature makes it much too expansive a genre to fit under the desk-sized microscope of modern poetics' study of literary art *qua* text. Drama's presence in the discipline is tolerated out of respect for historical ties, but its company is rarely sought. In fact, the dramatic text, always reeking just a bit of real bodies and things, must even represent something of an affront to students of literature raised on Romantic notions about the autonomy of the text. Experienced teachers of literary theory, poetry, novels, and short fiction often avow that it "never occurred" to them to teach plays, or that they feel "uncomfortable" when called upon to do so, for their textual training has ill prepared them to analyze the kind of text that a play is. As a result, drama is often only grudgingly admitted into the republic of literary genres at all, for literature is now expected to be "pure," that is, unsullied by anything "real," meaning nontextual.

We need consult only a few standard reference works for literary theory and criticism in our time to see the uncomfortable position into which drama had been elbowed by post-Gutenberg thinking. In his *History of Modern Criticism* (1981), René Wellek says simply that G. E. Lessing's belief in the centrality of drama within literature is due to a faulty notion of what literature is. Literature, for Wellek and for all the "modern *readers*"[4] on

---

3. See Bakhtin (1981, 1984a, 1986) and Godzich and Kittay (1987) for examples of this view.

4. The italics are mine.

whose behalf he claims to speak, is ideally lyric poetry; if Lessing had not been so blinded by "insensitivity," an outmoded Aristotelianism, and a transparent occupational bias, he would have recognized this too (1981, 1:164). What we find in J. A. Cuddon's *Dictionary of Literary Terms* (1991) is equally telling. Cuddon defines "literature" as the group of "works which belong to the major genres: epic, lyric, drama, novel, short story, ode" (505). When we consult his entries for these genres, we find, however, that the novel receives twenty-two pages of history, theory, and analysis; the epic rates nine and a half pages; both the lyric and the short story merit four pages each; and the ode elicits three and a half pages. Drama is dispensed with in exactly *three sentences,* two of which are not even about drama as a genre. Drama is *named* by Cuddon as one of the "literary genres," but is not treated equally with the others.[5]

Drama's misfit status within modern literary theory is faced more directly by Roman Ingarden in *The Literary Work of Art* (1973), but with equally puzzling results. A more exhaustive and painstaking analysis of "the basic structure and mode of existence of the literary work" (lxxi) could hardly be imagined. Ingarden begins by determining which objects fall under the heading of "the literary work," and although he soon amends the formula to include the "low-brow" genres as well, his definition of the category follows Cuddon's generic approach. Literary works for Ingarden are works from all the "literary genres," and his examples are the *Iliad,* Schiller's dramas, *The Magic Mountain.* Drama, in short, is used along with the other genres to *constitute* the category "literary art." Yet, some three hundred pages of analysis later, drama is found *not* to conform to the very class of objects it helped to define. Ingarden is forced to conclude that a play "is not a *purely* literary work in that entirely new means of representation, precluded by the essential nature of a purely literary work, appear in it: 1) real objects engaged in performing the function of reproduction and representation and 2) aspects appropriately formed and predetermined by the properties of these real objects, in which represented objectivities are to appear" (320). On the one hand, then, drama serves a vital function in defining the category of literature; on the other, it is not really literature at all——it is, in Ingarden's words, "a borderline case" (322).

In response to this marginalization by theorists and critics of literature,

5. From biographical information we learn that Cuddon is himself an avid theatregoer and playwright, so "anti-theatricalism" (see Barish 1981) is clearly not at work here. On the contrary, Cuddon's dictionary elsewhere shows more awareness of theatrical terms than most literary anthologies and surveys. The problem seems to lie rather with the oddness of drama as a literary genre.

twentieth-century theorists of drama and theatre have tended to take up one or the other of two extreme positions. In one particularly striking case both positions were taken up, in succession. I am thinking of David Cole's study *The Theatrical Event* (1975), and his *Acting as Reading* (1992). These two books may not be found on every theorist's bookshelf; but placed side by side, they create an accurate map of the course dramatic theory has charted in our time, from ritual to text.

As Cole himself is aware, these two works make mutually exclusive claims about what theatre is. The first of them, written at the height of the anti-text fever that swept both theory and practice at midcentury, locates theatre "within a pre-literate problematic of tribal ritual," and focuses on shamanism and possession experience (1992:76). The second "presents acting not merely within the framework of literacy and textuality but as, in its inmost essence, a mode of engagement with texts" (76). Although Cole makes a halfhearted attempt to explain away this about-face, his vague tropes about water, depths, oceans, and travels cannot hide the fact that he has, in the space of seventeen years, reversed his position on the relation of writing to theatre and theatre to literacy.

Cole's work does not really deserve to stand as the epitome of the discipline's theoretical confusion. But there is no denying that his wild swing from preliterate ritual to all-encompassing textuality is an accurate reflection of larger theoretical trends. His bibliographies tell the story of twentieth-century dramatic theory at a glance. In the 1970s, Cole's readings in comparative religion, anthropology, and psychology reflected the attempts made by so many Western theorists of drama to explore the extent of theatre's likeness to a variety of nonliterary, non-Western practices: theatre was found to have more in common with shamanism, Haitian voodoo, Tibetan mysticism, Ethiopian religion, and Songhay magic than with European literature. What did it matter that theatre had been deprived of its throne within the commonwealth of literary genres? Theatrical performance was more like religious possession, ritual healing, and psychopathology anyway. By the 1990s, however, Cole's readings in Derrida, Poulet, Iser, Barthes, and Jameson had apparently reglamorized the Western tradition as a source for theatrical theory. The true essence of theatre no longer had to be sought in "primitive" non-Western practices, and the shaman was abandoned in favor of the literary theorist. And so in Cole's more recent book we find that the essence of theatre is now "readerly": acting is reading; being an audience is being read to; and the stage is a site of performance texts, inscriptions, and reader responses. The incompatibility of these two versions of the essence of theatre is obvious. In the first case, theatre is a preliterary religious ritual; in the second case, it is indissolubly dependent on the existence of writing and literacy.

Although the flowering of theatre's romance with ritualism can be dated conveniently to the mid-twentieth century—say, to the 1970s of *The Theatrical Event*—antiliterary sentiments run deep in theatrical theory. Besides Cole's early readings in comparative anthropology, we find the writings of Hegel and Jane Ellen Harrison, both of whom were influential in encouraging modern theorists like Cole to wash their hands of literature altogether. Although not exactly a ritualist, Hegel was one of the earliest aestheticians to attack texts on principle as alien to theatrical performance. In his *Aesthetics,* Hegel argued that drama, being an embodiment of action, comes into contradiction with itself when read.[6] Hegel saw the theatre's only hope in a ban on printing: dramatic texts, to be true to themselves, should be enacted, seen in action, and not read at all (except by actors—and, evidently, by Hegelian philosophers). The impracticality, to say nothing of the arbitrariness, of Hegel's solution can be let pass. Hegel's pronouncement, however, did succeed in bringing into awareness one of the fundamental issues of theatrical theory, an issue that had never before been formulated in so radical a form. Aristotle, for example, seems to take for granted that plays are written, and that they are intended for performance, but he does not explore the theoretical implications of this bi-medial situation. Interested primarily in the plot, Aristotle does not appear to see the medium as affecting the message in any way. A plot heard is the same as a plot seen. If we know better today, and I think we do, we might credit Hegel with making the theatre's "written-ness" into the problem it has remained.[7] Regardless of how it has

---

6. "Drama is concerned to depict an action in all the reality of its actual presence" and "would fall into contradiction with itself if it were forced to remain limited to the means which poetry, simply as such, is in a position to offer" (Hegel 1975:1181). Hegel continues: "Indeed, in my opinion, no play should really be printed" (1184).

7. The history of theatrical theory is of course strongly marked by the debate about the relative merits of performance over the reading of plays. Castelvetro in 1576 was perhaps the first to contradict Aristotle explicitly and stress the primacy of performance: "Aristotle is of the opinion that the delight to be obtained from reading a tragedy is as great as that to be obtained from a performance of it; this I aver to be false" (*Poetica d'Aristotle vulgarizzata e sposta;* trans. and cited in Carlson 1984:48). Lessing has a special place in this history, thanks to his rigorous semiotic analysis of the limits of literary versus plastic media. For Lessing, the materiality of the theatrical sign puts limitations upon it from which literary representations are relatively free (see esp. Wellbery 1984:88). And later Hazlitt, equally sensitive to the phenomenal differences between text and performance, argued for the supremacy of the text: "The representing of the finest of [Shakespeare's plays] on the stage, even by the finest actors, is, we apprehend, an abuse of the genius of the poet, and even in those of a second-rate class, the quantity of sentiment and imagery greatly outweighs the

been solved, the problem of writing and its relation to performance, once revealed, could no longer be ignored, and soon came to occupy the energies of theatre theorists of all kinds, emerging in this century as perhaps *the* issue for theory and practice alike.

What Aristotle skipped lightly past, and Hegel pointed out, twentieth-century theorists began to lose sleep over. The closer they were looked at in theory, the more dissimilar texts and performances appeared. In terms of their sign systems, their phenomena, their temporal structures, in terms of the perceptual apparatus they activate and the social contexts that ground them in practice, texts and performances proved to be incommensurable objects when it came to theoretical analysis.[8] The seeming impossibility of theoretically reconciling theatre's textual and nontextual elements led some theorists to give up the attempt. Jiri Veltrusky (1977), for example, concluded that theatre's literary and nonliterary elements are so opposed in nature that drama and theatre must be viewed as two separate and irreconcilably different art forms. Any actor who has just learned a "drama" by heart in order to perform it in the "theatre" would of course scoff at this suggestion, since theatre and drama, in practice, are simply two different names for a continuous activity. It is only theory that has trouble reconciling them. And so long as texts are conceived according to the standards of post-Gutenberg thinking, the difficulty of reconciling them with performing bodies must seem acute.

With the advent of the ritual hypothesis, however, any perceived need to reconcile text and performance seemed to disappear. For advocates of ritualism such as Jane Ellen Harrison, as for precursors such as Frazer, Freud, and F. Max Müller, the stories we tell one another are not what they appear to be. Beneath the visible surface of myth lies a truer, more primal and deeply human reality. For Harrison, all our mythological "sayings" are really "doings" in disguise. Myths are "really" attempts to explain religious rituals no longer recognized as such. Applying her views about religion to drama, not by any means her area of expertise, Harrison concluded that "for Greece at least, only in orgiastic religion did drama take its rise."[9]

Despite its fictionality, the idea that drama was originally the worship

---

immediate impression of the situation and story" (1930–34 5:221–22). But Hegel made textuality into an explicit theoretical problem in a way that most closely anticipates the antitext trends of our time.

8. As Pavis describes the incommensurability of text and performance, "linguistic arbitrariness and stage iconicity cannot be reconciled or mutually canceled out by a common system" (1982:143).

9. Harrison 1991:568; orig. pub. 1903.

of a polyonymous "Year-Spirit" caught on. Certainly it was a much more exciting theory about the origins of drama than could be produced by such careful philologists as Oliver Taplin and Arthur W. Pickard-Cambridge. According to Robert Ackerman, Gilbert Murray's social connections may have had something to do with the theory's immunity to sound historical scholarship: because he knew the editor personally, Murray was able to get Harrison's ritual hypothesis into the *Encyclopaedia Britannica* before it could be subjected to unbiased scrutiny (1991:170). As a result, the ritual hypothesis received wider dissemination, and planted itself more deeply in the public imagination, than perhaps it deserved.

For Murray and followers such as Francis Fergusson (1949), characters like Oedipus, Orestes, and Hamlet were not realistic psychological portraits, but functioned rather as superficial masks for a single seasonal god of an ancient fertility rite. If theatre is "really" an ancient religious ritual disguised, then mythological characters are just decadent later additions, and the whole dramatic text is an irrelevant, concealing add-on. As Christopher Innes (1981) has shown, a similar belief in some primal disguised origin of theatre is at work throughout the century's avant-garde, anti-textual theories and theatrical experiments. As he notes, Artaud (1958), Grotowsky (1968), the Living Theatre, Barba (1990), Chaikin (1972), and Schechner (1971, 1973, 1976, 1977) all latched on in one way or another to the ritual hypothesis, and all concluded, in their disparate ways, that because theatre is an essentially irrational, preliterate phenomenon, writing can only pervert theatre's true calling. If theatre was originally a religious rite, a holy communion shared by initiates, then texts can only get in the way.[10]

Despite the shortage of evidence for the actual existence of such a religious ur-drama,[11] the hypothesis was welcomed as a panacea for all the theoretical uncertainties of the text-performance relation. The most tangible consequences of the theatre's enchantment with ritual were the many theatrical experiments, referred to earlier and discussed by Innes, in which practitioners ended up throwing the baby of theatre out with the bathwater of text.[12] Since Harrison and Murray's time, however, theorists of myth and ritual such as David Bynum and G. S. Kirk have argued that the early advocates of the ritual hypothesis were in any case demonstrably wrong in their

10. See Innes 1981 passim, esp. 257–58.
11. Pickard-Cambridge 1962:189; Else 1965b:7; Vickers 1973:33ff. Not surprisingly, Seaford's (1994) ritualistic study of ancient theatre must rely, to a disproportionate extent for such a long work, on Euripides' *Bacchai*.
12. See, for example, Kirby 1969; Benamou 1977; Schechner 1971, 1973, 1976, 1977; Artaud 1958.

claims that ritual always underlies myth. These are simply different types of phenomena, and their relationship to each other is much more complex than simply one of surface and depth or cause and effect (Kirk 1985:252). That myth and ritual, which tend to occur together at festivals and other social gatherings, are actually two different types of "social behaviour" is not, however, something that would be obvious to an anthropologist in the field; as Kirk suggests, "the ceremonial circumstances in which myths are most conspicuously recited naturally make the deepest impression on the direct observer" (1970:253). So we can understand why Western observers might have had a tendency to conflate the two and see the ritual as the crux of the event. Nevertheless, it can be shown that "the great majority of Greek myths were developed without any special attention to ritual" (Kirk 1985:253), and that "[Greek] rituals do not seem to generate myths except in rare and exceptional cases" (236). In fact, as Kirk has discovered through detailed cross-cultural analysis, most myths worldwide have no particular ritual connection whatever (1970:19). Sometimes existing myths are used to build up the etiology of a specific cult, and sometimes myths are invented to explain an ancient cult practice, but such direct connections between myth and ritual are rare.[13] And even where it does exist, "the relation between myth and ritual . . . is not a simple matter of cause and effect in either direction" (1985:252).

As Bynum (1981) explains, rituals are activities that communities use to symbolically mark their social customs, such as marriage; myths are the stories that people tell one another and do not necessarily have any particular ritual content at all. (Myths about sexual unions say nothing about *how* people celebrate marriage rites, or even *whether* they do.) Whereas rituals are by nature local, changeable, and in some cases superficial (Thomas 1996:191), it is rather in the telling of stories about experience that humans reveal something of their ultimate and often universalizable aspirations. According to Bynum, there are any number of different ritual methods of getting married, or being initiated into adulthood, or buried, or born into the community. These rituals, which vary from place to place and epoch to epoch, even within the same country (Thomas 1996:185), reveal almost nothing about the myths that coexist alongside them—myths about the creation of the world, relations between men and animals, between men and women, between people and nature or the supernatural, and so on. One community might ritually mark the birth of girls by a religiously sanctioned excision of their genitals; another might shower the mother in small pink

13. Kirk 1970:16, 18–19; also Kirk 1985:223–53.

gifts and force her to wear a hat made out of the ribbons from the wrapping paper. These rituals reflect local social conditions and values and do not usually produce myths, although they may well provide opportunities for enjoying those that already exist.[14] As Kirk points out, the natives of the Pacific Northwest practise the potlatch as one of their central rituals, yet have virtually no myths about potlatch situations (1985:248). This is because, in Kirk's words, "alongside the stream of religious imagination there runs a stream of purely narrative invention" which we call storytelling, or myth (1985:226).[15]

This complex relationship between myth and ritual was not grasped by the advocates of the ritual origins of theatre, and as a consequence they were unable to see theatre in its earliest days for what it was: a species of storytelling whose ritual associations were only circumstantial.[16] The theatre, of course, was not just any kind of storytelling: it was the first genre of storytelling to benefit from the preexistence of written stories, with all that that entailed. And it is precisely here that ritualism reveals its greatest weakness as a tool for theatrical theory. In addition to underestimating the autonomy and primacy of our narratological impulses, ritualism cannot grapple with a historical variable such as technology; indeed, many of ritualism's most influential ideas have depended on a willful discounting of technological differences between one culture and another. Instead, its insights were gathered from direct, ahistorical comparisons between anthropological data drawn from radically different cultures at various stages of technological advance. Concrete and culturally specific facts, such as whether the society in question learns from bards or from books, were not allowed to disturb the apparent symmetry. As Robert Weimann has argued in a discussion of the

14. One may perform a play in honor of a wedding, as the actors do in *Midsummer Night's Dream,* or attend a performance of *The Nutcracker* during the Christmas holidays, as we do today, or go to the theatre during the Festival of Dionysus, as was the practice in ancient Greece.

15. This distinction between myth and ritual is strongly confirmed by the circumstances surrounding the emergence of aboriginal theatre in Canada. Theatrical form did not emerge out of the potlatch or other Longhouse activities which continue to carry out such ritual functions as preserving social customs, affirming community solidarity, and celebrating local rites of passage. Such traditional ritual performances are "fully comprehensible only to the culturally initiated"; but dramas based on myths such as those of the Trickster can be enjoyed by any audience, not just the local one (Brask and Morgan 1992:x, xv). Brask and Morgan, who have studied the emergence of theatre in a number of aboriginal settings, conclude that native rituals are alien to the universalizing narrativity of theatrical performance (xiii).

16. For discussions of the circumstances that put theatre under the auspices of the Dionysian city festival, see Pickard-Cambridge 1962, 1968; Else 1965b; Gernet 1981; Segal 1986; Taplin 1978; Herington 1985; Vernant and Vidal-Naquet 1990.

224 ◆ *Dionysus Writes*

so-called ritual sources of Shakespearean theatre, "anthropological models" taken from preliterate "canoe plays" and "jungle hunting games" are less pertinent than they might appear: "At this level of culture mimesis arises out of a community in which there is little division of labour[;] the 'spectators' take part in the game or join in the acting. The unity of player and audience is complete" (1978:2). In short, such models are not actually "theatrical" in the sense intended by members of a literate society such as ours. Nor are they theatrical in the sense assumed by the ancient Greeks, who observed in their artistic activities a separation between audience and performer that was absent from their religious activities. And yet, as Kirk has shown, the method of the early ritualists was precisely this: to accumulate catalogues full of items that looked vaguely similar, but in practice, in their actual social contexts, were unrelated (1970:4).[17]

As Bynum has argued, this downplaying of specific cultural and historical differences continues to compromise the work of anthropologists. For example, Victor Turner and Clifford Geertz, whose comparative anthropology is often applied to theatre research, betray a typical tendency to treat traditional religious rituals as if they were culturally equivalent to literate artworks such as *Macbeth* and *Moby Dick* (Bynum 1981:142–63). As laudable as it is in itself, this impulse, to find human similarities despite seeming cultural differences, can badly botch its evidence if the latter is simply ignored. The mimetic dances of the Bambuti pygmies *may* have something to teach us about theatrical performances in Elizabethan London, but only if it is remembered that the purpose and meaning of a given type of social behavior can change over time—and especially under the impact of such powerful social and technological factors as the division of labor and literacy. When comparing anthropological material from different cultures, in other words, theorists must take care to give historical and technological differences the weight they deserve.

For as we have seen throughout this study, literacy changes things. One of the effects of literacy that we noticed for ancient Greece was a generalized de-specialization of performance personnel, an inauguration of performative amateurism in poetic storytelling. That this amateurism is typical of a specifically *theatrical* mode of public performance only becomes visible, however, through a *historical* analysis of changing speech styles, and hence has not been recognized or adequately appreciated by modern, comparative-minded theorists. As a result, many have drawn specious parallels between

---

17. Kirk describes this method as, "even by the indulgent view . . . rather reprehensible—although no one reached the point of successfully reprehending it" (1970:4).

theatre and shamanistic performance. Theorists such as Richard Schechner (1976) and the early David Cole (1975), intrigued by superficial phenomenological similarities, have described theatre as essentially shamanistic, and shamanistic performance as essentially theatrical. The list of reasons why this comparison is misleading is actually rather long, and includes such pivotal divergences as the presence in the one and the absence in the other of religious and ritual elements, and the absence in theatre and the presence in shamanic performance of direct audience involvement. Tao-ching Hsu describes the main difference between the actor and the shaman as follows: "The shamanesses worked on the spirits, not on the spectators; they tried to invoke gods, not amuse men; in fact, in some cases there might not be any spectators at all" (1985:200). But aside from these obvious functional dissimilarities, there is the crucial difference which is all too easily overlooked by those not attuned to the historical realities of technological change. This is the fact that, like other preliterate speech genres, shamanistic performance is the exclusive preserve of specially initiated practitioners. Unlike the actor, the shaman is divinely "chosen" for his performative function; unlike the actor, the shaman must also undergo a physical "initiation" that marks him for life as a select practitioner of a sacred and secret "vocation" (Conquergood 1992:45–49). The actor, on the contrary, in antiquity no less than in modernity, is anyone with a script. For this reason, shamanic performance, if comparable to any mythological activity—which is itself by no means self-evident—would bear more meaningful comparison to epic than drama, for the shaman, like the oral bard, is the physical embodiment of a traditional style and is considered the divinely authorized repository of esoteric knowledge and a special technique not available to everyone.

There may be something in theatre practitioners that naturally draws them toward the oldest, most universally attested anthropological evidence in their search for the meaning and function of their art. Or perhaps, as Jack Goody has suggested, an enchantment with primitive, preliterate models is typical of all literates, not just those interested in drama: "A perpetual trend of complex, written cultures is the search for, and to some extent identification with, the simpler cultures of the past. One only has to recall the attraction of 'savage' cultures for the eighteenth-century Rousseau. . . . A modern version of the same theme lies behind the search for the natural, the untouched, the oral . . . and representing in some of its guises the apotheosis of the oral and the renunciation of the written as the real source of truth" (1987:293). The fact that the Western theatre has *always* consisted mainly of written plays should be enough to dissuade us from taking this "apotheosis of the oral" too far.[18] But the historical record, as we have seen, stands in the way of our even flirting with it. Writing had already been practised in Greece for almost two centuries by the time theatre made its first appearance, and there is little to be gained by pretending otherwise.

Cole's later work, of course, implicitly acknowledges that the premises of ritualism simply do not jibe with the historical facts. As Cole had to grant eventually, even adherents to ritualist doctrine are wedded to writing despite their wishes: "One can argue endlessly about whether the actor can or should or might function as a 'social critic' (Brecht) or 'skilled worker' (Meyerhold) or 'secular saint' (Grotowsky) or 'signal[er] through the flames' (Artaud); but meanwhile there is no question that he *is* functioning as a reader. Every actor—whether he works for Robert Wilson or the Shubert organization, the Royal Shakespeare Company or the high school dramatics club—*reads*" (1992:3). This is Cole's belated recognition of the role played by reading in the actor's work. Far from simply recognizing it, however, Cole goes on to overestimate it. Like so many theorists in recent years, Cole ultimately exaggerates the extent to which a textual activity such as reading can be used to explain everything that goes on in theatres. For, as we soon discover in *Acting as Reading,* all theatrical activities are subsumable under the aegis of textuality. Theatre is now no longer conceived by Cole as nontext; it is now *all* text.

Like the ritual hypothesis, which was borrowed, inappropriately, from Harrison's religious studies, so too were the textually based theories of reading on which Cole depends co-opted from sources inattentive to the historical and practical realities of theatre. In taking over the methods and terminology of contemporary literary theory, Cole and others have thus imported into theatrical theory all of literary theory's discomfort with the nontextual aspects of drama. The explosion of interest in literary theory throughout the last few decades may have had the effect of rehabilitating writing as an intellectually respectable subject; but the new text fetish has produced results for theatrical theory which have proven as absurd as those bequeathed us by the previous avant-garde. Theorists from the late 1970s into the 1990s, apparently intoxicated by the cachet of textuality, were moved to describe even the stage spectacle as a "performance text" "written" by a "stage-writer," the director, and "read" by an audience.[19] In sum, the

18. My concern is exclusively with the Western theatrical tradition. That the situation is quite different in the East is acknowledged and discussed in Chapter 1.

19. See esp. Lyotard 1977, Ubersfeld 1978, Elam 1980, Pavis 1982, Svenbro 1990, Cole 1992. Nor is there any sign of change at this writing: a theatre conference at the University of Toronto's Graduate Centre for Study of Drama in 1997 was titled "The Performance Text."

theoretical pendulum had swung so far in the opposite direction that even corporeal performance came to be seen, by theatre practitioners who should have known better, as if it too were a text.

According to my findings throughout the foregoing chapters, the impact of writing cannot be underestimated in any account of the rise of theatre nor in any description of its practice today. But neither can this historical evidence be taken as a licence to do away with the text-performance problem by pretending that even performances are texts. Having followed Kierkegaard's advice and having traced this problem back to its home, to its first appearance in ancient Greece, we find ourselves in an especially good position to evaluate the extent to which readerly theories can serve as a satisfactory replacement for the postulates of ritualism. In his remarks about the actor's dependence on reading, Cole refers to the textual activities of theatre practitioners *today;* but reading and writing have become occupational necessities for virtually everyone. Had we simply examined the theatre's use of writing *today,* we would have proved nothing more than that our culture is dependent on written modes. This we already know. What we needed to ascertain was not the extent of writing's influence on cultural life today, but the extent of its role in constituting the theatre as an art form; and the only way to do this was to return to the moment when theatrical form visibly emerged.

Sixth- and fifth-century Greece proved to be an ideal laboratory for evaluating the extent of theatre's dependence on writing. Writing at this time was being widely used, but it had not yet displaced oral habits altogether. Better still, the beginning of the classic age of drama in Greece is a period in which traces of mainly oral performance styles can still be found. Drama appeared on the performance scene at a time when the oral recitation of poetry was still the expected norm for most audiences; and yet, even in the earliest theatrical performances of the fifth century, the distinctive marks of literacy are evident. Having followed the progress of the hybridizing shift from exclusively oral performance to the performance of literary drama, we have been able to see what theatre does and does not owe to writing.

For example, in my discussion of Kallias' *ABC Show* in Chapter 1, I suggested that the art of the theatrical actor was at least partly constituted through a transference of the arbitrary semiotic principle from writing to poetic performance. As semioticians such as Veltrusky (1964) and Elam (1980) have noted, one of the first conventions of theatrical space is that it treats the things that fill it as unmotivated signs: a sack of potatoes can represent a dead body, a boy can represent a girl, a crooked index finger can represent a chink in a wall.

Nevertheless, an awareness of this "alphabetical" freedom of people and objects on stage can easily lead to incorrect theoretical conclusions. And it has, if we can judge from those theorists in our time who have declared that theatrical performance must *itself* be treated as a kind of writing. Jean-François Lyotard claims that staging a play involves the rewriting, or transcribing, of the text by the director, who is described as a kind of "writer" himself (1977:90). Kier Elam conceives performance as a "text" (1980:3, 7, 12, 213). Patrice Pavis similarly describes the director as a "writer," and performance as a "stage writing" or "text" which can be "read" by the audience; even the actor's body can be "read like a text" (1982: 31, 55, 73, 78, 124, 135, 174). Anne Ubersfeld does likewise (1978:24), as does Marco De Marinis.[20] Jesper Svenbro describes stage presentation as a "vocal rewriting of the text,"[21] and from that deduces that Athenian audiences actually improved their *reading* skills by watching plays (1990:371ff.). Cole begins by questioning the appropriateness of the stage-as-quick-book[22] trope, but ultimately makes the surprising decision to retain it on the grounds that, since we commonly speak of "reading" "photographs, drawings, films," we should be able to speak of reading a performance text, especially since so many reputable theorists and poets have already done so (1992:200).

In the first place, conformity with past theoretical precedent, no matter how illustrious, is *not* adequate justification for maintaining a descriptive trope, particularly one so fraught with generic significance. In the second place, Cole should have been alert to the fact that "photographs, drawings, films" have one thing in common which theatrical performance does not have: as artistic objects they are all inanimate, fixed, disembodied tissues of signs. A theatrical performance, however, is patently not a text in this sense, which really means that it is not a text at all. One of the effects of the popularity of semiotic models, especially those of Barthes and Derrida, has been to expand our notion of what a text is. In the main this has been a positive development, providing critics and theorists with a consistent vocabulary for speaking about all kinds of cultural phenomena (rather than just about books). But the theatre differs from many other products of culture in one key respect: its special character consists in the fact that it combines, explicitly, both textual and nontextual phenomena. The theatre's distinctive combination, and even contrast, of text and non-text, cannot be argued away; and recognition of this unerasable duality is therefore essential for an accu-

---

20. As cited by Carlson 1984:501.
21. But "vocal rewriting" is a contradiction in terms.
22. "Quick" in the medieval sense of "living;" see Cole 1992:199.

rate understanding of the genre. By calling both the textual, and the living, nontextual aspects of theatrical practice by the same name, theorists obscure the differences between them, and leave themselves no room to discuss the relation between texts and bodies, a relation that could be said to constitute the essence of the art. Certainly my discussion of the nature of the actor/ student in Chapter 2 suggests that a clearly delineated text-body relation is essential to any analysis of theatrical representation.

A wholesale adoption of textual models also causes problems when "readerly" hermeneutics are used to analyze the audience's experience of theatrical performance. I am thinking in particular of Susan Bennett's dissertation, "The Role of the Theatre Audience" (1987), and again Cole's *Acting as Reading* (1992). Both of these works use varieties of "reader-response" criticism to describe theatrical processes. Relying on theorists of reading such as Wolfgang Iser (1978), Cole for example quotes, approvingly, such theoretical statements as the following: a text is "a sort of living organism" "formed out of living matter"; a text is "an organic web." [23] Or "the text is . . . a verbal body . . . that can be sounded, weighed"; the text is "a sort of human being." [24] Cole concludes that "to the extent that texts are experienced as others, reading tends to be experienced as interpersonal encounter" (13). Iser asserts that "a dialogue" exists between readers and their books, a "dyadic interaction" (80, 66). On the basis of such ideas, Cole theorizes that "texts are capable of standing in all the sorts of relations to their readers that one self may stand in to another": a book may serve the function of a "friend," "therapist," or "lover." Now, anyone who has had the pleasure of having a real friend, therapist, or lover is not likely to be convinced by this. But Cole is convinced, and goes on to say that "to be alone with a text . . . is already to be interacting with others." This is so because, thanks to reader-response criticism, "solitary reading is, at all moments, interaction with 'others'" (14). Reading is certainly *described* that way, but that does not make it true.

Their decision to equate corporeal performances with texts has led theorists such as Bennett and Cole to some fairly preposterous conclusions. Cole ultimately asserts that "it is scarcely an exaggeration to say that acting begins and ends in reading" (1992:8) and that reading and acting are *equally* physical activities (29). In the process of his analysis, he cannot help but falsify the nature of *both* acting and reading. In the first place, books are not what Georges Poulet says they are: "living, feeling, resisting" *people*. [25] Con-

---

23. Yuri Lotman as cited in Iser 1978:66.
24. Georges Poulet as translated and cited by Cole 1992:65; Iser 1978:154.
25. As cited by Cole 1992:39–40.

sequently, encounters with them are not dialogues but complex mono-logues. Books are mechanically reproducible, and often destructible without serious consequences, which actors, for better or for worse, are not. And it is of the nature of writing to have a deferred relation with its receiver, a rela-tion strictly opposed to the simultaneity with which performances are pro-duced and received. Furthermore, the word *audience,* when used of a text's readership, has an abstract, almost imaginary quality to it, whereas audi-ences of stage plays are real, present "collectivit[ies], acting here and now on one another and on the speaker" (Ong 1977:13). Theatre audiences, in short, occupy the same spatiotemporal context as the performers. As Ong observes further, texts are produced out of writers' *withdrawal* from direct immersion in a social situation (1977:57), a feature of writing (and reading, for that matter) which can hardly be predicated of acting. Writing can communicate over time and distance in the absence of both the sender of the message and any particular receiver, and again, this is something that theatrical actors do not normally have an ability to do. Theatrical performance involves the spa-tial and temporal co-presence of sender and receiver, and surely this is enough to guarantee that it cannot meaningfully be described as any kind of writing.[26]

The ritualist approach may have been unnecessarily prejudiced toward texts, but one cannot solve the problem of the relation of writing to the stage in this way either. By any definition of text that is meaningful in the context of theatre, the body of a live actor speaking in person to an equally live audience is not a textual phenomenon. From whatever point of view one wishes to adopt—structuralist, poststructuralist, semiotic, phenomeno-logical—performances cannot be equated with texts. They make meaning in different ways, produce different sorts of experiences, are composed of radically different sensory material, are consumed by audiences according to different principles, and communicate through different channels, different media. To call them both texts is an abuse of the language.

The textual approach constitutes a slight advance over that of the ritualists, for at least it acknowledges the everyday realities of theatre practice today and throughout history. But the advance is not a great one, since reading is not *all* that happens in theatres, nor is reading all that actors do. In response to our theoretical quandary—what is the relation of writing to the stage?—we have thus received two unsatisfactory answers in our time. The ritualists

---

26. In the case of broadcasts or films, this rule would seem to evaporate—which is precisely why it *does* make sense to speak of films and recordings as texts.

banished the text as irrelevant and obscurantist; the textualists have made it all the world. Neither of these theoretical extremes can account for the peculiar, sometimes troubled, always fertile cooperation between texts and bodies that we see in the Western theatre from its very beginnings; neither can usefully locate dramatic art within literature as a whole.

For in the final analysis, it is theatre's knowledge of but stubborn nonabsorption by writing which has guaranteed for it a special, even privileged position within the family of literary genres. Precisely because it is *not* textual itself, theatrical performance can "display" or represent writing in a way that a written medium itself cannot; in the theatre there is an "outside" of writing. In staging the Ionian alphabet for the Athenians, Kallias can both *use* a grammatological semiosis and *show* the difference between letters and bodies. The representing signs of a writing system cannot "get pregnant," as does Kallias' female writing student, who out of shame represents her baby with letters. This difference, between inanimate signs and real people, cannot be ignored theoretically. As Bert States observes, theatrical signs distinguish themselves from textual ones precisely in this way: "In the theatre [unlike in texts] there is always the possibility that an act of sexual congress between two so-called signs will produce a real pregnancy" (1985:20).

Writing is regularly *displayed* on stage, but theatre does not become writing by virtue of this. Methods of displaying writing range from Kallias' alphabet chorus, to the writing of "Thebes" on the scenery, to the pinning of Shakespearean love letters on trees, to Brechtian placards, to the multiplicity of avant-garde devices that have more recently been used for showing actors as readers.[27] For reasons similar to those already stated, directors can only be said, without sophistry, to be behaving as "writers" when they compose introductory notes for the playbill, or indicate therein that the performance will run without intermission.

As we see in *The ABC Show,* the theatre can represent writing, but it does this representing by means of a medium that is unambiguously *not* writing itself (i.e., actors' bodies and voices and real objects). Nevertheless, Kallias' letter/characters, who function on stage as signs for fictional personages or things that they themselves are not, do present us with a theoretical dilemma. If it is the nature of a sign *not* to be what it represents, what does this say about actors? If they represent passionate human beings, as they do in so many plays, does this mean that they must not be passionate human

27. See Cole's discussion of the readerly theatre of the Wooster Group, Daryll Chin, Robert Wilson, and La Mama's *Home Remedies* (1992:190–96). These productions actively explored, in performance, the phenomenology of reading by staging acts of reading, giant books, projected text, and so forth.

beings themselves? Diderot wrestled at length with this paradox, concluding at one point that actors must on some level be quite devoid of their own personality in order to represent other personalities (1957:16–20). The question goes further: Can men and women, who on stage represent men and women, albeit "other" ones,[28] even be said to function as signs at all, since at root they also *are* what they represent?

The answer involves the recognition that the actor remains a performer, even while she or he functions as a sign does. Like the epic rhapsode, and like the lyric performer, the actor is still *competing*—for the audience's love, for the prize, money, or fame. As a contestant in a festival agon, the actor is therefore still engaged in all the pragmatics of performance: exhibiting virtuosity, displaying bodily charms, flattering, seducing, shocking, moving the audience to tears and delighting in the effects. Plato's Ion provides us with a lovely description of the paradox of the actor, for whom the performative pragmatics of *pleasing* always underlie his semiotic activity of representing. The means of performance in drama may have become representational, but the end or goal remains "to please," and to do so through the agency of one's own present body.

To say that the actor preserves the performative function of the *aoidos* or rhapsode is therefore to say that he experiences the effects of his performance *as he performs.* Like other types of performer, the actor experiences the audience's enjoyment or disapproval simultaneously with his performance, which is to say that audience response will more or less directly affect the *way* he performs. And it is here that the difference between theatre and other literary arts makes itself most keenly felt. A text such as a novel is never a performance: the letters on the page do not get nervous before the reader's gaze or wither at the reader's restlessness, nor do they bloom before the reader's appreciative laughter, applause, cheers. This may seem obvious enough, but there have been many attempts among theorists of the disembodied literary arts to arrogate "performance" pragmatics to the novel. The most notorious of these is perhaps Bakhtin's insistence that novels are "plays . . . without footlights"—which in a Bakhtinian worldview makes them superior and more truly "dramatic" than plays (Wise 1989). Derrida also arrogates performance functions to texts in a number of discussions,[29] and Kristeva speaks of texts as theatrical performances as well (1989:185ff.). Cole has noticed that this affectation, by critics of texts, of a theatrical vocabulary

28. For an eloquent statement of this situation, see Handke 1969.

29. For example, the writer "put[s] things on stage . . . is on stage himself; writing is a theatrical "scene" (Derrida 1981:206, 290).

is rampant in critical camps from the New Critics to the phenomenologists of literary response: readers are said to "act out" the text, "impersonate" the characters, get "cast in roles," and so on (1992:23–29). Nevertheless, this use of performative metaphors to describe textual activities obscures the fact that written signs do not possess the same qualities as stage actors and objects: co-presence in a unique time-space context with a living audience, dialogic interaction with that audience, and an ever-changing corporeal, phenomenal reality. To call a textual artifact a performance is therefore no less mistaken than to call a performance a text.

Actors do indeed extend the arbitrary semiotic principle from page to stage, but they also preserve the performative function of the oral bard, who tries to delight the listener with his own present self. Although it is not easy to accept this, there would seem not to be any hard and fast rule that explains how these two functions interact in the actor's art. Some actors try to transcend their own personal oral-performative inclinations in pursuit of a perfectly transparent semiotic representation; others exploit their own deictic reality for use in the representation, as did the ancient actor who brought the ashes of a dead relative to the theatre with him in order to gain the audience's sympathy for his character by way of their sympathy for his real grief. For some performers, performative intentions and desires consist mainly of being beautiful and charming; others aim in performance above all to seduce their audiences, by various reality effects, into taking their representations for reality. In some cases the oral-performative and dramatic-semiotic functions enter into a conspicuous conflict. Sometimes this happens inadvertently—when an actor is poorly cast or does not understand the role—and sometimes to a purpose, as when she or he has decided to use the performative function to comment on or criticize the role as written. The exact nature of the balance struck between the two functions clearly varies greatly from performer to performer, play to play, even from one given moment in a given production to the next. As Brecht noted with his usual perspicacity, the actor, as performer, will always be taking up *some* attitude to his role (1964:37, 98, 137, 198). But between the Brechtian extremes of "naturalizing" the role (closing the gap as much as possible between semiosis and performance) and "alienating" it (deliberately widening the gap between the two), there are sure to be as many shades of gray as there are actors. Among North American "Method" actors, the assumption may exist that the performative function of the actor should merge with perfect equivalence into the representative function, but this is simply one style among many. In States's view, the nonrepresentational aspects of the stage presentation function by wounding the semiotic circuitry of the representation

(1985:12), but this view has no greater universality in the theatre than does its opposite. On the contrary, oral-performative phenomena are if anything more commonly used *in support* of semiotic functions: a comedian is cast in the role of a comedian; a pianist represents Mozart; real-life lovers are cast as lovers, or become lovers during rehearsal; memories of actual traumas are summoned up on stage; and so on.

One of the main reasons why the oral-performative and semiotic functions cannot be pitted against each other in any predictable, universally valid way is that the actor, in performing as his phenomenally real self, is even here involved in representations—not of the character but of himself. That is, he represents himself with an eye to gaining the audience's approval. How an actor, say, in Kallias' play chooses to represent the Ω of the script may be the product of his semiotic vision of the shape of the letter Ω, but it is also a function of how he wishes to show himself making an Ω, of what image of himself he wants the audience to have. In short, there is little that can be stated as axiomatic about the relation between an actor's own personal intercourse with his audience as a performer and his representation of absent signifieds. Only one thing can be said with certainty on the subject: that in representing the absent things that they are not, actors do so from the point of view of their own personal oral-performative present, which, as we saw in Chapter 3, they share with a judging audience, for better or for worse.

Cole's exploration of the role of reading in the actor's work usefully examines an area of theatre practice that has been too long neglected. Nevertheless, his approach is compromised by his use of a readerly hermeneutics which was developed for, and is better suited to, use in nonperformative genres such as the novel. And although Cole shrewdly observes that one of the central dialectics in theatre practice is between reading and "feeding the audience," he takes this "feeding," which is really but a convenient metaphor to describe the performer's need to "please," as a literal description of the atavistic pleasures lodged in reading. Thus, in effect, the root pleasure of performance for Cole can be traced back to the hidden psychological pleasures of reading—a very illogical and disappointing conclusion. It is certainly true that the actor, like the bard before him, aims to give pleasure; and we might add that bardic performance was originally intimately connected with actual feasting (Segal 1992:4–22).[30] But not all corporeal

---

30. It is interesting to reflect on the fact that of the surviving fragments of comedy, twenty-two are concerned with literate practices, while *hundreds* concern food. For this reason, the paradigmatic fragment from the lost fifth-century plays might well be that of the comic poet Plato: a Homeric parody in which a legendary hero stands on stage reading verbatim from a cookbook! (*Phaon* frag. 173 Edmonds 1957).

pleasures, on stage or off, are necessarily culinary. As we saw in Chapter 2, at least some of the pleasures of face-to-face discourse are connected with seduction and impregnation; others, as I suggested in Chapter 3, are connected with winning. Nor, in any case, can all of the pleasures of performance be seen as derivative of the pleasures lodged in reading. Western playwrights have undoubtedly all been readers, but actors and audience members may enjoy, and at various times probably have enjoyed, theatrical performance without having experienced the pleasures of reading themselves. Cole's theory is a perfectly illustrative case of the theoretical errors that must come of the uncritical use of (post-Romantic) literary theory in discussing theatrical phenomena. Modern literary theories tend to be characterized by a built-in bias in favor of print, a bias that strictly limits their use in dramatic theory.

As for the vexed question of theatre's place within literature, to conclude, with Ingarden, that drama is a "borderline" literary genre is at least not as inaccurate as to say that it is either preliterate or wholly textual; and yet it is not very helpful either. (The border of what?) In most modern dramatic theory, either theatre is categorized according to the prejudices of ritualism, and isolated from the rest of literature as an essentially nontextual art form, or theatre is absorbed so completely into the domain of textuality that its main generic features cease to be available for theoretical analysis at all.

Of contemporary theorists, Benjamin Bennett (1990) provides an analysis of drama's place within literature which is most in line with the evidence from ancient Greece. Bennett discusses theatre as an essentially literary event and drama as "the memory and the conscience of literature" (60). Drama for Bennett is "not merely one literary type among others, but rather is to literature as literature is to the whole of language, a focus of maximally intense self-reflection" (14). Bennett has regrettably chosen to retain a ritualist vocabulary, to conclude that "drama is the church of literature" (14), and to suggest that "the destiny of drama . . . is to become a ritual exercise in the ethics of reading" (54). But this is a quibble. For Bennett has ascertained, albeit through very different methods, what my own investigation into the historical genesis of theatre has discovered: that theatre "comes after" literature—not as an epigone but as an irritant. The special historical circumstances under which theatrical form was first constituted have determined that theatre must be located resolutely *within* literature, not as a "borderline case," but as the very genre that first inaugurated the practice we now take to be specifically "literary": a use of writing to tell a fictional story in which the text is demonstrably more than a record of an antecedent oral performance. But unlike the other literary arts that followed it, drama's peculiar *mode* of being-within-literature has determined that it always functions to some degree at the expense of literary dictates and models.

As we saw particularly in Chapter 2, whenever the technology of writing is put on stage, it is directly compared, and contrasted, with the real materiality of bodies and things. Plays and scenes that staged writing for the ancient Greeks nearly all suggest that writing has a built-in danger: that those who use it have a tendency to forget about the body, the organic body, which can never be reproduced in any text—or by any technology for that matter. Scenes of writing on the ancient stage show this forgetfulness of the body, and rebuke it—sometimes comically, sometimes with tragic seriousness. Because it conspicuously counters texts with bodies, writing with the corporeality of those who use it, the theatrical stage is unique in literate culture, able as it is to mount such a trenchant critique of the technology that produced it.

In fact, if this history of theatre's relationship with writing teaches us anything, it is that the theatre has a very special role to play in *all* technological revolutions. Unlike the art of the epic, for example, which was rendered culturally superfluous almost overnight by the advent of the alphabet, the theatre's function in a technological society cannot be exhausted, no matter what technologies we chance to invent. For unlike philosophical dialogues, novels, films, and all other representing media, the theatre puts real things, real bodies, real swollen feet beside and in opposition to all conceivable artificial representations of them.

As we move throughout theatre history, we find that no sooner does a new technology appear but the theatre puts it on stage. From Clytaemestra's smoke signals and Phaedra's letters, to Dr. Faustus's mechanical clock, to Prospero's books and star maps and astrolabes; from the locomotives of melodrama to the helicopters of *Miss Saigon;* from Cocteau's telephone to Beckett's tape recorder; from Svoboda's magic lantern projections to the live video rapiers of Robert Lepage—the theatrical stage has tested them all. Writing may have been the first technology to be subjected to critical scrutiny on the stage, but it was by no means the last. As new technological artifacts such as telephones and fax machines and computers continue to expand the range of our "natural" communication modes, the theatre continues not only to reflect their effects but also to provide a kind of corporeal analysis of them. Every time a character on stage picks up the phone or listens to his own voice on tape from an absent body, the theatre is carrying out its work of evaluating the changes wrought by technology upon our naturally occurring space-time categories, upon our bodily life. In the theatre, these space-time categories have never been entirely natural, since from the very beginning of the art form, Clytaemestra has received smoke signals from Troy, and men and women have communicated through writing from beyond the grave. But so long as the theatre remains *also* a genre in which real bodies communicate naturally in real time and space, such meditations on the impact of technology as the genre can mount will always retain the power to weigh, counteract, and even occasionally criticize new technologies without simply being absorbed by them. Of course, the dialectical nature of the natural-artifactual polarity guarantees that even our notion of theatrical "presence" may change—just as our notion of what constitutes a "unified" time, place, or action surely has been changed by the advent of satellite telephones and television and transcontinental flight. But the continued presence of real stuff on stage will also preserve for theatre, on behalf of literature generally, sufficient measures of naturalness to enact drama's ancient literary mandate: to provide an accurate aesthetic reflection of, as well as an effective bodily safeguard against, the use made by humans of all representing technologies—including writing.

Bibliography

Ackerman, Robert. 1991. *The Myth and Ritual School*. New York: Garland.

Allen, Thomas W. 1969 (1924). *Homer: The Origins and the Transmission*. Oxford: Clarendon.

Aristophanes. 1931. *The Comedies of Aristophanes*. The Athenian Society. Vol. 1. New York: Rarity Press,

———. 1982–85. *The Comedies of Aristophanes*. Vols. 3–5. Ed. Alan H. Sommerstein. Warminster, England: Aris Phillips.

Aristotle. 1927. *Poetics*. Loeb Classical Library. Cambridge: Harvard University Press.

———. 1941. *The Basic Works of Aristotle*. Ed. Richard McKeon. New York: Random House,

Arnott, Peter D. 1989. *Public and Performance in the Greek Theatre*. London: Routledge.

Artaud, Antonin. 1958. *The Theatre and Its Double*. Trans. M. C. Richards. New York: Grove Press.

Athenaeus. 1927. *The Deipnosophists*. 7 vols. Loeb Classical Library. Cambridge: William Heineman and Harvard University Press.

Auerbach, Erich. 1965. *Literary Language and Its Public in Late Antiquity and in the Middle Ages*. Trans. Ralph Manheim. New York: Bollingen Foundation.

Austin, J. L. 1975 (1962). *How to Do Things With Words*. Ed. J. O. Urmson and Marina Sbisa. Cambridge: Harvard University Press.

Ayrton, Michael. 1977. *Archilochus*. Trans. Michael Ayrton with essay by G. S. Kirk. London: Secker & Warburg.

Bakewell, Geoffrey. 1997a. "Metoikia in the *Supplices* of Aeschylus." *Classical Antiquity* 16, no. 2:205–24.

———. 1997b. " '*Eunous Kai polei soterios metoikos*': Metics, Tragedy, and Civic Ideology." Presented at "Crossing the Stages: The Production, Performance and Reception of Ancient Theatre," University of Saskatchewan, October 23.

Bakhtin, Mikhail. 1981. *The Dialogic Imagination*. Trans. Caryl Emerson and Michael Holquist. Austin: University of Texas Press.

———. 1984a. *Problems in Dostoevsky's Poetics.* Trans. Caryl Emerson. Minneapolis: University of Minnesota Press.

———. 1984b. *Rabelais and His World.* Trans. Helene Iswolsky. Bloomington: Indiana University Press.

———. 1986. *Speech Genres and Other Late Essays.* Trans. Vern W. McGee. Austin: University of Texas Press.

Barba, Eugenio. 1990. "Eurasian Theatre." Trans. Richard Fowler. In *The Dramatic Touch of Difference: Theatre Own and Foreign,* ed. Erika Fischer-Lichte et al. Tübingen: Gunter Narr Verlag.

Barish, Jonas. 1981. *The Antitheatrical Prejudice.* Berkeley: University of California Press.

Barnstone, Willis, and William E. McCulloch, trans. 1962. *Greek Lyric Poetry.* Bloomington: Indiana University Press.

Barthes, Roland. 1985. *The Grain of the Voice.* Trans. Linda Coverdale. New York: Hill and Wang.

Bauman, Richard. 1986. *Story, Performance, and Event: Contextual Studies of Oral Narrative.* Cambridge: Cambridge University Press.

Baumann, Gerd, ed. 1986. *The Written Word: Literacy in Transition.* New York: Oxford University Press.

Beck, Frederick A. G. 1964. *Greek Education.* London: Methuen.

———. 1975. *Album of Greek Education.* Sydney: Cheiron Press.

Beck, M. G. 1993. *Potlatch.* Seattle: Alaska Northwest Books.

Benamou, Michel, and Charles Caramello, eds. 1977. *Performance in Postmodern Culture.* Madison: University of Wisconsin–Milwaukee Press.

Bennett, Benjamin. 1990. *Theatre as Problem: Modern Drama and Its Place in Literature.* Ithaca: Cornell University Press.

Bennett, Susan. 1987. "The Role of the Theatre Audience." Ph.D. diss., MacMaster University.

Beye, Charles Rowan. 1987 (1975). *Ancient Greek Literature and Society.* Ithaca: Cornell University Press.

Bieber, Margarete. 1961 (1939). *The History of the Greek and Roman Theatre.* Princeton: Princeton University Press.

Blau, Herbert. 1992. *To All Appearances: Ideology and Performance.* New York: Routledge, Chapman and Hall.

Bowra, C. M. 1969 (1966). *Landmarks in Greek Literature.* Cleveland: Meridian.

Bowra, C. M., and T. F. Higham. 1950. *The Oxford Book of Greek Verse.* Oxford: Clarendon.

Brask, Per. 1992. "Recovering a Language." In *Aboriginal Voices: Amerindian, Inuit, and Sami Theatre,* ed. Per Brask and William Morgan. Baltimore: Johns Hopkins University Press.

Brask, Per, and William Morgan. 1992. *Aboriginal Voices: Amerindian, Inuit, and Sami Theatre.* Baltimore: Johns Hopkins University Press.

Brecht, Bertolt. 1964. *Brecht on Theatre.* Trans. J. Willet. New York: Hill and Wang.

Bristol, Michael D. 1985. *Carnival and Theatre: Plebeian Culture and the Structure of Authority in Renaissance England*. New York: Methuen.

Brockett, Oscar. 1982. *History of the Theatre*. Boston: Allyn and Bacon.

Burkert, Walter. 1966. "Greek Tragedy and Sacrificial Ritual." *Greek, Roman, and Byzantine Studies* 7:87–129.

Burn, A. R. 1960. *The Lyric Age of Greece*. London: Edward Arnold.

Burns, Alfred. 1981. "Athenian Literacy in the Fifth Century B.C." *Journal of the History of Ideas* 42:371–87.

Bynum, David E. 1981. "Myth and Ritual: Two Faces of Tradition." In *Oral Traditional Literature: A Festschrift for Alfred Bates Lord*, ed. John Miles Foley. Columbus, Ohio: Slavica Publishers.

Calder, William M. III, ed. 1991. *The Cambridge Ritualists Reconsidered*. Atlanta: Scholars Press.

Calhoun, George M. 1944. *Introduction to Greek Legal Science*. Oxford: Clarendon.

Carlson, Marvin. 1984. *Theories of the Theatre*. Ithaca: Cornell University Press.

———. 1990. *Theatre Semiotics: Signs of Life*. Bloomington: Indiana University Press.

Cartledge, Paul. 1978. "Literacy in the Spartan Oligarchy." *Journal of Hellenic Studies* 98:25–37.

Chadwick, John. 1990 (1958). *The Decipherment of Linear B*. Cambridge: Cambridge University Press.

Chafe, Wallace L. 1985. "Linguistic Differences Produced by Differences between Speaking and Writing." In *Literacy, Language, and Learning: The Nature and Consequences of Reading and Writing*, ed. D. R. Olson, N. Torrence, and Angela Hilyard. Cambridge: Cambridge University Press.

Chaikin, Joseph. 1972. *The Presence of the Actor*. New York: Atheneum.

Changeux, Jean-Pierre. 1988. "Learning and Selection in the Nervous System." In *The Alphabet and the Brain*, ed. Derrick de Kerckhove and Charles Lumsden. Berlin: Springer Verlag.

Christy, T. Craig. 1989. "Humboldt on the Semiotics of Writing." In *The Semiotic Bridge: Trends from California*, ed. Irmengard Rauch and Gerald F. Carr. Berlin: Mouton de Gruyter, 1989.

Clanchy, M. T. 1979. *From Memory to Written Record: England, 1066–1307*. Cambridge: Harvard University Press.

Cole, David. 1975. *The Theatrical Event*. Middletown: Wesleyan University Press.

———. 1992. *Acting as Reading: The Place of the Reading Process in the Actor's Work*. Ann Arbor: University of Michigan Press.

Cole, Douglas, and Bradley Lockner, eds. 1993. *To the Charlottes: George Dawson's 1878 Survey of the Queen Charlotte Islands*. Vancouver: University of British Columbia Press.

Cole, Susan Guettel. 1981. "Could Greek Women Read and Write?" *Women's Studies* 8:129–55.

Conacher, D. J. 1967. *Euripidean Drama*. Toronto: University of Toronto Press.

Conquergood, Dwight. 1992. "Performance Theory, Hmong Shamans, and Cultural Politics." In *Critical Theory and Performance*, ed. J. Reinelt and J. Roach. Ann Arbor: University of Michigan Press.

Coulmas, Florian. 1989. *The Writing Systems of the World*. Oxford: Basil Blackwell.

Craig, Edward Gordon. 1956. *On the Art of the Theatre*. New York: Theatre Books.

Cross, Frank Moore. 1989. "The Invention and Development of the Alphabet." In *The Origins of Writing*, ed. W. M. Senner. Lincoln: University of Nebraska Press.

Csapo, Eric, and William J. Slater. 1995. *The Context of Ancient Drama*. Ann Arbor: University of Michigan Press.

Cuddon, J. A. 1991. *A Dictionary of Literary Terms*. Oxford: Blackwell Reference.

Davison, J. A. 1962. "Literature and Literacy in Ancient Greece." *Phoenix* 16, no. 3:141–56

De Francis, John. 1989 (1984). *The Chinese Language*. Honolulu: University of Hawaii Press.

de Kerckhove, Derrick. 1979. "Sur la fonction du théâtre comme agent d'intériorisation des effets de l'alphabet phonétique à Athènes au Vᵉsiècle." *Les Imaginaires II*, no. 10/18:345–68.

——. 1981. "A Theory of Greek Tragedy." *Sub-Stance* 29:23–35.

——. 1982. "Écriture, théâtre, et neurologie" *Études Françaises* 18:109–28.

——. 1983. "Synthèse sensorielle et tragédie: l'éspace dans *Les Perses* d'Eschyle." In *Tragique et tragédie dans la tradition occidentale*, ed. P. Gravel and T. J. Reiss. Montreal:

——. 1988. "Critical Brain Processes Involved in Deciphering the Greek Alphabet." In *The Alphabet and the Brain*, ed. Derrick de Kerckhove and Charles Lumsden. Berlin: Springer Verlag.

de Kerckhove, Derrick, and Charles Lumsden, eds. 1988. *The Alphabet and the Brain*. Berlin: Springer-Verlag.

Delza, Sophia. 1969. "The Classic Chinese Theatre." In *Total Theatre*, ed. E. T. Kirby. New York: E. P. Dutton.

De Marinis, Marco. 1993. *The Semiotics of Performance*. Trans. Aine O'Healy. Bloomington: Indiana University Press.

Derrida, Jacques. 1973. *Speech and Phenomena*. Trans. David B. Allison. Evanston: Northwestern University Press.

——. 1976 (1974). *Of Grammatology*. Trans. Gayatri Chakravorty Spivak. Baltimore: Johns Hopkins University Press.

Diamond, Elin. 1992. "The Violence of the 'We': Politicizing Identification." In *Critical Theory and Performance*, ed. J. Reinelt and J. Roach. Ann Arbor: University of Michigan Press.

Diderot, Denis. 1957. *The Paradox of Acting*. New York: Hill and Wang.

Dillon, Matthew, and Lynda Garland. 1994. *Ancient Greece: Social and Historical Documents from Archaic Times to the Death of Socrates*. London: Routledge.

Diogenes Laertius. 1925. *Lives of Eminent Philosophers.* Trans. R. D. Hicks. London: Heinemann.

Dolan, Jill. 1992. "Practicing Cultural Disruptions." In *Critical Theory and Performance,* ed. J. Reinelt and J. Roach. Ann Arbor: University of Michigan Press.

Dolby, William. 1976. *A History of Chinese Drama.* London: Paul Elek.

Donkin, Ellen. 1992. "Mrs. Siddons Looks Back in Anger: Feminist Historiography for 18th-Century British Theatre." In *Critical Theory and Performance,* ed. J. Reinelt and J. Roach. Ann Arbor: University of Michigan Press.

Donlan, Walter. 1981. "Scale, Value, and Function in the Homeric Economy." *American Journal of Ancient History* 6:101–17.

Dover, K. J. 1972. *Aristophanic Comedy.* Berkeley: University of California Press.

Duggan, Joseph J. 1990. "Formulaic Language and Mode of Creation." In *Oral-Formulaic Theory: A Folklore Casebook,* ed. J. M. Foley. New York: Garland.

Eco, Umberto. 1977. "Semiotics of Theatrical Performance." *TDR* 21:

———. 1984 (1979). *The Role of the Reader.* Bloomington: Indiana University Press.

Edmonds, John Maxwell, ed. and trans. 1957. *The Fragments of Attic Comedy.* Vol 1. Leiden: E. J. Brill.

———. 1964. *Lyra Graeca.* Cambridge: Harvard University Press.

Ehrenberg, Victor. 1975. *From Solon to Socrates.* London: Methuen.

Eisenstein, Elizabeth. 1985. "On the Printing Press as an Agent of Change." In *Literacy, Language, and Learning: The Nature and Consequences of Reading and Writing,* ed. D. R. Olson, N. Torrence, and A. Hildyard. Cambridge: Cambridge University Press.

Elam, Kier. 1980. *The Semiotics of Theatre and Drama.* London: Methuen.

Ellen, William Henri. 1918. *Ibsen in Germany.* Boston: Gorham Press.

Else, G. F. 1965a. *Homer and the Homeric Problem.* Cincinnati: University of Cincinnati Press.

———. 1965b. *The Origin and Early Form of Greek Tragedy.* Cambridge: Harvard University Press.

Elsky, Martin. 1989. *Authorizing Words: Speech, Writing, and Print in the English Renaissance.* Ithaca: Cornell University Press.

Enders, Jody. 1992. *Rhetoric and the Origins of Medieval Drama.* Ithaca: Cornell University Press.

Erp Taalman Kip, A. Maria van. 1990. *Reader and Spectator: Problems in the Interpretation of Greek Tragedy.* Amsterdam: J. C. Gieben.

Felman, Shoshana. 1983. *The Literary Speech Act: Don Juan and J. L. Austin.* Trans. Catherine Porter. Ithaca: Cornell University Press.

Felperin, Howard. 1985. " 'Tongue-tied our queen?' The Deconstruction of Presence in *The Winter's Tale.*" In *Shakespeare and the Question of Theory,* ed. Patricia Parker and Geoffrey Hartman. New York: Methuen.

Fergusson, Francis. 1949. *Idea of a Theater.* Princeton: Princeton University Press.

Filewod, Alan. 1992. "Averting the Colonial Gaze: Notes on Watching Native The-
    atre." In *Aboriginal Voices: Amerindian, Inuit, and Sami Theatre,* ed. Per Brask
    and William Morgan. Baltimore: Johns Hopkins University Press.

Finkel, Leif H. 1988. "Neuronal Group Selection: A Basis for Categorization by the
    Nervous System." In *The Alphabet and the Brain,* ed. Derrick de Kerckhove
    and Charles Lumsden. Berlin: Springer-Verlag.

Finley, M. I. 1968 (1960). *Aspects of Antiquity.* New York: Viking.

——. 1983. *Politics in the Ancient World.* Cambridge: Cambridge University Press.

Finnegan, Ruth. 1977. *Oral Poetry.* Cambridge: Cambridge University Press.

——. 1990. "What Is Oral Literature Anyway? Comments in Light of Some African
    and Other Comparative Material." In *Oral-Formulaic Theory: A Folklore Case-
    book,* ed. J. M. Foley. New York: Garland.

——. 1992. *Oral Traditions and the Verbal Arts.* London: Routledge.

Fischer-Lichte, Erika, et al., eds. 1990. *The Dramatic Touch of Difference. Theatre
    Own and Foreign.* Tübingen: Gunter Narr Verlag.

Flickinger, R. C. 1973 (1918). *The Greek Theatre and Its Drama.* Chicago: University
    of Chicago Press.

Foley, John Miles. 1991. *Immanent Art: From Structure to Meaning in Traditional
    Oral Epic.* Bloomington: Indiana University Press.

Foley, John Miles, ed. 1981. *Oral Traditional Literature: A Festschrift for Albert Bates
    Lord.* Columbus, Ohio: Slavica Publishers.

——. 1986. *Oral Tradition in Literature.* Columbia: University of Missouri Press.

——. 1990. *Oral-Formulaic Theory: A Folklore Casebook.* New York: Garland.

Forte, Jeanie. 1992. "Focus on the Body." In *Critical Theory and Performance,* ed. J.
    Reinelt and J. Roach. Ann Arbor: University of Michigan Press.

Fowler, Robert L. 1987. *The Nature of Early Greek Lyric.* Toronto: University of
    Toronto Press.

——. 1991. "Gilbert Murray: Four (Five) Stages of Greek Religion." In *The Cam-
    bridge Ritualists Reconsidered,* ed. William M. Calder III. Atlanta: Scholars
    Press.

Frazer, Sir James George. 1951 (1922). *The Golden Bough.* New York: Macmillan.

Gagarin, Michael. 1986. *Early Greek Law.* Berkeley: University of California Press.

Garland, Robert. 1990. *The Greek Way of Life.* Ithaca: Cornell University Press.

Garner, Richard. 1990. *From Homer to Tragedy.* London: Routledge.

Garvie, A. F. 1969. *Aeschylus' Supplices: Play and Trilogy.* Cambridge University Press.

Gelb, I. J. 1952. *A Study of Writing: The Foundations of Grammatology.* Chicago: Uni-
    versity of Chicago Press.

Gentili, Bruno. 1988. *Poetry and Its Public in Ancient Greece.* Baltimore: Johns Hop-
    kins University Press.

Gernet, Louis. 1981. *The Anthropology of Ancient Greece.* Trans. John Hamilton, S.J.,
    and Blaise Nagy. Baltimore: Johns Hopkins University Press.

Gjerset, Knut. 1924. *History of Iceland.* New York: Macmillan.

Godzich, Wlad, and Jeffrey Kittay. 1987. *The Emergence of Prose.* Minneapolis: University of Minnesota Press.

Goethe, Johann Wolfgang von. 1986. *Essays on Art and Literature.* Trans. Ellen von Nardroff and Ernest von Nardroff. New York: Suhrkamp.

Goldhill, Simon. 1986. *Reading Greek Tragedy.* Cambridge: Cambridge University Press.

——. 1989. "Reading Performance Criticism." *Greece and Rome* 36, no. 2 (October):172–82.

——. 1990. "The Great Dionysia and Civic Ideology." In *Nothing to Do with Dionysus? Athenian Drama in Its Social Context,* ed. John J. Winkler and Froma Zeitlin. Princeton: Princeton University Press.

Goody, Jack. 1986. *The Logic of Writing and the Organization of Society.* Cambridge: Cambridge University Press.

——. 1987. *The Interface between the Written and the Oral.* Cambridge: Cambridge University Press.

Goody, Jack, ed. 1968. *Literacy in Traditional Societies.* Cambridge: Cambridge University Press.

Gredley, Bernard. 1984. "Greek Tragedy and the 'Discovery' of the Actor." In *Drama and the Actor,* ed. James Redmond. Cambridge: Cambridge University Press.

Green, Richard, and Eric Handley. 1995. *Images of the Greek Theatre.* Austin: University of Texas Press.

Grene, David. 1950. *Greek Political Theory.* Chicago: University of Chicago Press.

Grene, David, and Richmond Lattimore, eds. 1991–92. *The Complete Greek Tragedies.* Chicago: University of Chicago Press.

Grotowsky, Jerzy. 1968. *Towards a Poor Theatre.* New York: Simon and Schuster.

Hadas, Moses. 1954. *Ancilla to Classical Reading.* New York: Columbia University Press.

Hagège, Claude. 1988. "Writing: The Invention and the Dream." In *The Alphabet and the Brain,* ed. Derrick de Kerckhove and Charles Lumsden. Berlin: Springer Verlag.

Halpern, Barbara Kerewsky. 1990. "Genealogy as Oral Genre in a Serbian Village." In *Oral-Formulaic Theory: A Folklore Casebook,* ed. J. M. Foley. New York: Garland.

Handke, Peter. 1969. *Kaspar and Other Plays.* Trans. Michael Roloff. New York: Farrar, Straus and Giroux.

Harris, Roy. 1986. *The Origin of Writing.* London: Gerald Duckworth and Co.

——. 1989. "How Does Writing Restructure Thought?" *Language and Communication* 9, no. 2/3:99–106.

Harris, William V. 1989. *Ancient Literacy.* Cambridge: Harvard University Press.

Harrison, Jane Ellen. 1991 (1903). *Prolegomena to the Study of Greek Religion.* Princeton: Princeton University Press.

Harvey, F. D. 1966. "Literacy in the Athenian Democracy." *Revue des Études Grècques* 79, 2, no. 376/378:585–635.

Hatto, A. T., ed. 1980. *Traditions of Heroic and Epic Poetry.* 2 vols. London: Modern Humanities Research Association.

Havelock, Eric A. 1963. *Preface to Plato.* Cambridge: Belknap Press of Harvard University Press.

———. 1977. "The Preliteracy of the Greeks." *New Literary History* 8:369–91.

———. 1986. *The Muse Learns to Write.* New Haven: Yale University Press.

Havelock, E. A., and J. P. Hershbell, eds. 1978. *Communication Arts in the Ancient World.* New York: Hastings House.

Hazlitt, William. 1930–34. *The Complete Works.* Ed. P. P. Howe. 21 vols. London: J. M. Dent.

Hegel, G. W. F. 1975. *Aesthetics.* Trans. T. M. Knox. Oxford: Clarendon Press.

Heidegger, Martin. 1962. *Being and Time.* Trans. John Macquarrie and Edward Robinson. New York: Harper and Row.

Henderson, Jeffrey. 1990. "The Demos and Comic Competition." In *Nothing to Do with Dionysus? Athenian Drama in Its Social Context,* ed. John J. Winkler and Froma Zeitlin. Princeton: Princeton University Press.

Herington, John. 1985. *Poetry into Drama.* Berkeley: University of California Press.

Hermans, Hubert J. M., et al. 1992. "The Dialogical Self: Beyond Individualism and Rationalism." *American Psychologist* 47, no. 1 (January):23–33.

Herodotus. 1987. *The History.* Trans. David Grene. Chicago: University of Chicago Press.

Herondas. 1981. *The Mimes of Herondas.* Trans. Guy Davenport. San Francisco: Grey Fox Press.

Hesiod. 1967. *Fragmenta Hesiodea,* ed. R. Merkelbach and M. L. West. London: Oxford University Press.

———. 1973. *Theogony.* Trans. Dorothea Wender. London: Penguin.

Highway, Tomson. 1988. *The Rez Sisters.* Saskatoon: Fifth House.

Hsu Tao-Ching. 1985. *The Chinese Conception of the Theatre.* Seattle: University of Washington Press.

Hsun Lu. 1959. *A Brief History of Chinese Fiction.* Trans. Yang Hsien-Yi and Gladys Yang. Peking: Foreign Languages Press.

Humboldt, Wilhelm von. 1988 (1836). *On Language: The Diversity of Human Language Structure and Its Influence on the Mental Development of Mankind.* Trans. Peter Heath. Cambridge: Cambridge University Press.

Humphreys, S. C. 1978. *Anthropologies and the Greeks.* London: Routledge and Kegan Paul.

———. 1985. "Social Relations on Stage: Witnesses in Classical Athens." *History and Anthropology* 1:313–69.

Hunter, I. M. L. 1964 (1957). *Memory.* London: Penguin.

Ihde, Don. 1993. *Philosophy of Technology.* New York: Paragon House Publishers.

Immerwahr, Henry R. 1964. "Book Rolls on Attic Vases." In *Classical, Mediaeval, and Renaissance Studies in Honour of Berthold Louis Ullman.* Rome: Edizioni di Storia e Litteratura.

Ingarden, Roman. 1973. *The Literary Work of Art.* Trans. George G. Grabowicz. Evanston: Northwestern University Press.

Innes, Christopher. 1981. *Holy Theatre: Ritual and the Avant Garde.* Cambridge: Cambridge University Press.

Iser, Wolfgang. 1978. *The Act of Reading.* Baltimore: Johns Hopkins University Press.

Jaeger, Werner. 1960 (1939). *Paideia: The Ideals of Greek Culture.* Trans. Gilbert Highet. 3 vols. New York: Oxford University Press.

Jeffrey, L. H. 1990 (1961). *The Local Scripts of Archaic Greece.* Oxford: Oxford University Press.

Jones, John R. Melville. 1993. *Testimonia Numeria: Greek and Latin Texts Concerning Ancient Greek Coinage.* Vol. 1. London: Spink.

Jousse, Marcel. 1990. *The Oral Style.* Trans. Edgard Sienaert and Richard Whitaker. New York: Garland.

Kalmár, Ivan. 1985. "Are There Really No Primitive Languages?" In *Literacy, Language, and Learning: The Nature and Consequences of Reading and Writing,* ed. D. R. Olson, N. Torrence, and A. Hildyard. Cambridge: Cambridge University Press.

Kassel, Rudolf. 1965. *Aristotelis De Arte Poetica Liber.* Oxford: Oxford University Press.

Kirby, E. T. 1969. *Total Theatre.* New York: E. P. Dutton.

Kirby, Michael. 1982. "Nonsemiotic Performance." *Modern Drama* 25 (March):105.

Kirk, G. S. 1970. *Myth: Its Meaning and Functions in Ancient and Other Cultures.* Cambridge: Cambridge University Press.

———. 1985 (1974). *The Nature of Greek Myths.* Harmondsworth: Penguin.

Kirk, G. S., J. E. Raven, and M. Schofield. 1987. *The Presocratic Philosophers.* Cambridge: Cambridge University Press.

Knox, Bernard. 1968. "Silent Reading in Antiquity." *Greek, Roman, and Byzantine Studies* 9:421–35.

———. 1983. "Greece à la Française." *New York Review of Books* 30, no. 3:26–30.

Kobialka, Michael. 1988. "The Quem Quaeritis: Theatre History Displacement." *Theatre History Studies* 8:35–51.

Kraay, Colin M. 1976. *Archaic and Classical Greek Coins.* Berkeley: University of California Press.

Kristeva, Julia. 1989. *Language: The Unknown.* Trans. Anne M. Menke. New York: Columbia University Press.

Kurzon, Dennis. 1986. *It Is Hereby Performed: Explorations in Legal Speech Acts.* Amsterdam: John Benjamins.

Lafont, Robert. 1988. "Relationships between Speech and Writing Systems in Ancient Alphabets and Syllabaries." In *The Alphabet and the Brain,* ed. Derrick de Kerckhove and Charles Lumsden. Berlin: Springer-Verlag.

Lakoff, Robin. 1972. "Language in Context." *Language* 48, no. 4:907–27.

Lamberton, Robert, and John J. Keaney, eds. 1992. *Homer's Ancient Readers.* Princeton: Princeton University Press.

Lattimore, Richmond. 1964. *Story Patterns in Greek Tragedy.* Ann Arbor: University of Michigan Press.

——, trans. 1951. *The Iliad of Homer.* Chicago: University of Chicago Press.

——. 1977 (1965). *The Odyssey of Homer.* New York: Harper and Row.

——. 1992. "Introduction to *Iphigenia in Tauris.*" In *The Complete Greek Tragedies* ed. David Grene and Richmond Lattimore. Chicago: University of Chicago Press.

Lentz, Tony M. 1989. *Orality and Literacy in Hellenic Greece.* Carbondale: Southern Illinois University Press.

Lesher, J. H. 1992. *Xenophanes of Colophon: Fragments.* Toronto: University of Toronto Press.

Lévi-Strauss, Claude. 1982. *The Way of Masks.* Trans. Sylvia Modelski. Seattle: University of Washington Press.

Liddell, Henry George, and Robert Scott. 1983 (1859). *A Lexicon Abridged from Liddell and Scott's Greek-English Lexicon.* Oxford: Clarendon.

Linell, Per. 1988. "The Impact of Literacy on the Conception of Language: The Case of Linguistics." In *The Written Word: Studies in Literate Thought and Action,* ed. Roger Saljo. Berlin: Springer-Verlag.

Lloyd, G. E. R. 1990. *Demystifying Mentalities.* Cambridge: Cambridge University Press.

Lock, Andrew, ed. 1978. *Action, Gesture, and Symbol: The Emergence of Language.* London: Academic Press.

Loftus, Elizabeth F. 1979. *Eyewitness Testimony.* Cambridge: Harvard University Press.

——. 1980. *Memory.* Reading, Mass.: Addison-Wesley.

Logan, Robert. 1986. *The Alphabet Effect: The Impact of the Phonetic Alphabet on the Development of Western Civilization.* New York: St. Martin's.

Lord, Albert Bates. 1960. *The Singer of Tales.* Cambridge: Harvard University Press.

——. 1981. "Memory, Fixity, and Genre in Oral Traditional Poetries." In *Oral Traditional Literature: A Festschrift for Albert Bates Lord,* ed. John Miles Foley. Columbus, Ohio: Slavica Publishers.

——. 1986. "The Merging of Two Worlds: Oral and Written Poetry as Carriers of Ancient Values." In *Oral Tradition in Literature,* ed. John Miles Foley. Columbia: University of Missouri Press.

——. 1990. "Perspectives on Recent Work on the Oral Traditional Formula." In *Oral-Formulaic Theory: A Folklore Casebook,* ed. J. M. Foley. New York: Garland.

——. 1991. *Epic Singers and Oral Tradition.* Ithaca: Cornell University Press.

Lorimer, H. L. 1948. "Homer and the Art of Writing." *American Journal of Archaeology.* 52:11–23.

Luria, A. R. 1981. *Language and Cognition.* Ed. James V. Wertsch. Washington, D.C.: V. H. Winston.

Lyotard, Jean-François. 1977. "The Unconscious as *Mise-en-scène.*" Trans. Joseph Maier. In *Performance in Postmodern Culture,* ed. Michel Benamou and Charles Caramello. Madison: University of Wisconsin–Milwaukee Press.

Maitland, Frederic William, ed. 1891. *The Court Baron.* London: B. Quaritch.

Matejka, Ladislav, and Irwin Titunik. 1976. *Semiotics of Art: Prague School Contributions.* Cambridge: MIT Press.

May, Keith M. 1990. *Nietzsche and the Spirit of Tragedy.* London: Macmillan.

McLuhan, Marshall. 1964. *Understanding Media.* New York: McGraw Hill.

Meier, Christian. 1990. *The Greek Discovery of Politics.* Trans. David McLintock. Cambridge: Harvard University Press.

Miller, Paul Allen. 1994. *Lyric Texts and Lyric Consciousness.* London: Routledge.

Morgan, William. 1992. "The Trickster and Native Theatre: An Interview with Tomson Highway." In *Aboriginal Voices: Amerindian, Inuit, and Sami Theatre,* ed. Per Brask and William Morgan. Baltimore: Johns Hopkins University Press.

Moses, D. D. and Terry Goldie, eds. 1992. *An Anthology of Canadian Native Literature in English.* Toronto: Oxford University Press.

Mukarovsky, Jan. 1978 (1977). *Structure, Sign, Function.* Trans. John Burbank and Peter Steiner. New Haven: Yale University Press.

Müller, F. Max. 1976 (1881). *Selected Essays on Language, Mythology, and Religion.* 2 vols. New York: AMS Press.

Murko, Matija. 1990. "The Singers and Their Epic Songs." In *Oral-Formulaic Theory: A Folklore Casebook,* ed. J. M. Foley. New York: Garland.

Murray, Gilbert. 1907 (1897). *A History of Ancient Greek Literature.* London: Heinemann.

Myres, John L. 1958. *Homer and His Critics.* London: Routledge and Kegan Paul.

Nagler, A. M. 1952. *A Source Book in Theatrical History.* New York: Dover.

Nagler, Michael N. 1990. "The Traditional Phrase: Theory of Production." In *Oral-Formulaic Theory: A Folklore Casebook,* ed. J. M. Foley. New York: Garland.

Nagy, Gregory. 1981. "An Evolutionary Model for the Text Fixation of Homeric Epos." In *Oral Traditional Literature: A Festschrift for Albert Bates Lord,* ed. John Miles Foley. Columbus: Slavica Publishers.

———. 1986. "Ancient Greek Epic and Praise Poetry: Some Typological Considerations." In *Oral Tradition in Literature,* ed. John Miles Foley. Columbia: University of Missouri Press.

Natoli, Joseph, ed. 1989. *Literary Theory's Future(s).* Urbana: University of Illinois Press.

Nauck, August. 1964. *Tragicorum Graecorum Fragmenta.* With supplement by Bruno Snell. Hildesheim: Georg Olms Verlag.

Naveh, Joseph. 1988. "The Origin of the Greek Alphabet." In *The Alphabet and the Brain,* ed. Derrick de Kerckhove and Charles Lumsden. Berlin: Springer-Verlag.

Nietzsche, Friedrich. 1956. *The Birth of Tragedy.* Trans. Francis Golffing. New York: Doubleday.

Nilsson, Martin P. 1968 (1933). *Homer and Mycenae.* New York: Cooper Square.

O'Barr, William M. 1982. *Linguistic Evidence: Language, Power, and Strategy in the Courtroom.* New York: Academic Press.

Ober, Josiah, and Barry Strauss. 1990. "Drama, Political Rhetoric, and the Discourse of the Athenian Democracy." In *Nothing to Do with Dionysus? Athenian Drama in Its Social Context,* ed. John J. Winkler and Froma Zeitlin. Princeton: Princeton University Press.

Olson, David R. 1985. "Introduction." In *Literacy, Language, and Learning: The Nature and Consequences of Reading and Writing,* ed. David Olson, Nancy Torrence, and Angela Hildyard. Cambridge: Cambridge University Press.

———. 1988. "Mind, Media, and Memory: The Archival and Epistemic Functions of the Written Text." In *The Alphabet and the Brain,* ed. Derrick de Kerckhove and Charles Lumsden. Berlin: Springer-Verlag.

Olson, D. R., Nancy Torrence, and Angela Hildyard, eds. 1985. *Literacy, Language, and Learning: The Nature and Consequences of Reading and Writing.* Cambridge: Cambridge University Press.

O'Neill, John. 1985. *Five Bodies: The Human Shape of Modern Society.* Ithaca: Cornell University Press.

Ong, Walter J. 1977. *Interfaces of the Word.* Ithaca: Cornell University Press.

———. 1982. *Orality and Literacy: The Technologizing of the Word.* London: Methuen.

Orgel, Stephen. 1988. "The Authentic Shakespeare" *Representations* 21 (Winter):1.

Ostwald, Martin. 1986. *From Popular Sovereignty to the Sovereignty of Law: Law, Society, and Politics in Fifth-Century Athens.* Berkeley: University of California Press.

O'Sullivan, Neil. 1996. "Written and Spoken in the First Sophistic." In *Voice into Text: Orality and Literacy in Ancient Greece,* ed. Ian Worthington. Leiden: E. J. Brill.

Padel, Ruth. 1990. "Making Space Speak." In *Nothing to Do with Dionysus?,* ed. John J. Winkler and Froma I. Zeitlin. Princeton: Princeton University Press.

Page, Denys L. 1962. *Select Papyri.* Vol. 3. Cambridge and London: Harvard University Press and William Heinemann.

———. 1987 (1934). *Actors' Interpolations in Greek Tragedy.* New York: Garland.

Palmer, Richard. 1977. "Postmodern Hermeneutics of Performance." In *Performance in Postmodern Culture,* ed. Michel Benamou and Charles Caramello. Madison: University of Wisconsin–Milwaukee Press.

Parke, Herbert William. 1967. *Greek Oracles.* London: Hutchinson.

Parker, Patricia, and Geoffrey Hartman, eds. 1985. *Shakespeare and the Question of Theory.* New York: Methuen.

Parry, Adam, ed. 1971. *The Making of Homeric Verse: The Collected Papers of Milman Parry.* Oxford: Clarendon.

———. 1989. *The Language of Achilles and Other Papers.* Oxford: Clarendon.

Pausanias. 1965. *Description of Greece.* Trans. J. G. Frazer. New York: Biblo and Tannen.

Pavis, Patrice. 1982. *Languages of the Stage.* New York: Performing Arts Journal Publications.

Peacock, Sandra J. 1991. "An Awful Warmth about Her Heart: The Personal in Jane Harrison's Ideas about Religion." In *The Cambridge Ritualists Reconsidered,* ed. William M. Calder III. Atlanta: Scholars Press.

Petrone, Penny. 1990. *Native Literature in Canada: From the Oral Tradition to the Present.* Toronto: Oxford University Press.

Pfeiffer, Rudolf. 1968. *History of Classical Scholarship.* Oxford: Clarendon.

Pfister, Manfred. 1988. *The Theory and Analysis of Drama.* Trans. John Halliday. New York: Cambridge University Press.

Pickard-Cambridge, Arthur W. 1962 (1927). *Dithyramb, Tragedy, and Comedy.* Oxford: Oxford University Press.

———. 1968. *The Dramatic Festivals of Athens.* Oxford University Press.

Plato. 1955. *Hipparchus.* Loeb Classical Library. Cambridge: Harvard University Press.

———. 1962. *Ion.* Loeb Classical Library. Cambridge: Harvard University Press.

———. 1968. *The Republic of Plato.* Trans. Allan Bloom. New York: Basic Books.

———. 1986a. *Phaedrus.* Trans. C. J. Rowe. Warminster, England: Aris and Phillips.

———. 1986b. *Theaetetus.* Trans. Seth Benardete. Chicago: University of Chicago Press.

———. 1996. *Protagoras, Philebus, and Gorgias.* Trans. Benjamin Jowett. New York: Prometheus Books.

Podlecki, Anthony J. 1966. *The Political Background of Aeschylean Tragedy.* Ann Arbor: University of Michigan Press.

———. 1984. *The Early Greek Poets and Their Times.* Vancouver: University of British Columbia Press.

Pomeroy, Susan B. 1975. *Goddesses, Whores, Wives, and Slaves: Women in Classical Antiquity.* New York: Dorset Press.

Powell, Barry B. 1991. *Homer and the Origin of the Greek Alphabet.* Cambridge: Cambridge University Press.

Pratt, Mary Louise. 1977. *Toward a Speech Act Theory of Literary Discourse.* Bloomington: Indiana University Press.

Purdy, Anthony, ed. 1992. *Literature and the Body.* Amsterdam and Atlanta: Editions Rodopi B.U.

Raschke, Wendy J., ed. 1988. *The Archaeology of the Olympics: The Olympics and Other Festivals in Antiquity.* Madison: University of Wisconsin Press.

Redmond, James. 1984. *Drama and the Actor.* Cambridge: Cambridge University Press.

Reinelt, Janelle G., and Joseph R. Roach, eds. 1992. *Critical Theory and Performance.* Ann Arbor: University of Michigan Press.

Reynolds, L. D., and N. G. Wilson. 1968. *Scribes and Scholars.* Oxford: Clarendon.

Rhodes, P. J. 1986. *The Greek City States: A Sourcebook.* Norman: University of Oklahoma Press.

Richardson, N. J. 1992. "Aristotle's Reading of Homer and Its Background." In *Homer's Ancient Readers,* ed. R. Lamberton and J. J. Keaney. Princeton: Princeton University Press.

Ricoeur, Paul. 1981. *Hermeneutics and The Human Sciences.* Trans. John B. Thompson. Cambridge: Cambridge University Press.

Robb, Kevin. 1994. *Literacy and Paideia in Ancient Greece.* New York: Oxford University Press.

Rothenberg, Jerome. 1977. "New Models, New Visions: Some Notes toward a Poetics of Performance." In *Performance in Postmodern Culture,* ed. Michel Benamou and Charles Caramello. Madison: University of Wisconsin–Milwaukee Press.

Rowe, C. J. 1986. *Phaedrus: Translation and Commentary.* Warminster, England: Aris and Phillips.

Safire, William. 1992. *Lend Me Your Ears: Great Speeches in History.* New York: W. W. Norton.

Saljo, Roger, ed. 1988. *The Written Word: Studies in Literate Thought and Action.* Berlin: Springer-Verlag.

Sallis, John. 1991. *Crossings: Nietzsche and the Space of Tragedy.* Chicago: University of Chicago Press.

Sandys, Sir John Edwin. 1958. *A History of Classical Scholarship.* Vol. 1. New York: Hafner.

Sapir, Edward. 1949 (1921). *Language.* New York: Harcourt Brace.

Saussure, Ferdinand de. 1974 (1959). *Course in General Linguistics.* Trans. Wade Baskin. London: Fontana.

Schechner, Richard. 1971. "Actuals." *Theatre Quarterly* 1, no. 2 (Spring):49–66.

———. 1973. *Environmental Theatre.* New York: Hawthorne Books.

———. 1977. *Essays on Performance Theory.* New York: Drama Book Specialists.

Schechner, Richard, and Mady Schuman, eds. 1976. *Ritual, Play, and Performance.* New York: Seabury Press.

Schlegel, A. W. 1914. *Lectures on Dramatic Art and Literature.* Trans. John Black. London: Bohn Library.

Schlegel, Friedrich. 1880. *Lectures on the History of Literature.* London: George Bell and Sons.

———. 1957. *Literary Notebooks, 1797–1801.* Ed. Hans Eichner. London: Athlone Press.

———. 1968. *Dialogue on Poetry and Literary Aphorisms.* Trans. Ernst Behler and Roman Struc. University Park: Penn State University Press.

Schlesier, Renate. 1991. "Prolegomena to Jane Harrison's Interpretation of Ancient Greek Religion." Trans. Michael Armstrong. In *The Cambridge Ritualists Reconsidered,* ed. William M. Calder III. Atlanta: Scholars Press.

Schmandt-Besserat, Denise. 1989. "Two Precursors of Writing: Plain and Complex Tokens." In *The Origins of Writing,* ed. W. M. Senner. Lincoln: University of Nebraska Press.

Scinto, Leonard F. M. 1986. *Written Language and Psychological Development.* London: Academic Press.

Scribner, Sylvia, and Michael Cole. 1981. *The Psychology of Literacy.* Cambridge: Harvard University Press.

Seaford, Richard. 1994. *Reciprocity and Ritual: Homer and Tragedy in the Developing City-State.* Oxford: Clarendon.

Seale, David. 1982. *Vision and Stagecraft in Sophocles.* Chicago: University of Chicago Press.

Searle, J. R. 1975. "The Logical Status of Fictional Discourse." *New Literary History* 5:328.

———. 1992 (1969). *Speech Acts.* Cambridge: Cambridge University Press.

Segal, Charles. 1986. *Interpreting Greek Tragedy.* Ithaca: Cornell University Press.

———. 1992. "Bard and Audience in Homer." In *Homer's Ancient Readers,* ed. R. Lamberton and J. J. Keaney. Princeton: Princeton University Press.

Senner, Wayne M. 1989. *The Origins of Writing.* Lincoln: University of Nebraska Press.

Shakespeare, William. 1965. *The Complete Works.* Ed. W. J. Craig. Oxford: Oxford University Press.

Shrimpton, Gordon. 1997. *History and Memory in Ancient Greece.* Montreal: McGill–Queen's University Press.

Silk, M. S., and J. P. Stern. 1981. *Nietzsche on Tragedy.* Cambridge: Cambridge University Press.

Simon, John. 1975. *Singularities.* New York: Random House.

Slater, Niall. 1990. "The Idea of the Actor." In *Nothing to Do with Dionysus? Athenian Drama in Its Social Context,* ed. John J. Winkler and Froma Zeitlin. Princeton: Princeton University Press.

———. 1996. "Literacy and Old Comedy." In *Voice into Text: Orality and Literacy in Ancient Greece,* ed. Ian Worthington. Leiden: E. J. Brill.

Sommerstein, Alan H. 1982–85. *The Comedies of Aristophanes.* Vols. 3–5. Warminster, England: Aris and Phillips.

Sörbom, Göran. 1966. *Mimesis and Art.* Stockholm: Bonniers.

Stallybrass, Peter, and Allon White. 1986. *The Politics and Poetics of Transgression.* Ithaca: Cornell University Press.

States, Bert O. 1985. *Great Reckonings in Little Rooms: On the Phenomenology of Theatre.* Berkeley: University of California Press.

Steiner, Deborah Tarn. 1994. *The Tyrant's Writ: Myths and Images of Writing in Ancient Greece.* Princeton: Princeton University Press.

Steiner, George. 1977. *Language and Silence.* New York: Atheneum.

Stock, Brian. 1983. *The Implications of Literacy: Written Language and Models of Interpretation in the Eleventh and Twelfth Centuries.* Princeton: Princeton University Press.

Stockton, David. 1990. *The Classical Athenian Democracy.* Oxford: Oxford University Press.

Stone, George Winchester, Jr., and George M. Kahrl. 1979. *David Garrick.* Carbondale: Southern Illinois University Press.

Stott, John C., et al. 1993. *The HBJ Anthology of Literature.* Toronto: Harcourt Brace Jovanovich.

Street, Brian V. 1988. "Literacy Practices and Literacy Myths." In *The Written Word: Studies in Literate Thought and Action,* ed. Roger Saljo. Berlin: Springer-Verlag.

Stroud, Ronald S. 1989. "The Art of Writing in Ancient Greece." In *The Origins of Writing,* ed. W. M. Senner. Lincoln: University of Nebraska Press.

Svenbro, Jesper. 1990. "The 'Interior' Voice: On the Invention of Silent Reading." In *Nothing to Do with Dionysus? Athenian Drama in Its Social Context,* ed. John J. Winkler and Froma Zeitlin. Princeton: Princeton University Press.

Szondi, Peter. 1986. *On Textual Understanding and Other Essays.* Trans. Harvey Mendelsohn. Minneapolis: University of Minnesota Press.

———. 1987. *Theory of the Modern Drama.* Trans. Michael Hays. Minneapolis: University of Minnesota Press.

Taplin, Oliver, 1977. *The Stagecraft of Aeschylus.* Oxford: Oxford University Press.

———. 1978. *Greek Tragedy in Action.* London: Methuen.

Taylor, Insup. 1988. "Psychology of Literacy: East and West." In *The Alphabet and the Brain,* ed. Derrick de Kerckhove and Charles Lumsden. Berlin: Springer-Verlag.

Thomas, Carol G. 1977. "Literacy and the Codification of Law." *Studia et Documenta Historiae et Juris* 43:455-58.

———. 1996. "Wingy Mysteries in Divinity." In *Voice into Text: Orality and Literacy in Ancient Greece,* ed. Ian Worthington. Leiden: E. J. Brill.

Thomas, Rosalind. 1989. *Oral Tradition and Written Record in Classical Athens.* Cambridge: Cambridge University Press.

———. 1992. *Literacy and Orality in Ancient Greece.* Cambridge: Cambridge University Press.

Thomson, Peter. 1994. *Shakespeare's Professional Career.* Cambridge: Cambridge University Press.

Thucydides. 1954. *History of the Peloponnesian War.* Trans. Rex Warner. London: Penguin.

Todorov, Tzvetan. 1982a. *Theories of the Symbol.* Trans. Catherine Porter. Ithaca: Cornell University Press.

——. 1982b. "French Poetics Today." In *French Literary Theory Today,* ed. Tzvetan Todorov. Trans. R. Carter. Cambridge: Cambridge University Press.

Turner, E. G. 1951. *Athenian Books in the Fifth and Fourth Centuries B.C.* London: H. K. Lewis.

——. 1965. "Athenians Learn to Write: Plato *Protagoras* 326d." *Bulletin of the University of London Institute of Classical Studies* 12:65–67.

——. 1971. *Greek Manuscripts of the Ancient World.* Oxford: Clarendon.

Turner, Victor. 1974. *Dramas, Fields, and Metaphors.* Ithaca: Cornell University Press.

Ubersfeld, Anne. 1978. *Lire le théâtre.* Paris: Editions Sociales.

Udall, Nicholas. 1912. *Ralph Roister Doister.* Ed. C. G. Child. Boston: Houghton Mifflin.

Underhill, Ruth Murray. 1938. *Singing for Power.* Berkeley: University of California Press.

Vanderpool, Eugene. 1970. *Ostracism at Athens.* Cincinnati: University of Cincinnati Press.

Vansina, Jan. 1985. *Oral Tradition as History.* Madison: University of Wisconsin Press.

Veltrusky, Jiri. 1964. "Man and Object in the Theatre." In *A Prague School Reader on Esthetics, Literary Structure, and Style,* trans. Paul L. Garvin. Washington, D.C.: Georgetown University Press.

——. 1977. *Drama as Literature.* Lisse: Peter de Ridder Press.

Vernant, Jean-Pierre. 1978. "Ambiguity and Reversal: On the Enigmatic Structure of *Oedipus Rex.*" *New Literary History* 9 (Spring):475–501.

Vernant, Jean-Pierre, and Pierre Vidal-Naquet. 1990. *Myth and Tragedy in Ancient Greece.* Trans. Janet Lloyd. New York: Zone Books.

Vickers, Brian. 1973. *Towards Greek Tragedy.* London: Longman.

Vygotsky, Lev. 1978. *Mind in Society: The Development of Higher Psychological Processes.* Ed. Michael Cole et al. Cambridge: Harvard University Press.

——. 1992. *Thought and Language.* Trans. Alex Kozulin. Cambridge: MIT Press.

Wade-Gery, H. T. 1952. *The Poet of the Iliad.* Cambridge: Cambridge University Press.

Walter, Bettyruth. 1988. *The Jury Summation as Speech Genre.* Amsterdam: John Benjamins.

Webster, T. B. L. 1959. *Greek Art and Literature, 700–530 B.C.* Westport, Conn.: Greenwood Press.

Weijie, Yu. 1990. "Topicality and Typicality: The Acceptance of Shakespeare in

China." In *The Dramatic Touch of Difference: Theatre Own and Foreign,* ed. Erika Fischer-Lichte et al. Tübingen: Gunter Narr Verlag.

Weimann, Robert. 1978. *Shakespeare and the Popular Tradition in the Theatre.* Ed. Robert Schwartz. Baltimore: Johns Hopkins University Press.

Weiser, Joshua. 1992. "Indigenous Theatre." In *Aboriginal Voices: Amerindian, Inuit, and Sami Theatre,* ed. Per Brask and William Morgan. Baltimore: Johns Hopkins University Press.

Wellbery, David E. 1984. *Lessing's Laocoon: Semiotics and Aesthetics in the Age of Reason.* Cambridge: Cambridge University Press.

Wellek, René. 1981. *A History of Modern Criticism,* 1750–1950. Cambridge: Cambridge University Press.

Wheeler, Jordan. 1992. "Voice." In *Aboriginal Voices: Amerindian, Inuit, and Sami Theatre,* ed. Per Brask and William Morgan. Baltimore: Johns Hopkins University Press.

Whitaker, Richard. 1996. "Orality and Literacy in the Poetic Traditions of Archaic Greece and Southern Africa." In *Voice into Text: Orality and Literacy in Ancient Greece,* ed. Ian Worthington. Leiden: E. J. Brill.

White, Allon. 1993. *Carnival, Hysteria, and Writing.* Oxford: Clarendon.

Whiteman, Marcia Farr, ed. 1981. *Writing: The Nature, Development, and Teaching of Written Communication.* Lawrence Erlbaum.

Whitman, Cedric. 1951. *Sophocles.* Cambridge: Harvard University Press.

Wiles, Timothy J. 1980. *The Theatre Event: Modern Theories of Performance.* Chicago: University of Chicago Press.

Willcock, M. M. 1990. "The Search for the Poet Homer." *Greece and Rome* 37, no. 1 (April):1–13.

Winchester, Ian. 1985. "Atlantans, Centaurians, and the Litron Bomb." In *Literacy, Language, and Learning: The Nature and Consequences of Reading and Writing,* ed. D. R. Olson, N. Torrence, and A. Hildyard. Cambridge: Cambridge University Press.

Winkler, John J. 1990. "The Ephebes' Song: Tragoidia and Polis." In *Nothing to Do with Dionysus? Athenian Drama in Its Social Context,* ed. John J. Winkler and Froma Zeitlin. Princeton: Princeton University Press.

Winkler, John J., and Froma Zeitlin, eds. 1990. *Nothing to Do with Dionysus? Athenian Drama in Its Social Context.* Princeton: Princeton University Press.

Wise, Jennifer. 1989. "Marginalizing Drama: Bakhtin's Theory of Genre." *Essays in Theatre* 8, no. 1 (November):15–22.

Wood, Robert. 1976 (1769). *An Essay on the Original Genius of Homer.* Hildesheim: Georg Olms Verlag.

Woodbury, Leonard. 1976. "Aristophanes' *Frogs* and Athenian Literacy: *Ran.* 52–53, 1114." *Transactions of the American Philological Association* 106:349–57.

Worthington, Ian, ed. 1996. *Voice into Text: Orality and Literacy in Ancient Greece.* Leiden: E. J. Brill.

Yangzhong, Ding. 1990. "On the Insatiable Appetite and Longevity of Theatre." In *The Dramatic Touch of Difference: Theatre Own and Foreign,* ed. Erika Fischer-Lichte et al. Tübingen: Gunter Narr Verlag.

Yates, Frances A. 1966. *The Art of Memory.* Chicago: University of Chicago Press.

Zeitlin, Froma I. 1990. "Playing the Other: Theater, Theatricality, and the Feminine in Greek Drama." In *Nothing to Do with Dionysus? Athenian Drama in Its Social Context,* ed. John J. Winkler and Froma Zeitlin. Princeton: Princeton University Press.

Index

Performing Rites

Simon Frith

Performing

On the Value of Popular Music

Rites

Oxford University Press

1996

This book is for Gill.

Oxford University Press, Walton Street, Oxford OX2 6DP
Oxford New York
Athens Auckland Bangkok Bogota Bombay
Buenos Aires Calcutta Cape Town Dar es Salaam
Delhi Florence Hong Kong Istanbul Karachi
Kuala Lumpur Madras Madrid Melbourne
Mexico City Nairobi Paris Singapore
Taipei Tokyo Toronto
and associated companies in
Berlin Ibadan

Oxford is a trade mark of Oxford University Press

© Simon Frith 1996

British Library Cataloguing in Publication Data
Data available

Library of Congress Cataloging in Publication Data
Data available
ISBN 0-19-816332-0

Printed in the United States of America

Contents

Acknowledgments

The arguments in this book started as a course on the aesthetics of popular music at McGill University in Montreal in 1987. I'm grateful to my students for their help and tolerance, to the Graduate Program in Communications for inviting me to Canada, and to Will Straw and Sylvie Roux for all the talk, love, and music. I further developed my ideas (and took the opportunity to bury myself in a wonderful library) while a Senior Fellow at the Society for the Humanities, Cornell University, in 1991. I'm grateful to Jonathan Culler and Martin Hatch for this opportunity; to the students in my course on "The Good and Bad in Popular Culture"; to my fellow followers of pop fashion, Alex Doty, Karal Ann Marling, Rachel Bowlby, Jane Feuer, Nöel Carroll, and Sally Banes; and to Aggie Sirrine, Mary Ahl, and Linda Allen for making our time in the A. D. White House such fun. The first draft of the book was written while I was the visiting Bonnier Professor of Journalism at the University of Stockholm in 1994. My thanks to Peter Dahlgren and Mark Cormerford for their hospitality, to Marianne and Philippa Scheffold for a room of my own (in a house full of friendship), and to Johan Fornäs, Hillevi Ganetz, and Roger and Goral Wallis for sounds, food, and argument.

My graduate students at the John Logie Baird Centre since 1989 will, I hope, recognize how much they've contributed to my understanding of popular music, and I'm very grateful also to my colleagues John Caughie (for his unflagging enthusiasm for our work) and Sandra Kemp (for making me think properly about performance). None of this would be possible without the support of Margaret Philips, who, among other things, keeps us from taking ourselves too seriously.

In writing this I have become increasingly aware of my dependence on the work of IASPM (the International Association for the Study of Popular Music) and *Popular Music*. I'm proud to have been closely associated with both, and I hope that my intellectual debts to my fellow scholars are evident in what follows.

Many of my ideas on the value of popular music were first floated in my Britbeat column in the *Village Voice*, and I'm grateful to my editors there— Doug Simmons, Joe Levy, and Robert Christgau—for giving them a clearer shape. I've also learned much from my role as chair of the Mercury Music Prize—thanks to my fellow judges for the disputes, and to David Wilkinson, Robert Chandler, and Samm Gibson for the support. My editor at Harvard University Press, Lindsay Waters, has been more patient than even an academic author could expect; I'm grateful for his faith that there was a book here somewhere, and to Bruce Phillips at Oxford University Press for his graceful agreement.

As ever, my thoughts on music (and much else) have been much stimulated and challenged by my friends Jon Savage, Greil Marcus, and Gill Frith, and I am particularly in debt to a friend I've never met, Frank Kogan, for a correspondence that has made me, again and again, stop and rethink. Finally, Deborah Cameron and Wendy Wolf read my original manuscript with as sharp and critical eyes as I could wish—if the book now works it is thanks to their advice; if it doesn't it is due to my obstinacy.

Some of the material here first appeared in article form: "What Is Good Music," *Canadian University Music Review* 10(2), 1990; "The Good, the Bad, and the Indifferent: Defending Popular Culture from the Populists," *diacritics* 21(4), 1991; "Adam Smith and Music," *New Formations* 18, 1992; "Representatives of the People: Voices of Authority in Popular Music," *Mediterranean Music Cultures and Their Ramifications* (Madrid: Sociedad Española de Musicología, 1994); "What Is Bad Music?" *Musiken år 2002* 11 (Stockholm: Kungl. Musikaliska Akademien, 1994); "The Body Electric," *Critical Quarterly* 37(3), 1995; "Introduction: Performance Matters," *New Formations* 27, 1995; "Music and Identity," in Stuart Hall and Paul du Gay, eds., *Questions in Cultural Identity* (London: Sage, 1996).

Music Talk

The Value Problem in Cultural Studies

I used never to weep at Great Art, at Couperin or Kirkegaard, maintaining it was too multidimensional for the specific of tears. I wept at the rapid associative revelations of a Piaf, or at Lana Turner's soapy dilemmas. Crying was caused hence by entertainment, not masterworks.

Today tears dictate my first judgment of any works, their levels be damned. What counts is to be kinetically moved. And who says Edith and Lana aren't art—or, if they are, that Kierkegaard is more so?

Ned Rorem[1]

There is no way possible that Poison can EVER be on top. Them little underdeveloped chromoshoes don't got cock big enough to fuck an ant. So all you fucking whores out there who praise the ground Poison walks on are in shit. METALLICA RULES and that will never change.

Letter from LaDonna to *Metal Mania*, May 1990[2]

It was my third night in Stockholm, a very cold February night, and I'd gone to have supper with old friends, people I see maybe every two years, usually at conferences. There was one other guest, the professor in the department in which I was a visiting scholar, a man I hadn't met before. A few years older than I am, I'd guess; just as Johan Fornäs and Hillevi Ganetz are a few years younger. We talked, we ate, and about halfway through the main course, Johan said, "Let me play it to you!" and jumped over to the CD player.

The rest of the evening was driven by the dialectic of liking things. We ate, we talked, and at least some of the time (this wasn't an obsessive boys' night in, rock critics pouring over the runes) we argued about music. As hosts, Johan and Hillevi had the advantage—they could illustrate their claims (why someone could or couldn't sing; why the Flesh Quartet were Sweden's most amusing band; why Eva Dahlgren's latest album was more interesting than it first sounded). I could only respond—"Yeah, that's really good"; "No, I don't like that at all"—and write down titles, and ask occasionally, "Have you heard . . .? I must tape it for you."

A mundane and enjoyable evening, in short, not unlike Sunday evening suppers happening all over this and many other cities; and if the conversations elsewhere weren't necessarily about music they would almost certainly have been, at some point, about books or films or TV programs, about footballers or models or magazines. Such conversations are the common currency of friendship, and the essence of popular culture. We may have been a group of intellectuals, used to talking, to arguing publicly for our prejudices, but similar talk can be heard every day in bars and on buses, on football terraces and in school yards, as people wait at the hairdresser or take lunch in the office cafeteria, and have conversations about last night's TV, Take That's hit record, the new Clint Eastwood film, the latest headline in the *Sun*.

Part of the pleasure of popular culture is talking about it; part of its meaning is this talk, talk which is run though with value judgments. To be engaged with popular culture is to be discriminating, whether judging the merits of a football team's backs or an afternoon soap's plots. "Good" and "bad" or their vernacular versions ("brilliant," "crap") are the most frequent terms in everyday cultural conversation. I will be saying much more about this later, but to return to that Stockholm evening for a moment, two further features of our talk need noting. First, though all of us knew well enough that what was at issue was personal taste, subjective response, we also believed, passionately at times, that we were describing something objectively *in the music,* if only other people could hear it. Value arguments, in other words, aren't simply rituals of "I like/you like" (which would quickly become tedious, even in *Metal Mania*); they are based in reason, evidence, persuasion. Every music fan knows that moment of frustration when one can only sit the person down and say (or, rather, shout) despairingly, "But just listen to her! Isn't she fantastic!"

But if value judgments in popular culture make their own claims to objectivity (to being rooted, that is, in the quality of objects), their subjectivity can't be denied either—not, however, by banal reference to people having their own (essentially irrational) likes and dislikes, but because such judgments are taken to tell us something about the person making them. I was struck that evening in Sweden by how little the professor contributed to the talk about music (he talked engagingly about everything else), not, I think, because he was uninterested (I discovered later that he was a great jazz fan, a gifted amateur jazz pianist), nor because he didn't have things to say, but because he didn't really know me: he could not yet judge how an argument about music might affect the evening's good will.

In his pioneering sociological study of literary taste, Levin Schücking comments on the importance of books for the shifts in courtship rituals in late nineteenth century Germany: "Here, in reading together, the opportunity was gained of securing from the other's judgement of men and things an insight into thoughts and feelings; an insight likely to become the first bond between kindred souls."[3] And nowadays listening to music, watching television, and going to movies together serve similar functions. We assume that we can get to know someone through their tastes (eyeing someone's book and record shelves the first time we visit them, waiting nervously to see what a date says as we come out of a movie or a concert). Cultural judgments, in other words, aren't just subjective, they are self-revealing, and to become another person, to fake ourselves for whatever reason, means having to pretend to like things in which we find nothing valuable at all—a problem, as Pierre Bourdieu points out, for people attempting to *buy* cultural capital, and a secret shame, as Frank Kogan suggests, for those of us who have ever tried to impress new friends.

The point is not that we want friends or lovers just like us; but we do need to know that conversation, argument, is possible. In the pop world this is most obvious to musicians, who have to get along well enough to play together, who have to balance the creative/destructive effects of shared and different tastes, and who conduct the delicate business of coming together (and falling apart) almost entirely through stated pop judgments:

> Me and Graham thought that King was terrible but The Three Johns were great; we go down the pub and Malc and Chris thought King was great and hated The Three Johns—that said it all really so we split up.

> We were into bands like Bryan Adams and King, whilst Clint and Ad were into The Three Johns and The Shop Assistants. It was just no good.[4]

As Pat Kane (from Hue and Cry) concludes:

> Everybody has a theory of pop—not least those who make it. Even the least self-conscious of artists can be jolted into an extended analysis of "what's good about rock'n'roll," if you trade the wrong reference with them. There is a real evaluative disdain when two musicians react opposingly to the same source. "How can you

love/hate Van Morrison/Lou Reed/Springsteen/Stevie Wonder/ Kraft-werk? These people are/are not 'great popular music.' How can you say otherwise?" I have suffered (and inflicted) the worst aesthetic hauteur, as my opponent and I push each other to our fundamen-talist positions. You are a rocker, I am a soulboy; you find solace in raw-throated guitar release, I am consoled by the bubbling symmetry of a Muscle Shoals rhythm section. Different planets, Kiddo.[5]

For fans, whose musical values don't matter so much, or, rather, matter in different ways, with different consequences, trading pop judgments is a way to "flirt and fight." As Frank Kogan suggests, this means that for the pop listener (if not for the pop player) the stability of our judgments matters less than their constant deployment: as pop fans we continually change our minds about what is good or bad, relevant or irrelevant, "awesome" or "trivial" (our judgment in part determined by what happens to a sound in the marketplace, how successful it becomes, what other listeners it involves), but we never cease to believe that such distinctions are necessary "social pressure points, gath-ering spots for a brawl over how we use our terms. If our comparisons stood still, how could we have our brawl?"[6]

As I was leaving that supper party I got involved in a dispute about the Pet Shop Boys, which delayed me in the hall for another twenty minutes. "But *you* like disco!" said Hillevi, in mock dismissal, as I left. I got back to my room and put on *Very*.

It *is* a good record. What makes the Pet Shop Boys special is their sense of musical space. Using what is, in fact, a rather limited repertory of sounds (a thin lead voice; the most superficial resources of the digital synthesizer—sup-porting noise tends to be buried deep in the mix), the Pets conjure up a remarkable variety of soundscapes—the dance floor obviously, but also shops and cars and flats and dreams; on "To Speak is a Sin," for example, the discreet bar setting is prepared with the care of a high-class set designer and lighting cameraman.

One reason for the effectiveness of the Pets' approach to songs as scenes is that the duo realized from the start that computerized instruments freed sounds from a performance context. (Other electronic groups have, of course, come to the same conclusion—Kraftwerk and Yello most obviously. In this, as in their disco tastes, the Pets are continentally European; other British electro duos, Blancmange and Tears for Fears and even Erasure, have never quite shaken off a sense of being boy boffins in their bedrooms.) Most other forms of rock and pop bear the traces of their construction (of their ideal, imagined, construction, that is to say). Even on record a concerto means a concert hall, a chamber piece a drawing room, an opera an opera house; just as jazz means a jazz club, a big band a dance hall, a rock band a pub back-room or stadium. But because electronic sounds aren't produced like this, even in pop fantasy, they tend to be as much associated with musical consumption as musical production, consumption that isn't confined either to the disco or dance club (as later rave, house, and acid musics are) or to the living room, but describes, rather, the way in which all-around sounds are absorbed (like rap) into daily urban life. (And so in their "live" shows the Pet Shop Boys have had to go to great trouble, hiring filmmakers and stage designers, to put on musical events that don't feel like pop concerts at all.)

The Pets' musical appeal is rooted in this sense of mobile space, in the use of sounds which as both texture and hook surprise us by their very familiarity. But this sonic reassurance is overlaid with (or, perhaps, makes possible) an unusual pop sensibility: the Pet Shop Boys, unlike most rock groups, seem to be listening to their own numbers, to be picking up their own references and ambiguities. This means that their music is always funny (a surprisingly unusual quality in pop), most obviously here in the camp utopianism of their version of Village People's "Go West": Neil Tennant's effete voice sets off the chorus of butch baritones, whom I can't help hearing as a shipful of Russian sailors from a 1920s Soviet film. But there's also a profoundly regretful undertow to the Pets' ironies, a regret permanently lodged in the rhythmic hesitations of Chris Lowe's keyboard lines, in Tennant's flat tones. This means that Pet songs, for all their simple pop forms, are run through with emotional tension. "One in a Million" is thus a straightforward breaking-up song—if you've got to go, you've got to go—but with a chilling threat: only "one in a million men can change the way you feel," how sure are you that you'll find another one besides me? "Young Offender," an older man's love song to a younger one, leaves one confused as to which lover is, in the end, more physically, emotionally, and aesthetically vulnerable: "who will give who the bigger surprise?" "Dreaming of the Queen" shifts from the cheeky, silly image of "you and Her and I," joined at tea by Lady Di, to a sober sense of the romantic landscape of AIDS, as the Queen says (troubled mother), "I'm aghast, love never seems to last," and Di replies (worldly wise) that "there are no more lovers left alive."

Now this is to read images into the lyrics that may not be there (always a pleasure of pop), but the underlying, troubled feelings are there—in the sighing quality of the Pets' pop voice, in the brittle elegance of their arrangements. It's as if the Pet Shop Boys are both quite detached from their music—one is aware of the sheer craftiness of their songs—and completely implicated by it: they suggest less that they have been touched by the banality of love than by the banality of love songs; they seem to understand the fear as well as the joy of sex (fear and joy which always lie in the *anticipation* of the physical moment); they capture the anxiety of fun. Their gayness is less significant here (at least for a heterosexual fan) than their emotional fluency; it's as if the spaces they occupy are actually frozen moments in time, the moments just before and just after emotion (which is why this is disco music with an intensely intellectual appeal), the moments which the best pop music has always defined (nothing else can stop time like this). Listen to any Pet Shop Boys track and you know that they too have had their life reduced to a single catch in the voice, a single melodic phrase (here, for me, the opening of "Liberation") that must be played again and again. They know that in this sort of music it is such surface noise that resonates most deeply in our lives.

In writing about the Pet Shop Boys this way (wearing my rock critic's hat) I'm not actually saying much that I haven't already said to friends, Pet lovers and haters alike. Note the knowledge I'm assuming, about the Pets' own history and sexuality, about disco music, about other electronic sounds. Pop judgment is a double process: our critical task, as fans, is first to get people to listen to the right things (hence all these references to other groups and sounds), and only then to persuade them to like them. Our everyday arguments about music are concentrated on the first process: getting people to listen the right way. Only when we can accept that someone is hearing what we're hearing but just doesn't value it will we cede to subjective taste and agree that there's no point to further argument. Popular cultural arguments, in other words, are not about likes and dislikes as such, but about ways of listening, about ways of hearing, about ways of being.

The importance of value judgment for popular culture thus seems obvious, but it has been quite neglected in academic cultural studies. I will examine some of the reasons why in this chapter, but I should begin by confessing my own failure in this respect. I may have spent the last twenty years writing pop and rock criticism, judging records for a living, but I have tended to keep such arguments (plunging assertively into fan talk at the bar and in the record store) out of my academic work. I am well aware, to put this another way, of the reasons why value questions are difficult to raise in the cultural studies classroom, journal, and textbook. A couple of weeks after that supper party, for example, I argued in a graduate seminar that academics had a duty to make (rather than evade) value judgments when teaching popular culture. Not to say that Charles Dickens was better than Barbara Cartland (which I certainly believe) seemed to me to be not only dishonest and/or condescending to one's students, but also to evade an important analytic problem, how judgment works in all cultural spheres. Hillevi Ganetz, with whom I'd been arguing about the Pet Shop Boys just a few nights earlier, in a conversation in which we'd flung around "good" and "bad" words with ready abandon, strongly disagreed, saying that such a statement of personal preference had no sanctioned place in the classroom; it begged too many questions—"better" for whom or for what?

In the subsequent seminar discussion what became clear to me was that the issue wasn't really value but authority: the question was not whether Barbara Cartland (or the Pet Shop Boys) are any good or not, but who has the authority to say so. Now in everyday terms this isn't necessarily a problem—one could define popular culture as that cultural sector in which all participants claim the authority to pass judgment; no one needs to be licensed by study or qualification to speak "authoritatively." In practice, though, there clearly are people—loosely defined as "fans"—who do claim precisely that their superior knowledge, experience, and commitment give their judgments a particular weight: this is how both rock critics and season ticket holders to football games claim a special attention. There is such a thing, in other words, as popular cultural capital, which is one reason why fans are so annoyed by critics, not just for having different opinions but for having public sanction to state them.

Pierre Bourdieu's argument in *Distinction* is that the accumulation of cultural knowledge and experience—through education, as part of one's upbringing—enhances the richness and pleasure of the reading of cultural texts, not least because of the pleasure of displaying one's superior enjoyment and discrimination. His interest, though, is in the creation of a taste hierarchy in terms of high and low: the possession of cultural capital, he suggests, is what defines high culture in the first place. My point is that a similar use of accumulated knowledge and discriminatory skill is apparent in low cultural forms, and has the same hierarchical effect. Low culture, that is to say, generates its own capital—most obviously, perhaps, in those forms (such as dance club cultures) which are organized around exclusiveness, but equally significantly for the fans (precisely those people who have invested time and money in the accumulation of knowledge) of even the most inclusive forms—sports or soap operas, say. Such fans certainly do claim, with good justification, to have a richer experience of their particular pleasure than "ordinary" or "passive" consumers, and this is one reason why it is problematic to take fans as ordinary consumers, as models for popular cultural "resistance" (a concept to which I will return).[7]

But if there are forms of popular cultural authority—represented by fans, determined by institutions (critics, deejays, and A&R departments, for example, all explicitly engage in popular musical discrimination)[8]—these are not easy to exercise in the classroom, where everyday questions of the good and the bad are entangled with academic concepts of the high and the low.

In his book *Origins of Popular Style,* the musicologist Peter Van Der Merwe suggests that "reviewing the popular music of the twentieth century as a whole, most people would probably agree that some of it is excellent, some unbearable and most of it very indifferent. What the good, bad and indifferent share is a musical language."[9] Most people probably would agree with this; disagreement would be about which records and songs and performers were good, which bad, which indifferent. But, as Van der Merwe points out, aesthetic arguments are possible only when they take place within a shared critical discourse, when they rest on an agreement as to what "good" and "bad" music mean—the argument, that is to say, is not about the labels but about what should be so labeled.

Take, for example, the following confident statements. "Rock music," writes rightist cultural critic Allan Bloom in *The Closing of the American Mind,* "has one appeal only, a barbaric appeal, to sexual desire—not love, not *eros,* but sexual desire undeveloped and untutored . . . these are [its] three great lyrical themes: sex, hate and a smarmy, hypocritical version of brotherly love." [10] "The rock critic," writes leftist cultural critic Mark Crispin Miller in the *New York Review of Books,* "struggles to interpret something that requires no interpretation . . . tries to appraise and explicate a music whose artists and listeners are anti-intellectual and usually stoned, and whose producers want more than anything to own several cars."[11] Both writers seem remarkably assured that they know what rock means to its listeners and that the meaning of what they heard (I'm assuming, perhaps wrongly, that both men did listen to rock before holding forth about it) was transparent.

Compare now a different voice. At one point in *The Shoe,* Gordon Legge's fine novel about being a pop fan in Scotland in the 1980s, the central character asks,

> How could people get so worked up about relatives and cars when there were records? Records cut so much deeper. For him *Astral Weeks, Closer,* and *For Your Pleasure* (the three best LPs of all time, [he] said. No contest . . .) articulated the mundanity, despair and joy of existence . . . [He] said his records were the most important things in his life—more important than Celtic [football club] easily . . . It's just that football was easier to talk about for five hours down at the pub on a Saturday night.[12]

Legge's point, with which any pop fan must agree, is that the exercise of taste and aesthetic discrimination is as important in popular as in high culture but is more difficult to talk about. No, that should read: but is more difficult to talk about in terms that are recognized as aesthetic and discriminatory by high cultural authorities. This means that the glib, professional talkers, the Blooms and Millers (and I could multiply examples of such confident statements about the meaning of pop culture from both left and right) have the voices that are heard in the pulpit, the lectern, and the upmarket journal.

This remains the case even after the rise of cultural studies as an academic concern. Contemporary popular culture may now be a familiar topic on the curriculum, but in being constituted as a fit object for study it has become an oddly bloodless affair—the aesthetics of the popular continues to be at best neglected and at worst dismissed. One obvious reason for neglect is that cultural studies emerged from disciplines in which questions of taste and judgment were already kept well away from issues of academic analysis and assessment. Sociologists, anthropologists, and social and cultural historians have always been wary of proclaiming the activities they study as good or bad (such judgments are not their business); perhaps more surprisingly, "evaluation," as Barbara Herrnstein Smith suggests, was also long ago apparently "exiled" from literary criticism.[13]

As I've learned since becoming a professor of English, Smith is clearly right about this (the effects are most dramatic in the literature department–derived subject of film studies, in which students have to be taught in their first week that whether they think a particular film is any good or not is quite irrelevant to its proper analysis), but I wonder whether "exile" is quite the right metaphor here. "Deep entry" may be the more appropriate term, in honor of those Trotskyites whose infiltration of the Labour Party was so disguised that they could never do anything that might reveal that they were not, in fact, just like any other Labour Party members. So values are there in literary criticism, but they must never ever show themselves (or they will, indeed, be "exiled," or, in Labour speak, expelled). This is possible because of the underlying assumption in literary studies that every text studied in a course is valuable, by definition: what is English literature as an academic discipline if not the study of valuable literature? This assumption becomes clear at unexpected (unexpected by me, anyway) moments of staffroom conflict. We can't teach a course in *contemporary* literature, I'm told, we don't yet know which authors and titles are any good.[14] We can't offer a degree course in creative writing, I'm warned, we wouldn't know how to assess it—this from the only group of people in the country who make a full-time living from literary criticism.

It's not so much evaluation that has been exiled from literary criticism, then (and this is Herrnstein Smith's real point), as discussion of evaluation; value, to put this another way, is taken for granted (and is certainly not an issue open to student dispute in the classroom even if it is, as Deborah Cameron put it to me, "the very stuff of their corridor conversation"). Professors of cultural studies can't, one would think, make the same assumption that the underlying value of what they teach is proved by the fact that they teach it, although, even after little more than a decade, it's already surprisingly easy to point to a popular cultural canon, a selection of films, TV shows, ads, stars, performers, genres, sites, and events which are valued primarily for their richness as a subject of academic argument. In film studies, for example, most film teachers do now assume, as I think literature teachers do, that they teach "good films" even if, unlike literature teachers, they can't refer to quite the same general high cultural extra-academic agreement on this.[15] And while cultural studies lecturers themselves may not be deluded that a Barbara Cartland novel or Madonna video, a *Sun* front page or Kleenex ad is aesthetically valuable in itself (as against being effective or semiotically interesting or "good of its kind"), they rarely encourage classroom discussion about what, in this context, "aesthetically valuable in itself" might mean.

Culture as an academic object, in short, is different from culture as a popular activity, a process, and the value terms which inform the latter are, it seems, irrelevant to the analysis of the former. To give a simple example: when Judith Williamson, one of Britain's finest academic cultural theorists, became film critic for the *New Statesman* she immediately faced an insoluble problem. Her (academically derived) approach to films as texts meant treating them, discussing them, as finished, structured objects; readers, however, wanted reasons for watching (or missing) a movie *which didn't give away the plot!*[16]

In universities, then, just as in high schools (and however many pop icons are now pinned up on classroom walls) there is still a split between what Frank Kogan describes as the discourse of the classroom (with its focus on a subject matter) and the discourse of the hallway (with its focus on oneself and one's opinions about a subject matter and one's opinions about other people's opinions about a subject matter and one's opinions about other people).[17]

One consequence is what Joke Hermes calls "the fallacy of meaningfulness," the academic assumption that popular cultural goods must signify something (her research on women's magazines suggested that many of their readers actually valued them for their insignificance, because they were "easy to put down.")[18] Popular culture, to put this point another way, has as much to do with sociability, and how we talk about texts, as with interpretation, and how we read them. In Kogan's terms, in the hallway the question is not what does it mean but what can I do with it; and what I can do with it is what it means—interpretation is a matter of argument, of understanding wrought from social activity.

In the classroom, meanwhile (and despite first impressions), academic approaches to popular culture still derive from the mass cultural critiques of the 1930s and 1940s, and particularly from the Marxist critique of contemporary popular culture in terms of the production and circulation of commodities. For the Frankfurt School, analyzing the organization of mass production, on the one hand, and the psychology of mass consumption, on the other, commercial popular culture was worthless aesthetically, and Adorno and Horkheimer developed a number of concepts (such as standardization and repetition) to show why this must be so. In creating markets for their goods, cultural entrepreneurs developed manipulative sales methods that ensnared consumers in self-delusion, in the continual pursuit of false (and easily satisfied, easily dissatisfied) desire. "If one seeks to find out who 'likes' a commercial piece, one cannot avoid the suspicion that liking and disliking are inappropriate to the situation, even if the person questioned clothes his reactions in those words. The familiarity of the piece is a surrogate for the quality ascribed to it. To like it is almost the same thing as to recognize it." [19]

In broad terms, the analytic response to Frankfurt pessimism has been to accept the organizational account of mass cultural production, to ignore the complexities of Adorno's aesthetic theory, and to look for the redeeming features of commodity culture in the act of consumption. The task, beginning with American liberal sociologists in the 1950s (inspired by the émigré scholar Paul Lazersfeld, who opted to stay in the United States), was to find forms of mass consumption that were not "passive" and types of mass consumers who were not stupefied, to provide a sociology of watching and reading and listening. If it is through consumption that contemporary culture is lived, then it is in the process of consumption that contemporary cultural value must be located.

In the cultural studies tradition with which I am most familiar, British subcultural theory, this reworking of Frankfurt theory took on the particular form of identifying certain social groups with what we might call "positive mass consumption" (which became—and remains—the pithiest current definition of "popular"—as against mass—culture). The value of cultural goods could therefore be equated with the value of the groups consuming them—youth, the working class, women.

I want to make two points about this argument (which I have used myself in analyzing rock and roll). First, it remains a highly politicized approach to popular cultural value (this is the key Frankfurt inheritance), whether explicitly, as in the British use of terms like "resistance" and "empowerment," or implicitly, as in the American celebration of opinion leaders and taste publics in the name of a pluralist democracy. The importance of popular culture, in other words, is rooted here in its ideological effects; other ways of valuing a song or film or story, by reference to beauty, craft, or spectacle, are notable for their absence. Cultural value is being assessed according to measures of true and false consciousness; aesthetic issues, the politics of excitement, say, or grace, are subordinated to the necessities of interpretation, to the call for "demystification."

This is a way to solve the authority problem that lies at the heart of the difficulty of discussing cultural values in the classroom. The teacher now has the authority to explain why Madonna videos or *Aliens 2* matter—not by saying whether they're any good or not, but by assessing their ideological implications, which are, paradoxically (this approach began with the importance of what consumers *do*) all there in the text, for the academic analyst (like any good literary critic) to uncover. The 1990s thus saw a boom in the academic Madonna business—the books! the articles! the conferences! the courses! Scouring compulsively through all this material, I couldn't tell whether Madonna was a good singer (as well as a skilled media operative); whether she was an engaging dancer (as well as a semiotic tease); whether I'd actually want to play her records and videos as well as read about them.

In the classroom, then, when a popular text (a TV show or a shopping mall, a Madonna video or a Nirvana CD) is read positively, what's at issue is not its immediate qualities or effects, but the opportunities it offers for further interpretation, for a reading, for a reading *against the grain*. And from this perspective even the judgment that something—a Jeffrey Archer novel, an Andrew Lloyd Webber musical—is "bad" is really a political rather than an aesthetic assessment, a comment on markets, not form.

As cultural studies has established itself as an academic subject, particularly in the United States, there have been obvious signs that it has been "depoliticized," that the original, radical thrust of the Birmingham School in Britain, which was explicitly Marxist and developed cultural studies as a critique of conventional academic subjects like literature, history, and sociology, has been blunted. What was once an argument about cultural class, race and gender conflict, has been translated into a kind of celebratory political pluralism. But if this is depoliticization, it is so in a more complex way than it first appears. After all, John Fiske, who is usually held up as the villain in this narrative, still provides a radical, class-based account of American popular culture (his "populism" is quite different from the cheerful train-spotting version developed over the years at Bowling Green), and the academic rise of cultural studies has meant less a declining interest in cultural politics than its diffusion across a much wider media site—it sometimes seems that for Fiske every act of popular consumption is thereby "resistant."

From the value perspective, then, the problem of populist cultural studies is less its politics than its sociology, its assumption that the "popular" is defined by the market. The populist position is that whatever our (class-bound) personal tastes and values may be, we have to accept that sales figures, box office returns, and record charts tell us what "the people" want. It's only a residual academic elitism that leads us to celebrate the radical or avant-garde; if *The Price is Right* is more popular than *Twin Peaks,* for example, then it must be, culturally, more important. We, as intellectuals, may think *Hill Street Blues* or Martin Scorsese is good; but "the people" clearly use quite different value criteria—they choose *Blind Date* and Stephen Spielberg.

This equation of popular culture with market choice is problematic. It means that "popularity," by default, is consumption as measured by sales figures and market indicators—Nielsen ratings, the music charts, box office returns, best-seller lists, circulation statistics, and so on (figures that in turn become the regulators of popular cultural history). Even if such figures were accurate (which is doubtful), they provide no evidence as to why such goods are chosen by their consumers nor whether they are actually enjoyed or valued by them (it is a common enough experience to go to a blockbuster film, watch a high-rated TV program, read a best-selling book, or buy a chart record that turns out to be quite uninteresting). The elision between what sells and what is popular (the assumption that what sells is therefore "valuable") is obvious in Fiske's account of "popular discrimination," for example. He stresses rightly the inability of mass culture industries to predict or manipulate popular taste (as indicated by the vast number of "failed" records, films, TV shows, magazines, and so forth) but does not question the assumption that a market failure is by definition unpopular or that a market success has by definition a popular audience.[20] In accounts of popular music, at least, this is to ignore the significant unpopularity of certain stars (Meat Loaf, say, or Bryan Adams) and the popular influence of such market failures as Velvet Underground or Joy Division or Neil Young. If nothing else, consumer research among pop fans immediately reveals the intensity with which musics and musicians are loathed as well as loved, and to argue, like Dave Harker, that we need to rethink existing cultural accounts of the 1960s because the soundtrack of *The Sound of Music* topped the British album charts for more weeks than the Beatles, and of the 1970s because punk records sold far less than Elton John LPs, seems to me perverse.[21] Are market choices (as measured somewhat inaccurately by the culture industries' own research devices) really all we mean by "the popular"?

The analytical effect, at any rate, is contempt for the consumers supposedly being celebrated, for their varying tastes and interests. The populist assumption is that all best-selling goods and services are somehow the same in their empowering value (as they are in terms of exchange value); the populist suggestion is that we can somehow equate romance reading and *Star Trek* viewing, Madonna and metal fans, shoppers and surfers. The aesthetic discrimination essential to cultural consumption, and the considered judgments it involves—to buy the new Madonna record or not, to choose Janet Jackson instead—are ignored.

It is hard to avoid the conclusion that the more celebratory the populist study, the more patronizing its tone, an effect, I think, of the explicit populist determination to deny (or reverse) the usual high/low cultural hierarchy. If one strand of the mass cultural critique was an indictment of low culture from the perspective of high art (as was certainly the case for Adorno), then to assert the value of the popular is also, necessarily, to query the superiority of high culture. Most populist writers, though, draw the wrong conclusion from this; what needs challenging is not the notion of the superior, but the claim that it is the exclusive property of the "high."

To deny the significance of value judgments in popular culture (to ignore popular taste hierarchies) is also hypocritical. How often, I wonder, do populist cultural theorists celebrate popular cultural forms which they themselves soon find boring? How are their own feelings for the good and the bad coded into their own analyses? If, in my own cultural practice, I prefer Dickens to Barbara Cartland, Meat Loaf to U2, shouldn't I be prepared to argue the case for my values? Shouldn't I *want* other people to read Dickens rather than Cartland, to listen to Meat Loaf rather than U2? Shouldn't I be able to persuade them with classroom as well as hallway arguments? The problem is, precisely, how to do this, but to gloss over the continuous exercise of taste by the pop cultural audience is, in effect, to do their discriminating for them, while refusing to engage in the arguments which produce cultural values in the first place. This is, in the end, to reduce people to a faceless mass or market every bit as effectively as the mass cultural theorists against whom the populists are supposedly arguing.

This book is about taking popular discrimination seriously. It starts from two assumptions. The first is that the essence of popular cultural practice is making judgments and assessing differences. I'm not just thinking here of the marketing use of endless hit parades and best-seller lists but also of the ubiquitous use of competitions in the popular arts—talent contests, battles of the bands, and so forth—in which judgments, distinctions, and choices have to be publicly justified: to examine the question of value in popular culture is to examine the terms of such justifications. Take this description of music making in turn-of-the-century New Orleans:

> In the frequent "bucking contests" that took place between bands, it was the crowds of onlookers that decided when one band had fallen noticeably behind the other in quality. When that happened the people watching would crowd around the victorious musicians cheering and encouraging them to go on. The process by which the audiences determined which band was superior intrigued [Sidney] Bechet. He concluded it had to do with the fact that the audience was more than an audience, it was also participating: "how it was they could tell—that was the music too. It was what they had of the music inside themselves." It was always the people who made the decision. "You was always being judged."[22]

And half a century later Brian Jackson sat in the audience of a brass band contest in Yorkshire. Each band had to play the "test piece," which was therefore heard over and over again throughout the day: "There were a large variety of interpretations, and each of the twenty-two performances was argued out aloud as 'very musical' or 'bit pedestrian' or 'too much of a sameness.'"[23]

My second assumption is that there is no reason to believe a priori that such judgments work differently in different cultural spheres. There are obvious differences between operas and soap operas, between classical and country music, but the fact that the objects of judgment are different doesn't mean that the processes of judgment are. As Richard Shusterman has argued, the general distinctions usually drawn between high and low art don't stand up to close philosophical scrutiny. He examines, for instance, the suggestion that the pleasures of popular art are not "real" but fleeting, "that transience entails spuriousness, that gratifications are unreal and fraudulent if they later leave us hungry for more"—an argument that could equally well be applied to high art. And he goes on to ask if it is really possible, in practice, to differentiate high, intellectual aesthetic appreciation from low, sensuous bodily response; or to distinguish between a high engagement with real life and a low escape from it; or to make a clear contrast between high art's complex structures and low art's formless simplicity.[24]

For Shusterman the point is that low culture can be treated as if it were high culture—his analysis of Stetasonic's 1988 track, "Talkin' All That Jazz," is therefore designed to reveal its complexity, its philosophical content, its artistic self-consciousness, its creativity and form. This is a familiar strategy in rock criticism: one way of ascribing popular cultural value is to show that a successful record is, in fact, art. But Shusterman's strategy is subtler in that he wants to value low culture's "low" values too. Here he examines the old distinction (used, in different ways, by both Adorno and Fiske) between the "autonomy" of high art (which exists only for "artistic reasons," its value an effect, therefore, of its form) and the "function" of low art, which exists to serve some end (commercial, hedonistic) and is valued accordingly, by reference not to its internal features but to its *use*. Fiske accepts the distinction between form and function, but redefines it as a contrast between measures of quality and aesthetics, on the one hand, and measures of relevance and productivity, on the other.[25] High cultural audiences thus assume the value of an art object is contained within it; low cultural audiences assume that the value of an art object lies in what it can do for them.[26]

I'm not sure that this distinction can be sustained sociologically (as a statement of what audiences expect and do); I'll come back to this in the next chapter. In any case, Shusterman is not convinced that it can be maintained philosophically. He suggests, for example, that rap "not only insists on uniting the aesthetic and the cognitive; it equally stresses that practical functionality can form part of artistic meaning and value."[27] Rap's consciousness raising function lies in its aesthetic form, in other words, and vice versa.

Shusterman's suggestion that the aesthetic and the functional are inextricable from each other in the way we respond to and make sense of popular art is a kind of reverse echo of Pierre Bourdieu's point that the aesthetic interpretation of high art is, in fact, functional: it enables aesthetes to display their social superiority. My position is that it is not only the bourgeoisie who use aesthetic criteria for functional ends. If social relations are constituted in cultural practice, then our sense of identity and difference is established *in the processes of discrimination.* And this is as important for popular as for bourgeois cultural activity, important at both the most intimate levels of sociability (an aspect of the way in which friendships are formed and courtship organized), and at the most anonymous levels of market choice (in the way in which the fashion and advertising industries seek to place us socially by translating individual judgments of what we like and dislike into sales patterns). These relationships between aesthetic judgments and the formation of social groups are obviously crucial to popular cultural practice, to genres and cults and subcultures.

I want to end this chapter with a bolder assertion. As a matter of analytic strategy I believe that we should begin from the principle that there is no difference between high and low culture, and then see how, nevertheless, such a difference has become a social fact (the result of specific historical and social and institutional practices). This seems to me a more fruitful strategy than either taking the high/low difference for granted (whether from the elitist perspective of an Allan Bloom or the populist perspective of a John Fiske) or seeking to prove that it is spurious (as with Shusterman). Rather, I would argue, at least as a starting premise, that in responding to high and low art forms, in assessing them, finding them beautiful or moving or repulsive, people are employing the same evaluative principles. The differences lie in the objects at issue (what is culturally interesting to us is socially structured), in the discourses in which judgments are cast, and in the circumstances in which they are made.

It is arguable, for example, that there are a number of aesthetic/functional axes around which all cultural judgments work: believability (and its complex relations with both realism and fantasy); coherence (whether in terms of form or morality—and with a great variety of ways in which cause is taken to relate to effect); familiarity (and the constant problem of the new, the novel); usefulness—whether at the most material level (is that painting the right size, shape, and color for this space on this wall in this room?) or at the most spiritual (does this experience *uplift* me, make me a better person?).

What I'm suggesting here is that people bring similar questions to high and low art, that their pleasures and satisfactions are rooted in similar analytic issues, similar ways of relating what they see or hear to how they think and feel. The differences between high and low emerge because these questions are embedded in different historical and material circumstances, and are therefore framed differently, and because the answers are related to different social situations, different patterns of sociability, different social needs.

I remain enough of a sociologist, in short, to agree with Bourdieu that the interesting question is how to relate cultural judgments to material conditions (by reference to specific experiences, discourses, skills, and knowledge). And I remain enough of a Marxist to be wary of answers to this question which are static, undialectical, which suggest that the way things are is the way they have to be. The old leftist anxiety about the inadequacy of popular culture reflected an assessment of the *thinness* of the experiences which commercial art seemed to offer: this was a theme in Raymond Williams's work, for example, and was a central point in Richard Hoggart's *Uses of Literacy*.[28] But such arguments are as much about the thinness of people's everyday experience as about popular songs and magazines and films as such, and those contemporary novelists who best understand today's popular culture, Gordon Legge, say, or Bobbie Ann Mason, make clear that things like shopping malls and *NME* and top 40 music and reruns of *M.A.S.H.* matter so much because people's lives are otherwise tedious and desperate and sad.

In the end, then, the populist cultural studies line that popular consumer culture serves people's needs, and that by denigrating it we therefore denigrate those needs and thus the people themselves, misses the point. The issue is whether people's lives are adequate for human needs, for human potential. The political argument, in other words, concerns culture as reconciliation versus culture as transformation.[29] And this is the context in which the concept of "resistance" is so slippery. How should we distinguish between the ways in which people use culture to "escape," to engage in pleasures that allow them a temporary respite from the oppressive relations of daily life (a functional use of working class leisure that the bourgeoisie have always encouraged), and those uses of culture which are "empowering," which bring people together to change things?

This is partly an empirical and historical question—one would need to examine the role of popular culture in revolutionary as well as routine situations—and one can assume that what's at stake is not a simple matter of either/or: "resistance" shifts its meaning with circumstance. But it's also a question about where oppositional values come from, and how people come to believe, imaginatively, in something more than resistance. Culture as transformation, in other words, must challenge experience, must be difficult, must be *unpopular.* There are, in short, political as well as sociological and aesthetic reasons for challenging populism. The problem is how to do this while appreciating the popular, taking it seriously on its own terms. And I know this is where my own tastes will inform everything that follows, my own tastes, that is, for the *unpopular popular,* my own belief that the "difficult" appeals through the traces it carries of another world in which it would be "easy." The utopian impulse, the *negation* of everyday life, the aesthetic impulse that Adorno recognized in high art, must be part of low art too.

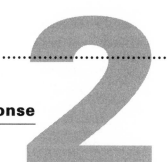

The Sociological Response

If a man has a big voice without knowing in the least how to use it, without having the most elementary ideas of the art of singing; if he produces a sound violently he is applauded violently for the *sonority* of this note.

If a woman possesses only an exceptional vocal range, when she produces, *a propos* or not, a *sol* or lower *fa* more like the dying moan of a sick person than a musical sound, or a high *fa* as agreeable as the yelp of a little dog when you step on his paw, that is enough for the whole hall to resound with acclamations.

. . . But, you will say, will anyone be bold enough to say that the public does not applaud, and very warmly, the great artists, masters of every resource of dramatic song, endowed with sensitivity, intelligence, virtuosity, and that rare faculty called inspiration? No; doubtless the public applauds *them* also. The public at that time resembles those sharks that follow a ship and which men fish for; it swallows everything—the piece of fat and the harpoon.

Hector Berlioz[1]

In *Contingencies of Value,* her book about high cultural evaluation, Barbara Herrnstein Smith suggests that "what we are doing in making an explicit judgment of a literary work is (a) articulating an estimate of how well that work will serve certain implicitly defined functions (b) for a specific implicitly defined audience (c) who are conceived of as experiencing the work under certain implicitly defined conditions."[2] This could equally well describe what's going on in the judgment of pop songs or TV shows, shopping centers or newscasters, and it suggests a sociology of aesthetic discrimination: to understand cultural value judgments we must look at the social contexts in which they are made, at the social reasons why some aspects of a sound or spectacle are valued over others; we must understand the appropriate times and places in which to voice such judgments, to argue them.

I'll return to the social settings of evaluation in Chapter 3. First I want to examine another aspect of Herrnstein Smith's argument: that value judgments also have a discursive context. They must be put into words, and in any fruitful aesthetic argument there must be agreement about what these words mean, however excited the disagreement about their application. In this chapter, then, I want to explore the discursive context of the aesthetics of popular music. And to introduce the discussion I will describe four examples of moments when discourses about music have clashed, when argument has indeed collapsed, when accounts of the "good" and "bad" in music have gone past each other to ridiculous or outraged effect.

My first example comes from the autobiography of John Culshaw, for many years head of the classical division of Decca Records. His autobiography is instructive in general terms because it takes it for granted that classical records are produced commercially. The tension between judgments of commercial value and judgments of musical value was thus ever-present in Culshaw's work. The nicest example concerns the original recording of Benjamin Britten's *War Requiem*. Culshaw was convinced of both its musical and its commercial worth—the *Requiem* was being given its first performance as part of the celebrations surrounding the rebuilding of Coventry Cathedral; its launch would be accompanied by a mass of radio, television, and press publicity. Unfortunately, Britten was not, historically, a best seller, and Decca's bosses were not convinced that any new classical music sold particularly well—its place in the Decca catalogue was a matter of prestige rather than profit. Culshaw therefore lost the internal argument about how many copies of the *War Requiem* to press; its run was the same as for previous Britten works.

As it turned out the pressing (which covered the North American as well as the European market) was far too small; the *War Requiem* sold out in a week. Culshaw had to wait several months for more copies (Decca's pressing plants were fully booked up with pop product), by which time the sales impetus had been lost. Furious, he confronted the man who had made the original pressing decision. The latter apologized and explained: "Daren't take the risk old boy. First thing of Britten's that's ever sold at all. Do you think you could talk him into writing another *Requiem* that would sell as well? We wouldn't make the same mistake twice."[3]

Culshaw tells this story to get a laugh, but it wouldn't be particularly funny if told about a pop composer—one only has to think of the industry kudos as well as huge sales that Virgin got for coming up with Mike Oldfield's *Tubular Bells 2* and Meat Loaf's *Bat Out of Hell II*, follow-up versions of supposedly "unique" rock compositions. In Decca's pop division, then, this was a perfectly reasonable comment—"Write another! We know how to sell it now!"—and what Culshaw is describing is an unbridgeable gap between commonsense assertions about the meaning of the *War Requiem* as product and as art. To put this another way, when an increasing tension between creative and sales processes began to be experienced within record companies' pop divisions too, toward the end of the 1960s, it was a sign that art discourses were beginning to be applied to "commercial" sounds.

My second anecdote comes from the biography of the novelist Radclyffe Hall, who also wrote pop lyrics. Her biographer quotes a correspondence she had in 1918 with William Davey, the chairman of Chappell and Company, then Britain's largest music publishers. Hall complained that she had received no royalties for her lyrics for "The Blind Ploughman," a song which had "swept the country." Davey replied as follows:

> I yield to no-one in my admiration of your words to "The Blind Ploughman." They are a big contributing factor to the success of the song. Unfortunately, we cannot afford to pay royalties to lyric writers. One or two other publishers may, but if we were to once introduce the principle, there would be no end to it. Many lyrics are merely a repetition of the same words in a different order and almost always with the same ideas. Hardly any of them, frankly, are worth a royalty, although once in a while they may be. It is difficult to differentiate, however. What I do feel is that you are quite entitled to have an extra payment for these particular words and I have much pleasure in enclosing you from Messrs Chappell a cheque for 20 guineas.[4]

This letter is interesting in a number of ways, not least for its revelation that Chappell was, apparently, routinely breaking the law—the Copyright Act of 1911 included lyricists in musical copyright regulations even though the music publishers had campaigned against this. In broad terms, though, the publisher's differentiation between the appropriate rewards for routine pop production and for individual craft skill did (and still does) have legal support. It is illuminating, for example, to follow plagiarism cases through the British courts since 1911. What criteria have judges established for proof of musical "originality"? From the start they took it for granted that anybody with even a modicum of musical skill could write a pop song, that there were only a limited number of note combinations that could be arranged to make

The Sociological Response

a popular tune. To prove plagiarism, then, it was not enough to show that two songs were the same; one had to prove that the person who "stole" your song had heard it before they wrote their own. Otherwise evidence that two pieces of pop music were identical simply reflected the fact that all pop composers were constrained by the same pop formulas.

The arguments here concern the role of individual authorship in establishing the value of a piece of music; the discursive clash reflects quite different accounts of what's meant by lyrical "creativity." I've always found, for instance, that students, deeply implicated in the romantic mythology of rock, are genuinely shocked by Sheila Davis's *The Craft of Lyric Writing*, the most intelligent and entertaining of all the "how to write a pop song" books. They seem to be shocked less by the baldness with which she lays out lyrical formulas than by the fact that so many of her formulaic examples come from canonical rock texts, texts which precisely stand for individual expressivity. What she implies, in short, is not just that Morrissey could write another "Heaven Knows I'm Miserable Now," but that anyone who had read her book could do it for him.[5]

The third argument I want to describe occurred a few years ago at an event I organized in Birmingham. We arranged for a young, local group who were booked to play in a city center hall that evening to come along at two o'clock in the afternoon. The sound crew (hired by the concert promoter) arrived early too, and carried out the soundcheck—setting up the amplification equipment, measuring the hall's acoustics, miking up the musicians—in public. The audience (a surprising number of whom were local musicians) sat in a circle around the mixing desk while the mixers explained, sound by sound, what they were doing.

When everyone was wired up and leveled off, the band ran through a complete song. As it finished somebody in the audience asked them to do it again "with the vocal mixed up because we couldn't really hear the voice." The engineers adjusted their levels, the band played the song again, and the audience agreed that they sounded much better. The mixers were asked the obvious question: "Why didn't you mix it like that the first time?" They replied, "because she [the band's lead singer] can't sing." And suddenly there was a raging argument between mixers and musicians about what constituted a "good sound." The mixers were categorical: musicians do not understand good sound. They're egomaniacal, concerned only to hear themselves; they have no sense at all of what is going on in acoustic space. Audience pleasure depends on sound "experts," professionals who are "detached." The musicians were equally categorical: all sound mixers are deaf; this is one of the reasons they become sound mixers. Instead of listening to music they simply look at lights and knobs and dials, adjusting them not by reference to musical effects but according to the rules of pseudo-scientific acoustic theory (the theory they'd been expounding all afternoon). The musicians felt more strongly than I'd realized that as public performers they were powerless (particularly when starting out), that sounds were imposed on them by engineers in the studio and on stage alike; and the afternoon collapsed into shouted abuse and walkouts.

The argument here was about professionalism, but it also involved conflicting accounts of the relationship between music and sound quality, as does my final example of value clash, the critical debate around the introduction of compact discs. CDs were first promoted, like previous technological innovations in sound recording, in terms of "fidelity." The sales pitch was that a digitally stored sound was more "faithful" to the sound and dynamics of the original (as if "live") performance than an analog recording could ever be. CDs' detractors, meanwhile, argued that digital sound storage was actually "unfaithful" to those musical forms (like rock 'n' roll) which were essentially "impure."

This argument didn't last long—partly because, in the end, CDs' appeal was their convenience and not their sound quality, and partly because rock critics soon discovered that CDs actually enhance the presence of the roughest of studio sounds. But what interests me here is less the technological evaluation of sound than the implicit disagreement about what it means to listen to a record. I was reminded of the earlier (and, to me, much more irrational) debate about the introduction of the vinyl LP. In the late 1940s Compton Mackenzie, founding editor of the British classical music magazine *The Gramophone*, argued against LPs, not simply because he resented having to replace an entire record collection, but also because of the LP's threat to what he considered to be a superior listening experience. The collector of 78 recordings had to be an "active" listener, had to use her imagination to hear the sound that was buried in the 78's bumps and crackles, had to keep jumping up to change the record, which could never be, then, background music. By contrast, Mackenzie suspected (accurately enough), LP listeners would be essentially passive, able to put their feet up, their thoughts aside, not needing to work at listening at all.[6] The same sorts of anxieties, I think, underlay rock critics' initial suspicions of CDs (and pop videos); we also believed that an "active" relationship between listener and record was being threatened by a new technology.

Such critical suspicions draw attention to a recurring discursive clash in twentieth-century popular music, in which nature is pitted against artifice, "true" music ("live" music) against "false" (studio or electronically manufactured) sounds. The most interesting reflections on the impossibility of this argument I've come across are gathered in a 1966 issue of *High Fidelity*, to accompany a polemical article by Glenn Gould. One point Gould wanted to establish (as part of his championing of recorded over live performance) was that whatever their public claims, record companies had inevitably to fake live music. Classical record producers, at least, had to persuade people that they were having the ideal—concert hall—experience of their music, in the restricted acoustic space of their homes.[7]

I've been describing examples here of musical arguments which broke down, whether in farce (as with the *War Requiem*), in retreat (as with Chappell's payment of Radclyffe Hall's royalties), in violence (as at the sound mixing seminar), or in deception (as with new sound technologies). They broke down not because of disagreement about the value of particular pieces of music, but because of disagreement about what it meant to "value" music in the first place. What I want to suggest, in other words, is that to understand what's at stake in arguments about musical value, we have to begin with the discourses which give the value terms their meaning. Musical disputes are not about music "in itself" but about how to place it, what it is about the music that is to be assessed. After all, we can only hear music as valuable when we know what to listen to and how to listen for it. Our reception of music, our expectations from it, are not inherent in the music itself—which is one reason why so much musicological analysis of popular music misses the point: its object of study, the discursive text it constructs, is not the text to which anyone else listens.

The question then becomes, what do people hear? What are the possibilities? I want eventually to suggest that these days music is heard through three overlapping and contradictory grids, grids mapped by what I call the art discourse, the folk discourse, and the pop discourse. But like all discursive practices, these are the effects of specific historical situations; they have to be rooted, that is to say, in the cultural landscape established by industrial capitalism in the nineteenth century and, in particular, by the high/low cultural constructs that we came across in Chapter 1. These constructs, after all, are implicated in the very idea of making aesthetic judgments, being discriminating, exercising taste, in the first place. So before coming back to art and folk and pop, I want to say something about the construction of the more general discourses of the high and the low. And I have a secondary purpose in choosing this approach: cultural historians have produced some of the most subtle (and best informed) analyses of popular culture, and yet their work remains oddly distanced from (and ignored by) cultural studies, a subject with, it seems, a cavalierly postmodern attitude to the past.

Peter Van Der Merwe argues that in nineteenth-century Europe musical categorizations revolved around three axes: musical literacy, social class, and aesthetic status. Aesthetic judgments, that is to say, rested on criteria that were both musical and social. On the one hand, this meant that the high/low distinction only came into play in what might be called a common musical field. Music hall was low culture in a way that folk music was not, because music hall could be seen as an impoverished or banal use of a musical language also employed by "serious" composers.[8] (The same distinction is apparent today in the different attitude of the classical music world to Western pop and to so-called "world musics," and in the academic distinction between music studied by musicologists and music studied by ethnomusicologists.) On the other hand, this meant that as the class structure got more complicated (particularly with the rise of a new sort of middle class), so did musical judgments, the ways in which high/low boundaries were defined.

One could put this another way: the high/low cultural boundary was partly defined by the choices made by people (composers, performers, listeners) within a shared musical context. It was only through such choices (the serious over the frivolous, the idealistic over the commercial) that the social significance of the judgment could be made clear. If such choice wasn't possible, if the different musics were simply, well, different (like different folk musics), then musical taste revealed nothing about one's aesthetic facilities at all (just as the habit of listening to one sort of religious music rather than another would be an effect of one's religious beliefs and not one's musical tastes). Dave Russell makes clear the resulting confusions of class, aesthetic, and musical differences in his history of popular music in England at the end of the nineteenth century. He quotes, for example, from the Reverend Haweis's *Music and Morals:* "Music is not to our lower orders a deep-rooted need, a means of expressing the pent-up and oppressive emotions of the heart, but merely a noisy appendage to low pastimes." And from the *Yorkshire Orchestra:*

Our bandsmen are all mechanics; some of them, no doubt fine specimens of humanity—rough, hard-working, honest fellows— deserving our highest admiration as mechanics, *but lacking the refinement of feeling or the ability to become efficient musicians.* The greatest delight many of them have is to wear a grand military uniform, so that they may parade in the streets at night, followed by a large crowd (usually composed of all the tag-rag and bobtail of the town) when "bang" goes the big drum, immediately followed by a terrific crash of nasty, coarse, brassy sounds, enough to terrify into fits our little ones, who are frequently awoke out of the first sleep by these noisy, thoughtless, brassy men.[9]

This has something of the same disdain as Mark Crispin Miller's view of rock musicians and fans quoted in Chapter 1, but it suggests the recurring anxiety of those who originally made such high/low distinctions that they were, in fact, spurious. As Van Der Merwe points out, the very effort that went into distinguishing classical music from parlor songs reflected a furtive pleasure in the latter (just as musicians frequently crossed the boundaries, whether as professionals, taking paid work where they could find it, or as amateurs, piano players and choral singers, shifting in and out of the classical and the popular repertoires).[10]

One aspect of this, as cultural historians have shown in entertaining detail, is the amount of work that had to go into the production of "high culture" as something special in the first place. William Weber, for example, suggests that in the eighteenth century there was little distinction between high and popular music (distinctions were only made in terms of musical literacy: some music needed performers and listeners with specific forms of musical training). But in the early nineteenth century, under the influence of Romanticism, with its concepts of "genius" on the one hand, and "the folk" on the other, German classical music came to be seen as high art, while other forms of composed music (Italian opera, for example) or virtuoso performances (soon to be embodied in Liszt) were seen as "popular." Such differences were institutionalized within what we would now think of as the classical music world: the "popular" music public going for novelty, stars, salons, and benefit shows; the "art" music public going to orchestral and chamber music concerts which put the emphasis on a musical canon, on composers and compositions (with choral music left to lower middle class amateur choirs).[11]

In other words, the nineteenth-century mapping of musical taste in Europe was bound up with shifting identities within the middle class. From the 1830s a high-status, affluent "popular" classical music public came to dominate musical institutions, and to merge with upper-class audiences, to adopt "art" musical values. Weber notes two aspects of this process in particular: first, the importance of music for middle-class family life, and for the social and courtship rituals that now began to integrate the bourgeoisie into landed capitalist families; and second, the increasing power of the professional musician in this marketplace (as performer, teacher, promoter, and publisher)—amateur musicians (the upper-class model) were displaced, and a new sort of musical "magnate" appeared. What we now recognize as the classical music world marked, in short, a simultaneous economic and aesthetic movement: "high culture" was commercialized and professionalized, but popular middle-class culture was infused with the ideal of transcendence. New boundaries now had to be drawn within the "popular": amateur music making was increasingly a lower middle class affair (as reflected in the history of the piano); entertaining music (music in cafés and dance halls and parks) was increasingly seen as "vulgar."[12]

Lawrence Levine has traced the same developments (under German influence) in the even more complicated musical class structure of the United States, showing how the cultural flexibility of eighteenth-century America gave way to the uplifting aesthetic ideology of the mid-nineteenth. "A concert given in Baltimore on September 12, 1796, attests to the prevalence of a musical ethos quite divergent from the one we have come to know, an ethos that thought it quite proper to follow a Haydn overture with the song 'And All For My Pretty Brunette,' and a Bach overture with the song, 'Oh, None Can Love Like an Irish Man.'"[13]

The development of a new musical ethos meant first promoting the concept of "a sacralized art," an "art that makes no compromises with the 'temporal' world, an art that remains spiritually pure and never becomes secondary to the performer or to the audience, an art that is uncompromising in its devotion to cultural perfection"—the words are taken from *Dwight's Journal of Music*—and then marking off this sort of cultural experience from all others.

> Thus by the early decades of this century the changes that had either begun or gained velocity in the last third of the nineteenth century were in place: the masterworks of the classical composers were to be performed in their entirety by highly trained musicians on programs free from the contamination of lesser works or lesser genres, free from the distractions of the mundane; audiences were to approach the masters and their works with proper respect and proper serious-ness, for aesthetic and spiritual elevation rather than mere entertain-ment was the goal.[14]

And Paul Di Maggio has shown how this aesthetic argument was fed into the development of a class-conscious American bourgeoisie: the distinction between high and popular culture, he writes, emerged in the second half of the nineteenth century "out of the efforts of urban elites to build organiza-tional forms that, first, isolated high culture and, second, differentiated it from popular culture." His examples are the Boston Symphony Orchestra (which sloughed off the Boston Pops) and the Boston Museum of Fine Arts. What became high art rituals, connoisseurship and so on, were, then, an aspect of bourgeois "distinction" which combined social, aesthetic, and ethical superiority: if art had become the experience of the transcendent and the ineffable, then it was also the exclusive property of "those with the status to claim that their experience is the purest, the most authentic."[15]

The problem, though, was to make this distinction stick, to hold on to high art as an exclusive property, particularly when it was, in fact, being made and consumed as a commodity in a marketplace. "The art must not be degraded," complained a columnist in London's *Music World* in 1845 in response to an announcement of cheap concerts. "To play the finest music to an audience which has been admitted at a shilling apiece is what I can never give consent to."[16]

And despite such calls to control taste by price, in England, at least, by the end of the nineteenth century "something very close to a mass musical culture had emerged—a sharing of common taste across a broad social range."

> Through the people's concert, the concert-hall, the music-hall, the choral contest, the brass band performance and other routes, Handel, Wagner and Donizetti to name but three, were known to many 'ordinary people': vaguely by some, intimately and expertly by a significant minority.[17]

This is not to deny that there was, by the end of the nineteenth century, a "Great Musical Schism" between classical and parlor music, but, rather, that the differences could not be easily mapped onto the class structure. Just as professional musicians of the time moved easily between opera and music hall pit bands, between winter seasons in symphony orchestras and summer seasons in pier shows, so listeners from all social spheres could be fans of Wagner and Vesta Tilley, choral music and comedy turns. Dave Russell describes concert bills in the late nineteenth century which match Levine's examples from late eighteenth century America, suggesting that the musical ethos had not, perhaps, changed as much as the aesthetic argument suggested: "A popular concert in Bradford in 1871 featured the music hall star The Great Vance, Miss Newbould, a local soprano, and the Halifax Glee and Madrigal Society; in 1897 visitors to the Bournemouth Winter Gardens could have heard the municipal orchestra follow Mendelssohn's *Ruy Blas* with a medley of Albert Chevalier's coster songs."[18] And Katherine Preston's study of professional musicians in Washington, D.C. at the end of the century suggests that the high/low distinction was really a matter of occasion. Orchestras which were available for anything from a family picnic to the opening of a new shop, from a steam trip to a fashion show, reserved their "elevated" music for elevated events. "At dances, for parades, in the theater, at athletic events, at private parties, and on excursion boats," the musicians played popular songs and dances, melodies from musical theater and operetta; at university commencements and official ceremonies they switched to classical, European sounds.[19]

"Highbrow and lowbrow lived in the same world," as Van Der Merwe puts it, and "quite often they were the same person." A fact that turn-of-the-century entrepreneurs were quick to exploit. In its 1934 obituary of Edward Elgar, the *Times* remembered what a "rage" his first (1904) symphony had been: "For some time the regular orchestras of London could not play it often enough, special concerts were arranged for it, [and] enterprising commercialists even engaged orchestras to play it in their lounges and palm courts as an attraction to their winter sales of underwear."[20]

To trace the social meaning of high and low culture, then, it is not enough to point to the aesthetic ideology of the urban bourgeoisie; we also need to look at the effects of mass cultural production, which marked out the emergence of bourgeois culture and worked on it (just as it marked out and worked on the urban proletariat). The "transcendent" meaning of classical music, for example, was both exploited and denied by its use in the new movie houses, just as it has been since by radio and record and television companies, as the background sound of advertisements and airplanes and shopping malls. And the mass cultural notion of stardom, combining a Romantic belief in genius with a promise to make it individually available as commodity (and merchandise) derives as much from the packaging of "high" artists as from the hype of the low. Levine describes, for example, how "three of the most popular European visitors to the United States in the first half of the nineteenth century—the Viennese ballerina Fanny Elssler, the Norwegian violinist Ole Bull, and the Swedish soprano Jenny Lind," were able "to assume a place in a cultural lexicon that cut through class and income." This wasn't just a matter of repertoire; it also meant that their names could be exploited in the most crass ways without it, apparently, demeaning their art. During her American tour in 1840–1842, "shops peddled Fanny Elssler brand boots, garters, stockings, corsets, parasols, cigars, shoe polish, shaving soap and champagne."[21]

Merchandising in the name of Jenny Lind (whose first American tour was masterminded by P. T. Barnum) was even more extensive, and it is certainly arguable that it was with "classical" rather than "pop" musicians that the music business came to understand the possibilities of mass marketing: if Elssler and Lind set the pattern for touring and merchandising, Caruso showed what it could mean to be a recording star and Toscanini what money could be made out of a radio station/record company tie-up (just as Pavarotti became a force for the spread of CDs and global multimedia exploitation). The case of Jenny Lind is particularly instructive because Barnum was so explicit about his use of her purity, her "transcendence" ("art in its sanctity," as Hans Christian Anderson described her voice) in his sales strategy:

> From a Swedish artist, [he] acquired a romanticized portrait of Jenny Lind for fifty dollars. He had it reproduced in newspapers and periodicals and handbills. He hired an English journalist who had heard Jenny Lind sing, and instructed him to grind out weekly news stories stressing her chastity, charity and European triumphs. These stories were released to the Press under a London dateline. Barnum encouraged publishers to bring out biographical pamphlets on his vocalist. Monthly magazines devoted completely to her were put on sale.

Barnum's strategy was triumphant. The *New York Tribune*'s music critic duly described how he and the enraptured first-night audience watched "the divine songstress, with that perfect bearing, that air of all dignity and sweetness, blending a childlike simplicity and half-trembling womanly modesty with the beautiful confidence of Genius and serene wisdom of Art, address herself to song." What Barnum was selling was the classical ideal.[22]

Three lessons can be learned, I think, from mass cultural history. First, if high culture is defined too simply as bourgeois culture, then it becomes an equally over-simple reflex to equate mass culture with the working class. In fact mass culture (if we define it as the culture made possible by technological change, by the use of the means of mass cultural production) has always been a form of middle-class culture, characterized by middlebrow concerns, marked by highbrow traces. As Janice Radway has shown in her studies of the Book of the Month Club, the rise of a mass culture at the beginning of this century actually meant a blurring of the distinctions between high and low, art and commerce, the sacred and the profane.[23] This was, indeed, a point made by Max Horkheimer and Theodor Adorno in *Dialectic of Enlightenment,* where they note that the culture industry compromises the vulgar and the absurd as much as it does the serious and the difficult: "The culture industry is corrupt not because it is a sinful Babylon, but because it is a cathedral dedicated to elevated pleasure . . . The fusion of culture and entertainment that is taking place today leads not only to a deprivation of culture, but inevitably to an intellectualisation of amusement."[24]

The implications of this for musical tastes are examined in detail in

Joseph Horowitz's *Understanding Toscanini*, an illuminating case study of what, following Dwight Macdonald, he calls midcult, "high culture diluted for mass sales and consumption."[25] Here we see how that mode of rapt, superior musical appreciation so laboriously constructed by Theodore Thomas and his followers in the nineteenth century was adapted to new media (record companies and the radio) and a new audience (the advertiser-friendly middle class). Radio, notes Horowitz, "feasted on great music"—and he's talking about commercial radio, American radio, not the BBC.

> Radio offered the Metropolitan Opera and the NBC Symphony on Saturdays, the New York Philharmonic and "The Ford Hour" on Sundays. As of 1939, these four well-known longhair broadcasts were said to reach more than 10 million families a week . . . and the weekday schedule might include more than a dozen live broadcasts of hinterlands orchestras, and studio recitals. Moreover, when the radio was off, the phonograph was on . . . RCA Victor's sales rose 600% between 1933 and 1938, with symphonic, not popular, releases leading the way.[26]

As Horowitz argues, what this "commercialization" of classical music involved was not simply an exercise in transforming something transcendent into something commonplace, nor was it an entirely cynical exercise in using "great music" as a source of prestige (just as obvious in the drive of every American town of reasonable size to have its own civic orchestra). There was also an idealism here: "to partake in great music's exclusivity was made a democratic privilege." The selling of classical music on radio and record was mediated by "musical appreciation," by instruction about how you, as an "ordinary" person, should listen to and therefore come to appreciate extraordinary music. And such an educational strategy was an aspect of the classical record market from the beginning (in Britain, for example, EMI funded *The Gramophone,* and ran classes for shop assistants, so that they could in turn educate record shoppers). Music appreciation followed the Great Books model of literary appreciation, and the record industry certainly looked to book publishing for guidance to records' market potential. In particular, pop music's appeal was taken to be unstable (especially after the collapse of record sales at the end of the 1920s); people had to be persuaded to build a "library" of recordings, to treat music-on-record as something to treasure and keep. Horowitz quotes *The Victor Book of the Symphony,* published by RCA in 1934: "The importance to music of modern methods of reproducing sounds is parallel to that of the printing press to literature, philosophy and the whole sum of the world's knowledge."[27]

Horowitz suggests that we should not overstate the aesthetic impact of midcult. If a minority of the new audience "purposely used music appreciation to enhance their social esteem and social rank," an equal minority undoubtedly "moved from music appreciation to understanding, fortified by 'active listening' and praxis." And for the majority of listeners what mattered "was the excitement of newfound experience, of an unsuspected passion whose rituals included record collecting, radio listening, and starting or supporting a first-class symphony orchestra." In other words, "adapting mass culture to the high cultural world" (or the reverse) meant, above all, developing new forms of sociability, and what is most striking is how much this depended on clubs and societies—the gramophone society, the book club, the film society, the rhythm club (the label in Britain for "jazz appreciation societies," which met in the 1930s and 1940s to listen to and discuss jazz records).[28] Paradoxically, in short, the rise of "mass culture" meant new forms of social activity, new ways of using aesthetic experience to define social identity.

My second historical point follows from this: if one effect of mass culture was to "discipline" the nineteenth-century urban "unrespectable," another, equally important, was to loosen up the nineteenth-century urban (or suburban) respectable. There is, by now, much illuminating historical work on the former process. In *Rudeness and Civility*, for example, John F. Kassan shows clearly how the rise of consumer culture, the "orderly spectacle," meant the decline of a participatory, communal leisure culture in American working-class neighborhoods, a move from "enthusiasm" to "disciplined spectatorship."[29]

But the other side of this story is the selling of "safe" ways for middle-class city dwellers (and the respectable working class) to enjoy the proletarian pleasures of noisy public behavior. Kathy Peiss, for example, suggests that the rise of mass culture (the cinema is a good instance) meant developing those aspects of working-class leisure that the middle class found attractive and shedding those things of which they disapproved. Mass culture meant "Polite Vaudeville," "regulated pleasure," for all classes; it was organized, in particular, around "hetero-sociability" and a new valorization of youth. Her example is Coney Island:

> Steeplechase incorporated into its notion of mass entertainment cultural patterns derived from working class amusements, street life and popular entertainment. Like them, the park encouraged familiarity between strangers, permitted a free-and-easy sexuality, and structured heterosocial interaction. This culture was not adopted

wholesale, but was transformed and controlled, reducing the threatening nature of sexual contact by removing it from the street, workplace and saloon. Within the amusement park, familiarity between women and men could be acceptable if tightly structured and made harmless through laughter. At Steeplechase, sexuality was constructed in terms of titillation, voyeurism, exhibitionism and a stress on a couple and romance.[30]

From this historical perspective, popular culture describes the process in which class and other group values and conflicts are *mediated* (rather than directly expressed), which is one reason why popular commodities (heavy metal music, say, or splatter movies, or the tabloid press) can be and often are simultaneously "transgressive" (of "respectable" values) and reactionary.

My third point follows: if mass culture is defined not against middle-class culture, against art, but as a way of processing it, then the crucial high/low conflict is not that between social classes but that produced by the commercial process itself at all levels of cultural expression, in pop as well as classical music, in sport as well as literature. High/low thus describes the emergence of consumer elites or cults, on the one hand (the bohemian versus the conformist), and the tension between artists and their audiences (the modernist and avant-gardist versus the orthodox and the mainstream), on the other. I'll come back to the value terms of these conflicts in Chapter 3; here I just want to reiterate a point well made by Geoffrey Nowell-Smith, who notes that because of the culture industries' inability to control taste themselves (for all their efforts), they have to rely on other "taste-forming machines" (or what in this chapter I'm calling discursive practices). It is for this reason that "traditional criteria of what is good and what is not" continue to be influential, and that "the culture industry can often be happier with art—or what passes for art—than with items of acknowledged junk culture like game shows and pop singles."

> The conservative critique of the culture industry—and some "left" critique as well—has focused on the way it has marginalized art and displaced it with commercial pap. This critique seems to me misplaced. Living art may well be marginal, thriving only in the interstices of society untouched by the culture industry. But what has replaced it in the mainstream is not just the novelty of popular culture. All too often the replacement for living art is dead art.[31]

This is the context in which I want to turn now to a more orderly, sociological approach to contemporary aesthetic discourse. My arguments are derived from two sociological models: Howard S. Becker's account of "art worlds" and Pierre Bourdieu's concept of "cultural capital."[32] Becker suggests that to understand art objects and people's response to them we have to understand the institutional and discursive processes (the art world) in which they are constructed as art objects, as works to which a particular sort of aesthetic response is socially appropriate. Bourdieu uses the concept of cultural capital to relate cultural values to social structural variables (social class variables in his case), to questions of power and hierarchy that Becker puts to one side. The reason different people engage with different art worlds has to do with the amount (and type) of cultural capital they possess. For Bourdieu, in other words, the aesthetic response can only be understood by reference to the social organization of taste which patterns people's lifestyle, morality, and habitus. Putting Becker and Bourdieu together (and extrapolating somewhat from what they actually say), I want to suggest that, in very broad terms, music is valued according to three types of discursive practice (related to Becker's three sorts of art worlds, to Bourdieu's three kinds of taste groups).[33]

The first art world I want to describe, the first taste group, is what I will call (although it is not an altogether satisfactory term) the bourgeois world (or what Bourdieu calls dominant culture). In terms of my argument in this book, the bourgeois art world is the world of classical (or art) music, the world of nineteenth-century high culture (and twentieth-century midcult) which I have already described.

The organizing institution of bourgeois musical discourse is, as Bourdieu argues, the academy, by which I mean the music departments of universities, conservatories, the whole panoply of formal arrangements and practices in which classical music in its various forms is taught and handed down the generations. Central to this world is the teacher/pupil relationship, the belief that musicians must serve an apprenticeship, must progress through fixed stages (like the Associated Board's instrumental grades in Britain) before they are "qualified" to play. (I'm always struck by the way in which concert program notes describe soloists in terms of their teachers, as if establishing a sort of *provenance* for their talent; jazz musicians, by contrast, are described by reference to whom they have previously played with.) As in the similarly academic fine art world, to compose or play without having the right credentials, without having had one's talent "passed on," so to speak, is to be labeled "primitive" or "naive." Kyle Gann suggests that in the United States the operative distinction for composers is thus that between the amateur and the professional. In Morton Feldman's words, "In music, when you do something new, something original, you're an amateur," while the professional composer

> writes a piece occasionally. It is played occasionally . . . His pieces are well made. He is not without talent. The reviews aren't bad. A few awards—a Guggenheim, an Arts and Letters, a Fulbright—this is the official musical life of America. You can't buck the system, especially if it works. And this system does work . . . These men are their own audience. They are their own fame. Yet they have created a climate that has brought the musical activity of an entire nation down to a college level.[34]

As Feldman (who sees himself as working in the unprofessional, "iconoclastic," passed-over-in-one's-lifetime tradition of Charles Ives and Edgard Varèse) makes clear here, the bourgeois music world faces a constant tension between its firm sense of musical tradition (which has to be preserved, documented, refined, and elaborated) and its equally firm belief in the value of creativity and the importance of the new and the original. And I would make a further point here, with specific reference to composition. The ideology is that the composer is answerable only to herself; she does not compose for an audience; she is, in this respect, free of the crowd-pleasing pressures that afflict the "hack." In practice, though, the "professional" composer (the composer, that is, whose living is composition) has to please an audience—teachers, grant givers, concert programmers, specialist record companies—which is in many respects more tightly in control of the "acceptable composition" than the so-called mass public. Truth-to-self, in other words, depends on others' approval until (just as in the pop world) one reaches a sufficient level of success (in terms of both esteem and earnings) to be "autonomous."[35]

The best account I know of these tensions is Henry Kingsbury's sensitive and revealing study of a music conservatory. The problem for the music student, suggests Kingsbury, is focused on the concept of "talent." Talent is something that students possess, it is talked about as something real, but it can only be recognized by someone else, by a teacher, and the paradox of music education is its underlying assumption that only the "talented" few can be taught what is in the end unteachable (because it is, in fact, a quality of the student). On the one hand, this confirms the importance of the teacher/pupil relationship—musical apprenticeship as a process of recognition by someone with the authority to recognize (and be recognized); on the other hand, it means that from the students' point of view their "talent" is never actually in their possession at all: it exists only in its validation by others. And this comes to the heart of the problem of tradition versus creation, or, in Kingsbury's terms, between playing music and playing notes, between technical skill (the ability to play the notes "correctly") and musical skill, the ability—the talent—to do what? To be recognized as talented! The problem (and a cause of great stress and paranoia at music schools) is that while talent is assigned and described individually, it only exists in the making of music as a social event; in Kingsbury's words, "musical meaning is social meaning."[36]

As we'll see in the next chapter, this makes for profound value conflicts between performers and audiences even as the applause for the performance rings out, but for the moment it is enough to say that the role of the academy is not simply to produce performers and to nurture "talent," but also to institutionalize a familiar way of thinking about music: as the creation of composing geniuses, embodied in sacred scores (texts guarded religiously by music scholars), faithfully but feelingly articulated by gifted performers to reverential audiences guided by enlightened critics.[37]

In terms of consumption too, then, the bourgeois art world depends on scholarship, on the accumulation of the knowledge of musical history and the compositional process without which score and performance cannot be understood. As Aaron Copland put it in a 1936–37 music appreciation course (later published as *What to Listen for in Music*),

> No composer believes that there are any short cuts to the better appreciation of music . . . It is very important for all of us to become more alive to music on its sheerly musical plane . . . The intelligent listener must be prepared to increase his awareness of the musical material and what happens to it . . . Above all he must, in order to follow the composer's thought, know something of the principles of musical form.[38]

The scholarly skills developed in university music departments—archive skills, reading skills, interpretive skills—are, then, just like those developed by art historians or literary critics. Their purpose is the same: to establish the canon, to come up with a coherent, linear historico-aesthetic narrative.[39] But to sustain the classical music world such academic skills must make their way out of the university to the general bourgeois public, which depends for its knowledge on a set of semi-academic institutions and practices—liner notes, music journals, newspaper critics, concert programmers, and classical music radio stations—which bridge the gap between high music scholarship and everyday domestic music listening.[40]

While laymen and women can thus gain access to the classical world, it remains strictly hierarchical. There is a clear distinction, that is, between the composer of a work and its performers, between performers and their audience; and the central bourgeois music event, the concert, offers (in its ideal) a transcendent experience, something special, something apart from the everyday world. As Thomas Russell put it in his best-selling 1942 book on the London Philharmonic Orchestra, "To leave a concert hall after a vital experience and fight for a seat in a bus or a train, to jostle for a place in a crowded café, surrounded by people *not blessed with the same experience* is to become aware of an anti-climax."[41]

The seriousness of the classical concert is both made possible by and registered in a series of performing conventions. Lawrence Levine has shown how sternly the nineteenth-century American audience had to be taught these conventions, taught to listen silently and respectfully, taught that the highest musical experience was, well, religious; in the twentieth century these listening conventions have been coded into the building and organization of concert halls themselves. In an illuminating comparison of musical performance in London's Royal Festival Hall and in a New Orleans jazz café, Christopher Jackman shows the elaborate extent to which audiences are now prepared for a spiritual experience in a classical venue, with its strict separation of bodily needs (toilets, bars, and cloakrooms) from musical uplift (No Drinks to be Taken into the Auditorium), and its careful use of staging and lighting to mark out the boundaries of the musical moment. In the jazz café the musicians employ a very different set of performing conventions (negotiating with the waitresses, for example, a balance between letting customers listen and hassling them for orders), and the difficulty of responding properly to a rock show in a concert hall is familiar: in Britain, at least, there is a ceaseless skirmish between the dancers in the aisles and the patrolling security staff.[42]

To summarize, then, bourgeois or what I shall now call the art music discourse is organized around a particular notion of musical scholarship, a particular concept of musical talent, and a particular sort of musical event, in which music's essential value is its provision of a transcendent experience that is, on the one hand, ineffable and uplifting but, on the other, only available to those with the right sort of knowledge, the right sorts of interpretive skills. Only the right people with the right training can, in short, experience the real meaning of "great" music.

The second source of evaluative musical discourse is what I'll term the folk music world (roughly speaking, what Bourdieu means by popular culture). The starting argument here is that the value of music has to be understood in terms of cultural necessity—ideally, there is no separation of art and life. The appreciation of music is therefore tied up with an appreciation of its social function. Many of the terms and arguments of this discourse are familiar from ethnomusicological studies of non-Western, non-capitalist cultures, but the point I want to make here is that the terms of folk culture are sustained in the ways in which people talk about popular music in the West too. How, then, is folk discourse sustained in societies in which folk music is, according to its own anti-modernist ideology, impossible?

The most sustained sociological answer to this question can be found in Niall MacKinnon's *The British Folk Scene,* a study which reveals two problems in particular. First, the folk values of the natural, the spontaneous, and the immediate are, in fact, only realized through a kind of subterfuge. The folk world, in MacKinnon's words, depends on "an elaborate construction of informality," an informality which operates as a form of "constraint" on performers and audiences alike. He describes folk's subtle performing conventions—the way stages are set and lit and amplified, the rules of when audiences should talk and when they should keep silent, the obligation on performers to "shrink from overtly stylised presentations of self," to avoid elaborate stage movements.[43] Second, such folk conventions only work because of their difference from the perceived rules of commercial pop. What's involved in folk performance, as MacKinnon puts it, is "a very conscious destroying and destruction of glamour."[44]

Now it's easy enough to be cynical about folk discourse, which seems to rest on an essential self-deception—that which is worked hard for is presented as coming naturally, that which is commodified is presented as communal. But this is not to say that folk ideology isn't (perhaps for just this reason) rhetorically very persuasive, and there are two further reasons for this. First, the folk world, like the classical world, in preserving its ideals puts a central emphasis on tradition. It has its own archives and archivists, its own scholars and scholarly magazines, its own instructive use of liner notes ("the record as teaching device").[45] The emphasis, though, is less on history and the accumulation of knowledge than on "purity" and the correct (traditional) way of doing things. Folk music is thus evaluated (and condemned—Dylan going electric) according to concepts of unchanging musical "truth."

Second, the folk world is organized around a set of performing rituals, not the rituals of bourgeois transcendence but nonetheless rituals that mark off the musical experience from everyday life. Folk discourse, in other words, can only be understood as a critique of quotidian commerce. Robert Cantwell describes how the 1950s folk revival in the United States drew on a vision of "the old Free America": "The revival made the romantic claim of folk culture—oral, immediate, traditional, idiomatic, communal, a culture of characters, of rights, obligations, and beliefs, against a centrist, specialist, impersonal technocratic culture, a culture of types, functions, jobs and goals."[46]

The most developed and important folk rituals are therefore the club and the festival. MacKinnon remembers his first—conversion—experience of the folk club: "People sang. They sang to each other, without a stage, without amplification, with no special clothes, and with no special flourish which said 'we are performers.'" And he goes on to describe how folk clubs attempt to minimize the distance between performer and audience, to provide a "different form of socialising in which active musical performance and participation [are] integrated."[47]

The folk festival describes a time (usually a weekend) and a space (usually outdoors) within which folk values—the integration of art and life—can be lived (and this is a form which is therefore used—for folk ends—by other musical genres, by rock, soul, and rave). Hence the strict festival conventions: the famous performer must come and have a drink with the audience in the tent after the show, and, often enough, take part in workshops; anyone in the audience must be able to stand up somewhere on the site—in a "club room"—and perform herself, informally; there is a constant attempt to deny the actual (commercial) separation of folk stars and folk fans. Folk festivals are more likely to be organized around a large number of small stages than one big spectacle; there is, as MacKinnon puts it, no "back room" for folk performers, no place to prepare themselves. Bruce Jackson describes how the Newport Folk Festival was remade in 1967–68: there was an increased emphasis on education sessions and workshops, a decreased use of microphones and stars, as the organizers sought to reestablish the gathering as a folk rather than a pop event. And Georgina Boyes notes how at the same time in Britain folk festivals offered "folk club members the chance to live the Revival lifestyle for days at a time."[48] In short, the folk festival seeks to solve the problem of musical "authenticity"; it offers the experience of the folk ideal, the experience of collective, participatory music making, the chance to judge music by its direct contribution to sociability.

The third source of musical discourse is the commercial music world (what Bourdieu would call majority culture), which I won't describe in detail here since I've dealt with it extensively elsewhere.[49] Its values are created by and organized around the music industry, around the means and possibilities of turning sounds into commodities—musical value and monetary value are therefore equated, and the sales charts become the measure and symbol of "good" pop music. The commercial music world is also organized around particular sorts of musical events—events (such as promotional concerts and discos) which offer a kind of routinized transcendence, which sell "fun." Fun is an escape from the daily grind (which is what makes it pleasurable) but is, on the other hand, integrated with its rhythms—the rhythms of work and play, production and consumption.

The tripartite structure I've suggested here of bourgeois, folk, and commercial music worlds, of high art, folk art, and pop art, is familiar enough, and one can readily observe the discourses in operation. Wilfrid Mellers's rock musicologies, for example, describe performers who start out as "folk" musicians, get absorbed into the "pop" process, and then emerge as "artists."[50] And in *Sound Effects* I suggested that in trying to distinguish the practices of rock from those of "commercial" pop, rock's '60s ideologists were obliged to draw on both folk values and art values.[51] Even more dramatically, the jazz critic Ernest Borneman suggests that

> every cycle of civilisation re-enacts the Fall of Man in every generation and on every level of experience. Awareness wrecks the naive innocence of a folk culture and divides it, like Cain and Abel, into embodiments of an ever widening conflict between the eclectic upper-class culture of the few and the epigonic cliché culture of the vast masses who have lost the innocence of a naive folk art without gaining the awareness of a fully developed aesthetic.[52]

In the end, then, what is involved here is not the creation and maintenance of three distinct, autonomous music worlds but, rather, the play of three historically evolving discourses across a single field—hence the sorts of disputes with which I began this chapter.[53] For musicians and listeners in the bourgeois, folk, and commercial music worlds alike, value judgments reflect a path being traced with some difficulty through the confusing noise of competing discourses. If, for example, the standard line of rock 'n' roll history is that an authentic (that is, folk) sound is continually corrupted by commerce, it could equally well be argued that what the history actually reveals is a commercial musical form continually being recuperated in the name of art and subculture.[54] In the folk world, similarly, the terms "authentic" and "artificial" are used to describe the same musical processes. Thus bluegrass, a musical form whose invention can be dated fairly precisely, stands now (in the annual summer season of bluegrass festivals) not just for the North American folk tradition but for the North American mountain and country traditions too.[55]

Art music makers also know well enough that their livelihoods depend on commercial logic, that art and commercial values have to be reconciled in practice if kept apart in rhetoric. This was the symbolic importance of Toscanini (and, indeed, of the development of the conductor as star), and one can still hear the argument at work on North American classical music radio stations: listen to the deejays imply in their reverent tones of voice that what is on offer is still a transcendent experience even if it is now punctuated by advertisements for insurance. As classical music becomes a ubiquitous part of the commercial soundscape—as the background hum of upmarket offices, shops, and telephones on hold—we are, in George Steiner's words, enveloped by "A Muzak of the sublime."[56]

But value discourses don't themselves work autonomously either: their terms were developed in relationship to each other; each discourse represents a response to the shared problems of music making in an industrial capitalist society; each can be traced back, therefore, to the late eighteenth century; and each can be found in the ways all sorts of musics have made sense of themselves in the twentieth century, whether in the Romantic mythology of rock or in the spiritual ambitions of the brass band movement, with its "sincere attempt to apprehend the good, the beautiful and the true," to help "mankind on an upward journey."[57]

It seems unduly restrictive, in short, to treat the classical, folk, and pop music worlds (as most analysts have) as if they were distinct objects of study; it is more fruitful, as Ruth Finnegan has argued, to treat them comparatively, tracing contrasting solutions to shared problems.[58] How are the different musics learned and taught, for example? How is skill defined? How are the lines drawn between the "amateur" and the "professional"? I'll return to these and other contextual questions in Chapter 3, but I can make the point here that a comparative sociology reveals far less clear distinctions between music worlds than their discursive values imply. And one of the most striking aspects of popular music history is that musics may anyway change their discursive meaning, may cross apparently firm cultural boundaries. As Ernest Borneman once argued, "All standards of musical criticism are abstractions from a previously developed and digested practice of music. Theory limps: it is always a step behind practice. A new music requires a new aesthetic rationalisation."[59]

And it first of all needs to be heard as a "new music." I've discussed elsewhere the ways in which pop was rethought as art in the 1960s and 1970s, so I'll focus here on the case of jazz.[60] Examining its initial reception in Britain, Howard Rye notes that one question critics had to answer (and to begin with answered quite differently) was to what extent this African-American music was continuous with what was already familiar from the nineteenth century—minstrelsy and Negro spirituals: "The inconsistency of responses underlies the absence of any established critical standards." But the issue, at least to begin with, wasn't so much the absence of standards as a confusion about which ones to apply. Thus Joe Jordon's Syncopated Orchestra, which made a brief British tour after appearing in a London revue, *Push and Go*, in 1905, was firmly placed in the perceived nineteenth-century black musical tradition:

> Jordon's Syncopated Orchestra at Newcastle's Empire Theatre are unquestionably one of the smartest combinations since minstrelsy was in its prime. They, numbering ten, present an entertainment anything but antiquated, and . . . sing and dance in a manner that entirely drives away dull care and compels one to be joyful.[61]

The Southern Syncopated Orchestra (which included Sydney Bechet) was described in rather different critical terms when it played in London fourteen years later, in 1919:

> This negro folk music is quite an art-music of its own and is of course best when interpreted by those who truly love and understand the spirit of it as these thirty-six players do. There is richness of melody, diablerie, merriment and some pathos interwoven, but the unique entertainment is one music lovers should not miss as it serves to demonstrate how very far from its original sources nine-tenths of the ragtime we get howled at us has strayed.

While in the words of another critic, "Mr Sydney Bechet's extemporised clarinette solo"—which was also impressing Ernest Ansermet—"compels admiration, so true is his ear and so rhythmical and vital his conception."[62]

The confusion over quite what to hear in this music—minstrelsy, folk culture, art, craft?—continued in Britain until the end of the 1920s, when *Melody Maker*'s critics changed the way they wrote about it—and therefore, presumably, the way they heard it—in the space of a few months.[63] Ron Welburn has examined the parallel discursive shift in American jazz criticism. In brief, in the 1920s, critics (music critics rather than jazz critics then) focused on "symphonic jazz" and ignored improvised ensembles. The early critics, that is to say, were interested in the ways in which jazz's "nonintellectual" elements (rhythm, showmanship) were being used by "serious" composers (like Stravinsky or George Gershwin) in "complex" musical structures; by the 1930s symphonic jazz was rarely treated sympathetically by either music or, now, jazz critics.[64]

There were two elements in this shift. First, it began to be argued (by Roger Pryor Dodge in *The Dancing Times* in 1929, for example) that jazz was not a folk music but an art music. It was already "composed"; its "nonintellectual" elements were therefore already being used to maximum artistic effect. Symphonic jazz was thus an arrogant nonsense. As Borneman, writing nearly twenty years later (when jazz's critical criteria were well established) puts it:

> There is no such thing as "symphonic jazz." By our standards, "symphonic" jazz is a term of abuse and not of praise. Bix Beider-becke's little piano pieces which have been compared to Debussy would therefore tend to make us doubt rather than confirm his value as a jazz musician. Gershwin's *Rhapsody in Blue, American in Paris, Concerto in F,* etc., may be admired for any amount of reasons but certainly not for "raising jazz to the level of symphonic music." Jazz has a function in its own right: any attempt at "raising" it can only result in lowering it to the level of a musical hybrid.[65]

When this sort of argument was first made, in the late 1920s, it was still assumed that jazz was a "primitive" art; its musical values were primitive musical values. The best jazz was the most "low down" jazz; it was best played by black jazz musicians and, in Dodge's words, by "those lower members of the white race who have not yet lost their feeling for the primitive." Jazz, in short, had to be understood as "a musical form produced by the primitive innate musical instinct of the negro," and the task of jazz critics was, in the words of B. H. Haggin in 1930, to oppose "arty refinement."[66]

And there was clearly a racial shift here: whereas before it was critically obvious that white jazz was better than black jazz because of its refinement, now the same musical description led to the opposite judgment: black jazz was better than white jazz because of its lack of refinement. But the argument had barely reached this position when critics had to make sense of Duke Ellington. Now what was recognized was a kind of appropriate refinement, a development and elaboration of the "nonintellectual" elements of jazz in ways which could not be understood as either "primitive" or "arty." And it was in making sense of Ellington, suggests Welburn, that jazz criticism developed its basic form, the record review, and a discourse which depended on formal and musical (not functional and sociological) analysis. Welburn cites the case of Robert D. Darrell, who wrote the first detailed praise of Ellington (as against Gershwin) in the *Phonograph Monthly Review* in 1927: "Duke Ellington's music, with its multi-thematic and improvisatory characteristics, provided Darrell a means of shaping and refining the language specifically of the record review and in general the evaluative tenets of jazz criticism."[67]

The sociological point, to conclude, is that we're dealing here with different sorts of music, whether jazz or rap, folk or rock, which are all, in one way or another, handling the issues thrown up by their commodification. (If we wanted to look at musics with really different sociological bases, we'd need to examine those with quite other functions than market exchange—religious music, for example, or military music, which cannot be discussed in art/folk/pop terms.) Whether we are looking at a composition student in a conservatory, a session player on a cruise ship, or a would-be rapper in the Bronx, we're looking at musicians faced with the same problems in deciding whether their music is any good or not. The issues concerned—the position of the artist in the marketplace, the relations of class and community, the tensions between technology and tradition, the shaping of race and nation, the distinction of the public and the private—are not confined to any one social group, to any one musical practice. Whether they become pressing or not depends on circumstances, not ideology. And it is to those circumstances that I will now turn.

Common Sense and the Language of Criticism

If he [the critic] studies music as an aspect of cultural anthropology he is not allowed to judge its value with the current standards of his own civilisation; faced with, say, the boat-songs of seventeenth century Dahomey, he is not in a position to say that song A is "better" than song B, or that singer X is "better" than singer Y. Similarly, on approaching a native American pattern of culture such as the jazz idiom and its tradition, it would be inadequate to say that "St Louis Blues" is a better piece of music than "Pistol Packin' Mama," or that Louis Armstrong is a better trumpeter than Clyde McCoy; instead, we will want to know how and why "St Louis Blues" and "Pistol Packin' Mama" came to exist, what function they perform in the American social pattern and, finally, why Armstrong is considered by our own musicians and critics as a better musician than McCoy.

Ernest Borneman[1]

Every trained pop musician and working pop critic would agree that Jimi Hendrix is a better, and a greater guitarist than Eddie Van Halen; that Frank Sinatra is a better singer than Eddie Fisher.

Jim Miller[2]

In Chapter 1 I suggested that value judgments are the common currency of popular culture. Anyone who's any sort of pop fan is used to the arguments involved—that's a good song, a good tune, a good sound, a good beat—but such judgments have been of surprisingly little interest to cultural theorists. What's going on when these remarks are made? What's being described? What's being inferred? What's the point of making this judgment of this record in these terms at this moment?

Recent theorists of popular meaning have tended to start from the quantitative measures of market research; these are taken to reveal, in themselves, a map of popular taste, an account of popular values (so that when *Billboard* alters its methods of compiling its charts, it's as if American music preferences have changed overnight). But even if they were accurate such measures wouldn't tell us why people chose to tune into a program, go to a movie, buy a CD, nor whether they enjoyed them, nor, indeed, what "enjoyment" might mean. A measurement of popularity, in short, is not a measurement of value.

Market researchers do use qualitative measures too, of course. Cultural producers are always keen to answer the missing questions—why people bought something, whether they enjoyed it, whether they'd buy it again—and television researchers have thus developed the Appreciation Index, and film researchers the use of response cards at previews. The problem with these methods is that their value terms are almost always determined by the researchers, not the respondents. "Appreciation" is indicated by checking boxes which may not describe how people usually think at all, a problem that market researchers then try to solve with focus groups, discussions driven by audience rather than research discourse. But focus groups are not the usual settings in which judgments are made either; they don't tell us much about the everyday process of appreciation, the pleasures of popular discrimination itself.

I haven't got any solutions to these methodological problems. There is some secondary evidence of how people like and rate things in the media themselves, in readers' letters (published and unpublished), in calls to television stations and in requests to radio programs, but these are self-selected samples of viewers and listeners with particularly strong feelings—and a reason for wanting to make them public.[3] This is a problem too with cultural studies' recent interest in self-declared fans, people who are certainly well enough organized to express their views—and, indeed, organize fan clubs in order to do so—but whose terms of judgment are, for just that reason, likely to be a bit peculiar (even if we accept, with the Vermorels, that this peculiarity is just an extreme and obsessive version of what we all do and feel anyway).[4]

I want to start this chapter, then, from a different source of popular criticism, from audience comments on films and film tastes gathered by the British research organization Mass-Observation in the 1930s and 1940s. Mass-Observation was itself a peculiar organization, founded by an anthropologist, a poet, and a filmmaker with two impulses: first, to document "ordinary" British life, to describe, from an anthropological standpoint, British mores, customs, and rituals as they were articulated in the everyday; second, to reveal the oddities, the *unconscious* foundation of British habits.

The methodological basis of its work was therefore to be a mixture of observation ("mass observers" were themselves "ordinary" members of the public, and the line between "observing" and spying or voyeurism was not always clear) and self-observation, through people's use of diaries and questionnaires.[5]

Mass-Observation certainly didn't solve the research problems of sampling or question-begging, but its data do seem to reflect the everyday more than other market research, to give a sense, that is, of how the different things in people's lives fit together. And Mass-Observation also did take for granted people's ability to account for their own actions; the observers were not much interested in the hidden "effects" of the media on people, in how the cinema, say, was changing the patterns of people's lives, their moral values, sense of reality, and so forth, without their knowing it.[6]

The Mass-Observation cinema surveys were designed to discover, like other sorts of research, why people went to the cinema and what sorts of films they enjoyed, but Mass-Observation was also interested in cinema-going as a ritual in itself, and observers were instructed to go to cinemas and take notes of behavior, of those aspects of the occasion that didn't have anything directly to do with the film. They were told to note when people laughed or talked, shouted out remarks or fell silent, to describe all the incidents that formed a night out.[7]

The evidence I want to look at comes from questionnaires handed out and comments elicited (with promises of free tickets) through newspaper advertisements. In 1938 cinema-goers in Bolton were asked to explain their preferences between British and American films; in 1943 a more widely distributed questionnaire asked people to name the best films they had seen in the previous year, and to explain their choices. For my purposes this evidence is interesting because it focuses on specific value judgments and asks people to account for them—the results are less useful, that is, as a measure of British cinema audience taste in 1938–1943 than as a source of evaluative discourse.[8]

It is clear, to begin with, that films were judged in terms of *technique, skill, and craft*. The question for viewers was whether something was done well (acting, most obviously), and there were also recurrent references to cinematic detail, to care (with scenery), and so on. Second, there were recurring evaluations in terms of the *expense* involved, by reference to production values. Cheapness (or tackiness) is a term of abuse, and there is clearly a tendency to value the *spectacular* (which, of course, has a long history in popular theater and melodrama).

These first two clusters of judgment revolve around what people perceived as having gone into the picture, which was well enough understood as an industrial product, a commodity depending for its success on both capital investment and box office returns. Audiences expected that their role as consumers would be taken seriously, and American films were constantly rated more highly than British ones for just this reason: they took moviegoers more seriously in terms of trouble taken (and costs run up). Hollywood has always been aware of this attitude, of course; boasting about how much money a film has cost is a routine part of the marketing process.

A third kind of evaluation referred to films' *truth-to-life,* their believability. This was usually stated in terms of characters (can I identify with them?) and was seen as an issue of both form and content. Judgments refer to conventions of realism (is an actor sincere? was an actress's response authentic? was the story well shaped? did it make sense?) and to experience—the viewer's life is compared to life on the screen, and vice versa.

Fourth, respondents referred to films' ability to *take-one-out-of-oneself,* to give them a quality of experience measured by the intensity of feeling. Judgments of this sort covered thrills and excitement, laughter and surprise (respondents noted that such experiences were quite likely to be matters of moments, found in visual gimmicks and stunt-laden scenes). The point is that entertainment should meet the promise of being different from the everyday.

There are obvious contradictions between the third and fourth criteria here, but these seem to be built into popular film values themselves. It's not that some people want to see films that are true to life and other people films that are different from the everyday; nor even that the same person wants to see one sort of film one day, the other the next. Rather, people want both sorts of qualities simultaneously, and this was evident in the fifth kind of value criterion: the positive evaluation of films in terms of *the range of experiences* offered: a good laugh and a good cry, realism and spectacle, truth and fantasy.

Finally, and again in apparent contrast to this, what is striking in these responses is the significance of *genre distinctions,* the use of genre markers to shape expectations about what kinds of pleasure a film may offer. The recurring negative evaluation only makes sense in these terms: people constantly referred to their *disappointment* in a film—it didn't live up to its promises, it wasn't what I was expecting. Such a judgment reflects people's easy familiarity with genre conventions, but also how they rate films by reference to other films, in terms of their knowledge of stars and directors and studios, of marketing strategies and trailers and billboards. And there is obviously a kind of popular cultural capital at play here too—we can draw a distinction between film fans and ordinary moviegoers, between expert and casual viewers (a distinction taken for granted in people's responses to the questionnaires).

There is a further point to make about this: in assessing their cinematic experience, people brought with them both a knowledge of the cinema and what it could do, and a knowledge of culture and what it could do. This is partly reflected in the way in which films are judged by reference to other cultural forms, to adapted books and quoted paintings. But it is also reflected in a more diffuse sense of the high and the low which runs through these questionnaire answers and which people applied to the films they saw. In everyday terms most of us distinguish between easy and hard listening, between light and heavy reading, between entertaining and serious viewing, and in the Mass-Observation surveys the cinema is thought to be primarily about entertainment and escape, and not usually, therefore, to offer "real" aesthetic experience, though some particularly good "art films" may be "demanding" in the right sort of way. There is, in short, a sense of indulgence (and even guilt) running through even the positive evaluations of films in these surveys (particularly by middle-class viewers), and the food metaphor is recurrent: cream cakes versus something good for you.

Which leads me to the final evaluative theme, the argument that a film should have a *moral*, should teach one something (especially if it hasn't been entertaining!), but also, and I think that's the significance of this term here, should have a *meaning*. The pursuit of a moral (a point, a closure) is, in academic cultural studies, seen as naive if not reactionary; it ensures that commercial popular culture, whatever the supposed content, remains orderly. On the other hand, in pursuit of such order, a popular reading often has to pursue what Jonathan Culler once called (with reference to the story of the Three Little Pigs) "improper questions," just as in their concern for the real, popular readers or viewers or listeners are often in pursuit of improper detail, of gossip, of anecdotal truth.[9]

The compulsion to explain the inexplicable, a recurring theme of popular narrative, has the effect of making the remarkable banal and thus, literally, even more remarkable. This is not a political impulse (politics starts from the material conditions in which people live, not with the cultural strategies that make those conditions livable), but it does generate a certain critical momentum, and much of what I've said here about popular values in moviegoing could, I think, be repeated for popular uses of music. Pop records too are assessed in terms of technique and skill and craft, with reference to things, details, done well. Pop records too are evaluated in terms of expense and spectacle, in terms of what has gone into their production, although of course in rock, to a greater extent than in film, there is also the counter-value of cheapness, the small scale, the "independent," which relates, in turn, to how music is judged as believable, true-to-life, sincere. And music is judged too in terms of its ability to take one out of oneself, to offer intense experiences, an overwhelming mood; and by reference to the range of experiences it offers, to genre expectations, to cultural hierarchy.

I'll come back to these points; in particular to the question of how such criteria can be applied to music, which does not appear to have a "content" quite like film or fiction. But before discussing how people talk about music, I want to say something more about the context of judgment. In the end, after all, even the Mass-Observation material is really only evidence of how people thought about film when thinking about it for the purposes of a survey. And what still concerns me are the social circumstances in which people make musical judgments in everyday life, in the usual processes of popular cultural activity.

In music making and listening practice, three social groups are of particular importance (though this obviously doesn't exhaust the musical world). First are the *musicians*.[10]

Of everyone involved in the popular music world, musicians most routinely use value judgments, and use them to effect. Musicians have to make a series of decisions—should I play this note, use this take, hire this musician, change the melody here, the order of the set there, shorten my solo, change the key; and these decisions rest on a constant process of evaluation—that's the wrong chord, the wrong tempo, the wrong sound, the wrong mix—and a constant process of encouragement: that's *good,* leave it! Such decisions are both individual, a reflection of one's own talent (musical talent describes, among other things, the ability to make the right decisions about what's good), and social—only other people, other musicians, can legitimate your decisions. And on the whole my own interviews with rock musicians confirm Borneman's account of jazz musicians' "critical standard,"

> which tends to accept jazz as a trade, a skill and an enjoyable activity. This is a purely pragmatic standard: good is what the good musicians play. Commercial success, instrumental skill, professional acclaim are accepted as self-evident proofs of good musicianship. There is no theory, no intellectual speculation, no nostalgia for the "good old days."[11]

In their study of musicians' experience of stress, Wills and Cooper found that the "prime concern of the popular musician is that he will not be able to play to the best of his ability." Stress is therefore associated with fears that

instruments and equipment won't work properly, that rehearsals were inadequate, that one might be too tired or ill to keep up (musicians are notorious
hypochondriacs). The basic point is that for the musician, the highest stress
factors are those that impinge directly upon *performance*.[12]

At the core of musicians' value judgments, then, are the values on which
successful performances depend: values concerning collaboration, the ability
to play with other people; the values of trust, reliability, a certain sort of
professionalism—even the most anti-professional punk band needs its members to turn up at rehearsals or gigs, to be in a fit state to take to the stage.
This is the context in which skill and technique become valued not as abstract
qualities but by reference to what must be done in a particular musical genre,
what fellow players can take for granted (classically trained musicians routinely report how difficult they first found it to play in rock bands; their
supposedly superior technical skills were irrelevant to the music they now
wanted to play; and the skills they really needed, for improvisation, were only
rudimentary). Similarly, as part of this collaborative work, musicians are
expected to have a certain basic knowledge of their instrument and of
technology—they need to be able to change a string, tune a drum, program
a sampler.

The second cluster of musicians' values emerges from the experience of
performance itself, and what interests me most here is how this leads, inevitably it seems, to a sense of alienation from the audience which becomes, in
turn, a kind of contempt for it.[13] This is, in one sense, a sociological response:
what is work for the musician is play for the audience; the very rhythm of
their lives is different, in terms of day and night, let alone status and attention.[14] But what's more significant here is that the bases of musical appreciation are also different, a necessary consequence of the power relation involved:
on the one hand, musicians learn to read and manipulate audiences, to please
them with tricks and devices that they, the musicians, despise; on the other
hand, the musicians experience rejection by audiences, often of the things
with which they are most pleased. As Art Hodes puts it neatly, "They don't
always applaud what knocks me out; they applaud what knocks them out."[15]
And in the words of a New York club date musician, "I can show you a dozen
different bands where the musicians are terrible. I mean, they can play, but
not well. But, they know when to play a certain song—when to do a rock set,
when to do a cha-cha, and get the people riled up so they have a good time.
Musicianship plays only a 50 percent role—the rest is knowing how to control
the people."[16]

Performance inevitably comes to feel like a compromise, a compromise
which is blamed on the audience.[17] But musicians are also, in my experience,

surprisingly quick to accuse each other of "prostituting" themselves, whether by following the whims of an employer, an audience, or a market. Earl Van Dyke, for example, notes that for Motown studio musicians in the 1960s, "Jazz was our first love. The reason why we worked at night was to take out all our musical frustrations from playing all that shit during the day in the studio."[18] The implicit assumption is that the most valuable noise is made without reference to anything but "the needs of the music."[19]

In this respect, I don't think there is any great divergence between the basic outlooks of musicians across different music worlds and genres (even if different musics have different "needs"). This relates to the point I made at the end of Chapter 2: musicians of all sorts face similar problems; the sociological question is how different musical values emerge in their solution. I'll consider four such problems here, the first of which is *learning*.

In all music worlds, learning music means learning to play a musical instrument; and in all music worlds, as far as I can tell, a distinction is made between being able to play an instrument, technically, and being able to "feel" it emotionally or instinctively—something which, by definition, cannot be taught. For popular musicians two issues arise here. One is the problem of voice. Singers, it seems, have a "natural" instrument, not simply in the fact that learning to sing for popular performance is not as obviously a technical problem as learning to play guitar or saxophone, but also because the voice is taken to define individuality directly—trying to play guitar just like Hendrix or Clapton is an honorable way into rock music-making; trying to sound just like Lou Reed or Poly Styrene would be thought silly. (Just as club date musicians strive to reproduce, as accurately as possible, the instrumental sound of, say, a Bruce Springsteen track, but would not pretend to put on Bruce's "voice.")

On the one hand, then, singers are not really musicians—their apprenticeship is different. Until 1979 they were not even eligible to join the American Federation of Musicians; as George Seltzer explains, "Before then, a singer with a band applied for AFM membership as a tambourine or cocktail drum player, a real farce."[20] On the other hand, in most pop groups the voice is central to the collective sound, to its popular appeal, and it is taken for granted that the singer will be the star, the center of public attention. The problematic relationship of singer and band feeds into disputes about creativity, as I'll discuss below.

But first I need to make another point about music learning: it is important that we dispose of the myth of the "untrained" pop performer. Pop musicians may be "unschooled" (although, as Rob Walser suggests, rather more have had formal music lessons than one might suppose), but they are not "unlearned," even if this is primarily a matter of learning by doing. And learning in all pop genres is a matter of imitation: the "master" is available in the grooves, and nearly every musician to whom I've spoken has rueful stories of teenage years spent listening to sounds on records and then trying to reproduce them, over and over and over again. As The Who's John Entwistle recalls, "I didn't know it was James Jamerson. I just called him the guy who played bass for Motown, but along with every other bassist in England, I was trying to learn what he was doing."[21]

Such imitation becomes, paradoxically, the source of individual creativity: without the master there to tell you what to do (as in the conservatory) it's up to the would-be musicians to put together what's heard and what's done, to come up with their own way of doing things (which, given the disparities of home and studio sound technology, is likely to be quite novel). At the same time, though, this means that in most popular music genres music-making emerges from obsessive music listening; a certain sort of "fandom" is thus built into the process—which is why when bands come together and fall apart, they do so (as we've seen) in the name of their various musical models, by reference to their record collections.

The second shared problem I want to examine is *rehearsing*. This is the moment when learning becomes social, when other people's judgments come into consideration, when musicians have to move from "messing around" to taking things seriously, from playing to playing together. It indicates, as Konstantin Economou argues, a new kind of "musical awareness," an awareness that takes into account an audience:

> The notion of musical awareness can be said to relate to a notion of socialization into a way of living, and thinking, like a "producer" of music, of making a transition from listener to creator. The production of your own [music] is an important step also in another sense. It highlights the fact that the music you make as a band [will] become more "public," and . . . subject to evaluation by others.[22]

On the one hand, then, musicians have to shift from a personal to a social value system: from trying to sound, to one's own satisfaction, like a record, to trying to sound right for the band, to everyone else's agreement. On the other hand, they have to face the brute fact that "talent" is unequally distributed: you can't always play what you want, but *she* can! The central sociological peculiarity of the popular music world, in short, is that it involves primarily music made by small groups: popular music-making is a small group experience.[23]

I'll come back to the general implications of this, but one aspect that needs special attention from a value perspective is *the audition*. Auditions are useful settings in which to observe musical judgments at work because they are here made explicit: musicians are being judged, discussed, against each other. In the pop world everyone has always been clear that this is not an entirely "musical" judgement. While certain sorts of abilities to do certain sorts of things are obviously a requirement, so is the right sort of person: someone who fits into a band's image and ethos and ambition, someone whose playing suggests a shared world view.[24]

It is sometimes assumed that this distinguishes pop from classical auditions, but, as we've seen, musical "talent" is a problematic concept everywhere, and one only has to look at the systematic exclusion of women from symphony orchestras until fairly recently to wonder what else was at issue besides musicality. Appearance, in particular, is an issue for all public performers. MacLeod notes the increasing importance of appearing young in the club date world, quoting a guitarist (in his early thirties): "Audiences like to *look* at a band . . . and they want to take it from what they see . . . they want it to reflect. People want to look at something and get a feeling of youth and vigour. That's what entertainment is all about."[25] And there are certainly areas of classical music performance too where how one looks is significant, just because the player (as in a rock or pop group) is going to be performing in highly visible circumstances. These days, opera singers, instrumental soloists, and conductors are chosen (by orchestras, record companies, and concert promoters) on the basis of a definition of talent that has as much to do with marketing as musical possibilities.[26]

Which brings me, finally, to the issue of *creativity*. None of my friends who have been through music school has ever been able to explain to me how or when the would-be classical musician decides between composing and interpreting other people's work, or whether the decision marks any sense of "failure." The art music world seems to occupy a position somewhere between the art college, on the one hand (where all students are expected to create their own work) and the literature department, on the other (where studying English literature is not held to mean writing it, even if it is assumed that good writing depends on good reading). In the art music world there is, in short, a paradoxical relationship between performer and contemporary composer: the former is more likely to make a living from music, is unlikely, in fact, to have any interest in contemporary composition, and yet in discursive terms the composer is the genius on whom the whole edifice rests.[27]

For most popular musicians the highest goal these days is obviously "creativity." Since the Beatles British rock bands, for example, have been expected to write their own material; in the United States "cover bands" are taken to be, by definition, inferior to their sources; Frederickson and Rooney have even argued that session players, playing to employer order, become, in effect, "non-persons."[28]

But there are complications to this ideology. If everyone is agreed that creativity (or originality) is a Good Thing, there is often bitter disagreement among musicians as to what musical creativity (or originality) *is*. One aspect of the resulting dispute is the tricky relationship in most pop genres of the "new" to the "formulaic." Another reflects the sociology of pop as a small group activity, and the resulting problems of individualism (which is when pop's own version of the composer versus the performer comes in, particularly when the songwriter is, as is often the case, the singer, the non-musician).[29] These issues are most clearly expressed, perhaps, in *negative* judgments.

For musicians, bad music seems to fall into two broad categories. First, *incompetent* music, music that is badly played, that reflects inadequate skill, technique, and so forth (the magazine of the British Musicians' Union has over the years carried articles and correspondence attacking, successively, rock 'n' roll, disco, punk, and rave music on just these grounds). But even here there's a confusion of a technical "objective" judgment—one can point to a player getting behind the beat, having erratic pitch, only being able to play two notes on the bass guitar—with an ideological, subjective one. The reason given for musicians' incompetence is either that they are *untutored* (which may mean, among other things, that they have "bad habits," that they are simply unable to do certain things because they haven't been taught how to) or that they are *unprofessional* (they're unwilling to learn proper techniques). If the former argument implies that bad musicians want to play differently but can't, the latter implies that there are pop genres in which "bad musicianship"—erratic pitch, wrong notes—is actually welcomed.

This argument spills over into a second sort of musician conception of bad music, that it is *self-indulgent*. I've often heard this criticism (not only from musicians, of course), and it seems to conflate at least three different sorts of description:

> *selfishness:* bad musicians forget that "good music" is a collective
> practice, and use performance to show off their own virtuosity
> or character, to dominate the microphone or sound mix, to play
> too long or too loudly. Such musicians don't properly offset their

musical colleagues, and the resulting music is "unbalanced" (this, as we've seen, is the sound mixers' view).

emptiness: bad musicians indulge in form at the expense of content, make music that "has nothing to say" but says it elaborately anyway. Their music is not made for any good reason but merely as a display of technical ability; such musicians play something only to show that they can. This is a common critique of "session musician music."

incomprehensibility: bad musicians play in a completely introverted way, for self-satisfaction or for therapeutic reasons, as a matter of private obsession. Their music is not communicative; it does not acknowledge or address an audience. This is the workaday musician critique of "arty" music, of the "new" jazz, for example, and of avant-garde rock.

As these arguments make clear, for most musicians, "creativity" cannot be judged in abstraction; it has to be defined in terms of music's perceived social and communicative functions. And there is a further complication here. In pop terms "originality" can be understood both as a kind of free-floating expressive individuality and as a market distinction, a selling point.[30] Popular musicians may, then, be trapped as well as freed by their "originality" (if it becomes just a moment of fashion), and in this world it is not even assumed that they will improve with age (as with jazz and classical performers). Does anyone—the Stones themselves?—believe that the Rolling Stones are a *better* band now than they were thirty years ago?

But I want to end this discussion on a different note, with the suggestion that when musicians talk about good and bad music they reveal an aesthetic as strongly rooted in ethical values and a sense of responsibility (to each other, to ideal listeners) as in technical values, the ability to make sounds that other people can't. Hence their use of the terms *right* and *wrong*.

John Miller Chernoff has written an eloquent account of what it means to be an African musician:

His musical creativity directly dramatizes his mind as it is balanced on the understanding that his individuality, like the rhythms that he plays, can only be seen in relationship. In the distinctive style of the expression which he must bring forward in the fulfilment of his complex social role, the personality of the musician becomes important in the sense that the quality and maturity of his aesthetic contribution either limits or expands the realization of a general concern, determining whether the people present constitute a community.[31]

Compare the more mundanely expressed thoughts of a Yorkshire brass bandsman:

Well, what always inspired me is that you have twenty-four men sweating and straining away, and for nothing. They don't get any money out of it. It's just to *make music better*. It's a movement . . . And if you're on your holidays, just find out where there's a band playing and go around and you've got friends. Lots of community spirit.[32]

A different sort of community, but the same belief that it is something *made sense of in music-making*. I'm reminded of how much of the local music described in Ruth Finnegan's *The Hidden Musicians* is made for charity, not just to raise money but also, again, to articulate a community (or, in the Milton Keynes context, many different communities). Popular musicians, who are on the whole unromantic about themselves and what they do, have a surprisingly moral attitude to what "music" should ideally be.

The case is very different for the second significant group to exercise judgment in the everyday pop process, the *producers*. I'm using this term loosely, to describe the broad range of people whose concern is to turn music and musicians into profitable commodities, and to draw attention to the recording studio as the place where the most interesting and influential musical value judgments are made.[33] But the studio is, in fact, only one site for the long chain of decisions which make up "the production of culture," as musicians lay down demo tracks (deciding on their best songs, their best versions, their best takes); as A&R departments determine which, if any, of the accumulated demos are any good, which need following up, which group or musician or song has any "potential"; as groups are signed and groomed and new decisions are made about song and image, about recording and the recording process, about releases and promotion; as the records go off to deejays and critics, to promoters and retailers, who in turn decide whether this group, this music, is worth playing or reviewing or booking or stocking; as consumers tune in, turn up, and make their own market choices.[34]

The point I want to make about this process is that at each stage, presumably, something—an act, a song, a record—has been judged positively; otherwise it wouldn't be passed along the line. And yet there is also a considerable dropout rate: the percentage of tracks or performances that are eventually rated positively by the public is tiny. The biggest fallout occurs at the beginning of the process (very few demos actually result in recording contracts) and at the end (fewer than one in ten releases command much of an audience). Two things follow. First, record companies spend a considerable amount of time producing "failures," and yet there are very few studies of these failures—the "public verdict" is allowed a retrospective authority. But, *at the time*, people in those record companies were making enthusiastic judgments. On what basis? How on earth, I used to wonder as a record reviewer, did *anyone* come to release this? Second, it's easy to use this model to set up a clash of art and commerce cast in terms of musicians versus the business (and one can see why from the musicians' point of view, as their demos are rejected, their releases "not properly promoted," the stress line falls like this).

There are a number of ways, however, in which this description doesn't work. To begin with, the musicians' relationship with a record company in the production of their sound is as much collaborative as combative, and, indeed, at least one aspect of A&R judgment concerns a group's collaborative potential, its professionalism. Both parties, in other words, expect art and commerce to be intertwined.[35] It is clear, moreover, that producers have a *more* romantic ideology of creativity (and creative success) than musicians; just as in the conservatory, the key term is "talent" (the key task its exploitation). And while company personnel know how exploitation works, talent remains mysterious, especially when the public fails to hear it. Record companies, or, at least, record company executives can, in fact, be surprisingly obstinate in sticking with their belief in a talent that hasn't yet been "recognized," and their value judgments are shot through with Romantic terminology—the musician as genius, music as ineffable, the musical experience as overwhelming. At the core of this, of course, is the problem I've already mentioned, the double articulation of originality, as the source of both art and profit (a double articulation defined by the copyright laws on which music as business depends).[36]

My second general point about industry values is that all producers' judgments rest, as Hennion argues, on an imputed audience. Each decision, at each step of the way (and this includes the musicians' original preparation of their demo) means a judgment both about the "quality" of the music and about its likely market. Sometimes these can be separated—in genre terms, for example: many demos are rejected because A&R teams decide that there is no market for "that kind of music." But often they are impossible to disentangle, they are part of the same evaluative process, and this means that the audience too is romanticized, its tastes and choices also treated as mysterious. There is a touching faith in the industry in anyone who can claim to read the audience, to be in tune with public taste (the usual measure of which is a previous success); such people carry a special authority in in-house arguments: they have a "good ear," and it takes many failures to offset the original success.[37]

But then record companies don't just produce cultural commodities and lay them out in the marketplace. They also try to persuade people to buy them, and this means telling the potential consumer why the product is valuable. The product, to put this another way, is laid out for us so as to *invite* assessment. The record company works to define the evaluative grounds, thus ensuring that we make the right judgment.

The problem for the record industry is that its best means of communication with its consumers are mediated: sounds reach us through radio, film, and television; stars reach us via newspapers, magazines, and video. And media people judge music according to their own criteria. Does it suit my playlist? My demographic? A skilled record company marketing department is, therefore, skilled in its handling of a complex of value frames, in its role in ongoing value arguments. I came to learn as a rock critic that press handouts weren't just designed to sell a sound to me, but also to persuade me to write about a record or artist in the right way, in the right discursive frame. Take, for example, Chrysalis's 1990 pitch for Child's Play:

> Good playing, solid songwriting, hard work and perseverance. Remember when these were the qualities that set apart a band destined for the big time? In a highly competitive market, these are still the elements that decide who will be in for the long haul—the kind of band that *earns* their success by winning over their fans' hearts as well as ears. That personal connection has been the key element in the success of Chrysalis recording artist Child's Play, whose powerful debut album is titled *Rat Race*.
>
> Drummer/vocalist John Allen pegs his band's music as "blue-collar rock" and that seems an apt description for their versatile sound. Child's Play's identity is not based on a specific musical idea, but rather on an attitude towards life and the struggle it involves. This is a band who have seen tough times and dry spells, and they reflect their deep-seeded determination with an aggressive hybrid of blues, metal, punk and good old rock and roll. Child's Play are more familiar with jeans and sweat than hairspray and eyeliner, and followers in their hometown of Baltimore, Maryland know they can count on the band to understand and even share their daily concerns.
>
> "We have a lot of songs that are 'pay your dues' or 'times are tough'

sort of ideas," Allen relates. "We all come from working-class backgrounds, so we've got the stories and inspiration to write songs about trying to get ahead. Our fans relate to our down-to-earth attitude. We write and sing about real-life stuff; the relationships that middle-class people go through."[38]

And this is what BMG had to say about Raging Slab, the same year:

> The band's first single, "Don't Dog Me," is a perfect representation of their classic hard rock style. Over a matched guitar lick, lead singer/songwriter/guitarist Greg Strempka howls the title as heavy white-boy-blues riffs not heard since the early '70s boil out of the speakers . . . From the dynamic melodicism of "Geronimo" to the aching balladry of "When Love Comes Loose" and ending up with the bruising double kickbass wallop of "Dig A Hole," the album is diverse. "We've been called Lynyrd Skynyrd meets Metallica," explains Greg, "which is not as unlikely or ridiculous as it first sounds. There's a great diversity in the band. We're capable of doing a lot of styles, but most of the time we do them all at once."[39]

What interests me here is less what these blurbs say—how they put the groups concerned into a story—but why they do so. My final point about producers, then, is this. They too mediate between performers and audiences. To put this another way: once rock and pop (or classical) performers are embroiled in the sales process they cease to have unmediated access to their listeners (even live performance is staged in the terms of a sales narrative). This situation is usually treated negatively: producers are seen to "interfere" in the proper communication of musician and audience. But this is not necessarily the case: they may, in fact, make that communication possible. At the very least (to come to the *consumer,* the third major player in the pop world), the musician is protected to an extent from having to answer the producer's obsessive question: "But what does the listener want?"

Academics have been no more successful in answering this question than market researchers, but they have confirmed two general principles as relevant to any answer: first, that what listeners want is determined by who they are; second, that what they want is an effect of the nature of "wanting." The first principle implies a connection between people's social and aesthetic values; the second suggests that aesthetic theory must be related to an account of fantasy. The first argument has been developed most systematically in terms of "homology," music interpreted as a coded expression of the social aims and values of the people to whom it appeals.[40] Fantasy-based theories focus, instead, on why a particular piece of music is appropriate for a certain kind of pleasure, on how it meets psychological needs.[41]

These arguments have been developed primarily in the study of youth music, and there is an obvious tendency to divide them up along gender lines: the appeal of boys' music explained by boys' social lives; the appeal of girls' music explained by their private fantasies. But the best academic accounts of youth music consumption show that these approaches must be combined to make sense.[42] If consumers (of all ages) value music for the function it fills, then that "function" must be defined both socially and psychologically.[43]

Given this, the question becomes how consumers' attitudes to music relate to musicians' values (compare, for example, Donna Weinstein's consumer-led analysis of heavy metal with Robert Walser's performer-led account),[44] which is to return to the issue of professional musicians' apparent contempt for their audiences (whatever their communal ideals). In exploring the musician/listener value gap now from the listener's side I want to begin from an argument about high cultural musicology.

In his stimulating exploration of the reason why what musicologists say about music appears to bear no relationship to how ordinary people hear it, Nicholas Cook argues that the problem is not the difference between two sorts of listeners, but between two sorts of music. He generalizes, that is to say, from a point Kathryn Bailey makes about a work by Webern: it consists of "two quite different pieces—a visual, intellectual piece and an aural, immediate piece, one for the analyst and another for the listener."[45] But what Cook goes on to suggest is that there is a similar difference between the music a composer writes (and a performer plays) and the music a listener hears: "What makes a musician is not that he knows how to play one instrument or another, or that he knows how to read music: it is that he is able to grasp musical structure in a manner appropriate for musical production—the most obvious (though of course by no means the only) example of such production being performance."[46]

And musicologists seek to "grasp" music this way too—in a manner appropriate for musical production, rather than for musical listening. (A similar point could be made about literary theorists since New Criticism; the descriptions of how a text works make much better sense to someone trying to write a poem than they do to someone reading it—a point of which T. S. Eliot, at least, was well aware.) As Cook puts it, "notes simply do not exist for the listener"; they hear sounds. And he concludes that a musical culture "is a tradition of imagining sound as music. Its basic identity lies in its mechanism for constituting sounds as intentional objects, from the level of a single note to that of a complete work. This means that the ubiquitous discrepancies between the manner in which musicians conceive music and that in which listeners experience it are endemic to musical culture. Indeed, they define it."[47]

In the pop music world it was obvious from the start that the object the musicologist defined was not the object the pop fan heard. But when William Mann's and Wilfrid Mellers' and Deryck Cooke's elaborately technical analyses of the Beatles were mockingly quoted (by musicologists and pop fans alike), it was never quite clear whom the laugh was against: the Beatles for being too simple to carry the weight of such words? Or the critics for so misunderstanding pop pleasures?[48]

What Cook suggests is that musicologists in fact misunderstand all listeners' pleasures; and what was really at issue in the 1960s was the nature of pop composition: did the Beatles really *write* like this, in Aeolian clusters and so forth? The orthodox musicological view of the time was bluntly stated by Sir Jack Westrup, in an editorial for *Music and Letters* in 1968:

> The world of pop is largely a featureless desert. It is hardly surprising that the life of a "pop" song is so short. This is not simply because most of the performers have unlovely and insignificant voices, which would be inaudible without the aid of a microphone. The reason lies rather in the appalling poverty of melodic invention, which is not relieved by a persistent rhythm or even by harmonic ingenuities which serious critics mistakenly attribute to the singers instead of the expert musicians who write the "backing."[49]

Only the arranger, the "expert" musician, did something that felt to Westrup like real composition; only the arranger organized notes on a page. And twenty-five years later Robert Walser can write an entirely convincing musicological analysis of heavy metal not because pop musicians now compose like classical musicians (though the processes are rather more similar than Westrup realized) but because Walser (himself a guitarist) knows how the rock composition process works, can "grasp" (in Cook's words) rock's "musical structure in a manner appropriate for musical production."[50] The question remains, though: does a technical understanding of what metal musicians do explain what metal audiences hear? Is what sounds right to the music's makers what sounds good to the music's listeners?

Enter the critic. In high cultural history, when at the beginning of the nineteenth century good music became autonomous, something conceived for its own sake, irrespective of audience response, then the critic became necessary as an expert, as someone who could explain the music to the public, teach it how to listen. The musician/listener gap was taken for granted and the critic was by definition on the artist's side, championing the new and the difficult. As a large-scale commodity culture emerged at the beginning of this century, though, the mediation role became equally significant the other way around: the mass audience had to be interpreted to producers, and the critic became the ideal consumer too.

Or at least, some critics did, because what really happened was a split, which helped define modernism, between writers on the side of the artist and writers on the side of the audience, and different discursive values emerged accordingly. For the former, as Levin Schücking notes of theater reviewers, the critical observation that "the play succeeded with the public" became a standard line in the scathing review, as German theater critics sought to ally themselves with experimental playwrights (and the future) against audiences (and the past).[51]

"The crowd liked them" remains a standard line in a scathing review.[52] Andrew Porter's 1990 *New Yorker* notice of the Met's *Ballo in Maschera,* for example, one of the most scathing reviews I've ever read (Porter begins by calling the production "a disgusting exhibition," "an obscenity," and "a circus"), suggests sarcastically that perhaps director Piero Faggioni "meant to mock and satirize the opera in question, the whole idea of opera, the Met, and a Met audience uncaring about music and easily pleased . . . If his aim was to make fun of *Ballo,* he missed the mark with the first-night audience. The show was acclaimed."[53]

Built into such criticism is a suspicion of popularity itself—in Schoenberg's words, "If it is art it is not for all, and if it is for all it is not art"—and, in particular, of the effects of the pursuit of popularity.[54] Such suspicion is equally common among critics writing about music that is, supposedly, commercial to begin with. Here is Ernest Borneman, for example, on the plight of jazz in the late 1930s, faced with "the opulence of the new music industry that had arisen phoenix-like out of the ashes of the depression":

So much money was invested in each "hit tune" that the investors could no longer permit it to be submerged in the contrapuntal intricacies of old-time jazz; thus harmonisation replaced counterpoint, arrangement replaced improvisation, and Tin Pan Alley tunes replaced folk tunes. So much money had at the same time been invested in each band that the band manager could no longer afford to let the musicians play as they liked. In the old days the musicians could take occasional busmen's holidays to play the music as they thought music should be played; they still made enough money to earn a living. But now they had to make money for a whole dragon's tail of hangers-on and go-betweens—managers, bookers, agents, pluggers, publicity men, girl singers and front men. To pay for these vast new overheads, the music had to be tailored to a much wider public than jazz had ever been able to attract. This process of making jazz intelligible to the moron was based on a simple recipe: Mix the phrasing of New Orleans jazz with the arrangement and orchestration of sweet jazz and the result will be swing music. The logic of the process was based on the assumption that the common denominator of all audiences is the lowest intelligence prevailing among them.[55]

Compare this to Ira Robbins, one-time editor of *Trouser Press* and long-time champion of "independent" American music, writing forty-five years later about the crisis facing the rock scene at the end of the 1980s:

Goals that were once considered standard—innovation, artistic effort, motivation beyond the pursuit of the market share—are no longer prized, and the mute, ignorant acquiescence of a generation raised on a steady diet of garbage rubber stamps the worst and the cheesiest, encouraging the record industry to search out and exploit ever inferior artists whose marketing skills increasingly outweigh their ability (or even interest) in making original (or even cleverly derivative) music. Singers who can't sing, bands who can't play, producers who do all the work and trivialize the artist, classic records borrowed wholesale, soundalike songwriting factories, superstars totally beholden to technology for their creations, Oz-like pop icons who hide behind a carefully groomed image—it all adds up to a total abandonment of the creative autonomy that once was the hallmark of the rock era.[56]

In short, the themes that haunted modernist writers and critics at the beginning of the century (their "high" cultural concern to be true to their art, to disdain mere entertainment, to resist market forces; their longing for a "sensitive minority" readership, for what Ezra Pound called "a party of intelligence") still haunt popular music.[57] What needs stressing, though, is that it is not just critics who hold these views, but also the readership for whom they write (and which they help define): music magazines like *Melody Maker* or *Rolling Stone* in the late '60s and early '70s, like *New Musical Express* in the mid to late '70s, like *Spin* in the '80s, were aimed at consumers who equally defined themselves against the "mainstream" of commercial taste, wherever that might lie. (And this goes back to a point I made in Chapter 2:

the most interesting aesthetic distinctions aren't those between the high and the low, but those between the select and the mainstream, the radical and the conservative.)[58]

For most rock critics, then (this was certainly my experience), the issue in the end isn't so much representing music to the public (the public to the musician) as creating a knowing community, orchestrating a collusion between selected musicians and an equally select part of the public—select in its superiority to the ordinary, undiscriminating pop consumer. The critic is, in this respect, a fan (most rock writers start on fanzines; most are, indeed, collectors), with a mission to preserve a perceived quality of sound, to save musicians from themselves, to define the ideal musical experience for listeners to measure themselves against. Ernest Borneman suggests that the jazz collector

> tends to identify enjoyment of this or that musician's style, or pleasure in listening to records from this or that period of jazz, with evidence of the musician's or the style's objective value. Collectors are impetuous, emotional, rarely interested in any music but jazz alone. The degree of musical illiteracy among them is astonishing to the academic critic . . . They attack the current name bands as "commercial" and consider all musicians inferior to their chosen idol.[59]

And even if, as critics, rock fans (and collectors) have to suggest some sort of "balance" in their opinions, the language of music criticism still depends on the confusion of the subjective and objective, on the championing not so much of music as of a way of listening to music. Roland Barthes famously remarked that music critics are obsessed with adjectives.[60] Henry Kingsbury notes their strange habit of imbuing notes with personality.[61] My favorite example of this is Norman Lebrecht's description of Harrison Birtwistle's music: "It is a totally personal sound—tough, gritty, even violent; and at the same time shy, warm and slyly humorous."[62] Such descriptive terms, designed to capture in words what the music sounds like, are also always implicitly theoretical, referring to a general account of how music works. In this there is no difference between the classical and the pop critic. Compare Lebrecht on Birtwistle, just quoted, and Robert Sandall on Lou Reed's *Magic and Loss*: "the deep reverberation of Mike Wasserman's slithery bass, the spry twang/cosmic howl of the guitars and the booming spaces around Michael Blair's drums."[63] In both cases the adjectives turn description into interpretation and are effective only to the extent that we are prepared to agree that, yes, this is how musical sounds mean.

In general, pop criticism uses adjectives to two ends: to relate the music to its possible uses ("Plaintive Malian folk-blues ballads for single voice and lonesome guitar. Fragile, delicately strummed, soothing and sorrowful. Good for a self-indulgent sulk in the small hours") and to place it generically ("Impressively trashy and abrasive punk'n'roll with chainsaw guitars, a jittery Cramps-style breakneck approach and angry Iggy vocals recorded over the CB, possibly. Looks like we got ourselves a convoy").[64]

In either case the purpose is consumer guidance, and the reviewer draws on conventional assumptions about what different sorts of music, different sorts of sound, are good for. Which is where the knowingness, the collusion of critic and reader, comes in. Such reviews are incomprehensible to anyone who is not already informed in the right way. Criticism, in other words, is not just producing a version of the music for the reader but also a version of the listener for the music. Take this quote (from a review of Teenage Fan Club's *Bandwagonesque*): "'December' is a fey, honey-dripping exercise in Chiltonese, 'Guiding Star' is the Jesus and Mary Chain attempting to write a No. 1 single for the Christmas of 1974, 'Star Sign' degenerates, after a glassy, ominous intro, into lily-livered Byrds-by-rote anaemia."[65]

I think these descriptions are, indeed, elegant and pithy ways of saying just what these tracks sound like, but they encode in a few words an extraordinary number of references to both pop history and pop motivation. Rock criticism, in short, makes arguments about audiences as well as about sounds, about the ways in which music works as a social event. This is most obvious, of course, in concert reviews, for ideological reasons neatly summarized by Geoffrey Himes: "Live performances have always been the most intense, most revealing experiences in pop music. That's where you can tell if an artist can really sing, really make you dance, really deliver an unfaked emotion or epiphany to a breathing audience."[66] The argument here hinges on the word "really," and it is a very peculiar argument: the suggestion that if an artist can make you dance on record she's not really making you dance is capped by the implication that record and radio listeners aren't really breathing!

If high critics tend to see the audience as accountable to the artist, rock critics are equally concerned to make the artist accountable to the audience. In the former case the critics' authority, the reason why anyone should take any notice of them, rests on their technical and historical knowledge of the music at issue, their academic credentials. In the latter case the critics' authority rests on their knowledge of the audience and its needs and values and this, in turn, rests on who the critic is. The self thus becomes a key part of rock critics' argument, a key term in their evaluative vocabulary; what's at issue is how the music engages them emotionally, and audiences are found wanting not just as philistines—refusing to listen to difficult and demanding sounds—but also as dull, unable to be moved by them.

Rock criticism is driven by the need to differentiate: music is good because it is different, different from the run of "mainstream" pop, different in the special intensity of feelings it brings about. It follows that most judgments of music are simultaneously explanations of music: the judgment is the explanation, the explanation is the judgment. Musical descriptions are routinely couched, for example, in sociological terms: "bad music" is so assessed by reference to a "bad" system of production or to "bad" social effects; critical evaluation works by reference to social institutions or social behavior for which the music simply acts as a sign.

I can clarify this by going through the most common critical arguments about musical production. There are two familiar positions. The first is that music is judged in the context of or by reference to a critique of mass production. Bad music is "standardized" or "formula" music. Good music is implicitly "original" or "autonomous," and the explanation built into the judgment depends on the familiar Marxist/Romantic distinction between serial production, production to commercial order, to meet a market, and artistic creativity, production determined only by individual intention, by formal and technical rules and possibilities.

Among other things, this means that "formula" or "standard" production that is not capitalist is not, in this discursive context, usually judged bad: the fact that all disco numbers in the late 1970s "sounded the same" is a mark of unhealthy (commercial) formulaic production; the fact that all folk songs collected in east Norfolk in the late 1870s sounded the same is a sign of their (healthy) roots in a collective, oral history. More generally, we could say that such "formula criticism" tends to be genre-centric: minor variations in teeny-bop music (the fact that the stars have different vocal registers, say) are taken to be quite insignificant; minor variations in rural blues guitar phrasings are taken to be of great aesthetic importance.

A second sort of criticism, which refers to production but without a Marxist edge, equates bad music with imitative music—again, the implicit contrast is with "original" or, perhaps, "individual" sounds; a record or artist is dismissed for sounding just like someone else (or, not least, for sounding just like their own earlier records or songs). The critical assumption is that this reflects a cynical or pathetic production decision; it is not just an accident or coincidence.

There are many variations on this sort of argument. The most interesting is the distinction between "the cover version" and "the version." The cover version is almost always heard as bad—this is now the usual attitude to the white pop versions of black songs and records in the 1950s, for example: Pat Boone's "Tutti Frutti" is probably the nearest thing to a consensual bad record in popular music history, a track that is both exploitative and feeble. (One aspect of learning to be a rock fan in the 1960s was, in fact, learning to prefer originals to covers. And this was, as I recall, something that did have to be learned: nearly all the records I had bought in the late 1950s had been cover versions.) The fact that Pat Boone's "personal stamp" was put on Little Richard's music is clearly a bad thing.

"Version," by contrast, refers to a situation in which the "copy" is taken to improve on the original, to render it "bad" by revealing what it could have been. Here, reversing the previous argument, black covers of white originals are routinely valued positively (Ray Charles singing "I Can't Stop Loving You"), and rock arrangers are taken to make pop songs more interesting (Vanilla Fudge's "You Keep Me Hanging On," Phil Collins' "You Can't Hurry Love"). The fact that Ray Charles puts his personal stamp on Don Gibson's song is obviously a good thing. Imitation, in short, is as much an ideological as a musical matter; the critical response depends on an account of who is imitating whom and for what attributed reason.

Musical judgments referring to production processes obviously depend on particular sorts of knowledge. To condemn a record as imitative, we must know (or know about) the "original"; to describe a song as "standardized" means that we have heard (or heard of) other songs of a similar type. Such knowledge may be more or less extensive, more or less valid; judgments in this respect often rest on what one might call hypothetical knowledge, on unexamined assumptions about record company, studio, and marketing decisions. Listeners read from a record how they think it must have been produced, and then condemn it (or not) accordingly. Hence the familiar enough experience (to which people are loath to admit) that we need to know who a record is by before we can evaluate it. But whatever knowledge we might need in order thus to label music good or bad, we are still, in the end, referring to the something "in the music" that led us down this discursive path in the first place. And the recurring musical judgment here seems to be in terms of excessive familiarity: a piece of music is bad because it uses musical clichés; because its development is easily predictable; because nothing happens.[67]

Critical musical judgments, in short, are almost always entangled with social explanations of why the music is good or bad, and much of our day-to-day argument about music is conducted in just this way: aesthetic judgments are tangled up with ethical judgments. One could argue further, though, that what's involved here is not an explanation of good or bad music as such (though that is how such judgments are presented) but a justification for using the labels "good" and "bad" in the first place, labels which are, in fact, assertions of personal taste and depend on a different system of musical meaning altogether.

Consumers' everyday judgments (as against critics' "considered" views) tend to take place in noisy situations, in free-wheeling conversations about musical meaning and value, and their terms and judgments are inevitably less consistent, less coherent, and less self-conscious than I have so far implied. In conversational criticism we certainly use terms which draw on articulated discourses, which deploy assumptions about art and folk and pop, which refer to the ways in which musicians speak and critics write; but we also, equally certainly, confuse them. Three everyday terms seem particularly significant here.

First, *authenticity*. This clearly relates to questions of production but not to a thought-through theory; "inauthentic," that is to say, is a term that can be applied evaluatively even within genres which are, in production terms, "inauthentic" by definition—fans can distinguish between authentic and in-authentic Eurodisco, and what is being described by implication is not how something was actually produced but a more inchoate feature of the music itself, a perceived quality of sincerity and commitment. It's as if people expect music to mean what it says, however cynical that meaning, and music can be heard as being "false" to its own premises. How do people hear music in such an ethical way? What is it about a record that makes us say, "I just don't believe it!" (my reaction to Paul Simon's *Graceland*, for example)? This is obviously related somehow to the ways in which we judge people's sincerity generally; it is a human as well as a musical judgment. And it also reflects our extra-musical beliefs—what I already knew about Paul Simon obviously had an effect on how I heard his music (and new knowledge—new music—might mean I changed my mind).

Second, *taste*. The question here concerns the musically appropriate. On the one hand, this is a functional question, whether narrowly (is the music right for this dance floor, this party, this film?) or broadly (is the music right for this situation—the Trammps' "Disco Inferno" for a gay funeral? Whitney Houston's "I Will Always Love You" for everyone else's?). Answers depend on one's assumptions about music's place or function in the artistic or social situations concerned. On the other hand, this is an ethical question about the suitability of popular music (as a form of entertainment) to deal with certain issues—disease and death, for example—and, in particular, to deal with them in an "entertaining" way (hence the common negative response to country music "maudlin" songs, to pop and rock commentaries on social and political affairs—Phil Collins on the homeless; Bono on Bosnia). Judgment, in short, rests less on what this particular music is than on an argument about what music in general should be. (And we can have quite contradictory responses to a song or record, disapproving of our own enjoyment!)

Third, *stupidity*. This is a very common term in popular discourse that is not often (or at least not in quite this way) articulated by professional critics. And it is an interesting term because it is not only applied to words or lyrics—people can and do find tunes and arrangements and sounds stupid too. What is meant here? Clearly the analogy is with the way we call a statement (or the person making the statement) stupid, a suggestion not just that their account of the world is wrong, but that it is also somehow demeaning, that it demeans us through our involvement, however unwilling, in the collusive act of listening (to someone making, say, a racist or sexist remark). Stupid music in this (non-academic) context is offensive because it seems to deny what we're capable of, humanly, rationally, ethically, aesthetically.

And that brings me to the essence of everyday musical value. I'm happy to concede that musical assessment is, as they say, a matter of taste, that it involves a judgment which depends on the particular (changing, irrational) social and psychological circumstances of the person making it. On the other hand, whatever the individual bases of our judgments, once made we do seek to justify them, to explain them, and my concern in this chapter has been to describe the discursive languages that are available to us, and to point out some of their problems. But the questions I want to stress now, the issues that I will focus on in the rest of this book, are different.

First, it is clear that we need concepts of good and bad music even if we know full well that we won't be able to agree on how the labels should be applied. The marking off of some tracks and genres and artists as "good" and others as "bad" seems to be a necessary part of popular music pleasure and use; it is a way in which we establish our place in various music worlds and use music as a source of identity. And "good" and "bad" are key words because they suggest that aesthetic and ethical judgments are tied together: not to like a record is not just a matter of taste; it is also a matter of morality.

Second, even though, as a sociologist, I've translated this evaluative process into a use of language, a matter of discourse, what's really at issue is feeling. In the end, "bad music" describes an emotional rather than an ideological judgment. We don't like a record; we then seek to account for that dislike (we don't, on the whole, arm ourselves with a grid of ideological consistency through which everything must pass before we feel it). Feelings, particularly feelings of like or dislike—for music, for people—are often surprising, contradictory, and disruptive; they go against what we're supposed to feel, what we'd like to feel. The important point here is not that critical judgment is always a process of justification (and not really explanation), but that the feelings it describes are real (and not just discursive).

When we label something as "bad music," then, it is because it is music that upsets or offends us, that we don't want to listen to. *Please* play something else! Do I *have* to listen to this? It grates, hurts, bores; it's ugly, it's painful; it's driving me *mad!* As Howard Becker once wrote, the problem for a sociologist of culture is that "people do not experience their aesthetic beliefs as merely arbitrary and conventional; they feel that they are natural, proper and moral."[68] And the word I would emphasize here is "feel." Nobody needs to be told what is good or bad music—you know it the moment you hear it.

Half a century after Mass-Observation investigated popular film values, the Music in Daily Life Project in Buffalo, New York, set out to ask equally ordinary people, "What is music about for you?"[69] The replies echo the themes of the moviegoers. Truth to life: "I like music by people who seem to have a grip on life, and they're not just selling themselves out or being superficial." "People hearing those songs know that they're real things, that really happened, not just someone sitting down and trying to write a hit." The significance of genre: "Rock is wild, violent, and everything I don't want to hear . . . Rock music is a cultural [*sic*] I don't care for." "It [country music] doesn't have too much relevance in my life."[70]

But what is most striking about the accumulated voices of people talking about music is the sense that music matters not just because it is (like film) a powerful force for taking one out of oneself, but also because it can take one deep inside. On the one hand, "Well, it is a . . . I suppose, a kind of tonic or medication of sorts. It enables me to feel better usually, even if it is a small piece or sad piece. I feel some sort of relief when I'm listening to music. I can be transported or get out of myself or my immediate surroundings and . . . take a journey on the melody." On the other hand, "It brings out feelings you didn't even know you had." "It gives me the same kind of happiness that being angry gives me. A kind of fierce feeling." "Without music, I would die . . . I just wouldn't be. I wouldn't have a personality . . . It just fills up every muscle and vein in my body." "Like it's either, um, music's gotta, it's gotta like . . . hit you a certain way like it's gotta . . . give you some kind of feeling like either if you're in a depressed mood, you want to be, you know, it helps you to be depressed."[71]

The problem, of course, is to explain how it does this, and the other recurring point here, one on which to end this chapter, is that musical talk is both necessary and useless:

A: I just think this is great . . . I don't know why I like it so much. And some of them I've listened to so many times that I sing along. (laughs) Like "Here Comes Jesus" in German.

Q: But why is it so great?

A: I don't know.

Q: Well, you have to tell me.

A: It's hard to explain . . . it's all feelings and emotions . . .

Q: You gotta tell me why, though.

A: I don't know why. (annoyed) Just like you don't know why your music is a particular way . . . even if I tried to tell you a million reasons, you know, like it reminds me of home or because of the key . . . even if I say all these things . . . (she stops and gasps as a new part of the piece starts, an oboe solo) Now this part is *sad.* (listens for a while)

Q: Why is this part sadder than the other part?

A: (glares) I'm getting annoyed.

Q: Why?

A: Because the fact is it *is* sad. It evokes certain feelings. It has and it probably always will. Why? Well I don't know why. I could talk about the notes or the voice or the oboe.

Q: Well, go ahead then.

A: But I feel no . . . I mean I feel somewhat of a . . . maybe I just want to enjoy it, I don't want to explain it. I don't want to start describing "what" and "why." I just like it and like to hear it . . . like to be moved by it. I feel no *need* to explain it . . . Maybe it's programmed into my genes so that a G-sharp really knocks me out.

Q: Okay, okay . . .

A: . . . It's not a scientific experiment. And I'm glad because I don't want to know . . . I don't want to know. I don't care.[72]

Genre Rules

> The little child is permitted to label its drawing "This is a cow—this is a horse" and so on. This protects the child. It saves it from the sorrow and wrong of hearing its cows and its horses criticized as kangaroos and work-benches.
>
> **Mark Twain**[1]

> **When we obtain a theory of genres we will then be able to see that every genre has its own specific objective laws which no artist can ignore without peril.**
>
> Georg Lukács[2]

There was a program on a college radio station in Ithaca when I was living there in early 1991 which described itself as "Pure American folk from singers who defy labels," and this self-contradictory statement can stand as the motto for this chapter, in which I will examine the role of labels in popular music and consider the seemingly inescapable use of generic categories in the organization of popular culture. These are so much a part of our everyday lives that we hardly notice their necessity—in the way bookshop shelves are laid out (novels distributed between romance, mystery, science fiction, horror, popular fiction, contemporary fiction, classics, and so on); in the way TV program guides classify the evening's entertainment (sitcom, game show, talk show, crime series, documentary); in the ways films are advertised and videos shelved (comedy, Western, horror, musical, adventure, adult); in the way magazines are laid out at newsagents (women's, children's, hobby, general interest, fashion, computers, music). Such labels are only noticeable, in fact, when we want a book or video or magazine *that doesn't fit* and suddenly don't know where to find it.

In this chapter I will argue that such labeling lies, in practice, at the heart of pop value judgments. I'll start (as with the examples already cited) with the use of genre categories to *organize the sales process.*

Genre distinctions are central to how record company A&R departments work. The first thing asked about any demo tape or potential signing is what *sort* of music is it, and the importance of this question is that it integrates an inquiry about the music (what does it sound like) with an inquiry about the market (who will buy it). The underlying record company problem, in other words, how to turn music into a commodity, is solved in generic terms. Genre is a way of defining music in its market or, alternatively, the market in its music. (Exactly the same could be said of the way publishers handle manuscripts and book ideas, film companies scripts, and television companies program proposals.)

Whatever decision is made generically (and this may mean serious argument, may involve composite or "crossover" markets, and thus may not be straightforward at all) will have a determining influence on everything that happens to the performer or record thereafter. A record company will, for example, immediately look at the spread of its acts. (Does it need something or something else of this sort? Will the new signing compete with or complement existing talent?) And once signed, once labeled, musicians will thereafter be expected to act and play and look in certain ways; decisions about recording sessions, promotional photos, record jackets, press interviews, video styles, and so on, will all be taken with genre rules in mind. The marketing and packaging policies, in other words, that begin the moment an act is signed are themselves determined by genre theories, by accounts of how markets work and what people with tastes for music *like this* want from it.

Initially, then, to understand how a genre label works—why these particular musical characteristics have been put together in this particular way— is to understand a reading of the market. In 1907, for example, the American music publisher Jerome H. Remick offered songs for sale under the following labels: ballad, cowboy song, novelty, Irish comic, coon song, Indian love song, waltz song, topical song, sentimental ballad, march song, and march ballad. In the same period E. M. Wickes, in his book *Advice to Songwriters,* distinguished between the ballad and the novelty song: the former included "the Semi-high-class, March, Rustic, Irish, Descriptive, and Mother"; the latter "Flirting, Juvenile, Philosophical, Comic, Irish, Production, Stage, Suggestive, and Ragtime."[3] As Nicholas Tawa points out, musical labels in Tin Pan Alley at this time sometimes referred "to subject or emotional content and sometimes to the basic music meter," sometimes to lyrical themes, sometimes to musical forms. The logic of labeling depends on what the label is for: publishing catalogues were written for amateur and professional singers who needed songs appropriate for their particular style or repertoire; advice manuals were written for would-be songwriters with different musical skills and linguistic facilities.

If the music industry has always used labeling procedures, then, they have never necessarily been clear or consistent. Genre maps change according to who they're for. And there is a further complication. The point of music labels is, in part, to make coherent the way in which different music media divide the market—record companies, radio stations, music magazines, and concert promoters can only benefit from an agreed definition of, say, heavy metal. But this doesn't always work smoothly, if only because different media by necessity map their consumers in different ways. Record retailers, for example, don't always organize their stock in the same way as record companies organize their releases (indeed, for reasons I'll come back to, retailers are likely to anticipate record companies in labeling new markets and redrawing old genre distinctions). Sometimes this has to do with immediate consumer demand (most stores have a category, "TV advertised," to cater for the market that results from such promotion regardless of the musical category involved). Sometimes it has to do with material conditions: how one organizes the racks depends on how many racks one has. And sometimes it reflects the fact that people shop in ways that are not easy to classify generically: my favorite sections in British record shops used to be those labeled "male vocal" and "female vocal," which were, in effect, residual light pop categories (all those singers who couldn't be filed under rock, soul, jazz, or nostalgia). Why in this category, unlike any other, was the musician's gender taken to be significant?

Record shopping is instructive in this context for many reasons. A committed music fan will soon find, for example, that she's interested in sounds that seem to fit into several categories at once, and that different shops therefore shelve the same record under different labels.[4] Or one can follow the emergence of new shelving labels—world music (which may or may not include reggae); rave (which may or may not include American imports). It's as if a silent conversation is going on between the consumer, who knows roughly what she wants, and the shopkeeper, who is laboriously working out the pattern of shifting demands. What's certain is that I, like most other consumers, would feel quite lost to go to the store one day and find the labels gone—just a floor of CDs, arranged alphabetically. This happens sometimes, of course, in the bargain-bin special offer sales, and while I approve in principle of the resulting serendipity, I mutter to myself all the time that it would have been much easier if somebody had sorted out these cut-outs before dropping them in a heap.

In terms of later embarrassment, record stores have the advantage that no one can remember how they once organized genre categories (rock 'n' roll as "novelty") or placed particular acts (Bob Marley as "folk"). And so the best evidence (except, possibly, *Billboard*'s chart terms) of how music business labels so often seem to miss the point can be found in the history of the Grammy Awards. In 1958, for example, the main pop categories were plain: record of the year; album of the year; song of the year; vocal—female; vocal—male; orchestra; dance band; vocal group or chorus (there were separate slots for country and rhythm & blues performers). In 1959 new titles included Performance by a Top 40 Artist and Folk Performance. In 1960 the Top 40 award became Pop Singles Artist; in 1961 there was, for the first time, an award for Rock and Roll Recording (which was won by "Let's Twist Again"). In 1964 the Beatles won the Grammy for Vocal Group of the Year; Petula Clark made the winning Rock and Roll Recording. By 1965 the latter category was labeled Contemporary (Rock and Roll); this became Contemporary Pop in 1968, Pop in 1971, and Pop, Rock, and Folk in 1974. In 1979 it was split between Pop (male and female vocal, group, instrumental) and Rock (male and female vocal, group, instrumental). One would, indeed, get a strange notion of popular music history from Grammy categories (and winners) alone. Soul Gospel appears from 1969, Ethnic or Traditional (including blues and "pure" folk) from 1970, disco (for one year only) in 1979. A Video award was made (rather more promptly) from 1981; the decade also saw, eventually, awards for metal, hard rock, and rap.[5]

I've always felt that the Grammies give one a good sense of how the American music industry would like to see the market even as, reluctantly and tardily, it has to adapt to the way the market really is. And the oddity of the Grammies lies in their subsequent air of fantasy: no one in any individual record company could afford to be so stupid about public tastes, but collectively and anonymously record companies can still show how they'd like things to be.

Back in the real world, the problem, at least for the record industry in the United States, is radio. Out of promotional necessity record companies must constantly adapt their product not to consumer taste as such, but to consumer taste as understood and organized by radio stations. From a British perspective just the names for U.S. radio formats seem exotic: Adult Contemporary (full service, gold-intensive, lite, music-intensive, adult alternative), AOR (album oriented rock), Beautiful Music, Big Band, CHR (Contemporary Hit Radio), classical, country, easy listening radio, gold (gold—classic rock), gospel, Hispanic, jazz, Music of Your Life, New Age, nostalgia, Quiet Storm, Urban Contemporary.[6]

The thinking behind such labels is captured in a *USA Today* story about the emergence at the beginning of the 1990s of so-called "adult Top 40," "hot adult contemporary," or "mix" stations, playing "top singles with grown-up appeal."

> "Standard Top 40 has gotten so extreme that mothers and daughters don't like the same music anymore," says Guy Zapoleon, national program director for the 12-station Nationwide Communications.
>
> Lots of stations are going with Mom, sacrificing the kids to rival stations. It's a money decision. In the radio business, the 25–55 age group is called the "money demographic" . . .
>
> Stations move into the adult Top 40 format from two directions. Some are former adult contemporary stations that now mix in many current releases with their soft fare from the past couple of decades for a "hotter" sound. Others are former standard Top 40 stations that have deleted the jarring extremes of teen-aimed tunes.
>
> Zapoleon says similar formats have sprung up in other eras when pop music has become fragmented, but were abandoned when superstar innovators with across-the-board appeal reunited listeners.[7]

The peculiarity of generic definitions in music radio terms is that programmers are using the sounds to put together an audience (or market or demographic) for delivery to advertisers. Sometimes the radio definition of this market-by-taste coincides with the record industry's (as with country music, for example); often it does not. Record companies can never be sure how radio programmers will classify a new sound (or whether that classification will make sense to record buyers). Genre labeling, in this context, becomes both slippery and powerful (given radio's control of the pop soundscape). It's as if radio programmers can create a territory by mapping it. And record companies can't find their way to market without that map; they don't even know where they may be going.[8]

The problem of radio-driven definitions of music is raised equally acutely (and more hilariously) when the state gets involved: both Canada and Britain, for example, have generic definitions built into broadcasting legislation. Canadian legislators took an interest in pop genres for two reasons. First, in a compromise between public service and commercial broadcasting principles, it was determined that while entrepreneurs could bid for licenses to run advertising-funded radio stations, the local population still had the right to a diversity of programming principles, to a range of different musics. Local licenses, then, are granted under principles of *balance:* would-be licensees have to declare (and stick to) a programming policy; the licensers have to ensure that each radio locality has the right mix of pop and rock and jazz and classical and country. To do this such categories have to be defined: when does the music on a so-called country station playlist, for example, cease to be "country"?

Second, for reasons of national cultural policy, broadcasters in Canada are subject to a content law: a percentage of the music played must be "Canadian" (written by Canadians, performed by Canadians, produced by Canadians, or some combination thereof). The difficulty here is that some musical genres have more Canadian material available than others; it didn't make sense to make the same Canadian content demands on, say, classical and country stations, or on rock and folk and jazz. To apply different quota regulations to different stations according to different genres meant, again, giving such generic definitions legal clout.

Canadian radio law thus defines music radio under the following headings:

> Category 6: *Music–General*
> Live or recorded entertainment music, extending from the advent of mass-produced recordings to the latest hits as defined in charts of recognized trade publications, including popular songs and compositions which fall under the headings "pop," "country-and-western," "rhythm and blues," "rock," "easy listening," "middle-of-the-road," "beautiful music," "mood," and "mainly for dancing"; popularized arrangements of classical music, jazz or authentic folksongs, music written in a folk idiom by present-day artists; songs of protest and political and social comment, humorous and satirical songs, chansonniers and chansonnettes, English music hall and North American vaudeville, individual excerpts from works for the musical stage, non-religious Christmas songs, popular music for films and television, and international pop songs; popularizations of folk idioms, such as Latin American, Hawaiian and Calypso, and the popular music of Canada's various ethnic cultures, other than authentic traditional folk music; for greater particularity, this category includes the following five subcategories:
> Subcategory 61: *General Popular*
> This subcategory includes all musical selections that fall within the terms of the general description for category 6 but are not included in subcategories 65, 66, 67, 68.
> Subcategory 65: *Rock and Rock-Oriented*
> This subcategory includes rock and roll, rhythm-and-blues, rock, country-rock, folk-rock, jazz-rock, and pop-rock, where the music is

characterized by a strong beat, the use of blues forms, and the presence of rock instruments such as electric guitar, electric bass, electric organ, or electric piano.

Subcategory 66: *Country and Country-Oriented*

This subcategory includes simple, guitar-accompanied "country," back country or "western" songs; orchestrated, citified or "town and country" songs, including those in a Nashville and country-pop styles; old-time fiddle music, breakdowns, hoedowns, jigs and reels other than those in subcategories 67 or 77; bluegrass music, and country yodelling.

Subcategory 67: *Folk-Oriented*

This subcategory includes music in a folk style composed by the troubadours and chansonniers of our time, popular arrangements of authentic folksongs, and popularization of folk idioms.

Subcategory 68: *Jazz-Oriented*

Music sung or played in a popular style by performers with a jazz background, including the work of the jazz-influenced dance bands, "cocktail" jazz and jazz improvisation when presented against a popularized orchestral background, but not including jazz-rock falling under subcategory 65.[9]

Several things are striking about the genre definitions here. First, because what is at issue is, supposedly, content (not market), the approach is basically musicological; rock, for example, is defined in terms of what it sounds like (beat, form, and instrumentation) rather by reference to who might listen to it. Second, even within such "objective" measures there are, nevertheless, ideological implications, as indicated by the use of the terms "authentic" and "popularized" with reference to folk and classical music. Such descriptive terms are not purely musical. Third, the boundaries between the various subcategories are, inevitably, imprecise, and an interesting question emerges: can a record be played on more than one sort of station? Does it thereby change its meaning?[10] Fourth, how can musical tastes ever change in this system? Can the legislators' "objective" account of musical meaning really be written over the much more fluid, "subjective" approach of radio listeners?

This question was posed in an even starker (and more ludicrous) manner in the British parliament. Here the legislative problem was both simpler and more difficult: how to distinguish between "rock" and "pop." The question also emerged from radio policy, and from a muddled compromise between public service principles and market forces. The 1980s Conservative government had decided to license three national commercial radio stations (previously, commercial operators had only been licensed to broadcast locally). Rather than just license the three highest bidders, though, the Tories too retained a belief in "balance." One station was to be talk, and one was to be "other than pop." More particularly, the first wavelength to be released, the only one of the three with FM access, was to be non-pop. The Thatcher government, which combined belief in the market with a strong sense of the state's right to enforce moral standards, had always been wary of simply opening up the airwaves to more "pop and prattle" (a phrase used by the minister then in charge of broadcasting policy, Douglas Hurd). What was involved here, in other words, wasn't just a matter of choice—listeners could already choose nationally from the BBC's Radio 1 (pop/rock), 2 (easy listening), 3 (classical), and 4 (talk)—but also a matter of value.

This became clear when the bidders for the station began to declare themselves. One of the most powerful was Rock FM, a consortium put together by Britain's leading rock promoter, Harvey Goldsmith, and the publishing company EMAP (publishers of Britain's leading rock magazine, Q). From their perspective rock was clearly "other than pop"; it meant "album-based music for adults" rather than "instant, singles-based music aimed at teenagers."[11]

This was not at all what the government had intended, and it hastily introduced an amendment to the Broadcasting Act. "Pop music" was now defined to include all kinds of music "characterised by a strong rhythmic element and a reliance on electronic amplification for their performance."[12] The amendment was introduced in the House of Lords, and the flavor of the resulting debate is captured in the following exchange. Earl Ferrars, for the government:

> It has been argued that rock music is not the same thing as pop music. I do not know whether it is or not. But I do know that it would be an odd result—and not, I am sure, what your Lordships intended—if a rock music or similar application were able to win the licence for the non-pop service . . . The somewhat intricate style of the amendment was thought appropriate because the parliamentary draughtsman thought that my definition of "pop," which was thump, thump, thump, would not be parliamentary or statutorily adequate.

The Viscount of Falkland, speaking on behalf of the record industry:

> Pop music, as it is understood by the music industry in this country and in the United States, now has a clear definition. There is a clear

understanding that pop music as such is music which is recorded in single versions mainly for a teenage market and which forms part of what is generally known as the Top of the Pops table. It is generally accepted that pop music is a single which is part of a market-based table or chart of 40. That may be even more esoteric to your Lordships, but that is the fact of the matter. It is well known that in this country there are other forms of music which have been grouped by the Government, or those who are helping to draw up the legislation, with those singles in the charts that I have described. That includes rock music to which the noble Earl referred . . . Noble Lords may wonder about the kind of music to which I refer. I shall simply mention two names. In this country there is an artist, who is I believe very popular with the Royal Family, called Phil Collins. He is an extremely successful rock artist and something of a film actor. His albums come within the term "rock." They are extremely successful and popular. In the United States there is a recording artist called Bruce Springsteen, known popularly as The Boss, who is a world-renowned artist in this kind of music. Sales of his records continue to boom. Rock goes into other areas, some of which are perhaps more limited in appeal. However, there is a world of difference between pop music and rock music and indeed many other forms of music which have the same thump, thump element. [Earl Ferrars: Thump, thump, thump, my Lords.] My Lords, I apologise; a thump, thump, thump element. That includes a great deal of ethnic music such as music of West Indian origin.[13]

The terms of this debate are clear. The British government (like the Canadian government) sought to define rock musicologically, in terms of form (thump, thump, thump); the industry (and Rock FM) sought to define it sociologically (by reference to its market) and ideologically (by describing its market function).[14] The problem with the sociological argument, as Earl Ferrars pointed out in the House of Lords, was that it didn't stand up to close analysis: both Phil Collins and Bruce Springsteen had released singles that were included in the "Top of the Pops Table." The British popular music world doesn't fall into neat pop and rock divisions, musically or sociologically; it is more logical to treat it as a market unity. And where the industry argument was powerful—with respect to ideology (Bruce Springsteen fans just know they're different from Kylie Minogue fans)—it made no legislative sense: how could one safely define music in terms of attitude? As the American critic Barry Walters puts it (commenting on *Rolling Stone's* list of "The

100 Best Singles of the Last Twenty-Five Years"), "Since the form pop music takes is more consistent than any other commercial art, quality is most often a matter of style, which eludes objective appraisal. The meaning, the ultimate value, of pop emerges out of the meeting between music and listener, an interaction that changes over time."[15]

Bruce Springsteen's music has, after all, already been recuperated as nostalgia (it's the classic radio accompaniment to ads for classic jeans and classic beer) and will, inevitably, become "lite," "gold," and "easy listening" in the years to come. If nothing else, then, the Lords pop/rock debate did make clear that generic labeling involves a complex interplay between musical, marketing, and ideological forces. This is obvious in the other sectors of the music business in which labels are essential: the music press, which is designed to appeal to pop fans generally but also to forge them into a newly com-mitted—ideological—readership; and clubs and club nights, which use music labels in their flyers and posters (Techno-Rave-Acid-Jungle) to attract a particular sort of crowd and thus to ensure a particular sort of evening.[16]

Readers and clubbers (unlike radio listeners) thus become an important part of the labeling process—a new genre is recognized by a new audience. The key ideological moment each year for music papers is the readers' poll, which serves as a public display of the magazine's success in forging a community out of its disparate consumers, a process which is particularly important (not least in maintaining advertising revenue) when a magazine changes its generic base (whether in response to reader interest or not). The British folk magazine *Southern Rag* redefined its brief in the mid-1980s, for instance, to include "roots" music (which referred less to musical form than to the spirit in which it was played—local, live, cheap rock and roll of all kinds) and ethnic sounds (the same spirit reflected in music from the Third World). The shift had more to do with what was happening on the live folk circuit (who was being booked into pubs and clubs; what folk musicians themselves found interesting and relevant) than with any obvious sense of reader dissatisfaction (or falling circulation). In changing its name to *Folk Roots*, in other words, in redefining "folk," the magazine was making a pitch for a *new* sort of reader who was thought to be out there. Publicity material now carried the endorsement of the *NME*, a rock paper: "*Folk Roots* is both modern, yet steeped in tradition; it has a historical importance, yet it is always hunting for the sounds of the future . . . *Folk Roots* does not have its finger in its ear, it has its finger on the pulse."[17]

Folk Roots went on to play a key role (alongside a handful of radio and club deejays and concert promoters) in defining—and putting together the market for—"world music," a genre label (in the United States the term was "world beat") which emerged from a 1987 meeting with eleven independent record labels:

> Whilst not all of these labels are devoted exclusively to World Music, they have united to bring recognition to the many diverse forms of music as yet unclassifiable in Western terms. Trying to reach a definition of "WORLD MUSIC" provoked much lengthy discussion and finally it was agreed that it means practically any music that isn't at present catered for by its own category, e.g.: Reggae, jazz, blues, folk. Perhaps the common factor unifying all these WORLD MUSIC labels is the passionate commitment of all the individuals to the music itself.

The object was to improve the music's sales situation: "The term WORLD MUSIC will be used to make it easier to find that Malian Kora record, the music of Bulgaria, Zairean soukous or Indian Ghazals—the new WORLD MUSIC section will be the first place to look in the local record shop."[18] But what was equally significant (hence *Folk Roots'* role) was the perception of the potential world music market as people drawn from the rock and folk audiences, people, that is, with a particular set of musical attitudes, needs, and expectations. Not all the music made in the world, after all, got to be "world music."[19]

I want to make two general points about this. First, in using genre labels to make the marketing process more efficient, record companies are assuming that there is a manageable relationship between musical label and consumer taste. This rests, in turn, on a set of assumptions about who these consumers are, in terms of age, gender, ethnicity, disposable income, leisure habits, and so forth. In broad market research terms, such assumptions are usually efficient enough. Record companies aren't stupid about the decisions they make as to how to package and market musicians—where to advertise world music or heavy metal records, say, or in which magazines and TV shows to place a would-be indie star or teen idol.

Nevertheless, what is going on here is an idealization, the creation of a *fantasy* consumer (the sort of fantasy consumer being invoked by the press releases I quoted in Chapter 3) and, in this, the industry follows tastes rather than forming them. (I can't think of an example of a musical genre created by a marketing machine, rather than given a hasty definition, like "world music," after its loose characteristics had already emerged through new consumer alliances.) As fantasies, then, genres describe not just who listeners are, but also what this music means to them. In deciding to label a music or a musician in a particular way, record companies are saying something about both what people like and why they like it; the musical label acts as a condensed sociological and ideological argument.[20]

The second general point follows from this: although we are ostensibly dealing here with sound qualities, it may be difficult to say what different acts or records in a genre have in common *musically*. This is obvious, for example, in the case of "indie" music. Such a label refers both to a means of production (music produced on an independent rather than a major label) and to an attitude, supposedly embodied in the music, in its listeners, and, perhaps most important, in the relationship between them.[21] It can therefore lead, in turn, to intricate (and fiercely debated) judgments as to whether a band "sells out," changes the meaning of its music, by appealing to a wider audience.[22]

It is difficult to explain how such arguments about genre boundaries work to people uninvolved with the genre in the first place, people ignorant, that is to say, of a basic (if unstated) agreement within a genre about what their music is *for*. To take another British example, "student music" (as record companies realize) must fit student life, fit the student rhythm of collective indulgence and lonely regret, boorishness and angst, and also draw on shared teen memories and the sense of exclusiveness that being a student (at least in Britain) still entails. Take this list of albums, for instance: *The Wall* (Pink Floyd), *The Joshua Tree* (U2), *Brothers in Arms* (Dire Straits), *Bat Out of Hell* (Meat Loaf), *The Queen is Dead* (The Smiths), *Love Over Gold* (Dire Straits), *Graceland* (Paul Simon), *Steve McQueen* (Prefab Sprout), *Sgt. Pepper's Lonely Hearts Club Band* (The Beatles), *Dream of the Blue Turtles* (Sting). At first sight (on first hearing) it would make little sense generically, and yet as "The Nescafe Student All Time Favourite Albums, 1988" it is explicable in terms of both range of sounds covered and the odd mix of the "classic" and the ephemeral (I doubt if students five years later had even heard the Prefab Sprout or Sting LPs).[23]

Similarly, "women's music," a sales label used in both Britain and the United States, is a category which jams together very disparate sounds. *WRPM* (Women's Revolutions Per Minute), the British women's music catalogue, is laid out in familiar ways (feminist/politics; spoken; classical; blues and jazz; folk and country; world/roots music; gospel; for young people; rock/pop/soul; humor—only "healing and ritual" is a category unlikely to be found in other general catalogues), and if the common denominator is that the music is made by women, the catalogue still excludes many different types of female performers. "Women's music" thus seems to describe something *brought* to a sound, whether that sound is "US synthesizer politico-pop" (Sue Fink), "theatrical brilliance and original anti-racist humour backed with disco music" (Frank Chickens), "soft rock and silky ballads" (Deidre McCalla), or "very sexy rock music" (Tret Fure). And if there are social tendencies here (the music is quite likely to be feminist, to be lesbian, to be independently produced, to be live or acoustic), none of these factors is determinate. Caroline Hutton describes *WRPM*'s principles as follows: "This catalogue is part of the process of change in our lives. The music, I hope, will touch you. It can heal, inspire, energise and give great pleasure to us all. Many of the lyrics will say a lot more about the world and our experiences than 'I love you baby.'"[24]

"Women's music," in short, is defined ideologically, and, more to the point here, it is defined *against* other ways of music-making. Like "indie," it is a category that only makes sense as an argument about "mainstream music" as well as about women; it describes what is not included—male-dominated music of all sorts. In fact, the logic of the label seems obvious enough, even (perhaps especially) to those people who don't much like "women's music" anyway.[25]

I'll come back to genres as ideologies shortly. First, a few words on the second way in which genre labels work in popular music evaluation: as a way of organizing *the playing process*.

Perhaps because of their lack of formal or academic music education, popular musicians are accustomed to using generic labels as a basic shorthand for particular sounds (or riffs or beats). This is obvious in the way in which musicians talk to each other in rehearsal or in the recording studio, in the instructions given to players or engineers about their musical and sound decisions. The basis of session players' reputations, for example, often rests on their ability to respond to such shorthand without explanation being needed. And one of the services that sampling devices and "sound banks" currently offer is precisely such generically labeled sounds, on demand, over the phone line.

In musical terms, the words used here are difficult to understand unless one already knows their meaning (a technically skilled but generically igno-rant musician would not be able to understand requests to "give it some funk!"; to "try a reggae bass!"; to "hit that Phil Collins hi-hat!"; to "fall into the Stock-Aitken-Waterman groove!"). Genre discourse depends, in other words, on a certain sort of shared musical knowledge and experience (think, for example, of the use of musical labels in the ads published by groups seeking a new member, or on the "musician wanted" cards pinned up in musical instrument stores). What is obvious from this language is that for musicians too, genre labels describe musical skills and ideological attitudes simultaneously.[26]

This is even more obvious in the third use of genre labels, as a way of organizing *the listening process*. In Chapter 3 I suggested that rock critics rarely describe music in formal language, but almost always through comparison: new sound X is described by reference to already known sound Y. Done well, this is an elegant and economical form of descriptive shorthand (a good critic could be defined as one who can make such comparisons both original and telling), and genre labeling is, from this critical perspective, an *implied* comparison (or set of comparisons)—generic labels are, in fact, among the critic's most essential tools.[27]

Deejays have probably been even more effective than journalists in defining new genres, "discovering" new markets (if only because they put their arguments to practical test, on the dance floor), though often all they are doing is routinizing terms taken from club chatter, and, in practice, it is virtually impossible to say where a new term (house, rave, rap, grunge) first came from. Genre origins remain a matter of elaborate and unresolvable debate. Or, to put this more sensibly, the genre labeling process is better understood as something collusive than as something invented individually, as the result of a loose *agreement* among musicians and fans, writers and disc jockeys. It is in fanzines, for example, that sounds are most systematically lined up with attitudes (musicians with audiences) and genres most earnestly argued about ideologically (and related to ways of life).[28]

Focal ideological figures and their programs, clubs, and magazines play, then, something of the same role in the formation of popular genre-consciousness as galleries in the formation of new movements in the fine arts. A new "genre world," that is to say, is first constructed and then articulated through a complex interplay of musicians, listeners, and mediating ideologues, and this process is much more confused than the marketing process that follows, as the wider industry begins to make sense of the new sounds and markets and to exploit both genre worlds and genre discourses in the orderly routines of mass marketing.[29] The issue then becomes how to draw genre boundaries. Genres initially flourish on a sense of exclusivity; they are as much (if not more) concerned to keep people out as in. The industry aim is to retain the promise of exclusivity, the hint of generic secrets, while making them available to everyone. It sometimes seems, indeed, as if a genre is only clearly defined (its secret revealed) at the moment when it ceases to exist, when it can no longer be exclusive. Fanzines, that is to say, are surprisingly often *launched* on the premise that the music they are celebrating no longer really exists.[30]

In looking at the various ways in which genre labels are used to organize music making, music listening, and music selling, I have been circling around the same point: popular music genres are constructed—and must be understood—*within* a commercial/cultural process; they are not the result of detached academic analyses or formal musicological histories.[31] For people who *live* in genres there are continuous questions to be answered about new acts and releases: does this fit my playlist, my roster, my review pages, my collection? And the answers are inevitably reached by measuring the new music against a notion of the real thing: is this really jazz or punk or disco or New Age? Authenticity is a necessary critical value—one listens to the music for clues to something else, to what makes the genre at issue valuable as a genre in the first place. The musical judgment is necessarily a social judgment: does this music understand the genre, is it true to it? For people who *study* genre, the questions are retrospective: how were these decisions made, what was it about these records that caused them to be labeled the same way, what do they have in common? The answers are much more formal: blues or punk or progressive rock are described in terms of the musical language they deploy; records are excluded from the definitions because they don't fit technically—have the wrong structure, beat, or orchestration.

The problem of these different approaches is apparent in the writing of genre histories, which matter both because what happens to genres over time is a crucial part of their meaning and because genre self-consciousness derives in the first place from an account (usually mythical) of its own past.[32] The crunch comes when the academic account is written over the mythical one—by *the collector*—and the history of the genre is rewritten in terms of a new purism. Now the critical question (most familiar, I suppose, in folk music) becomes what might be called formal authenticity: does this singer or song obey the genre's musicological rules?[33]

I'll come back to the issue of genre rules and their authority. Before that I need to refer to one of the few pieces of empirical research on the history of genres in everyday life, Ruth Finnegan's *The Hidden Musicians*. Musical labels are the key to Finnegan's map of "music-making in an English town," and I want to draw attention to two of her arguments in particular. First, Finnegan shows that to have a musical interest, a genre taste, is to engage in the set of relationships which give meaning to that taste. An individual's liking for punk or opera, for country music or progressive rock, whether as performer or audience, is a commitment to a taste community, the taste community, in fact, which defines what I earlier called a genre's "ideal consumer."[34]

Second, Finnegan, doing her social scientific duty, tries to relate the resulting genre ideologies to social characteristics, to class, age, gender, ethnicity, and so forth. Her question becomes: do social identities and needs map onto musical identities and needs? does a homological approach to musical values make empirical sense? Her answer is, perhaps surprisingly, no! While it was apparent, for example, that each new teenage generation had its own music (punk at the time of Finnegan's research), it was also clear that thereafter the enjoyment of such music was not confined to its own generation: old youth musics (rock 'n' roll, progressive rock, heavy metal, glam rock) were played by the people who had grown up on them *and* by musicians from subsequent generations (the rock 'n' roll scene thus included musicians of any age from 20 to 55). Ironically, the only music world whose members shared social class characteristics, the folk world (which was essentially middle class), was also the only music world with a clear class ideology: it defined itself as working class.[35]

Finnegan concludes that in relating music and society, we should reverse the usual sociological approach. Rather than looking for people's material conditions in their aesthetic and hedonistic activity, we should look at how their particular love and use of music inform their social situations. She suggests, for example, a distinction between musical activities that are continuous with people's other social ties (this is often how people come to be in choirs or amateur operatic societies, for example, and can explain tastes— running in the family—in country music or rock 'n' roll), and musical activities that are used by people to mark themselves off from their families or community (as with the middle-class punk or the orchestra member from a non-musical family). One can distinguish, similarly, between the degrees of ritual a musical life involves: the annual operetta or weekly folk night matter to their participants in different ways than the occasional participation in a disco or pub singalong. The use of music, in other words, can vary as to how important it is in defining one's social identity, how significant it is in determining one's friendships, how special it is in forming one's sense of self. The question of musical value is, as I suggested in Chapter 1, inevitably tied up with questions of sociability. And the significant social differences may be less those between genres than between degrees of commitment (or types of commitment) to them.[36]

What does seem clear is that it is through its generic organization that music offers people, even so-called passive at-home listeners, access to a social world, a part in some sort of social narrative, offers them what Finnegan calls "social pathways." In aesthetic terms, musical sounds, ideologies, and activities, musical texts and their implied contexts, cannot be separated. The pleasures popular music offers us, the values it carries (and I include classical music as popular here), have to be related to the stories it tells about us in our genre identities. Or, to put this the other way around, genre analysis must be, by aesthetic necessity, narrative analysis. It must refer to an implied community, to an implied romance, to an implied plot. In examining how the elements of popular music work (the sound, the lyric, the voice, the beat) we always have to take account of their genre coding: popular musical pleasures can only be understood as genre pleasures; and genre pleasures can only be understood as socially structured.

To conclude this chapter, then, I want to return to the question of genre rules, and the pioneering work of Franco Fabbri. Fabbri argues that a musical genre is a set of musical events (real or possible) whose course is governed by a definite set of socially accepted rules, and suggests that these rules can be grouped under five headings.[37]

First, *formal and technical rules.* These are the rules of musical form (to be classified as punk or country, a piece of music has to have certain aural characteristics)which include playing conventions—what skills the musicians must have; what instruments are used, how they are played, whether they are amplified or acoustic; rhythmic rules; melodic rules; the studio sound quality; the relation of voice to instruments (whether there's a voice at all); the relationship of words to music; and so forth. Such rules can be very loose (anything can be "rocked") or very tight (as in Canada's legal definition of authentic country music). But just as turning noise into "music" means knowing how to organize the sounds we hear in particular (conventionalized) ways, so to hear music generically (hearing this as punk, this as hard core; this as acid, this as techno) means organizing the sounds according to formal rules.

Second, *semiotic rules.* These are essentially rules of communication, how music works as *rhetoric;* such rules refer to the ways in which "meaning" is conveyed (referential meaning, emotional meaning, poetic meaning, imperative meaning, metalinguistic meaning, phatic meaning: Roman Jakobson's communicative functions). How is "truth" or "sincerity" indicated musically? How do we know what music is "about"? Consider, for example, how different genres (opera, folk, rock, punk) read singers: as the protagonists of their songs? As revealing themselves? Rules here, in other words, concern musical expressivity and emotion; they determine the significance of the lyrics— different genres, for example, having quite different conventions of lyrical realism: soul versus country, the singer/songwriter versus the disco diva. Rules here also concern issues like intertextuality (to what extent does the music refer to other music?) and the ways in which a genre presents itself as "aesthetic," "emotional," or "physical." Part of what is involved here is the placing of performer and audience in relationship to each other, the degrees of intimacy and distance. Such rules have practical effects. As Ola Stockfelt argues (quoting from Fabbri), "adequate listening" depends upon them: "The distance between musician and audience, between spectator and spectator, the overall dimension of [musical] events are often fundamental elements to the definition of a genre . . . often 'how you are seated' says more about the music that will be performed than a poster does."[38]

In short, as Fabbri admits, it is difficult to distinguish semiotic rules from the next category, *behavioral rules*, which cover performance rituals in a widely defined sense. These are gestural rules, then; they determine the ways in which musical skill and technique, on the one hand, and musical personality, on the other, are displayed—compare a Bruce Springsteen and a Kraftwerk concert, for example, or Erasure and the Mekons. Behavioral rules apply to audiences as well: an audience for the Cocteau Twins behaves differently from an audience for Nirvana. Lawrence Levine has a nice example of the misunderstandings that result when an audience behaves "wrongly":

> Ethel Waters, who began her career in 1917, did not sing before a northern white audience until the 1920s, and the sharp difference in audience reactions confused her and led her to conclude that she had been rebuffed when in fact she had scored a great success. "You know we took the flop of our lives just now," she told her partner, Earl Dancer. "Those people out front applauded us only because they wanted to be polite. Nobody stomped as they always do in coloured theatres when I finish my act. Nobody screamed or jumped up and down. Nobody howled with joy."[39]

Behavioral rules also concern offstage performance, behavior in interviews, packaged performance, the artist in videos and press photographs. Fabbri notes, for example, how different types of singers in Italy appear (or are packaged) differently on television:

> Traditional and sophisticated singers are in their element on television; their gestures are no different from those of the presenters . . . The pop singer is in his element too, but tends to overdo the smiles and raised eyebrows which reveal his underlying anxiety to please. The rock singer and the *cantautore* are uncomfortable on television: the former because television is too bourgeois, and is too small for his exaggerated gestures, and the latter because it is too stupid. Anyway, the *cantautore* must always give the impression of being uncomfortable in front of his audience, because privacy is his "true" dimension. In either case nervous tics are acceptable . . . The political singer hardly ever appears on television, and the gestures associated with him are those of the participant in a political meeting.[40]

Rules of conversation and etiquette apply here, guiding the meetings between performers and journalists, performers and concert organizers, performers and fans.[41] As Fabbri notes, the apparent spontaneity of offstage rituals is exposed by the laughter that breaks out when rules are broken—one of the pleasures of *Smash Hits,* the British teen pop magazine, is the way it insistently breaks behavioral rules, asking "serious" rock stars intimate teen-pop questions: what's in your handbag, what did you eat for breakfast, who do you fantasize about in bed? Behavioral rules apply to audiences off stage too: there are "appropriate" ways to listen to a record, to respond to it. And such rules are not just random, as it were; they reflect what performers (and listeners) are meant to be and thus how their "realness" as stars and communities is indicated.

The fourth category consists of *social and ideological rules.* These cover the social image of the musician regardless of reality (a heavy metal or hard core musician has to be "outrageous" socially in a way that a folk or classical musician does not), but also refer to the nature of the musical community and its relationship to the wider world. These are the rules concerning the ethnic or gender divisions of labor, for example, and, in general, reflect what the music is meant to stand for as a social force, its account of an ideal world as well as of the real one.

Finally, there are *commercial and juridical rules.* These refer to the means of production of a music genre, to questions of ownership, copyright, financial reward, and so on; they determine how musical events come into being, as well as the relations of musics to record companies and the recording process, and records to live concerts and the promotion process.

The problem of such a schematic overview (as Fabbri emphasizes) is that it implies a static picture of genres with clearly defined boundaries, whereas, in fact, genres are constantly changing—as an effect of what's happening in neighboring genres, as a result of musical contradictions, in response to technological and demographic change.[42] Fabbri notes too that the relative importance of the different sorts of rules varies from genre to genre. The "ideological" rules of punk, for example, were more important than those of Euro-disco, and Helfried Zrzavy has argued persuasively that the defining feature of New Age was less how it sounded than how it looked: it was "ultimately, the cohesion in the aesthetics of New Age cover art that established the genre's unmistakeable identity" as "a primarily visual musical genre."[43]

The final point to make here, though, is that one way in which genres work in day-to-day terms is in a deliberate process of rule testing and bending. As Charles Hamm has argued, popular musicians "work within a tradition that allows and even demands flexibility and creativity in shaping a piece. Genre is not determined by the form or style of a text itself but by the audience's perception of its style and meaning, defined most importantly at the moment of performance. Performers can thus shape, reinforce or even change genre."[44] It is out of such "transgressive" performances that genre histories are written: old genres "fail" when their rules and rituals come to seem silly and restrictive; new genres are born as the transgressions become systematic. The value question here is a particularly interesting one: how do people recognize a good example of a genre? As music that follows the rules so effectively that it is heard to *exemplify* them? Or as music that draws attention to the way in which a genre works by *exposing* the unstable basis of its rules? This is another version of a recurring question in popular cultural studies: how should we relate the pleasures of novelty and repetition? The answer will, of course, depend on the genre involved, but there is one general point to make: as we saw in the Mass-Observation surveys, the importance of all popular genres is that they set up expectations, and disappointment is likely *both* when they are not met *and* when they are met all too predictably.[45]

The value of Fabbri's approach here is that it clarifies how genre rules integrate musical and ideological factors, and why *performance* must be treated as central to the aesthetics of popular music. I could reorganize Fabbri's argument by dividing his rules more neatly into sound conventions (what you hear), performing conventions (what you see), packaging conventions (how a type of music is sold), and embodied values (the music's ideology). But this would be to break the connections (if only for analytic reasons) that Fabbri was concerned to emphasize. The particular way in which a guitarist gets a guitar note, for example (whether George Benson or Jimi Hendrix, Mark Knopfler or Johnny Marr, Derek Bailey or Bert Jansch) is at once a musical decision and a gestural one: it is the integration of sound and behavior in performance that gives the note its "meaning."[46] And if nothing else this makes it impossible to root explanations of popular music in consumption. It is not enough to assert that commodities only become culturally valuable when they are made "meaningful" by consumers: they can only be consumed because they are *already* meaningful, because musicians, producers, and consumers are already ensnared in a web of genre expectation.

To summarize my argument so far:

We can only begin to make sense of the aesthetics of popular music when we understand, first, the language in which value judgments are articulated and expressed and, second, the social situations in which they are appropriate. Value language is itself shaped by historical and social circumstance; and in the West, at least, how people think about popular music is an effect of the nineteenth-century industrialization of culture, and the use of music as a commodity. These historical developments put into play a set of assumptions about the "high" and the "low" and a way of making sense of cultural experience through the mutually defining discourses of art, folk, and commerce. We still live within these discourses, and it is impossible to understand what it means to value music without reference to the *ideological* baggage we carry around with us.

We can only make sense of musical value judgments, moreover, if we understand the circumstances in which they are made—and what they are made for. I have divided these circumstances up in orthodox sociological fashion: the processes of music making, selling, and consuming; but the general point (what these circumstances have in common) is that value judgments only make sense as part of an argument, and arguments are always *social* events.

Finally, in the world of popular music, ideological and social discourses are invariably put together *generically.* It is genre rules which determine how musical forms are taken to convey meaning and value, which determine the aptness of different sorts of judgment, which determine the competence of different people to make assessments. It is through genres that we experience music and musical relations, that we bring together the aesthetic and the ethical.

With these broad sociological assertions in mind, I will turn now to the music.

On Music Itself

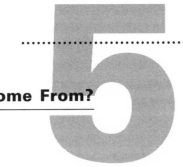

Where Do Sounds Come From?

The practice of making music with two or more simultaneous sounds is perhaps one of the great testimonies to the human struggle against boredom.

Richard Norton[1]

When [Georges] Auric composed the score for Jean Cocteau's film, *The Blood of a Poet*, he produced what is commonly known as love music for the love scenes, game music for game scenes, funeral music for funeral scenes. Cocteau had the bright idea of replacing the love music with the funeral, game music with the love, funeral with game.

Ned Rorem[2]

Musical evaluation as I've discussed it so far seems inevitably to mean thinking backwards: first the experience, the music; then the judgment, the account of the music. Even everyday criticism frames the music discursively *after the event,* as it were. The question I want to ask now is this: what was the event? And the question concerns cognition as well as evaluation: we have to recognize something as something (noise as music; music as genre) before we know what to do with it, how to assess it.[3] How does this cognitive process work? Even if we adopt Herrnstein Smith's account of evaluation at its most functional—so that the question "is it good?" really means "is it good *for* something or somebody?"—there is still the question of what the "it" is. And this leads us to the familiar question of philosophical aesthetics: is music, as music, meaningless? If so, where do the musical meanings coded into musical descriptions, conversations, genre distinctions, and critical assessments come from? How do people move from something they hear (a tone or a beat, an instrument or vocal quality) to some understanding of what it is "about"?

There are a variety of answers to this question, but we must begin by distinguishing music from noise. Music is an ordered pattern of sounds in the midst of a vast range of more or less disorderly aurality. Music is marked out as different from noise; as our sense of noise changes, so does our sense of music. In the twentieth century there has been not only a significant increase in the sheer quantity of noise, but also a shift in our underlying sense of silence: technology provides us with a permanent hum, a continued sonic presence. What does it mean to his music, as Philip Tagg once asked, that Mozart never heard a steam engine, a car, an aeroplane, a power drill, a ventilator, air conditioning, a refrigerator, a police siren, the central heating boiler, or the mains buzz; what does it mean for our listening to Mozart's music that we rarely hear the sound of horses' hooves on cobbles, a wood fire, the rustle of layers of petticoats? Is such noise entirely irrelevant to the meaning of his music?[4]

One of the effects of twentieth-century technology has certainly been to blur the boundaries between noise and music, as music, including (perhaps especially) classical music, has become part of the soundscape as "background noise," as a sound against which other sounds (such as conversation) are foregrounded (rather than vice versa).[5] The point here is simply that the meaning of music *as sound* depends, in the first place, on the quality of concentration with which it is attended. Music becomes music by being heard as such by the listener; it follows that to make music is not just to put sounds together in an organized way but also to ensure that these sounds *make their mark*.

An alternative way of relating musical meaning to non-musical sounds is in terms of imitation. At least some music "means" what it sounds like. It imitates nature; it works onomatopoeically. This can be a simple enough process. Gillian Anderson cites C. Roy Carter's 1926 manual, *Theatre Organist's Secrets*, in which he describes "how to imitate the following effects on the organ":

> The Snore, Laughter, Yell or Scream, The Kiss, R. R. Train, Aeroplane, Thunder and Rain Storm, Steam Whistle, Policeman's or Other Shrill Whistle, Prize-Fight Gong, Dog Bark, Dog Yelp, Cat Meow, Lion Roar, Cow's Moo, Rooster Crow, Pig Grunt, Cuckoo, Bag Pipes, Music Box, Banjo, Hand Organ, Accordion-Harmonic, Telegraph-Typewriter.[6]

Is what is being described here music (as opposed to a noise being made by a musical instrument)? Once imitation becomes a formal *organization* of noise, then the imitation is, by necessity, impressionistic. The music doesn't sound exactly like the real noise but gives an impression of it, whether the sea (Debussy's *La Mer*) or the Morse code of ticker tape (the TV news jingle). And once we're talking impressions we're talking conventions, agreements to hear certain musical combinations (particular instruments, textures, rhythms, melodies) as sounding "like" what they claim to represent. Storms as depicted by Wagner, the Doors, Vangelis, and Kate Bush sound no more like each other (or the real thing) than "onomatopoeic" sounds for animal noises (moo, woof, miaow) sound the same in different European languages.

Philip Tagg provides an entertaining example of the conventional (rather than imitative) way in which people hear music as "sounding like" nature:

> In at least twenty different seminars or courses during which *The Virginian* was under discussion, music students facing the question, "what's happening here?" after hearing only the first two bars almost unanimously responded "horses" or "riding" but were rarely able to give any unequivocal answers to the questions "where are the horses in these two bars?" or "how can you hear all those horses here?" This is not simply because the musical semiosis of horse hooves goes little beyond knocking coconut shells along the lines of the Monty Python gag at the opening of the *Holy Grail* movie. Or, to reverse the problem, unless you are watching a sped-up video of some novel trick taught to a show horse at the Spanish Riding School in Vienna, no horse actually puts its hooves to the ground in time with the initial *Virginian* rhythms . . . So if people hear horses after one or two bars, where are they in the music?[7]

Tagg's argument is that there is not a direct connection between real horse noise and musical horse noise. Rather, this interpretation is derived from a chain of the "representational" meanings of "musemes" (the basic musical elements that people actually hear, which may be instrumental sounds, melodic phrases, kinds of beat, or whatever). The *Virginian* theme thus combines a fandango rhythm (which moviegoers have learned to associate with Spanish/Mexican/Western America) and rimshots (which are associated with country and western dancing, with poor rural whites). "Fandango" plus "rednecks" equals "cowboys"; this is now a settled convention of Western film scoring, though it was presumably once learned—settled—by composers and audiences alike. We always hear these sounds together; we always thus hear "horses." In short, as Tagg puts it, "horses" in music follow not the iconic logic of *anaphones,* musical sounds "painting" natural sounds directly, but an indexical logic: musical sounds, as a matter of convention, *standing for* natural sounds. And the question is how such sonic conventions are established.[8]

The psychologist's answer is that there is a biologically necessary relationship between sounds and human responses to them, so that the meaning of the music *is* the response: "sleepy music," a lullaby, for example, is music which sends one to sleep; that is what this music—this sort of tune, this instrumental quality, this rhythm—means. If the response is the meaning, what triggers that response is physiology: the music makes us feel or do something directly. The baby doesn't interpret the song as a lullaby and therefore feel sleepy; the song just puts her to sleep. Not surprisingly, such biological claims have tended to focus primarily on the rhythmic quality of music, on the supposed effects of a regular beat on repeated body movements—on the heartbeat, the pulse, the gyrating hip, on sexual and nervous "agitation." It is by now a deeply rooted commonsense assumption that a funk beat necessarily *means* sex.

The problem with such arguments (I'll come back to sex and rhythm in Chapter 6) is their level of generality. From an ethnomusicological perspective, that is to say, there is no obvious relationship between human experience and musical sounds, between what we all feel as humans and how we express and evoke those feelings as members of particular societies. As Philip Tagg argues, the fact that all peoples make music doesn't mean that they all make the same music, any more than the fact that all peoples speak means that they speak the same language. In his illuminating study of musical accounts of death, Tagg shows that the "appropriate" sound of grief varies widely and can only be explained ideologically, in terms of social attitudes. In fact, as Tagg makes clear, there are very few universally understood aspects of musical expression, and these establish no more than extremely general types of bio-acoustic connections between musical structure and the human body and its acoustic and temporo-spatial surroundings. All evaluative and affective musical symbols are culturally specific.[9]

It may be true, in short, that in all cultures sounds must be louder the bigger the space they have to fill, that the human capacity to hold a breath or note is biologically determined, that more or less energetic noise (in terms of both tempo and volume) is necessarily associated with more or less energetic social activity—"nobody," as Tagg puts it, "yells jerky lullabies at breakneck speed," just as "nobody uses *legato* phrasing and soft or rounded timbres for hunting or war situations." But to turn such "bio-acoustic" facts into musical principles requires "rhythmic, metric, timbric, tonal, melodic, instrumental or harmonic *organisation*. Such *musical* organisation requires some kind of *social* organisation and cultural context before it can be created, understood or otherwise invested with meaning."[10] In other words, the biological approach to the meaning of music does not take us very far.

If music is meaningful in emotional terms it is therefore largely as an effect of cultural rather than psychological conditions. Enter musicologists, who have long argued that to understand music is to interpret stylistic codes, not to respond to physiological triggers. Take Susan McClary's ground-breaking project of a feminist musicology, for example.[11] One of McClary's concerns is to examine sexuality (a human universal) in classical music, and one of her crucial arguments is that the sexual meaning of music is necessarily metaphorical, that it necessarily reflects changing gender ideologies and changing compositional conventions. She notes the German encyclopedia definition of the sonata form: "Two basic principles are expressed in each of these two main themes; the thrusting, active masculine principle and the passive feminine principle." The first (masculine) theme is aggressive, has "thrust"; the second (feminine) theme is softer, has "give." To listen to a symphony is to listen to the masculine theme "quash" the feminine theme in a moment of triumphant "climax."[12]

This tells us as much about nineteenth-century sexual as musical dis-course, and it raises a key musicological question: if music is encoded this way, is that code a necessary part now of that music's meaning? McClary shows quite convincingly how "the celebration of [male] sexual desire, which culminates in a violent ejaculation, becomes virtually a convention of nine-teenth-century symphonic music," and what's at issue here is not biological necessity but cultural understanding. If, as McClary shows, the sexual mean-ing of a Beethoven symphony is an effect of a musical style, then to miss this meaning is to misread the code, but the question is whether to appreciate music is to understand it. Can we enjoy a piece of music without knowing what it means? Does such pleasure involve grasping that meaning— Beethoven's sexual aggression—*without knowing it?*

McClary argues that

> the principal innovation of tonality is its ability to instill in the listener an intense desire for a given event: the final tonic cadence. It organized time by creating an artificial need (in the real world, there is no reason one should crave, for instance, the pitch E; yet by making it the withheld object of musical desire, a good piece of tonal music can within ten seconds dictate even one's breathing). Further, tonal procedures strive to postpone gratification of that need until finally delivering the payoff—its violent release of pent-up ten-sions—in what is technically called the "climax," which is quite clearly to be experienced as metaphorical ejaculation.[13]

This is, I think, to raise two issues: on the one hand there is an argument about *musical structure* (to hear a piece of music as music is to hear sounds ordered in a particular way); on the other hand there is an argument about musical appreciation, about what we might call the listener's *interpretive freedom*.[14]

The first argument is that the structure of the music evokes feelings in listeners which are then given emotional and/or metaphorical interpretations. It is the music itself that sets up our sense of "tension," "incompletion," "dissatisfaction," and so forth, that conveys a sense of liveliness or languor, movement or rest. Such terms refer to our feelings on hearing the music (relate them to our usual narratives of emotion), but we are actually describing something caused by the experience of the sounds themselves, by our response to what is happening structurally.

The most eloquent general statement of this view can be found in Leonard Bernstein's Harvard lectures:

> That's one of the questions I'm most frequently asked by nonmusicians: why is the minor "sad" and the major "glad"? Isn't this proof of the "affective" theory of musical expression? The answer is no; whatever darkness, or sadness, or passion you feel when you hear music in the minor mode is perfectly explainable in purely phonological terms . . . this so-called "affective" phenomenon of the minor mode is not an extrinsic metaphorical operation at all; it is intrinsic to music, and its meaning is a purely musical one.[15]

Bernstein is making this argument in the context of a discussion of music as a communicative activity. His question is *how* does music communicate (which is, for him, a prior question to what it does), and his starting assumption is that it must "mean" the same thing to composer, performer, and listener, otherwise communication would be impossible. In investigating this problem Bernstein draws on linguistics, on Chomskyan linguistics, in particular, on a theory of what makes communication *possible:* an underlying human capacity to grasp the "deep structure" of the communicative process. Bernstein thus argues that the musical effects he is describing happen (at this "deep" level) whether or not we understand how they are caused. Chopin's *Prelude No. 4 must* make me feel "unsatisfied" (a feeling of which I give my own emotional interpretation) whether or not I understand Bernstein's technical analysis of why it must (which I don't). The effect is not the result of any particular process of musical education or socialization—we don't have to be *taught* to hear Chopin as sad—though we are talking about cultural rather than biological norms here. People from different musical cultures would, at least, have to learn to hear Chopin's preludes as music. Bernstein's point is that in doing so, in learning how to make sense of Western harmonic forms, they would also necessarily learn to hear the fourth prelude as sad music.

Bernstein's argument here is one taken for granted by film scorers, who are, among all popular music composers, perhaps the most concerned to use music to communicate particular feelings to a great range of people (to people with a great range of musical knowledge and experience). In his study of Bernard Herrmann's music, Graham Bruce therefore makes exactly the same point as Bernstein about the relationship of structure and feeling:

> Percy Scholes, speaking of the effect of the seventh chord in certain works by J. S. Bach, suggests that "All the mere triads gave a feeling of satisfaction in themselves; they were *Concords*. This 'chord of the seventh' gives a feeling of restlessness; the ear is dissatisfied until it has passed to the next chord and the seventh itself (C) has moved to the note below (B). This chord of the seventh, then, is a Discord—not necessarily, observe, a chord of harsh effect, but a chord that demands following in a certain way, i.e. 'Resolution.'"
>
> It is just this feeling of "restlessness" and "dissatisfaction," that Herrmann exploits as a means of creating musical suspense.[16]

Nöel Carroll has characterized such use of music in film as "modifying music—the music modifies the movie."

> Modifying music is one of the major uses of music in popular movies. It may be used to embellish individual scenes and sequences, or it may be integrated into leitmotif systems. Structurally, modifying music involves the use of movie elements—photography, narrative, dialogue and synchronized sound—as *indicators* that fix the reference of a shot, scene or sequence. The associated musical elements are *modifiers* which attribute expressive qualities to the referent, thereby characterizing it emotively as, for example, dreamy or jaunty.

More particularly,

> If adding music to the movie enhances one's expressive control over the action, it is also the case that the imagery intensifies the impact of the music by particularizing its affective resonance. The unnerving, shrieking strings in *Psycho* are cruel, painful, and murderous when matched with Norman Bates' descending knife. Here, the reference afforded by the movie elements serves to individuate the

emotive content of the music in the way that narrative and panto-mime do in ballet, and as words do in a popular song or opera.[17]

Carroll's is one of the more helpful analyses of film music, and I will return to it, but the points I want to stress here are, first, that he describes the working assumptions of both film scorers and film viewers (we do all understand the conventions) and, second, that he can therefore assume that certain musical elements do have, in themselves, predictable emotional effects. In his words, "modifying music, given *the almost direct expressive impact of music,* assures that the *untutored* spectators of the mass movie audience will have access to the desired expressive quality and, in turn, will see the given scene under its aegis."[18] Carroll is here, like Leonard Bernstein, drawing on an argument about the structure of classical music: "that the Prelude to *Tristan and Isolde* is expressive of yearning or that the 'Great Gate at Kiev' from *Pictures at an Exhibition* is expressive of majesty are part of the *incontestable* data of aesthetic theorizing."[19]

It is clear that musicological accounts of Western art music, musicological theories of classical musical codes, are essential for studies of popular music too. Take, for example, the film scorers' use of twelve-tone techniques, which are by now rather more familiar to cinema than concert hall audiences. The aspects of twelve-tone music that the classical public doesn't like—the lack of tonality which makes such dissonant music "difficult," "ugly," and "point-less"—are precisely those aspects which can be used by film scorers to their own ends, "for moments of tangled texture and stress." Fred Karlin and Rayburn Wright cite, as an example, Jerry Goldsmith's music for the scene in *The Omen* in which Mrs Baylock, the evil nanny, fights Gregory Peck:

> The music has the sound of twelve-tone procedures without being a strict application of the system . . . Bar 10 is a typical twelve-tone procedure. All 12 tones derived from the intervals of the original bass ostinato are heard without duplications. Much of the rest of the cue is constructed in the same way. To get the full impact of these relationships listen to the closing Ave Satani cue to hear the original ostinato and then listen to the fight with Mrs. Baylock.
>
> Whether used in technical strictness or not, the sense of twelve-tone lines and their resulting "harmonies" adds bite and tension to a film score when this quality is desired.[20]

The importance of such technical analysis for our understanding of how film music works is incontestable, but there are hints here of the problem with the structural approach to musical meaning: how free are listeners to make their own interpretation of what they hear? Karlin and Wright talk about film scorers' use of "the *sense* of twelve-tone lines," and this "sense" of twelve-tone as dissonant and tangled can only be derived from its relationship to the norms of tonality. Its meaning lies in aural contrast: it is an effect of musical expectations derived not simply from the structural imperatives of this or that piece, but also from a cultural or social sound experience, from a cultural or social listening position.

In her discussion of Janika Vandervelde's *Genesis II,* Susan McClary notes both that the composer had a clear sense of her piece (it opens "with what Vandervelde intends as a musical image of childbirth: the pulsation of a fetal heartbeat, the intensifying strains of labor, and the sudden emergence into a fresh and calm new world") and that different listeners hear Vandervelde's contrasting piano and string parts (representing women's and men's time) quite differently (in part because of their own position as men or women):

> There are listeners who quickly tire of the "minimalistic" clockwork [piano] and who identify more with the string parts when they break away. I know people who hear the clockwork as mechanistic, or as a beautiful yet inanimate mineral formation, against which the strings become the specifically human voice. Others (and here I must count myself) are attracted to or identify with the gentle ebb and flow of the cyclic clockwork and are unnerved by the violence wreaked upon it by the impulsive self-expressive strings.[21]

It is not accidental that McClary is describing here "new music," musical meanings which are not yet fixed. It's not so much that listeners disagree about the meanings of the musical elements of Vandervelde's piece as that they read its overall *argument* differently, place different weights on the relations between the elements. In his polemical attack on music criticism, Hans Keller writes:

> I have, in fact, always listened as uncritically as possible, especially to begin with, at the very moment when, in view of something new, the critic is expected to employ his critical capacities to the utmost. But at the outset, one has to discover what the artist has to say or is trying to say; how can we judge how he is saying it if we don't know what it is?[22]

My question is: how does such "discovery" work? For a pop fan the oddest aspect of new art music is the role of the program note of the author's intentions, a necessary part, it seems, of the listening experience. I'll quote two examples:

Mebasi for chamber orchestra.

Last fall, when I first heard the music of the Bibayak Pygmies of West Africa, I was immediately struck by their fascination with very gradual voice leading and polyrhythms—techniques which have recently fascinated me, also. "Mebasi" is their word for a festival vocal game in which singers compete with one another in long, modulated cries. I've borrowed the spirit of the game, as well as some of the music, to make a miniature chamber concerto featuring each instrument in competitive solos. Besides contesting one another, the musicians also engage a variety of sharp-edged, polyrhythmic pulses. Finally, the music self-destructs as a solo trombone hurls its African theme against hammer blows which gradually become unhinged— while composing, I imagined the unsynchronized gears and springs of a robot falling apart.[23]

Charmonium for harpsichord and chamber orchestra.

In the colorful language of elementary-particle physics, "charmonium" refers to the family of bound states of the charm quark and its antiparticle. As a musical title, then, it is deceptive: not only does the root "charm" in "charmonium" imply no aesthetic qualities or magic, but the cognate relationship to the Latin "harmonia" and its derivatives is strictly false.

Chordal fanfares of short repeated cells alternate with solo episodes in which "improvisatory" figures are spun out against a backdrop of converging or diverging chromatic lines moving at independent speeds. The resulting contrasts of rhythm and perceived *tempi* put me in mind of the paths of elementary particles as photographed in bubble- and streamer-chamber experiments, with some tracing great sweeping arcs while others whirl in tight spirals or dart mercurially; hence the title.[24]

Three points can immediately be made about such wordy approaches to musical meaning. First, they draw to our attention the fact that virtually all instrumental music has some sort of associated verbal description, even if only in its title. It may therefore be difficult to disentangle the way we interpret the meaning of a piece of music from the way we interpret its title. This is, perhaps, most intriguing for jazz, in which titles (*A Love Supreme, Sketches of Spain,* "Misterioso") work like labels to supply interpretive information, an indication of how to listen.

Second, though, it is not at all obvious that we can only *enjoy* a piece of music if we understand it according to the program note. Is a piece of music meaningless if we don't know what, in the words of the composer, it is about?

Which leads to a third question: not *does* our listening experience bear any relationship to an author's account of the music, but *can* it? To put this more strongly: is "interpretation" necessary for musical enjoyment? What does "misinterpretation" mean? Nicholas Cook notes that misinterpretations (or "false" labels) are not uncommon in classical music history. For example, the standard nineteenth-century interpretation of Beethoven's "Les Adieux" sonata was that it was about the parting and reunion of two lovers; now (as the result of proper historical data) we know that it concerned Archduke Rudolph's departure from and return to his dukedom. Did this "wrong" reading matter? What changed when the "correct" meaning was found: the music? The way people heard the music? Or simply the way they wrote about it?[25]

Arguments about musical meaning depend on shared understandings of musical codes (otherwise there would be nothing to argue about), and there can be no doubt that Western music listeners in the late twentieth century do take for granted a series of relationships between what they hear and what they feel. As Leonard Meyer has elegantly argued, this is what we mean by musical "acculturation."[26] We may not all have attended music schools, but we have all been to the movies; we may not be able to tell the difference between a major and a minor chord, but we do know when a piece turns sad. Musicologists can rightly claim, in short, to be able to relate the structural qualities of a certain sort of music to the emotional effects it has on its listeners; or, to approach this the other way around, we can examine instrumental music which is labeled as sad or angry or happy and find that such labels match specific structural qualities.[27] Such feelings *are* caused by the musical elements themselves, but through a process of conventional association.

From a sociological perspective, then, music listening can only occur in music cultures. To hear combinations of sounds as music, it is necessary to know something about the conventional meanings of agreed musical elements.[28] One obvious aspect of this is the way music quotes music—composers may evoke church bells or a marching band, folk music or popular tunes.[29] As Christopher Ballantine notes, such quotation isn't only a matter of using sounds for their "semantic connotations." By putting the quoted music in a new context, the composer can also indicate an attitude toward those connotations, through homage, celebration, pastiche, irony, and so on.[30] Quotation has been equally common in popular music, in the use of other genre clichés, for example, and is now essential to the use of sampling and the construction of music as montage.[31]

Further clues to everyday musical interpretation can be found in song lyrics. As Keir Keightley notes, because in practice song words are usually written after the music, this, ironically, "makes them a source of insight into common conventions of *musical* meaning."[32] I'll come back to this in Chapter 8. I want to focus here on film music—partly because it is a form which depends, for economic reasons, on quotation, and partly because film music enables us to *see* how musical/emotional coding works (a coding heavily dependent on the conventions of Western art music).

Film music is an oddly neglected area of popular music studies (and has been of even less interest to film scholars). I say "oddly," because if we include under the label the soundtracks of commercials on television, then it is arguable that this is the most significant form of contemporary popular music; or at least, of the popular understanding and interpretation of instrumental music. Perhaps for both these reasons—its neglect and its importance—it has also brought forth some of the most interesting and subtle academic accounts of how music works.[33]

The starting point for any study of the meaning of film music is that it depends on a relation of sound and drama. The cinema draws on both popular and art traditions—on vaudeville, melodrama, the circus, and pantomime, on one hand; on opera and ballet, on the other—and in very general terms I would suggest that in the former, popular forms, the music *accompanies* the action, is used to describe the action aurally, to identify characters, to "coax" extra emotion from the audience, and so forth.[34] In the latter, art forms, the music *produces* the action: in their different ways opera and ballet interpret the music, put sound into action.

Film music uses both strategies and, in doing so, raises intriguing questions about the relation of sound and image in the making of cinematic meaning. There's a common exercise in the teaching of film music composition in which a silent film image is shown: a woman walking down some stairs. As either a narrative or an emotional image this doesn't really mean anything (or rather, perhaps, can mean everything). Show the same clip with music, and according to the nature of the music the image takes on different meanings: play "suspense" music and we immediately know something is going to happen; melodramatic music and we know that something has already happened; within these frames the music can also indicate whether what's going to happen will be fearful or joyful (a killer or a lover at the bottom of the stairs) or indeed (as in a Herrmann score) both; whether what has happened is a matter of joy or grief (a mother living or dying).

What we hear can, then, be a more powerful source of meaning than what we see. In this exercise, it seems, the music is more meaningful than the photography; it provides us with the clues to the character and situation that allow us to read them. If the exercise were to be reversed, if the same piece of music were shown accompanying scenes of laughter or tears, violence or lovemaking, we would still be more likely to change our reading of the scene than of the music; if the music for a happy scene is violent or suspenseful, for example, then we assume that this scene won't last, that something else is going on.

The argument here is a commonplace in film music theory, which follows Robert Bresson's edict that "a sound always evokes an image but never the reverse," and Schopenhauer's that "suitable music played to any scene, action, event, or surrounding seems to disclose to us its most secret meaning, and appears as the most accurate and distinct commentary upon it."[35] But the question begged here is what Schopenhauer means by "suitable." Gillian Anderson quotes a 1922 manual for cinema organists which spelled out the possible pitfalls in this regard:

> If you are playing pictures, do so intelligently. To give you an idea of how easily a wrong number can be chosen for a scene, a man and a woman were shown on the screen in each other's embrace. The organist began playing a silly love song, only to find that the couple were brother and sister. Here is another example: during the last war an army of soldiers were shown marching in the distance. Immediately the organist began playing "Three Cheers for the Red, White and Blue." Naturally the audience rose to their feet only to find that they were greeting an army of German soldiers instead. The audience seeing their mistake gradually slipped into their seats but the organist tore madly though the number not noticing the difference. I once heard in a prominent theatre in one of the eastern cities, an organist play "I Am Always Chasing Rainbows" when Salome was chasing John the Baptist in the picture. There is no logical reason for anyone playing a drinking song such as "How Dry I Am" on an echo or cathedral chimes. Yet you hear it done and many other things equally as ridiculous. Persons of good taste would not be seen in a bathing suit at a church wedding, yet players do just as absurd things in the fitting of pictures.[36]

Where Do Sounds Come From?

The application of music to image can be "absurd" as well as "suitable," then. The domination of image by sound in the making of meaning may not be straightforward, may even seem ridiculous. The problem with that scoring exercise is that it is an exercise; in practice films have other sources of narrative meaning, whether immediate (what we *see* happen next) or in terms of expectation (about this star, this genre). Two points follow from this. First, the systematic use of certain sorts of music in films can change the meaning of that music: fairground music has been used in enough suspense or horror films, for example, that these sounds, which once presumably connoted happiness and play, now make one feel uneasy (just as it is difficult now for filmmakers to have a ringing telephone portend good rather than bad news, a relaxing rather than a disturbing conversation). Or, to cite a different sort of example: thanks to its use in Kenneth Anger's *Scorpio Rising* and David Lynch's *Blue Velvet,* that once rather bland and innocuous Bobby Vinton ballad now has a perverse erotic charge.

Second, to return to Nöel Carroll's argument about "modifying music," both sound and image are necessary for meaning making because they have different roles: the music gives us "vague" emotions (suspense, joy, fear, anger); the images provide us with the occasion for these feelings, their causes and thus their specific shape. As Carroll puts it, music is expressive of "emotive qualities but ones that are inexplicit, ambiguous and broad." To become explicit emotion must refer to something; the broad feeling must be focused on the relevant object on the screen or in the narrative.[37] Even in the case of the woman walking down the stairs, while the music may indicate to us roughly what we should feel about the situation (and, by projection, what she may also feel), it is, nevertheless, the visual image (and our visual imagination) that gives us the source for these diffuse feelings, and thus allows us to give them a precise shape. (And if the argument here is about film images it could equally well be applied to dancing bodies in ballet, and to the voices and words of pop songs: it is the extra-musical information which enables us to hear the music as *specifically* meaningful.)

One issue that is relevant here is the relationship of film and opera. One can obviously make a simple contrast in terms of power (though there are exceptions on both sides): in opera the composer is a more significant figure in determining the nature and meaning of the narrative than the librettist or the director; in film the director (and scriptwriter) are more significant in determining the nature and meaning of the narrative than the composer. There is, in consequence, a different relationship between sound and image, between the use of sound to bring out the meaning of what's seen (film), and of image to bring out the meaning of what's heard (opera).[38]

Despite these differences, film composers certainly draw on opera writing conventions, in at least two important respects. The first is the way in which musical meaning is constructed as structurally *internal* to a work. In film as in opera, for example, a musical sign may be attributed to a character, and this is what the sign (whether it is a fully developed leitmotif or simply the use of a particular instrument) means. And, in a more complicated process, an equation can be made (in film and opera alike) between narrative structure and musical structure, such that the musicological notions of tension, thrust, climax, dissatisfaction, and so forth are given a narrative translation through the stage or film plot: the "climax" of the music will come at the moment of triumph or death.

Second, musical meaning in film, as in opera, may be constructed symbolically; the musical element (whether instrument, melody, key, or harmonic principle) is used to stand for or symbolize an aspect of the plot (good or evil, male or female, class, ethnicity, character, culture or nature) in a way that is *not* necessarily coherent in terms of the soundtrack's overall musical structure.[39]

The difference between film and opera, then, is not that they use different devices, but that they organize them differently. In opera musical logic is supreme (though the great operas are precisely the ones in which musical and narrative logic, structural and symbolic meanings are integrated, as in Wagner); in films, narrative logic is supreme (though the great film scores are the ones in which musical and narrative logic, structural and symbolic meanings are integrated, as for Bernard Herrmann). Herrmann, in fact, deliberately changed his approach to musical structure so that his commitment to musical coherence might survive the demands of film narrative. As Graham Bruce puts it,

An even more radical challenge to the late nineteenth-century romantic style of Korngold and his colleagues was Herrmann's rejection of melody. Herrmann argued that, since the symmetrical span of a melody required a certain space to unfold, continual use of melody would require that a purely musical logic would prevail, the piece being governed by the predetermined shape of the melody rather than by the movements of the film narrative. Herrmann sought a more flexible unit, one which could interact fully with the filmic articulation. This he found in the short phrase, the brief musical module consisting of one or two measures, or sometimes as few as two notes. The possibilities which such flexible musical units offer for interaction with dialogue, narration, actor movement, camera movement, and editing are evident . . . [in] *The Magnificent Ambersons.*[40]

Or, as Herrmann put it himself, "a composer's first job is to get inside the drama. If he can't do that he shouldn't be writing the music at all."[41]

In short, from the scorer's perspective, the "meaning" of the music in a film is clearly a "musical meaning," derives from the organization of a musical structure, is an effect of the relations between notes, but now a "correct" reading is grounded not in a musical knowledge of that structure (in a study of the score) but in the accompanying organization on screen of the dramatic narrative. And, at the same time (which is what makes film scoring so interesting a challenge to musicians), our understanding of that dramatic narrative is determined by what we hear—is an effect of the musical process. This double process—meaning given by the *mutuality* of musical structure and dramatic narrative—is, as Nicholas Cook argues, perhaps most obvious (because, by necessity, most condensed) in television commercials. Cook describes the closing sequence of a commercial for the Prudential Building Society:

> The tempo gets slower and slower; the harmony outlines a classic II-V-I progression, and the melody rises towards the upper tonic cadencing an octave higher than it began. As I mentioned, the final phrase is the only one that is not arch-shaped, and its ascent to the upper tonic coincides with the appearance of the Prudential logo on the screen. In this way, a purely musical process is being used not just to highlight the product name, but to assert what is really the fundamental message of the commercial—a message that is not spoken (and indeed cannot quite be spoken), but to which everything in the commercial seems to lead with the force of inevitability: *Prudential is the [re]solution of all your problems.*

And Cook goes on to argue that in commercials generally, "Music transfers its own attributes to the story line and to the product, it creates coherence, making connections that are not there in the words or pictures; it even engenders meanings of its own. But it does all this, so to speak, silently."[42] Cook's point (following Claudia Gorbman) is that music doesn't simply bring meaning to images from the outside, as it were (through its semantic connotations); music, in its internal organization, acts to interpret what we see: *it allows meaning to happen.*

So far (starting from the opera analogy) I have been describing this process in structural terms, in terms of concepts like "coherence," which imply an *orderly* relationship between film score and film script. In sound practice, of course, most films (unlike most TV commercials) are much messier, much more *disorderly*. Michel Chion thus asks:

> What do sounds do when put together with a film image? They dispose themselves in relation to the frame and its content. Some are embraced as synchronous and onscreen, others wander at the surface and on the edges as offscreen. And still others position themselves clearly outside the diegesis, in an imaginary orchestra pit (non-diegetic music), or on a sort of balcony, the place of voiceovers. In short, we classify sounds in relation to what we see in the image, and this classification is constantly subject to revision, depending on changes in what we see. Thus we can define most cinema as "a place of images, plus sounds," with sound being "that which seeks its place."[43]

The "place" of music in film is usually defined functionally. Aaron Copland, for example, describes five broad functions: "creating atmosphere, underlining the psychological states of characters, providing background filler, building a sense of continuity, sustaining tension and then rounding it off with a sense of closure."[44] Bernard Herrmann explained that the music in a film could seek out or intensify the "inner thoughts" of a character; invest a scene with terror, grandeur, gaiety, or mystery; propel a scene forward or slow it down; lift dialogue into the realm of poetry; and act as "the communicating link between the screen and the audience, reaching out and *enveloping* all."[45] Michel Chion suggests that in the cinema, music "fits" or "enfolds" a scene like clothes "fit" or "enfold" a body.[46]

This last is a nice image, with its implication that film music (like clothes) both conceals the plot (the body) and expresses and reveals it; that the meaning of the music (like the meaning of clothes) has as much to do with the meaning of other musics (other clothes) as it has to do with the particular shape of this story (this body); that the shape of the narrative is, in fact, determined by the shape of its implied score (just as the nude in art is shaped by its implied clothes)[47]—this is particularly obvious in terms of genre (think, for example, how Ennio Morricone's fragmented scores for Sergio Leone's westerns determine how these stories must be told). In short, what the clothes metaphor makes clear is that film music has to be read semiotically, as part of a musical "fashion system," as well as by reference to the immediate clothing needs of this particular story.

Such an approach to film music, through its codes, is by now well developed; here I just want to summarize those themes that are relevant for popular music analysis, those codes that are used by popular musicians and composers whether they are writing for films or not.[48]

The first set of codes, *emotional codes,* concern the ways in which music is taken to signify feeling. The arguments here reflect the continuing influence of the compositional conventions of classical music on film scoring, and it is, in fact, difficult now to disentangle film and classical musical/emotional meanings. There are historical reasons for this, reflecting the way in which music was used in the "silent" film era. On the one hand, cinematic music was then live music, and the orchestral musicians employed, primarily classically trained, took their cues from the classical repertoire. Gillian Anderson has documented, for example, the astonishing range of orchestral overtures that were played at the beginning of each of the four daily film showings at the Rialto in New York between 1918 and 1921, and even in small, local cinemas the theater organist often prepared the audience for the show using similar works.[49] As a musical experience, early cinema was more like a popular classical concert than the burlesque or vaudeville from which its story conventions came.

On the other hand, classical music also became the root source for the music accompanying the pictures themselves. Classical music was, from early in American cinema history, used as "mood" or "modifying" music. Max Winkler recalls how, working for the orchestral music publisher Carl Fischer in the early 1910s, he found himself serving an increasing number of film exhibitors and theater managers, looking for suitable scores for their pianists and organists so as to prevent films from being shown with inappropriate or incoherent accompanying sounds. Interestingly enough, the problem was conceived as the poor fit between the popular tunes favored by the jobbing professional pianists employed in the smaller theaters and the "serious" emotions and situations being projected on the screen—"unsuitability," as we've already seen, combined an aesthetic and an ethical judgment. As the cinema began to take itself more seriously narratively, in other words, and sought to attract a better class of customer with proper stories and moral dramas (moving away from the earlier emphasis on novelty, voyeurism, and spectacle), so it began to take the musical accompaniment more seriously too. Winkler understood the situation in commercial terms:

> One day after I had gone home from work I could not fall asleep. The hundreds and thousands of titles, the mountains of music that Fischer's had stored and catalogued kept going through my mind. There was music, surely to fit *any* given situation in *any* picture. If we could only think of a way to let all these orchestra leaders and

pianists and organists know what we had! If we could use our knowledge and experience not when it was too late, but much earlier, before they ever had to sit down and play, we would be able to sell them music not by the ton but by the train-load![50]

Winkler thus invented the "cue sheet." He saw films before release and roughly scored them; theater managers bought from him a musical guide to each silent film they showed, a scene-by-scene breakdown suggesting the most appropriate accompanying music—which they could then, of course, also buy.

The question was where such music would come from. Initially Winkler thought in terms of original compositions. Unfortunately,

> Every scene, situation, character, action, emotion, every nationality, emergency, wind storm, rain storm and brain storm, every dancer, vamp, cowboy, thief and gigolo, eskimo and zulu, emperor and street walker, colibri and elephant—plus every printed title that flickered in the faces of the five-cent to twenty-five-cent audiences—had to be expressed in music, and we soon realized that our catalog of so-called Dramatic and Incidental Music was quite insufficient to furnish the simply colossal amounts of music needed by an ever-expanding industry . . .
>
> In desperation we turned to crime. We began to dismember the great masters. We began to murder the works of Beethoven, Mozart, Grieg, J. S. Bach, Verdi, Bizet, Tchaikovsky and Wagner—everything that wasn't protected by copyright from our pilfering.
>
> The immortal chorales of J. S. Bach became an "Adagio Lamentoso for sad scenes." Extracts from great symphonies and operas were hacked down to emerge again as "Sinister Misterioso" by Beethoven, or "Weird Moderato" by Tchaikovsky. Wagner's and Mendelssohn's wedding marches were used for marriages, fights between husbands and wives, and divorce scenes: we just had them played out of tune, a treatment known in the profession as "souring up the aisle." If they were to be used for happy endings we jazzed them up mercilessly. Finales from famous overtures, with "William Tell" and "Orpheus" the favorites, became gallops. Meyerbeer's "Coronation March" was slowed down to a majestic pomposo to give proper background to the inhabitants of Sing Sing's deathhouse. The "Blue Danube" was watered down to a minuet by a cruel change in tempo. Delibes' "Pizzicato Polka" made an excellent accompaniment to a sneaky night scene by counting "one-two" between each pizzicato. Any piece

using a trombone prominently would infallibly announce the home-coming of a drunk; no other instrument could hiccup with such virtuosity.[51]

Winkler's initiative meant that when "talking" pictures arrived, when integrated film scores were required, it was composers adept at using these nineteenth-century European bourgeois musical conventions who were seen as best fitted for the task. The emotional codes of nineteenth-century symphonic music, the particular sentimental use of tonal structures and harmonic rules, familiar in rough-and-ready form in the accompaniment of silent films, now became, more subtly because carefully composed for each movie, the norm of talkies too. And just as the earlier use of these conventions (rather than those of popular American entertainment) was a gesture at the emotional importance of what was being enacted on screen, so the use of classical music conventions in talkies reflected the belief that its "transcendent" and "universal" qualities could give the scenes it "enveloped" a *general* meaning. Everybody—working-class, middle-class, and upper-class characters, audiences in America and Europe—could kiss to this music; too obviously popular or vernacular musical forms would limit a scene, would be too indicative of divisive national and social identities.[52]

Within film music's emotional codes we need to distinguish two functions. First, there is music designed to tell the *audience* how to feel. Here we find most obviously the accepted rhetoric of symphonic music and the use of general mood musical signs. Music here can imply, among other things, the right audience attitude toward the film and toward their own feelings about the film (it can be used, that is, both ironically and intertextually; Bernard Herrmann used to quote from his own previous scores). In general terms, this use of music is *culturally determined:* it draws on what is assumed to be the audience's shared understanding of particular musical devices. The shift in film scoring in the 1970s and 1980s toward the use of marketable title cuts and youth-oriented scores (which brought to an end a composing career like Herrmann's) was not simply a matter of demographics or marketing. It also reflected, I think, a generational change in what was heard as the basic language of the emotions. For the rock generation popular music was as capable of expressing "serious" emotion as classical music; Jennifer Warnes and Joe Cocker as expressive of romantic intensity as ersatz Mendelssohn; John Barry as expressive of dramatic tension as ersatz Wagner.

The second function of emotional codes in film music is to tell us what the *characters in the film* are feeling. Here we find the most obvious use of operatic devices, leitmotifs, and so on, and here the codes are, in a sense, *composer determined*. The score itself, as I have already discussed, provides the context in which we read the significance of certain melodic or instrumental figures.

In the end, though, the most interesting (and powerful) aspect of film music is that it integrates these cultural and composer codes, dissolves the distinctions between "how I feel" and "how they feel." As in music generally, in interpreting film sounds emotionally we are, in effect, interpreting our own feelings on hearing them, and the effect is, as Herrmann suggested, "enveloping." Sartre, the philosopher of egoism, has given perhaps the best description of the cinema as a musical experience:

Above all, I liked the incurable muteness of my heroes. But no, they weren't mute, since they knew how to make themselves understood. We communicated by means of music; it was the sound of their inner life. Persecuted innocence did better than merely show or speak of suffering; it permeated me with its pain by means of the melody that issued from it. I would read the conversation, but I heard the hope and bitterness; I would perceive by ear the proud grief that remains silent. I was compromised; the young widow who wept on the screen was not I, and yet she and I had only one soul; Chopin's funeral march; no more was needed for tears to wet my eyes. I felt I was a prophet without being able to foresee anything; even before the traitor betrayed, his crime entered me; when all seemed peaceful in the castle, sinister chords exposed the murderer's presence. How happy were those cowboys, those musketeers, those detectives; their future was there, in that premonitory music, and governed the present . . . the virgin's desperate struggle against her abductor, the hero's gallop across the plain, the interlacing of all those images, of all those speeds, and, beneath it all, the demonic movement of the "Race to the Abysss," an orchestral selection taken from the *Damnation of Faust* and adapted for the piano, all this was one and the same: it was Destiny . . . What joy when the last knife stroke coincided with the last chord! I was utterly content, I had found the world in which I wanted to live, I touched the absolute. What an uneasy feeling when the lights went on; I had been wracked with love for the characters and they had disappeared, carrying their world with them. I had felt their victory in my bones; yet it was theirs and not mine. In the street I found myself superfluous.[53]

Nöel Carroll explains the same experience in cooler terms:

> In contrast to our encounters in everyday life, movie events have an unaccustomed intelligibility and lucidity; movies, that is, are so much more legible than life . . . Unlike our quotidian experience of events, the music constantly alerts us to the feeling with which we see. Where in life the affect that goes with an observation is so often unknown, in movies, we not only have some affect but also the appropriate affect tied to virtually everything we see, through modifying music . . . Reciprocally, the focusing function of the movie indicators renders the emotive content of the music more and more explicit, enhancing their clarity in yet another way.[54]

In short, through the use of emotional codes, film music has taught us how to see, while film images have taught us how to hear.

This leads me to the second semiotic dimension of film music, the *cultural code.* This is the use of music to tell us where we are; to reveal as economically as possible (so we can get on with the story) the basic social and cultural facts of the images we're seeing: place and time (geography and history), social setting (sociology and political economy). The most efficient means of musical shorthand is the use of generic conventions, whether these are indicated by melodic structures or by rhythmic rules or, most simply, by instrumentation (the quickest way of indicating, for example, that a film is set in China or Scotland, in Nashville or Paris). Such references may be crude (bagpipes, an accordion) or subtle—as in the indication of a moment in social experience by precise pop quotation (famously in *The Big Chill,* for example). Leith Stevens comments in these terms on his score for *The Wild One:*

> The characters of the play are young people, full of tensions, for the most part inarticulate about their problems, and, though exhibitionistic, still confused and wandering.
>
> These characteristics suggested the use of progressive jazz or bop (call it what you will) as an important segment of the score. This music, with its complicated, nervous searching quality, seemed best suited to complement these characters. This is the first score, to the writer's knowledge, to use contemporary jazz in actual scoring of scenes.[55]

This is obviously an area where questions of musical authenticity arise. Miklós Rózsa contrasts film and opera composing in terms of "realism":

The orientalism in *Aida, Samson and Delilah,* or *Queen of Sheba* is only used as color, and they are full-blooded romantic operas mirroring the style of the period of their creation with no attempt whatsoever to represent the true style of the period of their action. But the motion picture is different. It is realist and factual. It not only tries to capture the spirit of bygone eras but also tries to make believe that it projects before the eyes of the spectator the real thing.

On the other hand, having been assigned the score for *Quo Vadis,* and having researched the sounds, instruments, and composing conventions in Rome in the year 64 A.D. ("there is absolutely no record of any music of the classical times of Roman history"), Rózsa realized that "as the music for *Quo Vadis* was intended for dramatic use and as entertainment for the lay public, one had to avoid the pitfall of producing only musicological oddities instead of music with a universal, emotional appeal." At the same time, "the archaic sound had to be created with our modern instruments." In short, Rózsa had to *imply* archaism, through the use of familiar musical and instrumental conventions; "realism" in music, as generally, is a matter of representational conventions.[56]

The same issues are involved in the use of all the other devices of socio-musical representation—representations of race and class, gender and nation. Kathryn Kalinak describes the musical conventions developed in Hollywood to depict female sexuality:

Certain types of instrumentation, melody, harmony and rhythm came to denote certain types of women. These musical stereotypes helped to determine the audience's response to and evaluation of female characters, and like signposts, directed the audience towards the "correct" estimation of a woman's character . . . The fallen woman was characterized by a nucleus of musical practices which carried indecent implications through an association with so-called decadent musical forms such as jazz, the blues, honky-tonk, and ragtime. Instrumentally the fallen woman was characterized by a predominance of orchestral colors associated with popular jazz such as saxophones and muted horns; harmonically, by the inclusion of unusual harmonies, chromaticism and dissonance; rhythmically, by the use of dotted rhythms and syncopation; and structurally, by the use of portamento and blue notes.

The virtuous wife and mother, on the other hand, was characterized by musical practices with strong positive associations. Her instrumentation was orchestral, with the violins usually carrying the melody; the harmonies were lush, based on late nineteenth century models; the rhythms were even and lyrical; and the melodies often had an upward movement, or included upward leaps in the melodic pattern.[57]

Here, clearly, Hollywood taught us how to hear musical signs, through moral plots, even as it drew on our commonsense readings of sound settings.

Finally, film scorers may employ *dramatic codes*, use music for its narrative effect, to propel the action forward or hold it back. The music is neither telling us where we are nor what to feel about this, but, rather, helps us to place ourselves in the *unfolding* of the story. Film music, for example, can indicate how quickly time is passing, can suggest a spatial perspective, can tell us how close we are to the action.[58] One of the most interesting findings from Philip Tagg's listening tests is the extent to which people hear instrumental music "narratively" rather than "emotionally"; music is understood both in terms of specific physical movements (by boat or train, for instance) and by reference to a vaguer, narrative movement (toward a meeting, away from a confrontation).[59]

While such listening is clearly an effect of years of going to the cinema, it does not depend on specific cinematic images; and this is true of our understanding of film music's emotional and cultural codes too. Rather, such codes are free-floating; they inform *all* our music listening. We hear music in the cinema as if we were hearing it "in reality" (the film scorer's starting assumption), but we also hear music "in reality" as if we were in the cinema. Writing about cinematic sound realism more generally, Michel Chion asks: "If we are watching a war film or a storm at sea, what idea did most of us actually have of sounds of war or the high seas before hearing the sounds in the films?"[60]

And the same point could be made about music: if we are watching a melodrama or a suspense sequence, what idea did most of us actually have of the emotional meaning of this chord sequence, this tangle of strings, before hearing the sounds in the films? We are left with a wonderfully circular process: scorers bring sounds *to* films, for their everyday semantic connotations, from their roots in Western art music and musicology; listeners take musical meanings *from* films, from the cinemas in which we've learned what emotions and cultures and stories sound like.

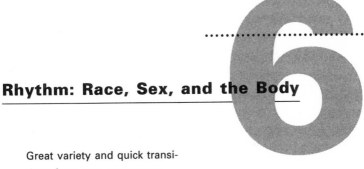

Rhythm: Race, Sex, and the Body

Great variety and quick transitions from one measure or tone to another are contrary to the genius of the beautiful in music. Such transitions often excite mirth, or other sudden and tumultuous passions; but not that sinking, that melting, that languor, which is the characteristical effect of the beautiful, as it regards every sense.

Edmund Burke[1]

The Red Hot Chili Peppers are putting the three most important letters back into FUNK, taking the piss out of the idiots who forgot what it was for in the first place and are being censored left, right and centre because of it.

"From our viewpoint it's impossible to ignore the correlation between music and sex because, being so incredibly rhythmic as it is, it's very deeply correlated to sex and the rhythm of sex, and the rhythm of your heart pounding and intercourse motions and just the way it makes you feel when you hear it. We try to make our music give you an erection."

Melody Maker[2]

Everyone seems agreed, the music's lovers and loathers alike, that rock and roll means sex; everyone assumes that this meaning comes with the beat. I don't, and in this chapter I suggest that if rock does sometimes mean sex it is for sociological, not musicological reasons. (And besides, as the Red Hot Chili Peppers' casual male chauvinism makes clear, in this context sex is an essentially sociological sort of thing, anyway.) Deliberately misreading the Chili's point, then, I will start this chapter with the concept of *fun*.

"Fun" can only be defined against something else, in contrast to the "serious" and the "respectable," and in musical discourses the opposition of "serious" and "fun" sounds (the aesthetic versus the hedonistic) involves both a moral-cum-artistic judgment and a distinction between a mental and a physical response. In classical music criticism, "fun" thus describes concerts which are not the real thing—benefit or charity shows, the Last Night of the Proms; the critical tone is a kind of forced, condescending bonhomie: "it was just a bit of fun!" In pop criticism "art" and "fun" define each other in a running dialectic—if 1970s progressive rockers dismissed first Motown and then disco as "only" entertainment, 1980s progressive popsters saw off rock's pretensions with the tee-shirt slogan "Fuck Art, Let's Dance!"[3]

As I noted in Chapter 2, the equation of the serious with the mind and fun with the body was an aspect of the way in which high culture was established in Europe and the United States in the nineteenth century. John Kassan quotes Mark Twain's description of the audience "at the shrine of St. Wagner" in Bayreuth:

> Absolute attention and petrified retention to the end of an act of the attitude assumed at the beginning of it. You detect no movement in the solid mass of heads and shoulders. You seem to sit with the dead in the gloom of a tomb. You know that they are being stirred to their profoundest depths; that there are times when they want to rise and wave handkerchiefs and shout their approbation, and times when tears are running down their faces, and it would be a relief to free their pent emotions in sobs or screams; yet you hear not one utterance till the curtain swings together and the closing strains have slowly faded out and died.[4]

Twain then watched the audience burst into "thunderous applause." Other observers, more ideologically correct Wagnerians, claimed that even after the performance there was just intense silence. Such complete physical control—or mental transportation?—did not become a classical concert convention (orchestras would be dismayed to get *no* applause at the end of a show), but the denial of any bodily response *while* the music plays is now taken for granted. A good classical performance is therefore measured by the stillness it commands, by the intensity of the audience's mental concentration, by the lack of any physical distraction, any coughs or shuffles. And it is equally important, as we have seen, to disguise the physical effort that goes into classical music-making—Wagner kept the orchestra hidden at Bayreuth, and "from early in his career ridiculed those who enjoyed '*looking* at the music instead of listening to it.'"[5]

A good rock concert, by contrast, is measured by the audience's physical response, by how quickly people get out of their seats, onto the dance floor, by how loudly they shout and scream. And rock performers are expected to revel in their own physicality too, to strain and sweat and collapse with tiredness. Rock stage clothes (like sports clothes) are designed to show the musician's body as instrumental (as well as sexual), and not for nothing does a performer like Bruce Springsteen end a show huddled with his band, as if he'd just won the Super Bowl. Rock acts conceal not the physical but the technological sources of their sounds; rock audiences remain uneasy about musical instruments that appear to require no effort to be played.

The key point here, though, is that the musical mind/body split does not just mark off classical from rock concert conventions; it also operates within the popular music domain. When rock (or jazz) acts move into seated concert halls, for example, it is often to register that the music is now "serious," should now be appreciated quietly. (I sometimes suspect that it is at such sit-down shows—for Leonard Cohen, say, or the Cure, or P. J. Harvey—that one best gets a sense of what the mid-nineteenth century battles over classical concert behavior were like, as the listening and the dancing sections of the crowd get equally annoyed with each other, and as the attendants struggle to keep *everyone* seated.) The underlying contrast here between listening with the mind and listening with the body is well captured by photography: the classical audience *rapt*, the rock audience *abandoned*; both sorts of listener oblivious to their neighbors, both with eyes shut and bodies open, but the classical listener obviously quite still, the rock listener held in the throes of movement.[6]

The question that interests me in this chapter, then, is how the musical mind/body split works. Why is some music heard as physical (fun), other music as cerebral (serious)? Is there nothing of the mind in the former? Nothing of the body in the latter? And in approaching these questions the first point to make is that just as "sin" is defined by the virtuous (or would-be virtuous), so fun (or music-for-the-body) is, in ideological practice, defined in contrast to serious music, music-for-the-mind. The Red Hot Chili Peppers' crude equation of musical pleasure, rhythm, and sex derives, in short, from a high cultural argument.

The musical equation of aesthetic/mind and hedonistic/ body is one effect of the mental/manual division of labor built into the Industrial Revolution, and into the consequent organization of education.[7] In the mid-nineteenth century this was mapped onto the original Romantic dichotomy between feeling and reason: feelings were now taken (as at Bayreuth) to be best expressed spiritually and mentally, in silent contemplation of great art or great music. Bodily responses became, by definition, mind-less. "The brain," wrote Frank Howes in the *British Journal of Aesthetics* in 1962, is associated with art music; "brainlessness" with pop. Popular music, agreed Peter Stadler, is music requiring "a minimum of brain activity."[8]

For Stadler, this isn't necessarily to devalue popular music, which (thanks to its rhythms) may well be sexy and humorous; jazz, in particular, he suggests, gives us direct access to bodily sensation; it is not a music that has to be interpreted, it is not a music *that has to be thought about*.[9] A decade later Raymond Durgnat celebrated rock in much the same way, as a music which in its use of rhythm was immediately, gloriously, sensual.[10]

The meaning of popular music is being explained here by intellectuals who value (or abhor) it because it offers them a different experience from art music. A telling example of such a celebration of otherness can be found in Guy Scarpetta's description of going with friends from the French art and music magazine *Art-Press* to see Johnny Halliday, the rock 'n' roll singer, perform in Nice. For these self-conscious intellectuals, the "flagrant" pleasure of the show began with the opportunity to slough off their class distinction, to identify with their generation, but what most struck these young men about this particular experience of "encanaillement" (or slumming) was the corporal presence of the music. Scarpetta heard in rock "une intensité organique, une force pulsionelle," saw in Halliday "une fantasmatique directement sexuelle." This was not something on offer from the essentially "conceptuel" Parisian avant-garde of the time—Halliday's performance was "fun," in short, because it stressed the physical pleasure of music in ways repressed elsewhere; for Scarpetta and his friends it articulated something otherwise forbidden.[11]

Two points emerge from this passage. First, it describes a musical experience which can only be understood in high cultural terms (it tells us nothing of what Halliday's low-class fans made of his music). The organization of high culture in terms of bourgeois respectability has meant, inevitably, the identification of low culture with the unrespectable (and obviously, in institutional terms, while high art took its nineteenth-century place in the secular temples of gallery, museum, and concert hall, low music continued to be associated with the bodily pleasures of the bar and the brothel).[12] By the beginning of this century, in other words, low music was both a real and a fantasy site for casting off bourgeois inhibitions.

The second point here concerns race. In 1922, forty years before Johnny Halliday's Nice concert, another French avant-garde intellectual, Darius Milhaud, was taken by a friend to a Harlem "which had not yet been discovered by the snobs and the aesthetes." As Bernard Gendron explains, "in a club in which 'they were the only white folks' he encountered a music that was 'absolutely different from anything [he] had ever heard before.'"

This surprising experience moved him from an exclusively formalist and experimentalist preoccupation with jazz to one tempered by a strong interest in its lyricism and primitivism. Such "authentic music," he was sure, had "its roots in the darkest corner of negro soul, the vestigial traces of Africa." It is in this "primitive African side," this "savage" "African character," "still profoundly anchored" in black North American music, "that we find the source of this formidable rhythmic, as well as of such expressive melodies, which are endowed with a lyricism which only oppressed races can produce."

Milhaud starkly contrasted the archaic lyricism of negro blues with the hyper-modernity, worldliness *(la mondanité)*, and mechanicalness, of white jazz.[13]

There is, indeed, a long history in Romanticism of defining black culture, specifically African culture, as the body, the other of the bourgeois mind. Such a contrast is derived from the Romantic opposition of nature and culture: the primitive or pre-civilized can thus be held up against the sophisticated or over-civilized—one strand of the Romantic argument was that primitive people were innocent people, uncorrupted by culture, still close to a human "essence."[14]

It's important to understand how this argument works, because it lies at the heart of claims about rock, rhythm, and sex. The logic here is *not* that African music (and African-derived musics) are more "physical," more "directly" sexual than European and European-derived musics. Rather, the argument is that because "the African" is more primitive, more "natural" than the European, then African music must be more directly in touch with the body, with unsymbolized and unmediated sensual states and expectations. And given that African musics are most obviously different from European musics in their uses of rhythm, then rhythm must be how the primitive, the sexual, is expressed. The cultural ideology produces the way of hearing the music, in short; it is not the music which gives rise to the ideology. Or, as Marianna Torgovnick puts it, "within Western culture, the idiom 'going primitive' is in fact congruent in many ways with the idiom 'getting physical.'"[15]

I can best illustrate this argument by quotation: the histories of both jazz and rock 'n' roll are littered with such racist readings. The Bloomsbury art critic Clive Bell, for example, complained in the *New Republic* in 1921 about the people "who sat drinking their cocktails and listening to nigger bands . . . Niggers can be admired artists without any gift more singular than high spirits: so why drag in the intellect?" For Bell, as D. L. LeMahieu notes, jazz represented a rebellion not only of "the lower instincts," but of "an inferior race" against European "civilization."[16]

Rhythm: Race, Sex, and the Body

In France after World War I, wrote the ethnographer Michel Leiris, a newly adult generation ("the generation that made Josephine Baker a star") colluded in "an abandonment to the animal joy of experiencing the influence of a modern rhythm . . . In jazz, too, came the first public appearances of *Negroes*, the manifestation and the myth of black Edens which were to lead me to Africa and, beyond Africa, to ethnography."[17] In the United States, as Lawrence Levine writes, "jazz was seen by many contemporaries as a cultural form independent of a number of the basic central beliefs of bourgeois society, free of its repressions, in rebellion against many of its grosser stereotypes. Jazz became associated with what [Aaron] Esman has called the 'vital libidinal impulses . . . precisely the id drives that the surperego of the bourgeois culture sought to repress.'" Young white musicians were attracted by jazz because it seemed to promise cultural as well as musical freedom; it gave them the opportunity "to be and express themselves, the sense of being *natural*."[18]

Ted Gioia has shown how these strands of white thought about black music—as instinctive, as free—became entangled in jazz criticism. The French intellectual ideology of the primitive, the myth of the noble savage, meant that jazz was heard as a "music charged with emotion but largely devoid of intellectual content," while the jazz musician was taken to be an "inarticulate and unsophisticated practitioner of an art which he himself scarcely understands." (As late as 1938 Winthrop Sergeant could write that "those who create [jazz] are the ones who know the least about its abstract structure. The Negro, like all folk musicians, expresses himself intuitively.") At the same time, young white musicians (and fans) had their own reasons for asserting that jazz was quite different from art music: "cerebral" became a term of jazz critical abuse ("energy" the contrasting term of praise). Robert O'Meally notes that John Hammond, for example, objected to Billie Holiday's work after "Strange Fruit" as "too arty." Holiday herself "felt that she had finally begun to discover herself as a singer."[19]

Gioia notes that the underlying body/mind split here—the supposed opposition of "inspired spontaneous creativity" and "cold intellectualism"—makes no sense of what jazz musicians do at all. *All* music-making is about the mind-in-the-body; the "immediacy" of improvisation no more makes unscored music "mindless" than the immediacy of talking makes unscripted speech somehow without thought. Whatever the differences between African- and European-derived musics, they cannot be explained in terms of African (or African-American) musicians' lack of formal training, their ignorance of technical issues, their simple "intuition" (any more than what European musicians do can really be described as non-physical).

The matrix of race, rhythm, and sex through which white critics and fans made ideological sense of jazz was just as important for the interpretation of rock 'n' roll. As Charles Shaar Murray writes in his illuminating study of Jimi Hendrix:

> The "cultural dowry" Jimi Hendrix brought with him into the pop market-place included not only his immense talent and the years of experience acquired in a particularly hard school of show business, but the accumulated weight of the fantasies and mythologies constructed around black music and black people by whites, hipsters and reactionaries alike. Both shared one common article of faith: that black people represent the personification of the untrammelled id—intrinsically wild, sensual, dangerous, "untamed" in every sense of the word.[20]

And Linda Martin and Kerry Seagrove's study of "the opposition to rock 'n' roll" shows how appalled 1950s observers automatically equated the rhythm of rock 'n' roll with savagery of various sorts, whether they were moralists like the Bishop of Woolwich ("the hypnotic rhythm and wild gestures in [*Rock Around the Clock*] had a maddening effect on a rhythm-loving age group"), high musicians like Sir Malcolm Sergeant ("nothing more than an exhibition of primitive tom-tom thumping . . . rock 'n' roll has been played in the jungle for centuries") or Herbert von Karajan ("strange things happen in the bloodstream when a musical resonance coincides with the beat of the human pulse"), or psychologists like Dr. Francis J. Braceland, director of the Institute of Living, who explained that rock 'n' roll was both "cannibalistic and tribalistic." The various strands of the argument were brought together in an editorial in the academic *Music Journal* in February 1958. Adolescents were, it seemed, "definitely influenced in their lawlessness by this throwback to jungle rhythms. Either it actually stirs them to orgies of sex and violence (as its model did for the savages themselves), or they use it as an excuse for the removal of all inhibitions and the complete disregard of the conventions of decency."[21]

The academic witnesses who lined up against rock 'n' roll (historians and anthropologists, psychologists and music analysts) conflated a number of different arguments about rhythm and the primitive. "Experts Propose Study of 'Craze,'" ran a rock 'n' roll headline in the *New York Times* on February 23, 1957, "Liken It to Medieval Lunacy, 'Contagious Dance Furies' and Bite of Tarantula." A Dr. Joost A. M. Meerlo, Associate in Psychiatry at Columbia University, explained that, as in the late fourteenth century, there was now a "contagious epidemic of dance fury." He himself had observed young people moved by a juke box to dance themselves "more and more into a prehistoric rhythmic trance until it had gone far beyond all the accepted versions of human dancing."

> Why are rhythmical sounds and motions so especially contagious? A rhythmical call to the crowd easily foments mass ecstasy: "Duce! Duce! Duce!" The call repeats itself into the infinite and liberates the mind of all reasonable inhibitions . . . as in drug addiction, a thousand years of civilization fall away in a moment . . . Rock 'n' roll is a sign of depersonalization of the individual, of ecstatic veneration of mental decline and passivity. If we cannot stem the tide with its waves of rhythmic narcosis . . . we are preparing our own downfall in the midst of pandemic funeral dances. The dance craze is the infantile rage and outlet of our actual world.[22]

The primitive in music (rhythm), the primitive in social evolution (the medieval, the African), and the primitive in human development (the infantile) are thus reflections of each other. In the words of the psychoanalyst Heinz Kohut, "the rocking of disturbed children and of schizophrenics, and the ecstatic rites of primitive tribes" are thus equally examples of the "regressive" function of rhythm. From a psychoanalytic perspective, people's pleasure in music is clearly "a catharsis of primitive sexual tension under cover." Under cover, that is to say, of melody and harmony. "The weaker the aesthetic disguise of such rhythmic experiences," the less "artistic" the music.[23]

Eric Lott suggests that in the United States, at least, what may be at issue here in terms of racial ideology is not so much the infantile as "the state of arrested adolescence . . . to which dominant codes of masculinity aspire . . . These common white associations of black maleness with the onset of pubescent sexuality indicate that the assumption of dominant codes of masculinity in the United States was (and still is) partly negotiated through an imaginary black interlocutor."[24]

And if "black culture in the guise of an attractive masculinity" was "the stock in trade of the exchange so central to minstrelsy," it was equally essential for the use value of rock 'n' roll. As Bernard Gendron has argued, "the claim that rock and roll brought real sexuality to popular music is usually understood to be related to the claim that it brought real blackness," and from this perspective it certainly does seem "reasonable to place [Jerry Lee] Lewis's 'Whole Lotta Shakin'' in the tradition of black-faced minstrelsy." "If 'Whole Lotta Shakin'' was to succeed in advertising itself as *white-boy-wildly-sings-black,* it had to do so quickly and simply. The result had to be a coarsely outlined cartoon of what it means to sing black. That is, the result had to be a caricature."[25]

The racism endemic to rock 'n' roll, in other words, was not that white musicians stole from black culture but that they burlesqued it. The issue is not how "raw" and "earthy" and "authentic" African-American sounds were "diluted" or "whitened" for mass consumption, but the opposite process: how gospel and r&b and doo-wop were *blacked-up*. Thanks to rock 'n' roll, black performers now reached a white audience, but only if they met "the tests of 'blackness'—that they embody sensuality, spontaneity, and gritty soulfulness."[26] As Gendron writes:

> The black pioneers of rock and roll were also driven to produce caricatures of *singing-black*. Chuck Berry, Little Richard, and Ray Charles . . . quite radically changed their styles as their audience shifted from predominantly black to largely white. Though all three began their careers by singing the blues in a rather sedate manner (at least by rock and roll standards), they later accelerated their singing speed, resorted to raspy-voiced shrieks and cries, and dressed up their stage acts with manic piano-pounding or guitar acrobatics. According to rock and roll mythology, they went from singing less black (like Nat King Cole or the Mills Brothers) to singing more black. In my judgement it would be better to say that they adopted a more caricaturized version of singing black wildly, thus paving the way for soul music and the British invasion.[27]

The problem of rock and roll arguments about rhythm and sex (the arguments still made by bands like the Red Hot Chili Peppers) is not just their racist starting point, but also their confusion about what's meant by rhythm, by musical rhythm in particular. The assumption that a musical "beat" is equivalent to a bodily beat (the heartbeat, the pulse) doesn't stand up to much examination (why isn't musical regularity compared to mechanical repetition—neither metronomes nor clocks are thought to rouse their listeners to a frenzy).

There is equally little evidence that Western readings of African rhythmic patterns as "sexual" have anything at all to do with their actual use, musical or otherwise. As John Miller Chernoff points out, "African music and dance are not performed as an unrestrained emotional expression." They are, rather, ways of realizing aesthetic and ethical *structures*. "Ecstatic" is, in fact, the most inappropriate adjective to apply to African music: "The feelings the music brings may be exhilarating but not overpowering, intense but not frenzied. Ecstasy as we see it would imply for most Africans a separation from all that is good and beautiful, and generally, in fact, any such loss of control is viewed by them as tasteless, ridiculous, or even sinful."[28]

In her study of African oral poetry, Ruth Finnegan notes similarly that "*cultural* factors help to determine what is appreciated as 'rhythmic' in any given group or period: it is not purely physical." If some oral poetry is bound up with a regular physical action (as in a work song), nevertheless "the rhythmic movements are accepted by current convention rather than dictated by universal physiological or material requirements." As Maurice Halbwachs once put it, "Rhythm does not exist in nature; it, too, is a result of living in society."[29]

The point here seems so obvious that it's surprising that it still has to be made: musical rhythm is as much a mental as a physical matter; deciding *when* to play a note is as much a matter of thought as deciding *what* note to play (and, in practice, such decisions are anyway not separable).[30] In analyzing the differences between African and European musics, then, we can't start from a distinction between body and mind; that distinction, while now an important aspect of musical meaning, is ideological, not musicological.

What are the alternatives? One common analytic strategy is to rework the nature/culture metaphor in terms of the simple and the complex: African music is simple, European music is complex. There is an obvious evolutionary claim here: European music, it is implied, was once simple too—that's what we mean by "folk music." Thus, although this argument may not be biologically racist (blacks as "naturally" more rhythmic than whites), it remains historically racist: African cultures, it seems, haven't yet "advanced" to the European level. In short, the association of the rhythmic with the primitive is retained: simple music is music driven by rhythmic rules; music becomes "complex" when it is concerned with melodic and harmonic structure.

Lawrence Levine notes a particularly lucid statement of the combined musical and social assumptions of this attitude in a 1918 issue of the *New Orleans Times-Picayune*. There were, the paper suggested, "many mansions in the houses of the muses." There was the "great assembly hall of melody," where "most of us take our seats." There were the "inner sanctums of harmony" where a lesser number enjoyed "truly great music." Finally, there was, "down in the basement, a kind of servants' hall of rhythm. It is there we hear the hum of the Indian dance, the throb of the Oriental tambourines and kettledrums, the clatter of the clogs, the click of Slavic heels, the thumpty-tumpty of the negro banjo, and, in fact, the native dances of the world."[31]

The different pleasures offered by the musically "simple" and the musically "complex" are, then, still being related to differences between body and mind. Leonard Meyer suggests that "the differentia between art music and primitive music lies in speed of tendency gratification. The primitive seeks almost immediate gratification for his tendencies whether these be biological or musical." Meyer's definition of "primitive" here refers to music that is "dull syntactically" rather than to music "produced by non-literate peoples," but it is difficult not to read the familiar equation of musical, social, psychological, and racial infantility into an assertion like the following:

> One aspect of maturity both of the individual and of the culture within which a style arises consists then in the willingness to forego immediate, and perhaps lesser gratification. Understood generally, not with reference to any specific musical work, self-imposed tendency-inhibition and the willingness to bear uncertainty are indications of maturity. They are signs, that is, that the animal is becoming a man. And this, I take it, is not without relevance to considerations of value.[32]

Musicologists themselves have criticized the simple/complex, African/European distinction in two ways. Some accept Meyer's broad descriptive terms but reverse his evaluative conclusions—the spontaneous, human expression of African communities contrasts positively with the alienated rationalism of the European bourgeoisie; improvised musical creativity is valued over rule-bound musical interpretation, "jes' grew" over "The Wallflower Order."[33]

Others dismiss Meyer's position as ethnocentric. The argument here is that African music is just as complex as European music, but complex according to its own conventions. Andrew Chester, for example, contrasts the "extensional" form of Western musical construction—"theme and variations, counterpoint, tonality are all devices that build diachronically and synchronically outward from basic musical atoms"—with the "intensional" development of non-European music: "In this mode of construction the basic musical units (played/sung notes) are not combined through space and time as simple elements into complex structures. The simple entity is that constituted by the parameters of melody, harmony and beat, while the complex is built up by modulation of the basic notes, and by inflection of the basic beat."[34]

What's still taken for granted in these arguments—that African music's "simplicity" is a sign of its superiority; that African music is complex in-its-own-way—is that African and European musics do work and mean differently. And this assumption, as Philip Tagg has argued, is still rooted in ideology rather than musicology, still concerns not different musical principles as such, but different institutional uses of these principles.[35]

Further, sweeping comparisons of "African" and "European" musics are decidedly unhistorical. Ernest Borneman makes the point most clearly:

> When I hear the enthusiast talking lightly of the "African roots" of jazz, I wonder invariably what part of Africa they are talking about. Africa is the largest of all continents. It has a greater variety of genetic and lingual groups than any comparable land mass. Negroes, generally considered the typical Africans, actually form a comparatively small part of the continent's population. Their music differs more profoundly from that of the Berbers in the North or the Bushmen in the South than the music of any two European nations ever differed from each other during the whole history of the European tradition. During the 325 years that have elapsed since the first Negroes reached America, African music has changed more deeply than our music between Palestrina and Schoenberg. And even within each lingually coherent group of African musics there is a complex gradation from folksong through dance music to the highly skilled and highly specialised activities of the professional dancers and musicians. These gradations are never stable over any length of time and within any single community: their patterns have altered so much over the last three hundred years that any parallel drawn between the present-day music of African and American Negroes is highly suspect in its applicability to the key period of the seventeenth century when American Negro music split off from its African roots.[36]

From an ethnomusicological point of view, then, an understanding of how rhythm works in African music has to begin with the question of how the music works in its particular historical and social contexts; it cannot be deduced from what it means to white listeners in quite different situations altogether.[37] And here two (related) arguments come into play, one concerning the *function* of music in African societies, the other having to do with *music-making practices.* Borneman, for instance, suggests:

> What we do know with a fair degree of accuracy is the strictly functional nature of seventeenth century West-African music and the complete absence of "art music" in the European sense of the term. All West-African music from the Gold Coast to the Ivory Coast had a strict purpose in the cultural pattern of the community. Each type of song was used by one group within the community, and by that

group alone, to exert an effect on another group or on the gods who controlled the affairs of the group . . . All social occasions had their distinct functional music . . . each forming a distinct pattern, but all of them united by a common quality: they could be danced as well as sung, and it was in their function as dance music that all these songs transcended the level of functionalism and were raised to the level of artistic integrity . . . Geoffrey Gorer in *Africa Dances* goes so far as to say that . . . "the West-African Negro is not so much the blackish man or the cannibal man or the primitive man as he is the man who expresses every emotion with rhythmical bodily movement."[38]

As Chernoff's 1970s studies make clear, what is being invoked here is not African nature but African society—"very few villagers can themselves play the drums . . . most 'drummers' rarely progress beyond the lesser drums," but "there is a special kind of sophistication to the ways that rhythms work in African music," there is a particular "sensibility," an "orientation to music and to life which defines the significant dimensions of excellence within the total configuration of a musical event."[39]

Music defined in these terms describes a form of *communication*. One aspect of this in some African cultures is the integration of verbal and physical means of expression. In Borneman's words, "language and music are not strictly divided." On the one hand, many African languages use what Europeans would regard as "sung" elements (variations of pitch, vibrato, and timing)—these elements are as essential to what an utterance means as the use of vowels and consonants; on the other hand, African musicians expect to "talk" instrumentally: African drummers, for example, vary the pitch, vibrato, and timing of their sounds just as skillfully as African singers. "It is high time," writes Borneman, "that the myth of African 'jungle rhythm' were put in perspective by the propagation of some concrete facts and data on the use of timbre in African music which is the invariable and inseparable complement of its rhythmical structure."[40]

The significance of rhythm for African music and culture, then, lies not in its simplicity and "directness" but in its flexibility and sophistication, not in its physical expressivity but in its communicative subtlety, its ability to make coherent *all* the movements of the body. As Richard Waterman once put it, "Essentially, this simply means that African music, with few exceptions, is to be regarded as music for the dance, although 'the dance' involved may be entirely a mental one."[41]

In his history of African-American culture and consciousness, Lawrence

Levine cites a study of schoolyard games in St. Louis in 1944 in which the researcher found that children were still singing and dancing to songs she remembered from the 1890s:

> Little Sally Water,
> Sitting in a saucer,
> Weeping and crying for someone to love her.
> Rise, Sally rise,
> Wipe off your eyes;
> Turn to the east,
> Turn to the west,
> Turn to the one that you love the best.

Young black children, however, sang their own version:

> Little Sally Walker,
> Sitting in a saucer,
> Weeping and crying for a nice young man.
> Rise, Sally, Rise;
> Wipe your weeping eyes.
> Put your hand on your hip,
> Let your backbone slip;
> Shake it to the east, O baby;
> Shake it to the west;
> Shake it to the one you love the best.

Not only the words but the gestures accompanying these play songs differed from those of the white children: "They have syncopated the rhythm, and they accompany the hand-clapping with a 'jazz' and 'swing' rhythm of the body." [42]

The point here is not that young black children were naturally more physical than white children, more "sexual" (though one can easily imagine disapproving white teachers and admiring white peers both thinking so), but that they were more rhythmically *articulate*, better able to bring together verbal and bodily expressive devices, bring them together, that is, under the name of "rhythm."

This is clearly an aspect of what is involved when white musicians learn to play black musics. Art Hodes remembers the process this way:

> Many times they'd ask me to play. I was kidded plenty. Someone would holler, "Play the blues, Art," and when I played they would laugh. Not mean, but they would laugh. That hurt but I couldn't blame them. I hadn't as yet learned the idiom. I was entranced by

their language but I hadn't learned to speak it. The next night I was there again, putting my nickels into that piano. That music did something to me. I can't explain. I had to hear it. That's one feeling that never left me. Jackson would say to me, "Art, I'll show you how to play the blues; just watch my hands." And I'd answer him, "No, don't teach me, just play." Because I knew I couldn't learn that way. I knew that I had to feel the blues myself and then they'd flow easily.[43]

It was not that Hodes had somehow to become black to play black, nor that the blues could only be expressive of a specifically racial experience, but rather that to "feel" the music he had to get *inside* it. And this is as true for listeners as players. How is this different for other sorts of musicians? The European, suggests Christopher Small, "tends to think of music primarily in terms of entities, which are composed by one person and performed to listeners by another." "Pieces" of music thus exist "over and above any possible performance of them . . . Composition and performance are separate activities, and the composer dominates the performer as the performer dominates the audience."

The African musician, on the other hand, thinks of music primarily as action, as process, in which all are able to participate. In so far as musical entities exist at all, they are regarded not as sacrosanct, but rather as material for the musicians, whose primary responsibility is to the listeners and to the occasion for which they have come together, to work on . . . Composition and performance are thus part of a single act which Europeans call improvisation but others call, simply, playing.[44]

Music, in other words, is defined by its performance, only exists *as it is performed.* This has profound aesthetic consequences. In general terms, it reflects

the idea that the arts, and especially that great performance art of music-dance-drama-masking-costume for which we lack a name, are vital means by which human identities and relationships are explored, affirmed and celebrated, and human societies criticized . . . [This idea] is not unique to Africa but it is without doubt there that it is most highly developed and best understood; it is the unique and precious contribution of Africans to human culture.[45]

More specifically, as Charles Keil has brilliantly argued, it means that we *can* distinguish between African and African-derived and European and European-derived musics aesthetically: not in terms of body and mind, the simple and the complex, or even the "intensional" and the "extensional" (though these terms come closer to what is at issue); rather, what's at stake is the difference between "embodied meaning" and "engendered feeling." The former term refers to the way in which the meaning of a piece of music is embodied "within" it, formally, structurally, and syntactically; the analytic assumption (this is the norm of Western musical aesthetics) is that it is in response to these embodied meanings that we, as listeners, "experience" music. Interpreting, feeling, and evaluating thus constitute a single process. But in musical cultures where the emphasis is on performance (not composition), there is "an on-going musical progress that can be subsumed under the general heading of 'engendered feeling.'" Obviously this distinction is not absolute (after all, European music is performed, African music has syntax; European music engenders feeling, African music embodies meaning), but there are, nonetheless, clear contrasts of aesthetic emphasis, differences in what is being referred to when music sounds "right."[46]

Alan Durant makes this point lucidly in a commentary on Pierre Boulez's disdain for improvisation. First, Boulez:

> Instrumentalists do not possess invention—otherwise they would be composers. There has been a lot of talk of "improvisation," but even taken in the best sense of the word it cannot replace invention. True invention entails reflections on problems that in principle have never been posed, or at least not in a manner which is readily apparent, and reflection upon the act of creation implies an obstacle to be overcome. Instrumentalists are not superhuman, and their response to the problem of invention is normally to manipulate what is stored in the memory. They recall what has already been played, in order to manipulate and transform it.

And this is Durant's comment:

> Boulez repeatedly implies that interest in music lies in posing and solving intellectual problems. But playing and listening to music are material activities, and also involve potential cross-fertilisation between intellectual, sensual and physical pleasures. For all its own unresolved conceptual difficulties, it has been a major accomplishment of improvised music that it has helped wrestle contemporary musical argument away from increasingly arid post-serialist debates over formal complexity and artistry into more direct consideration of issues of pleasure, which can come just as effectively from repe-

tition and simple contrast as from complex combination or trans-formation. The idea of taking pleasure as freely from repetition as from permutation and combination—which is fundamental to jazz, rock and most non-Western musics—challenges the *formalist* ideas of composers such as Berio and Boulez; and when these alternative ways of gaining pleasure then combine with pleasures of physical activity in *making* music, a challenge is also made to the distinction Boulez everywhere confidently assumes between categories of "in-strumentalists," "composers," and "audiences."[47]

In a "processual" aesthetic the decision of what (and when) is the "right" next note is a decision for which the musician has to take personal respon-sibility—but in a social setting. As Chernoff notes in his study of African drumming, "A rhythm which cuts and defines another rhythm must leave room for the other rhythm to be heard clearly, and *the African drummer concerns himself as much with the notes he does not play as with the accents he delivers.*"[48] African music may, then, be improvised, but it is not "made up on the spot, nor is it particularly loosely structured," and, as Keil suggests, from the musicians' point of view what matters most here is movement (not architecture), the perceived "vital drive" of what they are doing. Improvised music is, in this sense, a permanent *presence;* there's no time to wonder where it's going, where it has come from; the only thing to do is indicate where one is, now.

From this perspective, as Chernoff repeatedly emphasizes, "improvisa-tion" describes an ethical commitment to social participation rather than purely individual or "random" expression—"African music is improvised in the sense that a musician's responsibility extends from the music itself into *the movement of its social setting.*"[49] And listeners also have a responsibility—to engage with the music (rather than just to contemplate it), to follow the musicians' decisions as they are made, and to respond to them. On the one hand, this is because, as in any other communicative performance, the music's success, in rhetorical terms, depends on that response (and on the musicians' further response to it); on the other hand, it is because the combination of feeling, interpreting, and evaluating involved here depends on listeners en-tering into the *performing* process (rather than the compositional one). To put this another way, the only response that matters here is the first response: what we feel about the music is what it means; like the musicians, we don't have time to interpret the sounds first, and respond to them later. This comes back to Richard Waterman's point: the ideal way of listening to music is to dance to it, if only in one's head.[50] This is the only way, in Chernoff's words, "to mediate the rhythms actively," by engaging with the same vital drive as the musicians. Ron Brown, himself a Motown bassist, thus describes listening to James Jamerson:

> He had a unique ability to set your ear up in terms of listening to music. Like a rider on a horse, it would be like . . . he'd start you off at a nice galloping pace and race down the track; and all of a sudden, he'd take a right turn and throw you and you'd be out flying in space not knowing where you are. Then just before you touch the earth, he's right back there and you land in the saddle. You see, he had the ability to suggest to your ear where he wanted you to think that he was going . . . but then he wouldn't go there. But then somehow, he'd always manage to wind up back on his feet when beat one came around.[51]

One can imagine both technological and technical reasons why percussive skills might become central to a process-based musical aesthetic. In some societies the most complex musical instruments doubtless tend to be things that can be hit and plucked (rather than bowed or blown), while in all oral cultures musicians have to store their techniques and traditions in the body. Both playing and listening tend to deploy (and develop) an elaborate sense of rhythm, and the ability to make precise decisions about the timing of a note. Some African musicians are therefore certainly used to doing things that Western musicians are not—they hear complex polyphony in rule-bound, patterned terms; they maintain a complex rhythmic drive and structure without needing an external guiding force (a conductor or a metronome). A. M. Jones was startled to find that African musicians could "hear" time intervals as small as one twenty-fifth of a second: "When we Europeans imagine we are beating strict time, the African will merely smile at the 'roughness' of our beating."[52] Chernoff adds:

> I have a cousin who trained as a pianist to the point that she contemplated a professional career. During a discussion we had about African music, I asked her to beat a steady rhythm on a table top, and she of course did so quite well until I added the off-beats between her beats. She became so erratic in her beating, speeding up and slowing down, that she accused me, incorrectly, I would think, of deliberately syncopating my beats in an effort to confuse her. I replied that she should have been able to maintain her rhythm anyway. That such an apparently simple task should have presented her with such difficulties is an indication, particularly in view of her

specialization, that the Western and African orientations to rhythm are almost opposite.[53]

It should be obvious by now that the equation of rhythm and sex is a product of European high cultural ideology rather than of African popular musical practice. It is, in fact, the rhythm-focused experience of *music-in-the-process-of-production* that explains the appeal of African-American music and not its supposed "direct" sensuality. The body, that is to say, *is* engaged with this music in a way that it is not engaged with European musics, but in musical rather than sexual terms.

"In African music," writes Chernoff, "it is the listener or dancer who has to supply the beat: the listener must be *actively engaged* in making sense of the music; the music itself does not become the concentrated focus of an event, as at a concert."[54] John Blacking, who of all ethnomusicologists has argued this point most eloquently, concludes that rhythm describes not a sound but the *making* of a sound, the relationship with a "non-sound," the hand being lifted as well as the hand coming down on the drum skin.[55] If to describe either melody or harmony is immediately to move into an abstraction, the relationship of notes to each other in the imagination, to describe a rhythm is always to describe an action, to describe that which produces the sound (and, indeed, rhythmic description need not refer to *sounds* at all). Keil describes the jazz drummer's "attack" as "the type of contact the player makes with his instrument in the initial production of a note." What's at issue musicologically is the drummer's relationship to the musical pulse—"on top" or "laid back"—and the bass player's sonic mode of "plucking"—"chunky" or "stringy"; but such terms inevitably describe physical actions, the movements that create the sounds as much as the sounds themselves.[56]

What we mean by "feeling" in popular music (what Art Hodes meant by "feeling" the blues) is, then, a physical as much as a mental experience; "feeling" describes the way the body feels as it produces sounds, whether by hitting, plucking, or blowing things, or by singing (and, of course, even Western classical music involves physical feeling too—the first instruction in the middle-class piano lesson is to "relax," to "feel" the music). As John Blacking argued so persuasively, if grasping music means feeling it, then musical understanding is a bodily as well as a mental process (with which argument Stravinsky agreed, writing that "the sight of the gestures and movements of the various parts of the body producing the music is fundamentally necessary if it is to be grasped in all its fullness").[57]

People who play musical instruments,therefore, do hear music played on their instrument differently from the way people who don't play the instrument hear it—they listen with a felt, physical empathy. But my general point is that for the popular music audience the easiest way into the music is almost always rhythmically, through regular body movements (we can all participate in the music's percussive action, even if we have no instrumental skills at all). From this perspective, the difference between African- and European-based musics just describes the conventional requirements of different sorts of musical events: more participatory musics are more rhythmically complex (and harmonically simple); more contemplative musics are rhythmically simpler (and more harmonically complex).

It is in this context that one can begin to see clearly why "African" and "European" are somewhat arbitrary labels. The musical differences at issue (the focus on performative participation; the emphasis on structural cognition) are really differences between ideologies of *listening*. And, in the end, "structural cognition" is a peculiar approach to music even in Europe: it describes the high cultural ideal (but not necessarily normal listening practice) only of the last two hundred years or so.[58] In musical terms, which is the odder event: a classical music concert where we expect to see musicians bodily producing the music which we listen to thoughtfully, silent and still; or a club night at which we don't expect to see the musicians (or even the deejays) producing the sounds, but in which *our* physical movement is a necessary part of what it means to listen?

This is to reiterate that dance matters not just as a way of expressing music but as a way of listening to it, a way into the music *in its unfolding*— which is why dancing to music is both a way of losing oneself in it, physically, and a way of thinking about it, hearing it with a degree of concentration that is clearly not "brainless": "One who 'hears' the music 'understands' it with a dance, and the participation of the dancer is therefore the rhythmic interpretation which we have described as the aesthetic foundation of appreciation, the essential foothold on the music, so to speak."[59] In short, it is through rhythm, through decisions regarding when to move, at what pace, with what sort of regularity and repetition, that we most easily participate in a piece of music, if only by tapping our feet, clapping our hands, or just jigging our head up and down. And in terms of live performance this is certainly experienced both as *collective* participation, our movements tied in with those of other people, and as *musical* participation, our response (as in the classic African call-and-response tradition) a necessary part of the music in itself.[60]

Having said that, it is also true that *how* we enter music bodily and take pleasure in it is a matter of the discursive conventions and expectations we bring to it—"artless" movement (idiot dancing) involves as significant a statement about what music means as artful dance (like ballet).[61] And it is here, in what we bring *to* music rather than in what we find *in* it, that sexual suggestions lie. Dancing, after all, is, as Wendy Wolf put it to me, the socially sanctioned way of being physically *with* "someone you fancy." The sensual meaning of music, in other words, may be coded "in the rhythm," but how those codes are constructed, how rhythms are read, is a matter of cultural, not musical politics. Arguments about "sex" in music have always also been arguments about public behavior (and about the public which is so behaving).

The implicit suggestion about public and private music listening here is aesthetically misleading. Listening to classical music is taken to be a more private, "in the head" sort of experience than listening to heavy metal, head banging, even though empirically speaking the latter is probably a more private or at least individualized affair, whether the listener is using a walkman or has her ears shoved up against the speakers at a live show. In the same way, because sex is usually an intimate activity, "sexy" music (music to have sex by) is conventionally not, in fact, the rock 'n' roll that inspired teenagers to orgy in the 1950s or the Red Hot Chili Peppers to strip on stage today, but the yearning, lush balladry of Johnny Mathis and Luther Vandross, the Romantic porno-classical sounds of a Francis *"Emmanuelle"* Lai. (And it may reveal something of the poverty of the Chilis' sexual ideology that they associate good sex with a 4:4 beat.)

There's a familiar elision of categories in the usual rhythm/sex arguments: the mind is associated with individuality, the self; the body with the mass, the crowd, the public. African-American music is heard as more "bodily" because it is more collective (which does indeed make both historical and musical sense), but then descriptions of the music become confused with attitudes toward its collectivity. Music, to put this another way, is seen as "orderly" or "disorderly" by reference not to different types of audience participation but simply to different types of audience.[62]

The reason why rhythm is particularly significant for popular music is that a steady tempo and an interestingly patterned beat offer the easiest ways into a musical event; they enable listeners without instrumental expertise to respond "actively," to experience music as a bodily as well as a mental matter. This has nothing to do with going wild. Rather, a regular beat, some sense of order, is necessary for the participatory process which rhythm describes (we talk about the tempo being "strict" as a source of discipline). Rhythm, like dance, is always about bodily control (not the lack of it). Polyphony, for example, first came into European music, replacing the monody of plain chant, through peasant dances, which required mensuration and therefore made possible the rhythmic order on which polyphony depended. In Philip Tagg's words, "The more music is used in connection with bodily movements (dancing, working, marching, etc.) the *greater* the probability of regular tempo and periodicity."[63]

While different dance styles have different textures, different pulses and tempos, the most popular dance musics in the West during this century have used tightly repetitive rhythms and firmly fixed time signatures. "It is particularly difficult to dance to white rock music," concludes Chernoff, from his Africanist perspective, "because the main-beat emphasis is retained and the use of off-beat accentuation and multiple rhythms is restricted. There is no room inside the music for movement."[64]

This makes it all the more striking that the pleasures of rock music continue to be explained by intellectuals in terms of *jouissance,* the escape from structure, reason, form, and so forth. As should by now be obvious, what's involved in such assertions is not a musical (or empirical) judgment at all, but an ideological gesture, a deviant expression of respectable taste. So-called "hot" rhythms, that is to say, don't actually mean bodily abandon but signify it, signify it in a particular ideological context.

It may seem to follow from this that the erotics of pop has nothing to do with rhythm at all. But my argument is, rather, that it is an erotics of the orderly. The sexual charge of most pop music comes, in fact, from the tension between the (fluid) coding of the body in the voice (in the instrumental voice) and the (disciplined) coding of the body in the beat—hence the classic disco (and rave) sound of the soul diva mixed over electronic machines.[65]

In the end, music is "sexy" not because it makes us move, but because (through that movement) it makes us feel; makes us feel (like sex itself) intensely present. Rhythm, in short, is "sexual" in that it isn't just about the experience of the body but also (the two things are inseparable) about the experience of time.

Rhythm: Time, Sex, and the Mind

What else can one call these recordings of Holiday's? They lament, they celebrate, they philosophize, they cajole, seduce, satirize, protest, question, laugh, cry, shatter in vulnerability, or pose with stoic grace. And since they address aesthetic problems through the medium of improvisation, they propose to give the moment something it never has—order, which is the greatest contribution of jazz: it shows over and over that the present, the most anarchic region of experience, can be given perceivable form.

Stanley Crouch[1]

Music is movement, flow, time, and yet it is based on recurrence; all transmissible themes are potentially recurrent—the more so when transcribed; all music included in the sound continuum is repeatable; all melodies tend towards an end that may start a repeat . . . There can be a recurrence of motif, of theme and of combined intervals in a melody. Emotions and feelings from the past are re-evoked and moments recalled by and through music . . . music is nothing else but number and proportion (intervals, rhythm, timbres) and it is at the same time nothing else but lyricism, profusion and dream. It is all vitality, exuberance and sensuality and all analysis, precision and permanence.

Henri Lefebvre[2]

What all music offers us is a way of being present; what "music listening" means is the experience of "inner time." This, argues Alfred Schutz, is "the very form of existence of music"; it is what makes musical communication possible.

The flux of tones unrolling in inner time is an arrangement meaningful to both the composer and the beholder, because and in so far as it evokes in the stream of consciousness participating in it an interplay of recollections, retentions, protentions, and anticipations which interrelate the successive elements. To be sure, the sequence of tones occurs in the irreversible direction of inner time, in the direction, as it were, from the first bar to the last. But this irreversible flux is not irretrievable. The composer, by the specific means of his art, has arranged it in such a way that the consciousness of the beholder is led to refer what he actually hears to what he anticipates will follow and also to what he has just been hearing and what he has heard ever since this piece of music began. The hearer, therefore, listens to the ongoing flux of music, so to speak, not only in the direction from the first to the last bar but simultaneously in a reverse direction back to the first one.[3]

In terms of time, Schutz's point is this: our inner experience of time is not the same as the experience of real time. (And it can't be measured in the same ways—for a listener, as Schutz puts it, "it is not true that the time he lived through while listening to the slow movement was of 'equal length' with that which he dedicated to the fast one." Inner time is not so commensurable.) But for musical communication to work, different people's experiences of inner time (the composer's, the beholders') must match. They must live together, as it were, in a shared temporal continuum: "The beholder, thus, is united with the composer by a time dimension common to both, which is nothing other than a derived form of the vivid present shared by the partners in a genuine face-to-face relation such as prevails between speaker and listener."[4]

And whereas when reading "space-objects" we only need to reproduce a writer's thought processes in order to grasp her argument or meaning, in "time-objects" (such as music, dance, and poetry) understanding is *the same thing* as "the very polythetic constitutional process itself."[5] One cannot summarize or paraphrase a musical message, translate it into a different language. "And it will 'take as much time' to reconstitute the work in recollection as to experience it for the first time. In both cases I have to re-establish the quasi-simultaneity of my stream of consciousness with that of the composer."[6]

Schutz's final point is that in *playing* music together, musicians have to relate their inner time experience of the music to the physical actions which take place in "outer time" (the real time of the performance). The musicians' inner times must be shared and coordinated, whether by following each other's actions and expressions in a small group's performance, or by following a conductor or band leader—"his evocative gestures into which he translates the musical events going on in inner time, replace for each performer the immediate grasping of the expressive activities of all his co-performers."[7]

Schutz's account of musical communication is based on the model of the European chamber concert, and in applying it to popular music a number of questions arise. First, what are the communicative implications of *improvisation?* Chernoff suggests that "the most evident dynamic feature of African music is that the way the rhythms are established in relationship creates a *tension in time.*" In a polyrhythmic music, that is, listeners (and performers) have to "resist the tendency to fuse the parts," while "the tension of the rhythms works to make time seem to speed up or slow down." In effect, "African music is *both slow and fast.*" It doesn't have one inner time but many, and the listener's attention may shift from one pattern of repetition to another, from one performer to another, while being aware of the overarching community—the musicians here act together more like speakers in an unfolding conversation than like orchestral players, all and only concerned with the composer's thought. It would thus be impossible for African musical ensembles to have a conductor: their narrative is always in the process of *becoming* (and it is the musicians—and their audience—who must decide, as they go along, what it will become).

> The repetition of a style is important as a way of maintaining the tension of an ensemble's beat, and the duration of the style is important in terms of the crucial decision of when to change to get the maximum effect. In the timing of the change, the drummer demonstrates his own awareness of the rhythmic potential of the music and his personal control of its inherent power, but most important, *he demonstrates his involvement with the social situation* in a dramatic *gesture* that will play upon the minds and bodies of his fellow performers and his audience . . . As the music engages people to participate by actively and continuously integrating the various rhythms, a change at just the appropriate moment will pace people's exposure to the deeper relationships of the rhythms, involving an audience for different lengths of time with the various rhythms that have been judged to fit most properly . . . *The music is perhaps best considered as an arrangement of gaps where one may add a rhythm, rather than as a dense pattern of sound.*[8]

Second, what are the communicative implications of *crowd-pleasing?* To put it crudely, can music lie? On the one hand, the answer must be no: music works through the sharing of "inner time"; such sharing cannot rest on a deception. But, on the other hand, all communication, by definition, can be misunderstood; and such misunderstanding can, in turn, be manipulated. Jonathan Kramer usefully distinguishes between sounds that take their meanings from their place in a musical structure (climaxes, endings, recapitulations, and so on) and sounds that are, in fact, *gestures* at such moments *in themselves*, and not because of their structural position (the most obvious example is the "false ending"). Such sounds signify transition, climax, contrast, and so forth, but they do so conventionally (that's what these things usually sound like), without actually functioning as such in this particular score. Composers, in other words, can play with "gestures of time"; they can suggest a contrast *between* "absolute" and "gestural" time. A piece can "end" gesturally before it is actually over.[9]

Time gestures are particularly significant in pop songs, the appeal of which rests, in a sense, on their ability to project "inner time" beyond their material limits (as, for example, in the fade-out). Keir Keightley suggests that from this perspective there are "only two tenable genres of vocal popular songs, ballads and fast (or rhythm) numbers . . . ballads (slow songs) may be seen to involve a greater sense of the past, compared to the emphases on an enhanced and exclusive present in rhythm numbers (fast songs)." In organizing the appropriate rhetorical accounts of time—the ballad seeming to envelop everything that has already happened; the rhythm number expanding to fill the moment—pop songs are as dependent on musical as on lyrical devices.[10]

Kramer generalizes that all music has (or may refer to) at least two temporal continua: both an order of succession and the conventional meaning of gestures. Music's account of past/present/future can therefore be distinguished from the actual note order of earlier/simultaneous/later; in narrative (or rhetorical) terms, music's beginning, middle, and end is determined as much by gestural shape (its "theory" of time passing) as by the actual order of succession: "the time structure of music, at least of tonal music, can thus be profoundly multiple, paradoxical, and contradictory."[11]

Kramer, then, supplements Schutz's concept of inner time with a concept of "moment time"; he emphasizes the importance in music of the "now," an experience of the *continuous* present. Moment time, that is to say, makes memory impossible (or, the same thing, irrelevant): it doesn't offer rehearsals of what is to come or rehearings of what has been; it does not contain developments or returns or "expositions," the elements of musical communication that Schutz took for granted. Duration is divorced from content, from the memory of durations. Nonetheless, we cannot separate linearity and non-linearity completely: we hear the music in time, in succession, even if its meaning, its "impact" is non-linear, in moments: "Moment time may deny the waves of tension and release, of upbeats and downbeats, that are the essence of linear musical time. But in their place moment time offers its ultimate paradox: *Moment time uses the linearity of listening to destroy the linearity of time.*"[12] This is as pithy a description of disco as I know, and it helps to explain disco culture's obsession with the technology of time, with those devices (the double deck, the extended mix, the 12" single, the measured beats-per-minute) which enable moment time to be lengthened *non-linearly*, as it were.

What both Jonathan Kramer and the disco deejay understand is the importance of music as offering us an experience of *time passing*. In the most general terms, music shapes memory, defines nostalgia, programs the way we age (changing and staying the same).[13] But here I want to focus specifically on the musical experience itself, on Stravinsky's suggestion that "music is given to us with the sole purpose of establishing an order in things, including, and particularly the coordination between man and time."[14] Once music is "unencumbered," in Kramer's words, by plot, character, narrative, or representation, then it really is only about time, about "tonal relationships existing and transforming in time." For twentieth-century art composers, at least, music has meant *confronting* time.[15]

John Blacking goes on from Stravinsky's claim to argue that if "ordinary daily experience takes place in a world of actual time, [the] essential quality of music is its power to create another world of virtual time."[16] Music thus enables us to experience time aesthetically, intellectually, *and* physically in new ways. From this perspective (this is Stravinsky's point) music is essentially *about* time and its meaning. Swing, Gary Giddins once wrote, is "a graceful way of advancing time that suggests ironic distance from time itself." And if swing is unique for its grace (and irony), all music, I would say, is a way of advancing time that also implies a distance from time itself. Music, to put this another way, allows us to stop time, while we consider how it passes.[17]

The first point to make here concerns the basic peculiarity of "time" itself, as a concept which depends on spatial metaphors, on implications of distance (a *long* time ago; it will be happening *shortly*) and movement (the times they are a-changin')—even though, as St. Augustine puts it, "time is not the movement of a body," not even the regular movement of a body in space (the hands going around a clock) with which we "measure" it (measure, that is, both movement and length). The past is no longer here; the present has no duration by definition; the future is not here yet.

What, then, is time? I know well enough what it is, provided that nobody asks me; but if I am asked what it is and try to explain, I am baffled. All the same I can confidently say that I know that if nothing passed, there would be no past time; if nothing were going to happen there would be no future time; and if nothing *were*, there would be no present time.

Of these three divisions of time, then, how can two, the past and the future *be*, when the past no longer is and the future is not yet? As for the present, if it were always present and never moved on to become the past, it would not be time but eternity. If, therefore, the present is only time by reason of the fact that it moves on to become the past, how can we say that even the present *is*, when the reason why it *is* is that it is *not to be?* In other words, we cannot rightly say that time *is*, except by reason of its impending state of *not being.*[18]

Time, in short, does not exist. Nor does it exist at length. ("Its duration is without length. For if its duration were prolonged it could be divided into past and future. When it is present it has no duration.") Past and future exist only as the "present," in memory and anticipation. ("If the future and the past do exist, I want to know where they are . . . at least I know that wherever they are, they are not there as future or past, but as present . . . the present of past things is the memory; the present of present things is direct perception; and the present of future things is expectation.")[19] We can't "measure" the future (it does not exist), the past (it no longer exists), or the present (it has no duration). But we do measure time—"'How long did he speak?' we ask. 'How long did he take to do that?'" And such questions make clear that "what we measure is the interval between a beginning and an end." We can only measure something "in time" when it no longer exists in time; when it is over. We can only be measuring something "which remains fixed in memory."

For St. Augustine our sense of time depends on the mind performing three functions, "those of expectation, attention, and memory." And it is these which are being measured when we use spatial metaphors—"a long future is a long expectation of the future"; "a long past is a long remembrance of the past."[20] But even here the spatial metaphor is misleading: memory and expectation aren't so much long as full—the memory of a long time ago is a more encrusted memory than the memory of a short time ago; the further off the future, the greater the possible number of expectations. The question, perhaps a peculiar one, that this approach raises is this: how *long* is the present? More specifically, can music extend this? The answer, not so peculiar

Performing Rites

after all, is that if "the present" is actually defined by a quality of *attention*, then music does indeed expand the moment, by framing it. And it is precisely this "time attention" which defines musical pleasure.[21]

Edward Cone argues that rhythm is that aspect of music that connotes least outside itself, that most insistently draws our attention to "music it- self."[22] David Epstein adds that time is not "about" music (a way of describing "music itself"), it *is* music: "music *structures* time, incorporates it as one of its fundamental elements. Without time—structured time—music does not exist."[23] And I would add (following St. Augustine) that without music, structured music, time does not exist.

Repetition (which is central to our understanding of rhythm) is equally central to our understanding of time—it is only as things recur that there can be said to be movement *in time*. Musically speaking, repetition means repeating—referring to—elements of the music itself, and Richard Middleton distinguishes here between the "discursive" and the "musematic." In African-derived musics, "musemes" are repeated sound particles that provide the rhythmic "layers" of jazz and r&b. In white pop, "in music hall and Tin Pan Alley songs," rhythm is "an aspect of harmonic narrativity," while "in bour-geois song in general, sequence is a way of holding on to at least some of the power of repetition while, as it were, *cutting it down* to size, and *stitching it into* other structural processes. Sequence *composes* time (rather than marking time or obliterating it, as straight repetition, especially if musematic, seems to do)."[24] To be meaningful as a concept, then, time must be differentiated, and such demarcation "invokes two different orders of time: metrical—time unqualified by experience, marked off by mensural means external to a subject or living viewer; or experiential—time qualified by human experi-ence."[25]

Time is "perceived as intrinsically related to motion or flow," but musical "movement" can only be defined relative to a "constant" background (this is to echo Chernoff's point about African music). The issue here isn't subjective time (experiential, variable) versus objective time (metrical, fixed)—both of these are, as we've seen, constructed by the music—but what Epstein defines as "chronometric time" (mechanistic, evenly spaced) versus "integral time" (the unique organization of time in a particular piece). Like Kramer, if with a different approach to musical rhetoric, Epstein challenges the common sense of Schutz's "stream of consciousness." Given that "the temporal is intangible," we can only perceive Schutz's "inner time" of music in a "trained, *intelligent* act," as a kind of *deduction* from what we see and hear. Nothing done in music is ever "purely" rhythmic: even the simplest percussive instru-ments have pitch or timbre; even the most boring rock drummer has an individual percussive movement.[26] And nothing is completely unrhythmic—the human brain has a wonderful capacity for perceiving regularity in even the most randomly distributed noises (in the workplace, for example). "A beat," as Eisenberg puts it, "is like a Kantian category, a matrix that lets us perceive things as things instead of chaos."[27]

> Thus time in music poses a contradiction: in a world of physical sound, it is a basic element that is itself nonsonic, yet dependent for its statement and demarcation upon sound. More than any other musical dimension, time in music depends totally on forces outside its own proper domain—namely upon sound.[28]

It is clear by now that one problem of discussing musical time is the plethora of descriptive terms involved (a metaphorical abundance reflecting the problem that what is being described doesn't really exist). Even the simplest measuring words (describing the "rate" or "speed" of the music) such as "tempo" or "beat" really only refer to the recurrence of a particular sound or break or emphasis. As Robin Maconie puts it, "What the ear interprets as fast or slow has less to do with speed than with contour, contrast, texture, and rhythm." Musical tempo, in other words, is not something objectively *in* the music (a metronome setting, beats per minute) but an effect of the listener's (or player's or conductor's or deejay's or dancer's) "aural sensibility."[29]

Then there are words that refer to a quality of the production of sounds—"accent," "stress." These words describe "the tension of musical articulation." They refer to what Charles Keil and his colleagues call the "participatory discrepancies" in music making—"a PD is 'a slight human inconsistency' in the way that a musician executes rhythm, pitch and timbre"—and the immediate contrast being made here is between the human and the mechanical, between the drummer and the drum machine. David Epstein notes, for example, that Hollywood session musicians have problems with "click tracks"—no one can play "naturally or 'musically' in this fashion,"—while J. A. Prögler describes the various ways in which digital instrument makers have sought to "humanize" their programs, have become concerned with "'imperfections,' 'inaccuracies,' 'perturbations,' 'offsets,' 'adjustments,' 'shifts' and 'feel.'"[30]

Finally, there are words like "meter" and "rhythm" itself which refer to the resulting sound patterns, and thus seem to describe both musical events, things we actually hear as taking place in time, and something more abstract, the musical logic "behind" what we hear. On the one hand, as David Epstein notes, "rhythm" is thus "a primordially physical aspect of music, largely kinaesthetic and muscular," and dependent on musicians' intuitive judgments (the split-second decisions regarding when to bang or blow or bow). On the other hand, "rhythm" has come to mean, analytically, "the musical organization of time" encoded in the score structurally, as a matter of harmonic progression and resolution, pitch instructions, tension and release, principles of control.[31]

To grasp the "rhythm" of a piece of music (which is, in the end, to listen to it) means both participating actively in its unfolding and trusting that this unfolding has been (or is being) shaped—that it will lead us somewhere. It is at once a physical and mental process; it involves aesthetic and ethical judgments. By entering this world of "virtual" or "inner" time we effectively (willingly, trustfully) leave the world of "real" time: hence the common experience of music as timeless (the common use of music to achieve the state *of* timelessness).

In art music one recurrent concern of the avant-garde, whether modernist or postmodernist, Webern or Terry Riley, has been to reject both the classical account of musical time as leading to a resolution (whether in terms of cycle or goal) and the Romantic treatment of musical time as "destiny," and instead to use music to take control of time in the present, to intensify our perception of time-as-it-is-passed. The stress here is, as with Stockhausen, on time experienced through musical *action* (music as "not perpetually ready-made but perpetually to-be-made")[32] or, as with Cage, on time experienced as musical *process* (an effect of "random" sound choices). Either way, time is treated as "a frame to be filled," and how it is filled (actively, randomly) determines its shape (not vice versa). Music is thus a way of *experimenting* with time (to what else does "experimental music" refer?)—with chance events, order without sequence, sequence without order, juxtaposition without story. In Michael Nyman's words, "form thus becomes an assemblage, growth an accumulation of things that have piled up in the time-space of the piece." He cites an experiment by John Cage and George Brecht. They composed a piece in which each musician had to do two things, each once only, at a time of their own choice. The performance took place in the dark, so that performers couldn't see when someone was about to play or had played, couldn't anticipate what would happen next or, indeed, when the piece was "over" (the last sound made). Afterwards the performers were asked how long they thought they had been in the dark: "guesses ranged from four to twenty-four minutes: the actual duration had been nine minutes."[33]

So-called minimalist composers (like Nyman himself) developed a different defense against "teleological" music. If, in the latter tradition (the norm of Western classical music), everything leads to an end, with each work an "argument," the minimalists sought to compose "objectively," to put into play music that moved free of intent or human purpose, developed strictly according to formal logic. The emphasis is not on chance (and random sound events) but on mathematics (and necessary sound events), on quantitative rather than qualitative judgments. Minimalist music is thus "self-generating," neither expressive nor representational.[34]

Both chance and minimalist music require "aimless" listening too. The listener is placed in a virtual time which has no history (no story line), no architecture (no outline), no apparent beginning, middle, or end; there is neither musical resolution nor musical expectation, nothing to help us make narrative sense of what we hear. In Wim Mertens's words, minimalist music is thus a "field of intensity," a "free flow of energy," less a human statement than a kind of eternal force: the music was there before we started listening and will continue after we stop. In Philip Glass's words,

> When it becomes apparent that nothing "happens" in the usual sense, but that, instead, the gradual accretion of musical material can and does serve as the basis of the listener's attention, then he can perhaps discover another mode of listening—one in which neither memory nor anticipation (the usual psychological devices of programmatic music . . .) have a place in sustaining the texture, quality, or reality of the musical experience. It is hoped that one would be able to perceive the music as a . . . pure medium of sound.[35]

As Kramer argues, if the experience of "timelessness" actually describes an out-of-the-ordinary attention *to* time, this can, in turn, take different forms: he describes both a three hour experience which seemed like forty minutes, and a twenty-five minute performance which felt as if it had lasted two hours. In the latter case, a multimedia performance piece, Kramer experienced "a vastly extended present" because of "sensory overload" (the same metaphor as keeping busy in order "to fill time"); in the former case, listening to the "Vexations" section of Erik Satie's *Pages mystiques* (four eight-bar phrases played 840 times in succession), time initially got "slower and slower, threatening to stop."

> But then I found myself moving into a different listening mode. I was entering the vertical time of the piece. My present expanded, as I forgot about the music's past and future. I was no longer bored. And I was no longer frustrated because I had given up expecting. I had left behind my habits of teleological listening. I found myself fascinated with what I was hearing . . . True, my attention did wander

and return, but during the periods of attending I found the composition to hold great interest. I became incredibly sensitive to even the smallest performance nuance, to an extent impossible when confronting the high information content of traditional music. When pianists traded off at the end of their twenty-minute stints, the result was an enormous contrast that opened a whole new world, despite their attempt to play as much like each other as possible. What little information I found in the music was in the slight performance variability, not in the notes or rhythms.

I never lost touch with myself or my surroundings. Although I listened deeply enough to the music to accept its extended present, I never ceased to be aware of my mental and physical environment.[36]

There is in this respect a thin line between minimalist music and ambient music. Satie suggested that his "furniture music" (*musique d'ameublement*)

hopes to contribute to life the way a casual conversation does, or a picture in the gallery, or a chair in which one is not seated . . . We want to establish a music designed to satisfy "useful" needs. Art has no part in such needs. Furniture music creates a vibration; it has no other goal; it fills the same role as light and heat—as *comfort* in every form.[37]

Satie's concept of furniture music (like Brian Eno's idea of "music for airports") is more complex than it might at first seem. There are images of both culture and nature here (a chair, casual conversation; heat and light), the suggestion both that music shapes itself, usefully, to bodily needs, and that individual bodies are themselves absorbed into a kind of implacable sonic flow.[38] Virtual time here describes an experience of bodilessness, an indifference to materiality (minimal composers have a declared interest in Eastern religions), and Mertens notes the paradox that rhythmic regularity may well have exactly the same effect in dance music: disco, he suggests, also works like a "narcotic," "individuating" musical experience through repetition but leaving the listener/dancer "floating in cosmic soup," with no aims, no desires at all. Bodily excess—as at a rave: the sheer volume of the beat, brightness of the lights, intensity of the drugs, depth of the sweat and exhaustion—becomes bodily transcendence; an obsessively repetitive dance floor track like Kool and the Gang's "Get Down On It" is every bit as *mentally* absorbing as, say, Steve Reich's *Drumming*.[39]

But the most interesting aspect of the concept of "ambient" sound is the questions it raises about our experience of time as *space*. Kramer describes the ways in which experimental performers in the 1960s sought to focus audiences' attention on the present by blurring the distinction "between piece and environment." The model here, Cage's silent *4'33"*, made "music" out of the ordinary sounds of the environment simply by getting people to give them a special, concert-hall attention. Such pieces, Kramer notes, "may at first take advantage of listeners' expectations of what a concert should entail, but after the initial impact is gone their world remains as an unchanging entity to be explored during the extended present." Audiences found there was "nothing to listen to," and so got to hear Philip Glass's "pure sound event": "an act without any dramatic structure," referring to nothing outside itself.[40]

In dance culture the distinction between music and environment is blurred in other ways, by transforming space itself into a kind of moving sonic image. Lights and mirrors, darkness and deception, are used so that what one sees seems always an effect of what one hears; space becomes movement as dance hall, club, and warehouse are shaped by the dancing bodies that fill them; when silence falls, the setting disappears. The dancers are performers, programmed by the deejay; the music stops, play time—the *scene*—is over.[41]

As every clubber knows, to dance is not just to experience music as time, it is also to experience time as music, as something marked off as more intense, more interesting, more pleasurable than "real" time. To put this another way: how we experience time as music, as special, cannot be disentangled from how we hear time routinely, as ordinary; how we interpret time musically depends on how we make sense of it normally. Time passing, time returning, the rhythm of night and day, work and play, determine what it means to have time *free*, and musical time sense is thus as much a matter of history and sociology as of sound and rhythm.[42]

At the very least music is thus about temporal *possibility*; it suggests that time can be organized intentionally, as a matter of accent and stress, pulse and phrasing, rather than having to be experienced only as a matter of industrial discipline, or of menstrual and seasonal cycles, or of inexorable aging. But, further, music also works as a commentary on—an experiment with—our everyday experiences of time. As Philip Tagg suggests, it is in making and listening to music that we pay attention to—take pleasure in—temporal shifts from the static to the dynamic, the regular to the irregular, the quick to the slow, the empty to the full, the sudden to the gradual, the rough to the smooth.[43]

Popular music has a special interest in two common forms of time-experience in particular: boredom and fashion. To describe a situation as "boring" is to say that nothing is happening, nothing to engage our attention—time *drags*. Fashion, by contrast, "is the perception of a recurring process in time in which, while newness is seen as being of value, that which is new is constantly being swept away at a dizzying pace and replaced by a different newness. This is called 'industrialized eternal return.' In this sense, the essence of time is ephemerality and repetition."[44]

Popular music addresses these issues simultaneously. On the one hand, pop songs fill the hole that the bored stare into; fun is the time that one doesn't notice passing till afterwards. On the other hand, popular music works to stop time, to hold consumption at the moment of desire, before it is regretted. Even as it is enjoyed, though, popular music is confirming the premises on which its pleasures depend—that times change and nothing happens, that this is a momentary diversion. Pop is nothing if not fashionable (drawing our attention to its transience, to the ever-familiar shock of the new); and it is centrally—from cabaret to punk, from Billie Holiday to Kurt Cobain—*about* boredom, about the vanity of believing that cheap music is potent enough to take on nothingness.[45] From one perspective (Adorno's, say), pop music thus colludes with its own negation. A popular cultural critic like Abraham Kaplan argues that "popular art, far from countering boredom, perpetuates and intensifies it," while "there is a nostalgia characteristic of the experience of popular art, not because the work as a form is familiar but because its very substance is familiarity."[46]

But my conclusion is different. Music is not, by its nature, rational or analytic; it offers us not argument but experience, and for a moment—for moments—that experience involves *ideal time,* an ideal defined by the integration of what is routinely kept separate—the individual and the social, the mind and the body, change and stillness, the different and the same, the already past and the still to come, desire and fulfillment. Music *is* in this respect like sex, and rhythm is crucial to this—rhythm not as "releasing" physical urges but as expanding the time in which we can, as it were, *live in the present tense.*

Songs as Texts

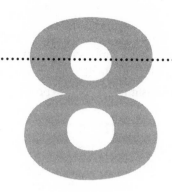

Building in any successful rock 'n' roll record is a sense of the power of the singer to say what he or she means, but also a realization that words are inadequate to that task, and the feeling of fulfillment is never as strong as the feeling of frustration. The singer goes as far as she or he can go; the singer even acknowledges the quandary, gives in to its tension, abandons words and screams. But the singer still comes up short; the performance demands the absolute lucidity it has already promised, a promise from which it is already falling back, and so an instrument takes over. It is a relief: a relief from the failure of language. The thrill is of entering a world where anything can be said, even if no one can know what it means.

Greil Marcus[1]

But people don't use songs according to anyone's intent. In the truest moments, songs like microbes—without intent, without brains—use people.

Greil Marcus[2]

Most contemporary popular music takes the form of song (even acid house), and most people if asked what a song "means" refer to the words. In examining what the words do mean we can follow two obvious strategies, treating songs either as poems, literary objects which can be analyzed entirely separately from music, or as speech acts, words to be analyzed in performance.

But in listening to the lyrics of pop songs we actually hear three things at once: *words,* which appear to give songs an independent source of semantic meaning; *rhetoric,* words being used in a special, musical way, a way which draws attention to features and problems of speech; and *voices,* words being spoken or sung in human tones which are themselves "meaningful," signs of persons and personality. In this chapter I will focus on words and rhetoric; in the following chapter I will consider the voice.

Until relatively recently, most academic analysts of Anglo-American popular music assumed, like commonsense listeners, that pop's meaning lay in the lyrics.[3] This is the tradition of content analysis, a tradition still faithfully followed in the pages of *Popular Music and Society;* and arguments about pop's political and social value are still more likely to refer to pop words than to pop sounds (think, for example, of the debate about rap). There are mundane reasons for this—fans, academics, and moralists alike are more used to dealing with verbal than with musical meaning, and find it easier to talk about (and censor).[4] But this does mean—and this is my starting point—that words matter to people, that they are central to how pop songs are heard and evaluated. In the most comprehensive survey I know of teenage use of music television, for example, the most cited reason for watching a video was not to see what the performers looked like but "in order to find out what the words mean."[5] Richard Rodgers made the essential point nearly fifty years ago: "For never does a song achieve any sort of public unless the words have at some point made a joint impact with the music on the individual and public ear . . . The old defensive and competitive cry of the composer, 'Nobody whistles the words!' is simply not true."[6]

What was clear to Rodgers, what remains obviously true, is that in everyday terms a *song*—its basic melodic and rhythmic structure—is grasped by people through its words, even if these words come to us in fits and fragments (or, more commonly and deliberately, in hooks and chorus lines); the best version of Queen's "Bohemian Rhapsody," for example, is Fuzzbox's a cappella reading, which translates all the instrumental bits into half-heard words too.[7]

Nicholas Tawa has shown how words—titles, hook phrases—became the basis of popular songs' market "punch" in the early days of Tin Pan Alley:

> E. M. Wickes said a good title can have punch and make the song into a hit. A title tag lingered in memory after one heard the piece; it conjured up related images and revived past recollections and associations. Some of the best titles were adverbial clauses, like "When the harvest days are over," "When the meadow lanes are green

again," and "Where the sweet magnolias bloom." Titles connected to the events of the day were valuable because they received free publicity. At any rate, a fine title suggested or conveyed a definite idea. It helped to attract the attention of performers, especially if they were selecting songs to be sent to them from a catalog. Amateurs in a music store would ask to see and hear a song whose title caught their eye.

Not surprisingly, the title was almost invariably used as a punch line by placing it in the first line and, less often, also towards the end of the chorus. Nearly without exception, it was set to one of the most appealing melodic phrases, and in most cases the most winning phrase, of the song.[8]

As this suggests, the words without the music were usually (quite literally) unmemorable. Unlike lyrical poems (a comparison to which I'll return), song words are only remembered in their melodic and rhythmic setting, as anyone knows who has followed the TV pop quiz question in which panelists are asked to identify a lyric that winds along the bottom of the screen as a plain print text. They usually can't, but it only takes a couple of notes of the music to be faded in and everyone (listeners at home too) can immediately recall it.

The first systematic content analysis of the American pop song that I know of was carried out by one of the Frankfurt School scholars in exile, J. G. Peatman, for Paul Lazersfeld's 1940s Radio Research project. Perhaps not surprisingly, Peatman found the same sort of standardization in song words that Adorno found in radio music: such a finding is, one could say, a necessary result of the coding process. The description of the pop song as a formula song is familiar enough in the music industry too. Tawa notes that even in the 1830s (when the modern song business began) critics accused the new songs of "a vitiating sameness," and Peter Etzkorn's study of professional songwriters in the United States in the early 1960s revealed that

> the composing activity of songwriters would seem to be constrained by their orientation towards the expectations of significant "judges" in executive positions in the music business whose critical standards are based on traditional musical clichés. In their endeavor to emulate the norms of successful reference groups, songwriters (even with a variety of backgrounds) will produce compositions virtually homogenous in form and structure, thereby strengthening the formal rigidity of popular music.[9]

One aspect of this in the early days, as Tawa notes, was that the song, as a commodity, had to have a particular sort of use value—it had to be *adaptable*.

A copy of a very popular song, "Anona," published in New York by Feist in 1903, advertises: "This famous composition is also published as an Intermezzo—Two Step—for Piano, also for Band, Orchestra, Mandolin, Guitar, Banjo, Zither, etc." The song's key, tempo, and dynamics were also flexible, thus freeing the performer and making a winning presentation dependent on his or her interpretation.[10]

The pop song "formula," in other words, was indeed (as the Frankfurt scholars argued) an effect of market forces. But content analysis has consistently revealed the way in which the pop formula is also dominated by a particular sort of romantic ideology. The pop song is the love song, and the implication, putting these two findings together, is that what pop songs are really about are *formulas of love*. Two analytic strategies can then be adopted. The first is to argue that these romantic formulas (and, in particular, the way they change over time) somehow *reflect* changing social mores, and thus give us useful evidence as to how "the people" regard love (and associated social mores). For Stuart Chase, for example, popular song "is the sum of all the patterns of behavior" which "keep the group from flying into a thousand fragments, and help it adapt to nature and survive its environment." Popular songs, from this perspective, express "commonly held values" and speak for "the millions who treasure them." "Popular recordings," as B. Lee Cooper has put it more recently, "are pieces of oral history."[11]

Alternatively, one can make a *contrast* between the standard pop account of love and something else, something more real and complex and individual. "Standard" lyrics, "sentimental" and "banal" words, are routinely measured against "realist" lyrics, against songs which deal with the actual world and lived emotions.[12] Lawrence Levine, replicating S. I. Hayakawa's famous 1955 study of American popular songs (which had been entitled, symptomatically, "Popular Songs versus the Facts of Life"), comes to much the same conclusion about both the sentimental vapidity of these songs and the contrasting "truthfulness" of the blues:

In a period when divorce rates were rising, family stability declining, pastoral life styles disappearing, bureaucratic impersonality and organization increasing, popular music constructed a universe in which adolescent innocence and naiveté became a permanent state. Men and women (often referred to in the songs as boys and girls) dreamed pure dreams, hopefully waited for an ideal love to appear (the gift of some beneficent power that remained undefined and unnamed), and built not castles but bungalows in the air complete with birds, brooks, blossoms, and babies.

Adults were being socialized to a world constructed out of childhood fantasies or, more accurately, adult views of childhood fantasies:

> You're right out of a book,
> The fairy tale I read when I was so high.
> No armored knight out of a book,
> Was more enchanted by a Lorelei than I.

As in the fairy tales, so too in popular songs, life was not purely idyllic. Reality was allowed to intrude: often lovers were faithless, promises broken, hopes unfulfilled. But the reality proved as insubstantial as the dream. Tears were shed and self-pity expressed, yet little was learned and less resolved. Fatalism prevailed and the fantasies went on and on.[13]

Levine compares white song lyrics with the blues, "the closest Negro equivalent to American popular music."

Any such comparison shows important and revealing differences. While both blues and popular music were dominated by lyrics concerning love, black consciousness of and attitudes towards this relationship differed considerably from those of the larger society.

The blues were far less pervaded by self-pity, the profound fatalism, and the very real disillusionment that marked American popular music.

For all their "pathos," then, the blues were "saved" from white narcissism "by the strong sense of humor and proportion which frequently prevented even the most pitiable lover from posturing." In the blues, "love seldom resembled the ethereal, ideal relationship so often pictured in popular songs. Love was depicted as a fragile, often ambivalent relationship between imperfect beings." It was, in other words, "portrayed realistically as a multidimensional experience."[14]

Levine concludes that the differences between black and white songs in the 1920s and 1930s had less to do with supposed differences between black and white sensibilities (or sexual behavior) than with the different uses and functions of popular music in different cultural settings, and his argument is thus subtler (and more convincing) than Hayakawa's (though he also has a tendency to leap from lyrical analysis to ideological effect without much pause for thought about how the songs were actually heard and used). Levine is clear, for example, that the lyrical contrasts he describes had as much to do with convention as intention: black song had different lyrical possibilities open to it because it served different purposes than white song, because it circulated in a different sort of cultural economy.[15]

Interviewed in *New Musical Express* in 1982, Elvis Costello made a similar point about the emotional constraints of pop formulas and functions, but put the emphasis on listeners being deprived of songs which articulate reality rather than being duped by songs into believing in daydreams.

> Most people, I think, are confused regarding their identities, or how they feel, particularly about love. They're confused because they're not given a voice, they don't have many songs written about them. On the one hand there's "I love you, the sky is blue," or total desolation, and in between there's this lack of anything. And it's never that clear-cut. There's a dishonesty in so much pop—written, possibly, with an honest intent—all that starry stuff. I believe I fulfil the role of writing songs that aren't starry eyed all the time.[16]

These are important arguments for any evaluation of song lyrics, and are familiar from both rock criticism and people's everyday accounts of why some songs are silly, others profound. At the same time, though, while the terms of such criticism may be familiar, their application often seems somewhat eccentric: one person's silly lyric touches another person's real feelings, and vice versa, particularly when we're talking about love songs. We need, in particular, to consider two further points about the sort of real/unreal argument used, in their different ways, by Levine and Costello.

First, it is important to remember that the distinction between "real" and "unreal" lyrics is, at least in part, arbitrary. Songs, after all, are not mostly general statements of sociological or psychological truth (as even Levine sometimes seems to imply); they are more likely to be examples of personal rhetoric.[17] And even in life (which is, after all, imbued by romantic ideology, organized sexually around the idea of "being in love"), one is more likely to say "I love you more than there are stars in the sky" than "there are ambiguities in the way I feel about you." The question becomes, in other words, why some sorts of words are *heard* as real or unreal, and to understand this we have to understand that how words work in song depends not just on what is said, the verbal content, but also on how it is said—on the type of language used and its rhetorical significance; on the kind of voice in which it is spoken.

Second, much of the argument that starts from lyrical content analysis assumes that the "content" (or "meaning") of songs as revealed by the analyst is the same as their content (or meaning) for other listeners. There is a very quick slippage in this analytic tradition from a summary of the lyrical content as revealed by academic survey to a moralistic denunciation of the effects of pop songs on their listeners—this is the strand of the argument that links Frankfurt School accounts of the psychology of consumption to Leavisite anxiety about the commercial corruption of childhood, which informs both Hayakawa's account of "demoralization" and Levine's account of "fatalism"; it is this argument that supports contemporary moralists' claims that heavy metal lyrics make white adolescents suicidal and that rap lyrics make black adolescents violent. All these things may be true, but they are certainly not demonstrated by content analysis alone.

There is, in fact, no firm empirical evidence that song words determine or form listeners' beliefs and values (any more than there is really much evidence that they reflect them). The few sociological investigations of teen-agers' response to song words show either that they don't understand them (as American researchers soon found to be the case with 1960s "protest" songs like "Eve of Destruction") or that they "don't really notice them" (semanti-cally, that is).[18]

What this suggests, I think, is the difficulty we face if, in interpreting how songs "mean," we attempt to separate the words from their use as speech acts. I would put the argument this way: song words are not about ideas ("con-tent") but about their expression. And I can best clarify this with two examples.

First, then, songs don't *cause* people to fall in love, but provide people with the means to articulate the feelings associated with being in love.[19] Levine's argument is, in a sense, back to front. It is not that love songs give people a false, sentimental, and fatalistic view of sexual relationships, but that romantic ideology requires such a view and makes love songs necessary (and the question that Levine really raises concerns the different place of romance in black and white American cultural histories). Historically speaking, after all, the love song *followed* the social diffusion of romantic ideology (rather than vice versa), and, interestingly, has had to take account of the male as well as the female investment in love (unlike other popular cultural forms, such as romantic fiction).

The realist critique of the love song is therefore problematic because of its implication that romantic fantasies aren't real. But people really do fall in love—really do engage, that is, in the pleasure of idealizing themselves and an other, fantasizing perfect and lasting relationships, equating sex and sympathy, sentimentalizing differences, and so on. The fact that love doesn't last, that the divorce rate is high, that passion causes as many pains as pleasures, doesn't mean that romantic fantasies aren't true, aren't felt, don't have consequences. If pop songs are narratives of love, and we do indeed fall in love, then songs are in this respect narratives of our lives, of the ways in which we engage in—and *realize*—fantasies. Silly love songs have certainly been as realistic—and helpful—in making sense of the romance in my life as so-called musical realism.

The second indication that songs concern not so much ideas as their expression can be found in the historical fate of "protest" songs. In pop terms, these don't function to convey ideas or arguments but slogans. And the paradox here is that the political power of a pop song—as a slogan—need not bear any relationship to its intended message at all. Irony, in particular, seems to be a doomed lyrical strategy. The Strawbs' 1973 single "Part of the Union," for example, was meant as an anti-union song, but its ironic chorus ("they can't get me, I'm part of the union!") became a gleeful picket line chant; while Tom Robinson's 1978 "Glad to be Gay," an ironic tag line to verses spelling out the oppression of homosexuals in Britain, became a triumphalist shout, and was even used as such by tipsy heterosexual students at the end of the Saturday night college disco. And I could point to numerous other examples of such lyrical drift: Pink Floyd's "We don't want no education," taken up as a slogan by black youth in South Africa, protesting about compulsory Afrikaans schooling; a pre-election Tory Party rally joining hands for John Lennon's "Imagine"; the Republican Party's attempt to hijack Bruce Springsteen's "Born in the USA" in the 1984 presidential election.[20]

This last example is particularly illuminating. "Born in the USA" is, lyrically, clearly a protest song. It is about growing up working class, being shipped off to fight in Vietnam and coming back to nothing—a standard scenario in American popular film and song, a populist formula. The lyrical theme was also tied to Springsteen's star persona—this was not his own story, but it was the story of the people with whom he identified, whom he was taken to represent (as indicated by his iconography on stage and album). The record did, then, lay claim to a certain sort of truth of veterans' experience, to a political realism. Formally, though, the song is organized around a chorus line—"Born in the USA!", a musical phrase which is, in rock convention (its texture, its rhythmic relentlessness, its lift), not bitter but triumphant. In other words, for a rock listener what comes across from this song is not the intended irony of the chorus line, but its pride and assertiveness. And it was as such a patriotic boast that Ronald Reagan wanted to use it. Although Springsteen dismissed this reading, in performance his own trappings (the American flag, the celebration of American working-class masculinity) could also serve to confirm it.[21]

Once we grasp that the issue in lyrical analysis is not words, but words in performance, then various new analytical possibilities open up. Lyrics, that is, are a form of rhetoric or oratory; we have to treat them in terms of the persuasive relationship set up between singer and listener. From this perspective, a song doesn't exist to convey the meaning of the words; rather, the words exist to convey the meaning of the song. This is as true of the "story song" or the *chanson* as of the most meaningless house or rave track, just as political and love songs concern not political or romantic ideas, but modes of political and romantic expression. Pop songs, that is, work with and on *spoken* language.

This means, first of all, that song language is used to say something about both the singer and the implied audience. Lyrical language is an important aspect of genre convention—the conversational colloquialism of the country song (a "storyteller" like Tom T. Hall reminiscing at the bar) works very differently from the raucous colloquialism of punk (a ranter like Joe Strummer agitating in the streets). Nicholas Tawa describes the linguistic conventions of the late nineteenth century commercial American popular song, conventions that were to be even more formulaically applied in twentieth-century Tin Pan Alley:

> Language is kept plain, graphic, relevant and concrete. Abstract and unusual references are avoided. Generally, an informal conversational tone is adhered to, and subject and expression are kept recognizable for easier comprehension. The title evokes the chorus; the chorus summarizes the content of the verse. The sense of each line is normally complete; the end of each line comes to a natural stop before a new line is taken up. The change from verse to chorus is managed so as not to perturb the listener, the latter appearing as a reasonable epilogue to the verse that has come before.[22]

But lyrical plain speaking may cover any number of linguistic variations. Peter Trudgill's study of "the sociolinguistics of British pop-song pronunciation" is illuminating in showing that it is not just words but also accents which situate singer and listener. Trudgill's starting point is the obvious one that British pop singers "employ different accents when singing from when they are speaking." The reason seems clear:

Most genres of twentieth-century popular music, in the western world and in some cases beyond, are (Afro-)American in origin. Americans have dominated the field, and cultural domination leads to imitation: it is appropriate to sound like an American when performing in what is predominantly an American activity; and one attempts to model one's singing on that of those who do it best and who one admires most.[23]

Such a sense of linguistic fitness is familiar in popular genres—folk singers adopt "quasi-rural" accents, white reggae singers a Jamaican lilt, European rappers New York street tones, and so on. But, as these examples make plain, such "language modification" does not always work. In the case of British pop singers' "American" voices, "one obvious measure of their lack of success is that many American listeners are utterly unaware that this is what British singers are trying to do." The problems here are manifold: for British singers to copy their vocal models accurately (often Black and/or Southern singers rather than "Americans" in general) they would need "sufficient access" (and the analytic ability) to work out the rules of their preferred linguistic behavior, and the discipline to modify their own pronunciation accordingly. As this was hardly the case, voices that were heard as "American" by British listeners still seemed—in their very peculiarity!—obviously British (or, at least, non-American) to Americans. Trudgill adds that "from around 1964 on, British singers generally began trying less hard to sound like Americans," as "British pop music acquired a validity of its own." Singers now sought to cross class barriers rather than the Atlantic. Punk, for example, introduced "features associated with low-prestige south of England accents":

The use of these low-status pronunciations is coupled with a use of nonstandard grammatical forms, such as multiple negation and the third-person singular *don't*, that is even higher than in other subgenres of pop music, and the intended effect is assertive and aggressive. There is also clearly an intention to aid identification with and/or by British working-class youth, and to appeal to others who wish to identify with them, their situation and their values.[24]

The desire to sound low-class English did not so much replace the desire to sound American as compete with it, and different groups handled the conflict differently. (Trudgill confirms linguistically my critical belief that the Stranglers weren't really a punk band: their "Americanisms" meant that "they closely resemble[d] 'mainstream' groups in their linguistic behaviour.")

The conflict is between a motivation towards a supposedly American model, and a motivation towards a supposedly British working-class model—which can be glossed as a conflict between "how to behave like a genuine pop singer" and "how to behave like British urban working-class youth."[25]

Which is a good a summary as one could have of the aesthetic dilemma of British rock, which has mostly been performed anyway by nice boys from the suburbs.

Two final points from Trudgill are relevant here. First, as he makes clear, linguists cannot explain why in particular cases particular choices are made in pronunciation—why is this word American-inflected, this one not? Since these are acoustic choices—decisions as to what words will *sound* like—we obviously have to consider other, musical reasons why a singer or lyricist might decide that "this sounds right." Second, Trudgill notes that "pop-music is a field where language is especially socially symbolic, and typically low in communicative function, high on the phatic and self-expressive." In other words, the use of language in pop songs has as much to do with establishing the communicative situation as with communicating, and more to do with articulating a feeling than explaining it.[26]

I can make the same point following a different route, from the study of rhetoric. There is, from this perspective, an inevitable tension in the popular lyric between its colloquial, vernacular language and its use in a "heightened," elevated way, framed by music. A pop song is ordinary language put to extraordinary use. Two issues arise from this.

On the one hand, the popular performer has a recurring problem of *sincerity*. In popular cultural terms, good talkers are mistrusted as well as admired: people who have a "way with words"—the seducer, the salesman, the demagogue, the preacher—are people with power, and the power to use words is a power to deceive and manipulate.[27] Sincerity may then be best indicated by an *inability* to speak (as in soul vocal convention) or through an aural *contradiction* between the glibness of the lyric and the uncertainty of the voice (as in much male country music).

On the other hand (and in other genres), singers and writers may deliberately use heightened language to draw attention to their art, to their individual sensibility. Here there is a deliberate use of non-colloquial language (as in Bob Dylan's early songs, for example), or else ordinary words are "framed," held up and examined, everyday clichés liberated by being taken literally or turned inside out.

Either way, songs can be used to explore the relationships of *different* languages—different ways of speaking—and in pop terms this has often meant challenging linguistic hierarchies, subverting the way words are used to dominate—"song texts," as Roland Barthes put it, "provide a framework for permissive language behavior."[28] This was obviously an aspect of the imitation of African-American and working-class accents by British pop singers, but voices can also be made to move between languages within a song. This was a key aspect of Gracie Fields' comic technique as a music hall singer;[29] and it is now a crucial component of rap, a song form which is word-rich in its obsession with the empowering and disempowering effects of language.[30]

Take Public Enemy's "Don't Believe the Hype."[31] As with "Born in the USA," the power of this lies in its chorus phrase—"Don't Believe the Hype!"—a slogan that could be of use to listeners in all sorts of circumstances. But the line is also an intervention in the debate about Public Enemy's music itself, about the meaning of rap, about the value of African-American male youth culture. The song is an *argument*, drawing on rap's conventional use as a form of conversation—between performer and performer, between performer and audience, between performer and media. And this is the context in which power is being defined as *a way with words*. Rap as a necessarily mass mediated form, a commodity, is in effect releasing all the forces of contemporary communications technology onto language, onto the clichés of corporate and political power (appropriated directly, via sampling), onto the vitality of the slang and the fragmented, reactive, ugly, utopian language of the streets. A rap like "Don't Believe the Hype" is significant less for its logical unfolding than for its investment of key words with force. And given the nature of these words—their obvious coding as urban black—they are being invested with urban black force; they are at once a threat and a promise, according to who's listening.

This brings us back to the point of the protest song. The most significant political effect of a pop song is not on how people vote or organize, but on how they speak. And this becomes a particularly interesting (and complex) effect in a rap, which foregrounds the problematic relationship of sung and spoken language. Rap acts like Public Enemy imply that such musical (or poetic) devices as rhythm and rhyme are material ways of organizing and shaping feeling and desire; they offer listeners new ways of performing (and thus changing) everyday life.

Lyrics, to put this another way, let us into songs as stories. All songs are implied narratives. They have a central character, the singer; a character with an attitude, in a situation, talking to someone (if only to herself). This, as Leon Rosselson argues, is one reason why songs aren't poems. The only way they can be introspective is if "the 'I' in the song is a fiction," and the lyric is about introspection. "Song," in this respect, "is theatre."

> The language of song, like the language of drama, is not a literary language; it embraces the idioms and rhythms of everyday speech while looking for ways of enriching that language . . . Song, like drama, is about the invention of characters and stories; people—not issues, arguments, slogans, abstractions or soul-searching—are at its centre. And because people do not live in a vacuum, song, like drama, is at home in the public arena.[32]

The most obvious narrative song is the French *chanson*. In Ned Rorem's words, "Fluid states of mind are what French popular songs portray: they have always told stories that develop in a straight line, *a-b-c*, towards a delicious or catastrophic resolution. Which is why their words haunt us more than their melodies. French song is thus not bound to set forms: the subject imposes the pattern. Often the music shifts to (or is entirely within) a regular 3/4—the dance of experience."[33] Rorem points out that generically the *chanson* derives from the troubadour epic via the "naturalistic *fin de siècle* café-concert narrations of Yvette Guilbert." It was always as much a verbal as a musical form. Edith Piaf's songs

> spoke of love fermenting into murder, then of redemption and of love's return in heaven. They spoke of Sunday fairs in the squalid Vincennes park as reward for the barmaid's six-day week. They spoke of injustice in Pigalle's underworld—what Parisians call *le milieu*. They told also, like Jerome Kern's song "Bill," of life sustained through fidelity to the unfaithful, but, unlike "Bill," that life was prolonged more through words than music. More as *littérateuse* than as *musicienne* is the Sparrow recalled today, as she was applauded in her prime.

Chanson singers, in other words, effectively "'talk' their tunes, beguiling through anecdote rather than through a formal development of sound."[34]

But this is not a simple matter of telling a story; or, rather, telling a story is not a simple thing to do. As Ginette Vincendeau argues, the *chanteuses* also took a part *within* their narratives: on the one hand, the imagery of the songs (which had an obvious cinematic source in terms of both character and setting) determined *how* they were performed—the singer lit and staged as if she too were on screen; on the other hand, the singers were taken to live the same lives as their characters, with the same melodramas, the same oppressions, the same romance, the same sadness. Edith Piaf's stories were authenticated by her own story; and her story was as much shaped by her songs as were those of her lyrical protagonists. People flocked to her shows not just to hear good tales well told, but also for the spectacle of *narrative-in-action,* for the sight of someone hanging onto life, pummeling and defying it, by putting it into words. And this pleasure was, from the beginning, imbued with nostalgia.[35]

It is notable that when *chanson* has been taken up by rock singers it has been as theatrical song—David Bowie sings Jacques Brel songs as if they were written by Brecht and Weill; Marc Almond treats them as high camp. For both Almond and Bowie the "character" of the song, the person they enact, is the *chansonnier* himself; and (putting aside the generic peculiarities of the *chanson*) this is a point that can be generalized: to sing a song is to tell a story, and to tell a story is to be a storyteller. One of pop's principle pleasures is being buttonholed in the first place.

In the British (as opposed to the French) tradition popular music has always featured the character song, a form which links music hall artists like Marie Lloyd and Gracie Fields to a cabaret act like Noel Coward, and which has been the most obviously "British" component of rock from Ray Davies and Mick Jagger to Elvis Costello, Morrissey, and Blur. The lyrical and narrative convention here is to use a song to portray a character while simultaneously drawing attention to the art of the portrayal. The singer is playing a part, and what is involved is neither self-expression (the equation of role and performer, as in *chanson* or the blues) nor critical commentary (as in the German theater song) but, rather, an exercise in style, an ironic—or cynical—presentation of character *as* style. The art of this sort of singing becomes a matter of acting, and there is always a question concerning the singer's relationship to his own words (an obvious question for Mick Jagger, for example).

Elvis Costello, probably the best contemporary writer of character songs, uses a person (and in this context even "his own character" is clearly an act) and a situation to encapsulate particular sensations—lust, jealousy, meanness, betrayal—but, at the same time, his songs are about the enactment of those sensations, about the embarrassment, humiliation, and frustration of trying to make such feelings known. Even at their most emotionally intense Costello's songs are self-conscious (a self-consciousness reflected, most obviously, in the drawing-attention-to-itself cleverness of his word schemes). For Costello, character songs are not so much (as Rosselson would have it) about people as about characterization.

A different approach to lyrical narrative can be found in the African-American blues tradition, which works less with incidents building to a climax or through gestures shaping a character than by the accumulation of images as feeling. For obvious historical reasons the expressive African-American use of the English language, originating in slaves' talk, has always been metaphorical, has always been dependent on double meanings, on allusion, indirection, and puns, on symbolism, and on the surrealism of language organized as *sound*.[36] And this leads to the central question about the song as a form of persuasive communication. What does it mean to *sing* words? How is their meaning changed from when these same words are spoken?

As I've already suggested, to sing words is to elevate them in some way, to make them special, to give them a new form of intensity. This is obvious in the use of singing to mark off religious expression from the everyday use of words. But note also our discomfort at hearing banal conversation sung. Opera (and oratorio) composers have always faced the problem of what to do with those words which are needed to move the audience from one (heightened) scene to another: hence the stylization of the recitative, which confirms musically the conventional distinction between "ordinary" talk and the emotion of song—however realist an opera or musical might otherwise be, it is a humorous device to get someone to sing, say, "Pass the salt!" One of the few attempts to defy this convention, the Jacques Demy/Michel Legrand musical film *Les Parapluies de Cherbourg,* opens with a man going into a garage and singing his request for his car (which is being serviced); the uneasy (and usually laughing) audience suddenly realizes that everything here is going to be sung. I love this film (and *Les Demoiselles de Rochefort*) because the effect *is* soon magical: sung, the most ordinary transactions seem to float across the pastel backdrops.[37]

Another way of getting at the difference between talking and singing is our own practice. Most people are happier to talk in public than to sing; singing (in a seminar, for instance) is a source of embarrassment. There are obviously social reasons for this—we're taught to speak in ways we're not usually taught to sing; talking has, in that respect, been naturalized (and there remain places and situations in which it is equally embarrassing to speak publicly, just as there are situations—a drunken party or a sports event or in church—where singing seems natural). But whatever the sociological reasons, the fact is that most of us experience singing (unlike speaking) as a *performance* (to see this just visit a *karaoke* bar).[38] A performance in two respects: singing draws a different sort of attention to the words, the "special" effect I've already noted; and it draws a different sort of attention to the singer, hence the embarrassment. Singing seems to be self-revealing in a way that speaking is not.

This is a paradoxical situation: by singing words we subject them to a control that they're not used to: they have to take their part in a rhythmic and melodic frame; how and where they are pitched is suddenly an open question. And so we, as their users, experience a loss of control—we may not be able to do what we want with the words (or with the sounds of our voices). To sing is to feel vulnerable (and to be a trained singer, to enjoy singing in public, is, precisely, to feel in control). Singing seems both less natural than speaking (involves a different, less familiar sort of self-consciousness) and at the same time more natural—more bodily, more exposing, more revealing of who we "really"—naturally—are.

I'll come back to issues of voice, subjectivity, and embarrassment in the next chapter; here I want to focus on the effect of singing on language. The challenge of setting words to music is that two principles of the organization of sound have to be made to cohere. The rhythm of speech, the way in which a stress pattern is determined by syntax, is not necessarily appropriate to the rhythm of music, which follows its own structural rules. Similarly, the sound of the word that is necessary semantically (to make a statement meaningful) may not be the sound of the word that is desirable musically, to make the musical statement attractive. As Dryden once complained (about his libretto for Purcell's *King Arthur*), "the Numbers of Poetry and Vocal Musick, are sometimes so contrary, that in many places I have been oblig'd to cramp my Verses, and make them rugged to the Reader, that they may be harmonious to the Hearer."[39]

There is a distinction, in Stockhausen's words, between words as "speech-symbols" and words as "sound-symbols," although, as he points out, words-as-sound-symbols can, in fact, take on their own semantic significance, as marks of ritual expression, for example—this is particularly obvious in relig-ious music, where the meaning of words becomes their meaning as sounds. (It is, likewise, difficult to avoid hearing intelligible words in vocal sounds: we find a meaning for songs sung in a strange language, and spontaneously interpret Lewis Carroll's "Jabberwocky" or Hugo Ball's Dada "Seepferdschen und Flugfische.")[40]

In pop terms this problem is routinely solved by rhyming—the craft of the lyricist is find the word which both sounds and means right, and one sort of pop pleasure is simply observing the cleverness with which this is done. The theater song tradition, for example, from Gilbert and Sullivan to Stephen Sondheim, is in part a celebration of the lyricist's artifice. A song like "Bewitched" (from *Pal Joey*) cannot just be discussed in terms of emo-tional realism: the song is about a mood (love as lust) and a situation (older woman/younger man), but it expresses the character of its singer (a character, in this case, in a musical play) and, even more overtly, the nature of her performance, her performance not just as an actress in a play but also as a singer to an audience. In the end the song is about a use of language; it draws our attention to its puns and rhymes, to the way this piece of spontaneous stage business was crafted lyrically—through repetition, contrast, changing verbal pace.[41]

The relation of spoken and sung language has undoubtedly been explored most fruitfully in African-American music, both because song was culturally important for so long as a means of expression of all sorts, and because, for the same oppressive historical reasons, oral (rather than print) culture remained for so long the source of social identity. By the turn of this century blues singers could draw on an accumulated store of lyrical resources: phrases, images, and clichés, elevated and mundane, stylized and familiar. As Levine notes:

> Many pages could be filled with familiar floating lines like these which appeared in different arrangements and contexts in song after song: I'm worried now but I won't be worried long; Got de blues but too damn mean to cry; Out in dis wide worl' alone; Brown-skin woman, she's chocolate to de bone; I got de blues an' can't be satisfied; I got a rainbow tied 'roun my shoulder; You don't know my mind; I'm laughin' to keep from cryin'; Woke up this mornin', blues all around my bed; Look down that lonesome road; I been down so long, it seems like up to me; If you don't think I'm sinking look what a hole I'm in.[42]

Words here are used as aphorisms (another way of making ordinary words special, framing them); or, in a reverse process with the same effect, common phrases which have lost their metaphorical power are taken seriously and so recharged. But this isn't just a matter of linguistic politics. "Ordinary language" also stands here for a kind of accumulated knowledge, a shared way of being (and a shared way of being denied political, cultural, and human rights), and blues singers have certainly treated language like this, as cultural memory. As Levine explains:

> The blues allowed individuals greater voice for their individuality than any previous form of Afro-American song but kept them still members of the group, still on familiar ground, still in touch with their peers and their roots. It was a song style created by generations in the flux of change who desired and needed to meet the future

Performing Rites

without losing the past, who needed to stand alone and yet remain part of the group, who craved communication with and reassurance from members of the group as they ventured into unfamiliar territories and ways.[43]

Rap offers another sort of example, also deriving from a musical use of spoken language rather being a lyrical form as such. Its origins lie in long-established rituals of insult in which language is subjected to rules of rhyme and meter, is treated with the skill with words that is a necessary aspect of an oral culture (where stories and songs have to be stored in the mind and the body, not on the page or in print). If, in rap, rhythm is more significant than harmony or melody, it is rhythm dependent on language, on the ways words rhyme and syllables count.[44]

As insults became more and more elaborately rhymed (in Philadelphia "jones" was the local ritual term), more surreal metaphorically, more personalized in their use of the put-down, so, noted Ulf Hannerz in the 1960s, they came closer and closer to "song jones." Words were increasingly chosen, that is to say, for their sound (for their sound in a particular voice, according to a specific rhythm of contempt) rather than for their meaning.[45] And whatever other explanations anthropologists or historians or psychologists might come up with for the insult ritual, its most obvious function is to develop participants' verbal skills—skills not just in verbal invention or virtuosity, but also in what one might call verbal discipline, the ability to follow rules of rhyme and meter. In this respect, an insult form like "the dozens" must be related to other verbal skills that are a part of African-American linguistic culture—the toastin' and testifyin' that have equally fed into rap.

I'll come back to the importance of these verbal performing skills in Chapter 10. What I'd like to note here, as a final twist to the discussion of how words are made fit for music, is that musical forms have, in practice, adapted themselves to languages, to ways of speaking. This is particularly obvious in the global movement of rock music. There are clearly ways in which rock musical conventions, in terms of melodic form, use of verse/chorus, mode of vocal attack, and so on, reflect—or at least gesture at—patterns of Anglo-American and Afro-American speech (as Trudgill's analysis made clear). These musical conventions may not be appropriate for other languages. The use of rhyme as the basic rhythmic device in rock lyrics, for example, creates problems for those languages (like Italian) which don't usually finish sentences with "hard," blunt-edged consonants. This is one reason why most non-English-speaking rock musicians compose in English (it is not just their pursuit of international sales)—and why punk was liberating for young bands in, say, Finland: the "ugliness" and incoherence of the punk sound meant that Finnish words sounded good sung too![46]

Genre sound rules, in other words, are as important in deciding what words can be sung as genre rules of what it is right to sing about—rock sung in, say, an upper-class English accent doesn't just sound unconvincing in terms of character, it also sounds wrong as a noise. And this seems a suitable point from which to turn finally (and I have deliberately left this issue till last) to a consideration of song lyrics as poetry.

In the academy, to study special or elevated uses of language is to study poetry, and from early on in rock history the highest critical compliment—the way to take lyrics seriously—was to treat them as poetry, as print texts. During the 1970s a spate of college-aimed rock poetry books appeared, with claims so heartfelt that it is impossible to resist the temptation of quotation:

> Then the phenomenon of rock burst forth. It was perhaps crude and unpoetic in its infancy, but as the sixties progressed, lyrics of increasing sophistication and skill appeared. Once more, the lyric voice is flowering. The great creative energy of man's stubborn attempt to penetrate the meaning of his existence is surging forth in voices from the streets, voices that weave the sounds of the present with the age-old questions of man in relation to his *loved one*, his *society*, and the *cosmos*.[47]

Or, again,

> Over the past few years there has indeed emerged something we can call "the poetry of rock," something that at times can be quite good. The beginnings, of course, were far from promising. Despite the fertile sources on which rock music of the 1950s drew, it was musically innovative and vibrant but lyrically almost unbelievably banal and trivial. If it contained any poetry at all, that poetry was pedestrian adolescent doggerel full of unrefined slang and trite neoromantic convention. But in the early 1960s there burst upon the scene a number of exceptionally talented artists, perhaps even poets, who managed to bring together in various degrees all the many elements of what we now call rock and to make something of quality.[48]

Now in one respect what we see here seems familiar: the high cultural judgment of pop. Pichashe compares the Stones' "No Expectations" favorably to the treatment of similar themes in country songs because "the Stones' song is not sentimental at all . . . The reaction of the singer, like the tone of the song, is a refreshing change from the gush we'd expect to get in this situation." And Bob Sarlin, having defined "song poetry" as a new form, and contrasted it with the "slick" and "insincere" Cole Porter, and the "self censorship," "stock imagery," and "worthlessness" of rock 'n' roll (song poetry's values are derived from the folk refusal to compromise), admits to his doubts about Don McLean's "American Pie": "I would be suspicious of a record or a song that appeals to everyone." He can't help concluding that McLean's work, like Carole King's, is "shallow."[49]

But in the end the rock-as-poetry books don't really value their chosen lyrics in terms of contemporary literary critical arguments but, rather, according to the middlebrow criteria that New Criticism successfully drove out of the academy in the 1930s.[50] There's not really much difference, in other words, in their understanding of poetry, between these 1970s accounts of rock lyrics and Theodore Dreiser's comments on his brother Paul's successful popular songs at the beginning of the century. Theodore admired Paul's "sighings over home and mother and lost sweethearts and dead heroes such as never were in real life . . . They bespoke . . . true poetic feeling for the mystery and pathos of life and death, the wonder of the waters, the stars, the flowers, accidents of life, success, failure."[51]

For more sophisticated approaches to lyrics as poetry—for close textual reading, the pursuit of ambiguity, the reference of lyrical devices to poetic history, the focus on form rather than feeling—we have to turn to Dylan studies, to Michael Gray's *tour-de-force ragout* of pop criticism, New Criticism, and Leavisism, *The Art of Bob Dylan* ("this calculated lack of specificity becomes, in Dylan's hands, a positive entity grown out of and beyond the specific; and it opens up the way for the recreation of many different universal relationships") or to Aidan Day's more theoretically and thematically austere *Jokerman* ("the present book concentrates on providing close readings of individual lyrics selected principally from that side of Dylan's lyrical writing which takes up questions of identity").[52]

Day starts from the assumption that although Dylan's lyrics are written to be sung, they nonetheless contain the "poetic richness of signification" and "density of verbal meaning" that characterize modernism; Day is therefore concerned primarily with "the semantic properties of the words of the lyrics," which "excludes consideration of the expanded expressive range belonging to performances of those lyrics." He concentrates on "obscurities in structure and verbal texture," on the "indirectness of language in the stanzas," on the "density of allusion and pun," on "lyrics whose framing of the multiform and bizarre energies of identity constitutes Dylan's most distinctive achievement."[53]

Day is helpfully clear here about the assumptions that inform most academic studies of rock lyrics. What is taken for granted is that (modern) poetry is something read, not something heard; that it is defined by page layout rather than by performing voice—and Derek Attridge has pointed to the irony of the fact that "high" poetry became primarily a visual form at precisely the moment when "the easy availability of recordings and recording devices" gave the human voice "a cultural centrality" it hadn't had since "printing became the dominant representation of language."[54]

There may well be cause and effect operating here: high cultural authority is, for all sorts of reasons, more easily challenged and subverted by the spoken than by the written word. But I want to take another point from Attridge: to treat the distinction between poetry and lyric as a distinction between the written and the spoken word is aesthetically misleading. There is, to put this another way, a continuity between poetry and song, rather than a clear division. Between the two lie various sorts of "performed" language, whether "oral poetry" as technically defined by anthropologists, or public and formalized uses of words for special ends as in nursery and playground and advertising rhymes; whether in insult rituals like the dozens, or in poetry "recitals." It is, after all, precisely the refusal to draw a clear boundary between poetry and song that has made African-American musicians so important for twentieth-century mass culture.

There are two contexts in which the "crossover" between poetry and song has been usefully explored. The first is the problem of the art music setting of "high" verse. Edward Cone, for example, makes the point that poetry as read is much more "open" for the reader, in terms of both sound and pace, than poetry as heard (whether being read aloud or set to music). The reader makes her own decisions about "speed, emphasis, tone, accent and inflection." Now obviously the poet plants clues or instructions—the original choice of words was partly made to cause the reading to work one way or another; but Cone argues, I think rightly, that in reading (unless the poem is a nonsense poem—and this is the definition of a non-sense poem) we balance sonic logic against semantic logic: we're trying to make sense of the poem as we read it, we're thinking about it, thinking back about it, rereading a line accordingly, shifting our emphases: the reading is the interpretation, and it is as much affected by a posited meaning behind the words as by the words themselves. A performance of the poem doesn't allow such flexibility; once a verse is set to music, "the mind is so to speak chained to the vehicle of the moving sound." We can't stop the music. We have to move from beginning to end and be satisfied with what we immediately perceive; our compensation is that the music makes the words more "vivid." A musical setting of a poem, then, is a *choice* of meaning given a special intensity, such that, in Mark Booth's words, the "content" of the song becomes its effect, becomes what it makes us feel.[55]

Such intensity no more guarantees that this is the "correct" or "best" reading of the poem, than the fact that it is being read aloud by its author. In Ned Rorem's words, "a poet declaiming his own verse is no more definitive, no more *inevitable,* than some composer's setting of that verse." Rorem recalls arranging Elizabeth Bishop's poem "Visits to St. Elizabeth's" for performance by a mezzo-soprano. "The tact of Elizabeth's disappointment was touching," but she eventually explained what she felt about it:

> My complaint is that it sounds too hysterical. I hadn't imagined it that way, somehow. Yes, I had thought of a male voice, I suppose— but I don't believe that is what bothers me. It is the fast tempo and the increasing note of hysteria. Because the poem is observation, really, rather than participation . . . something like that. Two friends have said rather the same thing to me. It is awfully well sung, nevertheless. I don't know whether it could be *slowed* down, or not? Probably not.[56]

Bishop's problem, as Rorem ruefully notes, is that "poets' work ends with their poems," and one difference between a poem and a lyric is that whereas both only exist when they are performed, the former can never be fixed by or to a performance. Every reader will perform it differently, and the poet herself cannot determine that her performance will be definitive (she can't even ensure that the voice, the "I" in which she speaks her poem when writing it, will be the voice that anyone will use when reading it). Bishop was shocked to hear Rorem's setting only because she wasn't used to hearing what her readers made of her verse: *every* reading the poem has had might be just as shocking![57]

Rorem puts it like this: "poetry is self-contained, while lyrics are made to be sung and don't necessarily lead a life of their own." And he adds that "when 'real' poets write with song in mind they fail both as poets and lyricists because, in 'helping' the composer, they overindulge in presumably felicitous vocables that emerge as self-conscious banality."[58] Which is to echo a point made by a lyricist, P. G. Wodehouse: "If I write a lyric without having to fit it to a tune, I always make it too much like a set of light verse, much too regular in meter. I think you get the best results by giving the composer his head and having the lyricist follow him."[59]

This leads us to the second way of thinking about music and poetry. The question is not now how musicians understand poetry, but how poets understand music. Northrop Frye notes that what is conventionally called "musical poetry" describes poetry with a particular sort of sound: sensuous, languorous, alliterative. Poets such as Poe or Swinburne are said to write verse that "flows" over us, envelops us, like music. But, Frye suggests, this actually describes the most unmusical sort of poem. Poetry that works as music should be concerned not with sound but with rhythm; it should be interested in "throwing the ear forward," not in encouraging us to bask in the words' presence. To be musical, poetry needs a dance rhythm, discordant textures and stressed accents, not balanced vowels and "a dreary, sensuous flow of sound."[60]

In considering the transitions from spoken English to poetry to music, Frye raises two different issues. One concerns poetry as such: a poet, that is to say, occupies a space *between* music and speech; she chooses words for reasons to do with both meaning and sound, to satisfy what she wants to say as well as the formal conventions of how she wants to say it. The more the choice is concerned with sonic rather than semantic factors, the more "musical" the verse. Frye's point is that the "musical" choice here is not simply a matter of sound (a sensuous decision) but also of movement. What's really involved in "musical poetry," then, is a poet trying to impose a performance on us, trying to persuade us to follow a certain sort of interpretive logic. As the poet John Ashbery puts it, "What I like about music is its ability of being convincing, of carrying an argument through successfully to the finish, though the terms of this argument remain unknown quantities. What remains is the structure, the *architecture* of the argument."[61] There is, in short, an issue of rhetoric here too: poets aren't the only people for whom sound-patterns are significant for meaning. We can recognize a sales patter or a sermon or a seduction without needing to understand the language (as any European tourist can testify). And lyricists are as interested in using these rhetorical devices as in following so-called "poetic" conventions.

A "rhythmic" poem, one which causes us to beat time whether through reading emphasis or with a literal tapping of the foot, occurs, in Attridge's words, not because a rhythmic structure, such as a melody, has been imposed upon the language, but because the language, read aloud (even read aloud "in our heads") produces "a rhythmic organization that encourages regular muscular movement." Our appreciation of what's expected of us rhythmically when faced with an order of words thus depends as much on our general knowledge of language as spoken as on our educated experience of poetry as written, and Attridge notes (like Frye) the particular rhythmic sophistication of English speakers because of "the coexistence, in some degree of tension, of *two* series of energy pulses in speech—those that produce the syllables, and those that augment certain syllables with stress. Both these series of pulse incline toward rhythmic repetition, but in the random syllabic arrangements of prose, neither can be fully satisfied."[62]

English is, in this sense (and unlike, say, Japanese), an inherently rhythmic, or at least syncopated, language, and this is the linguistic context in which music imposes on words its own way of reading, through its own production of rhythmic stress, its own power over how syllables are sounded, a power which may determine, in turn, what those words mean, syntactically, semantically, and rhetorically. And in this respect Frye's pitching of words-as-meanings against words-as-sounds seems too simple. A statement may be heightened in its intensity precisely because, musically, it departs from its "natural" linguistic rhythm.

The point is that as speakers we create meaning through stress; music creates stress; therefore music creates meaning. As a spoken phrase, for example, "she loves you" shifts its narrative meaning (if not its semantic sense) according to whether the emphasis is placed on "she" (rather than someone else), "loves" (rather than hates), or "you" (rather than me or him). In setting the words to music the Beatles had to choose one stress, one dominant implication. The song becomes the preferred reading of the words.

Rhythm, as Attridge explains it, is also relevant to my earlier point about how people grasp and remember songs—as words via music, as music via words. What's actually involved here is the way we grasp something *bodily*, store it physically so that we can reproduce it physically, by using our voices. Such grasping is, as Attridge suggests, an embodied perception of periodicity, but the point to stress is that this is a perception (not reality). It is periodicity as measured not by a metronome but by a sort of recognition via meaning (which is why words matter)—and for most of us such song memories are incomplete: we can reproduce songs internally, for ourselves, but wouldn't be able to reproduce them, to sing them, for anyone else.

And this brings me to my final point, the reason why lyrics aren't poetry and why no song words, in my opinion, stand up as print texts. Good song lyrics are not good poems because they don't need to be: poems "score" the performance or reading of the verse in the words themselves, words which are chosen in part because of the way they lead us on, metrically and rhythmically, by their arrangement on the page (a poem is designed to be read, even if in an out-loud performance, and such reading directions are just as much an aspect of "free" as of formally structured verse forms). Lyrics, by contrast, are "scored" by the music itself. For a lyric to include its own musical (or performing) instructions is, as Ned Rorem observes, to over-determine its performance, to render it infantile.

Ruth Finnegan makes the same point about the difference between oral and written poetry. Because oral poetry is performed in particular ritualized ways, part of its meaning and effect is taken from the performing context, from the "live" emotional atmosphere, the immediate pleasures of identification and suspense which are, in a sense, *tangible* (oral poetry is almost inevitably therefore flat and monotonous when written down and read). The performance, in other words (as with a song), is a necessary aspect of its "poetic" quality. Oral poetry doesn't need the devices written poetry must use to hold the reader's attention; that is the job of the poet herself, *as performer.*[63]

Good lyrics by definition, then, lack the elements that make for good lyric poetry. Take them out of their performed context, and they either seem to have no musical qualities at all, or else to have such obvious ones as to be silly (this goes as much for Lorenz Hart and Cole Porter as for Bob Dylan and Elvis Costello, as much for Curtis Mayfield and Smokey Robinson as for Hank Williams and Tom T. Hall). And this is most obvious (to return to Greil Marcus) in those songs in which the pleasure—the exhilaration—comes from the singer's failure to integrate musical and semantic meaning. The best pop songs, in short, are those that can be heard as a *struggle* between verbal and musical rhetoric, between the singer and the song.

The Voice

Let us imagine for this double function, localized in one and the same site, a single transgression, which would be generated by a simultaneous use of speech and kissing: *to kiss while embracing, to embrace while speaking.* It would appear that such a pleasure exists, since lovers incessantly "drink in speech upon the lips of the beloved," etc. What they delight in is, in the erotic encounter, the play of meaning which opens and breaks off: the function *which is disturbed:* in a word: *the stammered body.*

Roland Barthes[1]

We came to listen to that voice of difference likely to bring us *what we can't have* and to divert us from the monotony of sameness.

Trinh T. Minh-ha[2]

"Yeah," Scott said, "a singer like Ella says, 'My man's left me,' and you think the guy went down the street for a loaf of bread or something. But when Lady says, 'My man's gone' or 'My man's left me,' man, you can see the guy going down the street. His bags are packed, and he ain't never coming back. I mean like *never.*"

Tony Scott on Billie Holiday[3]

Look at a song's lyrics on the page: whose "voice" is there? Who's talking? The answer seems to start with the pronouns, the "shifters," not just the "I," the apparent speaker, but the "you" and "we" and "she" which reveal various things about the speaker. Even without an explicit "I," that is, we have an implicit one, someone who's doing the addressing: "*you've* got a lot of nerve, to say that *you're* my friend." The "voice" in the printed lyrics is thus articulated by the text itself, by a process that is both self-expressive and self-revealing, both declared openly and implied by the narrative.[4]

But even from the reader's point of view there's more to the voice than this. The printed lyric is already a double act, both the communicative process it describes or enacts—the "I" of the lyric speaking to the "you" of the lyric—and the communicative process it entails, writing and reading. As readers do we necessarily become the "you" of the writer's "I"? Do we take onto ourselves her love or contempt? Do we have to take a place in her story? The answer is obviously no; or, at least, there are certainly other options. We can refuse to become involved at all, read the lyric as an overheard conversation between other people, take it to be reported speech, put quotation marks around it. Or we can read it as if speaking it, become the "I" ourselves. (I think it would be impossible to read Bob Dylan's "Positively 4th Street" as if we were the "you" at issue—and this is a song positively *obsessed* with the word. The pleasure of these lines is as a means of sounding our *own* feelings of contempt and hauteur.)

How we read lyrics is not a completely random or idiosyncratic choice. The lyricist sets up the situation—through her use of language, her construction of character—in a way that, in part, determines the response we make, the nature of our engagement. But once we say that, we admit that there's another "voice" here, the voice of the lyricist, the author, the person putting the words in the "I's" mouth, putting the protagonists into their lyrical situation. And the authorial voice can be more or less distinctive; we may recognize—respond to—that voice (Cole Porter, Elvis Costello, Morrissey, P. J. Harvey) even when reading a lyric. "Voice" in this sense describes a sense of personality that doesn't involve shifters at all, but is familiar as the special way a person has with words: we immediately know who's speaking.

Now stop reading the lyrics, and listen to the song. Whose voice do we hear now? Again there's an obvious answer: the singer's, stupid! And what I argue in the rest of this chapter is that this is, in fact, the stupid answer. We hear the singer's voice, of course, but how that voice relates to the voices described above is the interesting question. To sing a lyric doesn't simplify the question of who is speaking to whom; it makes it more complicated.

In *The Composer's Voice*, Edward Cone asks whose voice we hear when we listen to a Schubert setting of a poem by Goethe. We hear a singer, Thomas Allen say, with a distinctive physical voice; we hear the protagonist of the song, the "I" of the narrative; we hear the poem's author, Goethe, in the distinctive organization of the words and their argument; and we hear Schubert, *in whose voice* the whole thing is composed.[5] And this last definition of voice, as the stylistic identity of the composer, is undoubtedly the dominant definition of "voice" in classical music criticism: a Schubert song is a Schubert song, regardless of whose words he has set to music and which singer is singing them. Schubert's "voice" thus refers to a personal quality—a quality of his personality—apparent in all his musical work.[6]

Even in this phrasing, though, a new question is raised. What is the relationship between Schubert's characteristics *as a composer* (his distinctive use of musical language which can be traced across different works, enabling us to speak of his musical "identity" and "development") and his characteristics *as a person?* This is, of course, to raise the long-debated question (long debated in literary criticism, at any rate) of the relationship between someone's life and their work. This issue tends to be put aside in music criticism because of the belief that music is a more directly emotional form of expression than literature, and is therefore more directly (or unconsciously) revealing of the composer's character. One of Anthony Storr's casual comments can thus be taken as typical: "The listener doesn't even have to be able to read music to recognize Haydn's robustness and humour, combined with his capacity for deep feeling."[7] Is music really so transparently expressive of personality? Is a voice?

The same questions can be addressed to popular music. What is the relationship between the "voice" we hear in a song and the author or composer of that song? Between the voice and the singer? This relationship has, of course, different complications in different genres, but two general issues arise immediately. First there is, as in classical music, the problem of biography: what is the relationship of life and art? On the whole, pop fans are less simple-minded than classical music critics about this. While one can certainly find Hollywood biopix of pop stars (Oliver Stone's *The Doors*, say) to match its biopix of classical composers—the life pouring out in the sounds—this tells us more about Hollywood (and the attempt to turn Jim Morrison into a Real Artist) than it does about pop music.

The up-front star system means that pop fans are well aware of the ways in which pop performers are inventions (and the pop biographer's task is usually therefore to expose the "real" Bob Dylan or Madonna who *isn't* in their music). And in pop, biography is used less to explain composition (the writing of the song) than expression (its performance): it is in real, material, singing voices that the "real" person is to be heard, not in scored stylistic or formulaic devices. The pop musician as interpreter (Billie Holiday, say) is therefore more likely to be understood in biographical terms than the pop musician as composer (Mark Knopfler, say), and when musicians are both, it is the performing rather than the composing voice that is taken to be the key to character. As Robert O'Meally asks about Billie Holiday, "She was the greatest jazz singer of all time. With Louis Armstrong, she invented modern jazz singing. Why do these accounts [all the books about her], which tell us so much about her drug problems, no-good men, and supposedly autobiographical sad songs, tell us so little about Billie Holiday, artist?"[8]

And the answer is because as listeners we assume that we can hear someone's life in their voice—a life that's there despite and not because of the singer's craft, a voice that says who they really are, an art that only exists because of what they've suffered. What makes Billie Holiday an artist from this perspective is that she was able to give *that which she couldn't help expressing* aesthetic shape and grace.[9] Compare Gregory Sandow on Frank Sinatra:

> Even before Kitty Kelley's unauthorized biography it was hardly a secret . . . that Sinatra hasn't always been the nicest of guys. So it's a commonplace of Sinatra criticism to separate Sinatra the artist from Sinatra the man. But I've always thought that his character slips through in his performance . . . And in fact it slips through precisely because of his art. Because he *is* an artist, he can't help telling a kind of truth; he can't help reaching towards the root of everything he's felt. He makes his living singing love songs; like any great popular singer, he can expand even a single sigh in those love songs into something vast. But he's also got his own story to tell, a story that goes far beyond what any love song could express: it's a story a little bit about triumph, partly about a lust for power, often about loss, and very much about humiliation and rage.[10]

The first general point to make about the pop voice, then, is that we hear singers as *personally* expressive (even, perhaps especially, when they are not singing "their own" songs) in a way that a classical singer, even a dramatic and "tragic" star like Maria Callas, is not. This is partly a matter of sound convention. As Libby Holman once put it, "My singing is like Flamenco. Sometimes, it's purposefully hideous. I try to convey anguish, anger, tragedy, passion. When you're expressing emotions like these, you cannot have a pure tone."[11]

In classical music, by contrast, the sound of the voice is determined by the score; the expression of anguish, anger, tragedy, and passion is a matter of musical organization. As Umberto Fiore writes, "In this context, the voice is in fact an instrument: bass, baritone, tenor, soprano and so forth. Individual styles can only *improve* these vocal masks, not really transgress them . . . the creation of a person, of a character, is substantially up to the music as such; if truth is there it is a *musical* truth."[12]

But if we hear the pop singer singing "her self," she is also singing a song, and so a second question arises: what is the relationship between the voice as a carrier of sounds, the singing voice, making "gestures," and the voice as a carrier of words, the speaking voice, making "utterances"? The issue is not meaning (words) versus absence of meaning (music), but the relationship between two different sorts of meaning-making, the tensions and conflicts between them. There's a question here of power: who is to be the master, words or music? And what makes the voice so interesting is that it makes meaning in these two ways simultaneously. We have, therefore, to approach the voice under four headings: as *a musical instrument;* as *a body;* as *a person;* and as *a character.*

I'll begin with the voice as a musical instrument. A voice obviously has a sound; it can be described in musical terms like any other instrument, as something with a certain pitch, a certain register, a certain timbral quality, and so forth. Voices can be used, like any other instrument, to make a noise of the right sort at the right time. Both these terms (right sort, right time) are apparent in the most instrumental use of the voice, as "backup." Here the singers' sound is more important than their words, which are either nonsensical or become so through repetition; and repetition is itself the key to how such voices work, as percussive instruments, marking out the regular time around which the lead singer can be quite irregular in matters of pitch and timing, quite inarticulate in terms of words or utterances.[13]

Even in this case, though, the voices can't be purely sound effects; at the very least they also indicate gender, and therefore gender relations (the aggressive-submissive attitude of the Raelettes to Ray Charles; the butch male choral support for Neil Tennant on the Pet Shop Boys' "Go West"), and it is notable that while rock conventionally uses other male voices, other members of the band, to sing close harmonies, backup singers are almost always female—and remarkably often black female at that.[14] This raises questions about the voice as body to which I'll return; but in talking about the voice as musical instrument I'm not just talking about sound, I'm also talking about skill and technique: neither backup nor lead singers simply stand on stage or in the studio and open their mouths. For the last sixty years or so, popular singers have had a musical instrument besides their voices: the electric microphone. The microphone made it possible for singers to make musical sounds—soft sounds, close sounds—that had not really been heard before in terms of public performance (just as the film closeup allowed one to see the bodies and faces of strangers in ways one would normally only see loved ones). The microphone allowed us to hear people in ways that normally implied intimacy—the whisper, the caress, the murmur. O'Meally notes the importance of the mike for the development of Billie Holiday's singing style, "as she moved from table to table in speakeasies . . . Whether in clubs or on recording dates, she continued to deliver her lyrics as if only for one or two listeners whom she addressed face to face."[15]

The appearance of the female torch singer and the male crooner had a number of consequences both for musical sexuality (crooners were initially heard as "effeminate" and unmanly, for example; the BBC even banned them for a time) and for what one might call musical seduction (radio advertisers took immediate note of "the performer's capacity to make each member of the audience perceive the song as an intimate, individual communication," and Rudy Vallee quickly became "one of the biggest radio and advertising successes").[16] As Bing Crosby, probably the greatest musical entrepreneur of the twentieth century (or at least the one with the best understanding of the implications of technology) realized, crooning made a singer the perfect salesman of his own song.[17]

This wasn't a matter of singers just going up to a microphone and opening their mouths, either. Mike technique had to be learned. Take the case of Frank Sinatra:

> As a young singer, he consciously perfected his handling of the microphone. "Many singers never learned to use one," he wrote later. "They never understood, and still don't, that a microphone is their instrument." A microphone must be deployed sparingly, he said, with the singer moving in and out of range of the mouth and suppressing excessive sibilants and noisy intakes of air. But Sinatra's understanding of the microphone went deeper than this merely mechanical level. He knew better than almost anyone else just what Henry Pleasants has maintained: that the microphone changes the very way that modern singers sing. It was his mastery of this instrument, the way he let its existence help shape his vocal production and singing style, that did much to make Sinatra the preeminent popular singer of our time.[18]

One effect of microphone use is to draw attention to the technique of singers *as singers* in ways that are not, I think, so obvious in classical music or opera, as they move with and around the instrument, as volume control takes on conversational nuances and vice versa.[19] Another is to draw attention to the *place* of the voice in music, to the arrangement of sounds behind and around it, as the microphone allows the voice to dominate other instruments whatever else is going on.[20] Consider these three descriptions of the popular musical voice.

Gregory Sandow on Alex Stordahl's arrangements for Frank Sinatra:

> I didn't know if I'd ever heard music at once so rapt and so shy. I searched for images. Could the arrangements be like waiters in a

restaurant? They took on shape only when they emerged briefly into view to fill pauses in Sinatra's phrasing; they might have been clearing plates away, making room on the table for the next course to be served. Or better still, were they like a wife? That made sense. Stordahl's arrangements, I decided, were like an adoring wife who says nothing in public but works patiently at home, cooking, mending, tending a spotless refuge for her man . . . but it might be more accurate to say that they're like a perfect dance partner, or, better still, like a woman lost in a dream because she's dancing with a perfect man.

Violins introduce "Embraceable You," and I hear her open her arms to surrender. "Embrace me," he sings; she lets him guide her, and, after an all but imperceptible breath, nestles more closely in his embrace. Now he sings ". . . my sweet embraceable you," and in response she whispers, almost to herself, "Oh YES, Frank." "Embrace me," he goes on, and she anticipates his step, moving with him almost before he knows where he himself will go. Then she hears him pause for an instant as he sings "my silk . . . and laceable you"; she waits, suspended, secure that when he resumes he'll know exactly what to do. "I'm in love with you, I am," he croons, and when from far in the distance she hears him add "and verily so," she closes her eyes and dances almost in place, hardly moving in his arms.[21]

Aidan Day on Bob Dylan:

Typically, the voice engages the line of the melody but its simultaneous jarring, atonal separation from the music, together with the relentless subordination of musical elements to the exigencies of verbal order, opens a space which registers a distance and unease involving both singer and listener. The singing voice at once solicits and rebuffs. The gratifications it offers are uncomfortable ones. It is a pattern of invitation and rejection in which the audience—alienated from easy absorption into the music and denied relaxation—is required to attend closely to the transactions between voice and words. While the voice impinges distinctively on the listener, it simultaneously seeks to refuse an unthinking capitulation to itself and to the sense of what it is singing. It is a pattern which places special demands upon an audience, expecting it to participate actively—and to risk itself—in the play of meaning.[22]

And Glenn Gould on Barbra Streisand:

> With Streisand . . . one becomes engaged by process, by a seemingly
> limitless array of available options . . . Like [Elizabeth] Schwarzkopf,
> Streisand is one of the great italicizers; no phrase is left solely to its
> own devices, and the range and diversity of her expressive gift is such
> that one is simply unable to chart an a priori stylistic course on her
> behalf. Much of the *Affekt* of intimacy—indeed, the sensation of
> eavesdropping on a private moment not yet wholly committed to its
> eventual public profile—is a direct result of our inability to anticipate
> her intentions.[23]

Although the voices described here are only ever heard, only exist, as
musical instruments, as sounds in arrangements of sounds, each of these
writers treats the voice as something which *has a relationship*—with an
orchestra for Sinatra, with an audience for Dylan, with the music itself, the
melody, for Streisand; the voice, that is to say, is described as if it existed—
could be heard—apart from the sounds that it does make, apart from what
we do hear. The implication is that all singers thus put "their own shape" on
the music, and it is the meaning of "their own" that interests me.

What these critics hear, to put this more plainly, is a *willed sound,* a sound
that is this way because it has been chosen so, could have been something
else. As Edward Cone suggests, a voice can never really be heard as a wordless
instrument; even when we listen to a singer in a language we do not understand, a singer making wordless sounds, scat singing, we still hear those
sounds as words we do not understand, or as sounds made by someone who
has *chosen* to be inarticulate.[24] "She accompanied herself on the piano," we
observe; not "she accompanied herself on vocals." And the matching term,
unaccompanied, which used to appear on popular concert bills, raises a
broader question still: when singing, do you accompany the music, or does
the music accompany you?

This helps explain, I think, the special status of the voice as a concept in
both musical and literary analysis. On the one hand, a musician's "voice"
need not be restricted to the voice in a physical sense: when jazz performers
are said to "speak" with their instruments, it is this same quality of willed
sound which is being described—which is why it is trickier to claim that
classical musicians, constrained in some respects by the score, have individual
"voices" (rather than styles): even Glenn Gould didn't really "speak" on his
piano (even if he sang along with it). On the other hand, to hear or read a
"voice" in a text is to assign *intention* to what we hear or read. "Authorless"

texts are those—like newspaper headlines or advertising jingles—however carefully crafted don't bear this imprint of individual articulation.

Even when treating the voice as an instrument, in short, we come up against the fact that it stands for the person more directly than any other musical device. Expression with the voice is taken to be more direct than expression on guitar or drum set, more revealing—which is why when drums and guitars are heard as directly expressive they are then heard as "voices." And this argument has legal sanction. Lawyers in cases of musical theft assume that a voice is a personal property, that it can be "stolen" in a way that other instrumental noises cannot (James Brown's vocal swoop is recognizably his immediately; a guitarist has to prove that a melodic riff, a composition rather than a sound, is unique). The most interesting legal rulings in this context concern soundalikes, cases in which the voices used ("Bette Midler," "Tom Waits") weren't actually theirs, and yet because they were recognizably "the same" could nevertheless be adjudged to invade the stars' "privacy," to steal their "personality." To recognize a voice, the courts ruled, is to recognize a person.[25]

Consider now the next element of this process, the voice as body. The starting point here is straightforward. The voice is a sound produced physically, by the movement of muscles and breath in the chest and throat and mouth; to listen to a voice is to listen to a physical event, to the sound of a body. This is, of course, true for the sound of other instruments too, but whereas what's involved there is the relationship between the body and something else—a string or reed or piano key or drum set—the voice draws our attention to something happening to the body itself; which is why we don't think of the microphone as a musical instrument: we don't expect voices to need anything outside the body in order to be heard. And this is clearly one reason why the voice seems particularly expressive of the body; it gives the listener access to it without mediation.

The effects of "the body in the singing voice" have been explored most famously by Roland Barthes, in his essay on the "grain" of the voice, where he argues that different timbral qualities have differential bodily implications. This point is usually taken up in rock criticism as a celebration of "the materiality of the body speaking its mother tongue," in terms of the "voluptuous pleasure of its signifier-sounds," but it is just as important to take note of the other side of Barthes's argument, his suggestion that there is such a thing as an "ungrained" voice, a voice that conceals its own means of physical production. This might, for example, be one way of describing those backup singers, further drawing attention to their peculiarity: here we have three ging "grainlessly," while a physically awkward male

e are further distinctions to be made here. We
... physically produced: we assign them qualities of
d, more specifically, we listen by performing, by
...ilently, tentatively) those muscular movements for
...with a singer by pushing the words up against the
... she does. A "grained" voice might, then, simply
...describe a voice with which, for whatever reasons, we have physical sympathy: "I am sitting in the Met at Leontyne Price's recital in 1985 and Price's vibrations are *inside my body*, dressing it up with the accouterments of interiority."[27]

The voice as direct expression of the body, that is to say, is as important for the way we listen as for the way we interpret what we hear: we can sing along, reconstruct in fantasy our own sung versions of songs, in ways we can't even fantasize instrumental technique—however hard we may try with our air guitars—because with singing, *we feel we know what to do*. We have bodies too, throats and stomachs and lungs. And even if we can't get the breathing right, the pitch, the note durations (which is why our performances only sound good to us), we still feel we understand what the singer is doing in physical principle (this is another reason why the voice seems so directly expressive an instrument: it doesn't take thought to know how that vocal noise was made).

This relates to a second point, that the voice *is* the sound of the body in a direct sense. Certain physical experiences, particularly extreme feelings, are given vocal sounds beyond our conscious control—the sounds of pain, lust, ecstasy, fear, what one might call inarticulate articulacy: the sounds, for example, of tears and laughter; the sounds made by soul singers around and between their notes, vocal noises that seem expressive of their deepest feelings because we hear them as if they've escaped from a body that the mind—language—can no longer control.[28]

Jonathan Swift put his own sardonic gloss on this three hundred years ago:

> Now the art of canting consists in skilfully adapting the voice to whatever words the spirit delivers, that each may strike the ears of the audience with its most significant cadence. The force or energy of this eloquence is not to be found, as among ancient orators, in the disposition of words to a sentence, or the turning of long periods; but, agreeably to the modern refinements in music, is taken up

wholly in dwelling and dilating upon syllables and letters. Th
frequent for a single vowel to draw sighs from a multitude, a
a whole assembly of saints to sob to the music of one solitary .
But these are trifles, when even sounds inarticulate are observ
produce as forcible effects. A master workman shall blow his nose
so powerfully as to pierce the hearts of his people, who were disposed
to receive the excrements of his brain with the same reverence as the
issue of it. Hawking, spitting, and belching, the defects of other men's
rhetoric, are the flowers, and figures, and ornaments of his. For the
spirit being the same in all, it is of no import through what vehicle
it is conveyed.[29]

One way in which we hear the body in the voice, to put this more
positively, is in the sheer physical pleasure of singing itself, in the enjoyment
a singer takes in particular movements of muscles, whether as a sense of
oneness between mind and body, will and action (a singer may experience
something of the joy of an athlete) or through the exploration of physical
sensations and muscular powers one didn't know one had (and the listener,
like the sports spectator, enjoys the experience partly by proxy, but also
aesthetically, with awe at the sheer grace of, say, Aaron Neville not exactly
singing "Tell It Like It Is," but *holding* its notes, turning them over for our
admiration).[30]

One effect of such pleasure is that for many singers what they are singing,
a word, is valued for its physical possibilities, what it allows the mouth or
throat to do. The singer finds herself driven by the physical logic of the sound
of the words rather than by the semantic meaning of the verse, and so creates
a sense of spontaneity: the singing feels real rather than rehearsed; the singer
is responding (like the listener) to the musical event of which they are part,
being possessed by the music rather than possessing it. The most obvious
device here (listen to Otis Redding live, for instance) is repetition, a syllable
being savored, sung again, sung with different consonants, tossed up against
different harmonies; but singers may slow things down as well—the young
Elvis Presley, for example, seemed to bask (like one of Swift's cantors) in the
sheer voluptuousness of his own vocal noise.[31]

Hovering around all of these approaches to the voice as body is the
question (Barthes's question) of music and sexuality: what makes a voice *sexy?*
What gives a voice its erotic charge? How does the attraction of a singing
voice relate to sexual attraction? Gender is obviously one issue here. We've
learned to hear voices as male and female (in terms of a biologically based
but not determining low/high register, for example), and the singing voice

arries these codings with it (which means that a performance artist like Laurie Anderson confuses the-body-in-the-voice no end by using a vocoder to give herself a "masculine" pitch, while Diamanda Galas threatens biological certainties with the sheer range of her vocals).[32]

What, then, is the significance of mainstream rock's generic preference for high-pitched male voices like Robert Plant's, for the articulation of a "hard" rock sound as a man straining to reach higher? In the spring of 1994 Canada's Crash Test Dummies had a worldwide hit with "Mmm Mmm Mmm Mmm," and no one doubted that a major reason for its success was the novelty of Brad Roberts's bass voice, his swollen vowels, the noise rumbling back down in his throat. This was manly singing, authoritative and a bit potbellied. And what made "Mmm Mmm Mmm Mmm" stand out was not that this sound is unusual as such (lots of men must sing in this deep-voiced way) but that it was unusual in today's radio soundscape. Roberts's voice is, by current pop standards, a freak.[33]

In other music contexts the high male voice has been regarded as freakish. Wayne Koestenbaum argues from his operatic perspective that the falsetto is "among the greatest of singing shames." "Long before anyone knew what a homosexual was," he writes, "entire cultures knew how to mock men who sang unconventionally high."[34] And Gary Giddins suggests that

> in American pop song and jazz, the baritone has ruled since the mid '20s, when Bing Crosby sang his first solos with Paul Whiteman and was celebrated for his virility and naturalness. The tenors he displaced were considered effete or affected—unnatural. The very few pop tenors who have appeared in recent decades were treated as novelties and worse: often they were adolescents (Wayne Newton, a castrato-manqué) or lunatic throwbacks (Tiny Tim and his ukulele).[35]

It's easy enough to spot the "unnatural" and "effeminate" rock use of the falsetto too: Frankie Valli's delirious high-pitched recollection of his father's advice in "Walk Like a Man"; Jimmy Somerville's appearance as a cherub in Sally Potter's *Orlando*. But the point is that such readings are matters of convention, not biology. A falsetto is, after all, a man's voice (there's no such thing as female falsetto); and the Crosby who, according to Giddins, "was celebrated for his virility and naturalness" was also the crooner the BBC sought to ban for "going against nature" and Cardinal O'Connell denounced for being "degenerate" and "effeminate."[36]

"Natural" voices, masculine and feminine, are defined culturally and must be understood structurally, as sounds heard against other sounds, and in rock history low, not high, voices have seemed structurally odder, a Captain Beefheart more idiosyncratic than a Jon Anderson. There are some obvious reasons for this. The high voice is heard as the young voice, and rock is a youth form—Frankie Lymon and Michael Jackson remain the teen male models. And one of the lasting effects of doo-wop was to break the male voice up into its component parts such that the combination of *all* its sounds, from low to high, defined masculinity. This remains the norm of male rock group singing, the boys in the band harmonizing above the lead, oohing and aahing just like a bunch of girls (but, of course, not heard like girls at all).

On the other hand, there have been few falsetto rappers so far, and if the youth and doo-wop roots of rock accustomed us to the sound of the high-pitched male voice, it was in a specific expressive context: as the sound of seduction, of intimacy, of the private man. For Britain's soul-inflected singers in particular (Mick Hucknell out of Jackie Wilson and Smokey Robinson) a high voice means not effeminacy (man as woman) but *a ladies' man,* and we now take it for granted that a male voice will move up a pitch to register more intense feeling, that the more strained the note, the more sincere the singer.

What seems odd about this is the relationship of body and voice and sex. It's as if in rock convention (*pace* Roland Barthes and the Barthians) the sexiest male voice is the least bodily—the heaving bosom of the Neapolitan baritone now seems "male" in a decidedly unsexy way (and Demis Roussos's high-pitched tremor thus comes across far more lasciviously than Pavarotti's big-chested tenor). But then Elvis Presley, probably as sexy a male pop singer as there has ever been, for a long time sought (via Dean Martin) to be an Italian balladeer; and what is apparent from his early records is that Presley was, in fact, his own doo-wop act, his bass no more unnatural than his falsetto. I'm perpetually seduced by his voice, and start to wonder: as a man-fan, what am I being seduced by? What am I being seduced for?

There's a simple point here: we hear voices as male or female and listen to what they say accordingly—according to our own sexual pleasures and preferences (which is why gay and lesbian singers can subvert pop standards by *not* changing the words: Ian Matthews bubbling that "I met him on a Monday and my heart stood still"; Mathilde Santing realizing that "I've grown accustomed to her face").[37] The possibilities for confusion here between "natural" and "conventional" voices of desire are well realized in X-Ray Spex's "Oh Bondage Up Yours!"[38] This is one of the most important tracks from the heyday of U.K. punk; its lyric refers both to the sexual bondage items worn by punks for shock value and to a generalized feminist anger. But the politics of the song lies in its voice—which is drawn to one's attention by the spoken intro: this is a "little girl" determined to be heard. And part of our "hearing" is negative, relates to what the voice is not. It is not "feminine"; it is not sweet or controlled or restrained. Such rawness also serves to register the track's punk authenticity—there is no need to assume that this sound reflects the limits of Poly Styrene's own voice; its "unmusicality" is crafted. It is necessary for the song's generic impact. There is, in short, a clear *collusion* here with the listener. The song addresses an "other"—"Up Yours!"—but on our behalf. We can only identify with the singer, with the voice, with the aggression. And if the politics here is a sexual politics, a gender politics, a politics of female identity and desire, then male listeners too are being offered the exhilaration of female de-bondage.

X-Ray Spex deliberately challenged the taken-for-granted reading of "male" and "female" voices both biologically—in terms of what girls do "naturally" sound like—and ideologically—in terms of what girls should naturally sound like. But there was a further question in their music too (or at least in their way of performing their music): does a voice have to be embodied? Must it be gendered? Can a singer *change sex?*

Sean Cubitt has made the point that the simultaneous emergence around the turn of the century of the telephone, the gramophone, and the radio meant that people became accustomed, for the first time ever, to hearing a voice without a body (previously such an experience would have meant the supernatural, the voice of God or the devil).[39]

But, of course, in practice we don't hear telephone or radio or recorded voices like this at all: we assign them bodies, we imagine their physical production. And this is not just a matter of sex and gender, but involves the other basic social attributes as well: age, race, ethnicity, class—everything that is necessary to put together a person to go with a voice. And the point to stress here is that when it comes to the singing voice *all* such readings have as much to do with conventional as "natural" expression, with the ways in which, in particular genres, singing voices are coded not just as female, but also as young, black, middle class, and so forth. In fact, the popular musician's hardest problem has been to develop conventional sounds for the *disembodied* voice—whether the ethereal voice (which is, nevertheless, female—the Cocteau Twins' Elizabeth Fraser) or the heavenly choir (ditto—Morricone's I Cantori Moderni d'Alessandroni); whether the computer voice (which is, nevertheless, male—Kraftwerk) or the collective voice of religious submission (ditto—the Stanley Brothers).[40]

This last strategy is the most interesting (and most successful) because it suggests that to disembody a voice is to rob it of individuality, and this leads directly to the question of vocal identity, to the *voice as a person*. How does a voice signify a person? What is the relationship of someone's vocal sound and their being? As I've already noted, the voice is usually taken to be the person (to imitate their voice is a way of becoming that person—hence the art of the impressionist), and the voice is certainly an important way in which we recognize people we already know (on the telephone, for example). But it is also a key factor in the way in which we assess and react to people we don't know, in the way we decide what sort of person they are, whether we like or dislike, trust or mistrust them. This is one reason why we often think we "know" a singer as part of what we mean by "liking" their voice (and why, similarly, we may feel we "know" the author of a book we like: we hear in it a particular sort of voice).

But having said this, I must add some qualifications. First, a voice is easy to change. As a matter of personal identity it is easier to change, indeed, than one's face (or one's body movements). And this is not just a matter of "acting" in the formal sense. People's voices change over time (as they adapt to the sounds of surrounding voices, to accents, and so forth; the shifting quality of people's voices in class terms, as they are upwardly or downwardly socially mobile, has often been noticed in Britain), and, more to the point, people's voices change according to circumstances—at home or in school, in the office or in bed, with friends or strangers (just listen to how people adapt their voice on the telephone, according to who is at the other end).

The voice, in short, may or may not be a key to someone's identity, but it is certainly a key to the ways in which we change identities, pretend to be something we're not, deceive people, lie. We use the voice, that is, not just to assess a person, but also, even more systematically, to assess that person's sincerity: the voice and how it is used (as well as words and how they are used) become a measure of someone's truthfulness.

In popular music, two points about this are striking. First, "truth" is a matter of sound conventions, which vary from genre to genre. What becomes clear in David Brackett's detailed comparison of Billie Holiday's and Bing Crosby's versions of "I'll Be Seeing You," for example, is that it is almost impossible to hear both of them as sincere: the assumptions that lie behind a reading of Holiday's voice as "witheringly" sad entail our hearing Crosby's voice as "shallow." If Holiday sings "for real," then Crosby, as Brackett puts it, gives "the impression of someone playing a role in a film"; while someone hearing Crosby as reassuringly direct and friendly could only hear Holiday as mannered. How we hear a musical voice, in other words, is tied into how we hear music.[41]

Second, one of pop's pleasures has always been singers taking on other people's voices, and I don't refer here simply to parody or pastiche but also to what Bernard Gendron describes as caricature, the taking on of another voice not as homage or mockery or pretense, but in order to draw attention to its specific characteristics (in the same way that a good comic impressionist doesn't just imitate someone's voice but uses its individual shape to reveal something about its owner). This is most obvious in the white use of black voices in rock and roll history, from Jerry Lee Lewis's "Whole Lotta Shakin' Goin' On," which, as Gendron says, "presents itself as white-boy-wildly-singing-and-playing-black," to Mick Jagger's "I'm a King Bee," which, we might say, presents itself as white-boy-lasciviously-slurring-and-playing-black-sex. No listener could have thought that either Lewis or Jagger was black; every listener realized that they wanted to be.[42]

Which leads me to my second general point about vocal deception: if a voice can be made to change to deceive other people, it can also be used to deceive ourselves. Our "internal" experience of the voice, that is to say, the way we hear ourselves, may not at all resemble how it sounds "externally," to other people (which is why most people are genuinely shocked—and appalled—when they first hear themselves on tape). "Putting on voices" is not something we only do as part of a specific public performance (in a *karaoke* bar, say), or in a specific act of deception; it is, rather, a normal part of our *imaginative* activity. And, as Jonathan Rée has suggested, it may in fact be difficult to know "one's own voice" amidst the babble of the different voices in which we talk to ourselves: "You glimpse the possibility that it is quite arbitrary to try to mark off certain of your vocal performances and nominate them as one voice, the voice that really belongs to you: do you really possess an ownmost, innermost voice which has the power to clamp quotation marks round the others and shrug them off as 'funny'?"[43]

This question seems pertinent too for our experience of hearing voices, of listening to song. The musical pleasure lies in the play we can make of both being addressed, responding to a voice as it speaks to us (caressingly, assertively, plaintively), and addressing, taking on the voice as our own, not just physically, as I've already discussed—singing along, moving our throat and chest muscles appropriately—but also emotionally and psychologically, taking on (in fantasy) *the vocal personality* too.

This is the context in which the voice as character becomes significant. In taking on a singer's vocal personality we are, in a sense, putting on a vocal costume, enacting the role that they are playing for ourselves. But a singer's act in this respect is complex. There is, first of all, the character presented as the protagonist of the song, its singer and narrator, the implied person controlling the plot, with an attitude and tone of voice; but there may also be a "quoted" character, the person whom the song is about (and singers, like lecturers, have their own mannered ways of indicating quote marks). On top of this there is the character of the singer as star, what we know about them, or are led to believe about them through their packaging and publicity, and then, further, an understanding of the singer as a person, what we like to imagine they are really like, what is revealed, *in the end,* by their voice.

Such a multiplicity of voices can be heard in *all* pop forms, whatever the generic differences in how they are registered—whether by Tom T. Hall or Johnny Rotten always "being themselves," by Dory Previn being "The Lady with the Braids" (complete with nervous laughter), or by Frank Sinatra being himself being a late-night melancholic in "One for my Baby"; whether, to be more dramatic, in Patti Smith's rock and roll chronicle, "Horses," in the Chi-Lites' strip cartoon, "Have You Seen Her," or in Meat Loaf's big brother act, "Objects in the Rear View Mirror May Appear Closer Than They Are."[44]

What we take for granted, listening to all these songs, is that they involve *layers* of interpretation, and that in pop it is therefore all but impossible to disentangle vocal realism, on the one hand, from vocal irony, on the other. How does one read, for example, Randy Newman's concert performance of "Lonely at the Top"? Here we have not just a cult singer/songwriter pretending to be a superstar (listen to the audience laugh with him) but also a highly successful writer/composer pretending to be a failure (listen to him laugh at his audience). Or take Michelle Shocked's "Anchorage," the meaning of which, as Dai Griffiths argues, depends on "whether you hear in Anchorage, a place in Alaska, the natural voice of the letter writer, or in 'Anchorage,' a song by Michelle Shocked, the crafted voice of the songwriter." And the pleasure of this lies in the fact that we actually hear *both Anchorage and "Anchorage" at once.*[45]

This returns us to the point from which I started: all songs are narratives; genre conventions determine how such narratives work; words are used to define a voice and vice versa.[46] In one respect, then, a pop star is like a film star, taking on many parts but retaining an essential "personality" that is common to all of them and is the basis of their popular appeal. For the pop star the "real me" is a promise that lies in the way we hear the voice, just as for a film star the "real" person is to be found in the secret of their look. This naturally leads to the issue of performance, but first I want to address two final matters relating to the voice itself: the question of interpretation, and the use in pop music of voices speaking/singing to each other.

In his discussion of the classical song, Edward Cone, as we've seen, distinguishes a song's composer, performer, and protagonist. A number of analytic questions follow from this. For example, does a performer need to know what she's singing about? If she sings the notes correctly and expressively, according to classical convention, as instructed by the composer in the score, will this *in itself* have the character effect the composer intended?[47] Cone proposes an analytic distinction: a protagonist's character is determined by the composer (by the way the music is constructed) but interpreted by the performer, and the question becomes what the relationship is of these two processes: what does an interpreter *do?* Cone also suggests that in responding to this question for themselves, listeners effectively make a choice: either to focus on the music, the piece performed, the character as composed, or on the performance, the performer, the character as interpreted. And he implies that one of the key differences between the art and the pop aesthetic can be found here: the classical concert performance is designed to draw attention to the work; the pop performance is designed to draw attention to the performer.[48]

Does this distinction stand up to pop scrutiny? I would argue, rather, that the pop performer draws attention to performance itself, to the *relationship* between performer and work. Take the case of the torch song, the "elegy to unrequited love," which is, perhaps, the clearest example of the pop singer's interpretive art. John Moore has suggested that the torch singer is best heard as an emotional expert—not an expert on emotions as such (the assumption of the form was that such emotions were universal) but an expert on their expression. Although the torch singers presented particular feelings describing particular situations (romantic illusions and disillusion), our pleasure in the songs lies not in the drama of the event, but in the way the singers explore the nuances of the feeling; torch singing is for both singer and listener an essentially narcissistic art. Torch song lyrics were therefore just signs of the feelings that the singer was to explore through the way they were sung. The music set up a "sense of sadness," the words a "verbal space" within which a voice could tell a story; and the singer applied herself—her critical, musical faculties—to the pleasures and difficulties of interpreting feelings, atmosphere, verse.[49]

Torch singing, in short, was a highly disciplined skill; it was certainly not about "direct" emotional expression or self-abandon. It involved reflection on feeling, not the feelings themselves—Billie Holiday, writes Martin Williams, "had the ability of a great actress to keep a personal distance from both her material and her performance of it"—and part of the sexual charge of the torch song came from the fact that not only were these women singers, as the lyrical protagonists, almost always reflecting on the behavior of men, they were also, as interpreters, reflecting on the words of men. These songs, then (and perhaps this is Cone's point), clearly "belong" to their singers, not their writers. Interpretation in this context does not mean realizing what the composer (or, rather, his music) meant, but using the music to show what interpretation means. Billie Holiday's voice, writes Robert O'Meally, whatever the song she sang, "was always, *always* the heroine."[50]

"Is there actually such a thing as the love song," asks Edward Cone, "outside the conventions of the love song itself?" And the answer is no, with the proviso that conventions are only the beginning of musical expression, not its end, and thus different singers (Ruth Etting and Helen Morgan, Billie Holiday and Bryan Ferry) can take the same words, the same tune, the same situation ("Body and Soul," "These Foolish Things") and use them to provide quite different accounts of love itself, its permanence and transience, its sweetness and humiliation. Voices, not songs, hold the key to our pop pleasures; musicologists may analyze the art of the Gershwins or Cole Porter, but we hear Bryan Ferry or Peggy Lee.[51]

My final question concerns vocal difference: what is the relationship *between* voices in popular song? After all, since the mid-sixties the group (rather than the solo singer) has dominated Anglo-American popular music (at least in terms of male voices), and if such groups more often than not have a "lead" singer we rarely hear his voice completely unaccompanied. We are, that is, accustomed to the idea of a "group voice"—the appeal of both the Beatles and the Beach Boys rested on their (quite different) blend of male voices; while, to take a different genre example, the male vocal trio (on the model of the Impressions) was central to the development of reggae in the 1960s and 1970s.

Such use of voices (rather than voice) can be pushed in two directions. In male group tradition, whether traced from gospel, barbershop, doo-wop (or their intermingling), the emphasis has been, in Keir Keightley's words, on singing as "social co-operation, the submission of individuality to the service of a larger corporate structure," and the "rational" organization of male voices as *sounds*—Lennon and McCartney thus sang "as one" (and it was only later, when we and they wanted to take these songs seriously as art, not pop, that anyone could hear Beatles numbers as "a Lennon song," "a McCartney verse").[52]

In female group tradition, by contrast (and I am deliberately exaggerating this contrast here; in practice male and female groups are not so distinct), different voices are used differently, in a conversational way (which in another trajectory, out of insult ritual, also leads to rap). The voices on tracks like the Shangri-Las' "Leader of the Pack" or the Angels' "My Boyfriend's Back" function as each other's audience; the chorus, dramatically, comments on the story and the action, encouraging the lead singer, disbelieving her, egging her on. Here "corporate identity" is indicated less by harmony singing than by the sharing out of the lead voice itself, and there is a direct continuity between the Shirelles' 1958 "I Met Him on a Sunday" and Salt-n-Pepa's 1991 "Let's Talk About Sex."[53]

As a label, "girl groups" (which may include groups of boys) describes a form which is, by its nature, *dramatic:* girl group records feature—focus on—vocal rhetoric and its effects. And, though less obviously, so does the pop duet (a form which has been somewhat devalued by the current fashion of reviving old stars' careers by getting them to sing along with new stars to no dramatic effect at all). In country music, for example, the man/woman duet is usually conflictual; the male and female voices are registered separately, present their different points of view, with the chorus harmonies suggesting just a temporary truce (the classic pairing here was Conway Twitty and Loretta Lynn). In soul the duet was usually used as a way of intensifying feeling, as a means of seductive talk, male and female voices moving in and to musical and sexual union (listen, for example, to Marvin Gaye and Tammi Terrell).[54]

In rock the most effective duets work not so much with realist effects (a man and woman quarreling or making up) as with star quality and across genre lines. Sinead O'Connor, for example, has been used to brilliant effect as a voice *querying* what's being said by a rapper, on the one hand (in her song with M. C. Lyte, "I Want (Your Hands on Me)"), and by a country singer, on the other (on Willie Nelson's version of Peter Gabriel's "Don't Give Up")—and I defy anyone to listen to her first entry on the latter track without a shiver of recognition that *this* person (with all we know about her) should be telling Willie Nelson (with all we know about him), should be telling him, so surely, so sweetly, to survive.[55]

Performance

10

One minute into this performance and she's not wearing
her heart on her sleeve: all of
her internal organs are draped
over her body like a hideous
new skin. Blood seeps through
her pores; stigmata break out
all over, making signs no one
can read. By marshalling an
array of blues and soul man-
nerisms, she contrives an act
that in certain moments—and
you can hear them coming—
ceases to be any kind of act at
all. The means of illusion produce the real, and the real is
horrible, but so vivid you
couldn't turn away to save
your life, or the singer's. It's no
fun: there's an instant in the
last chorus of the performance
when Joplin's voice goes . . .
somewhere else, and it's simply not credible that the music
then ends with an ordinary
flourish people can cheer for.
How did she get back?

**Greil Marcus on Janis Joplin's performance of
"Ball and Chain" at the Monterey International
Pop Festival, 1967**[1]

**At one extreme, one finds that the per-
former can be fully taken in by his own
act; he can be sincerely convinced that
the impression of reality which he stages
is the real reality. When his audience is
also convinced in this way about the
show he puts on—and this seems to be
the typical case—then for the moment at
least, only the sociologist or the socially
disgruntled will have any doubts about
the "realness" of what is presented.**

Erving Goffman[2]

My argument in this book is not just that in listening to popular
music we are listening to a performance, but, further, that "listening" itself is
a performance: to understand how musical pleasure, meaning, and evaluation
work, we have to understand how, as listeners, we perform the music for

ourselves. In this chapter I want to explore in detail how pop performance works. One problem here is what is meant by a "performance," particularly now that "the performative" is a familiar term in the literary critical lexicon. I should stress, then, that I am less interested in theories of text than of context, less interested in performance as a means by which a text is represented, "licensed," or made "excessive" than in performance as an experience (or set of experiences) of sociability (it has always seemed to me ironic that the academic effect of Jacques Derrida's musings on what it means to treat a text as an event has been the systematic study of events as texts).[3]

I'm sure, similarly, that postmodern theorists (also much concerned with performance issues) have more to learn from a study of popular music than popular music theorists have to learn from postmodernism. Nick Kaye, for example, concludes the most systematic survey of the "postmodern" in dance and theater by tentatively identifying the term with "an unstable 'event' provoked by a questioning that casts doubt sharply upon even itself," but his relentless attention to the institutionally defined avant-garde means that at no time does he stop to consider to what extent such instability and questioning have always been an aspect of popular performance—something as much to do with the social basis of the event as with the intentions or principles of the performers.[4]

My position, in brief, is that before trying to make sense of performance as a way of working with a text, we should first be sure we understand how performance is different, how it is "non-textual." What makes something a "performance" in the first place? What are its conditions of existence? How does performance-as-acting relate to performance-as-role-playing? What is the difference between performance on stage and performance off stage? Such questions are central to any discussion of performance in popular culture, in which the most interesting phenomenon is, precisely, the shifting boundary between the "staged" and the everyday.[5]

Sticking with a high cultural theory for a moment, then, what would it mean to treat popular musicians as performance artists? Noël Carroll has usefully suggested that the concept of performance art, as developed in the 1960s, is best understood as the entangling of two rather different practices and aesthetics.[6] On the one hand, the term described fine artists using their bodies, themselves, as the material of their art. In terms of art theory what mattered here was the *medium:* art became something living, moving, and, by its nature, changing. Work and artist were "for the time being" the same thing, and the space of art was redefined as a moment or period or *event:* now the work stopped when the artist's show was over. This was, nevertheless, still effectively an *objectifying* process, objectifying the artist herself, whose very being (her shape, her look, her "willed" acts) were constrained by the work's formal requirements. The unsettling question became: where is the "subject"?

On the other hand, performance art described stage performers (actors, dancers) who now took themselves and their bodies as the objects or sites of narrative and feeling. Such performers no longer "acted out" (or "in") a playscript or choreographic score, but effectively *subjectified* themselves: the implication of their work (which depended, as we will see, on a degree of collusion from the audience) was that what was happening on stage was determined only by the nature, shape, technique, body, and will of the performers themselves, which meant, among other things, a new emphasis on the process of putting together and taking apart a *persona*. Such performance involved the dialectic of coherence and incoherence.

Put these two lines of development together—objectifying the artist as the medium of the art; subjectifying the artist as the site of the narrative—and it is clear why performance art called into question a series of binary oppositions set up or assumed by the academic arts (though not, I think, by the popular arts): subject/object, mind/body, inside/outside. I'll come back to these distinctions in pop music terms shortly, but first I want to note two more general issues that emerge from this account of performance art.

First, the term "performance" defines a social—or communicative—process. It requires an audience and is dependent, in this sense, on interpretation; it is about meanings. To put this another way, performance art is a form of rhetoric, a rhetoric of gestures in which, by and large, bodily movements and signs (including the use of the voice) dominate other forms of communicative signs, such as language and iconography. And such a use of the body (which is obviously central to what's meant here by performance art) depends on the audience's ability to understand it both as an object (an erotic object, an attractive object, a repulsive object, a social object) and as a subject, that is, as a willed or shaped object, an object with meaning. Rhetorically, then, performance art is a way not of acting but of posing: it takes for granted an audience's ability to refer these bodily movements to others (in this respect, as in others, Madonna is the most self-consciously "arty" of pop performers, but by no means pop's only performance artist).

My second general point follows from this: the performance artist depends on an audience which can interpret her work *through its own experience of performance,* its own understanding of seduction and pose, gesture and body language; an audience which understands, however "instinctively" (without theorizing), the constant dialogue of inner and outer projected by the body in movement. For performance art to work it needs an audience of performers; it depends on the performance of the everyday.[7]

From a socio-historical perspective it would doubtless be relevant here to point to the increasing significance of performance in everyday life as an effect of urbanization and the decline of intimacy (more and more of our dealings are with people we don't know), as an effect of industrial capitalism (we no longer derive our identity from productive labor), as an effect of commodity fetishism (our consumption is now a matter of imagination, not need).[8] But whatever the material basis for contemporary performance, it is clearly culturally based. Western performance art only makes sense in terms of Western performing conventions—conventions shaped as much in the home and on the street as in the theater and the gallery.

What this means, in turn, is that the body-in-communication in performance art holds in tension not simply the subjective and the objective (the art question), but also the private and the public (the everyday question). In our experience (or imagination) of our own bodies, that is to say, there is always a gap between what is meant (the body directed from the inside) and what is read (the body interpreted from the outside); and this gap is a continual source of anxiety, an anxiety not so much that the body itself but its meaning is out of our control. In most public performances the body is, in fact, subject to a kind of external control, the motivation provided by a score or a script or a routinized social situation, which acts as a safety net for performer and audience alike. It is this safety net which the performance artist abandons, and one can therefore conclude that the essence of performance art is, in the end, embarrassment, a constant sense of the inappropriate. If, in conventional theater, one is embarrassed only when someone forgets a line or is suddenly "out of character," in performance art one is on the edge of embarrassment all the time because the performer is not "in character" to begin with (and the nervous tension among the audience at a "performance" as opposed to a "performance of a play" is palpable).

So far I have been describing performance "art," something defined in the gallery, on the one hand, and the theater, on the other. Performance itself, though, has a history in low cultural spaces too, and I'm sure that performances in popular places and genres (in the music hall and vaudeville, popular song and comedy) are much more akin to performance art than to "legitimate" art or theater. If performance artists in the 1960s turned to such popular forms as stand-up comedy and burlesque, wrestling and the circus, this was not just a postmodern breakdown of high/low cultural barriers; it was also because they had something to learn.[9]

Two aspects of this need further discussion. First, in describing something as a "live" performance we are drawing attention to a situation in which thinking and doing are simultaneous: we are watching willed activity in which it is the will that is active, so to speak. To put this another way, *all* live performance involves both spontaneous action and the playing of a role. This is obvious enough in live music: it must involve a *combination* of improvisation and note-following, with the extremes being a well-drilled orchestra (in which each player still has to will each note, just so) and a free-form solo invention (which must make a gesture at musical expectations even in flouting them). The interesting comparison here is with sports, in which performers may well feel most in control, most free, when, technically, they are playing most correctly.

The sports example is also a reminder that one of the recurring pleasures of popular culture is the difficult or spectacular act, the drama of which lies precisely in its liveness, in the resulting sense of risk, danger, triumph, virtuosity: we need to see things which we know must be live (even if we also know, as in the case of a James Brown show, that for such things to work they must be elaborately planned and rehearsed—they must always work, that is, *in exactly the same way*). What's valued here is not (as in high culture) seeing something unique, but seeing something difficult, something that *takes work*. Far from wanting the means of production to be concealed, the popular audience wants to see how much has gone into its entertainment. Performance as labor is a necessary part of the popular aesthetic.

The second point I want to make here about popular performance concerns "framing." Performance may only make sense through the everyday, but "public performance" also describes something marked off from the everyday, something in which when the everyday does appear it is as a joke, an intruder (which also means, to reverse the argument, that when the everyday turns out to have been a performance, to have been literally framed, by a viewfinder, it comes as a shock: "Smile, please! You're on *Candid Camera!*"). Public "framing," in short, involves the application of the sort of genre rules I've already discussed, rules which determine how both performer and audience should behave (rules which we can see enacted in even the most domestic of home videos).

As the anthropologist Richard Bauman has pointed out, it follows that there is not necessarily a clear distinction in terms of setting between the "staged" and the everyday. What is at issue, rather, is how activities are "staged" *within* the everyday. Thus a way of speaking can, in itself, signify a performance (which describes both an action and an event) by putting an "interpretive frame" around itself, such that listeners no longer treat what is being said as part of normal conversation. In everyday terms the most obvious example of this is probably the joke: joke telling is certainly a performance, even if it occurs within a casual conversation (or within another sort of performance altogether, a lecture, say)—hence people's claims that they "can't tell jokes." What does such "telling" involve?[10]

The relationship between the conversational and the performative is complex, then, involving not just a particular use of language but also a claim to be competent in such use, and an assumption that one's audience is also so competent, or, at least, able to recognize one's talking skills. Unlike ordinary conversation, that is, a performance can be good or bad; it is evaluated. It follows some sort of formal rule, and the anthropologist's question becomes how such a performance is "keyed". How do we know that it is a performance? That it has begun? That it is over?

The answers obviously relate to the genre rules I discussed in Chapter 4, but Bauman also makes three general points that are important here. First, he notes that in anthropological terms a performance may range, in principle, from the completely "novel" (spontaneous invention) to the completely fixed (a traditional religious rite). In practice, as I've already suggested, nearly all performances lie somewhere between these two extremes, and Bauman's point is that this is what enables an audience to *judge* them: by measuring what's original, personal to this performance, against the conventions of the perfor- mance form in general. This is one of the problems, of course, for "original" performance art: no one knows how to tell if it's any good or not. And this isn't just a problem for the audience. The success of a performance for a performer can, in the end, only be measured by the audience response (this is what makes it a performance, a kind of oratory). A joke that gets no laughs, a song that gets no response, is a bad performance by definition.

Bauman's second point follows from this: a performance is "an emergent structure"; it comes into being only as it is being performed.[11] As the dance theorist George Beiswanger puts it, performing is a "kind of activity, peculiar to art-making, in which doing and thinking are so aligned that thinking proceeds to deploy what the doing is to be, and doing provides the thinking with a manifest presence. What is thought out is precisely what is done, the thought-out dance and danced-out thought being one and the same . . . dances are events brought forth by performing."[12]

Finally, like Beiswanger, Bauman suggests that performance is an "en- hancement," involving a heightened "intensity" of communication: it makes the communicative process itself, the use of language and gesture, the focus of attention. And if for the performers this means prestige (for a good performance, for their skill), for the judging audience too it means an increased sense of *control* over the usual flow of communication: performance is, in this context, a way of standing back from content and considering form. Thus pop listeners are always aware of the tension between an implied story (content: the singer in the song) and the real one (form: the singer on the stage), while pop performers use this tension to destabilize the concepts of content and form in the first place. Björk's "There's More To Life Than This," for example, a track from her fine *Debut* album, was "recorded live at the Milk Bar toilets," and the drama of her performance, its sense of immediacy—a "secret" moment of song snatched from an evening of public display—is more significant for our listening pleasure than the excuse for it, a *faux-naive* on-the-spot song *about* sneaking away from the party. The image that sticks in the mind is not from the song ("we could go down to the harbour and jump between the boats") but from its singing, Björk hiding out in the bathroom.[13]

It is arguable, then, that in this self-conscious games-playing with the musical "event" we have exemplified not the postmodern but the popular. Whereas in both high and folk cultures, performing rules tend to be naturalized (so that everybody carefully avoids noting what a very peculiar event a classical concert or a folk festival is), in popular performance the rules (and the comic or shocking possibility of breaking them) are always on the surface of performance itself.[14] Peter Bailey thus argues brilliantly that the central performing trope in late nineteenth century music hall was a kind of *knowingness*, a *collusion* between performer and (implied) audience, between audience and (implied) performer, which was both inclusive and exclusive, worrying and reassuring.[15]

Bailey's key point is that the best performers in the music halls constructed their own audiences, their own colluders, by using a mode of address which both flattered the audience's social competence and acknowledged its social wariness, its feeling that it might *get things wrong,* a feeling played on by almost every comedian. (Bailey notes the routine use of a butt in the crowd, someone who could stand for cultural incompetence.) More specifically (and it is this which makes knowingness peculiar to the music hall—other forms of popular performance use other forms of collusion), music hall comics could work in the belief that the audience understood what was *not* said, could systematically use both innuendo and parody-by-inflection or, usually, both, as "respectable" English was spoken in a way that mocked its conventions in the very act of using them (which is, again, to come close to the idea of "postmodern" performance).[16]

For contemporary popular music, though, the most significant linguistic source of performing conventions is undoubtedly "talking black," the "speaking behavior" of African-American and African-Caribbean communities described by Roger D. Abrahams, in which there is not (as in European and European-American cultures) a clear distinction between "dramatic-type performance" and "other types of interactional behavior." Rather, workaday talk and conversation are *constantly* framed as performance, as the language used becomes formalized, as speakers "get into it," as the street itself becomes the site of a "constant self-dramatization," "an entertainment of each by the other." Abrahams notes that such "performing by styling" involves the use of body as well as verbal language: "to stylize is to call attention to formal and formulaic features" of both what one says and how and in what situation one is saying it (at home or in public; as a man or a woman; to an audience of men or women; and so forth).[17]

As Abrahams further notes, black slang (often misunderstood when taken over into white talk) systematically describes performance as a collective process—"doing your own thing" means taking your own part in a group drama; to "dig it" means not to understand, to get beneath, but to get involved, to get into. And it is this everyday experience of vernacular performance which has made African-American culture so important as a source of popular performing expertise, of popular performing style.[18]

I argued in Chapter 9 that the meaning of pop is the meaning of pop stars, performers with bodies and personalities; central to the pleasure of pop is pleasure in a voice, sound as body, sound as person. The central pop gesture, a sung note, rests on the same inner/outer tension as performance art: it uses the voice as the most taken-for-granted indication of the person, the guarantor of the coherent subject; and it uses the voice as something artificial, posed, its sound determined by the music. The star voice (and, indeed, the star body) thus acts as a mark of both subjectivity and objectivity, freedom and constraint, control and lack of control. And technology, electrical recording, has exaggerated this effect by making the vocal performance more intimate, more self-revealing, and more (technologically) determined. The authenticity or "sincerity" of the voice becomes the recurring pop question: does she really *mean* it?

And there is an additional point to make here. In the gallery world, one important reason for taking up performance art was its impermanence: the performance artist mocked the ideology of transcendence and the exploitation of art as property (though, of course, tapes of performances were soon marketed). In the pop world, recording made a performance a property from the start (and what happened in a studio in 1935, on a stage in 1965, is now sold as a jazz or rock "classic"), but the most important "permanent" element of pop music culture is not the event but the star. A performance is always, that is to say, a performance in a history of performances; an "image" (like a stylistic "voice") describes change within continuity.

This raises a number of questions about the listening (or spectating or consuming) process—we don't, after all, consume the stars but their performances. If the singer's voice makes public (makes manifest, makes available) the supposed sounds of private (personal, individual) feeling, then these public gestures are consumed privately, fitted into our own narratives, our own expressive repertories.[19] Similarly, if all songs are narratives, if they work as mini-musicals, then their plots are a matter of interpretation both by performers attaching them to their own star stories *and* by listeners, putting ourselves in the picture, or, rather, placing their emotions—or expressions of emotion—in our own stories, whether directly (in this situation, in this relationship, now) or, more commonly, indirectly, laying the performance over our memories of situations and relationships: nostalgia, as a human condition, is defined by our use of popular song.[20]

Just as a singer is both performing the song and performing the performance of the song, so we, as an audience, are listening both to the song and to its performance. For me this is a literal process: to hear music is to see it performed, on stage, with all the trappings. I listen to records in the full knowledge that what I hear is something that never existed, that never could exist, as a "performance," something happening in a single time and space; nevertheless, it *is now* happening, in a single time and space: it is thus a performance and I hear it as one, imagine the performers performing even when this just means a deejay mixing a track, an engineer pulling knobs.[21]

Even without such naiveté, I think it can be argued that the "act" of singing is always contextualized by the "act" of performing; and if the latter, like any other stage role, is put together behind the scenes, the former takes place in public: we see and hear the movement in and out of character; we watch this aspect of the performance *as a performance*. The way singers put roles on and off—"the next song is a slower number"—works differently in different genres, but all methods (irony, earnestness, virtuosity, craft pride, humor)[22] draw attention to the singers' knowledge of what is going on, to their knowledge of our knowledge of what is happening. It's as if the "as if" of the song performance is foregrounded in order to naturalize the "as if" of the musical performance. A skilled rock and role player like Bruce Springsteen seems to adopt the same attitude to his songs, to his band, and to his own performance as the audience itself, and in taking our place, living our reality, he thus enacts his own star persona, as *one of us*.

And it is here that we begin to get interesting divergences from (or glosses on) performance as performance art. For a star is also (to use the industry's own language) an "act"; performance is not as self-revealing as it may seem. To begin with, because pop is primarily a song form, because it involves the use of voice and words, so it is also a dramatic form: pop singers don't just express emotion but also play it (as I argued in Chapter 8, pop songs are, in this respect, more like plays than poems). But pop singers are unlike play actors (though similar to film stars) in two respects.

First, as we've seen, they are involved in a process of *double enactment*: they enact both a star personality (their image) and a song personality, the role that each lyric requires, and the pop star's art is to keep both acts in play at once. This is most obvious in the plainest narrative forms, such as music hall or country music, where performers employ a variety of techniques (more obvious on stage than in the recording studio, though used there too) to move in and out of character. Interruption thus becomes a basic vocal device: the performer's skill is to objectify an expressive gesture at the very moment of its expression, to put quotation marks around it. The singer (Elvis Presley, say) becomes his own audience: is it really *me* singing that? (In country music, with its excessively self-conscious equation of realism and formalism, a central place in this process is occupied by songs about the past: the singer in her present persona responds to the naïveté or ambition of her past self, as expressed in the song; the performer is thus the singer and not-the-singer simultaneously, just as—and this is essential to country ideology—the past is both the present and not the present.)

The second complication in the pop singer's enactment of the pop star is that she (unlike the opera singer, say) is also the site of desire—as a body, and as a person (the film star analogy still holds). In performance, then, in the playing of their various song parts, instead of "forgetting who they are," singers are continuously registering their presence. (This is, perhaps, most obvious for performers who are most remote—Whitney Houston, for example.) Singing, as an organization of vocal gestures, means enacting the protagonist in the song (the right emotions for this part), enacting the part of the star (the moves in keeping with the image), *and* giving some intimation of a real material being—a physical body producing a physical sound; sweat produced by real work; a physicality that *overflows* the formal constraints of the performance.

This raises questions about the sexuality or erotics of performance, and its relation to possession (why do audiences dress up like the stars?), though the issue that most immediately concerns me (one that is raised by performance artists too) is this: what does it mean to make a spectacle of oneself? In the last chapter I suggested that discussion of the voice as body would always be haunted by questions of sexuality. So are discussions of the body as body. To put it simply (to return to the everyday), to perform for an audience as a woman means something different than to perform for an audience as a man—different both in terms of the *social* connotations of what it means for a woman to show her body publicly, to pose, and in terms of the power play of sexual desire.[23] As Susan McClary puts it, a woman's problem is how to keep control of herself in a space, the stage, patrolled by an objectifying sexual gaze conventionalized by hundreds of years of patriarchal command. The female performer is inevitably much more self-conscious than a male performer in that she has to keep redefining both her performing space and her performing narrative if she is to take charge of her situation.[24]

McClary's heroine in this respect is Laurie Anderson; most recent feminist discussion of the issue has focused on Madonna.[25] But women performers in all musical genres have always been conscious of what it means to be spectacularly female. As a country singer, Dolly Parton, for example, doesn't only play on a male notion of femininity, but in *performing* the signs of vulnerability—the little-girl voice, the giggle, the nervous flounce—makes their meaning problematic. Parton's remarkable vocal range—in terms of volume/power rather than pitch as such—draws attention to her art as a singer as much as to her life as a woman. As is typical in country music, her voice (as opposed to her body), though a clearly physical sound, becomes the sign, the trademark even, of her stardom, the meaning around which all her other signs (the hair, the breasts, the gowns) are organized. The song of dependence (common in her repertoire and often self-written) is therefore so obviously crafted, so clearly designed to display vocal skill rather than an emotional state, that at the very least Parton's audience has to consider her lyrical sentiments as ironic. (It is not surprising that she built up a strong camp following.)[26]

By contrast, the English music hall star Gracie Fields, an ungainly, "homely" woman by showbiz standards, took on character roles much more specifically than Parton did and, like other music hall stars, mixed sentimental ballads with comic story songs. By spoofing her voice (rather than her looks), by displaying her vocal range (in terms of style as well as pitch) as a bit of a joke, Fields became endearing, beloved—"Our Gracie"—as a kind of favorite aunt or big sister. (This meant, among other things, that in her films Fields, unlike Parton, always, only, played herself.)[27]

By contrast again (although less of a contrast than one might imagine), Millie Jackson uses the different conventions of soul feeling and the insult ritual to set up another sort of collusive relationship with her audience—or at least with its female part, speaking for it, drawing on innuendo and the unsaid to unfold a conversation that could be taking place in the launderette and then moving dramatically back to the reality of her presence, on stage, with a band, microphone, lights. Like Fields, Jackson's movement from comic routine to ballad implies that, in the end, the comedy is the assumed role, the ballad the real feeling. The message, for all the ideological aggression, is orthodox: all men are shits (laughs) but we love them anyway (sighs). Her strutting public performance acts out a private resignation.[28]

Two issues are significant here, I think. The first is *embarrassment.* Performing involves gestures that are both false (they are only being put on for this occasion) and true (they are appropriate to the emotions being described, expressed, or invoked). Even the most stylized performer, the one with the most obviously formal and artificial gestures, is expressing the self, displaying in public sounds and movements usually thought of as intimate; what the audience wants to see, as Roland Barthes puts it, is "a convinced body, rather than a true passion."[29] In judging a performer we are, as an audience, measuring her gestures against our sense of what she's really like, off stage (what her voice and body really do, in this sort of situation), and even if, from the singer's point of view, this makes it even more important to maintain a clear separation or distance between self and personality, nevertheless, what's on offer is a kind of vulnerability: we might not like her (and in most pop genres performance is, specifically, about being liked).[30]

The performer's problem here is that however carefully crafted the star persona, in performance a real body is involved: singing is not necessarily or even desirably pretty—singers sweat, they strain, they open their mouths wide and clench their throats. To make the necessary musical sounds, singers have to do things (or simulate doing things) which may not "fit" the star body, the star persona. As Koestenbaum says of opera singers, "Singers look like freaks unless they control themselves, and this possibility of looking grotesque is appealing if you choose (as I am choosing) to embrace rather than to reject a stereotypical freakishness."[31]

Performers always face the threat of the ultimate embarrassment: *the performance that doesn't work.* (I have painful memories from my rock critic days of support acts orchestrating an audience response that isn't there, a singalong in which no one else is singing; that was just embarrassing, we muttered in the interval bar.) The appropriateness of a gesture, in other words, can be decided only by its effect. (This is a normal aspect of everyday performance too: a risked intimacy—an endearment, a caress—is always a risked embarrassment; it's the response which decides whether it was, indeed, fitting.)[32]

On the other hand, we also know from everyday life that the way to deflate embarrassment is through self-mockery—we hastily pretend that the gesture was a joke, was meant ironically. As audiences too we often decide (with delight or disdain) that a performer has gone "over the top." This is, in part, the effect of the music in making expressed feelings more intense: a stage performer gets the same sort of emotional charge from her soundtrack as a screen performer gets from his. And music's enveloping effect applies to the audience too: the world can only now be perceived in this emotional state, and the narcissism of the singer, exploring her own feelings, becomes our own. We forget ourselves in the music as part of a condition of collective self-indulgence; we are alienated, as Sartre would put it, in the collective ego.[33] But, further, over-the-top artists deliberately set gestures free from their appropriate setting. The great pop performers (whether Judy Garland or Shirley Bassey, Mick Jagger or Prince) don't so much enact emotional roles as hold their enactments up before us in fragments, so we can admire the shape of the gesture itself.

It is no accident that such performers are camp idols, are beloved (following Susan Sontag) in terms "of artifice, of stylization." Such performers seem to have grasped the camp point that the truth of a feeling is an aesthetic truth, not a moral one; it can only be judged formally, as a matter of gestural grace. "Sincerity," in short, cannot be measured by searching for what lies *behind* the performance; if we are moved by a performer we are moved by what we *immediately* hear and see.[34]

This brings me to the second theme I want to pick up here, *seduction*. Guy Scarpetta suggests that a singer is in the same trade as a prostitute, publicly offering a bliss that can only be experienced privately.[35] We realize that the singer is making us an offer ("Know me!") that is essentially false, yet is true to our fantasy of what the offer might be, that it might be just for us ("To know me is to love me"). The listening fantasy, to put this another way, is that we control the music (the sexual exchange) when, in fact, the performer does. The seductive voice mediates between nature (the real person about whom we fantasize) and culture (the performing person we get); it draws attention both to the social construction of our desire, to its artificiality, and to our obdurately subjective reading of it. The presence of even a recorded sound is the presence of the implied performer—*the performer called forth by the listener*—and this is clearly a sensual/sexual presence, not just a meeting of minds.[36]

What, then, is the role of the body in our understanding of musical performance and musical response? How does the body itself (as separate from the voice) communicate and react? Paul Eckman has usefully suggested that in considering so-called body language, we should move analytically from universal, unconscious, spontaneous bodily "utterances" through a spectrum of socialized body movements to the most stylized, conventionalized, and posed.[37]

First there are the direct physical expressions of emotional states—fear, ecstasy, delight, anger, aggression, timidity, and so forth. There does seem to be a repertory of physical and facial expressions (to go with the vocal noises described in Chapter 9) which are simply human (though we also read them onto animals). In responding to such bodily signs (a baby's smile; an audience's laughter; a friend's fear) we both read their bodies as indicating their emotional state and experience their emotions by reproducing the same bodily and facial movements for ourselves (by smiling, laughing, holding our bodies in the same state of tension).

This is the essence of what John Blacking calls "fellow feeling" (and, for him, a necessary aspect of musical communication). Such movements are, significantly, the hardest to act (it is difficult to laugh or cry to order), and actors normally need to be in the right character or narrative situation to do so—to be, that is to say, in the right state of fellow feeling. Nowadays, Blacking suggests, we tend to feel such "oneness" with other people only in specifically framed situations (as an aspect of particular sorts of hedonistic or religious or aesthetic experience; at climactic moments of love or achievement): "Similar somatic states seem to be induced by drink or drugs or fasting; but I think it would be more correct to say that such devices do not induce the state so much as help suppress the cultural rules that have inhibited their natural expression."[38] And this is obviously relevant to the way in which popular performance is framed, precisely with the promise of such fellow feeling. The usual cultural constraints on expression are suspended, and at the height of enjoyment at a rock concert (or football match), one can and does hug strangers, leap into the mosh pit, turn cartwheels on the floor. Such body movements feel spontaneous, unmeaningful of anything except a diffuse joy.

Second, there are what Eckman calls "illustrative movements," movements tied to the content of a verbal narrative, to the flow of speech. These can be quite unconscious (or "integrated") movements—the hand movements we make (and can't help making) when we speak, as a kind of commentary on what we say: an emphasis here, a shrug there (and tones of voice, bodily *sound* adapted to the nature of what we're saying, are obviously an aspect of this). But even if such movements are unconscious, they are certainly not universal; they are as culturally specific as the languages in which we speak. The point here is not simply that different languages use the body differently (so that one can distinguish French, Italian, and English speakers by sight as well as sound) but also that the same bodily movements may mean different things in different cultures. (A nodded head can be "yes" or "no"; eye contact a mark of respect or contempt. How to touch someone else's body is in most societies the subject of elaborate rules of power and decorum.)

In performance terms, we could also label the "semi-conscious" or intentional acting out of a described emotion as illustrative: in conversation, that is, we find ourselves mimicking the state we describe (in saying we felt sad we "sadden" our face, and so on), and such mimicry (which quickly becomes conventionalized) becomes the basis for the enactment of emotion in mime and pantomime (in the exaggerated bodily and facial movements of the silent screen actor and actress).

Eckman's third category is bodily manipulations, movements in which one part of the body does something to another part. Here we find an odd mixture of our most unconscious movements, nervous tics like head scratching, nose picking, mouth rubbing, nail biting, and so on—actions that we both can't help doing and are embarrassed to be caught at—and the most conventionalized, the language of insults, insulting, it seems, precisely because they draw attention to bodily functions.[39]

Finally there are what Eckman calls emblems, symbolic body movements which have specific (often verbal) meanings that can only be understood by people who know the interpretive rules, the code (and such body language is often, indeed, an aspect of membership in a secret or exclusive society). Obvious examples are making the sign of the cross, auction bidding, the Masonic handshake, and the referees' rulings in American football. Such movements are entirely conventionalized, which is to say that they make no reference whatsoever either to an emotional state or, indeed, to the body as such. It is simply being used as an instrument to write with, as a site to write on.

Two issues emerge from this approach to the performing body. First, at the core of our understanding of body language must be the knowledge that even the most direct form of human expression—the unmediated articulation of fear, anger, ecstasy, and so on—can always be faked (as in the faked orgasm restaurant scene in the film *When Harry Met Sally*). To call something a language is to say that it can be used for lying, and this is a particularly disturbing aspect of body language because its "truth" is tied into our own *unable-to-be-helped* response: someone's "appearance" of laughter or anger is enough to cause our laughter or fear *for real.*[40]

This takes us back to the script as safety net and to the potential for embarrassment when it is removed. A staged performance is framed by a suspension of fellow feeling or, perhaps, by a kind of enactment of it: we know the performer is acting anger, so we act our fearful response. In performance art, though, we don't know if this is an act, and an element of our fear is therefore real—maybe she, Millie Jackson, is going to come to my table and ask my partner about my own sexual performance (and there will be further embarrassment when I reveal my fear of humiliation just as she reveals that this was only an act, after all). Or, alternatively, perhaps she, Judy Garland, is not just acting grief but is really crying, which is to embarrass us in a different way, on her behalf. This is a particularly complex issue given that in performance body language is necessarily a combination of direct and conventional expression.

It is clear, moreover, that questions of gender and sexuality must be central to any account of body language, if only because the body is the key to the social meaning of both. On the one hand, sexual differences are directly read from physical differences (A has visible breasts, B doesn't; A is a woman, B a man); on the other hand, these biological differences are coded culturally into different *uses* of the body which have nothing to do with biology at all. And it is because men and women are seen to move differently that trans-gressive performance becomes possible, as a fertile form of sexual lying.[41]

So far I've been talking about the body as an expressive site or medium, assuming that an internal state or statement is externalized as a body shape or movement which is then interpreted, given meaning, by reference to the intention or feeling that produced it. And this is certainly one way in which we routinely listen to music and read performers. But we need to consider also the body's relationships *outside,* its place in the material world.

To begin with, take clothes. Clothes offer the body its most intimate traffic with the outside world (a point brilliantly made in *Paris Is Burning*), and there is by now a well-established literature that treats clothes (or fashion) as a language too. The implication here is that it is the clothes themselves that do the talking; beneath them is a kind of universal (if aged and gendered and racialized) body. This is the Emperor's New Clothes model: clothes are the way the body speaks; without them it has nothing to say. Hence the pop significance of dressing up, making up, Madonna's endlessly "revealing" costumes.

But as Anne Hollander has argued so persuasively, the relationship of clothes and body is more complex than this model implies.[42] Bodies themselves bear the imprint of clothes. Social signs, that is, are written on the body itself, on its shape, its size, its texture, its curves and bones and flesh and hair. Stage clothes, stage costumes, don't necessarily *transcend* physical circumstances (think of those clodhopping British glitter bands of the early 1970s like Sweet and Slade), and band uniforms depend, for their effect, as much on the musical relationships between a group's members as on their design features. How musicians look—how casual, how smart—clearly affects how at first we hear them (and most pop fans quickly realize that the most casual clothes are carefully chosen: it's the *same* ratty T-shirt every night). But we don't just experience a musician's body as costumed. As Ornette Coleman explains,

> For me, clothes have always been a way of designing a setting so that by the time a person observes how you look, all of their attention is on what you're playing. Most people that play music, whether it's pop, rock or classical, have a certain kind of uniform so they don't have to tell you what you're listening to. I always thought that if this was the case, why wouldn't I try to design from the standpoint of the opposite of that? Have the person see what you have on and have no idea what you were going to play. I'm not playing to represent what I'm wearing, and I'm not dressing to represent what I play.[43]

The point here is that the musician's body is also an instrument. Much of the discussion of body language treats the body as an autonomous object, something defining its own space. In fact, though, much (if not most) body movement is determined by other bodies (by parents and children and lovers and friends) and by the use of tools (whether at work or play). The use of the body as an instrument involves, in fact, two components. On the one hand, the *material* we work on determines our movements (when writing, cuddling, driving, sewing)—in musical terms the instrument we play thus determines the instrument our body must be (standing up, sitting down, bowing or blowing, hitting or pulling).[44] On the other hand, our movements are also determined by our *purpose* (to write a letter, comfort a child, go to the store, make a shirt, play a certain sort of note).

To describe body movement, then, is to describe both *what* is being done and *why* it is; to read body movements, to interpret them, is always to put them in a story. The same physical acts may be described as writing or doodling, as caressing or harassing; we refer here not to what we see but to what we infer (because of the situation, the characters, the plot). And the further complication here is that bodily movements (this is particularly obvious for musicians) depend on physical capacities, on learned competence. The body can't always do what we want it to, and what we see may mark a *failure* of purpose.

In pop terms, the most commonly learned form of musical movement is dance, and the most familiar setting for performing anxiety the dance floor. The starting question here is a simple one: what does it mean to move to music? Among performers (I'll come back to the audience shortly) we can distinguish between techniques of *interruption* and techniques of *enslavement,* between devices that signal listening to music by disrupting it, and devices that signal listening to music by being absorbed in it. In some musical genres the spontaneity of a show is indicated by the performers' mistakes, their broken strings, their false starts and ruffled endings; in others the musicians' total engagement with what they're doing is indicated by the precision of their changes, the perfection of their harmonies. Then there's the question of what musicians do when they are not playing: is their interest in their colleagues' sounds best shown by movement or stillness, by concentration or abandon? Silent singers perform their continuing stage role in various ways, but most deliberately move as musicians (rather than as listeners), grab castanets rather than go into a choreographed routine.[45]

The relationship of "listening" to music and "moving" to music is, in short, a matter of convention, as is what sort of movement to make; even a spontaneous response has to be coded as "spontaneous." The next question is when does a movement-to-music become a dance-to-music, and there are two issues here: the nature of the connection between what's heard and what's done, and the question of form, the relationship between one movement and another—how free are we to move, how do we know what movement is appropriate? The issue here is control: dancing is to walking, one might say, as singing is to talking. When dancing we subject our body movements to musical rules (we are less free than when we walk), and yet in our very self-consciousness we seem to reveal more clearly our physical sense of our selves; we are more self-expressive. As Francis Sparshott puts it, "Dance, then, is a mode of behaviour in which people put themselves rhythmically into motion in a way that transforms their sense of their own existence in a way that is at once characteristic and strongly qualified according to the dance performed."[46]

The art and ballet critic Adrian Stokes once noted that to add music to a scene is to frame it, to make the movements in it (people walking to and fro) look different, less natural. As spectators we become more aware of people's body movements (trying without thinking to relate them to a musical shape), and they look to us themselves more self-conscious. Movement to music seems more willed than movement without it; more thought is going into it—when to put one's foot down, when to pause and turn—and even when holding still one's posture now seems more consciously crafted. The analogy that comes to mind here is listening to a strange tongue: we distinguish between someone babbling and someone speaking an unknown language according not to what we hear but to what we assume about what we hear: language, unlike babble, is taken to be ruled, the words consciously chosen for their meaning. Adding music to a scene gives all the movements in it an implied intention: babble becomes speech, a walk becomes a dance, even if we don't understand it.[47]

Dance is not simply a heightened or more intense form of movement, then; rather, it is movement which *draws attention to itself,* in the very act of ceding control to the music—this is the difference between a movement that coincides with a beat and a movement that submits to it. (In the video of "Papa Don't Preach," for example, when does Madonna stop walking to the rhythm and start dancing to it?)[48] For Adrian Stokes, a balletomane, the question becomes: is a ballet dancer totally in control of her movements (all of which are decidedly unnatural, depending on years of training, skill, and self-discipline) or totally out of control of them (with *everything* she does determined by the score and the choreographer)? The dancer's technique, that which allows her body to do whatever the dance requires, is precisely that which allows her to forget about her body altogether and just think the music (the parallel with sport is again applicable here: the unnatural fitness to which a soccer player brings his body enables him to forget it, as a body, when he's playing—which no doubt explains why soccer players, like dancers, are recurrently injured: they also forget what frail things their bodies really are).

Dance, in short, is willed movement (people only dance on hot bricks by analogy), but it is also unnecessary movement, an end in itself rather than a means to another end (like walking to the store for milk or passing the ball to the inside right).[49] Dance movements are chosen for aesthetic rather than functional reasons—dancing to the store isn't the quickest way to get there, and dancing back may well mean dropping the bottle; there's an analogy here with the poetic use of language: describing the fire in sonnet form is not the most efficient way of clearing the building, even if the sonnet is still about the fire, just as dance is still about moving across a space. The anthropologist Roderyk Lange thus describes dance as "poeticised" walking—a form of movement in which we are "carried" by the music, and experience an "unusual degree of continuity" in our actions. They relate to each other now according to the logic of shape and sound rather than means and ends; again there's an obvious analogy with the "poetic" use of language, words chosen for the logic of a poem's rhythm, shape, and sound, not just to convey meaning.[50]

What makes a dance movement attractive or, to use the key word, graceful? To some extent such a judgment depends on genre conventions, but whether we're describing Margot Fonteyn or Michael Jackson, Cyd Charisse or John Travolta, Will Crooks or Siobhan Davies, the common factor seems to be ease of movement, a sense of bodies become somehow *immaterial*—as if the music flows through them without any physical hindrance at all. As Sarah Jeanne Cohen notes, "To be dramatically compelling on stage, the dancer cannot allow *involuntary* movement to distract the viewer."[51] The dancer, in other words, conceals her efforts, draws attention to the created form rather than the process of creation.

On the other hand (given the aesthetic of effort), at the populist end of dance there clearly is pleasure to be taken in virtuosity and spectacle, in high leaps and difficult turns.[52] The work that goes into these is certainly not concealed, and this is as true for Russian ballet dancers as for New York break dancers.

Sally Banes describes what happened to break dance when it became "art":

> The media hype about break dancing has changed both its form and its meaning. So to talk about break dancing you have to divide it into two stages: before and after media. Before the media turned breaking into a dazzling entertainment, it was a kind of serious game, a form of urban vernacular dance, a fusion of sports, dancing, and fighting whose performance had urgent social significance for the dancers. After media, participation in break dancing was stratified into two levels: professional and amateur. For the pros, break dancing had become a theatrical art form with a technique and vocabulary that, like ballet's, could be refined and expanded. On this level, competition took on new meaning. It was no longer a battle for control of the streets, for neighbourhood fame, or to win your opponent's "colors" (tee-shirt with crew insignia). Now cash prizes, roles in Hollywood movies, and European tours were at stake. For the amateurs, the element of competition had diminished. The appeal was a mixture of getting physically fit, tackling the challenge of breaking's intricate skills, and even becoming more like street kids, who've suddenly become stylish thanks to the meteoric vogue of hip hop.[53]

In tracing the way the meaning of break dance changed as it moved from an amateur to a professional setting, Banes raises general questions about the differences between various forms of stylized movement. What is the difference, for example, between dance and gymnastics? Answer: the different factors controlling the body's moves: music rather than equipment, choreographic convention rather than competitive rules. What makes dancing dif-

Performing Rites

ferent from ice dancing? Answer: in principle, nothing (ice dancing is mostly performed as a competitive sport, but that is not necessary to the form). But we're beginning to touch now on the aesthetic problem at the heart of dance analysis: if dance is a communicative art, what does it communicate, what is it about? Why, as Sparshott asks, should we attend to it? What, for example, do we mean by a good dancer? What are we describing? A physical skill? The dancer's ability to make us feel that she is somehow exempt from the law of gravity? Or something else—an interpretive skill, the ability to use the body to say something?[54]

In terms of physical display, there was a direct continuity between break dance as street and as theater art, but in terms of dance meaning there was an equally clear change of focus. As Banes notes, its "body symbolism" had made break dancing "an extremely powerful version of two favorite forms of street rhetoric—the taunt and the boast," but such rhetoric lost its point once staged for the art audience: the dance now represented the boast and the taunt, rather than being them.[55]

When we talk about dance we are almost always talking about movement to music.[56] The question therefore comes back to this: does a dancer, any sort of dancer, express the music, or respond to it? If, as Lange suggested, to dance is to let oneself to be carried by the music, to be moved by it (rather than by where one wants to go), then in what sense is this a personal matter? Does one have a heightened sense of oneself when one dances, or no sense of oneself at all? I don't know the answer to that question (both, I think), but one does, without a doubt, have a heightened, more intense, above all more concentrated sense *of the music.* Dancing (if not watching dancing), is, in this respect, a form of enhanced listening, which is why a good club deejay can play a club as if choreographing a dance (and why disco dancers on the floor are no more dancing apart than ballet dancers on the stage).

A question still remains, though: how do dancers know how to listen to the music, what to listen for? And clearly the answer depends on the genre. Conventions of dance performance are genre-based; they follow a combination of stylized and naturalized movements, of learned and spontaneous responses. (In my own experience, it is in learning how to dance to a music—watching what other people are doing and copying them—that we learn how best to listen to it.) And conventions also determine what the dance is "about." In classical ballet, after all, the dancer is not just dancing the music, but dancing a character, a narrative role, and Edward Cone thus distinguishes the "art dance" from the "natural dance" and the "ritual dance." But certain pop performers too (Madonna, Prince, Mick Jagger, most obviously) dance a part, dancing *to* the music but *in* character, and much vernacular dance has used mime, the dancer representing the movements of an animal, a work process, a social type.[57]

Dance is an ideological way of listening; it draws our attention (not least in its use of space and spaces) to arguments about its own meaning (think of the difference between classical, modern, and postmodern ballet, between ballroom and break dancing, between a hop and a rave). And dancing, like listening, doesn't come naturally: to dance to music is not just to move to it but to say something about it—whatever else the performer may tell us from stage, what they really think about their music is shown by how they move to it. The meaning of heavy metal is best articulated by head-banging, male bonding in futility, just as the most profound statement of what Motown meant in the twenty-fifth anniversary Motown TV show was Michael Jackson's glide across the stage in front of footage of old Jackson 5 stagecraft, a movement both exhilaratingly free and frighteningly precise.

It is somewhat ironic, then, that in self-consciously studying "performance," cultural analysts have paid far more attention to pop videos than to stage shows. There are various reasons for this: performance is taken to be a postmodern topic, pop videos are taken to be a postmodern medium, and so the two naturally go together; videos are now ever-present in the home: they're probably the way most teenagers now see most performances, and they're certainly the way most academics do; the most interesting contemporary performers (that is to say, Madonna) use music video as their performing medium, and therefore video is the source of pop's most interesting performance practices.

There's truth in all these assumptions, but there's also (as so often with postmodern theory) a willful ignorance of history: videos are analyzed as if pop stars didn't perform before there was a camera to record them (and as if pop's performing conventions weren't long ago established in both cinematic and televisual terms). The pop video is important, in other words, not because it compels musicians to perform in quite new ways (though it may sometimes do this), but in the way it necessarily draws on (and therefore brings to our attention) established performing conventions and adapts them to new technological and selling circumstances.[58]

From my perspective, then, music videos are less interesting as minifilms, as visual narratives, than as ideal types of performance, as visual frames, and the most obvious differences between video styles reflect musical rather than filmic conventions. As we've seen, different pop genres offer quite different accounts of the relationships between performer and audience, performer and song, performer and performer. These distinctions must be articulated in video: a credible heavy metal musician looks and acts quite differently than a credible country star.[59] And, just as important, a heavy metal crowd registers its pleasures quite differently than country music fans do. In framing performance for television, pop videos (like TV music shows before them) pull away from the stage (if only metaphorically) to show the auditorium as well. They reveal as much about the meaning of the music in the shots of people listening to it as in the footage of the people playing it.[60]

My conclusion from this is that videos are ideologically important not because they bring new concerns to pop performance (and certainly not as some sort of postmodern disruption of musical narratives) but because they enable musicians (or their record companies) to translate their performing ideals into televisual terms directly, without having to be mediated by the established norms of TV entertainment. However, two innovative aspects of video production are worth noting. First, video performance isn't restricted to the usual performing settings. While most videos do, in fact, set their stars front stage and in the recording studio or back stage and in the rehearsal room, they also move them out of a musical context—into the everyday (the street, the home); into the fantastic (the dream, the wilderness). And what makes such movement coherent is not the song (the closer the match between setting and lyric, the more banal the video) but the performer (whose ability to impose herself on all visual circumstances parallels the ability of the live performer to impose herself on all musical circumstances, to register the continuity between sad and happy song, rocker and ballad).

As video stars, pop performers have to play themselves. They are not acting out stories (videos are not operas). Video foregrounds the performance of music rather than the music itself. We don't take the musicians to be interpreting the song; rather, our response is to interpret the musicians. Video performers are taken to be the authors of what we see (videos are not watched as examples of either directors' or songwriters' art), which is why video was an empowering medium for female acts, whatever the sexist or "objectifying" visual elements involved.[61] Pop videos, in short, foreground performance-as-seduction and forestall performance-as-embarrassment. If nothing else (and this relates to the long history of music photography, framing the musician as pinup as well as stage star), video is now a key component in our understanding of music as erotic.

Technology and Authority

Not the voices of animals but their entrails are important to us, and the animal to which music is most indebted is not the nightingale but the sheep.

Eduard Hanslick[1]

The life of the touring blues musician, Charles Keil has observed, furnishes all the loneliness and jealousy he needs to sing the blues authentically. It is a strong extract of modern life. The recording situation is an even stronger and more representative extract. The glass booths and baffles that isolate the musician from his fellow musicians; the abstracted audience; the sense of producing an object and of mass-producing a commodity; the deconstruction of time by takes and its reconstruction by splicing—these are strong metaphors of modern life. Their mirror images in the listener's experience are solitude; the occlusion of the musician; the use of music as an object and a commodity; the collapse of a public architecture of time and the creation of a private interior design of time. Since they contradict everything that music-making once seemed to be, they are paradoxes.

Evan Eisenberg[2]

Who said that musicians are the only ones that can make music?

Hank Shocklee[3]

In its most basic definition, the technology of music simply refers to the ways in which sounds are produced and reproduced. From this perspective the history of music can be divided into three stages, each organized around a different technology of musical storage and retrieval.[4]

In the first (or "folk") stage, music is stored in the body (and in musical instruments) and can only be retrieved through performance. Music is either marked off from the everyday as ritual and ceremonial, or is so totally integrated into everyday social practices (work song, for example, or lullabies) as to be part of their meaning. In the second (or "art") stage, music is stored through notation. It can still only be retrieved in performance, but it also has now a sort of ideal or imaginary existence (against which any individual performance can be measured—and found wanting). Music becomes a potentially sacred experience; it gives us access to the transcendent (and, as in the appreciation of classical music, the musical mind is thus elevated over the musical body). In the final (or "pop" stage), music is stored on phonogram, disc, or tape and retrieved mechanically, digitally, electronically. This transforms the material experience of music: it can now be heard anywhere; it is mobile across previous barriers of time and space; it becomes a commodity, a possession. And yet ideologically—as a matter of interpretation and fantasy—the old values remain (presence, performance, intensity, event), and listening to recorded music becomes contradictory: it is at once public and private, static and dynamic, an experience of both present and past. In the world of recordings there is a new valorization of "the original." It is as if the recording of music—its closeup effect—allows us to recreate, with even greater vividness, the "art" and "folk" experiences which the recording process itself destroys.

It is clear, for example, that recording technology (particularly following electrical recording and the development of magnetic tape) allowed classical record producers to claim that their work represented the perfect (or impossible) musical object embedded in the score. Using tape splices, retakes, remixes, and so on, it became possible for a performer like Glenn Gould to set aside the usual "hazards and compromises" of concert performance, and to take to the recording studio "in a quest for perfection."[5]

Walter Legge, the pioneering British classical record producer, thus claimed,

> I was the first of what are called "producers" of records. Before I established myself and my ideas, the attitude of recording managers of all companies was "we are in the studio to record as well as we can on wax what the artists habitually do in the opera house or on the concert platform." My predecessor, Fred Gaisberg, told me: "We are out to make sound photographs of as many sides as we can get during each session." My ideas were different. It was my aim to make records that would set the standards by which public performances and the artists of the future would be judged—to leave behind a large series of examples of the best performances of my epoch.[6]

This involved not only "artificial" events in the sense of assembling performers just for the recording session, in halls and studios organized for recording-suitable acoustics, but also the creation of ideal performances from the fragments of real ones, from the assemblage of different takes and re-recordings. Records made available musical experiences which were unrealizable "live." At Decca in the 1950s and 1960s, for example, John Culshaw "demonstrated that the three-dimensional spatial illusion created by stereo could be used to sharpen dramatic focus, that varied acoustical ambience could articulate and colour individual scenes." Benjamin Britten "actually composed into [the *War Requiem*] the effects of placement and distance that Culshaw and his team had become so expert at realizing."[7]

The debate on classical music technology orchestrated by Glenn Gould in *High Fidelity Magazine* in 1966 focused on the question of the recording as a musical object: was it an event (a real or fake live performance) or a work (a score, the piece of music itself)? The resulting arguments reflected the ongoing implications of classical music ideology: on the one hand, the orchestral concert had been held up for well over a century as being, in itself, the transcendent musical experience; on the other hand, the recorded works at issue were pieces of music composed long before recording technology was available, pieces of music long familiar *as* live performance. Even in the 1960s, then, the classical music world was wary of musical perfection achieved through studio "cheating," and the suggested analogy between a much spliced or over-dubbed record and a much revised or edited manuscript (see the quote by Babbitt below) didn't quite work: we don't measure our individual experience of reading a book against even an imaginary public reading.[8] The 1960s arguments would have been different (as they were in pop and rock) if the classical works at issue hadn't already had a "live" existence quite apart from their recording. (As we'll see, there are doubts about recording technology in all musics that are ideologically committed to performance as collective *event*.)

Take the suggested elevation of the work as it "ought" to exist, as it *could* exist, above any particular performance of it. Milton Babbitt, composer:

> I can't believe that people really prefer to go to the concert hall under intellectually trying, socially trying, physically trying conditions, unable to repeat something they have missed, when they can sit home under the most comfortable and stimulating circumstances and hear it as they want to hear it. I can't imagine what would happen to literature today if one were obliged to congregate in an unpleasant hall and read novels projected on a screen.[9]

Adorno, interestingly, used a similar analogy in arguing that opera is a musical form best suited to the LP:

Shorn of phoney hoopla [the hoopla of both live stagings and radio and television opera broadcasts], the LP simultaneously frees itself from the capriciousness of fake opera festivals. It allows for the optimal presentation of music, enabling it to recapture some of the force and intensity that has been worn threadbare in the opera houses. Objectification, that is, a concentration on music as the true object of opera, may be linked to a perception that is comparable to reading, to the immersion in a text. This offers an alternative to that which opera does in the best case—and which is just what an artwork ought not do—that is: cajole the listener. The form of the gramophone record comes into its own as a form of sound figures. The ability to repeat long-playing records, as well as parts of them, fosters a familiarity which is hardly afforded by the ritual of performance. Such records allow themselves to be possessed as one previously possessed art-prints . . . LPs provide the opportunity—more perfectly than the supposedly live performances—to recreate without disturbance the temporal dimension essential to operas . . . The form of the LP makes it possible for more than a few musically engaged people to build up such a museum [of opera] for themselves. Nor need they fear that the recorded works will be neutralized in the process, as they are in opera houses. Similar to the fate that Proust ascribed to paintings in museums, these recordings awaken to a second life in the wondrous dialogue with the lonely and perceptive listeners, hibernating for purposes unknown.[10]

"Liveness," in short, whether defined in social or physiological terms, is *not* essential to musical meaning.

On the other hand, it is equally clear that to record a work is just as much to interpret it as to perform it in any other way. Glenn Gould himself defended tape-splicing in these terms: "One cannot ever splice style—one can only splice segments which relate to a conviction about style." But one can then criticize engineers for "misinterpreting" the music, for being poor "performers." Goddard Lieberson, record company executive:

I don't believe the engineer should intrude between the composer, or performer, and the listener and suddenly make you hear a flute or trumpet. I think the next step will be a regression back to the old days, with fewer microphones placed further away both to give perspective and to let the ears listen on their own. If a composer wants to write the other way, he should frankly call his piece a String

Quartet for Four Instruments and Four Microphones; that is quite a different sound than for instruments alone.[11]

The question begged here is the relationship between the "perspective" of the recording studio, that of the concert hall, and that of the living room. Even if people want the concert hall experience in their homes, the living room is a different acoustic setting, and the acoustic organization of the sounds must therefore change, even if only to have the same effect, to give "the illusion of the concert hall illusion" as RCA's Richard Mohr calls it. Gould quotes the pianist Claudio Arrau as objecting to concert hall recordings on the grounds that "stratagems . . . designed to fill acoustical and psychological requirements of the concert situation, are irritating and anti-architectural when subjected to repeated playbacks." The problem here is not just a shift of musical space (from concert hall to living room) but a change in musical time (from an experience of the unique to an experience of the repeated).[12]

And musical space-time is, as we have seen, itself an ideological construct. LeMahieu quotes a 1926 *Gramophone* review of *Adeste Fideles,* one of the first Columbia releases using electronic recording technology: "The result overwhelmed me. It was just as if the doors of my machine were a window opening on to the great hall in which the concert was held."[13] Obviously what was at critical issue here was the acoustic status of the "as if": a statement of an ideal, not an actuality. Meanwhile, from a popular cultural perspective, Philip Brophy suggests (with reference to the move from silent to talking pictures) that "sound may have set dramatic film back on a course of *theatrical mechanics* due to its reinstatement of the human voice in the narrative space."[14] We take it for granted now, that is, that the voice will dominate the film soundtrack (just as we take it for granted that the voice will dominate the song soundtrack). Films or records for which this isn't true sound "difficult" or shoddy, badly produced and badly mixed, whether deliberately or not. But, again, what's at issue isn't a "natural" sound badly recorded, but an ideological acoustic hierarchy, in which some sounds are just "naturally" more important.

Gould thus argues against live recordings as being, by their nature, "archive" recordings: they reveal in documentary fashion something about their times—how Beethoven was interpreted *then*—but they are therefore "indisputably of and for their time. They spurn that elusive time-transcending objective which is always within the realization of recorded music."[15]

While technology may liberate the music work from its performance in one way, it opens it up to new possibilities of humiliation in another. In Gould's words, "at the centre of the technological debate, then, is a new kind of listener—a listener more participant in the musical experience. The emergence of this mid-twentieth-century phenomenon is the greatest achievement of the record industry." Consumer choice means we decide what to listen to from among our records. (The gramophone, wrote Percy Scholes in 1924, "allows every man to decide for himself.") It means we decide which tracks to play and in which order. And it means we decide how loudly to play them, with what balance (left to right), what tone (treble to bass), what mix.[16]

Even in the 1960s, before digital recording and domestic equalizing devices, Goddard Lieberson was disturbed by the implications:

> I believe the listener should leave his phonograph alone; if he wants to get into the picture, let him play the piano. I would like to see a standard set with phonographs whereby even the volume could not be changed. Then you would finally have what the artist wanted. If you carried the opposite to its ultimate, you would end up with a printed piece of music to be played mechanically, with instructions to the customer to set his own tempo and dynamics; then everybody would be his own Beethoven interpreter.[17]

The folk arguments about technology and the "original" sound are different. Charles Keil, for example, argues that "in class society the media of the dominant class must be utilized for [a vernacular] style to be legitimated." In the 1920s, for example, the new media of radio and records seemed to "call forth" new forms of "ethnic" music (his examples are polka and blues), distinct American sounds that "could not be created and legitimated without being part of the new mainstream channels of communication." Polish musicians had to produce something that would still sound authentically Polish to their Polish immigrant communities *on the radio.* "The legitimating function of records and radio for blues is less clear," according to Keil, but he suggests that there is evidence that "all the best known blues artists from 1930 forward learned as much or more from records as from oral transmission." Evan Eisenberg pushes this point further with respect to jazz:

> I will argue that records not only disseminated jazz, but inseminated it—that in some ways they created what we now call jazz. It is important to remember, first of all, that numbers were often "composed" just before a recording session. As record companies did not like to pay royalties unless they had to, published tunes were avoided; but if one of the musicians came up with a tune, that came under his flat fee. So even regularly performing bands, when they recorded, often put aside their well-worn, worked-out routines and threw

together fresh ones . . . Armstrong said of Oliver, "When he started makin' records, he started bein' a writer. Ha ha ha!"[18]

In considering the relationship between technology and origin in vernacular culture, Keil himself makes two important points. First, rather than a "folk" style developing "naturally," as it were, out of sight or hearing of the media until it becomes too big or noisy to be ignored (the supposed rock 'n' roll story, for example), it actually develops *in* the soundscape mapped by the media—whether providing different pleasures to those of mainstream mass culture, or offering opportunities to local media entrepreneurs (providing "residual cultural resources" for "petty capitalists"). Noting the emergence of distinctively "rough" polka and blues styles in the 1950s, Keil asks, "Does the simultaneous opening up of the radio and record industries invite the 'down-home' blues and 'village' polkas out of the little taverns and into a redefined and more subtly mediated public space, or do these rough and ready styles rudely push themselves forward from the bottom up?"[19]

Second, Keil takes up Nietzsche's suggestion that Apollonian and Dionysian arts emerge from "the separate art worlds of *dreams* and *intoxication*." Keil suggests that in the vernacular art worlds of polka and blues, there were, indeed, two aesthetics. Rather than the recording achieving the perfection that the performance couldn't (the Glenn Gould model), the recording offered one sort of pleasure (the perfection of a form, a dream state) while live performance offered another (the pleasure of a process, risk and excitement, intoxication). Keil was originally curious about why there was so little live recording of polka and blues: was it really true, as it seemed, that these vernacular communities (unlike the classical audience) didn't want their records to represent live events?

> I suspect that the perfectionism in blues and polka recordings is an expression of people's preferences, musicians and their audiences wanting the cleanest and most sophisticated versions of their music in public space. Once norms are established, "recorded blues" and "recorded polkas" [recorded down-home blues; recorded honky-tonk-style polkas] take on a perfectible Apollonian dreamlife of their own. In polkas, for example, bands routinely record with upright string bass and a regular piano twenty years after these instruments disappeared from live performance because "that's the way polka records should sound." Many polka bands rehearse only when they have a recording session to prepare; the shared tradition of evergreen standards can sustain any band in live performances without rehearsing and through any changes in personnel.[20]

Kenneth Goldstein comes to similar conclusions from his experience as a folk record producer for the Riverside, Electra, and Folkways labels in the 1950s and 1960s: "I had to figure out what my responsibilities were to (1) the public, which is a record that is good to listen to, easy to listen to, straight through; (2) to the folklorist, an actual representation, an ethnographic record, if you will; and (3) to the singer, which is the best that he bloody well can do, which is what the singer wants to present to the world." Goldstein quickly identified primarily with the singers: "They had heard records, all of them had heard records. They didn't hear background noises on those records. That became the standard to them for what a good record was." The singers, in short, wanted the best possible sound in formal terms (Keil's perfection), and "there was never a question to me about splicing if it made the performance better."[21]

The basic point here is that in popular (unlike classical) forms, live and recorded practices are not necessarily seeking to realize the "same music" (even if people's expectations about what a band can and should do may carry over from one form into the other—one of the great pleasures of a pop concert is hearing the "hits": songs with which we have a long and sometimes profound intimacy suddenly sound both just the same and quite different). There is a sense, as Keil suggests, in which the record in popular music takes on the role of the score in art musics—as a kind of register of what the music is *ideally*—but then the music's live performance takes on its own value as a unique, audience-involving *contingent* experience: "the normative recordings intensify live performance as something extraordinary, abnormal, and magical as well."[22] And, put like that, this is obviously true for classical music too.

The arguments explored by Glenn Gould in the art music world and by Charles Keil in the folk or (his preferred term) people's music world address the same underlying question: how has musical experience been changed by recording technology? What are its aesthetic effects? It is important to note right away that the issue is not just about the transformation of music making and listening by the invention of recording—we can't simply divide the technological history of music into the periods before and after Edison.

On the one hand, we need to remember that recording is in fact an aspect of the long history of *musical instruments* (with the player piano—a much more important music machine culturally than is now remembered—acting as a kind of bridge between "productive" and "reproductive" instruments). Alan Durant notes that "with the exception of promotional and review literature, discussions [of new sound technologies] tend to be vague on matters of practical detail; they are rarely anchored in close attention to the music-making techniques they claim to be about, or to the terminology and relations of work which will define whatever new conditions of music emerge."[23] The point here is not simply that we should avoid technological determinism, but that musical technologies always describe means of sound production as well as reproduction—musicians, that is to say, are as significant for their development as consumers (even as the meaning of what it is to be a "musician" changes). Technology, in short, is a means of communication, and what people want to say has its own effects on the means they have to say it. As Durant points out, *all* musical instruments have a history "related to ideas of what they should sound like and when and how they should be played, as well as to economic and technical conditions of how they can be manufactured."[24]

On the other hand, the internal developments of recording processes themselves have been every bit as significant aesthetically as the first capture of the voice in the machine. The pursuit of "high fidelity," the best recording as the most "faithful" to the "original" sound, has thus been an increasingly misleading description of the recording process, a description rooted in the original wax processes (when the recording made, indeed, a highly imperfect reference to a performance which the listener had to imagine for herself, to reconstruct from these crackly notes).[25] Electrical recording (and amplification) broke the previously necessary relationship between the sound and the body; tape recording broke the previously necessary relationship between a musical object in space and a musical object in time. Recording perfection ceased to refer to a specific performance (a *faithful* sound) and came to refer, as we've seen, to a constructed performance (an *ideal* sound). The "original," in short, ceased to be an event and became an idea.

A number of difficult and contradictory points follow from this. Take the idea of "permanence" and history. The early ideology of recording stressed that music was now being made to last; there was much talk of subsequent generations, posterity, and so forth; performers could "speak" to future generations like writers. LeMahieu quotes Sergei Rachmaninov from 1931, "Formerly, the artist was haunted by the knowledge that with him his music must also vanish into the unknown. Yet, today, he can leave behind him a faithful reproduction of his art." In practice, though, as LeMahieu goes on to observe, the technological improvements in recording, plus the drive to high turnover and lowered production costs characteristic of mass production, meant that "old" records were soon heard as outdated, primitive, unlistenable; they broke, ceased to be produced, became rare items, of interest only to collectors.[26]

Enter the CD. Or, rather, enter digital technologies, which allow engineers to retrieve the information "packed into the grooves of waxen discs in the land before tape." Gary Giddins cites the example of a 1925 Sidney Bechet sarrusophone solo (the only one in jazz recording history): on the original record "he produced a clamorous rumble suggesting the kind of internal combustion caused by bad diet"; on the remastered digital version "you can hear the staccato tonguing and the ebullient control; the overall impression, once of frenzy, is now of audacious wit."[27]

Here the "original" sound was in the "original" recording, but was inaudible, because of the surface noises and crackles, because no equipment could get at it. Now the surface noise can be eliminated; now the information can be retrieved. This is, though, still to assume that we can distinguish between the original sound and its recording. In fact, practically speaking, that sound only existed—only exists—as a recording: the distinction between the noise that is necessary and noise that is unnecessary to an old recorded performance is an aesthetic as well as a technical judgment. Remastered records, whether from the jazz or the classical back catalogue, may still hold up the ideal of some historical "live" performance, but in fact they are providing something new: a performance reconstructed according to today's sound values. David Schiff has thus rightly observed that "analog recordings of avant-garde pieces sound 'older' than digital recordings of early music," while Keith Johnson, one of America's leading digital audio engineers, explains why his job is not just technical:

> If I've done my job, there's what I call a "thereness." You really have that sense like the performer is *there;* there's a human element. And there's something magical about that when it really works.
>
> Once I've gone through the digital system, if everything is working right in the digits, the most obvious thing that happens right away is that the human element seems to be more distant. The artist doesn't seem to be quite as present, and the recording has become kind of cold and hard and analytical on the digital playback. It'll be very quiet, it'll be very pure, it'll have a very low distortion, it'll be very clean—it'll have those features—but in a way that's an awfully high price to pay for silence. The analytical character—what I call a dull, brittle character—in my mind takes away more than I would like to have taken away.[28]

The question is who now has the power to decide what the original performance sounded like. As Johnson makes clear, the sound judgment that determines what we hear on such CDs is that of neither the original musicians nor the original studio producer/engineer but of the contemporary remaster.[29] The "original" sound that is being revealed in such cases is certainly not that, whatever else it may be.

Technology and Authority

Whatever the complications of music's recording history, we can, I think, reach some general conclusions about its social effects. First, music is now *everywhere* (an effect still best symbolized, perhaps, by soldiers' use of portable gramophones to play the latest metropolitan hits at the front in the First World War). Music no longer needs to be framed by a special place or time (it is, in this respect, no longer necessarily an event). It increasingly moves, one might say, from foreground to background. As Glenn Gould puts it, recordings do not depend, like concerts, "upon the mood of a special occasion." They are suitable as background, and, as such, music can now draw upon "an incredible range of stylistic reference," sounds which have a new validity precisely because they are out of context, "unobtrusive." Most commentators take this as music's loss of power—the more it's heard, the less it means. Background music has no sense of history or authority; it is anonymous, artificial, electronically enhanced, and so forth. It encourages "regressive" hearing in Adorno's terms—"alienated, narcotized listening"; listening that is, in Joseph Horowitz's words, "mentally supine."[30]

Gould disagreed:

> Those who see in background music a sinister fulfilment of the Orwellian environment control assume that it is capable of enlisting all who are exposed to it as proponents of its own vast cliché. But this is precisely the point! Because it can infiltrate our lives from so many different angles, the cliché residue of all the idioms employed in background becomes an intuitive part of our musical vocabulary. Consequently, in order to gain our attention any *musical* experience must be of a quite exceptional nature. And, meanwhile, through this ingenious glossary, the listener achieves a direct associative experience of the post-Renaissance vocabulary, something that not even the most inventive music appreciation course would be able to afford him.[31]

There is, in fact, less and less sense of music being "appropriate" to certain times and places (except in occasional tones of outrage—most noisily expressed, in my experience, by European tourists surrounded by blaring local radios in the foothills of the Himalayas). At the same time music has become entirely mobile: it can follow us around the house, from living room to kitchen and bathroom; on journeys, as "in car entertainment" and "the walkman effect"; across national and political boundaries; in and out of love and work and sickness.

The second aspect of this is the sheer *quantity* of music that is now around—the same work, the same event, the same performance, is endlessly repeatable, it is never lost; and music from all sources, from a hundred years ago, from a hundred thousand miles away, is equally available. The "past" of music is endless re-experienced in its presence; the most distant or strange music is heard in our most familiar surroundings. Simply in its accumulation music ceases to be special. It can no longer be defined against the everyday as something unusual; music *is* now the everyday (and silence becomes the mark of the special moment: a minute's silence to observe death; the silence in a film which accompanies the most intense tension or ecstasy).

A third point is that the musical experience has been *individualized*. Music is no longer a necessarily social or collective affair materially (though it may be in the imagination). There seems to be a long-term trend here: the street and concert hall piano of the mid-nineteenth century giving way to the domestic piano of the late nineteenth century which, in turn, gave way to the living room record player and radio, to the bedroom transistor and Dancette, to the boombox, Walkman, and Discman. One aspect of this is obviously the commodity effect: we can now possess music as obsessively, as madly, as music once possessed us. On the one hand, we have the collector (the collector as traveler and anthropologist, gathering up other people's music; the collector as archivist, tracing lineage, genealogies, catalogue numbers; the collector as investor, in pursuit of the odd, the rare, the first pressing—exchange value as use value).[32] On the other hand, we have what one might call the domestic stage manager: we can now decide for ourselves when and where to hear music, which music to hear, which sounds go together, how sounds will sound.

Musical taste, in short, is now intimately tied into personal identity; we express ourselves through our deployment of other people's music. And in this respect music is more like clothes than any other art form—not just in the sense of the significance of fashion, but also in the sense that the music we "wear" is as much shaped by our own desires, our own purposes, our own bodies, as by the intentions or bodies or desires of the people who first made it. Koestenbaum notes that the early phonograph was sold as "a kind of confessional" or as a mirror reflecting "your soul—and what is hidden deep within it." Eisenberg quotes his friend Nina: "'When I play a record,' she once told me, 'it's as though someone else were expressing my feelings. When I play the piano, it's as though I were expressing someone else's feelings.'"[33] Public sounds are thus brought into private situations and given new meanings: the domestic interior becomes a vaudeville stage, the vaudeville stage a domestic interior.

This means, in turn, a new dialectic in music: absence of performer/presence of performer (absence of audience/presence of audience) as against the classical, score-based dialectic of absence of composer (in the performance)/presence of composer (in the notes). Dave Laing reminds us how peculiar it first seemed to listen to "a voice without a face," and Adorno concluded that "what the gramophone listener actually wants to hear is himself, and the artist merely offers him a substitute for the sounding image of his own person which he would like to safeguard as a possession. The only reason that he accords the record such value is because he himself could also be just as well preserved. Most of the time records are virtual photographs of their owners, flattering photographs—ideologies."[34]

One question raised here concerns the relationship of visual and aural pleasures. Adorno argued in 1928 that

> male voices can be reproduced better than female voices. The female voice easily sounds shrill—but not because the gramophone is incapable of conveying high tones, as is demonstrated by its adequate reproduction of the flute. Rather, in order to become unfettered, the female voice requires the physical appearance of the body that carries it. But it is just this body that the gramophone eliminates, thereby giving every female voice a sound that is needy and incomplete. Only there where the body itself resonates, where the self to which the gramophone refers is identical with its sound, only there does the gramophone have its legitimate realm of validity: thus Caruso's uncontested dominance. Wherever sound is separated from the body—as with instruments—or wherever it requires the body as a complement—as is the case with the female voice—gramophonic reproduction becomes problematic.[35]

This is suggestive, if wrong—even as Adorno was writing, American female singers like Bessie Smith and Ethel Waters were making records on which they hardly sounded "needy and incomplete," and John Corbett has more recently suggested that in recording culture the look (or body) of the performer is replaced by the look of the record and record-playing equipment itself. ("For it is the lack of the visual, endemic to recorded sound, that initiates desire in relation to the popular music object.") We listen by way of the treasured record jacket, in a form of "fetishistic audiophilia" (the hi-fi freak), or as collectors with our cherished objects, those slithers of plastic themselves.[36]

On the other hand, as Philip Brophy points out, technology has also transformed the sound of *live* musical performance and changed audiences' sense of themselves in that sound. If, in classical music, the concert and the record are distinctive acoustic events (the problem is the relationship between them), the rock aesthetic, at least, is as much based on the technology of concert amplification as on studio equipment. "Live" rock music has thus become music that is super-live! "Electrical amplification," in Brophy's words, "is integral to the cultural and social growth of Rock. It changed not only the sound of instruments but also the scale of the live event which contained them, thereby determining the nature of the audience experience." For Brophy, the audience was thus amplified every bit as much as the musicians: "The guitar 'feedback' of the latter 60s *symbolizes* a distortion of audience 'feedback' pre-Beatles: both deal with an overload in the producer/production/product chain . . . If noise is essentially an overload of sounds, then Rock truly is noisy. In effect, the sound of its live concert—produced by audience-performer feedback and amplified electric instruments—is the *noise* of spectacle; the *noise* of communicated signals and audible responses."[37]

Brophy thus traces the role of the live rock recording in training consumers "how to become listeners and how to recognise themselves in the recordings," which were, in effect, recordings of their own performances (not those of the musicians, who might just as well be recorded in the studio). The record becomes the ideal performance in terms of its ideal staging—"the fusion of the best performance with the best response"—and if the best performance can be faked by the tape splicer, so can the best staging be faked by the digital engineer:

> Today, record production still speaks the essential technical dialect of digital delay and digital reverb: the two seminal components in creating space, location, perspective and dimension in sound in *post-production*. In effect, this is like a Frankenstein experiment in reviving the dead (with—surprise—electricity) . . . The void space of the studio is thus reconstructed through the *effecting* of sounds, making them occur in phantom spaces which do not exist within the physical confines of the actual studio.[38]

As Brophy suggests, "the sound of a space" thus becomes "more desirable and more effective than an actual space," and, one might add, following Adorno, that its desirability lies in the sense that this is *our* sound, the sound of the listener—the audience—in that space. "You are there!"

From another perspective one could add, finally, that we also have a new socio-technological form of music, *public records*: musical events, social gatherings, discos, and clubs in which sounds on disc are the entertainment.[39] Here, whether in terms of volume, spectacle, sociability, or emotional intensity, the private fantasies of record listening are, in a sense, enacted, felt *for real.* Dancing in public—listening in public—thus seems to be *more* expressive of how we feel about our music, more truthful, than dancing, listening, alone.[40]

From the listener's perspective, technology has clearly affected not just where and when and how we listen to music, but also what we hear. For a start, we now hear music in much more detail than ever before. This is not just a matter of sound quality (the elimination of extraneous noises; the "closeness" of sounds through headphones and speakers contrasted with the distant acoustic tones heard at the back of a hall), but also because we can now stop sounds, listen to them again and again, break them up into parts for analysis. In popular musical terms, this has meant, in particular, concentration on the "personal" touches of specific performers; music is heard in new ways as expressive of personality. Star quality in music, as we've seen, is thus a perception of intimacy. And the point here is not just that details of sounds lost in live settings, imperceptible in the passing of a musical event, become available through a new sort of technological attention (just as a TV playback and slow motion enable us to see the detail of a goal which is otherwise experienced only as a blur and a desperately rationalizing memory) but also that such sounds were heard in the twentieth century *for the first time*—as the pioneering recording engineer Fred Gaisberg suggested, recording revealed "tones hitheto mute to us."[41]

Similarly, amplification has enabled us to hear the detail of loud sound in quite new ways, and if the distinction between music and noise depends on our ears being able to find order in chaos, then technology, in allowing us to attend to previously indistinguishable sonic detail, has greatly expanded our sense of what music is and can be—at high as well as low volume. This is, perhaps, most obvious in popular music in the habit of listening, as it were, from the bottom. As Philip Brophy notes:

> The lineage of Caribbean music is founded on bass: from ska (the Caribbean distortion of East Coast R'n'B) to reggae (the latter being the first major instance of subsonic bass intruding upon white rock's favoured mid-range aural spectrum) to black disco (which continental Europe technologically colonized into Eurodisco and sold back to white America) to the eventual bass explosion in Eighties' hip hop. This explosion is regional: booming drum machines, pounding disco bass drums, cheesy subsonic synthesizer bass lines and creative distortions of bottom-end effects travelled from the East Coast (the New

York state of electro, rap, hip hop, Latin hip hop) throughout the nation (Chicago house and acid, Detroit techno, Miami bass) and over to the West Coast (LA hard core rap and jack-beat swing). And on it will go.[42]

At the same time we also now take for granted a kind of musical sonic *purity.* This relates to the history of recording technology referred to earlier, to the audio-engineer's drive to get rid of "extraneous" sounds, the hiss and crackle of the recording itself, the rumbles and pop of amplification. The implication is that we can now get to the kernel of the "musical sound" itself—the sound that no one before recording technology had ever actually heard (however well designed the room, however well behaved the audience, a live concert is always awash with small noises, small movements, of the people, of the building).[43]

The ideology of musical "purity" is what links the digital sound mixer to the piano tuner, and I don't need to repeat the points I've already made about the resulting confusion between musician and technician, between aesthetic and engineering sound decisions. What is clear is that Glenn Gould's championing of the perfect recording over the imperfect live performance is misleading insofar as it implies that the "perfection" of the record is a strictly musical matter. Joseph Horowitz points out that as classical recordings moved away from the simulation of live performances, so the resulting "good" sound reflected as much a technological or engineering ideal as the determination now to realize the *composer's* best intentions. Recordings "were engineered and edited to ensure clarity, precision, and brilliance," and these values began to be pursued by conductors like Toscanini (using live performance to sell the recorded sound) in the concert hall too. We ended up, in Eduard Steuermann's words, with "the barbarism of perfection."[44]

Making music has always involved not just the planning of notes on paper, but also the realization of those notes as sounds *in particular settings,* particular aural spaces. And if a musical score is obviously an unfinished object, its realization dependent on specific sound judgments made in specific sound settings (judgments by a conductor or record producer considering the audio-dynamics of the performing space), then so is the pop record. The music it stores is also only realized in specific settings—a radio transmission, a dance club, one's living room. It will sound different accordingly, whether as determined by a choice of record company mixes or as the listener shifts volume and tone controls.[45]

Music thus has a new effect on space. The recording studio (note the term—referring not just to the painter's *atelier* but also, as Keir Keightley puts it, to "a carpeted den") was a new musical location, and the record listener was given a new musical place: we're now somehow (thanks to the use of reverb, delay, and all the other engineering tricks) *in* the music, not constrained by the concert hall model of listening *at* it.[46] Whatever the familiar ideology of "active" (concert) listening and "passive" (home) listening, acoustically it is, in fact, as record listeners that we seem to be musical participants.[47]

Jonathan Tankel argues that the remix engineer creates a new work in reconceptualizing a record's "sonic atmosphere." This is a more drastic act than rearranging an existing tune because it changes the essence of what we hear—a remix is, in this respect, akin to a jazz player's improvisation on a standard tune: "Remixing *is* recoding, the reanimation of familiar music by the creation of new sonic textures for different sonic contexts . . . The remix recording creates a new artifact from the schemata of previously recorded music. It is *prima facie* evidence of Benjamin's contention that to 'an ever greater degree the work of art reproduced becomes the work of art designed for reproducibility.'"[48]

We certainly do now hear music as a *fragmented* and *unstable* object. The earliest phonographs had varying and unreliable speeds (had to be wound up, were quickly wound down); music became something to which things happened (rather than just being in itself the happening). As we have taken power over music on records, as they have become ubiquitous (every entrepreneur using music for her own ends), so the musical work has ceased to command respectful, structural, attention. All music is more often heard now in fragments than completely; we hear slices of Beatles songs and Bach cantatas, quotes from jazz and blues. Such fragmentary listening may have as much to do with—may be particularly suited to—industrialization and urbanization as with recording technology as such. Michael Ondaatje imagines Buddy Bolden reminiscing as follows:

> When I played parades we would be going down Canal Street and at each intersection people would hear just the fragments I happened to be playing and it would fade as I went further down Canal. They would not be there to hear the end phrases . . . I wanted them to be able to come in where they pleased and leave when they pleased and somehow hear the germs of the start and all the possible endings at whatever point in the music I had reached *then*. Like your radio without the beginnings or endings. The right ending is an open door

you can't see too far out of. It can mean exactly the opposite of what you are thinking.[49]

If listening to a piece of music from beginning to end is these days unusual, the exception rather than the rule, this presumably has some effect on our sense of musical progression. At the same time, because *all* our experiences of time are now fragmented and multilinear, fragmented music is also realistic music (this is Ondaatje's point); it represents experience grasped in moments. One aspect of this is, in Hosokawa's words, to direct "the listener's attention to 'sound,'" what is heard immediately, rather than to "music," notes as they make sense in a structure. "Technology," Kramer concludes, "has liberated listeners from the completeness of musical form." (Just as film has liberated us from the completeness of visual form.) Composers, knowing now that their music will be repeated on record and radio, no longer have to build "repeatability" into the score, into each performance. In the popular music aesthetic, at least, Hosokawa suggests, "perception of sound is more important than consideration of the 'composition' as an entity in and of itself." Hence the rise in the 1980s of popular music made up of fragments, of samples: "Such quoting establishes a connection that builds authenticity, a kind of italicizing that identifies the author, *by means of authorship, as it undoes it.*"[50]

The commonsense (Romantic) belief that recording technology has systematically undermined the authority of the composer is thus more problematic than it may at first seem. Consider these remarks by Milton Babbitt:

Somebody will ask those of us who compose with the aid of computers: "So you make all these decisions for the computer or the electronic medium, but wouldn't you like to have a performer who makes certain other decisions?" Many composers don't mind collaborating with the performer with regards to decisions of tempo, or rhythm, or dynamics, or timbre, but ask them if they would allow the performer to make decisions with regard to pitch and the answer will be "Pitches you don't change." Some of us feel the same way in regard to the other musical aspects that are traditionally considered secondary, but which we consider fundamental. As for the future of electronic music, it seems quite obvious to me that its unique resources guarantee its use, because it has shifted the boundaries of music away from the limitations of the acoustical instrument, or the performer's coordinating capacities, to the almost infinite limitations of the electronic instrument. The new limitations are the human ones of perception.[51]

There seem to be three issues here. First, the question of musical *origins*. Today all sounds from all sources can be relatively easily taken apart (through digital sampling) and reassembled; none of them therefore any longer carries any necessary realist or expressive weight (which becomes, instead, an ideological judgment). All sounds, that is, carry an equal value as signs; there is a flattening out of even the difference between human and non-human sounds; natural and unnatural noise; intended and found sounds; music and noise. No sound, in short, can any longer guarantee truth (no folk sound, no proletarian sound, no black sound).[52] However, one can also interpret this both as a new form of imitative realism (as accurately reflecting the noise of the contemporary street) and as a new opportunity for compositional freedom (Babbitt's point) as all physical constraints on sound making are removed.

Second, the question of the musical *author*. What's startling here is that just as it seems that a "self" can no longer possibly be expressed in the ever more socially and technically complex processes of pop production, so artistic authority is rediscovered—in the person of the producer, the engineer, the image maker, the deejay. We're not only desperate but still successful in finding voices in the machine—hence, for example, the academic idolization of Madonna.[53]

Third, the question of the musical *object*. There's no doubt here that the fetishization of the recording has meant the demystification of the work. Even in classical music, the accumulation of versions (now available, thanks to CD, for continuous historical comparison) has led to what I'll call *interpretive relativism*: everyone can hear that the readings of scores change, that the "ideal" performance is variable (old recordings are odd or incomplete or just plain "wrong" in the same way as old readings of literature or art). Our sense of the "timelessness" of great music has thus become the belief (eagerly fostered by the music industry) that it must be continually updated.[54]

In popular music, where the focus is on the work-as-performance rather than the work-as-score, the recording effect that interests me is different. (The CD here has, in fact, confirmed the "timelessness" of classic jazz and rock tracks.) Digital storage has reinforced the feeling both that music is never finished (with every cut the starting point for a variety of mixes) and that it is never really *integrated*—we are always aware of the parts that make up the (temporary) whole.[55] Multi-track recording, that is to say, has had a long-term aesthetic effect: we now hear (and value) music as layered; we are aware of the contingency of the decision that put this sound here, brought this instrument forward there. It's as if we always listen to the music *being assembled,* and the paradox is that pop listeners thus have a clearer sense than classical listeners of music in composition (music as it is conceived, that is, by a composer).

For Milton Babbitt the promise of technology was to give the composer complete control of his composition even through the contingencies of its performance. Technology offered a solution to longstanding problems of musical power and authority. But what's clear from a popular music perspective is that technology doesn't so much resolve the politics of musical meaning as change the context—the sense of musical time and space—in which the traditional arguments take place, the arguments *about* the transcendent and the contingent, about the freedom of artistic intention, the freedom of listener response. If we should resist easy arguments about technological determinism (the machines making meaning), so we should resist equally eager arguments about technological fertility (everything now possible). As Chris Cutler has long argued, even if musical technology in the abstract did make new—"liberated"—ways of composing and performing and listening possible, it doesn't work in the abstract, but as a commodity force, a matter of equipment to be bought and sold, and there are powerful interests (the electronics industry) working to ensure that whatever else may happen to music it remains a source of profit.[56] The detailed effects of technology may be unpredictable (nothing is used in the way the industry expected), but the general trend is undeniably conservative. What is most startling about the history of twentieth-century sounds is not how much recording technology has changed music, but how little it has. If music's meanings have changed, those changes have taken place within the framework of an old, old debate about what musical meaning can be.

Why Music Matters

The Meaning of Music

But much of Schumann and Chopin, saving some of the fine tumultuous pieces, should be laid aside for a while. Of Wagner, too, there is much question. Indeed, the morbidity, the servile melancholy, the frenetic sexuality, the day-dreaming flight from reality that permeates much of the music of the nineteenth century cannot be regarded as fit for a class with a revolutionary task before it.

Charles Seeger[1]

With its major tonality and foreshortened melodic range, "Tom Dooley" is a kind of sober, almost a pious duty, like planting a tree. With the simplicity of a bugle call, its tune climbs sadly in four nearly identical phrases from a grave fifth below the tonic to a weary second or third above it, where it pauses to rest. Lingering in one of the two chords, tonic or dominant, that resignedly bear away the stanza.

Robert Cantwell[2]

All truly meaningful music is a swansong.

Friedrich Nietzsche[3]

My argument in this book rests on a simple enough premise. As a sociologist I'm happy to assume that "meaning" can only be defined institutionally: the term describes not simply discursive conventions—agreements to agree—but regulated forms of social behavior. Arthur Danto's philosophical point—"To see something as art requires something the eye cannot decry—an atmosphere of artistic theory, a knowledge of the history of art: an artworld"—is the guiding principle of the sociology of culture too.[4]

To grasp the meaning of a piece of music is to hear something not simply present to the ear. It is to understand a musical culture, to have "a scheme of interpretation." For sounds to be music we need to know how to hear them; we need "knowledge not just of musical forms but also of rules of behaviour in musical settings."[5] The "meaning" of music describes, in short, not just an interpretive but a social process: musical meaning is not inherent (however "ambiguously") in the text. As Lucy Green argues persuasively, "Both experience of the music and the music's meanings themselves change complexly in relation to the style-competence of the [listener], and to the social situations in which they occur . . . music can never be played or heard outside a situation, and every situation will affect the music's meaning."[6]

John Cage's suggestion that "the wisest thing to do is to open one's ears immediately and hear a sound suddenly before one's thinking has a chance to turn it into something logical, abstract, or symbolical" is therefore futile: to adopt such a listening position is, in itself, a social gesture; what we hear will therefore already be meaningful.[7] Ola Stockfelt has shown how the meanings of musical works (Mozart's Symphony No. 40 is his example) change as they enter new "listening situations," as listeners apply different "modes of listening," appropriate for concert hall, walkman, car, cinema, café, sports contest, or airplane waiting to take off. The "appropriate" here is partly a social matter:

> For example, to dance during a symphony concert (which is practically impossible because of the fixed seats, etc.) is to commit a *gaffe*, a breach of social convention, even if one is hearing Viennese waltzes or other music originally meant to be listened to in connection with dancing. It is likewise inappropriate to sink into prolonged intramusical contemplation when one is squeezed into a 7–11 type convenience store.[8]

But it's also partly an ideological matter. Even if nowadays "one can listen to march music in the bathtub and salon music in the mountains," nevertheless specific musical styles are still "implicitly bound to specific environments and specific relationships between the performer and the listener," and it is not true to say that "all music has an equal relation to each different environment." A rave track on the BBC Radio 1 breakfast show still means something different from the rock ballads played around it, still refers to an *ideal* listening situation, still constructs one sort of musical space even as it is being heard in another one altogether.[9]

Once fantasy enters the picture the sociological model gets complicated. One can (I do) love rave music without ever having been to a rave, and this changes the argument I've been making. If the standard sociological position is that (real) social processes determine what music means, now the suggestion is that a musical experience "means" by defining (imagined) social processes. I'll discuss this further in the final chapter. Here I want to focus on one issue, the question of value. Sociological orthodoxy, following Bourdieu, is that "aesthetic" listening is itself a socially determined process, describes a particular sort of listening behavior in a particular sort of listening situation, means the right sort of listeners pursuing the right sort of listening aims. Rose Subotnik notes, for example, that her students hear the "Soldiers' March" from Stravinsky's *Histoire du Soldat* as better than Sousa's "Washington Post March" not because they like it any better (nor because they know what the pieces are), but because the Stravinsky piece signals "art music" and is therefore listened to in a specific way, with an ear for complexity, authority, and so forth.[10]

As Kyle Gann puts it,

> You like Milton Babbitt's music? It's probably not so much because you can hear the way he juggles hexachords as the fact that 12-tone music expresses the "serious-intellectual" values of the scientific/academic community you identify with . . . I like new music, successful or not, that tries things never heard before; I want to think of myself as independent, as having escaped the inauthenticity of mass consciousness.[11]

The suggestion here is that the conventional high cultural way of evaluating what one hears is a way of declaring who one is: a listener of distinction. And it is then a short step (the step Bourdieu takes) to explaining the meaning of music entirely in terms of its social function, its organization of taste. I have two problems with this position. First, it seems to deny (or ignore) the difference between the musical experience and other sorts of cultural processes. Music may, indeed, be used (or articulated) in functional terms, but that does not account for the undeniable ways in which it moves us, does not explain the ways in which to listen to music is, indeed, to be taken *out* of oneself (and one's society). Second, the argument about taste may undermine high culture's eternal categories, but it preserves high/low cultural difference: the implication is that the popular audience is unconcerned with aesthetic evaluation, with individual distinction. This is nonsense—all cultural life involves the constant activity of judging and differentiating—but, further, it is to miss the point that the peculiarity of the musical experience—its specialness as a form of sociability—makes it necessarily an aesthetic matter. In John Blacking's words, "Music is essentially about aesthetic experiences and the creative expression of individual human beings in community, about the sharing of feelings and ideas."[12]

For popular music listeners just as much as for classical music listeners, "good music" describes something unusual, unusual because it cannot easily be explained away in terms of everyday social practice, as a matter of class or commerce or functional routine. Which is why, when popular musical values are articulated, they are so often phrased in art musical terms (terms devised specifically to account for the meaning of music as music). This is Alec Wilder, for instance, waxing Romantic: "Arlen, like Rodgers, reveals in his melodies a deep rooted need to express himself. In both men there is a very personal, almost private approach to creation, rather than the professional capacity to contrive and produce reasonable facsimiles of the real thing."[13] And this is Keir Keightley expanding the boundaries of the pop musical text by drawing on any number of high critical conventions: "The 'thrilling sadness' mentioned above is produced in/by the song [The Beach Boys' "All Summer Long"] at a number of levels: the passing shift from major to minor, the falling movement of the group and the resistance and alienation of the falsetto, the situation of the lyric in traditions of summer songs concerned with passing seasons and moments of loss, the fragmentary construction of an imaginary montage, as well as other, less easily specified elements. The construction of both the lyric and the album cover in particular may be situated with traditions of criticism which see melancholy and loss as associated with fragments."[14]

This is the sociological paradox: musical experience is socially produced as something special; the importance of music is therefore taken to be that its meaning is not socially produced, is somehow "in the music." Pop fans too have an aesthetic mode of listening. Pop fans too believe that music derives its value "from its inner and private soul."[15]

It is not surprising, then, that the aesthetic theory developed in art music to distinguish what real musicians (and listeners) do from the market exchanges between pop's producers and consumers should provide the terms (and arguments) in which popular music becomes meaningful too. The error in high cultural attitudes toward low music is the condescending assumption that popular listening describes a quite different sort of experience. In his impeccably liberal humanist *Music and the Mind*, for example, Anthony Storr, while constantly stressing that Western art music is just one form of expression among many others "equally valid," also casually assumes that "much popular music today" is "trivial" and "monotonous," popular only because its listeners are "unsophisticated."[16] Or take this passage from Roger Scruton: "Consider modern pop music, and compare it with New Orleans Jazz and ragtime, and then with the folk music, African and American, from which both derive; you will see therein a tragic history of decline. Aggression and fragmentation have come in place of comfort and community."[17]

I find myself bristling at this not because of the aesthetic judgment involved (I'd happily argue for the value of aggression and fragmentation in art, certainly as against comfort—and, given his brand of conservatism, "community" means something rather different to Scruton than it does to me), but because of Scruton's obvious ignorance of the musics mentioned. He presumes that a high theorist can talk about the meaning of low music without listening to it, without liking it, without needing to know anything much about it at all. But then the concept of expertise, the relationship of knowledge and pleasure, is unclear in all musical worlds. As Nicholas Cook puts it, "What I find perplexing, and stimulating, about music is the way in which people—most people—can gain intense enjoyment from it even though they know little or nothing about it in technical terms."[18]

And so I find myself bristling equally when I read this:

> It is, for example, extremely important to hear Led Zeppelin's "The Crunge" (from *Houses of the Holy*) not only as a more-sophisticated-than-usual instance of heavy metal, but also as a sarcastic commentary on James Brown's more involuted performances. This is not simply collateral knowledge about the piece; it involves hearing certain modulations and syncopations in special ways. One who does not hear this has yet to understand the piece totally.[19]

Is such understanding necessary? This question has perplexed me ever since I became a rock critic and realized that I had no hesitation about pronouncing authoritatively on new releases and live performances while, formally, I could offer no convincing theoretical account of musical value at all. My questions in this book reflect personal as well as sociological curiosity: how do people come to value and assess particular sounds and styles and stars? How does music give pleasure (or pain)? In what terms do I make sense of my musical experiences? Where do these terms come from? What *is* musical understanding? "To understand music," suggests Peter Kivy, "seems in significant part to be able to describe it," and for the rest of this chapter I want to consider the problems of such description.[20]

In the eighteenth century argument about musical meaning focused on the relative value of instrumental and vocal or operatic works. The problem of instrumental music lay in its apparent inadequacy as a means of "imitation":

> Instrumental Music, though it may, no doubt, be considered in some respects as an imitative art, is certainly less so than any other which merits that appellation; it can imitate but a few objects, and in even those so imperfectly, that without the accompaniment of some other

art, its imitation is scarce ever intelligible: imitation is by no means essential to it, and the principle effects which it is capable of producing arise from powers altogether different from those of imitation.[21]

And most commentators assumed that instrumental music was therefore inferior to music accompanied by words or gestures.[22] It took the Romantic move—from theories of imitation to theories of expression—to reverse this judgment. In the nineteenth century instrumental music came to be valued above vocal music for its ability to release feeling "from the confinements of prosaic everyday reality," that is, from its attachment to particular objects or states.[23] By 1828, in his *Lectures on Music,* Hans Georg Nageli was celebrating instrumental music *because* it neither represents nor imitates. Music, he suggested, has no content but is simply "a being at play," and it is this which enables it to move the listener, to invoke "indefinite and ineffable feelings": "The soul hovers, carried along by this play of forms, in the whole immeasurable realm of emotions, now ebbing, now flowing up and down, plunging with the gently echoing breath of tones to the utmost depths of the heart and then soaring again with the rising impetus of tones to supreme feelings of bliss."[24]

For Adam Smith, writing fifty years earlier, such an appreciation of music necessarily involved intellectual understanding: we don't so much feel music's emotional meaning as admire its emotional shape.[25] Even when we contemplate a painting, he suggests, something clearly representational, we don't simply see what's represented; rather, we see how the picture differs from its object while suggesting it. We marvel, that is, at the skill with which one thing has been made to represent another. In contemplating instrumental music, which is not representational, we marvel at its order and method—and thus at the order and method of the mind itself: "Whatever we feel from instrumental music is an original and not a sympathetic feeling: it is our own gaiety, sedateness or melancholy; not the reflected disposition of another person."[26]

As Kevin Barry shows, Adam Smith here followed other eighteenth-century philosophers in valuing music for those qualities that discredited it to the empiricists—its obscurity, instability, and incompleteness. Because music is experienced temporally, what we perceive is always in a state of becoming. For James Usher this was why music, rather than painting, is sublime. The aesthetic experience is constituted by desire, a state of mind in which an object is known by its absence, in which the contemplation of perfection is not tainted by the flaws of its material presence. Music expresses this contemplative principle best. Its significance depends on absence, on sound already gone or yet to come; its "perfection" is always a matter of memory and anticipation.[27]

Adam Smith himself was less interested in the sublime than in the beautiful. The value of instrumental music (like the value of art in general) lay for him in its integration of the intellectual and the sensual. If music was the highest form of art, this was because it offered the most complete experience of the harmony of thought and feeling. The difference between the "nobler works of Statuary and Painting and the phenomenon of Nature," Smith wrote, is that the former "carry, as it were, their own explication along with them, and demonstrate, even to the eye, the way and manner in which they are produced."[28] Similarly,

> a well composed concerto can, without suggesting any other object, either by imitation or otherwise, occupy, and as it were fill up, completely the whole capacity of the mind, so as to leave no part of its attention vacant for thinking of anything else. In the contemplation of that immense variety of agreeable and melodious sounds, arranged and digested, both in their coincidence and in their succession, into so complete and regular a system, the mind in reality enjoys not only a very great sensual, but a very high intellectual pleasure, not unlike that which it derives from the contemplation of a great system in any other science.[29]

Smith is anticipating here one strand of Romantic thought—the belief in "absolute music." "Must not purely instrumental music create its own text?" asked Friedrich von Schlegel in 1798. "And is not its theme developed, confirmed, varied and contrasted, just as is the object of a sequence of philosophical speculation?" Or, as Jules Combarieu put it a hundred years later, music "is the art of thinking in sounds."[30]

In her study of the rise to dominance of the nineteenth-century concept of the "musical work," Lydia Goehr suggests that Adam Smith's writings "mark a transitory phase."[31] The transition was from the analysis of music as rhetoric to the analysis of music as art. Central to this change in perception were two metaphorical shifts. First, music began to be described in terms of space rather than time. Second, aesthetic attention moved from the listening subject to the musical object. By 1892 Edward Baxter Perry was writing in *Music* that "silence is to music what light is to painting—the first absolutely essential condition, upon which all its effects and impressions depend . . . The slightest noise, even involuntarily produced . . . blurs the outline of the work, like a shadow falling across a picture."[32]

Both of these changes meant the clear elevation of the intellectual over the sensual response. For Eduard Hanslick, the most influential champion of the new approach, "aesthetic value in music" meant "experiencing a piece of music as a kind of beautiful object through 'the voluntary and pure act of contemplation which alone is the true and artistic method of listening.'"[33] Hanslick argued—and this took him beyond Smith's position—that the value of music lay in the formal qualities of the work itself, and not in the quality of the listener's experience. Musical appreciation is thus a matter of reason (or, in Hanslick's terms, science); it means knowing what to listen to, rather than how to feel about it. In his words, "Certainly with regard to beauty, imagining is not mere contemplating, but contemplating with active understanding, i.e. conceiving and judging."[34]

This argument has had two obvious consequences. First, it has moralized the musical experience: it is now customary to distinguish "good" and "bad" listeners; musicology in the nineteenth century became a study not of how people did listen to music but of how they ought to. Second, this moral distinction was rooted in a distinction of mind and body, which became, in turn, a way of distinguishing between "serious" and "popular" listeners, between ideal and "flawed" listening. Rose Subotnik describes the effects of being taught to listen properly:

> In my college harmony course, use of piano was forbidden. Whereas scoreless listening was unheard of in my university education, soundless keyboards were fairly common . . . In numerous seminars on early music I transcribed reams of manuscripts of which I never heard a note or discussed the musical value. As a music major, and later as a teacher, listening to scratched and otherwise dreadful monophonic recordings, I developed a strategy of listening which I have never entirely shaken, whereby I mentally "correct" for inadequacies of sound or performance that distract from my structural concentration . . . Yet I am not at all sure that any of this structural discipline has made me a more competent listener than my brother, who travels eight hours a week to the opera houses of New York to hum the tunes and listen to certain sopranos.[35]

The nineteenth-century shift from music as rhetoric to music as art meant devaluing the listener's role in musical judgment. As Mark Bonds shows, in the eighteenth century the purpose of music had been to "elicit an intended emotional response," "to move, persuade and delight the listener," and musical "form" thus referred to qualities of "coherence and persuasiveness." In this context, the listener had been "the only true arbiter" of musical value. Now the arbiter became the work (and its composer):

As an organism, the musical work is an object of contemplation that exists in and of itself. As an oration, the musical work is a temporal event whose purpose is to evoke a response from the listener. We can be moved by both modes of experience; but the metaphor of the oration necessarily emphasizes the temporality of the work, the role of the listener, and the element of aesthetic persuasion, whereas the model of the biological organism has no need to account for a work's effect upon its intended audience. Indeed, the audience, for all practical purposes, is irrelevant to the organic model. The organic metaphor implies that the standards by which any given work is to be judged will be found within the work itself.[36]

Lydia Goehr suggests that we must understand the nineteenth-century definition of the musical work as a "regulative concept," that is, it meant not only a rewriting of musical history (to turn eighteenth-century composers into artists) but also the formulation of behavioral rules for both musical performers and audiences.[37] But while there is certainly plenty of evidence that such regulation was an aspect of developing bourgeois cultural practice, at the same time the difficulty of enforcing such rules suggests that, hard as they might try to suppress their feelings, even the most respectable listeners were still hearing music sensuously.

No doubt it is the sheer aesthetic obstinacy of music listeners (and players) which accounts for musicologists' occasional contemptuous tone. Hanslick set the pattern:

Slouched dozing in their chairs, these enthusiasts allow themselves to brood and sway in response to the vibrations of tones, instead of contemplating tones attentively. How the music swells louder and louder and dies away, how it jubilates or trembles, they transform into a nondescript state of awareness which they naively consider to be purely intellectual. These people make up the most "appreciative" audience and the one most likely to bring music into disrepute. The aesthetic criterion of intellectual pleasure is lost to them; for all they would know, a fine cigar or a piquant delicacy or a warm bath produces the same effect as a symphony.[38]

In its materiality, music, in Kant's words, "lacks good breeding," and the final logic of the music-as-music position is that it should be neither heard nor played, only contemplated. Sound, mused Adorno, is a "layer of music" using historically conditioned resources—instruments and technology and performers—which "bear the imprint of social ideology and allow the 'neutralisation' of structural individuality." "Why can't music go out the same way it comes into a man," wondered Charles Ives, "without having to crawl over a fence of sounds, thoraxes, catgut, wire, wood and brass?"[39]

Ives voices here the note of Romantic individualism that originally undermined accounts of music as oration and helped define the "serious" as the "unpopular." In his 1802 life of J. S. Bach, Johann Forkel suggested that "the public merely asks for what it can understand, whereas the true artist ought to aim at an achievement which cannot be measured by popular standards. How, then, can popular applause be reconciled with the true artist's aspirations towards the ideal?"[40] And Schoenberg believed that "those who compose because they want to please others, and have audiences in mind, are not real artists . . . They are merely more or less skilful entertainers who would renounce composing if they did not find listeners."[41]

Popularity is defined here not just by reference to quantity (the size of the audience) but also to quality (the nature of the response). The proper listener—the listener paying aesthetic attention—has to translate a temporal experience into a spatial one. Music has to be appreciated organically, in terms of its internal structure, and the question becomes how we can grasp an architecture from the immediate flow of sounds. "The listener," Heinrich Kostlin declared sternly in 1879, "needs a firm observation post from which he can review the march-past of those harmonies, like a general reviewing his troops on parade."[42]

Structural listening is necessarily dependent on music's spatial representation, on the score. "By legislating for pitch," notes the composer Robin Maconie, "notation could be said to have freed musical invention from the tyranny of the ear," just as "regulation of time values in its turn liberated player and composer from the limitations of memory and the tyranny of succession."[43]

But the score isn't the music, and in what is still the most interesting analytic exploration of musical "autonomy," Roman Ingarden suggests that the nineteenth-century argument involved two elements: the score, which fixes the work but does not constitute a musical experience nor even part of it; and an infinite set of performances, each one a distinct and unique experience, but nevertheless drawing its meaning from its "truth" to the score. Given that in practice no single performance is judged to be "the absolute, faultless, genuine embodiment of the score," least of all the first performance or the composer's own version, the musical work can only be said to exist in its potential. As Ingarden puts it, a musical work is an *intentional object*—it originates in a creative act which gives the score its purpose—and a *schematic object*—the score leaves open different possibilities of completion, aesthetically significant areas of indeterminacy.[44]

A musical work, in short, is neither real (it is not defined simply by its performances) nor ideal (it is brought into existence by material processes of composition and realization); it is neither the score nor its realization, but the relationship between the two. Bringing music into aesthetic line with the other arts in the nineteenth century meant building an "imaginary museum of musical works," a concert hall equivalent of the galleries in which the meaning of painting and sculpture was being redefined.[45] And the power of this metaphor is reflected in the musicological approach to popular music: the first task is transcription, the translation of sound into score, whether the score of an imaginary event (most contemporary recorded music is not performed but constructed) or an improvised one (Ornette Coleman is said to have looked aghast at a transcription of one of his solos, knowing that he would be quite unable to play it).[46]

From this perspective, musical listening is, by definition, a double process, involving both the immediate experience of sound and an abstract, comparative exercise of judgment. Music turns out to be, after all, an imitative art: a performance is an imitation of a score. But the possibility of such imitative listening depends on certain material conditions. To put it simply, a musical work must be heard repeatedly, and it was both a cause and an effect of the new approach to music in the nineteenth century that people began to think in terms of the musical repertoire (the imaginary museum), to take it for granted that "great" music was regularly performed music. In the eighteenth century even the most committed listener would not have expected to hear any particular piece more than once—it had to do its aesthetic work immediately.

My own conclusion from these philosophical arguments is that the aesthetics of twentieth-century popular music relates more obviously to eighteenth-century interests in oration, performance, and gesture than to the nineteenth-century concern with structure, but the question underlying the last two hundred and fifty years' debate about music remains: what does a listener to music actually *do*? Adam Smith wrote at a time when there was confidence—at least among intellectuals—that this question could be answered by systematic self-analysis, and it is, perhaps, unfortunate that since then experimental psychology has displaced the philosophy of the mind. "The intense influence of music upon the nervous system is fully accepted as fact by psychology as well as physiology," wrote Hanslick in 1854. "Unfortunately an adequate explanation of this is still lacking."[47] And, as John Sloboda comments, it is nowadays equally unfortunate that "musical reception, the one area of music psychology in which research is flourishing, should be characterised by a relative insensitivity to the problem of relating research findings to normal musical listening."[48]

So what is "normal" listening? It is noteworthy that the two great European rationalists of the early twentieth century, Freud and Lenin, were both disturbed by their response to music. Lenin was reluctant to listen to Beethoven because the music made him want to pat people on the head; Freud remarked that his pleasure in art lay in comprehension: "Whenever I cannot do this, as for instance with music, I am almost incapable of obtaining any pleasure. Some rationalistic, or perhaps analytic, turn of mind in me rebels against being moved by a thing without knowing why I am thus affected, and what it us that affects me."[49]

Laurence Kramer has suggested that to call music "meaningless" is a response "less to an absence of thought than to the presence of danger."[50] The danger—the threat posed by music and dance to aesthetics—is not so much the absence of mind as the presence of body. The ideology of the musical work leads, as we've seen, toward a repression of the sensual. In the words of one psychoanalyst, "it is a prerequisite to the *aesthetic* response to musical art work that we free ourselves of [such] sensuous feelings and let the work exert its influence unimpeded, in the full beauty of its aesthetic form."[51]

But, in the words of another, the musical experience is an essentially sensual "pleasure in motion": "The joyous freedom and inexplicable obedience to will in the play of musical movement is, according to my opinion, a regressive repetition and idealised intensification of bodily pleasure in that early period of infancy, when the discovery of limbs is followed by the gradual mastery of the whole body."[52]

The obvious solution to the contradiction here is to integrate the intellectual and the sensual. This strategy lay behind Adam Smith's refusal to refer the value of music to anything extra-musical. Music, argued Smith, may evoke feelings, but only as objects for contemplation. To feel music directly is to understand it less well than to concentrate on how these feelings are produced. To put it another way, music which is designed to arouse feeling is clearly inferior to music which stimulates feeling *through* thought. The latter works by suggesting nothing "that is different from its melody and harmony."[53]

There are a number of strands in this argument, but the most important is the suggestion that what we hear as the "sensuality" of music is actually the effect of following musical "thoughts." Rather than an immediate sensual response, and then its contemplative interpretation, musical listening means grasping a piece intellectually and then taking sensual pleasure in the "movement" of the mind. Music offers, it seems, the experience of *feelings under control*, and this model has become the norm (in various guises) of classical music ideology. Consider, for example, these remarks by Deryk Cooke:

> We may say then that, whatever else the mysterious art known as music may eventually be found to express, it is primarily and basically a language of the emotions, through which we directly experience the fundamental urges that move mankind, without the need of falsifying ideas and images—words or pictures. A dangerous art in fact . . . But under the guidance of the intellect and enlightened moral sense, it is surely as safe as anything human can be—as safe at least, shall we say, as religion or science.[54]

Two questions remain. First, why should following the motion of music be described as an *emotional* activity? And, second, if "the musical experience" is so clearly rooted in subjectivity, how can we say that anyone's response to music is "wrong"? The fact that most people don't hear (or describe) music as the movement of sounds that is represented by the score does not mean that they don't hear (and reflect pleasurably upon) music—sounds moving. "When we come down to the fundamental musical experience," concedes Cooke, "the transformation of sound into emotion, the professional is as tongue-tied as the layman."[55]

It was established in the eighteenth century that there couldn't be a direct link between sound and feeling. Sir William James pointed out that "no man, truly affected with love or grief, ever expressed the one in an acrostic, or the other in a fugue." James Beattie asked: "What is the natural sound of devotion? Where is it to be heard? What resemblance is there between Handel's 'Te Deum' and the tone of voice natural to a person expressing, by articulate sound, his veneration of the Divine Character and providence?"[56]

On the other hand, neither can it be denied that music makes us feel, nor that we can label those feelings—as gaiety, tranquillity, or melancholia, in Adam Smith's example. The eighteenth-century move was therefore to distinguish between general and specific feelings. Music, suggested Archibald Alison, was "limited indeed in the reach of its imitation or expression and far inferior to language, in being confined to the expression only of general emotions, but powerful within these limits beyond any other means we know, both by the variety which it can afford, and the continued and increasing interest which it can raise."[57]

For Hanslick, who believed that the content of music was simply "tonally moving forms," it thereby embodied "the motion of feeling, abstracted from the content itself, i.e. from what is felt." Music concerns the "dynamic of feeling" rather than feeling itself, and Hanslick made a telling analogy with dance: "The more it abandons the beautiful rhythmicity of its forms, in order to become gestures and mimicry to express specific thoughts and feelings, the more it approaches the crude significance of mere pantomime."[58]

Two different sorts of distinction are being made in these attempts to define emotion abstractly. On the one hand, the suggestion is that musical emotion is profound but vague—we have the feeling but not its occasion; in Adam Smith's terms, music doesn't make us sad but makes us feel sadness; in von Hartmann's words, "Music reveals ineffable depths of the emotional life, such as poetry simply cannot express, whereas poetry presents not only the emotion itself but a perception of the situations, characters and actions that determine the emotions."[59] This is, as we saw in Chapter 5, the working assumption of film scorers, who use music to arouse the general feelings which the audience then interprets according to the film's narrative; we are first made to feel and then given a reason for doing so. For Hollywood pragmatists, it doesn't much matter why certain sounds cause certain feelings, it's enough that they do. But the question remains as to how the analogy between musical and emotional shapes works—and whether there is anything more to this than an analogy.

The second way of approaching this is to suggest not that music somehow expresses the shape of feelings, but, rather, that in describing musical experiences we are obliged to apply adjectives, and that we therefore attach feeling words conventionally and arbitrarily to what is, in fact, a purely aural experience. This would explain why, for example, in music (unlike the other arts) a child prodigy can move us. As Max Dessoir says, "Children of eight can perform prodigies of understanding, performing, even creating music . . . There is virtually no parallel to this in the other arts, since even the most gifted can only gradually acquire that understanding of the world and of humanity which is needed by the poet and the painter. Music, on the other hand, has no essential need of any relationship with reality."[60]

But what interests me here is another point—not music's possible meaninglessness, but people's continued attempts to make it meaningful: to name their feelings, supply the adjectives. In the early nineteenth century the French critic François Joseph Fétis noted that

> with the large audience, colouring will always pass as expression, for unless it consist of individuals capable of forming an abstract ideal—something not to be expected of a whole auditorium, no matter how

select it may be—it will never listen to a symphony, quartet, or other composition of this order without outlining a programme for itself during the performance, according to the grandiose, lively, impetuous, serenely soothing, or melancholy character of the music.[61]

The issue here, to return to my starting point, is that to ascribe meaning to a musical work is to provide a certain sort of *description*. Roland Barthes may have been contemptuous of the use of adjectives in bourgeois music criticism, but music is, in fact, an adjectival experience. Henry Kingsbury notes, for example, that "in the bulk of contemporary theoretical texts, music is not so much an entity occasionally described with anthropomorphic terms as it is itself an anthropomorphic, figurative representation." He quotes Heinrich Schenker, the guru of structural analysis: "We should get accustomed to seeing tones as creatures. We should learn to assume in them biological urges as they characterize living beings."[62]

Kingsbury is interested in the way in which music theorists assign motives and character to "the music itself" (rather than to the performers who produce the music, or to the composer who wrote it), and Frank Sibley has developed this argument, showing how important figurative adjectives are to musical analysis, adjectives which can't be read as implicit descriptions of either music makers or listeners. He quotes Hanslick, who referred to "those imposing and sombre pyramids of sound of the old Italian and Dutch schools, and the finely chased salt cellars and silver candlesticks, so to speak, of venerable Sebastian Bach."[63] Sibley's point is that "purely musical" descriptions (more or less technical accounts of what is "actually" heard) "fail to articulate what, following others, I have been calling the 'character' and qualities of music, and do little to explain why music may engage us as appreciative listeners—which is why non-musicians and musicians alike employ figurative characterizations."

As Sibley suggests, someone could describe a piece of music perfectly accurately in technical terms while being quite unable to appreciate it; while someone quite unable to read music can perfectly well convince us that they've "understood" a work: they make sense of our own experience of it through their figurative description. This is the job of the rock critic, for example.

This view, that grasping the character of a piece involves hearing it in such a way that some possible extra-musical description(s) would be appropriate to our experience, would stand sharply opposed to the belief that extra-musical description is always improper. Much that is centrally appealing about music would be, paradoxically, essentially extra-musical.[64]

Two points follow from this. First, such descriptions must be "apt" rather than true. An inapt description is evidence of a musical misunderstanding, and Sibley suggests that description here is something like an actor's or director's interpretation of a dramatic role: each musical description may be personal, but it can, nevertheless, be used as evidence of whether someone has understood the work (in this respect describing a piece of music is analogous to playing it). Conversation—argument—about musical meaning is, then, possible: the adjectives describe the music and not people's responses to it; they are not a way of declaring how we feel (declarations that no one could deny). Second, though, "we do not grasp, realize, or perceive the character of music—or of faces, paintings or scenery—in words or in anything else . . . *Having* grasped its character, however, or while trying to, we may try to describe it in either [musical or figurative] terms."[65] And our skill here will be as much a skill with words as a skill "at listening."

The point to stress here is that this use of adjectives is not confined to professional writers about music and professional talkers about music, to musicians and critics. Rather, it is a necessary aspect of all musical listening; it defines the musical experience. John Sloboda remarks on

> someone who has just listened to a performance of a long and complex symphonic work. It is quite possible that he or she cannot recall a single theme from the work (I have often been in this situation myself), yet he or she certainly remembers *something* about the work, and can make some appropriate response to it. When this response is expressed in words it characteristically contains remarks about the substance of the music which are neither descriptive ("it was loud") nor reactive ("I liked it") but embody an attempt to *characterize* the music through metaphor ("it had the feeling of a long heroic struggle triumphantly resolved"). It seems less significant that people often disagree about their characterizations than that they nearly always have *some* comment to offer. This is not an arbitrary reaction, but a genuine attempt to describe some real thing or experience.[66]

Music does not have a content—it can't be translated—but this does not mean that it is not "an object of the understanding."[67] Or, to put it another way, the gap in music between the nature of the experience (sounds) and the terms of its interpretation (adjectives) may be more obvious than in any other art form, but this does not mean that the pleasure of music doesn't lie in the ways in which we can—and must—fill the gap. "After playing Chopin," wrote Oscar Wilde,

> I feel as if I had been weeping over sins that I had never committed, and mourning over tragedies that were not my own. Music always seems to me to produce that effect. It creates for one a past of which one has been ignorant, and fills one with a sense of sorrows that have been hidden from one's tears. I can fancy a man who has led a perfectly commonplace life, hearing by chance some curious piece of music, and suddenly discovering that his soul, without his being conscious of it, had passed through terrible experiences, and known fearful joys, or wild romantic loves, or great renunciations.[68]

To follow the history of music theory since Adam Smith is to follow an attempt to constitute both a definition of music and a way of listening. The peculiarity of this history is that it has, in a sense, been successful discursively and unsuccessful materially—in the academy, at least, people talk about music in ways which make little sense of how they listen to it. We take it for granted, for example, as I noted at the beginning of this chapter, that a clear distinction can be made between "serious" music and music as entertainment, or, at least, between serious listening and listening as entertainment. But in practice, as a listener, I'm much less clear about this difference. Can I really distinguish between the pleasure that I take in Bartok and the pleasure that I take in Hüsker Dü? Am I describing something quite different when I say that I'm moved by Fauré's *Requiem* and by Sharon Redd?

The debate about musical meaning in which Adam Smith took part was a debate about what we should say about music. Aesthetic argument is a matter of lexical regulation. "We may doubt," writes Roman Ingarden, "whether so-called dance music, when employed only as a means of keeping the dancers in step and arousing in them a specific passion for expression through movement, is music in the strict sense of the word."[69] But the point of music, whether in club or concert hall, is, precisely, to flout the strict sense of the word, and Roger Scruton has thus argued that "dancing to music is an archetype of the aesthetic response":

> When we dance to music we move in response to it, with the same dispassionate absorption with which we move to another's dancing . . . and our more "civilized" habits in the concert hall are in many ways like truncated dances, in which our whole being is absorbed by the movement to which we attend, inwardly locked in incipient

gestures of imitation. There is no doubt in our feeling that the object of this imitation is a human life, presented somehow through the music. We could not remove this thought from our response without destroying the whole place of music in our culture.[70]

Scruton suggests that the "aesthetic character of music" can be grasped in a variety of ways—by listening to it, playing it to oneself, performing it for others, moving to it. This differentiates music from other art forms, and Scruton concludes that to get at the peculiarity of music "we should not study listening, which has so much in common with reading and looking, but dancing, which places music in the very centre of our bodily lives." Anthony Storr, writing from a psychologist's point of view, makes a similar point: "The formalist analysts are trying to make the appreciation of music purely cerebral, whereas music is rooted in bodily rhythms and movement." Echoing Scruton, he notes that music, unlike poetry or paintings, "makes us want to move our bodies."

> If music is rooted in the body, and closely connected with bodily movement, even though modern listeners in the concert hall may have to inhibit such movement, then Schopenhauer's view that both our experience of the body and our experience of music possess a depth, an immediacy, and an intensity which cannot be obtained in other ways becomes comprehensible and persuasive.[71]

For Storr, the psychologist, the point here is that music affects our emotions bodily as well as engaging our feelings mentally. He cites Darwin: "So a man may intensely hate another, but until his bodily frame is affected he cannot be said to be enraged."[72]

For Scruton, the philosopher, the argument is put more coolly:

> In responding to the meaning of a piece of music, we are being led through a series of gestures which gain their significance from the idea of a community that they intimate, just as do the gestures of a dance. As with a dance, a kind of magnetic field is created which shapes the emotions of the one who enters it. We move for a while along the orbit of a formalized emotion and practise its steps. Our truncated movements [in listening without dancing] are also acts of attention: we do what we do in response to the sounds that we hear, when we attend to them aesthetically . . . And if it is worth anything, the music does not leave us there [with the little fragments of human life that musical elements may suggest], but leads us on, through its own powers of development. As we move with these elements, there-

fore, we are lead by our sympathies into a wholly new totality: a musical bridge is created, spanning distant reaches of human life.[73]

I've used these two anti-pop thinkers deliberately to show that even for them the meaning of music comes back to emotion, the body, movement, dance (all the things that are supposed to characterize African rather than European musics). But I want to return, finally, to a sociological point. Different musical activities (listening, playing, performing, dancing) produce different aesthetic objects. In particular, as Nicholas Cook has argued so effectively, the music produced by the composer must be distinguished from the music produced by the listener (with performers, critics, and analysts occupying uneasy positions between the two).[74]

This is reflected in the academic study of popular music: musicology produces popular music for people who want to compose or play it, sociology produces popular music for people who consume or listen to it; these approaches are different because they are concerned with different sorts of musical experience (which is why, in this chapter, I've been more concerned with the writings of philosophers and psychologists than with those of music analysts and sociologists). Cook quotes Schoenberg:

> Music is an art which takes place in time. But the way in which a work presents itself to a composer . . . is independent of this; time is regarded as space. In writing the work down, space is transformed into time. For the hearer this takes place the other way round; it is only after the work has run its course in time that he can see it as whole—its idea, its form and its content.[75]

I'll quote Ned Rorem:

> For myself, I no longer hear new music except visually: if it pleases me, I inscribe it on a staff in the brain, photograph that notation, take it home, and develop the film which can be preserved indefinitely. This manner of musical recall is not, I think, unusual to many composers.[76]

And what's at issue here is not just different musical practices, different musical experiences, different musical situations, but a single musical culture *defined by such differences.*[77] As Roland Barthes put it,

> I record myself playing the piano; initially, out of curiosity to *hear myself;* but very soon I no longer hear myself; what I hear is, however pretentious it may seem to say so, the *Dasein* of Bach and of Schumann, the pure materiality of their music; because it is my utterance,

the predicate loses all pertinence; on the other hand, paradoxically, if I listen to Horowitz or Richter, a thousand adjectives come to mind: I hear *them* and not Bach or Schumann.—What is it that happens? When I listen to myself *having played*—after an initial moment of lucidity in which I perceive one by one the mistakes I have made—there occurs a kind of rare coincidence: the past of my playing coincides with the present of my listening, and in this coincidence, commentary is abolished: there remains nothing but the music (of course what remains is not at all the "truth" of the text . . .)[78]

Toward a Popular Aesthetic

13

What, after all, do I put down when I put down notes? I put down a reflection of emotional states: feelings, perceptions, imaginings, intuitions. An emotional state, as I use the term, is compounded of everything we are: our background, our environment, our convictions. Art particularizes and makes actual these fluent emotional states. Because it particularizes and because it makes actual, it gives meaning to *la condition humaine*. If it gives meaning it necessarily has purpose. I would even add that it has moral purpose.

Aaron Copland[1]

The Beatles were all ours, from a Northern town, and we in our provincial towns all over the country could understand them.

Carol Dix[2]

The academic study of popular music has been limited by the assumption that the sounds somehow reflect or represent "a people." The analytic problem has been to trace the connections back, from the work (the score, the song, the beat) to the social groups who make and use it. What's at issue is homology, some sort of structural relationship between material and cultural forms. From this perspective musical meaning is socially constructed; our musical pleasures are defined by our social circumstances. Marxist and Weberian musicologists alike argue that music is a form of ideological expression, not just in broad institutional terms (how it is played and heard), but also aesthetically, through the expressive dependence of the organizing principle of the music as a structure of willed sounds on the organizing principle of society as a structure of power. As the semiotician

Theo van Leeuwen puts it, "Music can be seen as an abstract representation of social organization, as the geometry of social structure."[3]

The problem of the homological argument, as van Leeuwen himself notes, is that "music not only represents social relations, it also and simultaneously enacts them"; and too often attempts to relate musical forms *to* social processes ignore the ways in which music is *itself* a social process. In other words, in examining the aesthetics of popular music we need to reverse the usual academic argument: the question is not how a piece of music, a text, "reflects" popular values, but how—in performance—it produces them.[4]

Let me make this point in a different way, by quoting at length an exemplary piece of pop criticism, Frank Kogan's fanzine celebration of Spoonie Gee (written sometime in the mid-1980s).

> "Spoonin Rap" and "Love Rap" by Spoonie Gee are my favorite American-made records of the last ten years. They came out about five years ago, "Spoonin Rap" in late '79 and "Love Rap" in '80. I've never read a review of either.
>
> Rap music centres on the human voice. The voice is a rhythm instrument as well as a melodic one, capable of emphasizing beats as if it were a set of drums. Spoonie Gee bears down hard on the words, achieving a mesmerizing intensity akin to hard rock—yet he also puts a hanging drawl in his phrasing. So he sounds tough and funky/graceful simultaneously. His first producers, Frank Johnson and Peter Brown of Sound of New York and Bobby Robinson of Enjoy Records, were smart enough to emphasize Spoonie's voice: "Spoonin Rap" is just bass and drums, sound effects and voice; "Love Rap" is just voice, drums and percussion.
>
> On the basis of his voice alone, the way it balances coolness with angry passion while keeping a dance beat, Spoonie is a major artist; in addition, he's a writer. His lyrics are as intense as his singing, and embody the same tensions. Example: both "Spoonin Rap" and "Love Rap" start with detailed and explicit bragging—about how cool and sexy he is, about how the girls go for him, how they're impressed with his rapping and his car. He puts on his eight-track. He makes love to the girl in his car. In his Mercedes. The seat's so soft, just like a bed. At the moment of sexual triumph the lyrics make a jarring change, as if there's a second song hidden behind the first, as if the bragging were a set-up for something else. "Spoonin Rap": "Then I got the girl for three hours straight / a'but I had to go to work a'so I couldn't be late / I said, 'Where's your man?' She said 'He's in jail'

/ I said 'A'come on baby cuz you're tellin' a tale / Cuz if he comes at me and then he wants to fight / See I'm a get the man good and I'm a get him right . . .'". "Love Rap": "When I got into my house and drove the female wild / The first thing she said is 'Let's have a child' / I said 'No no baby I only got time / To make a lot of money and to save my pride / And if I had a baby I might go broke / And believe me to a negro that ain't no joke.'" And then it's like the first part of the song, but turned inside out—the guys and girls are drawn to his flashy clothes and car only so they can rip him off and leave him in the gutter. The girls are gonna play him for a fool . . . Then it shifts back to what a great lover he is, nice descriptions of his girl friends. "Spoonin Rap" shifts around in the same way. It's about how cool he is, about how sexy women are; then it's about don't do dope, don't steal, you'll go to jail and they'll fuck you in the ass. Then it's about jumping the turnstile and the cop pulls a gun but he doesn't shoot.

There's a lot of precedent in black lyrics for jarring emotional juxtapositions—in the blues particularly, also in Smokey Robinson's deliberate paradoxes. But the nearest emotional equivalent isn't in black music, it's in punk—early Stones, Kinks, Velvets, Stooges, Dolls—where a song will seem to be one thing, then be another. The ranting part of "Love Rap" could be Lou Reed in one of his bad moods—except that, unlike a Jagger or a Reed, Spoonie hasn't cal-culated—may not even be aware of—his juxtapositions. Which adds to his power. The feelings have great impact because they come from an unexpected source. If Spoonie were in punk or rock his alienation and rage would fill an expectation of the genre. In disco, they seem truer.

. . . Spoonie's not one of us. He has nothing to do with punk culture or post-punk culture. I don't know if I could carry on an interesting conversation with him, if we could find any cultural or moral common ground. But there is a common ground . . . However much I admire current heros like Mark Smith and Ian Mackaye, people I identify with, I know they don't make music as strong as this. Listening to Spoonie is like hearing my own feelings, and I have to confront my own fear. This means maybe that I'm not really unlike him. Maybe I'm more like him than I am like you.[5]

I've quoted this at length, partly because this is how it works as criti-cism—the move from description to emotion to identity—and partly to show how the concerns of this book (the ease and necessity of evaluation, the consideration of voice and genre, text and performance, knowledge, truth and feeling) can be focused on one artist, on a couple of tracks. What Kogan assumes—what I assume—is that music gives us a way of being in the world, a way of making sense of it: musical response is, by its nature, a process of musical identification; aesthetic response is, by its nature, an ethical agreement. The critical issue, in other words, is not meaning and its interpretation—musical appreciation as a kind of decoding—but experience and collusion: the "aesthetic" describes a kind of self-consciousness, a coming together of the sensual, the emotional, and the social *as* performance.[6] In short, music doesn't represent values but lives them. As John Miller Chernoff concludes from his study of drumming in Ghana,

> African music is a cultural activity which reveals a group of people organizing and involving themselves with their own communal relationships—a participant-observer's comment, so to speak, on the processes of living together. The aesthetic point of the exercise is not to reflect a reality which *stands behind it* but to ritualize a reality that is *within* it.[7]

And if music is particularly important in the history of black identities, such value is not confined to diasporan African cultures.[8] Philip Bohlman, for example, has explored the role of chamber music in forming German Jewish identity, in both articulating cultural values and enacting a form of collective commitment to them. In this context the scored basis of "absolute music" is as socially fecund as the improvised basis of jazz:

> Viewed from a performative perspective, the absence of specific meaning within the text allows meaning to accrue only upon performance, thus empowering any group—for example, an ethnic community—to shape what it will from absolute music. A gap therefore forms between the content of chamber-music repertories and the style of performance situations. It is within the mutability allowed by style that differences in meaning and function of music arise, thereby transforming chamber music into a genre that can follow numerous historical paths. These paths may be as different as, say, the ethnic associations in Israel and the practices of amateur music making found in many American academic communities. Clearly, such cases reflect different attitudes towards both the repertories of chamber music and the communities that lend the music its distinctive functions and form its different histories.[9]

And Gina Arnold describes how in the American indie scene in the 1980s, "deep in the heart of our very own small towns, we took the tools of our culture and hewed them into our very own road . . . Nirvana has dragged us all up along with them, and now here we stand, looking down at the past, at a mental map of our traversal of the route that brought all this to pass."[10]

In responding to a song, to a sound, we are drawn (haphazardly, as Arnold suggests) into affective and emotional alliances. This happens in other areas of popular culture, of course; in sports, for example, or in fashion and style—social constructions which provide keys to the ways in which we, as individuals, present ourselves to the world. But music is especially important for our sense of ourselves because of its unique emotional intensity—we absorb songs into our own lives and rhythm into our own bodies. In John Blacking's words, "Because music is concerned with feelings which are primarily individual and rooted in the body, its structural and sensuous elements resonate more with individuals' cognitive and emotional sets than with their cultural sentiments, although its external manner and expression are rooted in historical circumstances."[11] Music, we could say, provides us with an intensely subjective sense of being sociable. Whether jazz or rap for African-Americans or nineteenth-century chamber music for German Jews in Israel, it both articulates and offers the immediate *experience* of collective identity.[12]

Paul Gilroy remarks that while growing up he was "provided by black music with a means to gain proximity to the sources of feeling from which our local conceptions of blackness were assembled."[13] But he also notes that "the most important lesson music still has to teach us is that its inner secrets and its ethnic rules can be taught and learned," and as a child and teenager I also learned something about myself—took my identity—from black music (just as I did later, in the disco, from gay music). What secrets was I being taught?

First, that identity comes from the outside, not the inside; it is something we put or try on, not something we reveal or discover. As Jonathan Rée puts it, "The problem of personal identity, one may say, arises from play-acting and the adoption of artificial voices; the origins of distinct personalities, in acts of personation and impersonation."[14] And Rée goes on to argue that personal identity is therefore "the accomplishment of a storyteller, rather than the attribute of a character . . . The concept of narrative, in other words, is not so much a justification of the idea of personal identity, as an elucidation of its structure as an inescapable piece of make-believe."[15]

Identities are, then, inevitably constrained by imaginative forms—"structured by conventions of narrative to which the world never quite manages to conform," in Kwame Anthony Appiah's words[16]—but also freed by them. As Mark Slobin suggests, cultural imagination is not necessarily restricted by social circumstances: "We all grow up with *something*, but we can choose just about *anything* by way of expressive culture."[17] And as I have argued elsewhere, with reference to literary forms and social identities (black writing, women's writing, gay writing), the question is not whether such writing can be mapped back onto the reader (reading as a woman, a man, a black) but whether literary transformation—the process of writing *and* reading—doesn't subvert all sociological assumptions about cultural position and cultural feeling.[18]

This seems an even more obvious question to ask about popular music, of which the dominant forms in all contemporary societies have originated at the social margins—among the poor, the migrant, the rootless, the "queer."[19] Anti-essentialism is a necessary part of musical experience, a necessary consequence of music's failure to register the separations of body and mind on which "essential" differences (between black and white, female and male, gay and straight, nation and nation) depend.

It follows that an identity is always already an ideal, what we would like to be, not what we are. In taking pleasure from black or gay or female music I don't thus identify as black or gay or female (I don't actually experience these sounds as "black music" or "gay music" or "women's voices") but, rather, participate in imagined forms of democracy and desire, imagined forms of the social and the sexual. And what makes music special in this familiar cultural process is that musical identity is both fantastic—idealizing not just oneself but also the social world one inhabits—and real: it is enacted in activity. Music making and music listening, that is to say, are bodily matters; they involve what one might call *social movements*. In this respect, musical pleasure is not derived from fantasy—it is not mediated by daydreams—but is experienced directly: music gives us a real experience of what the ideal could be.

In his discussion of black identity, Paul Gilroy argues that it is neither "simply a social and political category" nor "a vague and utterly contingent construction" but "remains the outcome of practical activity: language, gesture, bodily significations, desires."

> These significations are condensed in musical performance, although it does not, of course, monopolise them. In this context, they produce the imaginary effect of an internal racial core or essence by acting on the body though the specific mechanisms of identification and recognition that are produced in the intimate interaction of per-

former and crowd. This reciprocal relationship serves as a strategy and an ideal communicative situation even when the original makers of the music and its eventual consumers are separated in space and time or divided by the technologies of sound production and the commodity form which their art has sought to resist.[20]

And once we start looking at different musical genres we can begin to document the different ways in which music works materially to give people different identities, to place them in different social groups. Whether we're talking about Finnish dance halls in Sweden, Irish pubs in London, or Indian film music in Trinidad, we're dealing not just with nostalgia for "traditional sounds," not just with a commitment to "different" songs, but also with experiences of alternative modes of social interaction. Communal values can only be grasped as musical aesthetics in action.[21] "Authenticity" in this context is a quality not of the music as such (how it is actually made), but of the story it is heard to tell, the narrative of musical interaction in which the listeners place themselves.

We all hear the music we like as something special, as something that defies the mundane, takes us "out of ourselves," puts us somewhere else. "Our music" is, from this perspective, special not just with reference to other music but, more important, to the rest of life. It is this sense of specialness (the way in which music seems to make possible a new kind of self-recognition, to free us from everyday routines, from the social expectations with which we are encumbered) that is the key to our musical value judgments. "Transcendence" is as much part of the popular as of the serious music aesthetic, but in pop transcendence articulates not music's independence of social forces but a kind of alternative experience of them. (Of course, in the end, the same is true of "serious" music too.)

Music constructs our sense of identity through the experiences it offers of the body, time, and sociability, experiences which enable us to place ourselves in imaginative cultural narratives. Such a fusion of imaginative fantasy and bodily practice marks as well the integration of aesthetics and ethics. John Miller Chernoff has eloquently demonstrated how among African musicians an aesthetic judgment (this sounds good) is necessarily also an ethical judgment (this is good). The issue is "balance": "the quality of rhythmic relationships" describes a quality of social life.[22]

Identity is necessarily a matter of ritual: it describes one's place in a dramatized pattern of relationships—one can never really express oneself "autonomously." Self identity *is* cultural identity; claims to individual difference depend on audience appreciation, on shared performing and narrative rules.[23] Such rules are organized generically: different musical genres offer different narrative solutions to the recurring pop tensions between authenticity and artifice, sentimentality and realism, the spiritual and the sensual, the serious and the fun. Different musical genres articulate differently the central values of the pop aesthetic—spectacle and emotion, presence and absence, belonging and difference.

In her study of music making in the town of Milton Keynes, *The Hidden Musicians*, Ruth Finnegan persuasively argues that these days people's voluntary, leisure activities are more likely to provide their "pathways" through life than their paid employment. It was in their musical activities that her town dwellers found their most convincing narratives; it was in their aesthetic judgments that they expressed their most deep-seated ethical views.[24]

This is, perhaps ironically, to come to the aesthetics of popular music as performance by way of a spatial metaphor: what makes music special—what makes it special for identity—is that it defines a space without boundaries. Music is the cultural form best able both to cross borders—sounds carry across fences and walls and oceans, across classes, races, and nations—and to define places: in clubs, scenes, and raves, listening on headphones, radio, and in the concert hall, we are only where the music takes us.

In this book I have suggested ways in which we can use a sociology of music as the basis of an aesthetic theory, how we can move from a description of popular music as a social institution to an understanding of how we can and do value it. One of my working assumptions has been that people's individual tastes—the way they experience and describe music for themselves—are a necessary part of academic analysis. Does this mean, in the end, that the value of popular music is simply a matter of personal preference?

The usual sociological answer to this question is that such preferences are themselves socially determined—that individual tastes are really examples of collective taste, reflecting consumers' gender, class, and ethnic backgrounds—and I don't want to deny that our cultural needs and expectations are, indeed, materially based. All the personal terms I have been using (identity, emotion, memory) are, of course, socially formed. But this is only part of the story. Pop tastes do not just derive from our socially constructed identities; they also help to shape them.

For the best part of this century, pop music has been an important way in which we have learned to understand ourselves as historical, ethnic, class-bound, gendered, national subjects. This has had conservative effects (primarily through nostalgia) as well as liberating ones. What music does (all music) is put into play a sense of identity that may or may not fit the way we are placed by other social forces. Music certainly puts us in our place, but it can also suggest that our social circumstances are not immutable (and that other people—performers, fans—share our dissatisfaction). Music is not in itself revolutionary or reactionary. It is a source of strong feelings which, because they are also socially coded, can come up against common sense. It may be that, in the end, I want to value most highly that music, popular and serious, which has some sort of disruptive cultural effect, but my argument is that music only does this through its impact on individuals, and that this impact is obdurately social.

I began this book at a dinner party in Stockholm. I'm ending it in a hotel room in Berlin. Across the street is the Hard Rock Café, and the local bars feature '50s and '60s North American pop. I desultorily watch the pop video shows on German television, but only Ace of Base's "Eyes of a Stranger" (intrigue on the Stockholm underground) holds my attention. I trawl the dial on my walkman and, pushing past the ubiquitously ingratiating Elton John, find things I do want to hear. Beethoven's Violin Concerto, played faster than usual so that the moments when the soloist returns to earth and the rest of the string section are there to catch her seem more exhilarating, more reassuring, than ever. A New Orleans version of "Nobody Loves You (When You're Down and Out)" with, I think, Louis Armstrong on trumpet, shaping pathos so lovingly that it becomes something else, a refusal of the human spirit to be laid low. Old pop songs with unexpected resonance: Rick Astley solemnly marking time to a cheap '80s disco beat; Cat Stevens' "Father and Son," well-meaning '70s advice; Whitney Houston swinging through a ballad like a trapeze artist. A big, brassy *schlager,* oompah music with a hint of Viennese mockery. German-Turkish music, the ululating voice picked out by a techno pulse. And then, spine-tingling coincidence, a track from Portishead's *Dummy,* a new British album with a strong critical buzz, to which I'd been listening on tape as I sat around in airports.[25]

This is my favorite track on *Dummy,* "Sour Times." The sampled sound from a Lalo Schifrin *Mission Impossible* LP places the track in space, not time, in the suspended space of the traveler, caught between West and East, past and future. Beth Gibbons' voice—high, sweet, thin—has the tone of a torch singer's but not the anxiety. She sounds matter-of-fact (like the Dutch singer Mathilde Santing), feminine without tears. And all the time behind her a babble of noise, the talk of the 1990s British dance floor, the movement of traffic between soul and house, white and black, Europe, America, the Caribbean, background and foreground. I decide that no record better captures the pop aesthetic at this time, in this place—not for its utopian (or dystopian) vision, but for its determination to be heard, to give cultural confusion a social voice. And I wish there were someone here to play this to.

"Human attitudes," Percy Grainger once argued, "and specifically human ways of thinking about the world are the results of dance and song."[26] I cast my mind back a few days. Another night and I'm in a small town in the British midlands, at a charity event in a community center. There's locally prepared Mexican food and a salsa band from Birmingham—the singer from South America (country unspecified), the musicians local session players. I meet people I haven't seen for a decade, friends from punk promoting days in Coventry. This is a community brought together by shared political interests (to benefit the environment and education in Nicaragua) but fused together, on the dance floor, by the obstinate insistence of the rhythms (this is a good salsa band) and by the sexual charge of the vocals. Memories dance with the music too—old ideological bust-ups and alliances, parties and love affairs. A flash of the lights offers a snapshot, of bodies held in motion, parents and children, friends and enemies, the successful and the unsuccessful, of where we've been together. This is what I mean, I think, by music both taking us out of ourselves and putting us in place, by music as both a fantasy of community and an enactment of it, by music dissolving difference even as it expresses it. The sounds on that Leamington dance floor, like the sounds now in this Berlin hotel room, are at the same time rootless, cut free from any originating time and place, and rooted, in the needs, movement, and imagination of the listener.

Another coincidence: "La Bamba" is on the radio. "La Bamba" was the encore spot of the salsa night, a track whose winding forty-year journey from 1950s Mexican Los Angeles to 1990s Berlin and Leamington Spa, through the mass media of rock 'n' roll, radio, TV, Hollywood, is matched by its winding journey through our own bodies, through the memories of what we once wanted to be that make us what we are. "La Bamba," I think restlessly, this is where I came in.

Notes

Index

Notes

1. The Value Problem in Cultural Studies

1. Ned Rorem, *Settling the Score* (New York: Harcourt Brace, 1988), p. 258.
2. Thanks to Frank Kogan for this quote.
3. Levin L. Schücking, *The Sociology of Literary Taste* [1931] (London: Kegan Paul, 1944), p. 32.
4. Ex-members of the band From Eden, who went on to form, respectively, Pop Will Eat Itself and The Wonder Stuff. Quoted in Martin Roach, *The Eight Legged Atomic Dustbin Will Eat Itself* (London: Independent Music Press, 1992), pp. 18, 89.
5. Patrick Kane, *Tinsel Show: Pop, Politics, Scotland* (Edinburgh: Polygon, 1992), p. 59.
6. Frank Kogan is quoted here, as elsewhere in this chapter, from private correspondence.
7. For further discussion of some of these issues see Sarah Thornton, *Club Cultures: Music, Media and Subcultural Capital* (Cambridge: Polity, 1995). And see Pierre Bourdieu, *Distinction: A Social Critique of the Judgement of Taste* [1979] (London: Routledge, 1984). The most illuminating application of Bourdieu's ideas to popular music is Mats Trondman, "Rock Taste—on Rock as Symbolic Capital. A Study of Young People's Music Taste and Music Making," in Keith Roe and Ulla Carlsson, eds., *Popular Music Research* (Göteborg: Nordicom-Sweden, 1990).
8. For the last three years I've chaired the judging panel of the Mercury Music Prize (for the British "album of the year"). My fellow judges have all been authoritative music industry types, and much of my understanding of how argument works in everyday musical evaluation is drawn from our disputatious shortlisting sessions (I was unable to convince my colleagues, for example, to put the Pet Shop Boys' *Very* on the 1994 shortlist).
9. Peter Van Der Merwe, *Origins of the Popular Style* (Oxford: Clarendon Press, 1989), p. 3.
10. Allan Bloom, *The Closing of the American Mind* (New York: Simon and Schuster, 1987), pp. 73–74.
11. Mark Crispin Miller, "Where All the Flowers Went." Reprinted in his *Boxed In: The Culture of TV* (Evanston, Ill.: Northwestern University Press, 1989), p. 175.
12. Gordon Legge, *The Shoe* (Edinburgh: Polygon, 1989), p. 36. The three albums listed were recorded by Van Morrison, Joy Division, and Roxy Music.
13. Barbara Herrnstein Smith, *Contingencies of Value* (Cambridge, Mass.: Harvard University Press, 1988).
14. As Derek Scott has pointed out, this sort of argument has proved problematic in the music academy too. The music of Sir Arthur Sullivan, for example, has done rather

better in terms of "longevity" than that of Schoenberg: how long should we wait for the latter to be properly appreciated "by posterity"? See Derek B. Scott, "Music and Sociology for the 1990s: A Changing Critical Perspective," *Musical Quarterly* 74(3) (1990): 389.

15. For the value issue in film theory see David Bordwell, *Making Meaning: Inference and Rhetoric in the Interpretation of Cinema* (Cambridge, Mass.: Harvard University Press, 1989). For the peculiar (and peculiarly British) concept of "quality television" see Charlotte Brunsdon, "Problems with Quality," *Screen* 31(1) (1990).

16. Many thanks to Judith Williamson for discussing her experience with me. Her collected film criticism is published as *Deadline at Dawn* (London: Marion Boyars, 1993).
    I discuss the problems of treating popular culture as an academic object in much greater detail in *Pearls and Swine: Instituting Popular Culture* (Manchester: Manchester University Press, forthcoming).

17. Frank Kogan, *Why Music Sucks* 7, 1991, pp. 3–4.

18. See Joke Hermes, *Reading Women's Magazines: An Analysis of Everyday Media Use* (Cambridge: Polity, 1995).

19. Theodor W. Adorno, "On the Fetish Character in Music and the Regression of Listening" [1938], reprinted in *The Culture Industry,* ed. J. M. Bernstein (London: Routledge, 1991), p. 26.

20. See John Fiske, "Popular Discrimination," in James Naremore and Patrick Brantlinger, eds., *Modernity and Mass Culture* (Bloomington: Indiana University Press, 1991).

21. See Dave Harker, "Still Crazy After All These Years? What *Was* Popular Music in the 1960s?" in Bart Moore-Gilbert and John Seed, eds., *Cultural Revolution? The Challenge of the Arts in the 1960s* (London: Routledge, 1992), and "Blood on the Tracks: Popular Music in the 1970s," in Bart Moore-Gilbert, ed., *The Arts in the 1970s: Cultural Closure?* (London: Routledge, 1994).

22. Lawrence Levine, *Black Culture and Black Consciousness* (New York: Oxford University Press, 1977), p. 233.

23. Brian Jackson, *Working Class Community* (London: Routledge and Kegan Paul, 1968), p. 34.

24. Richard Shusterman, *Pragmatic Aesthetics: Living Beauty, Rethinking Art* (Oxford: Blackwell, 1992), pp. 179, 183–187, 193–200. David Novitz argues equally persuasively that we also cannot distinguish high and low art in terms of formal difference (the complex vs. the simple), effective difference (the challenging vs. the confirming), or creative difference (individual vs. collective production). See his "Ways of Artmaking: The High and the Popular in Art," *British Journal of Aesthetics* 29(1) (1989).

25. See Fiske, "Popular Discrimination."

26. For a typical assertion of the assumptions here take this comment, in *The Independent,* on the financial support by the Grateful Dead's Phil Lesh (through the group's Rex Foundation) for recordings by "forgotten" and "neglected" twentieth-century British composers: "Most significant of all, it has opened a dialogue between creative musicians on opposite sides of the commercial schism, dissolving the difference between those who make music for instant gratification and those who patiently await the verdict of eternity." Norman Lebrecht, "The Grateful and the Dead," *The Independent Magazine,* June 22, 1991, p. 60.

Of all rock groups, the Grateful Dead (and their fans) probably think the least in terms of "instant gratification."

27. Shusterman, *Pragmatic Aesthetics,* pp. 212–213.

28. See Richard Hoggart, *Uses of Literacy* (London: Chatto and Windus, 1957), and Raymond Williams, "Culture Is Ordinary," [1958] in his *Resources of Hope* (London: Verso, 1989).

29. The clearest statement of this problem in recent cultural studies (clear at least in part because she is quite unable to resolve the contradiction) is Janice Radway's *Reading the Romance* (Chapel Hill and London: University of North Carolina Press, 1984).

2. The Sociological Response

1. Quoted (from *A travers chants*) in Carol MacClintock, ed., *Readings in the History of Music in Performance* (Bloomington: Indiana University Press, 1979), pp. 430–432.

2. Barbara Herrnstein Smith, *Contingencies of Value* (Cambridge, Mass.: Harvard University Press, 1988), p. 13.

3. John Culshaw, *Putting the Record Straight* (London: Secker and Warburg, 1981), p. 317.

4. Lovat Dickson, *Radclyffe Hall at the Well of Loneliness* (London: Collins, 1975), pp. 45–46. Thanks to Gill Frith for this reference.

5. Sheila Davis, *The Craft of Lyric Writing* (Cincinnati, Ohio: Writer's Digest Books, 1985).
   Carl Dahlhaus describes the same sort of discursive clash in the historically shifting aesthetic of classical music: "The concept of originality which grew up in the late eighteenth century established itself in the nineteenth as an unquestioned aesthetic doctrine, whereas the idea of *ars inveniendi*, the theory of musical invention which was taken for granted in the seventeenth and earlier in the eighteenth, was condemned in the nineteenth as if it were a blasphemy against the cult of genius. Until the end of the eighteenth century a musical idea could be a platitude, something quite commonplace, without attracting the charge of being meaningless; convention—recognizable dependence on precedent—was still regarded as aesthetically legitimate." Quoted in Janet M. Levy, "Covert and Casual Values in Recent Writings About Music," *Journal of Musicology* 6(1) (1987): 25.

6. This was already the case, of course, for radio listeners, and it was a problem of which the BBC, at least, was well aware: much of its music programming policy under John Reith in the 1920s and early 1930s was designed to promote "active" listening.
   The Gramophone (like the BBC's *Radio Times*) is a rich source of examples of how bourgeois musical discourse changed to meet changing technological and commercial circumstances. See D. L. Le Mahieu, "*The Gramophone*: Recorded Music and the Cultivated Mind in Britain between the Wars," *Technology and Culture* 23(3) (1982).

7. As Richard Mohr, musical director of RCA Victor's Red Seal label, puts it, "The ideal for a phonograph record is the concert hall illusion or rather the illusion of the concert hall illusion because you can't transfer the concert hall into the dimensions of a living room. What you can do is record a work so that you think you're in a concert hall when you listen to it at home." See Glenn Gould, "The Prospects of Recording," *High*

Fidelity Magazine, vol. 16, April 1966, p. 49. My thanks to Paul Thèberge for bringing this to my attention.

8. Robert Stradling and Meirion Hughes suggest that a similar distinction within classical music itself was put into play by the BBC at the end of the 1920s, when it created the "categories of 'light' and 'light classical' music, which had previously been unknown." "Light composers" like Ketèlby and Coates could no longer appear on the same programs as "serious" composers such as Holst and Vaughan Williams. See *The English Musical Renaissance* (London: Routledge, 1993), pp. 89–90.

9. Dave Russell, *Popular Music in England, 1840–1914* (Manchester: Manchester University Press, 1987), p. 4.

10. Peter Van Der Merwe, *Origins of the Popular Style* (Oxford: Clarendon Press, 1989), pp. 16–19.

11. William Weber, *Music and the Middle Class: The Social Structure of Concert Life in London, Paris and Vienna* (London: Croom Helm, 1975), pp. 19–21.

12. Ibid., pp. 30–38, 60, 85–88, 113.

13. Lawrence M. Levine, *Highbrow/Lowbrow* (Cambridge, Mass.: Harvard University Press, 1988), p. 107.

14. Ibid., pp. 120, 146.

15. Paul Di Maggio, "Cultural Entrepreneurship in Nineteenth Century Boston. Part II: The Classification and Framing of American Art," *Media Culture and Society* 4(4) (1982): 317. And see Di Maggio, "Cultural Entrepreneurship in Nineteenth Century Boston: The Creation of an Organizational Base for High Culture in America," *Media Culture and Society* 4(1) (1982).

16. Quoted in Weber, *Music and the Middle Class,* p. 26.

17. Russell, *Popular Music in England,* pp. 6–7.

18. Ibid., pp. 7–8.

19. Katherine K. Preston, *Music for Hire: A Study of Professional Musicians in Washington (1877–1900)* (Stuyvesant, N.Y.: Pendragon Press, 1992), pp. 241–242.

20. Quoted in Jeremy Crump, "The Identity of English Music: The Reception of Elgar 1898–1935," in Robert Colls and Philip Dodd, eds., *Englishness: Politics and Culture, 1880–1920* (London: Croom Helm, 1986), p. 167. And see Van Der Merwe, *Origins of the Popular Style,* pp. 3–4, and Russell, *Popular Music in England,* pp. 7–8.

21. Levine, *Highbrow/Lowbrow,* p. 108.

22. See Irving Wallace, *The Fabulous Showman* (London: Hutchison, 1960), pp. 120–122. For Barnum's own account see *Struggles and Triumphs of P. T. Barnum By Himself* [1882] (London: Macgibbon and Kee, 1967), chap. 9. His Jenny Lind story is an uncanny preview of the Beatles' "invasion" of America to come.

23. Janice Radway, "The Scandal of the Middlebrow: The Book of the Month Club, Class Fracture and Cultural Authority," *South Atlantic Quarterly* 89(4) (1990). See also Joan Shelley Rubin, *The Making of Middlebrow Culture* (Chapel Hill and London: University of North Carolina Press, 1992).

24. Max Horkheimer and Theodor W. Adorno, *Dialectic of Enlightenment* [1944] (London: Allan Lane, 1973), p. 143.

25. Joseph Horowitz, *Understanding Toscanini* (New York: Alfred A. Knopf, 1987), p. 7. For Horowitz's analysis of classical music as mass music (and middle-class sociability)

in the postwar period, see his study of Van Cliburn, *The Ivory Trade: Piano Competitions and the Business of Music* (Boston: Northeastern University Press, 1990).

26. Horowitz, *Understanding Toscanini*, pp. 197–198.

27. Ibid., pp. 202, 208–209. And see T. W. Adorno's "Analytical Study of the NBC *Music Appreciation Hour*," reprinted in *Musical Quarterly* 78(2) (1994).

28. See Horowitz, *Understanding Toscanini*, p. 224. For the gramophone societies in Britain in this period, loosely organized by *The Gramophone* to encourage classical music appreciation among new listeners, see Le Mahieu, "*The Gramophone*: Recorded Music and the Cultivated Mind."

29. John F. Kassan, *Rudeness and Civility: Manners in Nineteenth Century Urban America* (New York: Hill and Wang, 1990), pp. 252–256. The best study of the same process in Britain remains Peter Bailey, *Leisure and Class in Victorian England* (London: Routledge and Kegan Paul, 1978).

30. Kathy Peiss, *Cheap Amusements: Working Women and Leisure in Turn-of-the-Century New York* (Philadelphia: Temple University Press, 1986), p. 136.

31. Geoffrey Nowell-Smith, "On Kiri Te Kanawa, Judy Garland, and the Culture Industry," in Naremore and Brantlinger, eds., *Modernity and Mass Culture* (Bloomington: Indiana University Press, 1991), p. 78.

32. Howard S. Becker, *Art Worlds* (Berkeley: University of California Press, 1982); Pierre Bourdieu, *Distinction: A Social Critique of the Judgement of Taste* [1979] (London: Routledge, 1984). For an earlier sociological approach which, drawing on Schutz, implicitly employs concepts of both art worlds ("musical cultures") and cultural capital ("musical competence") see Derrick F. Wright, "Musical Meaning and its Social Determinants," *Sociology* 9(3) (1975). A musical culture, Wright suggests, involves "knowledge not just of musical forms and interpretative schemes but also of rules of behaviour in musical settings." It means knowing "how, when and where to hear music" (p. 428).

33. I sometimes wonder whether my compulsion to think in threes is an effect of the BBC's division of my music listening experience into Radios 1, 2, and 3 (or, before that, the Home Service, the Light Programme, and the Third Programme), but my folk/art/pop distinction is, in fact, routine in the field, as I'll describe. Van Der Merwe, for example, defines "parlour music" by contrast to "art" music, on the one hand, and "folk" music, on the other, while Booth and Kuhn, using a very different musicological model, also come up with a tripartite division of folk/art/pop, which they root in different economic bases of support and transmission (art music is defined as patronized music). Musical forms can then be related to the constraints imposed by different production/transmission systems, in terms of levels of complexity and novelty, the nature of the audience, who's paying for the music, and so on. See Gregory D. Booth and Terry Lee Kuhn, "Economic and Transmission Factors as Essential Elements in the Definition of Folk, Art and Pop Music," *Musical Quarterly* 74(3) (1990).

34. Quoted in Kyle Gann, "Pulitzer Hacks," *Village Voice* (date unknown), p. 84.

35. I owe this point to Gregory Sandow. The great majority of art music professionals, of course, are players and not composers, but they face a similar problem in earning a living: *someone's* got to pay their way, and Cyril Ehrlich has argued that the necessity to give lessons to make a living had an entirely debilitating effect on art music culture

in Britain (he is thinking specifically about piano lessons, which became a normal part of middle-class childhood for 75 years or so from the turn of the century). See Cyril Ehrlich, *The Music Profession in Britain since the Eighteenth Century* (Oxford: Clarendon, 1985), chap. 6.

36. Henry Kingsbury, *Music, Talent and Performance: A Conservatory Cultural System* (Philadelphia: Temple University Press, 1988).

37. I take this list from Kingsbury, *Music, Talent and Performance*, pp. 17–18. He also includes as a conservatory characteristic "highly privatised teacher-student dyads."

38. Quoted in Horowitz, *Understanding Toscanini*, p. 212.

39. For a scathing account of how the pantheon of Great British Composers of the twentieth century was thus constructed, in "a selection process in which something less abstract than aesthetic judgement was involved"—on down the crown of the road march Parry, Elgar, and Vaughan Williams; out on the sidelines sit Rutland Boughton, Samuel Coleridge Taylor and Sir Arthur Sullivan—see Stradling and Hughes, *The English Musical Renaissance*, chap. 6.

40. In *Understanding Toscanini*, Joseph Horowitz is entertainingly rude about the "music appreciation" broadcasts and books issued by such American classical music popularizers as Walter Damrosch in the 1920s and 1930s, seeing their approach as banal, parochial, and run through with an oily religiosity (pp. 203–210). Intellectuals were similarly quick to laugh at the ignorance and deplore the pronunciation of the presenters on Britain's first national commercial radio station, Classic FM, which was designed (successfully) to capture the popular audience for classical music that the BBC had eschewed. On the other hand, it remains striking that on newspaper arts pages it is still assumed that critics of popular forms (TV, film, and to some extent pop) need know nothing about such forms except as consumers: their skill is to be able to write about ordinary experience. Critics of high art forms, by contrast—music, art, and even literature—are expected to be educated in the form (book critics by having written books themselves). Music critics, in other words, are still seen as deriving their authority from their education rather than their individual sensibility or writing skills.

41. Quoted in Stradling and Hughes, *The English Musical Renaissance*, p. 234. Their emphasis.

42. Christopher Jackman, "Some Sociological Issues of Live Music Performance," Ph.D. thesis, Department of Sociology, Brunel University, 1992. For further thoughts on concert conventions see Christopher Small, "Performance as Ritual: Sketch for an Enquiry into the True Nature of a Symphony Concert," in A. L. White, ed., *Lost in Music*, Sociological Review Monograph 34 (London: Routledge, 1987). For the complex negotiations between bandleader and caterer on the New York private party circuit see Bruce A. Macleod, *Club Date Musicians* (Urbana and Chicago: University of Illinois Press, 1993), pp. 97–100.

43. Niall MacKinnon, *The British Folk Scene* (Buckingham: Open University Press, 1993). Direct quotes are from pp. 81, 94, and 112.

Compare Robert Cantwell's argument from the United States: "As Dave Guard [of the Kingston Trio] recalls, the untutored, but far from amateur, vocal sound [of the 1950s folk revival] was the conscious production of professional coaching in phrasing, vowel sounds, and speech accent." See his "When We Were Good: Class and Culture in the Folk Revival," in Neil V. Rosenberg, ed., *Transforming Tradition* (Urbana and Chicago: University of Illinois Press, 1993), pp. 43–44.

44. MacKinnon, *The British Folk Scene,* p. 81.
45. For the significance of these resources for folk "revivals" see Rosenberg, *Transforming Tradition,* passim. The liner-note quote is from Kenneth S. Goldstein, "A Future Folklorist in the Record Business," p. 109.

   The original folk revival in Britain, at the beginning of the century, was heavily dependent on Cecil Sharp's exercise of authority through the English Folk Dance and Song Society; he and his trained teachers took on "the role of expert in the legitimation of performance." See Georgina Boyes, *The Imagined Village* (Manchester: Manchester University Press, 1993), p. 105.
46. Cantwell, "When We Were Good," p. 57.
47. MacKinnon, *The British Folk Scene,* pp. 19, 40, 53.
48. Boyes, *The Imagined Village,* p. 241; Bruce Jackson, "The Folksong Revival," in Rosenberg, *Transforming Tradition,* pp. 76–77. And see MacKinnon, *The British Folk Scene,* pp. 57, 72.
49. Simon Frith, *Sound Effects* (New York: Pantheon, 1981).
50. See, for example, Wilfrid Mellers, *Twilight of the Gods* (London: Faber and Faber, 1973) (on the Beatles); *A Darker Shade of Pale* (London: Faber and Faber, 1984) (on Bob Dylan); and *Angels of the Night* (Oxford: Basil Blackwell, 1986) (on popular female singers).
51. Frith, *Sound Effects,* chap. 3.
52. Ernest Borneman, *A Critic Looks at Jazz* (London: Jazz Music Books, 1946), p. 48.
53. I'm assuming here (unlike Bourdieu) that we can't map these discourses onto social class, or trace "homologies" between aesthetic values and social situations. If nothing else, the historical work on high and low culture should make the critic wary of treating mass culture (and all these discourses concern mass culture) in simple class terms.
54. Charles Keil has suggested that commercial media have been important in legitimating ethnic musics in the United States, in providing them with that weight, that history, that assures their "authenticity." See "People's Music Comparatively: Style and Stereotype, Class and Hegemony," *Dialectical Anthropology* 10 (1985).
55. See Robert Cantwell, *Bluegrass Breakdown* (Urbana: University of Illinois Press, 1984).
56. George Steiner, *In Bluebeard's Castle: Some Notes Towards the Re-definition of Culture* (London: Faber and Faber, 1971), p. 92.
57. Quoted (from a bandsmen's magazine) in Brian Jackson, *Working Class Community* (London: Routledge and Kegan Paul, 1968), p. 25. For Romanticism and rock see Simon Frith and Howard Horne, *Art into Pop* (London: Methuen, 1987), chap. 2. For the historical origins of these various ideals see Morag Shiach, *Discourse on Popular Culture* (Cambridge: Polity, 1989).
58. See Ruth Finnegan, *The Hidden Musicians: Music-Making in an English Town* (Cambridge: Cambridge University Press, 1989).
59. Borneman, *A Critic Looks at Jazz,* p. 12.
60. See Frith, *Sound Effects,* and Frith and Horne, *Art into Pop.*
61. Howard Rye, "Fearsome Means of Discord: Early Encounters with Black Jazz," in Paul Oliver, ed., *Black Music in Britain* (Milton Keynes: Open University Press, 1990), p. 47.

62. Quoted in Rye, "Fearsome Means of Discord," p. 49.

63. See Simon Frith, "Playing with Real Feeling—Jazz and Suburbia," *New Formations* 4 (1988).

64. See Ron Welburn, "Duke Ellington's Music: The Catalyst for a True Jazz Criticism," *International Review of the Aesthetics and Sociology of Music* 17 (1986).

65. Borneman, *A Critic Looks at Jazz*, p. 14.

66. Welburn, "Duke Ellington's Music," pp. 114–115.

67. Ibid., p. 122.

3. Common Sense and the Language of Criticism

1. Ernest Borneman, *A Critic Looks at Jazz* (London: Jazz Music Books, 1946), p. 7. Borneman the jazz fan doesn't always follow the advice of Borneman the anthropologist. While he does attempt to establish an "objective" criterion of jazz value, which depends first on establishing what "makes this music different from all other forms of music," and second on asserting that "the best musician is the one who shows the least compromise with alien forms of music; who gives the widest development to the traditional framework; who shows the greatest variety within the unity of the chosen idiom" (p. 14), his views often stray across such clear generic boundaries and express obvious "subjective" views—"in jazz, as in all art, the great masterpieces are invariably lucid, serene and perfectly poised" (p. 15); "Tin Pan Alley tunes are not only poorly invented and generally in bad taste, but also insufficient in rhythmic, melodic and harmonic tension to provide a musical stimulus for jazz improvisation" (p. 16).

2. From a letter commenting on my arguments in this chapter.

3. For a useful discussion of the methodological issues raised here for taste research, see Jackie Stacey, "Textual Obsessions: Methodology, History and Researching Female Spectatorship," *Screen* 34(3) (1993).

4. See Fred Vermorel and Judy Vermorel, *Starlust: The Secret Fantasies of Fans* (London: W. H. Allen, 1985); and Lisa A. Lewis ed., *The Adoring Audience: Fan Culture and Popular Media* (London and New York: Routledge, 1992).

5. One observer, interested in courtship routines, was unceremoniously chased off the beach by angry lovemakers, and Graham Greene made full use of the spy/observer confusion in *The Confidential Agent* (London: William Heinemann, 1939). For an early overview of M-O's findings see Mass-Observation, *Britain* (Harmondsworth, Middlesex: Penguin, 1939).

6. For an example of this sort of research, see Herbert Blumer, *Movies and Conduct* (New York: Macmillan, 1933). Even in the Lynds' Middletown research, the emphasis tended to be more on cinema's effect on social mores, or, rather, on the Lynds' reading of this, than on Middletowners' own account of their movie pleasures—see, for example, Robert Lynd and Helen Lynd, *Middletown* (New York: Harcourt, Brace and Company, 1929), pp. 267–268.

7. See Jeffrey Richards and Dorothy Sheridan, ed., *Mass-Observation at the Movies* (London: Routledge, 1987). There are obvious precursors here of the way television researchers in the 1970s began to concentrate on television viewing as a social practice, one which might have very little to do with what was on the screen, and which was

shaped by particular sorts of domestic relationships. For a useful survey of the arguments see Dave Morley, *Television, Audiences and Cultural Studies* (London: Routledge, 1992).

8. There is some supporting evidence that the tastes described by the Mass-Observation projects were typical in a questionnaire survey carried out through *Picturegoer* a few years later. See J. P. Mayer, *British Cinemas and Their Audiences* (London: Dennis Dobson, 1948), pp. 153–244. Mayer looks at the film preferences of a sample of 50 moviegoers (the earlier part of the book concerns the effect of moviegoing on people's lives as revealed by their "motion picture autobiographies").

9. On this point see Robert B. Ray, "The Twelve Days of Christmas: A Response to Dudley Andrew," *Strategies* 3 (1990): 284.

10. There is not much academic research on popular musicians, but the few existing studies are rather good. In the United States Howard Becker's work on dance musicians became the model for a number of subsequent studies. See Howard S. Becker, *Outsiders* (Glencoe, N.Y.: Free Press, 1963); Robert A. Stebbins, "The Jazz Community: The Sociology of a Musical Subculture," Ph.D thesis, University of Minnesota, 1964; Robert R. Faulkner, *Hollywood Studio Musicians: Their Work and Career in the Recording Industry* (Chicago: Aldine-Atherton, 1971); H. Stith Bennett, *On Becoming a Rock Musician* (Amherst: University of Massachussetts Press, 1980).

   In Britain Mavis Bayton's "How Women Become Rock Musicians," Ph.D. thesis, University of Warwick, 1989, provides a useful corrective to Bennett's picture of an entirely masculine world, and there are two outstanding anthropological studies of local music making: Ruth Finnegan, *The Hidden Musicians* (Cambridge: Cambridge University Press, 1989), and Sara Cohen, *Rock Culture in Liverpool* (Oxford: Clarendon Press, 1991).

   All these studies (not least for methodological reasons) deal with the journeymen and women of the popular music world rather than with its stars, though Robert Walser's *Running with the Devil: Power, Gender and Madness in Heavy Metal* (Hanover and London: Wesleyan University Press, 1993) does something to redress the balance. He, like any serious researcher on this topic, is reliant on the magazine *Musician,* by far the best source of information on rock star values. See the interviews collected in Bill Flanagan, *Written in My Soul* (Chicago: Contemporary Books, 1986).

11. Borneman, *A Critic Looks at Jazz,* p. 12.

12. Geoff Wills and Cary L. Cooper, *Pressure Sensitive: Popular Musicians under Stress* (London: Sage, 1988), pp. 80–81.

13. A point first made by Howard S. Becker. See "The Professional Dance Musician and His Audience," *American Journal of Sociology* 57(2) (1952).

14. For an early sociological description of this problem see Carlo L. Lastrucci, "The Professional Dance Musician," *Journal of Musicology* 3(3) (1941).

15. Art Hodes and Chadwick Hansen, *Hot Man: The Life of Art Hodes* (Urbana and Chicago, University of Illinois Press, 1992), p. 109.

16. Bruce MacLeod, *Club Date Musicians: Playing the New York Party Circuit* (Urbana and Chicago: University of Illinois Press, 1993), p. 92.

17. As one of Wills and Cooper's interviewees puts it, "Most people regard musicians as one step up the 'social ladder' from rapists and muggers, and it's this 'alienation' from the non-musician that I believe creates most of the problems. The prolonged experi-

ence of being regarded as 'unclean' by 'civilians' is what causes the musician to retreat into himself, and causes a build-up of neuroses which can all-too-easily lead to a nervous breakdown. This is compounded by many facts . . . There is no standard set. The public wouldn't know a good player from a bad one, the media largely promote mediocrity, and the Musicians' Union have no set standard to conform to: pay your subs', and you're in! In any other profession, it's a fair bet that as you become more skilful, you move up, and do better quality work. Not so for the musician." Quoted in *Pressure Sensitive*, p. 46.

18. Quoted in Dr. Licks, *Standing in the Shadows of Motown: The Life and Music of Legendary Bassist James Jamerson* (Wynnewood, Pa.: Dr. Licks Publishing, 1989), p. 41.

19. It is interesting to read John Culshaw's views on this. From his perspective as a classical music producer, he concluded that it was the *situation* of performer/audience that was bad for music: "I really doubt that anyone plays better with an audience than without. They may think they do. But actually they only feel better. Listen to a transcription of a recorded concert that had the audience feeling 'My God, that was wonderful' and you will find that it really wasn't that good. But it was an occasion, like a funeral, and one is excited and moved by having been part of the audience. When somebody buys the record he feels that he has been swindled if he doesn't go crazy like the audience of 2,000 to 3,000 that was present and so he doesn't apply his usual critical faculties . . . He is a conditioned dog." Quoted in Glenn Gould, "The Prospects of Recording," *High Fidelity Magazine*, vol. 16, April 1966, p. 54.

20. They were more likely to be represented by American Equity. See George Seltzer, *Music Matters: The Performer and the American Federation of Musicians* (Metuchen, N.J.: Scarecrow Press, 1989), p. 263.

21. Quoted in Dr. Licks, *Standing in the Shadows of Motown*, p. xiii.

22. Konstantin Economou, *Making Music Work* (Linkoping, Sweden: Linkoping University, 1994), p. 200.

23. For an interesting sociological description of how this feels from the inside, see H. L. Goodall, Jr., *Living in the Rock N Roll Mystery* (Carbondale and Edwardsville, Ill.: Southern Illinois University Press, 1991).

24. As Economou's research suggests, young musicians, like any other young fans, value their idols as standing for "a certain way of looking at life." This is what the music (and the musical genre concerned) is taken to mean; such meanings must be shared by one's fellow players in a group. See Economou, *Making Music Work*, pp. 101, 202–205.

25. Quoted in MacLeod, *Club Date Musicians*, p. 141.

26. Many thanks to Greg Sandow for this point.

27. Norman Lebrecht observed Rodney Friend, leader of the BBC Symphony Orchestra, getting increasingly irritated as he rehearsed a piece by Harrison Birtwistle: "'The only pleasure I get,' expostulated Friend, unable to fathom the structure of the music sitting on his stand, 'is actually being able to play it from beginning to end more or less accurately.' . . . Both men, beneath the professional courtesies, were exceedingly angry. Friend felt he was being forced to abuse his instrument; Birtwistle heard his music being attacked." Norman Lebrecht, "Knights at the Opera," *The Independent Magazine*, May 18, 1991, p. 59.

28. Jon Frederickson and James F. Rooney, "The Free-Lance Musician as a Type of Non-Person: An Extension of the Concept of Non-Personhood," *Sociological Quarterly* 29(2) (1988).

29. In British critical ideology the ideal creative force is thus taken to be the guitarist/singer writing partnership—Jagger/Richard, Morrissey/Marr.

30. The resulting confusions in Britain's "indie-rock" scene are well brought out in Cohen's *Rock Culture in Liverpool*.

31. John Miller Chernoff, *African Rhythm and African Sensibility* (Chicago and London: University of Chicago Press, 1979), pp. 126–127.

32. Quoted in Brian Jackson, *Working Class Community* (London: Routledge and Kegan Paul, 1968), p. 25. Emphasis in the original.

33. For sociological studies of the recording studio see Edward R. Kealy's "From Craft to Art: The Case of Sound Mixers and Popular Music" (*Sociology of Work and Occupations* 6 [1979]), which shows how professional values shifted in the 1960s as sound engineers took on a more self-consciously artistic (rock-derived) attitude to their work; and Antoine Hennion's "The Production of Success: An Antimusicology of the Pop Song" (*Popular Music* 3 [1983]), a subtle account of Paris recording studios which draws attention to the ever-present arbitrating role of the person not there, the consumer, as everyone present tries to judge sounds against what she or he might like.

34. For a lucid and instructive account of "the production of culture" in country music, showing how at each stage the "work" at issue—the piece of music—becomes a different discursive object, see John Ryan and Richard A. Peterson, "The Product Image: The Fate of Creativity in Country Music Songwriting," in J. Ettema and D. Whitney, eds., *Individuals in Mass Media Organisations* (Newbury Park, Calif.: Sage, 1982).

35. I'm generalizing here both from my own conversations, and from Keith Negus's excellent study of the British recording industry, *Producing Pop* (London: Edward Arnold, 1992), which suggests that the key value clash is not that between musicians and companies, but between A&R and marketing departments, which define musical value differently and are equally eager to claim sales success for themselves (and blame market failure on each other).

36. For record company Romanticism see Jon Stratton, "Capitalism and Romantic Ideology in the Record Business," *Popular Music* 3 (1983). For copyright law, see Simon Frith, ed., *Music and Copyright* (Edinburgh: Edinburgh University Press, 1993).

37. Nicholas Tawa notes the importance of the man with an ear "like the public's" (and the actual commercial unreliability of his taste) for song publishers in turn-of-the-century Tin Pan Alley. See Nicholas Tawa, *The Way to Tin Pan Alley: American Popular Song, 1866–1910* (New York: Schirmer Books, 1990), p. 42.

38. Chrysalis Records Press Release, August 29, 1990.

39. BMG press release for Raging Slab, January 16, 1990.

40. See, for example, Paul Willis, *Profane Culture* (London: Routledge and Kegan Paul, 1978); and Dick Hebdige, *Subculture: The Meaning of Style* (London: Methuen, 1979).

41. See, for example, Vermorel and Vermorel, *Star Lust*; Sheryl Garratt, "Teenage Dreams," in Sheryl Garratt and Sue Steward, *Signed, Sealed and Delivered* (London: Pluto, 1984); and Sue Wise, "Sexing Elvis," *Women's Studies International Forum* 7 (1984).

42. See, for example, Donna Weinstein, *Heavy Metal: A Cultural Sociology* (New York: Lexington, 1991); Johan Fornäs, "Popular Music and Youth Culture in Late Modernity," in Keith Roe and Ulla Carlsson, eds., *Popular Music Research* (Göteborg: Nordicom-Sweden, 1990).

43. One of the more interesting examples of such a "functional" aesthetic concerns the South Korean genre of the "demo-song," songs used for demonstrations (and therefore banned by the state): "Generally speaking, demo-songs fall into three types. First, the lyric song, which has the Korean structure of feeling. What is important here are the words, which describe Korean political reality. We generally sing these songs in the bar or at home alone. Second, the folk song, translated into contemporary terms. We always sing the folk song before the political demonstration, along with group dances which represent unity. Here what is important is not the lyric but the empowering rhythm. Finally the direct demo-song. We sing these songs when we take part in a demonstration and fight the police and the army. The songs in this category are lyrically political but contain simple and repetitive rhythms. What is significant about demo-songs is not pleasure or fun but an experience in which I, the song, and reality become one. Of the three types I like the lyric song best, since such songs are most emotionally affecting. The more the grief expressed, the deeper the song's echo." Quoted, with thanks, from an unpublished essay by Chang Yun Joo.

44. Weinstein, *Heavy Metal*; Walser, *Running with the Devil*.

45. Nicholas Cook, *Music, Imagination and Culture* (Oxford: Clarendon Press, 1990), pp. 58–59. Compare Kyle Gann: "At a conference two years ago, I overheard a professor, who had just delivered a lecture on the structure of an Elliott Carter orchestral work, admit to a colleague that while Carter's music analyzes beautifully on paper, you can't hear in the music the nice things you've analyzed. His colleague sorrowfully agreed." (Kyle Gann, "Pulitzer Hacks," *Village Voice* [date unknown], p. 84.)

    The Italian musicologist Gino Stefani makes a similar distinction in terms of the different sorts of "musical competence" involved, contrasting "popular" competence and "high" competence in terms of a grid of interpretive codes moving from the general/functional to the formal/specific. See Gino Stefani, "A Theory of Musical Competence," *Semiotica* 66(3) (1987). I'm not convinced that there's a continuity here, rather than two quite different conceptions of music. My favorite example of what (to an ordinary listener) seems like musicological madness is cited by Janet M. Levy in "Covert and Casual Values in Recent Writings about Music," *Journal of Musicology* 6(1) (1987). This is Charles Rosen on Beethoven and "his continuous attempt to strip away, at some point in each large work, all decorative and even expressive elements from the musical material—so that part of the structure of tonality is made to appear for a moment naked and immediate, and its presence in the rest of the work as a dynamic and temporal force suddenly becomes radiant . . ." As Levy asks, what on earth does this mean? (p. 16).

46. Cook, *Music, Imagination and Culture*, p. 85.

47. Ibid., p. 223.

48. See William Mann, "What Songs the Beatles Sang . . .," *The Times*, December 27, 1963; Deryck Cooke, "The Lennon-McCartney Songs," *The Listener*, February 1, 1968; Wilfrid Mellers, *Twilight of the Gods* (London: Faber and Faber, 1973).

    As to who was laughing at whom, I can't resist quoting at length Glenn Gould's brilliant musicological review of Petula Clark. Parody? Serious? Or both?

But for Tony Hatch, tonality is not a worked-out lode. It is a viable and continuing source of productive energy with priorities that demand and get, from him, attention. "Downtown" is the most affirmative diatonic exhortation in the key of E major since the unlikely team of Felix Mendelssohn and Harriet Beecher Stowe pooled talents for "still, still with Thee, when purple morning breaketh, / When the bird waketh and the shadows flee" . . . Motivically, "Who Am I?" plays a . . . game of reverse "Downtown"-ism. The principal motivic cell unit of that ebullient lied consisted of the interval of a minor third plus a major second, alternating, upon occasion, with a major third followed by a minor second. In "Downtown," the composite of either of these figures, the perfect fourth, became the title motive and the figures themselves were elongated by reiterated notes ("When/you're/a/lone/and/life/is"), shuffled by commas ("down-town, where") ("to help, I") (["Pret]-ty, how can"), and constantly elaborated by the sort of free-diatonic transpositioning which seems entirely consistent with the impro-visatory fantasies of youth.

In "Who Am I?", however, the same motive, though introduced and occasionally relieved by scale-step passages ("The build-ings-reach-up—to-the-sky") is most often locked in a diatonic spiral—the notes F-E-C and C-A-G serving to underline "I walk alone and wonder, Who Am I?" Furthermore, the bass line at this moment is engaged with the notes D-G-E and G-E-A, a vertical synchronization of which would imply a harmonic composite of the title motive. Now, admittedly, such Schoenbergian jargon must be charily applied to the carefree creations of the pop scene. At all costs, one must avoid those more formidable precepts of Princetonian Babittry such as "pitch class," which, since they have not yet forded the Hudson unchallenged, can scarcely be expected to have plied the Atlantic and to have taken Walthamstow studio without a fight. Nevertheless, "Downtown" and "Who Am I?" clearly represent two sides of the same much-minted coin. The infectious enthusiasm of the "Downtown" motive encounters its obverse in the somnambulistic systematization of the "Who Am I?" symbol, a unit perfectly adapted to the tenor of mindless confidence and the tone of slurred articulation with which Petula evokes the interminable mid-morning coffee-hour laments of all the secret sippers of suburbia. ("Petula Clark," *High Fidelity*, November 1967. Quoted from Tim Page, ed., *The Glenn Gould Reader* [1984] [London: Faber and Faber, 1987], pp. 300–307.)

49. J. A. Westrup, Editorial, *Music and Letters* xlix(1), January 1968.
50. See Walser, *Running With The Devil*, passim.
51. Levin L. Schücking, *The Sociology of Literary Taste* [1931] (London: Kegan Paul, 1966), p. 57.
52. And it raises a recurring laugh among musicians. Bruce MacLeod notes that "the phrase 'Best band I've ever heard' has become a standard in-joke among club date musicians, who use it as an ironic response to questions about how the music was at a recent job. The reply makes it clear that it was pretty bad, although the audience liked it—as usual." (MacLeod, *Club Date Musicians*, p. 152.)
53. Andrew Porter, "Opera," *The New Yorker*, November 12, 1990, pp. 108–109.
54. Schoenberg quoted in Scott, "Music and Sociology for the 1990s," p. 389. Nicolas Slonimsky records an early example of this (and of the fact that "new music always

sounds loud to old ears") in a review of the first London performance of Beethoven's Ninth Symphony: "Beethoven finds from all the public accounts that noisy extravagance of execution and outrageous clamor in musical performances more frequently ensures applause than chastened elegance or refined judgement. The inference, therefore, that we may fairly make, is that he writes accordingly." See Nicolas Slonimsky, *Lexicon of Musical Invective* [1953] (Seattle and London: University of Washington Press, 1969), p. 18.

55. Borneman, *A Critic Looks at Jazz*, p. 52.

56. Letter to the *Voice Pazz and Jop Music Supplement*, March 5, 1991, p. 7.

57. For an entertaining and helpful account of these arguments among turn-of-the-century writers see Peter Keating, *The Haunted Study: A Social History of the English Novel, 1875–1914* (London: Secker and Warburg, 1989).

58. Perhaps the most striking feature of the resulting standoff between the aesthete and the philistine is that for both sides the other is feminine. The woman as materialist corruptor of the artist is a consistent theme of Henry James's stories and of subsequent bohemian mythology (in Bob Dylan's early songs, for instance), just as the high cultural description of mass culture as feminine by theorists from Horkheimer and Adorno to Baudrillard is echoed in rock fans' contemptuous dismissal of commercial pop as "teenybop." (See Andreas Huyssen, "Mass Culture as Woman: Modernism's Other," in his *After the Great Divide* (Bloomington: Indiana University Press, 1986.)

Meanwhile, from the philistine side, the American bandmaster John Philip Sousa once stressed to a Houston reporter that "the people who frequent my concerts are the strong and healthy. I mean healthy of both mind and body. These people like virile music. Longhaired men and shorthaired women you never see in my audience. And I don't want them." (Quoted in Levine, *Highbrow/Lowbrow*, p. 238.) Nicholas Tawa suggests that the philistine treatment of high art as "effete" was a central theme of the late nineteenth century popular song (see Tawa, *The Way to Tin Pan Alley*). This equation of high art with sissiness and perversion remains familiar in populist prose.

59. Borneman, *A Critic Looks at Jazz*, p. 13.

60. See Roland Barthes, "The Grain of the Voice" [1972] in *The Responsibility of Forms* (Berkeley and Los Angeles: University of California Press, 1991), p. 267: "If we examine the current practice of music criticism (or of conversations 'on' music: often the same thing), we see that the work (or its performance) is invariably translated into the poorest linguistic category: the adjective."

61. Kingsbury, *Music, Talent and Performance*, p. 87.

62. Lebrecht, "Knights at the Opera," p. 57.

63. Robert Sandall, "Lou Reed's *Magic and Loss*," Q, 65 (February 1992).

64. Reviews by Stephen Dalton from the "Short Circuit" album round-up, *New Musical Express* (date unknown).

65. Simon Reynolds, "Smells Like Teen Spirit," *Village Voice*, December 3, 1991, p. 69.

66. *Voice Pazz and Jop Supplement*, March 5, 1991, p. 7.

67. The most common arguments about musical effects are rather different. Popular music has, for example, been held responsible for sexual arousal and/or hysteria; delinquency and violence; despair and suicide; fascism and political mindlessness; sexism and homophobia; bourgeois ideology generally (and romantic heterosexualism in particular).

Such readings tend to be made by people from outside the music worlds concerned, and they therefore don't depend on any pop or rock knowledge at all (which is why such arguments so often seem plain silly to the fans and musicians themselves). Despite (or maybe because of) this, such arguments, unlike production arguments, tend to be remarkably effective materially, in terms of labelings, bannings, and censorship. The effects critics do influence what music is and can be produced and heard, and a necessary part of such judgments is, indeed, the assertion that something "should be done": stop Skrewdriver concerts! Ban Shabba Ranks tracks from the radio! This even though very little evidence usually exists that the music has the effects it is purported to have, whether on crowd behavior, individual attitudes, social beliefs, or whatever. It follows, paradoxically, that effects criticism focuses much more closely than production criticism on the music itself. The "effects" of the music, that is to say, have to be deduced from the music itself because there is no independent evidence of them. In this context "the music itself" is reduced to a rather small number of effective elements: rhythm; lyrics; performance.

68. See Howard S. Becker, "Art as Collective Action," *American Sociological Review* 39 (1974).

69. See Susan D. Crafts, Daniel Cavicchi, and Charles Keil, *My Music* (Hanover and London, Wesleyan University Press, 1993).

This is not Charles Keil's first venture into such research. In 1965 he "sponsored a contest in *Spear* magazine . . . which had a wide circulation in various levels of Nigerian society . . . Readers were asked to respond in thirty words or less to the question 'Who is your favourite musician—and why?'" The results are reported as an appendix to Chernoff, *African Rhythm and Sensibility*. The following quotes indicate the variety of technical and functional judgments:

"My favourite musician is I. K. Dairo. He begins moderately, sings moderately, ends moderately. No mixing of language. No mumble. Different tones, tunes, and beating in each music. His tunation, tone and beating moulded together keep music unfaded" (p. 174).

"My favourite musician is Mr Cardinal Jim Rex Lawson because his music can make the unhappy to be happy and a divorced couple to be reengaged and an angry lion to be calmed" (p. 174).

"Jim Lawson is my favourite . . . The underground sound of instruments thrills even a mad person to dance and escape madness meanwhile" (p. 175).

"In fact the moment I am annoyed with my girlfriend or feel unhappy with everything on earth and fed up with life, but as soon as I put on my radio and hear I. K. Dario's music, I will be just very happy and forget all sorts of bad thinking and start kissing my girlfriend" (p. 178).

"The late Jim Reeves is my music idol. His cool sentimentality, his heart-awakening compositions, the voice and the instruments which make you feel the angels around, surely win your heart" (p. 177).

70. Crafts, Cavicchi, and Keil, *My Music,* pp. 61, 168, 140, 144.

71. Ibid., p. 49 (and compare pp. 69, 103, 118, 137) and pp. 193, 85, 90–91.

72. Ibid., pp. 97–98.

4. Genre Rules

1. Quoted in Nicholas Tawa, *The Way to Tin Pan Alley: American Popular Song, 1866–1910* (New York: Schirmer Books, 1990), p. 85.
2. Quoted in Christopher Ballantine, *Music and Its Social Meanings* (New York: Gordon and Breach, 1984), p. 26.
3. Cited in Tawa, *The Way to Tin Pan Alley,* p. 162.
4. I always enjoy looking for my brother's records in strange record stores: as an "avant-garde" guitarist who has performed in a great variety of idioms, Fred Frith may turn up as jazz or rock or contemporary classical, as alternative, New Age, or Euro pop.
5. This information was taken from *Variety: The Complete Book of US Show Business Awards* (New York: Garland, 1985). Thanks to Alex Doty for bringing this to my attention.
6. This list was taken from Ken Barnes, "Top 40 Radio: A Fragment of the Imagination," in S. Frith, ed., *Facing the Music* (New York: Pantheon, 1988).
7. David Zimmerman, "Adult Top 40 Makes Waves in Radio," *USA Today,* date unknown.
8. There's a particular problem here of genre boundaries. On the one hand, radio stations are loath to play anything too different from their basic sound (the first principle of programming is to ensure that no one is moved to switch off); on the other hand, neither do they want to seem too exclusive (the second principle is to entice the straying listener to stay). The effect (as many a bemused European visitor will testify) is that, for all the fine demographic distinctions, American commercial radio stations sound much the same. This is not much help to record sellers—and helps explains the rise of MTV, which maps the music market in much more record company–friendly ways.
9. Government of Canada, *Loi sur la Radiofusion,* 1983, Schedule II, Content Categories and Subcategories, pp. 2573–4. On Canada's insistence, Canadian content requirements were not an issue in the Free Trade Agreements between Canada and the United States and Mexico. Thanks to Will Straw for clarification of Canadian radio policy.
10. For an interesting answer see Line Grenier, "Radio Broadcasting in Canada: The Case of 'Transformat' Music," *Popular Music* 9(2) (1990).
11. The words of EMAP's David Hepworth, quoted in Judy Rumbold, "Rock plays it riff and ready," *Media Guardian,* September 10, 1990.
12. The Independent Radio Authority, which is responsible for awarding broadcasting licenses, later put its own gloss on this clause, by defining music recorded or composed before 1960 as "non-pop music" even if it was both strongly rhythmic and amplified.
13. House of Lords *Weekly Hansard,* October 16, 1990, columns 752–754. The amendment was passed and accepted by the House of Commons; the FM license was awarded to Classic FM, a classical music station.
14. The rock/pop distinction was, in fact, taken from sociology—see my *Sound Effects* (New York: Pantheon, 1981). The ideological implications were obvious in media discussion at the time. Judy Rumbold quotes Danny Kelly, then editor of *New Musical Express* (now editor of *Q*): "Pop is bought by teenage girls. Rock is bought by everybody else." And Mark Fisher, then Labour Party spokesman for the Arts: "Pop music is rock music without the sex or soul." See Judy Rumbold, "Rock plays it riff and ready."

15. Barry Walters, "A Better Best Top 100," *Village Voice*, September 6, 1988, p. 73.

16. See Jason Toynbee, "Policing Bohemia, Pinning Up the Grunge: The Music Press and Generic Change in British Pop and Rock," *Popular Music* 12(3) (1993); and Sarah Thornton, *Club Cultures* (Cambridge: Polity, 1995).

17. *Folk Roots* press release, March 7, 1988. Readers' letters pages become particularly interesting (and angry) when a magazine moves genre boundaries—as in *The Wire*, the British jazz magazine, which extended its definition of jazz to cover all "interesting" contemporary music at about the same time as *Southern Rag* became *Folk Roots*.

18. Quoted from the first WORLD MUSIC press release, n.d. [1987]. And see Peter Jowers, "Beating New Tracks: WOMAD and the British World Music Movement," in Simon Miller, ed., *The Last Post: Music after Modernism* (Manchester: Manchester University Press, 1993), pp. 61–64.

19. I discuss this in much greater detail in "The Naked and the Dead," in Georgina Born and David Hesmondhalgh, eds., *Western Music and Its Others* (Berkeley: University of California Press, forthcoming).

20. This becomes a particularly complex argument in the marketing of "crossover" acts, when the same music has to be sold as fulfilling different functions for different audiences. The crossover appeal of Michael Jackson's *Thriller* to a rock audience, for example, depended on a particularly subtle mix of Eddie Van Halen's guitar against Jackson's voice.

21. For discussion of these issues in an American context see Holly Kruse, "Subcultural Identity in Alternative Music Culture," *Popular Music* 12(1) (1993); and Stephen Lee, "Re-examining the Concept of the 'Independent' Record Company: The Case of Wax Trax! Records," *Popular Music* 14(1) (1995).

22. In Britain a reliable sign of an "indie" band is that its albums top the charts on release and then fall straight out—such bands have devoted followers but fail to cross over.

23. The list is based on a questionnaire funded by Nescafe and administered by student radio stations. I'm taking the information from a press release dated October 1, 1988.

24. Quotes from *WRPM*, Autumn 1991. Thanks to Caroline Hutton for making this available to me.

25. For an example of an ideological category bringing together some even odder bedfellows, see Janos Marothy, *Music and the Bourgeois, Music and the Proletarian* (Budapest: Akadémiai Kiadó, 1974), pp. 536–538. At one point Marothy discusses "new folk singers" or "political folk singers," musicians who are not "lured by the commercial showbusiness" but "continue the proletarian folk tradition in the original spirit . . . so as to make it part and parcel of the conscious socialist movements of our modern age." These singers included Merle Travis (U.S.A.), Ernest Busch (Germany), Yves Montaud (France), Ewan McColl (Britain), and, from Italy, Margot and the Cantachronacle movement (which at this time included Italo Calvino). Some enterprising political nostalgic should put together a celebratory CD.

26. This is obvious, for example, in the musicians' conversations recorded in Sara Cohen, *Rock Culture in Liverpool* (Oxford: Clarendon Press, 1991).

    In an article examining the blurred boundaries between contemporary rock and art musics (and the increasing use of the term "new music"), Kyle Gann quotes Robert Ashley's simple formula: "Anything over five minutes is classical music, anything under that is rock." But even such an objective measure turns out to have an evaluative underpinning. Ashley explains that "Over five minutes a piece begins to need a structural foundation to hold together on a deeper-than-surface level." Add the suggestion that art music is also defined by its concert setting, a setting providing the necessary quietness, concentration, and intimacy, and we're back with a distinction that is really about art music's *superiority* to rock. See Kyle Gann, "Boundary Busters," *Village Voice*, September 3, 1991, p. 87.

27. Every critic is ambitious to fix a genre with a new label, to *conventionalize* a set of comparisons. My best attempt was the term "Hip Easy Listening," used in *Time Out* in April 1977 to describe Californian soft rock—Fleetwood Mac, etc. It was, however, redundant; the American radio label AOR described the same sort of music more efficiently. For a useful discussion of the same process in the book trade, see Susanne Kappeler, *The Pornography of Representation* (Cambridge: Polity Press, 1986), pp. 116–122.

28. Hence, for example, the continuing importance of *Maximum Rock'n'Roll* for the American since-punk scene, or the role of such little magazines as *Girl Germs* and *Girlymag* in the making of Riot Grrrl.

29. This clearly relates to the long-established truism of postwar popular music history that small, local, independent entrepreneurs pick up on new sounds and markets first (are "closer to the streets"). The majors only come in when new money-making possibilities are confirmed—the pattern from rock 'n' roll to rave.

30. Sarah Thornton makes this point about London's '90s dance club magazines, like *Boys' Own*—see *Club Cultures*. I am also indebted for the arguments here to Franc Donohoe's unpublished study of industrial music and Seona Slevin's unpublished work on Riot Grrrl.

31. For an excellent discussion of parallel arguments about the use of genre labels in film theory see Steve Neale, "Questions of Genre," *Screen* 31(1) (1990).

32. This is, perhaps, most obvious in country music. In Katie Stewart's words, "So it is that in country music the saddest of sad songs have come to represent the source or origins of 'country' as an other world or lyrical space that some people, and not others, inhabit. The music is filled with self-referential images of 'places' and 'types of people.' It fashions lyric images into a country world by indiscriminately mixing the metaphoric with the literal or the allegorical with the actual so that the subjects and objects of the songs appear as if in quotes and the categories themselves become objects of discussion to be reproduced, carried to excess, parodied, or taken to heart." Katie Stewart, "The Narrative Poetics of American 'Country' Lament: A Re-presentation of Country Music's Lost Love and Appalachia's Litanies of the Dead," unpublished paper, n.d., pp. 16–17. And see Aaron Fox, "The Jukebox of History: Narratives of Loss and Desire in the Discourse of Country Music," *Popular Music* 11(1) (1992).

33. See Paul Oliver's comments on the problems bequeathed by blues collectors to historians of African-American popular music: "Perceiving the blues as central to black secular song has had the effect of minimizing and even totally ignoring other vocal traditions, or of placing them in a relationship dependent upon their bearing on blues." Paul Oliver, *Songsters and Saints: Vocal Traditions on Race Records* (Cambridge: Cambridge University Press, 1984), pp. 3–12.

34. See Ruth Finnegan, *The Hidden Musicians* (Cambridge: Cambridge University Press, 1989), passim.

35. Ibid., pp. 68–69. One problem with Finnegan's research is that Milton Keynes is a rather white town, and she is not therefore able to say much about music and ethnicity. Common sense suggests that there are close ties between ethnicity and musical tastes and activities, though even here perhaps not as clear-cut as might be thought. For the relationship of different ethnic groups to reggae and ragga worlds see Simon Jones, *Black Culture, White Youth* (London: Macmillan, 1988); and Les Back, "X Amount of Sat Siri Akal! Apache Indian, Reggae Music and Intermezzo Culture," *New Formations* 26 (1995).

36. The second flaw of Finnegan's study is the lack of attention she pays to the media and what one might call genre's fantasy communities. How such fantasies work varies from genre to genre, and they affect musicians (who may or may not have ambitions for wider audiences) differently than consumers (who are involved in this wider world just by buying its artifacts, its sounds and its media). No musical scene these days, least of all most of those with which Finnegan was concerned, is simply local. For an important discussion of these issues see Will Straw, "Systems of Articulation and Logics of Change: Communities and Scenes in Popular Music," *Cultural Studies* 5 (1991).

37. Franco Fabbri, "A Theory of Musical Genres: Two Applications," in David Horn and Philip Tagg, eds., *Popular Music Perspectives* (Göteborg and London: IASPM, 1982), p. 52.

38. Ola Stockfelt, "Adequate Modes of Listening," *Stanford Humanities Review* 3(2) (1993): 160.

39. Lawrence Levine, *Black Culture and Black Consciousness* (New York: Oxford University Press, 1977), pp. 232–233.

40. Fabbri, "A Theory of Musical Genres," p. 70.

41. For an illuminating discussion of how such behavioral rules, such expectations of "good manners," constrain performers and audiences in the folk club, see Niall MacKinnon, *The British Folk Scene* (Buckingham: Open University Press, 1993).

42. Jeff Todd Titon notes, for example, the ways in which blues singers changed their off-stage stories to meet the behavioral conventions of their new white "revival" audiences in the 1960s, while Mark Fenster has documented the effects of video promotion on behavioral and semiotic rules in country music. See Jeff Todd Titon, "Reconstructing the Blues: Reflections on the 1960s Blues Revival," in Neil V. Rosenberg, ed., *Transforming Tradition* (Urbana and Chicago: University of Illinois Press, 1993), p. 234; and Mark Fenster, "Genre and Form: The Development of Country Music Video," *Popular Music* 7(3) (1988).

43. Helfried C. Zrzavy, "Issues of Incoherence and Cohesion in New Age Music," *Journal of Popular Culture*, 24(2) (1990): 39, 51.

44. Charles Hamm, "Genre, Performance and Ideology in the Early Songs of Irving Berlin," *Popular Music* 13(2) (1994): 149.

45. This is not just an issue in popular music. Hans Keller, most acerbic of classical music critics, once commented that: "The background of a composition is both the sum total of expectations a composer raises in the course of a piece without fulfilling them, and the sum total of those unborn fulfilments. The foreground is, simply, what he does instead—what is actually in the score . . . The background boils down to form, which many pieces have in common, and which can be found in the textbooks; the

foreground is the individual structure, which happens instead of the form, unless the music is a bore and fulfils all expectations—in which case you can write it yourself after the first few bars; you don't need a composer for it." Quoted in Storr, *Music and the Mind*, p. 85.

46. For a particularly interesting example of this argument, see James Parakilas, "Classical Music as Popular Music," *The Journal of Musicology* III(1) (1984). Parakilas compares performing conventions in "classical music" ("the classical style of playing Beethoven is not Beethoven's style of playing but a style about Beethoven," p. 7); "early music" (in which "style" ideally becomes "inaudible"); and "new music" (in which the composer's "style" has to be "discovered"). Parakilas's point is not just that one can't separate how these musics are played and heard from ideological arguments about their meaning (about the meaning of performance) but also that "performance" in this context has to be widely defined. Early music performers, for example, talk to the audience, drawing attention to their performance; classical performers act as if what they do is already approved by "authority"—it needs no justification; the unpredictable reception of new music, by contrast, makes "concert notes" of particular significance. Parakilas concludes that there are many uses of classical music: "Each use makes classical music popular in a different way, and every form of popularity feeds the others" (p. 13), while noting that the most common use of the music today is as "background," for reasons that haven't really been examined empirically. Because of its wordlessness? Its familiarity? Its prestige? But the theoretical question is this: how can the same music be the subject of both the most concentrated and the least concentrated listening? Is the "same" music really part of two quite different genres? Or do the boundaries of the classical genre need rethinking?

5. Where Do Sounds Come From?

1. Richard Norton, *Tonality in Western Culture* (University Park, Pa.: Pennsylvania University Press, 1984), p. 105.

2. Ned Rorem, *Settling the Score* (New York: Harcourt Brace, 1988), p. 357.

3. As Richard Norton puts it with reference to Western art music: "tonality is a *decision* made against the chaos of pitch" (his emphasis). See Norton, *Tonality in Western Culture*, pp. 4–5.

4. See Philip Tagg, "Reading Sounds: An Essay on the Soundscape and Music, Knowledge and Society," unpublished paper, 1986, p. 5. The most profound study of music from this perspective remains Murray Schafer, *The Tuning of the World* (New York: Alfred A. Knopf, 1977). For more recent work see Helmi Järviluoma, ed., *Soundscapes: Essays on Vroom and Moo* (Tampere: Department of Folk Tradition, 1994).

5. Ronald Radano thus suggests that Muzak is "a sonic form standing at the nexus of music and noise . . . a natural ambient music-noise of the indoor public environment . . . Muzak becomes a shadow—a likeness of music—for which the formalist arguments of value and quality are simply irrelevant." Ronald M. Radano, "Interpreting Muzak: Speculations on Musical Experience in Everyday Life," *American Music* 7(4) (1989): 457. And see Joseph Lanza, *Elevator Music: A Surreal History of Muzak, Easy Listening and Other Moodsong* (New York: St. Martin's Press, 1993); and James

Parakilas, "Classical Music as Popular Music," *The Journal of Musicology* III(1) (1984).

Deborah Cameron has pointed out to me in this context that "the age of the musical foreground" (and silent, contemplative listening) may actually be the historical anomaly. Court musicians, for example, primarily produced background sounds for other activities, and eighteenth-century opera goers seemed to have moved, talked, and dined throughout the performance.

6. Quoted in Gillian B. Anderson, "The Presentation of Silent Films, or Music as Anaesthesia," *The Journal of Musicology* 5(2) (1987): 269.

7. Philip Tagg, *"The Virginian,"* from unpublished work in progress (with Robert Clarida), p. 7.

8. Rom Harré (who also refers to storms and horses) suggests that "in acquiring one's competence as a listener (and a composer) one accumulates a repertoire of musical devices, with, so to say, standard meanings in the culture." He is not, though, very clear as to where these meanings come from. See "Is There a Semantics for Music?" in Michael Krausz, ed., *Music and Philosophy* (Oxford: Clarendon Press, 1992), pp. 206–207.

9. Philip Tagg, "'Universal' Music and the Case of Death," *Critical Quarterly* 35(2) (1993): 76.

10. Ibid., pp. 74–45. (His emphases.)

11. See, in particular, Susan McClary, *Feminine Endings: Music, Gender and Sexuality* (Minneapolis: University of Minnesota Press, 1991). For a useful overview of the subsequent academic debate about musicology, gender, and sexuality, see Paula Higgins, "Women in Music, Feminist Criticism, and Guerilla Musicology: Reflections on Recent Polemics," *Nineteenth Century Music* XVII(2) (1993). The most crusty (and least convincing) male response to McClary's arguments was undoubtedly Pieter C. Van Den Toom, "Politics, Feminism and Contemporary Music Theory," *Journal of Musicology* IX (1991). And see Ruth A. Solie's "What Do Feminists Want? A Reply to Pieter Van Den Toom" in the same issue.

12. Susan McClary, "Comment: Getting Down Off the Beanstalk," *Minnesota Composers' Forum Newsletter,* February 1987, no page numbers. For a later version of this essay see *Feminine Endings,* chap. 5.

13. McClary, "Comment." And see *Feminine Endings,* pp. 77–78.

14. I find McClary's figurative musical descriptions immensely suggestive, but I do wonder sometimes where the adjectives come from—the "sluttish" second theme in Tchaikovsky's Fourth Symphony, for example. For helpful discussion of McClary's work in these terms see Mary Ann Smart's review of *Feminine Endings* in *Journal of Musicological Research* 14(1/2) (1994), and Charles Rosen, "Music à la Mode," *New York Review of Books,* June 23, 1994.

15. Leonard Bernstein, *The Unanswered Question: Six Talks at Harvard* (Cambridge, Mass.: Harvard University Press, 1976), pp. 178–179.

16. Graham Bruce, *Bernard Herrmann: Film Music and Narrative* (Ann Arbor: UMI Research Press, 1985), p. 118.

17. Nöel Carroll, *Mystifying Movies* (New York: Columbia University Press, 1988), pp. 218–219, 222.

18. Ibid., p. 223. (My emphases.) For the views of film scorers themselves on this, see the

interviews in Irwin Bazelon, *Knowing the Score: Notes on Film Music* (New York: Arco, 1975), and Royal S. Brown, *Overtones and Undertones: Reading Film Music* (Berkeley: University of California Press, 1994).

19. Carroll, *Mystifying Movies,* p. 219. (My emphasis.)

20. Fred Karlin and Rayburn Wright, eds., *On the Track: A Guide to Contemporary Film Scoring* (New York: Schirmer, 1990), pp. 228–236.

21. McClary, "Comment."

22. Hans Keller, *Criticism* (London: Faber and Faber, 1987), p. 153.

23. Note by Stephen Taylor, "New Music by Cornell Composers," February 23, 1991.

24. Note by Brian Robison, "New Music by Cornell Composers," February 23, 1991.

25. Nicholas Cook, *Music, Imagination and Culture* (Oxford: Clarendon Press, 1990), p. 171.

And composers may be no more reliable in fixing their own music's meaning. Haydn's biographer, G. A. Griesinger, asked him what he was trying to "express" in his music: "He said that he oftentimes had portrayed moral characters in his symphonies. In one of his oldest, *which, however, he could not accurately identify,* 'the dominant idea is of God speaking with an abandoned sinner, pleading with him to reform. But the sinner in his thoughtlessness pays no heed to the admonition.'" (My emphasis.) Quoted in David P. Schoeder, *Haydn and the Enlightenment* (Oxford: Clarendon Press, 1990), p. 125.

26. See Leonard B. Meyer, *Emotion and Meaning in Music* (Chicago: University of Chicago Press, 1956).

27. See, for example, Deryck Cooke, *The Language of Music* (Oxford: Oxford University Press, 1959).

28. Philip Tagg uses "listening tests" to get at how musical connotations work empirically. He is interested, on the one hand, in measuring to what extent people's musical interpretations are shared (does everyone hear this melody as "angry"?) and, on the other, what elements of the music carry this implication (which combinations of melody, harmony, instrument, beat). See Philip Tagg, "Analysing Popular Music: Theory, Method and Practice," *Popular Music* 2 (1982). For an illuminating example of Tagg's analytic use of his method see *Fernando the Flute: Musical Meaning in an Abba Mega-Hit* (Liverpool: Liverpool University Institute of Popular Music, 1991).

For an earlier version of the listening test (using a more directed set of questions than Tagg's, based on Charles Osgood's "semantic differential test") see Charles Keil and Angeliki Keil, "Musical Meaning: A Preliminary Report. (The Perception of Indian, Western and Afro-American Musical Moods by American Students)," *Ethnomusicology* X(2) (1966). And for an important critique of the method, arguing that musical interpretation also derives from how people "frame" the music, derives that is from the *social* circumstances of listening, and not just from the possible (fixed) semantic codes of the music itself, see Steven Feld, "Communication, Music, and Speech About Music," *Yearbook for Traditional Music* 16 (1984).

29. David Schoeder notes the same use of quotation from folk, church, and dance music in Haydn, and suggests that Haydn's "extraordinary achievement" was thus "to devise procedures for instrumental music that would allow it an intelligibility previously thought possible only if words were present." See Schoeder, *Haydn and the Enlightenment,* pp. 74, 68–71, 146–157.

30. Christopher Ballantine, *Music and Its Social Meanings* (New York: Gordon and Breach, 1984), p. 73, and see his analysis of Charles Ives' *Central Park in the Dark*, p. 87.

Robert Stradling and Meirion Hughes point out that folk quotations are the basis for assertions of music's supposed national expressiveness. They quote random examples from BBC Radio 3 program notes: "The music [of Guy Ropartz] gives off the authentic flavour of Brittany—indeed its last movement is based on a Breton folk tune." "Nielsen's music utilised a great deal of material from his island homeland of Fünen . . . which is why it sounds so Danish." And add George Bernard Shaw's tart comment: "Grieg's music does not remind me of Norway, perhaps because I have never been there."

31. Rap thus self-consciously draws attention to the act of quotation itself. As Paul Gilroy suggests, "the aesthetic rules that govern it are premised on a dialect of rescuing, appropriation and recombination that creates special pleasures." These are pleasures in which "aesthetic stress is laid upon the sheer social and cultural distance that formerly separated the diverse elements now dislocated into novel meanings by their provocative aural juxtaposition." See Paul Gilroy, "Sounds Authentic: Black Music, Ethnicity, and the Challenge of a *Changing* Same," *Black Music Research Journal* 10(2) (1990): 128–131; and compare Ballantine's analysis of Bob Dylan's use of vernacular musical quotes, his "way with signs," in *Music and Its Social Meanings*, p. 105.

32. Keir Keightley, "The History and Exegesis of Pop: Reading 'All Summer Long,'" M.A. thesis (Communications), McGill University, 1991, p. 15.

33. The pioneering work on film music from the direction of film studies was Claudia Gorbman's *Unheard Melodies: Narrative Film Music* (Bloomington and London: Indiana University Press and the BFI, 1987); and, from the direction of musicology, Philip Tagg's *Kojak: 50 Seconds of Television Music* (Gothenberg: Institute of Musicology, 1979). I have learned most of what I understand about film music from Gorbman and Tagg, as much through conversation as through their published work, and I hope that what follows does justice to their suggestions.

34. I take this list from David Mayer, "The Music of Melodrama," in David Bradby, Louis James, and Bernard Sharratt, eds., *Performance and Politics in Popular Drama* (Cambridge: Cambridge University Press, 1980), p. 62.

35. Schopenhauer quoted in Carroll, *Mystifying Movies*, p. 216; Bresson quoted in Jonathan Rosenbaum, "Sound Thinking," *Film Comment*, Sept.-Oct. 1978, p. 40.

36. Quoted in Anderson, "Presentation of Silent Films," p. 279.

37. Carroll, *Mystifying Movies*, p. 220.

38. Pop videos are thus much more like operas than like films, a point to which I'll return in Chapter 11.

39. For this approach to opera (drawing on the semiotics of Charles William Morris and C. S. Pierce), see Fritz Notske, *The Signifier and the Signified: Studies in the Operas of Mozart and Verdi* (The Hague: Martinus Nijhoof, 1977). Notske shows, for example, how Mozart uses the flute in his operas "as the disturber of balance, serving the intrigue and often revealing subconscious desire" (p. 125). And he analyzes the way Verdi uses the "musical figure of death" unconventionally, thus "renewing" its meaning as a topos (pp. 171, 214). From Notske's semiotic point of view, the meaning of music is not "intrinsic" to the text, but produced in the reading of it; from his perspective

the "sign giver" or composer is no more significant for the interpretation of a work of art than any other reader.

For discussion of relations between musical and narrative structure from the film composer's perspective (film composition as a craft), see George Burt, *The Art of Film Music* (Boston: Northeastern University Press, 1994).

40. Bruce, *Bernard Herrmann*, p. 216.
41. Quoted in John Broeck, "Music of the Fears," *Film Comment* 12 (1976): 56–60.
42. Nicholas Cook, "Music and Meaning in the Commercials," *Popular Music* 13(1) (1994): 35, 38.
43. Michel Chion, *Audio-Vision: Sound on Screen* [1990] (New York: Columbia University Press, 1994), p. 68.
44. This list taken from Carroll, *Mystifying Movies*, p. 216.
45. Quoted in Broecks, "Music of the Fears." (My emphasis.)
46. Chion refers to "la façon dont la musique *tombe* sur l'image (comme une robe tombe sur un corps)." Michel Chion, *Le Son au Cinéma* (Paris: Cahiers du Cinéma/Etoile, 1985), p. 119.
47. For this argument see Anne Hollander, *Seeing Through Clothes* (New York: Viking, 1978).
48. For this approach to film music see Gorbman, *Unheard Melodies;* Tagg, *Fernando the Flute;* Simon Frith, "Hearing Secret Harmonies," in my *Music for Pleasure* (Cambridge: Polity, 1988); Anahid Kassabian, "Songs of Subjectivities: Theorizing Hollywood Film Music of the 80s and 90s," Ph.D. thesis, Stanford University, 1993.
49. Anderson, "The Presentation of Silent Films," pp. 274–275. And see Preston, *Music for Hire*, pp. 93–96.
50. Max Winkler, "The Origin of Film Music," in James L. Limbacher, ed., *Film Music from Violins to Video* (Metuchen, N.J.: Scarecrow Press, 1974), p. 17.
51. Winkler, "The Origin of Film Music," pp. 21–22.
52. For an extremely interesting discussion of the impact of classical music on Hollywood in the 1930s see Caryl Flinn, *Strains of Utopia* (Princeton, N.J.: Princeton University Press, 1992). Flinn stresses the class and historical/nostalgic basis of this music, but underplays, I think, the use of the argument from "transcendence" that was at this time also selling classical music to middle-class America on record and radio.
53. Quoted in Anderson, "Presentation of Silent Films," pp. 261–262.
54. Carroll, *Mystifying Movies*, pp. 223–224.
55. Leith Stevens, "The Wild One," in Limbacher, ed., *Film Music from Violins to Video*, pp. 120–121.
56. Miklós Rózsa, "Quo Vadis," in Limbacher, ed., *Film Music from Violins to Video*, pp. 147–153.

One of the more interesting aspects of such conventions concerns "diegetic" music, music which is produced as part of the screen action itself, whether directly, by actor as performer, or as part of the setting (in the use of a radio or jukebox, for example). Do we believe that the performer is really playing the music (as in bio-pics of classical composers) or that he is "enacting it," but for real (as in bio-pics of pop performers)? What is the different effect? What is meant by realism here? See, for example, Charlie Gillett's comments on the Tina Turner bio-pic, *What's Love Got To Do With It,* "Truth and Tina," *Sight and Sound* 4(1) (1994): 64. For a general discussion of this issue see Irene Kahn Atkins, *Source Music in Motion Pictures* (East Brunswick, N.J.: Associated Universities Press, 1983).

57. Kathryn Kalinak, "The Fallen Woman and the Virtuous Wife: Musical Stereotypes in *The Informer, Gone with the Wind,* and *Laura*," *Film Reader* 5 (1982): 76–77. And see her *Settling the Score: Music and the Classical Hollywood Film* (Madison: University of Wisconsin Press, 1992.

58. For film music's "representation symbolique du temps" see Charles J. Boilès, "La Signification dans la Musique de Film," *Musique en Jeu*, 1975, pp. 74–75. For music and space see Chion, *Audio-Vision*, chaps. 2–3.

59. See Philip Tagg, "*The Virginian*," passim, and Alan Williams, "The Musical Film and Recorded Popular Music," in Rick Altman, ed., *Genre: The Musical* (London: Routledge and Kegan Paul/BFI, 1981).

60. Chion, *Audio-Vision*, p. 107.

6. Rhythm: Race, Sex, and the Body

1. Edmund Burke, *A Philosophical Enquiry into the Origin of our Ideas of the Sublime and the Beautiful* [1757] (Oxford: World's Classics, 1990), p. 112.

2. *Melody Maker,* March 9, 1988.

3. In the 1990s, the message was reversed again. Tee shirts now read: "Fuck Dance, Let's Art!"

4. Quoted in John F. Kassan, *Rudeness and Civility* (New York: Hill and Wang, 1990), p. 246.

5. Ibid., p. 246. Even today, performers or conductors who draw attention to themselves physically are thought to be a little vulgar—"Flash Harry" was the unaffectionate nickname for the British conductor Malcolm Sergeant, for example.

6. The rock equivalent to the classical experience is, I suppose, the psychedelic show: I remember the 1960s Grateful Dead audience, for example, as surprisingly quiet— "spaced out." But then this was a drug experience, and the mind/body split didn't hold.

7. Carl Dahlhaus notes that in the nineteenth century "the folk" and "nature" thus came to be connoted musically simply as a contrast to the orderly, romantic model of classical composition. See *Realism in Nineteenth-Century Music* [1982] (Cambridge: Cambridge University Press, 1985), p. 107.

8. Frank Howes, "A Critique of Folk, Popular and 'Art' Music," *British Journal of Aesthetics* 2(3) (1962); Peter Stadler, "The Aesthetics of Popular Music," *British Journal of Aesthetics* 2(4) (1962).

9. This seems to have been a well-established view among British educators. A 1945 textbook for youth club leaders concerned about their charges' low musical tastes explained that jazz "required no thought for its understanding, and relies entirely for its appeal on rhythm and sentiment." "One of the great weaknesses of jazz," the author elaborated, "is that it appeals only to the motor activities of man (i.e. as a stimulant to dance), or to the sentiment of the heart (i.e. sex) and is seldom, if ever, related to the head . . . Jazz expresses no great truths or depth of emotion, but is a stimulant to

the cheaper and more superficial sensations." Desmond Macmahon, *Youth and Music* (London: Thomas Nelson, 1945), pp. 89–90.

10. Raymond Durgnat, "Rock, Rhythm and Dance," *British Journal of Aesthetics* 11(1) (1971). This still seems to be the established aestheticians' view of rock—see, for example, Bruce Baugh, "Prolegomena to an Aesthetics of Rock Music," *The Journal of Aesthetics and Art Criticism* 51(1) (1993).

11. Guy Scarpetta, *L'Impureté* (Paris: Bernard Grasset, 1985), p. 77–78. Compare Ned Rorem: "In November 1961, the evening before I left France, Nora Auric took me to hear Johnny [Halliday] at the Olympia. Still ignorant of Presley—of Presley's *art* if you will—I was sceptical about meeting it second hand. Yet from the moment that handsome kid appeared and for the solid hour of his gyrations, Nora and I were as drugged by the mass hysteria loosened by his superbly whorish musicality as were the five thousand adolescents that jammed the hall." (*Settling the Score*, p. 257. Note the word "whorish.")

12. I'm not just thinking of jazz here. The late nineteenth century British music hall was constantly condemned by middle-class moralists as a haunt of prostitutes.

13. Bernard Gendron, "Jamming at La Boeuf: Jazz and the Paris Avant-Garde," *Discourse* 12(1) (1989–90): 11–12.

14. For a stimulating antidote to this (still widely believed) myth of the primitive, see Robert Farris Thompson's overview of African and African-American art and philosophy, *Flash of the Spirit* (New York: Random House, 1983). This is not to say that Western myths don't themselves feed into African musical ideologies. Among the replies in *Spear* to Charles Keil's 1965 question about Nigerian musical tastes was this: "Roy Chicago is my favourite musician and has been since February 1962. There is yet to appear a musician to equal his exhilarating brand of music which is peculiarly African. The absence of such music in Europe, psychologists claim, is responsible for so many Psychic cases over there. With Roy's music about the place, even the most reserved of persons forgets being shy and really does let go." Quoted in John Miller Chernoff, *African Rhythm and African Sensibility* (Chicago and London: University of Chicago Press, 1979), p. 177.

15. Marianna Torgovnick, *Gone Primitive: Savage Intellects, Modern Lives* (Chicago: University of Chicago Press, 1990), p. 228.
    Even a such a well-respected blues writer as Samuel Charters casually refers (in *The Country Blues*) to "the direct expression of sexuality in black culture," thus eliding a point about conventional differences between African-American and European-American expressive cultures, with a suggestion that in black cultures (but not white cultures) sex just comes naturally. For a general discussion of such assumptions in blues writing, see Jeff Todd Titon, "Reconstructing the Blues: Reflections on the 1960s Blues Revival," in Neil V. Rosenberg, ed., *Transforming Tradition* (Urbana and Chicago: University of Illinois Press, 1993).

16. D. L. LeMahieu, *A Culture for Democracy: Mass Communication and the Cultivated Mind in Britain Between the Wars* (Oxford: Clarendon Press, 1988), pp. 116–117.

17. Quoted in Torgovnick, *Gone Primitive*, p. 111.

18. Lawrence Levine, *Black Culture and Black Consciousness* (New York: Oxford University Press, 1977), pp. 293, 295. His emphasis.

19. Robert O'Meally, *Lady Day: The Many Faces of Billie Holiday* (New York: Arcade, 1991),

p. 154; and see Ted Gioia, "Jazz and the Primitivist Myth," in his *The Imperfect Art: Reflections on Jazz and Modern Culture* (New York and Oxford: Oxford University Press, 1990), pp. 30–31; Kathy J. Ogren, "Prudes and Primitives: White Americans Debate Jazz," in her *The Jazz Revolution* (New York and Oxford: Oxford University Press, 1989); and Neil Leonard, *Jazz and the White Americans: The Acceptance of a New Art Form* (Chicago: University of Chicago Press, 1962).

20. Charles Shaar Murray, *Crosstown Traffic* (London: Faber and Faber, 1989), p. 78.

21. Quoted in Linda Martin and Kerry Seagrove, *Anti-Rock: The Opposition to Rock'n'Roll* (Hamden, Conn.: Archon Books, 1988), p. 53. Other quotes from pp. 35, 47, 51.

   One of the more bizarre variations of the arguments here can be found in the liner notes by Dr. Sigmund Spaeth ("America's Most Popular Speaker and Writer on Music") to *Rock and Roll*, volume 1 in The Music Appreciation Library. (Volume 2 contained the *Sleeping Beauty* ballet suite, and volume 3 Beethoven's Fifth and Schubert's Unfinished Symphonies). Spaeth writes: "This highly controversial but immensely popular type of music is as characteristic of our times as comic books, western films and gangster who-dun-its. It has been called everything from a sublimation of rhythm to a reversion to savagery, and its adherence to current codes of violence is unmistakeable." Spaeth goes on to argue that musically there is nothing new about rock and roll at all. He concludes: "The violence of syncopated percussion is perhaps most obvious in 'Rock and Roll' but it also utilizes the established patterns of Boogie and revels in discord as enthusiastically as a Schoenberg or a Varèse. It is actually close to jungle music, and as such it completes a cycle which went the rounds of Rag Time, Jazz, Swing, Boogie, Be Bop and 'Progressive' back to a primitive glorification of Rhythm as such. Similarly the formulas of classicism followed the cycle of romanticism to the Modern, Ultra-Modern and Atonal styles, only to return at last to so-called 'Neo-classicism,' with Bach and Beethoven still its models." Thanks to John Street for drawing this to my attention.

22. Milton Bracker, "Experts Propose Study of 'Craze,'" *New York Times*, February 23, 1957, p. 1. Thanks to Dave Marsh and Greil Marcus for drawing this to my attention.

23. Kohut thus questions the artistic value of Ravel's *Bolero*, while also noting that as "modern" art music has no discernible rhythm so it offers no discernible pleasure! See Heinz Kohut, "Observations on the Psychological Functions of Music," *Journal of the American Psychoanalytic Association*, V(3) (1957): 391. A decade later Pinchas Noy confirmed this psychoanalytic equation of the "primitive," the "rhythmic," and the "infantile." See "The Psychodynamic Meaning of Music. A Critical Review of the Psychoanalytic and Related Material. Part II," *Journal of Music Therapy* 4(1) (1967): 14–16.

24. Eric Lott, *Love and Theft* (New York and Oxford: Oxford University Press, 1993), p. 53.

25. Bernard Gendron, "Rock and Roll Mythology: Race and Sex in 'Whole Lotta Shakin' Going On,'" University of Wisconsin, Center for Twentieth Century Studies Working Paper No. 7, Fall 1985, pp. 5, 7, 9.

26. Alice Echols, "White Faces, Black Masks," *Village Voice*, February 15, 1994, p. 92. Echols notes that even in the 1930s light-skinned black jazz musicians (Billie Holiday, for instance) were still required, on occasion, literally to black-up, to darken their skins so as to be recognized as "black."

27. Gendron, "Rock and Roll Mythology," p. 10.

28. Chernoff, *African Rhythm and African Sensibility,* pp. 150, 141.

29. Ruth Finnegan, *Oral Poetry* (Cambridge: Cambridge University Press, 1977), pp. 91–92. Halbwachs is cited by Alfred Schutz (who disagrees with his position), "Making Music Together," in *Collected Papers, Volume 2* (The Hague: Martinus Nijhoff, 1964), p. 164.

30. See Maurice Bloch, "Symbols, Song, Dance and Features of Articulation," *Archives Européennes de Sociologie,* 15(1) (1974). Bloch argues that all formalized or ritualized means of communication (all art) involves (through the use of repetition, in particular) a *restriction* on available choices of sounds and gestures (which now must form a pattern). In this respect, "art is an inferior form of communication" (p. 72). On the other hand, "when nearly all this generative potential of language (or bodily movement) has been forbidden, removed, the remaining choices left are so simple that they can suddenly be apprehended consciously. Creativity has suddenly become controllable, hence enjoyable." (As against those everyday communicative processes that are complex and unconscious) (p. 73). *All* performance is consciously structured, whatever the communicative rules or communicative elements involved.

31. Lawrence Levine, *Highbrow/Lowbrow* (Cambridge, Mass.: Harvard University Press, 1988), pp. 220–221.

32. Quoted in Charles Keil, "Motion and Feeling through Music," *The Journal of Aesthetic and Art Criticism* 24 (1966): 347.

33. For the most sophisticated version of this argument see John Shepherd, *Music as Social Text* (Cambridge: Polity, 1991), chaps. 6–8. For the most persuasive see Ishmael Reed's history of "jes grew," *Mumbo Jumbo* (New York: Doubleday, 1972).

34. Andrew Chester, "Second Thoughts on a Rock Aesthetic," in Simon Frith and Andrew Goodwin, eds., *On Record: Rock, Pop, and the Written Word* (New York: Pantheon, 1990), p. 315. Richard Norton makes a similar distinction between "high" and "low" music, noting that in popular song one doesn't listen for "the uniqueness of its harmonisation": "Harmonic utterance is collectively understood in such music as a formal structure in which components other than harmonic ones are utilised as a means for individual expression." (Norton, *Tonality in Western Culture,* p. 229.)

35. See Philip Tagg, "Open Letter: Black Music, Afro-American Music and European Music," *Popular Music* 8(3) (1989); and Van Der Merwe, *Origins of the Popular Style.* It is interesting to note how Aaron Copland moves in his Norton Lectures from a description of rhythm as "the most primitive element in music," to a discussion of the richness and variety of the American composer's unique rhythmic heritage. Aaron Copland, *Music and Imagination* (Cambridge, Mass.: Harvard University Press, 1952/1980), pp. 71, 83–90.

36. Ernest Borneman, *A Critic Looks at Jazz* (London: Jazz Music Books, 1946), p. 29.

37. The pioneering anthropologist in this respect was A. M. Jones, whose first essay on African drumming was published in 1934. His work is gathered in *Studies in African Music* (Oxford: Oxford University Press, 1959). For an exhaustive treatment of the problems of musical description raised here, see Simha Arom, *African Polyphony and Polyrhythm: Musical Structure and Methodology* [1985] (Cambridge: Cambridge University Press, 1991).

38. Borneman, *A Critic Looks at Jazz,* p. 30.

39. Chernoff, *African Rhythm and African Sensibility,* p. 92.

40. Borneman, *A Critic Looks at Jazz,* pp. 8, 31.

41. Quoted in Charles Keil, "The Theory of Participatory Discrepencies: A Progress Report," *Ethnomusicology* 39(2) (1995).

42. Levine, *Black Culture and Black Consciousness,* p. 198.

43. Art Hodes and Chadwick Hansen, *Hot Man* (Urbana and Chicago: University of Illinois Press, 1992), p. 24.

    Alec Wilder makes a similar point: "If a film composer is asked to write 'storm' music as one of the many cues in a movie score, no one is surprised to find he can do it. For it is primarily a trick. Maybe he hates both storms and music describing them. But his profession demands that he be able to devise and contrive.

    "But a swinging song is much more than a trick. For if you don't feel it, in fact love it, you can't write it. Oh you may write an imitation, but it will sound false and phony." (Wilder, *American Popular Song,* p. 119.)

44. Christopher Small, *Music of the Common Tongue* (London: John Calder, 1987), pp. 45–46.

45. Ibid., p. 480.

46. Keil, "Motion and Feeling through Music," pp. 338–339. For his later thoughts on the issues here see Charles Keil, "Participatory Discrepancies and the Power of Music," *Cultural Anthropology* 2(3) (1987), and "The Theory of Participatory Discrepancies."

47. Alan Durant, "Improvisation in the Political Economy of Music," in Christopher Norris, ed., *Music and the Politics of Culture* (London: Lawrence and Wishart, 1989). Boulez suggests elsewhere that left to their own devices players will always produce clichés—"If the player were an inventor of forms or of primary musical material, he would be a composer. If he is not a composer, it is because he is by choice and capacity a performer; so that if you do not provide him with sufficient information to perform a work, what can he do?" Pierre Boulez, *Orientations* [1981] (Cambridge, Mass.: Harvard University Press, 1986), p. 461.

48. Chernoff, *African Rhythm and African Sensibility,* p. 60. His emphasis.

49. Ibid., p. 67. My emphasis.

50. "Could it be that in some cultures children learn to dance before (or even while) they learn to listen?" asks Charles Keil ("Motion and Feeling through Music," p. 339). Watching friends' children, I'd say this was true in all cultures, and this has implications which Keil does not spell out. Could it be that insofar as the high cultural audience makes the right contemplative concert response it is not really having a *musical* experience; and that insofar as it has a musical experience this is not purely contemplative? I'll return to this point in Chapter 12.

51. Quoted in Dr. Licks, *Standing in the Shadow of Motown,* p. 95. And see Chernoff, *African Rhythm and African Sensibility,* p. 95.

52. Quoted in Gunther Schuller, *Early Jazz: Its Roots and Musical Development* (New York and Oxford: Oxford University Press, 1968), p. 22.

53. Chernoff, *African Rhythm and African Sensibility,* p. 54.

54. Ibid., p. 50.

55. John Blacking, *How Musical Is Man?* (Seattle and London: University of Washington Press, 1973), p. 27.

56. See Keil, "Motion and Feeling through Music," pp. 341–343.

57. Quoted in Keil, "Motion and Feeling through Music," p. 339.

58. For this point see Henry Pleasants, *Death of a Music? The Decline of European Tradition and the Rise of Jazz* (London: Victor Gollancz, 1961), p. 172.

59. Chernoff, *African Rhythm and African Sensibility*, p. 143. And see Robert Farris Thompson, "An Aesthetic of Cool: West African Dance," *African Forum* 2(2) (1966). From the other side of this process, O'Meally suggests that Billie Holiday's "incredibly poised sense of rhythm" derived from her early experience of having to respond vocally to the immediate rhythmic demands of juke joint dancers; see *Lady Day*, p. 38.

60. Zora Neale Hurston distinguished white and Negro dance in these terms: "The difference in the two arts is: the white dancer attempts to express fully; the Negro is restrained, but succeeds in gripping the beholder by forcing him to finish the action the performer suggests." See her "Characteristics of Negro Expression," in Nancy Cunard, ed., *Negro* (London: Nancy Cunard at Wishart and Co., 1934), pp. 41–42.

61. For a brilliant discussion of "the politics of dancing" in the post-punk era, see Will Straw, "The Booth, The Floor and The Wall: Dance Music and the Fear of Falling," *Public* 8 (1993). As Straw notes, "In any number of interviews in the early 1980s, musicians spoke proudly of their music as being about thinking *and* dancing," implying both that "thinking music" (i.e., indie-post-punk) wasn't usually danceable and that "dancing music" (i.e., disco) was usually thoughtless: "In fact, one did *think* on the dance floor of the early 1980s post-punk club; but, in thinking, one was mapping out the acceptable ranges of gesture and expression. Post-punk dancing was shaped in no small measure by the lingering and horrific memory of two precursors: the free-form obliviousness of late-hippy dancing and the extravagant displays of disco. The self-conscious control required of postures in order that they not recall these earlier moments lent itself easily to the conviction that dancing was now an activity with intellectual substance. Thus there is a smooth passage from the sense of dance as that which involves a thoughtful constraint to the belief that it might embody a disciplined militancy" (p. 177).

62. Concert hall bouncers will thus confidently tell you (with no evidence at all) what sort of music causes trouble, by which they mean what sort of music draws a "troublesome" crowd, a crowd which is overly black or young or proletarian.

63. See Philip Tagg, "Understanding Musical Time Sense," *Festschrift for Jan Ling* (Göteborg: Institute of Musicology, 1984).

64. Chernoff, *African Rhythm and African Sensibility*, p. 148. And see Richard Dyer, "In Defence of Disco" [1979], in Frith and Goodwin, *On Record*.

65. See Simon Frith, "The Sound of *Erotica*: Pain, Power and Pop," in Lisa Frank and Paul Smith, eds., *Madonnarama: Essays on Sex and Popular Culture* (Pittsburgh: Cleis Press, 1993).

Will Straw suggests that "records such as these perpetuate one of the central aesthetic principles of dance music: that high-end sounds (vocals, strings and so on) represent the playful, outrageous moments within dance music, and that for the connoisseurist, credible exercises happen at the low end, in the bass and percussion. The former endow records with their novel singularity, the latter anchor them within an ongoing history of styles."

Even within dance music, then, we find the familiar, gendered opposition of immediate response and informed appreciation: "Dance music culture's association of the feminine with the commercial and the debased is further evidence of that culture's status as one of the last modernist artworlds." (Straw, "The Booth, The Floor and The Wall," p. 181.)

7. Rhythm: Time, Sex, and the Mind

1. Quoted in Robert O'Meally, *Lady Day: The Many Faces of Billie Holiday* (New York: Arcade, 1991), p. 52.
2. Henri Lefebvre, *Everyday Life in the Modern World* [1968] (London: Allen Lane, 1971), pp. 19–20.
3. Alfred Schutz, "Making Music Together," in *Collected Papers, Volume 2* (The Hague: Martinus Nijhoff, 1964), pp. 171, 170.
4. Ibid., pp. 171–172, 175. For a similar argument about "dance time" and "real time" see David Michael Levin, "Balanchine's Formalism," in George Beiswanger, Wilfried A. Hofman, and David Michael Levin, "Three Essays in Dance Aesthetics," *Dance Perspectives* 55 (Autumn 1973). Levin is equally concerned with how a dance "communicates," and shows that to "understand" a modern dance, audiences have to experience the dancers' movements in the choreographer's time (not according to the clock)—it is the *dance* which determines whether a movement is fast or slow, rough or smooth, willed or "accidental."
5. Note Schutz's inclusion of poetry here: his point, with which I agree, is that what is semantically meaningful about a poem, its content, is not its meaning *as a poem*, which is its meaning as a timed object, a performance (even in one's head). The poem as poem only exists as experienced in inner time.
6. Schutz, "Making Music Together," p. 173. Interestingly, though, the composer will almost certainly not experience this stream of consciousness herself until she hears the first performance.
7. Ibid., p. 177. Schutz thus notes the difficulty of making music with someone one can't see. His example is the blind musician, but this also raises questions about contemporary recording studio practices and the communicative role of the producer.
8. John Miller Chernoff, *African Rhythm and African Sensibility* (Chicago and London: University of Chicago Press, 1979), pp. 95–97, 112–114 (his emphases). In his 1952 Norton Lectures at Harvard, Aaron Copland similarly distinguished "American" from European rhythmic sensibility. For Europeans, he suggested, rhythm is always applied to a phrase; for Americans rhythm is "disembodied," works as a frame or continuous possibility. Americans could work with—imaginatively hear—"minute metrical units" that Europeans couldn't. Europeans, in short, can't swing: "Of course you cannot stay off the beat unless you know where that beat is." (*Music and Imagination*, p. 87.) The contemporary British rock audience is still apt to clap on the on rather than the off beat, with dire rhythmical consequences.
9. Jonathan D. Kramer, *The Time of Music* (New York: Schirmer Books, 1988), pp. 140, 150–151. Kramer borrows from Judy Lochead the useful analogy of "breakfast," which is defined as both the first meal of the day (one can have anything for breakfast) but also by its conventional content (restaurants advertise "all-day breakfasts"; one can eat "breakfast" as a meal at 10 P.M.).
10. Keir Keightley, "The History and Exegesis of Pop," M.A. thesis (Communications), McGill University, 1991, pp. 28–29.

11. Kramer, *The Time of Music*, p. 161. I think one can delete Kramer's defensive "at least."

12. Ibid., p. 219. (His emphasis.) The concepts of moment and linear time help explain the process Michel Chion describes, the use of sound in the cinema to enable us to perceive *time in the image*—what we hear determines how we read time in the moving picture: as exact or vague, going forward or back, dramatic or stuck. See Chion, *Audio-Vision* [1990] (New York: Columbia University Press, 1994), pp. 13–14.

13. In this respect music, as Jacques Lacan noted, is not "without analogy" to psychoanalysis, and musical understanding, we might add, is not without analogy to the analyst's grasp of the unconscious. In André Michel's words, "Music, then, ceases to be only the sublimation of the sensible and becomes the perception of the sublime." "Psychoanalysis of Music," *Music Review* XI(4) (1950): 276. And see Lacan, "De l'objet musical dans le champ de la psychanalyse" [1974], *scilicet* 617 (1976), p. 334. For elaboration of the same point with regard to Freud's own account of musical and psychoanalytic time, see Jacques Caïn and Anne Caïn, "Freud, 'Absolument Pas Musicien . . . ,'" in Jacques Caïn, Anne Caïn, et al., *Psychanalyse et Musique* (Paris: Société d'Édition, 1982), pp. 134–136.

14. Quoted in John Blacking, *How Musical Is Man?* (Seattle and London: University of Washington Press, 1973), p. 26.

15. See Kramer, *The Time of Music*, p. 167.

16. Blacking, *How Musical Is Man?*, p. 27.

17. Gary Giddins, *Rhythm-A-Ning* (New York: Oxford University Press, 1985), p. 246. Carolyn Abbate asks of nineteenth-century opera, "Can music, though it exists always in the present moment, create the sound of pastness? . . . Can music possess—aside from discursive space—the human, epistemological or moral complexities of a narrating voice?" (*Unsung Voices* [Princeton: Princeton University Press, 1991], p. 54). The convolution of her answers (yes and yes) reflects the problems of the "long tradition of musical analysis rooted in Hanslick's aesthetics of form" which "would argue that repetition actually creates structure, architecture, and hence stasis: time frozen" (p. 55). In popular music temporal gestures, rooted in repetition, work to make the music simultaneously past and present, to place the listener both inside and outside it. My favorite example of this narrative process remains Abba's "The Day Before You Came" (Epic, 1982), tedium recollected in tranquillity (or, rather, in emotional turmoil!), and its subtle adaptation to the even more mechanical banalities of electro-pop by Blancmange (London, 1984).

18. St. Augustine, *Confessions* [397–398] (Harmondsworth: Penguin, 1961), Book XI, section 14; and see section 24, pp. 264, 273.

19. Ibid., Book XI, sections 15, 18, 20, pp. 266–269.

20. Ibid., Book XI, section 28, p. 277.

21. One aspect of this, as Philip Tagg notes, is that "faster" pieces of music tend to be thought longer than they really are (in clock time), slower pieces judged shorter—more seems to be happening in the former; our attention is more engaged. And this is what we mean by something taking "more time." "Understanding Musical 'Time Sense,'" in *Festschrift for Jan Ling* (Göteborg: Institute of Musicology, 1986), p. 30.

22. See Edward T. Cone, *The Composer's Voice* (Berkeley: University of California Press, 1974). One complication in the study of popular music is that "rhythm" is taken to describe particular sounds—drums, bass, percussion—and a particular kind of beat,

and these don't just draw our attention to the music itself, but have all the ideological and physical connotations I discussed in Chapter 6.

23. David Epstein, *Beyond Orpheus: Studies in Musical Structure* (Cambridge, Mass.: MIT Press, 1979), p. 55.

24. Richard Middleton, *Studying Popular Music* (Milton Keynes: Open University Press, 1990), pp. 269, 272–275, 281. The suggestion that repetition might obliterate time echoes Roland Barthes's argument that "to repeat excessively is to enter into loss, into the zero of the signified." Barthes features "extravagant repetition" (formal, literal, obsessive repetition) in his semiotic erotics—the unexpected is now "succulent in its newness." *The Pleasure of the Text* [1975] (London: Jonathan Cape, 1976), p. 42.

25. Epstein, *Beyond Orpheus*, p. 55.

26. One reason why both avant-garde art composers and dance music producers have found electronic sounds interesting is that they seem to offer the possibility of sounds which are, in a sense, purely rhythmic. Stockhausen, for example, once claimed that "electronic music has liberated the inner world, for one knows that there is nothing to be seen outside oneself and that there can be no sense in asking with what and by what means the sounds and acoustical forms are produced." (Quoted in Evan Eisenberg, *The Recording Angel: Explorations in Phonography* [New York: McGraw-Hill, 1987], p. 134). But then electronic sounds soon connoted "electronics," sounds produced by machines, with (at least in the rock world) a whole series of implications about their "coldness" and inhumanity.

27. Eisenberg, *The Recording Angel*, p. 236.

28. Epstein, *Beyond Orpheus*, p. 57.

29. Robin Maconie, *The Concept of Music* (Oxford: Clarendon Press, 1990), p. 70. And see Philip Tagg: "The basis for all such conceptual units of musical duration is *recurrence*, either as repetition or reprise (the latter implying that there are *changes* which mark the recurrence), i.e. the measure and manner in which the same or similar musical structure can be regarded by a given musical-cultural community as establishing a pattern of occurrence." "Understanding Musical 'Time Sense,'" p. 23.

30. Epstein, *Beyond Orpheus*, p. 97 (note 14), and see p. 75; Allen Farmelo, "The Completing Consequences of Groove," and J. A. Prögler, "Searching for Swing: Participatory Discrepancies in the Jazz Rhythm Section," both in *Ethnomusicology* 39(2) (1995).

31. Epstein, *Beyond Orpheus*, pp. 55, 195–196. For an example of the "rhythm" of a piece being deduced from a structural reading of its score, see Ray Jackendoff and Fred Lerdahl, *A Generative Theory of Tonal Music* (Cambridge, Mass.: MIT Press, 1983), pp. 283–285. Though these authors do refer to what people hear, this "listening" is deduced from what would be necessary to make sense of the music structurally rather than from what people do actually think they're hearing when they listen.

32. Henri Pousseur, "Music, Form and Practice," in Herbert Eimert and Karlheinz Stockhausen, eds., *Die Reihe—Speech and Music* [1960] (Bryn Mawr, Pa.: Theodore Presser, 1964), pp. 80–82.

33. Michael Nyman, *Experimental Music: Cage and Beyond* (London: Studio Vista, 1974), p. 12, and see pp. 2, 26.

34. This argument is the theme of Wim Mertens, *American Minimal Music* (London: Kahn and Averill, 1983). For a highly critical review of Mertens's position see Gregory Sandow, "Minimal Thought," *Village Voice* (date unknown), which suggests that the

book is "full of confusion and mistakes." Sandow is particularly unconvinced by the suggestion that American minimalist music lacks "structure and direction," an argument which, for Sandow, reflects the weakness of Mertens's musical analysis rather than an insight into minimalist philosophy. Technically Sandow is probably right; emotionally I'm with Mertens: his argument does make sense of how at least this "unmusical" listener makes sense of minimalism. In terms of a close structural analysis the music of Philip Glass, Steve Reich, and Terry Riley undoubtedly does "develop," but such development is not what its listeners listen for.

35. Quoted in Kramer, *The Time of Music*, p. 376.

36. Ibid., pp. 378–381.

37. Quoted in Nyman, *Experimental Music*, p. 31.

38. New Age clearly draws on both minimalist and ambient sounds and ideas. For Brian Eno's ongoing thoughts on these issues see his occasional magazine, *Opal*.

39. Kool and the Gang, "Get Down On It," De-Lite 12", 1974; Steve Reich, *Drumming*, Elektra/Nonesuch LP, 1987.

40. See Kramer, *The Time of Music*, pp. 382–384. Philip Glass is quoted on p. 384.

41. Gary Jardim's *Blue: Newark Culture, Volume Two* (Orange, N.J.: De Sousa Press, 1993) contains an oral history of club music in Newark in which the dance floor is routinely treated as a stage setting. Jardim's interviewees remember how Richard Long constructed "the sonic environment" of the Zanzibar in Newark and the Paradise Garage in Manhattan (p. 94), while Kevin Hedge ("Growing up with Club") and Ace Mungin ("The Roots of Club in Newark") argue that the pioneering art of such deejays as Larry Levan was as "programmers"—their skill, in Jardim's words, was "to take the crowd on a journey." As he notes (p. 145), the essentially theatrical nature of the dance club also meant its use of all the "elements of style pioneered in the pre-disco gay club scene."

For disco/club/rave settings in Britain, see Sarah Thornton, *Club Cultures* (Cambridge: Polity, 1995). The politics of space has always been central to public dancing—in Britain, at least, there is a long history of the state seeking to regulate the dance floor (most recently, in 1994, in legislation seeking to prevent the unauthorized rave). See also Will Straw, "Systems of Articulation, Logics of Change: Communities and Scenes in Popular Music," *Cultural Studies* 5(3) (1991), which shows how important the (abstract) concept of "the scene" is for dance cultures.

42. Tagg, "Understanding Musical 'Time Sense,'" is illuminating on these issues. It should be stressed here that there is, from this perspective, no such thing as "real time," and composers who seek to work with it are therefore already involved in an ideological project. There is a significant difference, for example, between John Cage's and Olivier Messiaen's understandings of God and nature, and therefore of their musical uses of "natural time"—see Bayan Northcott, "Notes on the Music of Time," *The Independent*, May 25, 1991. Robert Morgan makes the further point that if music were really to use "ordinary" time then it would cease to be music, which is defined by a "special" temporal attention. Even Cage's *4′31″* is, after all, necessarily timed—what makes it a musical composition is that it does *not* take place in real time; the music here is not the environment but the environment as framed by Cage and his audience. (The arguments here obviously parallel those about art as that which is looked at as art.) See Robert P. Morgan, "Musical Time/Musical Space," *Critical Inquiry* 6 (1980).

43. Tagg, "Understanding Musical 'Time Sense,'" p. 30.

44. Shuhei Hosokawa, *The Aesthetics of Recorded Sound* [in Japanese] (Tokyo: Keisó Shobó, 1990), English summary, p. 6.

45. The best discussion of boredom in rock is Jon Savage's *England's Dreaming* (London: Faber and Faber, 1991). And see Ilene Strelitz, "'Repetition' as Cultural Rebellion: 'Boredom,' the Avant-Garde and Rock and Roll," *OneTwoThreeFour* 4 (1987).

46. Abraham Kaplan, "The Aesthetics of Popular Arts," in James B. Hall and Barry Ulanov, eds., *Modern Culture and the Arts,* 2nd ed. (New York: McGraw-Hill, 1972), p. 55.

8. Songs as Texts

1. Greil Marcus, "Speaker to Speaker," *Artforum,* March 1987, p. 11. Compare Wayne Koestenbaum: "At the opera, we must forget that language and music aren't mutually exclusive. *We want the border between music and words to exist, so that opera can erase the border in an act of apparent transgression*" (his emphasis). *The Queen's Throat: Opera, Homosexuality, and the Mystery of Desire* (London: GMP, 1993), p. 177.

2. Greil Marcus, "Days Between Stations," *Interview,* April 1994, p. 70.

3. For a general survey of academic approaches to pop lyrics see my "Why Do Songs Have Words?" in *Music for Pleasure* (Cambridge: Polity, 1988).

4. For a hilarious account of the FBI's desperate search for the real meaning of the lyrics of "Louie Louie," see Dave Marsh, "Combating Merchants of Filth: The Role of 'Louie Louie,'" in *Louie Louie* (New York: Hyperion, 1993), chap. 10.

5. Keith Roe and Monica Löfgren, "Music Video Use and Educational Achievement," *Popular Music* 7(3) (1988): 311. And compare Rom Harré: "Recently the lead singer of the Moody Blues explained why pop music needed the visual images that have been introduced through the use of pop video. The audience is forced to contemplate, according to him, 'what the songs really mean.'" (Harré, "Is There a Semantics for Music?", in Krausz, ed., *Music and Philosophy,* pp. 212–213.)

6. Richard Rodgers, "Introduction," in Oscar Hammerstein II, *Lyrics* (New York: Simon and Schuster, 1949), p. xiv.

7. Fuzzbox, "Bohemian Rhapsody," on the *What's the Point* 12" EP, WEA 1987.
   In an article in *Revue Philosophique* in 1939 ("La Mémoire collective chez les musiciens"), Maurice Halbwachs argues that for non-musicians—who can't remember music through the score—musical memory *has* to be attached to a "metamusical" experience: "The melody of a song is remembered because the words—a social product—are remembered." Cited in Alfred Schutz, "Making Music Together," in his *Collected Papers II: Studies in Social Theory,* ed. Arvid Broderson (The Hague: Martinus Nijhoff, 1964), p. 164.

8. Nicholas Tawa, *The Way to Tin Pan Alley* (New York: Schirmer Books, 1990), p. 166. And titles, as we've seen, are equally important for selling instrumental music.

9. K. Peter Etzkorn, "Social Context of Songwriting in the United States," *Ethnomusicology* VII(2) (1963): 103–104. And see J. G. Peatman, "Radio and Popular Music," in P. F. Lazersfeld and F. Stanton ed., *Radio Research* (New York: Duell, Sloan and Pearce, 1942–1943); Tawa, *The Way to Tin Pan Alley,* p. 84.
   Contemporary manuals remain clear that the "craft" of songwriting is to come up

with formulaic variations—see, for example, Sheila Davis, *The Craft of Lyric Writing* (Cincinnati, Ohio: Writer's Digest Books, 1985), passim.

10. Tawa, *The Way to Tin Pan Alley,* pp. 84, 90.

11. Chase is quoted in Tawa, *The Way to Tin Pan Alley,* p. 87. And see B. Lee Cooper, *Popular Music Perspectives: Ideas, Themes, and Patterns in Contemporary Lyrics* (Bowling Green, Ohio: Bowling Green State University Popular Press, 1991), p. 4. Cooper is here less interested in love songs than in the expression of social attitudes. His analysis of the pop treatment of education, for example, reveals that "Public education is clearly not respected in contemporary songs. Worse than that, it is openly ridiculed and condemned" (p. 17).

 For attempts to trace changes in American sexual mores through pop song lyrics see, for example, H. F. Mooney, "Popular Music since the 1920s," *American Quarterly* 20 (1968); J. T. Carey, "Changing Courtship Patterns in the Popular Song," *American Journal of Sociology* 74 (1969); R. R. Cole, "Top Songs in the Sixties: A Content Analysis," *American Behavioral Scientist* 14 (1971).

12. Among lyricists themselves the argument has had much more to do with formal craft. America's theater songwriters of the 1920s and 1930s seem to have despised the Tin Pan Alley tunesmiths not for their romantic ideology but for their incompetence. Lorenz Hart, for example, accused the Alley hacks of "sloppy versification, sophomoric diction, clichés, maudlin sentiments, and hackneyed verbiage." Quoted in Rhoda Koenig, "Prowling with the Alley Cats," *Independent,* August 26, 1992, p. 13. And James T. Maher suggests that in terms of "plot, situation and characterization" there was no real difference between theater and pop songs in the 1930s: theater songs were no more sophisticated about love; theater audiences no more "discriminating or subtle." Theater songs were, nevertheless, more interesting because of the "ambience, tradition and discipline" of the theater itself, which had a tradition of encouraging innovation and an audience which expected a "special quality" in the music for a theater night out. See Maher's introduction to Alec Wilder, *American Popular Song: The Great Innovators 1900–1950* [1972] (New York: Oxford University Press, 1990), pp. xxxi–iv.

13. Lawrence W. Levine, *Black Culture and Black Consciousness* (New York: Oxford University Press, 1977), p. 273. And see S. I. Hayakawa, "Popular Songs *vs* the Facts of Life," *Etc* 12 (1955).

14. Levine, *Black Culture and Black Consciousness,* pp. 274–283.

15. For a similar point about expressive conventions in African-American literature see Richard Wright's classic essay, "The Literature of the Negro in the United States," in *White Man, Listen!* (Garden City, N.Y.: Doubleday, 1957).

16. *New Musical Express,* August 21, 1982, p. 10.

17. As I. A. Richards put it in a different debate, "It is evident that the bulk of poetry consists of statements which only the very foolish would think of attempting to verify . . . Even when they are, on examination, frankly false, this is no defect." Quoted in James Anderson Winn, *Unsuspected Eloquence: A History of the Relations between Poetry and Music* (New Haven: Yale University Press, 1981), p. 303.

18. See J. P. Robinson and P. M. Hirsch, "Teenage Responses to Rock and Roll Protest Songs," and R. S. Denisoff and M. Levine, "Brainwashing or Background Noise? The

Popular Protest Song," both in R. S. Denisoff and R. A. Peterson, eds., *The Sounds of Social Change* (Chicago: Rand McNally, 1972). Such research is replicated at regular intervals, and with similar results, in *Popular Music and Society.*

19. For this argument see Donald Horton, "The Dialogue of Courtship in Popular Song," *American Journal of Sociology* 62 (1957).

20. For this incident see Dave Marsh, *Glory Days: Bruce Springsteen in the 1980s* (New York: Pantheon, 1987), pp. 254–266.

21. Bruce Springsteen, "Born in the USA," on *Born in the USA* LP, CBS 1984. For further discussion of this issue see Simon Frith, "Representatives of the People: Voices of Authority in Popular Music," in *Mediterranean Music Cultures and Their Ramifications* (Madrid: Sociedad Espanola de Musicologia, 1994).

22. Tawa, *The Way to Tin Pan Alley,* p. 95.

23. Peter Trudgill, "Acts of Conflicting Identity," in his *On Dialect: Social and Geographical Perspectives* (Oxford: Basil Blackwell, 1983), pp. 141–144.

24. Ibid., pp. 154–155. And see pp. 145, 148–150.

25. Ibid., p. 159. And see also p. 157.

26. Ibid., p. 159.

27. Levine notes that "every study of black urban communities and oral culture" shows ability with words to be as highly valued as physical strength—see *Black Culture and Black Consciousness,* p. 349.

28. See Roland Barthes, "Music, Voice, Language" [1977] in *The Responsibility of Forms* (Berkeley and Los Angeles: University of California Press, 1991), pp. 279–285.

29. I discuss Gracie Fields' vocal technique in more detail in "Northern Soul—Gracie Fields" in *Music for Pleasure.*

30. Most rappers would agree, I think, with Henri Lefebvre: "Language endows a thing with value, but in the process it devalues itself. Simultaneously it makes everyday life, is everyday life, eludes it, disguises and conceals it, hiding it behind the ornaments of rhetoric and make-believe, so that, in the course of everyday life, language and linguistic relations become *denials* of everyday life." Henri Lefebvre, *Everyday Life in the Modern World* [1968] (London: Allen Lane, 1971), pp. 120–121.

31. Public Enemy, "Don't Believe the Hype," on *It Takes a Nation of Millions to Hold Us Back,* Def Jam, 1988.

32. Leon Rosselson, "More Than Meets the Ear," *Poetry Review* 82(4) (1992/3): 8–9.

33. Ned Rorem, "The More Things Change: Notes on French Popular Song," *Settling the Score* (New York: Harcourt Brace, 1988), p. 251.

34. Ibid., p. 253.

35. The argument here is taken from Ginette Vincendeau, "The *Mise-en-Scène* of Suffering—French *Chanteuses Réalistes,*" *New Formations* 4 (1987). And see Adrian Rifkin, *Street Noises: Parisian Pleasure 1900–1940* (Manchester: Manchester University Press, 1993), chap. 2.

36. On African-American uses of English see, for example, Geneva Smitherman, *Talkin and Testifyin: The Language of Black America* (Boston: Houghton Mifflin, 1977).

37. *Les Parapluies de Cherbourg* (Jacques Demy, France, 1964); *Les Demoiselles de Rochefort* (Jacques Demy, France, 1967).

38. Ruth Finnegan makes the point that such "framing" or "italicizing" also distinguishes

an oral poetic performance from ordinary speech, and in oral societies "ordinary" people are presumably equally embarrassed to "perform" poetry in public. See Ruth Finnegan, *Oral Poetry* (Cambridge: Cambridge University Press, 1977), pp. 25–26.

39. Quoted in Winn, *Unsuspected Eloquence*, p. 242. Compare the eighteenth-century view of *The Spectator:* "That nothing is capable of being well set to Musick, that is not Nonsens." (The reference here is to Italian opera.) Quoted in John Hollander, *The Untuning of the Sky: Ideas of Music in English Poetry, 1500–1700* [1961] (New York: W. W. Norton, 1970), pp. 382–383.

Winn notes that Dryden followed Renaissance humanism in distinguishing between poetry as masculine (and reasonable) and music as feminine (and sensual). He believed, in short, "that music is foreign, effeminate, destructive of sense, and success-ful only when imitating the passions" (p. 244). This was to echo a long-standing ecclesiastical argument. St. Augustine, as Winn points out, had distrusted music (and rhetoric) as pagan virtuosity which drew attention to itself (rather than obediently following formal rules of expression) (p. 50), and Wayne Koestenbaum adds that in feeling "guilty" when he was "more moved with the voice than with the ditty," Augustine was clear that music meant "languor and effeminacy," that words should be "master." As it was, music was "turning them in the wrong way," and Koestenbaum puts his own gloss on the sexual politics involved here: "music reverses, inverts, and sodomizes language." See Koestenbaum, *The Queen's Throat*, pp. 183–184, 188; and, for the medieval belief that music is a "distraction, as the irresistible Siren song that lures the helpless conscience to its wreck," Hollander, *The Untuning of the Sky*, p. 110. Hollander also traces the sixteenth- and seventeenth-century imagery of music as "effeminate" (pp. 257–258) and anti-reason (pp. 382–383).

It is interesting to note, in this context, that Alec Wilder assumes in his classic study of twentieth-century popular song the opposite proposition, that music brings good order to unruly words. Writing on Jerome Kern, he reflects that "it would have shocked him to see the world he had helped to create turn into a littered carnival ground for the untutored, undisciplined, insensitive young player-performer-writer. The ominous cloud of anarchy moving over the musical landscape would certainly have troubled such an orderly mind, such a gentle, lyric, controlled talent." Wilder, *American Popular Song*, p. 86.

40. Karlheinz Stockhausen, "Music and Speech," in Herbert Eimert and Karlheinz Stock-hausen, eds., *Die Reihe—Speech and Music* [1960] (Bryn Mawr, Pa.: Theodore Presser, 1964), p. 58. For Hugo Ball and the problems of "pure verbal music" see Winn, *Unsuspected Eloquence*, pp. 320–321.

41. "Bewitched," words and music by Lorenz Hart and Richard Rodgers, 1946. In this song Hart deliberately breaks the rule formulated by Oscar Hammerstein II: "a rhyme should be unassertive, never standing out too noticeably," for "if a listener is made rhyme-conscious, his interest may be diverted from the story of the song." Quoted in Philip Furia, *The Poets of Tin Pan Alley: A History of America's Great Lyricists* (New York and Oxford: Oxford University Press, 1990), p. 185.

42. Levine, *Black Culture and Black Consciousness*, pp. 206–207.

43. Ibid., p. 238.

44. For the history of "the dozens" as verbal ritual (this term dates back to at least the

1890s), see John Dollard, "The Dozens: Dialectic of Insult," *American Imago* 1 (1939); and Roger D. Abrahams, "Playing the Dozens," *Journal of American Folklore* 75 (1962). Later discussions can be found in Smitherman, *Talkin and Testifyin,* pp. 118–128, and Levine, "The Ritual of Insult," *Black Culture and Black Consciousness,* pp. 344–358. While the origins of the particular tradition of insult ritual out of which rap emerges are almost certainly African, similar rituals, such as the Scottish "flytting," can be found in European cultures too. See Ken Simpson, "The Legacy of Flytting," *Studies in Scottish Literature* XXVI (1992). David Toop's *Rap Attack 2: African Rap to Global Hip Hop* (London: Serpent's Tail, 1991) remains the best study of rap in its historical context.

45. Ulf Hannerz, *Soulside: Inquiries into Ghetto Culture and Communication* (New York: Columbia University Press, 1969), pp. 129–135.

46. Kitagawa Junko notes that Kuwata, singer/writer for the Japanese rock band Southern All Stars, "first composes melodies with nonsense syllables that sound like English words, and finishes up with lyrics in Japanese after completing the melody." See "Some Aspects of Japanese Popular Music," *Popular Music* 10(3) (1991): 306.

47. Barbara Ferris Graves and Donald J. McBain, *Lyrical Voices: Approaches to the Poetry of Contemporary Song* (New York: John Wiley, 1972), p. vii. The most represented poet in this collection, with eight songs, is Donovan, followed by Leonard Cohen with seven; Dylan and Lennon/McCartney have three each.

48. David R. Pichashe, *Beowulf to Beatles and Beyond: The Varieties of Poetry* (New York: Macmillan, 1981), p. xiii (from the introduction to the first, 1972, edition).

49. Bob Sarlin: *Turn It Up! I Can't Hear the Words* (New York: Simon and Schuster, 1973). The quotes are taken from the Coronet edition (London, 1975), introduction and pp. 163, 176–177. See also Pichashe, *Beowulf to Beatles,* p. 275. And for a later version of the genre, see Matt Damsker, ed., *Rock Voices: The Best Lyrics of an Era* (New York: St. Martins Press, 1980) (which includes "American Pie"). Damsker has four songs each from Dylan, Joni Mitchell and Bruce Springsteen, three from John Prine, and two each from the Beatles and Leonard Cohen.

50. See Craig S. Abbott, "Modern American Poetry: Anthologies, Classrooms and Canons," *College Literature* 17(2/3) (1990).

51. Quoted in Tawa, *The Way to Tin Pan Alley,* p. 98.

52. Michael Gray, *The Art of Bob Dylan* (London: Hamlyn, 1981), p. 143. (This is the second edition of *Song and Dance Man,* London: Hart-Davis, MacGibbon, 1972.) Aidan Day, *Jokerman* (Oxford: Blackwell, 1988), p. 1.

53. Day, *Jokerman,* pp. 3–7.

54. Derek Attridge, "Rhythm in English Poetry," *New Literary History* 21 (1990): 1035. For a literary study of Dylan's words which does take account of their performance, see Betsy Bowden, *Performed Literature: Words and Music by Bob Dylan* (Bloomington: Indiana University Press, 1982).

55. Edward T. Cone, "Words into Music: The Composer's Approach to the Text," in Northrop Frye, ed., *Sound and Poetry* (New York: Columbia University Press, 1956), pp. 8–9, 15. And see Mark W. Booth, *The Experience of Songs* (New Haven: Yale University Press, 1981). See also Pierre Boulez, *Orientations* (Cambridge, Mass.: Harvard University Press, 1986), pp. 180–198.

56. Ned Rorem, "Poetry and Music," in *Settling the Score*, pp. 294–295. Rorem's emphases.

57. There's obviously an analogy here with the adaptation of books for film and television: the screened reading often seems wrong to us; the filmed version seems to deprive us of interpretive freedom (while adding "intensity," just like the musical adaptation of a poem).

58. Rorem, "Poetry and Music," p. 294. And see Jonathan Rée, "Funny Voices: Stories, Punctuation and Personal Identity," *New Literary History* 21 (1990). Rée notes that novelists have few resources to determine how a character's speech will be read/performed compared with those of a composer, who can determine pitch, voice type, metronome setting, and so forth (p. 1047), but, nonetheless, writers do use language, sentence structure, and punctuation to make a reading a reading aloud (p. 1049), and if, in Barbara Herrnstein Smith's words, "poems are pictures of utterances," then, Rée suggests, novels may be thought of as "pictures of oral storytelling" (p. 1056).

59. Quoted in Furia, *The Poets of Tin Pan Alley*, p. 39.

60. Or as Daniel Webb put it in 1769: "Strong passions, the warm effusions of the soul, were never destined to creep through monotonous parallels; they call for a more liberal rhythmus; for movements, not balanced by rule, but measured by sentiment, and flowing in ever new yet musical proportions." Quoted in Winn, *Unsuspected Eloquence*, p. 256. And see Frye, *Sound and Poetry*, p. xiii; and, for many illuminating thoughts on music, poetry, meter, and rhythm, C. Day Lewis, *The Lyric Impulse* (London: Chatto and Windus, 1965), and Charles O. Hartman, *Jazz Text: Voice and Improvisation in Poetry, Jazz and Song* (Princeton, N.J.: Princeton University Press, 1991).

Winn points out that poets have consistently misunderstood what it means to be "musical." For example: "The Romantic poets loosened their syntax in the name of a more 'musical' poetry, a stylistic change which made their poetry *less,* not more, like the music of their contemporaries, the Viennese classical composers, arguably the most syntactical music in Western history" (pp. 269–270).

61. Quoted in Hartman, *Jazz Text*, p. 169. My emphasis. Robert Pring-Mill shows how Spanish-American "committed poetry" (which is, given its political ends, "unequivocally univocal in its purpose—with even its intentional ambiguities and ironies contributing to an 'intended meaning' aimed at an 'intended audience'") depends for its political effects on popular song *forms,* which give its arguments the force of aesthetic necessity. See *"Gracias a la Vida": The Power and Poetry of Song* (London: Queen Mary and Westfield College), The Kate Elder Lecture, 1990. Quote taken from p. 12.

62. Attridge, "Rhythm in English Poetry," pp. 1022–23. And note Claud Brown's comment (with reference to the specific rhythmic qualities of African-American English) that "spoken soul has a way of coming out metered without the intention of the speaker to invoke it." "The Language of Soul," in Richard Resh, ed., *Black America* (Lexington, Mass.: D. C. Heath, 1969), p. 244.

63. Finnegan, *Oral Poetry*, p. 126. And for the problems of this for the literary history of the lyric, see María Rosa Menocal's richly suggestive *Shards of Love: Exile and the Origins of the Lyric* (Durham, N.C., and London: Duke University Press, 1994), especially chapter 11, a lucid discussion of, among other things, Eric Clapton's "Layla."

9. The Voice

1. Roland Barthes, *Roland Barthes by Roland Barthes* [1975] (New York: Farrar, Straus and Giroux, 1977), p. 141. His emphases.
2. Quoted in Ellie M. Hisama, "Postcolonialism on the Make: The Music of John Mellancamp, David Bowie and John Zorn," *Popular Music* 12(2) (1993): 99. Her emphasis.
3. Quoted in Robert O'Meally, *Lady Day: The Many Faces of Billie Holiday* (New York: Arcade, 1991), p. 52.
4. The song line is from Bob Dylan's "Positively 4th Street," 7" single, CBS, 1965. For the use of shifters see Alan Durant, *Conditions of Music* (London: Macmillan, 1984), pp. 201–206.
5. I could add a further complication here: what is going on when a composer writes *in someone else's voice?* Elgar's *Enigma Variations,* for instance, originated in "a domestic evening" when the composer was messing around with a piece, "playing it in the different ways his friends might have done had they thought of it." As Elgar later explained: "I've written the variations each one to represent the mood of the 'party'— I've liked to imagine the 'party' writing the var[iation] him (or her) self and have written what I think they wd have written—if they were asses enough to compose—it's a quaint idea and the result is amusing to those behind the scene and won't affect the hearer who 'nose nuffin.'" Elgar was here using music not exactly to describe his friends but, in a sense, to be them—and this act of *impersonation* suggests that he, like Cone, did in the end think of music as being the composer's voice. See Francis Sparshott, "Portraits in Music—a Case Study: Elgar's 'Enigma' Variations," in Michael Krausz, *The Interpretation of Music* (Oxford: Clarendon Press, 1993), p. 234.
6. Edward T. Cone, *The Composer's Voice* (Berkeley: University of California Press, 1972), chap.1. But see also Carolyn Abbate, *Unsung Voices: Opera and Musical Narrative in the Nineteenth Century* (Princeton, N.J.: Princeton University Press, 1991): "To Cone's monologic and controlling 'composer's voice,' I prefer an aural vision of music animated by multiple, decentered voices localized in several invisible bodies" (p. 13). For Abbate, the "voices" in music "manifest themselves . . . as different *kinds* or modes of music that inhabit a single work. They are not uncovered by analyses that assume all music in a given work is stylistically or technically identical, originating from a single source in 'the Composer'" (p. 12; her emphasis). I return to this argument later in the chapter.
7. Anthony Storr, *Music and the Mind* (London: HarperCollins, 1993), p. 117. Storr also tells us that "Wagner's personality was charismatic and so is his music" (p. 120).
8. O'Meally, *Lady Day,* p. 97.
9. As David Brackett notes, "It is difficult to determine whether our response [to her voice] is based on what we know about Holiday's life, or on a socially mediated construction of affect conveyed by certain musical gestures." Either way, to repeat O'Meally's point, few entries on her "in even the most scholarly jazz history books" fail to refer to "her struggles with drugs and personal relationships." See David Brackett, *Interpreting Popular Music* (Cambridge: Cambridge University Press, 1995), p. 62.
10. Gregory Sandow, "Tough Love," *Village Voice*, January 13, 1987, p. 71.

11. Quoted in John Moore, "'The Hieroglyphics of Love': The Torch Singers and Interpretation," *Popular Music* 8(1) (1989): 39.

12. Umberto Fiore, "New Music, Popular Music, and Opera in Italy," unpublished paper, n.d., p. 4. His emphasis.

An opera buff like Wayne Koestenbaum might challenge this distinction. He has no doubts, for example, about Callas's individuality: "No note she sings remains the same; she changes voice *inside* the note, as if to say: 'Try to catch me, to name me, to confine me in your brutal classifications'" (his emphasis). But even for Koestenbaum the opera singer's "self" only emerges at moments of musical crisis: "at the moment of vulnerability and breakdown, the diva proves that the seamless singing has been masquerade, and now her cracked and decayed, raucous and undisguised self is coming out." Koestenbaum, *The Queen's Throat* (London: GMP, 1993), pp. 146, 127. In pop, "cracked and decayed" voices are always available.

It could also be argued that as Maria Callas became more obviously "personally expressive," so she became more of a pop than an opera singer (an effect of her marketing as a recording star). See Réal La Rochelle's illuminating *Callas: La Diva et le Vinyle* (Montréal: Les éditions Triptyque, 1987).

The problem of "how emotional expressivity is induced in song performance" when "the pitch parameter is restricted by the score" has interested psychologists too. How do we hear one performance as more "expressive" than another when the same notes have been sung? The point here seems to be that the singer's skill is "the ability to portray by acoustical means the particular emotional ambience embedded by the composer in the song," and not to bring their own, personal means of emotional expression to it (thus "dressing a song in an inappropriate ambience"). If classical singers do nevertheless use familiar rhetorical gestures ("expressive" singing is, in acoustic terms, more "agitated" than "unexpressive" singing), these are, in a sense, personally empty: the emotional meaning is in the music itself. We don't hear the singer as angry, anguished, and so forth, but the music. For an interesting discussion of these issues see Johan Sundberg, Jenny Iwarsson, and Håkon Hagegård, "A Singer's Expression of Emotions," paper presented to the Vocal Fold Physiology Conference, Korume, Japan, April 1994.

13. I'm describing here the use of voices in rock's mainstream gospel-derived tradition. Ray Charles and the Raelettes were undoubtedly the key influence (listen, for example, to "I'm Moving On" on *The Genius Sings the Blues*, London-Atlantic, 1961); Van Morrison is probably the best rock exponent (live, at least), taking advantage of his consequent "freedom from utterance" to use his voice as if it were a saxophone.

14. As was parodied by Lou Reed in "Walk on the Wild Side." There are male backup traditions too: not just the male voice choir used by the Pet Shop Boys, but also in black and white gospel—Elvis Presley used the Jordonnaires throughout his career, and even the vocally democratic doo-wop increasingly featured lead/backup male voices as it reached the pop charts (Dion and the Belmonts, for example; Frankie Lyman and the Teenagers). Gladys Knight's Pips, on the other hand, always came across as a simple gender role reversal. In country music the dominant gender convention is of the star male lead voice being tracked by an anonymous female backing voice, with the man all the way, but always just off center, a sweetener and a restraint—listen, for example, to how Emmylou Harris traces the desire behind Gram

Parsons' voice on his "solo" LPs, *GP* (Reprise, 1973) and *Grievous Angel* (Reprise, 1974).

15. O'Meally, *Lady Day*, pp. 31–32.

16. For the BBC see my "Art *vs* Technology: The Strange Case of Popular Music," *Media Culture and Society* 8(3) (1986): 263. For advertising see Roland Marchand, *Advertising the American Dream: Making Way for Modernity, 1920–1940* (Berkeley: University of California Press, 1985), p. 109.

17. "Significantly enough," as Bernard Gendron writes, "Crosby's singing style actually evoked the ire of spokespersons for moral purity, with Boston's Cardinal O'Connell referring to it as 'immoral and imbecile slush,' 'a degenerate low-down sort of interpretation of love,' and 'a sensuous effeminate luxurious sort of paganism.'" See Gendron's "Rock and Roll Mythology: Race and Sex in 'Whole Lotta Shakin' Going On,'" Working Paper 7 (Milwaukee: University of Wisconsin, Center for Twentieth Century Studies, 1985), p. 4.

18. John Rockwell, *Sinatra* (New York: Random House, 1984), pp. 51–52.

19. This generalization is perhaps too sweeping (Glenn Gould, for example, compares Barbra Streisand to Elizabeth Schwarzkopf in this respect), and there are clearly styles of classical singing—coloratura, for example—in which the performer draws attention to her vocal technique (and to not much else). But then that is probably the reason why Cecilia Bartoli is the only classical soprano I adore.

20. One of the most obvious distinctions between pre- and post-microphone singing relates to this: in the original big bands the voice is featured as just a (minor) instrument, the words sung briefly, after one long instrumental workout and before another. By the end of the big band era, the instrumental break had become the punctuation, a fill between the second vocal chorus and the third vocal verse.

21. Sandow, "Tough Love," pp. 71, 73.

22. Aidan Day, *Jokerman* (Oxford: Blackwell, 1988), p. 2.

23. Glenn Gould, "Streisand as Schwarzkopf," in *The Glenn Gould Reader*, pp. 309–310. Compare Gary Giddins on Ella Fitzgerald: "even when she recorded Tin Pan Alley muck, she could empower certain notes with a shivery reflex, *disassociating* the singer from the song yet giving the song a kick all the same." "Joy of Ella," *Village Voice*, April 27, 1993, p. 90. My emphasis.

24. Cone, *The Composer's Voice*, p. 78.

25. See Jane M. Gaines, "Bette Midler and the Piracy of Identity," in Simon Frith, ed., *Music and Copyright* (Edinburgh: Edinburgh University Press, 1993).

26. Quotes from Barthes, "The Grain of the Voice," in *The Responsibility of Forms* (Berkeley: University of California Press, 1991), pp. 276, 270, 271.

27. Koestenbaum, *The Queen's Throat*, p. 43. Barthes's essay does, in fact, read more like a heartfelt and elaborate defense of his taste (for Panzéra; against Fischer-Dieskau) than as a particularly convincing account of different vocal techniques as such.

28. This relates, I suppose, to a Lacanian psychoanalytic view of musical pleasure, though I do not find Lacan's own words on music particularly illuminating. See, for example, his "De l'objet musical dans le champ de la psychoanalyse" [1974], *scilicet* 617 (1976). From the perspective of a kind of Lacanian socio-linguistics, Barbara Bradby and Brian Torode argue that: "the lyrics of the modern popular song permit a man to fantasise addressing a woman as love-object in terms of rocking a crying baby to hush

it. This use of lullaby language exploits the words of the absent mother in order to silence the present lover." "Song-Work," paper presented at the British Sociological Association Conference, Manchester, 1982. And see their "Pity Peggy Sue," *Popular Music* 4 (1984), and, in the same issue, Sean Cubitt, "'Maybelline': Meaning and the Listening Subject"—"the real object of desire flees before us like Maybelline's Cadillac" (p. 222).

29. Jonathan Swift, "A Discourse Concerning the Mechanical Operation of the Spirit" [1704], in *A Tale of the Tub and Other Satires* (London: J. M. Dent [Everyman], 1909), pp. 180–181.

30. Aaron Neville's "Tell It Like It Is" was originally released as a single in 1966. A live version (recorded at Tipitina's, New Orleans, in 1982) is included on the Neville Brothers' *Neville-ization,* Black Top/Demon Records, 1984.

31. For Otis Redding, listen to *Live in Europe,* Atlantic LP, 1972. Elvis Presley's pleasure in his own voice is best captured on *Elvis: The First Live Recordings* (RCA, 1984), live recordings from the Lousiana Hayride in 1955–56, and *Essential Elvis Presley,* vols. 1–3 (RCA, 1986, 1989, 1990), studio outtakes from his early RCA and Hollywood days. It is here (singers responding to themselves) rather than with backup singers (responding to a leader) that we get, paradoxically, the musical version of Erving Goffman's "response cries," the noises people make in conversation in response to someone else. Goffman suggests that such cries "do not mark a flooding of emotion outward, but a flooding of relevance in," but in musical terms the voice suggests both such movements simultaneously. See Erving Goffman, *Forms of Talk* (Oxford: Basil Blackwell, 1981), p. 121.

32. We don't always get a singer's sex "right," though in my experience this is *not* usually an effect of pitch (the Laurie Anderson effect)—women's low voices and men's high voices are still heard as women's and men's voices; see the discussion of falsetto that follows in this chapter. The misjudgment seems, rather, to relate to genre expectation—the only singer I've known people systematically to misread is Jimmy Scott, and this seems to have more to do with his (torch singing) style than with his (not particularly high) pitch—listen, for example, to *Dream* (Sire, 1994).

33. Crash Test Dummies, "Mmm Mmm Mmm Mmm" (RCA, 1993).

34. Koestenbaum, *The Queen's Throat,* p. 165. He also suggests that "cultural folklore convinces us that we can tell someone is gay by voice alone" (p. 14).

35. Giddins, "Joy of Ella," p. 90.

36. Deborah Cameron has pointed out to me that there is actually a dispute among phoneticians concerning the "female falsetto"—how else would we describe what Minnie Riperton does with her voice on her 1974 Epic hit, "Lovin' You," for instance? And for a stimulating discussion of the special erotic appeal of the *low* female voice see Terry Castle, "In Praise of Brigitte Fassbaender (A Musical Emanation)" in her *The Apparitional Lesbian: Female Homosexuality and Modern Culture* (New York: Columbia University Press, 1993).

37. Ian Matthews, "Da Doo Ron Ron," Philips 7" single, 1972; Mathilde Santing, "I've Grown Accustomed to Her Face," on *Mathilde Santing* 10" LP, Idiot, 1982.

38. X-Ray Spex, "Oh Bondage Up Yours!", Virgin single, 1977.

39. Sean Cubitt, "Note on the Popular Song," unpublished, 1983. Koestenbaum suggests that film musical ghosts (Marni Nixon singing for Audrey Hepburn in *My Fair Lady*

and for Deborah Kerr in *The King and I*) are further examples of "singing without a body, singing from an erased place in the universe." *The Queen's Throat*, p. 11. And Wendy Wolf reminds me that part of the appeal of the pop video is that it re-embodies the pop voice.

40. Record references: Cocteau Twins, "Aikea Guinea," 12" EP, 4AD 1985; Ennio Morricone, *Once Upon a Time in the West*, Soundtrack LP, RCA 1969; Kraftwerk, "The Robots," on *The Man Machine* LP, Capitol 1978; the Stanley Brothers and the Clinch Mountain Boys, *The Columbia Sessions, 1949–50*, Rounder LP, 1980.

41. See Brackett, *Interpreting Popular Music*, chap. 2, for a detailed discussion of Crosby's and Holiday's contrasting "musical codes," and for critical responses to them. And compare Bernard Gendron's account of the white pop "dilution" of black rock 'n' roll songs in the 1950s: Gendron, "Rock and Roll Mythology," pp. 6–7.

   I am reminded in this context of the wonderful moment when Martin Hatch, who had till then, as a good ethnomusicologist, sat equably through all the music I'd played during a course at Cornell on the "good and bad in popular culture," leapt out of his seat on hearing Bryan Ferry's version of "These Foolish Things" (one of my favorite ever tracks) and exclaimed: "*Now* I believe in bad music!"

42. Gendron, "Rock and Roll Mythology," p. 7. Gendron suggests that we can also hear black performers like Chuck Berry, Little Richard, and Ray Charles caricaturing their own styles: "According to rock and roll mythology, they went from singing less black (like Nat King Cole or the Mills Brothers) to singing more black. In my judgement, it would be better to say that they adopted a more caricaturized version of singing black wildly, thus paving the way for soul music and the British invasion" (p. 10).

   For a more general discussion of race and musical caricature, see Eric Lott, *Love and Theft: Blackface Minstrelsy and the American Working Class* (New York and Oxford: Oxford University Press, 1993). Record references here are Jerry Lee Lewis, "Whole Lotta Shakin' Goin' On" (Sun, 1957), and the Rolling Stones, "I'm a King Bee," on *The Rolling Stones* (Decca, 1964). There's no doubt too that white rock 'n' roll fans enjoyed the danger of sounding "black" in the safety of their own heads. The (much less obvious) phenomenon of black singers sounding "white" has hardly been studied.

43. Jonathan Rée, "Funny Voices: Stories, Punctuation and Personal Identity," *New Literary History* 21 (1990): 1053.

44. Record references are to Dory Previn, "Lady with the Braid," on *Mythical Kings and Iguanas* (UA, 1971); Frank Sinatra, "One for My Baby," on *Frank Sinatra Sings for Only the Lonely* (Capitol, 1958); Patti Smith, "Land," on *Horses*, Arista LP, 1975; the Chi-Lites, "Have You Seen Her" (Brunswick, 1971); Meat Loaf, "Objects in the Rear View Mirror May Appear Closer Than They Are," on *Bat out of Hell II* (Virgin, 1993).

45. Dai Griffiths, "Talking About Popular Song: in Praise of 'Anchorage,'" in Rossana Dalmonte and Mario Baroni, eds., *Secondo Convegno Europeo di Analisi Musicale* (Trento: Universita degli Studi di Trento, 1992), p. 356. Record references: Randy Newman, "Lonely at the Top," on *Randy Newman/Live* (Reprise, 1971), and Michelle Shocked, "Anchorage," on *Short Sharp Shocked* (Cooking Vinyl, 1988).

46. Carolyn Abbate suggests that in classical music "narrative" should be taken to describe a specific musical *act*, "a unique moment of performing narrative within a surrounding music" (*Unsung Voices*, p. 19). I've been suggesting here that in pop the voice always does this act, but that is not necessarily the case, and Abbate's argument could

certainly be applied to pop's instrumental-narrative moments, whether they're performed by an improvising player like, say, Keith Richards, or by a calculating producer, like, say, Phil Spector.

47. Is it better, for example, for an opera to be sung in the language in which it was composed, which "sounds" right but may not be linguistically comprehensible to either singers or audience; or to translate the libretto into, say, English, which means that Anglophones now know what is being sung but the vocal *sounds* are no longer those in which the opera was originally composed? I would always opt for the first approach, but then words have always been the least of my musical pleasures.

48. Cone, *The Composer's Voice*, p. 119–121. For further consideration of this issue, with reference to instrumental interpretation, see Jerrold Levinson, "Performative *vs* Critical Interpretation in Music," in Krausz, *The Interpretation of Music*.

49. See John Moore, "'The Hieroglyphics of Love.'" I take the concept of "verbal space" from Griffiths, "Talking About Popular Song," p. 353. For technical discussion of interpretive singing see Will Friedwald, *Jazz Singing: America's Great Voices from Bessie Smith to Bebop and Beyond* (New York: Scribners, 1990). For the torch singer's art listen to Chris Connor's "All About Ronnie" (1954), on *Out of this World* (Affinity, 1984), or Jerry Southern's "I Thought of You Last Night" (1952), on *When I Fall in Love* (MCA, 1984).

50. O'Meally, *Lady Day*, p. 198. His emphasis. Martin Williams is quoted on p. 43.

51. Cone, *The Composer's Voice*, p. 53. Record references: Billie Holiday, "These Foolish Things" (1936), on *The Billie Holiday Story Volume 1* (CBS, n.d.); Bryan Ferry, "These Foolish Things," on *These Foolish Things* (Island, 1973).

52. Keightley's discussion concerns the Beach Boys—see "The History and Exegesis of Pop," p. 128.

53. The Shangri-Las, "Leader of the Pack," Red Bird single, 1964; the Angels, "My Boyfriend's Back," Smash single, 1963; the Shirelles, "I Met Him on a Sunday," Tiara/Decca single, 1958; Salt-n-Pepa, "Let's Talk About Sex," Next Plateau single, 1991.

54. Record references: Loretta Lynn and Conway Twitty, *Lead Me On* (MCA, 1971); Marvin Gaye and Tammi Terrell, *Greatest Hits* (Motown, 1970).

55. Records cited: Sinead O'Connor and M. C. Lyte, "I Want (Your Hands On Me)," Ensign 12" single, 1988; Willie Nelson, "Don't Give Up," on *Across the Borderline*, Columbia LP, 1993. For discussion of the former see Katrina Irving, "'I Want Your Hands On Me': Building Equivalences Through Rap Music," *Popular Music* 12(2) (1993): 117–120.

10. Performance

1. Greil Marcus, "Days Between Stations," *Interview*, October 1993.

2. Erving Goffman, *The Presentation of Self in Everyday Life* [1959] (Harmondsworth: Penguin, 1971), p. 28.

3. For the distinction between "textual" and "contextual" performance theories see Graham F. Thompson's very useful "Approaches to 'Performance,'" *Screen* 26(5) (1985): 81.

4. Nick Kaye, *Postmodernism and Performance* (London: Macmillan, 1994), p. 144.

5. See Thompson, "Approaches to 'Performance,'" p. 88. I'm also obviously indebted in

what follows to the work of Erving Goffman—for an exemplary study see his lecture on "The Lecture" in *Forms of Talk*.

6. Noël Carroll, "Performance," *Formations* 3 (1986).

7. As Erving Goffman famously put it, "All the world is not, of course, a stage, but the crucial ways in which it isn't are not easy to specify." *The Presentation of Self*, pp. 77–78.

8. John Kassan, for example, suggests that embarrassment (or its avoidance) became the key to public behavior in the nineteenth-century American city, because of the unstable context of honor, shame, and reputation. See John F. Kassan, *Rudeness and Civility: Manners in Nineteenth Century Urban America* (New York: Hill and Wang, 1990), pp. 114–115.

9. See Sally Banes's excellent study of this period, *Greenwich Village 1963: Avant-Garde Performance and the Effervescent Body* (Durham, N.C.: Duke University Press, 1993).

10. See Richard Bauman, "Verbal Art as Performance," *American Anthropologist* 77 (1975).

11. Which makes it different from a literary text. It may be true, as I discuss in Chapter 12, that books too only come into being when read, but they can and are studied as if they were always already structured, so to speak.

12. George Beiswanger, "Doing and Viewing Dances: A Perspective for the Study of Criticism," in George Beiswanger, Wilfried A. Hofman, and David Michael Levin, "Three Essays in Dance Aesthetics," *Dance Perspectives* 55 (Autumn 1973): 8.

13. Björk, "There's More To Life Than This," on *Debut*, Bapsi/One Little Indian LP, 1993.

14. Anne Lederman argues persuasively that folk musicians' use of a "deliberately dramatic, *staged* presentation" of their music on tour or in the recording studio enables them to assume that their "ordinary" (though equally rule-bound) performances in "informal" settings, or in their own communities, just come naturally. See "'Barrett's Privateers': Performance and Participation in the Folk Revival," in Neil V. Rosenberg, ed., *Transforming Tradition* (Urbana and Chicago: University of Illinois Press, 1993). Charles Keil makes a similar point about polka bands' performing norms in "People's Music Comparatively," *Dialectical Anthropology* 10 (1985).

15. Peter Bailey, "Conspiracies of Meaning: Music Hall and the Knowingness of Popular Culture," *Past and Present* 144 (1994).

16. Bailey relates the music hall use of linguistic humor to the nineteenth-century disciplining of working-class talk in general, by factory, office, and school, and to the legal policing of music hall speech, in particular.

17. Within street conversation Abrahams thus distinguishes the casual *running it down* from the "aggressive, witty performance talk" of *signifying*. Within signifying one can distinguish *talking smart* ("serious, clever, conflict talk") from *talking shit* (nonserious, all-join-in contest talk). Talking smart (which can be further divided into the "overtly aggressive" *putting down* and the "covertly aggressive" *putting on*) "arises within conversational context yet is judged in performance (stylistic) terms." Talking shit (which can be further divided into "nondirective" *playing* and "directive" *sounding*) is "performance interaction, yet built on a model of conversational back-and-forth." And we can further add to this picture the variations of women's talk *talking tough* and *talking sweet*. See Roger D. Abrahams, *Talking Black* (Rowley, Mass.: Newbury House, 1976), Figure 1, p. 46, and, for the general argument here, pp. 5–89. Zora Neale Hurston, who long ago observed that "drama" defined the "Negro expressive

self," described Negro boys and girls walking past each other on the street as "little plays by strolling players." See "Characteristics of Negro Expression," in Nancy Cunard, ed., *Negro* (London, 1934), p. 39.

18. For further discussion of this argument, in terms of the nineteenth-century appeal of minstrelsy, see Eric Lott, *Love and Theft* (New York and Oxford: Oxford University Press, 1993).

19. See Donald Horton, "The Dialogue of Courtship in Popular Song," *American Journal of Sociology* 62 (1957) for one account of this process.

20. For this point see Mark W. Booth, *The Experience of Songs* (New Haven: Yale University Press, 1981), chap. 11.

21. Alfred Schutz suggests that all musical experiences, however "mediated," whatever the variations of "intensity, intimacy and anonymity," refer to the "vivid present" that performers and listeners share in face-to-face relations. "Making Music Together," p. 174.

22. In the early 1970s the British folk scene became an unexpected source of stand-up comics—Billy Connolly, Mike Harding, Jaspar Carrott.

23. Even in the most "respectable" of the performing arts—classical theater, the ballet—female performers (like artists' models) were taken in the nineteenth century to be akin to prostitutes, while one could argue that an important strand of performance in the low arts, such as vaudeville and music hall, blues and jazz, has been the continuing, deliberate emphasis on the performer's off-stage *propriety*.

24. In this respect, female stage performers have an advantage over women with the everyday problem of walking down the street. See Susan McClary, *Feminine Endings* (Minneapolis: University of Minnesota Press, 1991), chap. 6. David Schiff suggests that McClary doesn't push her argument far enough here: "Opera is performance art, and one in which female performers do not merely 'enact' a male drama but essentially rewrite it in performance . . . If performers were given their rightful place in the history of music, it could easily be shown that Callas exerted a far greater influence on the course of opera in the past forty years than any composer did. Might not feminist musicology profitably shift the focus away from a male-controlled cultural product to a female-centered cultural process and celebrate these issues of feminine dominance? Our notion of music would be appropriately challenged and enriched." (David Schiff, "The Bounds of Music," *New Republic,* February 3, 1992, pp. 35–36.)

Or, as Wayne Koestenbaum puts it, "Since the most electrifying singers were often women and castrati, the emphasis on performance undid opera's masculinity" (*The Queen's Throat* [London: GMP, 1933], p. 182).

25. The most entertaining collection of Madonna essays is Lisa Frank and Paul Smith, eds., *Madonnarama* (Pittsburgh: Cleis Press, 1993).

26. Listen, for instance, to Dolly Parton, *Best of Dolly Parton,* RCA LP, 1970.

27. Listen, for example, to Gracie Fields, *Stage and Screen,* EMI/World Record Club, n.d., which includes a live recording of her show at the Holborn Empire, October 11, 1933.

28. Listen, for example, to Millie Jackson, *Live and Uncensored,* Spring/Polydor, 1979.

29. Roland Barthes, *Roland Barthes by Roland Barthes* [1975] (New York: Farrar, Straus, and Giroux, 1977), pp. 177–178.

30. And as J. O. Urmson points out, in paying to see a performance we also expect that the star (Madonna, say) will, in good faith, continue to *be herself* (whatever the new

theme or costume). See his "The Ethics of Musical Performance," in Krausz, *The Interpretation of Music.*

31. Koestenbaum, *The Queen's Throat,* p. 168.

32. Which is not to say that the respondent isn't just as embarrassed by the misjudgment as the performer.

33. To be excluded from this excitement (the rock critic's common condition) is, oddly, to be embarrassed not for oneself but for everyone else. The point here is that intense or abandoned listening involves a loss of physical control—think of the ugliness of the audience in concert photos—and it is this which embarrasses: to be the only person to clap at the end of the first movement, the only person to leap to one's feet screaming. It is not embarrassing (well, I was never embarrassed) to be the only person taking notes.

34. See Susan Sontag, "Notes on 'Camp'" [1964] in her *Against Interpretation* (New York: Delta, 1966), p. 277.

    Camp strategy has been a useful solution to the male performing dilemma: how to make oneself an object of adoring—feminizing—attention while signaling clearly that *I'm still in charge!* For an interesting analysis of the camp basis of Mick Jagger's performance style, for example, see Sheila Whitely, "Mick Jagger: An Analysis of Sexuality, Style and Image," in Sheila Whitely and Stan Hawkins, eds., *Sexing the Groove: Representations and Identity in Popular Music,* forthcoming. For a general survey of the influence of camp sensibility on pop history see Jon Savage, "Tainted Love: The Influence of Male Homosexuality and Sexual Deviance on Pop Music and Culture since the War," in Alan Tomlinson, ed., *Consumption, Identity and Style* (London: Routledge, 1990).

    As Gary Jardim notes in his account of the Newark/New York 1970s and 1980s dance clubs, the same sort of "fascination with illusion and theater" and "grand sense of playfulness" fed into the *audience* performance that defined disco: "The elegant flow motion, the shuffle beat, the love spirit—they were all elements of style pioneered in the pre-disco gay club scene." See "Al Murphy and the Club Music Aesthetic in Newark," in Gary Jardim, ed., *Blue: Newark Culture, Volume Two* (Orange, N.J.: De Sousa Press, 1993), p. 145.

35. Guy Scarpetta, *L'Impureté* (Paris: Bernard Grasset, 1985), pp. 207–208. In Britain gossip about each successful new teenybop band is always the same: X or Y used to be *a rent boy!*

36. For graphic accounts of such calling forth see Fred Vermorel and Judy Vermorel, *Starlust* (London: W. H. Allen, 1985), and, for further discussion of what they mean, my "Afterthoughts" in Simon Frith and Andrew Goodwin, eds., *On Record* (New York: Pantheon, 1990).

37. See Paul Eckman, "Biological and Cultural Contributions to Body and Facial Movement," in John Blacking, ed., *The Anthropology of the Body* (London: Academic Press, 1977).

38. John Blacking, "Towards an Anthropology of the Body," in Blacking, *The Anthropology of the Body,* p. 7.

39. Sally Banes notes that the young break dancer in New York in the early 1980s, in attempting to be as "intricate, witty, insulting or obscene as possible," would "perhaps present his ass to his opponent in a gesture of contempt. Through pantomime, he

might extend the scatological insult even more graphically, pretending to befoul his opponent." Sally Banes, "Breaking," in Nelson George et al., *Fresh* (New York: Random House, 1985), p. 94.

40. As Erving Goffman notes, in judging whether someone else's performance is sincere or phony we pay special attention "to features of performance that cannot be readily manipulated." If they are, then we feel particularly deceived. *The Presentation of the Self*, p. 66.

41. Though what the truth is here is a difficult question to answer—see, for example, Jennie Livingstone's film about New York's transvestite balls, *Paris Is Burning*. "Driving the mechanism of these performed identities," as Peggy Phelan puts it, "is a notion of 'the real.'" These men-performing-as-women express real erotic desires (and invoke real erotic response): "Underneath the image of these visible women is a man, but it is extremely difficult to say what a man is. Underneath the film there is a performance but it is extremely difficult to say what the performance 'means.'" (Peggy Phelan, *Unmarked: The Politics of Performance*, London and New York: Routledge, 1993, pp. 96, 102.) And see Marjorie Garber, *Vested Interests: Cross-Dressing and Cultural Anxiety* (New York and London: Routledge, 1992), pp. 158–159.

42. Anne Hollander, *Seeing Through Clothes* (New York: Viking, 1978).

43. Quoted in Greg Tate, *Flyboy in the Buttermilk* (New York: Simon and Schuster, 1992), p. 115.

44. See John Baily, "Movement Patterns in Playing the Herati *dutr*," in Blacking, ed., *The Anthropology of the Body*.

45. "Stage dancer" is a specific band role in Britain, and has been at least since the days of Madness.

46. Francis Sparshott, *Off the Ground: First Steps to a Philosophical Consideration of the Dance* (Princeton, N.J.: Princeton University Press, 1988), p. 206.

47. See Adrian Stokes, *Invitation to the Dance* (London: Faber and Faber, 1942), p. 13.

48. As Sparshott points out, Adam Smith long ago noted that the type of movement valued in dance would be frowned on as "ostentatious" in ordinary life. See *Off the Ground*, p. 277. For a subtly choreographed move from walking to dancing see also the opening scene of *West Side Story* (thanks to Wendy Wolf for this example).

49. Like Francis Sparshott, I can't resist quoting here a 1588 account of what the function of dance might be: "Dancing is practised to make manifest whether lovers are in good health and sound in all their limbs, after which it is permitted to them to kiss their mistress, whereby they may perceive if either has an unpleasant breath or exhales a disagreeable odour as of bad meat; so that in addition to divers other merits attendant on dancing, it has become essential for the wellbeing of society." ("Thoinot Arbeau" or Father Jean Tabourot, quoted in *Off the Ground*, p. 22.)

50. See Roderyk Lange, "Some Notes on the Anthropology of Dance," in Blacking, ed., *The Anthropology of the Body*, p. 243. Sarah Jeanne Cohen notes another distinction here between dance and sport: "For dance, both performer and audience shift into a special time-space dimension. This is not the case with sport." *Next Week, Swan Lake: Reflections on Dance and Dancers* (Hanover, N.H.: Wesleyan University Press, 1982), p. 66.

51. Cohen, *Next Week, Swan Lake*, p. 54. My emphasis.

52. It could be argued, I think, that the emphasis on effort (as against grace) is gendered—

in classic ballet, at least, men show the work that goes into their routines while women conceal it. Cohen suggests, though, that virtuosity, at least, should be seen as a personal rather than a gender quality, its "exuberance" reflecting the sense that the dancer is "rebelling" against "restrictions of form," so that our attention is drawn to the "tension" between dancer and music rather than, as is more usual, to their unity. See *Next Week, Swan Lake,* p. 75.

53. Banes, "Breaking," p. 83.

54. For discussion of these issues see Sparshott, *Off the Ground,* pp. 207–214.

55. See Banes, "Breaking," p. 87.

56. "To say that music is one of the essentials of dance is not to say that every dance must have a musical accompaniment. It is rather that some music is expected, even it be only a drum, and if there is no music, the dance is danced *in the absence* of music." (Sparshott, *Off the Ground,* p. 173. His emphasis.)

57. Edward T. Cone, *The Composer's Voice* (Berkeley: University of California Press, 1972), pp. 140–144. For the use of imitative or symbolic body movements in break dancing see Banes, "Breaking," p. 97.

58. For the most lucid and intelligent discussion of music video see Andrew Goodwin, *Dancing in the Distraction Factory: Music Television and Popular Music* (Minneapolis: University of Minnesota Press, 1992).

59. See Mark Fenster, "Genre and Form: The Development of the Country Music Video," and Robert Walser, "Forging Masculinity: Heavy-Metal Sounds and Images of Gender," in Simon Frith, Andrew Goodwin, and Lawrence Grossberg, eds., *Sound and Vision: The Music Video Reader* (London: Routledge, 1993).

60. It could be argued, in fact, that live audiences long ago learned how to respond to music from television—American programs like *American Bandstand* and *Soul Train* and British programs like *Ready Steady Go* and *Top of the Pops* were as significant in showing audiences as musicians at work. And the effect of such programs as the British music hall show *The Good Old Days* or the American country show *Hee-Haw* was undoubtedly to define (and mythologize) what it meant to enjoy live music hall or country shows.

61. For this argument see Lisa A. Lewis, "Being Discovered: The Emergence of Female Address on MTV," in Frith et al., *Sound and Vision.* Barbara Bradby has suggested that video allows male directors to "fragment" the female body just as record producers once fragmented female voices. My argument is that the viewer (and listener) still takes the (female) performer rather than the (male) director to be the source of musical meaning. See Bradby's "Sampling Sexuality: Gender, Technology and the Body in Dance Music," *Popular Music* 12(2) (1993).

11. Technology and Authority

1. Eduard Hanslick, *On the Musically Beautiful* [1854] (Indianapolis: Hackett, 1986), p. 72.

2. Evan Eisenberg, *The Recording Angel* (New York: McGraw-Hill, 1987), p. 158.

3. Quoted in Harry Allen, "Invisible Band," *Village Voice Electromag,* October 1988, p. 11.

4. As Shuhei Hosokawa has argued most eloquently, music can thus be treated as a form of information; the technologies at issue are information technologies—oral trans-

mission was supplemented by written information (the score), which was then supplemented by writing "sound with sound" (in the grooves), which was then supplemented by writing digitally (electronic instructions stored in hyperspace). See Hosokawa, *The Aesthetics of Recorded Sound* (Tokyo: Keisó Shobó, 1990), English summary, p. 2.

5. Glenn Gould, "The Prospects of Recording," *High Fidelity Magazine,* vol. 16, April 1966, p. 53.

6. Elizabeth Schwarzkopf, *On and Off the Record: A Memoir of Walter Legge* (London: Faber and Faber, 1982), p. 16. Legge mostly worked for EMI; his views were echoed by his colleague in Britain's other major classical music recording company from the 1930s to the 1960s, John Culshaw. See Culshaw's *Putting the Record Straight,* and David Hamilton, "Electronic Maestros," *New York Review of Books,* May 13, 1982.

7. Hamilton, "Electronic Maestros," p. 38.

8. For the record/book analogy see John McClure in Gould, "Prospects of Recording," p. 52.

9. Quoted in Gould, "Prospects of Recording," p. 47. This comment has often been reiterated—equally in vain—by rock musicians and critics, particularly since the rise of stadium rock concerts in which large sections of the audience hear a distorted or distant sound and can't see anything at all.

10. Theodor W. Adorno, "Opera and the Long-Playing Record" [1969], *October* 55 (1990): 64–66. Adorno is partly contrasting long-playing to "short-playing" records in this piece; he relates the latter to their epoch, "the desire for highbrow diversion" (see, for example, Thomas Mann's *The Magic Mountain*) and suggests that "this sphere of music is finished: there is now only music of the highest standards and obvious kitsch, with nothing in between. The LP expresses this historical change rather precisely."

11. Quoted in Gould, "Prospects of Recording," p. 49. And see p. 52.

12. Mohr quoted in Gould, "Prospects of Recording," p. 49; Arrau quoted on p. 52.

13. D. L. LeMahieu, *A Culture for Democracy* (Oxford: Clarendon Press, 1988), p. 85.

14. Philip Brophy, "The Architecsonic Object: Stereo Sound, Cinema and *Colors*," in Philip Hayward, ed., *Culture, Technology and Creativity in the Late Twentieth Century* (London: John Libbey, 1991), pp. 107–108.

15. Gould, "Prospects of Recording," p. 54. There's no doubt that in rock too live recordings are "dated"—sound like archive recordings—in ways not necessarily true of studio recordings of the same music. It's as if they don't offer the same acoustic possibilities to changing ears; as if they do, in Gould's terms, capture just one, historically specific, spatio-temporal idea.

16. See Gould, "Prospects of Recording," p. 59. Scholes is quoted in LeMahieu, *A Culture for Democracy,* p. 87. I've always suspected that the CD's remote control was more significant for CD sales than its sound qualities, though it's not yet clear whether Personics ("You Pick the Songs! We Make the Tape!") will be a long-term commercial success. (The Personic catalogue for spring 1991 featured suggestions of tracks to include on tapes put together for loved ones in the Gulf War: "Sounds of Home," "Persian Gulf Blues," "Americana Songs." Personal choice, in other words, came prepackaged.)

17. Quoted in Gould, "Prospects of Recording," p. 59. In fact, the potential for active consumption is rarely matched by the practice: people are more likely to frequency-

hop than make up their own radio programs; to line up their CDs rather than to re-record tracks in a new order; to leave their hi-fi dials in much the same positions whatever music is playing.

18. Eisenberg, *The Recording Angel,* p. 144. And see Charles Keil, "People's Music Comparatively: Style and Stereotype, Class and Hegemony," *Dialectical Anthropology* 10 (1985): 124. The significance of records as resource and inspiration for both jazz and blues musicians is routinely noted in their biographies. For example, "Like many jazz artists of the twentieth century, including Lester Young and Charlie Parker, [Billie] Holiday received an important part of her musical education from records. By the time she was twelve, she had never left Baltimore but she had heard and studied closely the leading jazz artists of the world" (Robert O'Meally, *Lady Day* [New York: Arcade, 1991], p. 67).

19. Keil, "People's Music Comparatively," p. 125. For the simultaneous emergence of rock 'n' roll, examined from a similar perspective, see Richard A. Peterson, "Why 1955? Explaining the Advent of Rock Music," *Popular Music* 9(4) (1990). For a more general discussion of how recording technology determined popular concepts of the musically "authentic," see my "Art *vs* Technology: The Strange Case of Popular Music," *Media Culture and Society* 8(3) (1986).

20. Keil, "People's Music Comparatively," pp. 128–129.

21. Kenneth S. Goldstein, "A Future Folklorist in the Record Business," in Rosenberg, *Transforming Tradition,* pp. 118–121. Goldstein takes up another implication of the notion of good form here: "My experience has been that most people want to present themselves to the world formally, not informally." For folk singers, then, recorded "truth" was not something that made them sound "natural" but something that made them sound as they would most like to be heard. Goldstein saw his role in this respect as akin to that of the high street studio photographer, not snapping candid shots, but going to whatever technological trouble it took to capture people's *sense of themselves.*

22. Keil, "People's Music Comparatively," p. 129.

23. Alan Durant, "A New Day for Music? Digital Technologies in Contemporary Music-Making," in Hayward, ed., *Culture, Technology and Creativity,* p. 177.

24. Durant, "A New Day for Music?", p. 178.

25. For a useful summary of the ways in which early gramophones were sold in these terms domestically—"The mission of the Victrola is purely one of transmission"—see Holly Kruse, "Early Audio Technology and Domestic Space," *Stanford Humanities Review* 3(2) (1993). But even in these sales pitches, as Kruse notes, records were defined as "truthful" and "correct" in ideological as well as technical terms. Parents were told that these records would educate and uplift their children, keep them from becoming accustomed to "poor" music.

26. LeMahieu, *A Culture for Democracy,* p. 89.

27. Gary Giddins, "Computer Wars," *Village Voice,* December 8, 1992, p. 84.

28. Quoted in Harry Allen, "It Just Ain't Steak," *Voice Electromag,* October 1989, p. 7. Johnson also talks about digital recording giving the listener "a violin *sound* or a voice *sound.* It is, in fact, the sound of those instruments, but you can't reach in and pick out the individual instruments." See also David Schiff, "The Bounds of Music" (*The New Republic,* February 3, 1992), p. 32.

29. Aesthetic arguments about the results—what the music "should" sound like—are, in

practice, quickly overlaid here by accusations of remix engineers' sheer incompetence and of record companies' routine cheapness. There are too many CD "versions" of jazz and rock classics which have simply cut out crucial bits from the vinyl versions (Louis Armstrong's trumpet missing from his own recordings!) or completely misunderstood songs' acoustic dynamics (George Martin had to be called in to supervise a revised digital remix of the Beatles' *oeuvre*, while Jimmy Page made sure he took control of Led Zeppelin's digital reworkings himself).

For a useful round-up of jazz argument on this issue see Peter Pullman, "Digital Doldrums: Do CD Reissues Honor Jazz History or Mangle It?" *Voice Rock & Roll Quarterly*, March 1991.

30. Joseph Horowitz, *Understanding Toscanini* (New York: Alfred A. Knopf, 1987), p. 230.
31. Gould, "Prospects of Recording," p. 62.
32. The common feature of all the various record-based pursuits of "authentic" musical culture in this century (whether we look at blues or folk, jazz or "world music") is the constitutive role of the collector. "A dialectical energy of acquisitiveness and fantasy fuelled the [blues] revival," writes Jeff Titon, and the same point could be made about any of the other folk movements. Titon, "Reconstructing the Blues," in Rosenberg, *Transforming Traditions*, p. 226.

For an early account of the pleasures (and fetishism) of record collecting in the jazz world, see Stephen W. Smith, "Hot Collecting," in Fredric Ramsey and Charles Edward Smith, eds., *Jazzmen* (New York: Harcourt Brace, 1939).

33. Eisenberg, *The Recording Angel*, p. 162. And see Koestenbaum, *The Queen's Throat*, pp. 49–55.
34. Theodor W. Adorno, "The Curves of the Needle" [1928], *October* 55 (1990): 54. And see Dave Laing, "A Voice without a Face: Popular Music and the Phonograph," *Popular Music* 10(1) (1991). Adorno is referring implicitly here to the origins of the phonograph (in Edison's concept) as a *voice* preserving machine—for use in dictation, for example. The question becomes why it didn't develop (like the camera) as a tool for domestic records—baby's first words, alongside baby's first photo. Certainly in its early days the idea that one's voice could be preserved—and therefore possessed—apart from the body, as it were, intrigued writers. A. E. W. Mason, for example, tied the denouement of one of his detective stories *(The House of the Arrow)* around the victim's ability to speak, on phonograph record, after his death.
35. Adorno, "The Curves of the Needle," p. 54. Given that manufacturers have to make general choices about what sounds best, it is worth noting that radios and record players are usually designed to reproduce well the male rather than the female voice (just as film stock was developed to deal with white rather than black skin tones).
36. John Corbett, "Free, Single and Disengaged: Listening Pleasure and the Popular Music Object," *October* 54 (1990): 84–85.
37. Philip Brophy, "You Are There: Notes on 'Live' Music," unpublished paper, 1987, pp. 2–3.
38. Ibid., pp. 4, 5, 7.
39. Katherine Preston notes the very early selling of coin-operated phonographs in these terms: "These instruments will prove a great attraction in hotels, depots, church fairs, and all places where many people congregate." (Quoted in Preston, *Music for Hire*, pp. 236–237.) And it is arguable that the juke-box saved the record industry from the

effects of the depression in the 1930s. For the history of the use of records as public entertainment in Britain, see Thornton, *Club Cultures*.

40. Eisenberg notes that "when a number of people (a number greater than two) assemble in someone's home for the sole purpose of listening to records, they are much less likely to be family than friends, drawn together by an elective affinity." (*The Recording Angel*, p. 72.) The implication, I think, is that the *individual* identity that records define within the home needs public confirmation from outside it.

41. Quoted in LeMahieu, *A Culture for Democracy*, p. 84.

42. Brophy, "The Architecsonic Object," pp. 109–110. And see Frith, "Art *vs* Technology," for other examples of technology *expanding* our sense of music.

43. Michel Chion notes the implications of this distinction for how we read sound in film: "Take one image and compare the effect of a music cue played on a well-tuned piano with the effect of a cue played on a slightly out of tune piano with a few bad keys. We tend to read the first cue more readily as 'pit music,' while with the second, even if the instrument isn't identified or shown in the image, we will sense its concrete presence in the setting." *Audio-Vision*, p. 116.

44. Quoted in Horowitz, *Understanding Toscanini*, p. 415.

45. Jonathan Tankel, for example, describes the difference between the original Bob Clearmountain mix of Bruce Springsteen's "Dancing in the Dark," "coded for radio and home stereo," and the Arthur Baker remix, "recoded for the dance floor and the boom box." Jonathan David Tankel, "The Practice of Recording Music: Remixing as Recoding," *Journal of Communication* 40(3) (1990): 42–43.

46. For a subtle exploration of the issues here, relating them to the question of how we are placed by a film in cinematic space, see Philip Brophy, "The Architecsonic Object." The Keightley quote is from "The History and Exegesis of Pop" (M.A. thesis, Communications, McGill University, 1991), p. 78. Eisenberg notes how the introduction of stereo complicated listeners' understanding of "the phenomenology of the phonograph," "by adding a spatial, and hence a visual, aspect that at once clarified and confused . . . The exaggerated stereo effects used by rock producers serve not to project musicians in exterior space, but to direct listeners' attention to different zones of interior space." *The Recording Angel*, pp. 64–65.

47. John Corbett argues that one CD effect is to de-spatialize sound, to "conceal" music. A CD is an object with no material or visual presence, no posited spatial metaphor—digital music is music as time only. We could perhaps relate this to arguments about computer information generally—music too is now stored in hyperspace, as virtual sound. On the other hand, it could also be argued that music is used in computer games (as in animated films and pop videos) as a way of rooting sensations that might otherwise float spatially free. See Corbett, "Free, Single and Disengaged."

48. Tankel, "The Practice of Recording," p. 44.

49. Michael Ondaatje, *Coming Through Slaughter* (Toronto: General Publishing Co., 1976), pp. 93–94.

50. Steve Jones, "Critical Legal Studies and Popular Music Studies," *Stanford Humanities Review* 3(2) (1993): 88. His emphasis. And see Hosokawa, *The Aesthetics of Recorded Sound*, English summary, p. 8; Kramer, *The Time of Music*, pp. 45, 50, 69–70.

51. Quoted in Gould, "Prospects of Recording," p. 58. Babbitt interestingly echoes here a prediction made by Donald Tovey in the early days of recording: "There is nothing

to prevent the individual production of music directly in terms of the phonographic needle. That is to say, the composer, untrammelled by the technique of instruments, will prescribe all producible timbre in whatever pitches and rhythms he pleases, and will have no more direct cooperation with the craftsman who models the phonographic wave-lines, than the violinist may with Stradivarius." Quoted in Schutz, "Making Music Together," p. 165.

And see Alan Durant, "A New Age for Music?", p. 185: "At face value then, what this aspect [MIDI] of the technology leads to is extension and enrichment of traditional compositional processes, by offering solutions to problems of inaccurate, incomplete, or technically impossible performance, and by allowing for intensive scrutiny, manipulation and repair of anything entered into the machine."

52. For a useful account of current digital recording practices see Jeremy J. Beadle, *Will Pop Eat Itself? Pop Music in the Soundbite Era* (London: Faber and Faber, 1993), chap. 6. For general discussion of the issues here see Steve Jones, *Rock Formation: Music, Technology and Mass Communication* (Newbury Park, Calif.: Sage, 1992).

53. The best discussions of the issues here are Andrew Goodwin, "Sample and Hold: Pop Music in the Digital Age of Reproduction" [1988], in Frith and Goodwin, *On Record;* and Paul Théberge, "The 'Sound' of Music: Technological Rationalization and the Production of Popular Music," *New Formations* 8 (1989).

Now that the performance information embodied in a disc can be stored as MIDI data and used to drive other computers, music makers can also in effect compose new works *without knowing.* It would be possible, for example, as James Wyman suggests, to take a recorded performance (by Vladimir Horowitz, say, on a MIDI'd Yamaha grand piano), and use the resulting information "to play some sound other than a piano." See James Wyman, "It's MIDI Time," *Village Voice Electromag,* March 1989, p. 16. Sound can also be used in terms of "hypermedia" or a "hypertext," to drive images and written texts too.

54. One of the more ironic effects of such updating is the pursuit of the "authentic" performance: period instruments played in period settings and acoustics, brought to you by the magic of digital recording. (Thanks to Deborah Cameron for this point.)

55. There are aspects of this that I am too old to understand. How, for example, do people listen to CD singles, with their four or five versions of the same track? All through? Different mixes chosen on different occasions, in different moods? One version the favorite and programmed to repeat? The industry assumes this last habit; the other mixes are there for radio and/or club use. In practice I suspect that consumers "choose" the version familiar from club or radio play anyway. I remain a 7" single fetishist who never even played the B-side.

56. See Chris Cutler, "Necessity and Choice in Musical Forms, Concerning Musical and Technical Means and Political Needs" [1982], in his *File Under Popular* (London: RR Megacorp, 1991).

12. The Meaning of Music

1. Quoted (from a 1934 issue of *Modern Music*) in Joseph Horowitz, *Understanding Toscanini* (New York: Alfred A. Knopf, 1987), p. 267n.

2. Robert Cantwell, "When We Were Good: Class and Culture in the Folk Revival," in

Neil V. Rosenberg, ed., *Transforming Tradition* (Urbana and Chicago: University of Illinois Press, 1993), p. 38.

3. Quoted (from *Human, All-too-human*) in Julian Young, *Nietzsche's Philosophy of Art* (Cambridge: Cambridge University Press, 1992), p. 76.

4. Danto is quoted in Joseph Margolis, "Music as Ordered Sound: Some Complications Affecting Description and Interpretation," in Michael Krausz, ed., *The Interpretation of Music* (Oxford: Clarendon Press, 1993), p. 150. (Danto's article, "The Artworld," was published in *Journal of Philosophy* in 1964.) Compare Alfred Schutz's earlier sociological argument that musicians' ability to perceive the music in a score is founded not "on the conventional character of the visual signs," but rather on the "musical culture against the background of which the reader's or performer's interpretation of these signs takes place." See Schutz, "Making Music Together," p. 167.

5. My argument here is taken from Derrick F. Wright, "Musical Meaning and Its Social Determinants," *Sociology* 9(3) (1975): 424, 428.

6. Lucy Green, *Music on Deaf Ears* (Manchester: Manchester University Press, 1988), pp. 141, 143.

7. Quoted in Jonathan D. Kramer, *The Time of Music* (New York: Schirmer Books, 1988), p. 384.

8. Ola Stockfelt, "Adequate Modes of Listening," *Stanford Humanities Review* 3(2) (1993): 158.

9. Ibid., p. 159. For further discussion of how music "defines its own space but does so by moving through this space in its own unique manner," how "musical space, then, is a space of relationships," and how this relates to the "actual physical space in which music is performed," see Robert P. Morgan, "Musical Time/Musical Space" (*Critical Inquiry* 6 [1980]). Morgan observes that while people do read scores for pleasure, they don't read them like books (unless actually performing or preparing a performance) but skip back and forth "in the score's space" (p. 537).

10. Rose Rosengard Subotnik, *Developing Variations: Style and Ideology in Western Music* (Minneapolis: University of Minnesota Press, 1991), pp. 239, 249.

    In her discussion of the relationship between the "musical" and "extra-musical" meanings of musical pieces, Lydia Goehr suggests that the "aesthetic character of a work" might be "derived or extrapolated, without derogatory connotation, from its historical character." In other words, what we hear as music's aesthetic value is not a quality *in* the music, but describes how we understand it in the framework of a historically specific interpretive musical culture. See Lydia Goehr, "Writing Music History," *History and Theory* 31(2) (1992): 194.

11. Kyle Gann, "What Normal People Hear," *Village Voice*, July 28, 1992, p. 86.

12. John Blacking, *"A Common-Sense View of All Music"* (Cambridge: Cambridge University Press, 1987), p. 146.

13. Alec Wilder, *American Popular Song* (New York: Oxford University Press, 1990), p. 289.

14. Keir Keightley, "The History and Exegesis of Pop," M.A. thesis, McGill University, 1991, p. 146.

15. I take this phrase from Goehr, "Writing Music History," p. 191.

16. Anthony Storr, *Music and the Mind* (London: HarperCollins, 1993), pp. 63, 76, 179.

17. Roger Scruton, "Notes on the Meaning of Music," in Krausz, *The Interpretation of Music*, p. 197.

18. Nicholas Cook, *Music, Imagination and Culture* (Oxford: Clarendon Press, 1990), pp. 1–2.

19. Robert Kraut, "Perceiving the Music Correctly," in Krausz, *The Interpretation of Music*, p. 113.

20. See Peter Kivy, *Music Alone* (Ithaca, N.Y.: Cornell University Press, 1990), p. 97.

21. Adam Smith, "Of the Nature of that Imitation which takes place in what are called the Imitative Arts" [1777?], in *Essays on Philosophical Subjects*, ed. W. P. D. Wightman and J. C. Boyne (Oxford: Clarendon Press, 1980), pp. 206–207.

22. See Carl Dahlhaus, *Esthetics of Music* [1967] (Cambridge: Cambridge University Press, 1982), p. 24.

23. See James A. Winn, *Unsuspected Eloquence* (New Haven: Yale University Press, 1981): "Renaissance thinkers had considered music inferior to poetry because its meaning was vague; later thinkers preferred music for that very vagueness" (p. 198).

24. Quoted in Dahlhaus, *Esthetics of Music*, p. 28.

25. Compare John Norris's 1678 "Letter Concerning Love and Music." Norris argued that music was an intellectual rather than a sensual pleasure because of "the Harmony and Proportion of Sounds." Music is "an Abstract and Intelligible Thing, and the Pleasure of it arises not from any Bodily Movement . . . but from the Soul itself contemplating the Beauty and Agreement of it." (Quoted in John Hollander, *The Untuning of the Sky* [New York: W. W. Norton, 1970], pp. 296–297.)

    Norris and Smith anticipate Peter Kivy—the expressiveness of music is explained by "the congruence of musical 'contour' with the structure of expressive features and behavior." See Peter Kivy, *The Corded Shell* (Princeton, N.J.: Princeton University Press, 1980), pp. 22–30, 50–52, 77. Music thus offers us the cognition of feelings rather than the feelings themselves (I take the latter position to be that of Susanne K. Langer and her followers).

26. Smith, "Of the Nature of that Imitation," p. 198.

27. Kevin Barry, *Language, Music and the Sign* (Cambridge: Cambridge University Press, 1987), pp. 60–61.

28. Smith, "Of the Nature of that Imitation," p. 185.

29. Ibid., p. 204.

30. Friedrich von Schlegel, "Fragments from *Das Athenaum*" [1798–1800], reprinted in P. Le Huray and J. Day, eds., *Music and Aesthetics in the Eighteenth and Early Nineteenth Centuries* (Cambridge: Cambridge University Press, 1981), p. 247; Jules Combarieu, "Music, Its Laws and Evolution" [1907], reprinted in Bojan Bujic, *Music in European Thought 1851–1912* (Cambridge: Cambridge University Press, 1988), p. 211.

31. Lydia Goehr, *The Imaginary Museum of Musical Works* (Oxford: Clarendon Press, 1992), p. 154.

32. Quoted in John F. Kassan, *Rudeness and Civility* (New York: Hill and Wang, 1990), p. 243. For the best account of the shift from music as rhetoric to music as object, see Mark Evan Bonds, *Wordless Rhetoric: Musical Form and the Metaphor of the Orator* (Cambridge, Mass.: Harvard University Press, 1991), and, for a more general discussion of what was involved here, Donald M. Lowe, *History of Bourgeois Perception* (Chicago: University of Chicago Press, 1982).

33. Cook, *Music, Imagination and Culture*, p. 15.

34. Eduard Hanslick, *On the Musically Beautiful* [1854; 1891] (Indianopolis: Hackett, 1986), p. 4.

35. Rose Rosengard Subotnik, "Towards a Deconstruction of Structural Listening: A Critique of Schoenberg, Adorno and Stravinsky," in E. Narmour and R. A. Solie, eds., *Explorations in Music, the Arts and Ideas* (Stuyvesant, N.Y.: Pendragon Press, 1988), p. 120.

36. Bonds, *Wordless Rhetoric*, p. 145, and see pp. 54, 68, 95, 133. The identification of music with rhetoric was, of course, another reason for the empirical philosophers' suspicion of it. For them, music was one of those arts of persuasion which, in Locke's words, "are for nothing else but to insinuate wrong ideas, move the passions, and thereby mislead the judgement, and so indeed are perfect cheats." (See Hollander, *The Untuning of the Sky*, p. 176.)

37. Goehr, *Imaginary Museum*, pp. 121, 178.

38. Hanslick, *On the Musically Beautiful*, p. 59. As a brooding, swaying pop fan, one of my pleasures in reading contemporary musicology has been to note the recurrent hostility of these professionals to the "amateur" listener—an interesting concept in itself. For musicians' resistance to the Hanslick line see Robert Francès, *The Perception of Music* [1958] (Hillsdale, N.J.: Lawrence Erlbaum Associates, 1988), p. 227.

39. Kant quoted in Le Huray and Day, *Music and Aesthetics*, p. 163; Adorno in Subotnik, "Towards a Deconstruction," pp. 104–105; Ives in Goehr, *Imaginary Museum*, p. 229.

40. Quoted in Goehr, *Imaginary Museum*, p. 210.

41. Quoted in Cook, *Music, Imagination and Culture*, p. 182.

42. Heinrich Adolf Kostlin, *Die Tonkunst* [1879], reprinted in Bujic, *Music in European Thought*, p. 154.

43. Robin Maconie, *The Concept of Music* (Oxford: Clarendon Press, 1990), pp. 116–117.

44. Roman Ingarden, *The Work of Music and the Problem of Its Identity* (London: Macmillan, 1986), pp. 117 and 151–152, and see the introduction by the translator, Adam Czerniawski, p. xii.

45. For this term see Patricia Carpenter, "The Musical Object," *Current Musicology* 5 (1967): 68; and Goehr, *The Imaginary Museum*, p. 173.

 Joseph Horowitz's *Understanding Toscanini* shows why the conductor consequently became the object of adulation. (He suggests that American orchestras had "consolidated a museum identity as showcases for dead masters" by 1870; pp. 134–135.)

46. For an ingenious attempt to transcribe—and so analyze—a studio track see Stan Hawkins, "Prince: Harmonic Analysis of Anna Stesia," *Popular Music* 11(3) (1992). The Coleman story is cited in Cook, *Music, Imagination and Culture*, pp. 158–159.

47. Hanslick, *On the Musically Beautiful*, p. 51.

48. John A. Sloboda, *The Musical Mind. The Cognitive Psychology of Music* (Oxford: Clarendon Press, 1985), p. 153.

49. Lenin is cited by Maxim Gorky in *Lenin on Literature and Art* (London: Lawrence and Wishart, 1967), p. 270; Freud is quoted in Pinchas Noy, "The Psychodynamic of Music, Part 1," *Journal of Music Therapy* 3(4) (1966): 127.

50. Laurence Kramer, *Music as Cultural Practice, 1800–1900* (Berkeley: University of California Press, 1990), p. 4.

51. G. Revesz quoted in Pinchas Noy, "The Psychodynamic Meaning of Music, Part II," *Journal of Music Therapy* 4(1) (1967): 11. My emphasis.

52. Richard Sterba, "Toward the Problem of the Musical Process," *The Psychoanalytic Review* 33 (1946): 41.

53. Smith, "Of the Nature of that Imitation," p. 201.

54. Deryk Cooke, *The Language of Music* (Oxford: Oxford University Press, 1959), p. 272. And see Roger Scruton, *The Politics of Culture and Other Essays* (Manchester: Carcenet Press, 1981), pp. 69, 87; and Nelson Goodman, *Languages of Art* (Oxford: Oxford University Press, 1969), pp. 255–265.

55. Cooke, *The Language of Music*, p. 205.

56. Sir William James, "Essays on the Poetry of Eastern Nations" [1772] and James Beattie, "An Essay on Music and Poetry as they affect the Mind" [1776], both reprinted in Le Huray and Day, *Music and Aesthetics*, pp. 145, 151.

57. Archibald Alison, *Essays on the Nature and Principles of Taste* [1790], reprinted in Le Huray and Day, *Music and Aesthetics*, p. 151.

58. Hanslick, *On the Musically Beautiful*, p. 23, and see pp. 20, 29.

59. Eduard von Hartmann, *The Philosophy of the Beautiful* [1887], reprinted in Bujic, *Music in European Thought*, p. 174.

60. Max Dessoir, "Aesthetics and General Theory of Art" [1906], in Bujic, *Music in European Thought*, p. 383. The best account of these issues remains Kivy, *The Corded Shell*.

61. Winn, *Unsuspected Eloquence*, p. 274. Winn notes that Berlioz, Lizst, and other mid-nineteenth-century composers accepted that "such programmatic hearing was inevitable," and provided their own program notes. In his study of a brass band contest in Yorkshire more than a hundred years later, Brian Jackson observed that the test piece was given a story in the program notes by the contest organizers—the composer had refused to supply one. See *Working Class Community* (London: Routledge and Kegan Paul, 1968), pp. 30–36.

62. As Kingsbury also notes, Leonard Meyer, writing from quite a different theoretical perspective, suggested that "in following and responding to the sound gestures made by the composer, the listener may become oblivious of his own ego, which has literally become one with that of the music." (A description that echoes Adam Smith.) See Henry Kingsbury, *Music, Talent and Performance* (Philadelphia: Temple University Press, 1988), pp. 171–177.

63. Frank Sibley, "Making Music Our Own," in Krausz, *The Interpretation of Music*, p. 165.

64. Sibley, "Making Music Our Own," p. 169. As he adds, the use of figurative description to characterize experience is not confined to music—such adjectives are a way in which we make sense of all aesthetic and, indeed, "natural" objects.

65. Ibid., pp. 175, 172.

66. Quoted in Cook, *Music, Imagination and Culture*, p. 160. Note also Roger Scruton's comment: "Surely it is this relation which most needs explaining: the relation between a listener, a piece of music, and a state of mind or character, which obtains whenever the listener *hears* the state of mind *in* the piece." ("Notes on the Meaning of Music," p. 197.)

67. See Kivy, *Music Alone*, p. 66.

68. Quoted (from *The Critic as Artist*) in Jan Mukarovsky, *Aesthetic Function, Norm and Value as Social Facts* (Ann Arbor, Mich.: University of Michigan, Department of Slavic Languages and Literature, 1970), pp. 76–77.

69. Ingarden, *The Work of Music*, p. 46.

70. Scruton, "Notes on the Meaning of Music," p. 199.

71. Storr, *Music and the Mind*, pp. 78, 149; Scruton, "Notes on the Meaning of Music," p. 200. And see David Lidov, "Mind and Body in Music," *Semiotica* 66(1/3) (1987): "Music is significant only if we identify perceived sonorous motion with somatic experience." If in graphic arts the basic reference point is "similarity" (and theories of representation), in music it is "causation," an interaction with the body (p. 70). Carolyn Abbate (drawing on Gustav Mahler) notes that deafness, "as a metaphor for loss of understanding," describes "the experience of observing moving forms with a sense of their emptiness." In Mahler's own words, "life becomes horrible to you, like the motion of dancing figures in a brightly-lit ballroom, into which you are peering from the outside, in the dark night—from such a distance that you can't hear the music they dance to!" (See Abbate, *Unsung Voices*, pp. 124–125.)

72. Storr, *Music and the Mind*, p. 183.

73. Scruton, "Notes on the Meaning of Music," p. 201.

74. "What makes a musician is not that he knows how to play one instrument or another, or that he knows how to read music: it is that he is able to grasp musical structure in a manner appropriate for musical production—the most obvious (though of course by no means the only) example of such production being performance." (Cook, *Music, Imagination and Culture*, p. 85.)

75. Ibid., p. 40.

76. Ned Rorem, *Settling the Score* (New York: Harcourt Brace, 1988), p. 228.

77. "A musical culture is a tradition of imagining sound as music. Its basic identity lies in its mechanism for constituting sounds as intentional objects, from the level of a single note to that of a complete work. This means that the ubiquitous discrepancies between the manner in which musicians conceive music and that in which listeners experience it are endemic to musical culture. Indeed, they define it." (Cook, *Music, Imagination and Culture*, p. 223.)

78. Roland Barthes, *Roland Barthes by Roland Barthes* [1975] (New York: Farrar, Straus and Giroux, 1977), pp. 55–56.

13. Toward a Popular Aesthetic

1. Aaron Copland, *Music and Imagination* (Cambridge, Mass.: Harvard University Press, 1952/1980), p. 111.

2. Carol Dix, *Say I'm Sorry to Mother: The True Story of Four Women Growing Up in the Sixties* (London: Pan, 1978), p. 40.

3. Theo van Leeuwen, "Music and Ideology: Notes Towards a Socio-semiotics of Mass Media Music," in Terry Threadgold, ed., *Sydney Association for Studies in Society and Culture Working Papers* 2(1) (1988): 29–30. Van Leeuwen is drawing here on John Shepherd and his colleagues' pioneering *Whose Music? A Sociology of Musical Languages* (New York: Transaction Books, 1977).

4. As Bruce Johnson remarks, what sounds "right" musically is therefore not just a matter

of music. A performer can be true to the sociability of an event while getting her notes quite wrong—in most popular genres we expect musicians to take risks, to make "mistakes." See Bruce Johnson, "Klactoveesedstene Music, Soundscape and Me," in Helmi Järviluoma, ed., *Soundscapes* (Tampere: Department of Folk Tradition, 1994), pp. 42–43.

5. Frank Kogan, "Spoonie Gee," *Reasons for Living* 2 (1986). "Spoonin' Rap" by Spoonie Gee (Sound Around Town, 1979); "Love Rap" by Spoonie Gee (Bobby Robinson Music, 1980).

6. Which inevitably means performance as narrative: "Someone once said that while Coleman Hawkins gave the jazz saxophone a voice, Lester Young taught it how to tell a story. That is, the art of personal confession is one jazz musicians must master before they can do justice by their tradition. I couldn't relate to Cecil's music until I learned to hear the story he was shaping out of both black tradition and his complex 'life as an American Negro.'" Greg Tate, *Flyboy in the Buttermilk: Essays on Contemporary America* (New York: Simon and Schuster, 1992), p. 25.

7. John Miller Chernoff, *African Rhythm and African Sensibility* (Chicago and London: University of Chicago Press, 1979), p. 36 (his emphasis). Compare Christopher Waterman on *Jùjú:* "Jùjú history suggests that the role of musical style in the enactment of identity makes it not merely a reflexive but also a potentially *constitutive* factor in the patterning of cultural values and social interaction. Yoruba musicians, responding creatively to changes in the Nigerian political economy, fashioned a mode of expression that enacted, in music, language, and behaviour, a syncretic metaphoric image of an ideal social order, cosmopolitan yet firmly rooted in autochthonous tradition. This dynamic style configuration, consonant with Yoruba ideologies of the 'open hierarchy' as an ideal pattern of aesthetic and social organization, allowed jùjú performance to play a role in the stereotypic reproduction of 'deep' Yoruba values during a period of pervasive economic and political change." Christopher A. Waterman, "*Jùjú* History: Toward a Theory of Sociomusical Practice," in Stephen Blum, Philip V. Bohlman, and Daniel M. Neuman, eds., *Ethnomusicology and Modern Music History* (Urbana and Chicago: University of Illinois Press, 1991), pp. 66–67.

8. See Paul Gilroy, "It Ain't Where You're From, It's Where You're At . . .," *Third Text* 13 (1990–91), and "Sounds Authentic: Black Music, Ethnicity, and the Challenge of a *Changing* Same," *Black Music Research Journal* 10(2) (1990).

9. Philip V. Bohlman, "Of *Yekkes* and Chamber Music in Israel: Ethnomusicological Meaning in Western Music History," in Blum, Bohlman, and Neuman, eds., *Ethnomusicology and Modern Music History,* pp. 259–260. For the practices of amateur music making in American academic communities, see Robert A. Stebbins, "Music Among Friends: The Social Networks of Amateur Musicians," *International Review of Sociology* 12 (1976).

10. Gina Arnold, *Route 666: On the Road to Nirvana* (New York: St. Martin's Press, 1993), p. 227.

11. John Blacking, *"A Commonsense View of All Music"* (Cambridge: Cambridge University Press, 1987), p. 129.

12. For another example of this process see Donna Gaines's graphic study of young people's use of music in American suburbia, *Teenage Wasteland* (New York: Pantheon, 1991).

13. Gilroy, "Sounds Authentic," p. 134.

14. Jonathan Rée, "Funny Voices: Stories, 'Punctuation' and Personal Identity," *New Literary History* 21 (1990): 1055.

15. Ibid., p. 1058. This is to echo Nietzsche's argument in *The Gay Science* that "the process of creating the self is an *artistic* process, a task of ordering the events in one's life that in some respects is analogous to the writing of a *Bildungsroman,* a story of the growth of personality from naivety to maturity, and in other respects is analogous to the task of constructing a character that will engage the esteem and attention of the reader." (Julian Young's summary in *Nietzsche's Philosophy of Art* [Cambridge: Cambridge University Press, 1992], p. 107.)

16. Kwame Anthony Appiah, *In My Father's House* (London: Methuen, 1992), p. 283.

17. Mark Slobin, *Subcultural Sounds* (Hanover and London: Wesleyan University Press, 1993), p. 55. In Nazi Germany, for example, music was used to differentiate youth groups in relation to the German state: against the Hitler youth were placed both the "Edelweiss Pirates," who used German pop music in a consciously working-class gesture against National Socialism and *volk* sounds, and the "swingers," who used English language jazz and a sense of international modernism. (See Detlev J. K. Peukert, "Young People: For or Against the Nazis?", *History Today,* October 1985.)

18. Simon Frith, *Literary Studies as Cultural Studies: Whose Literature? Whose Culture?* (Glasgow: University of Strathclyde, 1991), p. 21.

19. I take this point from Veronica Doubleday's review of Martin Stokes's *The Arabesk Debate* in *Popular Music,* 13(2) (1994).

20. Gilroy, "Sounds Authentic," p. 127.

21. Helen Myers quotes Channu, a village singer in Felicity, Trinidad: "Indian music sounds much sweeter. Whatever the Indian sing and whatever music they play, they don't do it of a joke. It's a serious thing for whoever understand it. It brings such serious feelings to you. Calypso they only sing. You might hear calypso. You will just feel happy to jump up. But if you hear a real technical piece of Indian music, you might sit down stiff and still, and you might be contrasting so much that you mightn't know when it start or when it finish." ("Indian Music in Felicity," in Blum, Bohlman, and Newman, eds., *Ethnomusicology and Modern Music History,* p. 236.)

    Myers notes (p. 240) that "in the past, villagers have tended to select Indian models for their temple repertory and for other religious contexts. They have selected Western models, including calypso, soca and disco, for dance and other entertainment music." For these Trinidadians, "Indianized pieces, borrowed from a twentieth-century urban Hindi culture," are therefore heard as "more authentic than the local Westernized repertory, a reflection of their New World heritage."

    And see Sara Cohen's current research on ethnic communities in Liverpool for further anthropological insight into how musical identities work.

22. Chernoff, *African Rhythm and African Sensibility,* pp. 125, 140.

23. As Appiah puts it: "The problem of who I really am is raised by the facts of what I appear to be: and though it is essential to the mythology of authenticity that this fact should be obscured by its prophets, what I appear to be is fundamentally how I appear to others and only derivatively how I appear to myself." (*In My Father's House,* p. 121.)

24. Ruth Finnegan, *The Hidden Musicians* (Cambridge: Cambridge University Press,

1989). And see Robert A. Stebbins, *Amateurs: On the Margin between Work and Leisure* (Beverly Hills and London: Sage, 1979).

25. Portishead, *Dummy,* Go-Beat, 1994.
26. Blacking, *"A Commonsense View of All Music,"* p. 60.

Index